Ha

Digital Dissertations
and Theses

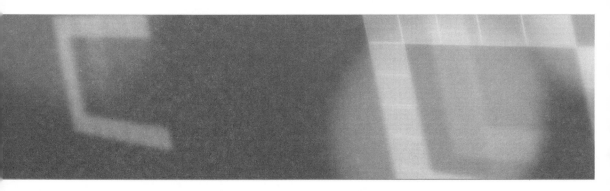

The SAGE
Handbook of
Digital Dissertations
and Theses

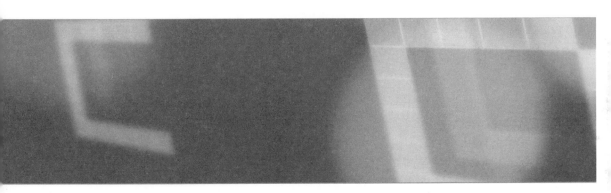

Edited by

Richard Andrews, Erik Borg,
Stephen Boyd Davis,
Myrrh Domingo and
Jude England

Los Angeles • London • New Delhi • Singapore • Washington DC

Introduction and Editorial Arrangement © Richard Andrews,
    Erik Borg, Stephen Boyd Davis, Myrrh Domingo and
    Jude England
Chapter 1 © Erik Borg and Stephen Boyd Davis
Chapter 2 © Richard Andrews and Jude England
Chapter 3 © Richard P.J. Freeman and Andrew Tolmie
Chapter 4 © Helen Beetham, Allison Littlejohn and
    Colin Milligan
Chapter 5 © Lesley Gourlay
Chapter 6 © Zoë Beardshaw Andrews
Chapter 7 © June E. Parnell
Chapter 8 © Jude Fransman
Chapter 9 © Dylan Yamada-Rice
Chapter 10 © Bronwyn T. Williams and Mary Brydon-Miller
Chapter 11 © Brian Fitzgerald and Damien O'Brien
Chapter 12 © Pauline Hope Cheong

Chapter 13 © Myrrh Domingo
Chapter 14 © Gunther Kress
Chapter 15 © Mine Doğantan-Dack
Chapter 16 © Anna-Marjatta Milsom
Chapter 17 © Susan Melrose
Chapter 18 © Juliet MacDonald
Chapter 19 © Michael Schwab
Chapter 20 © Joanna Newman
Chapter 21 © Martin Rieser
Chapter 22 © Lisa Stansbie
Chapter 23 © Ilana Snyder and Denise Beale
Chapter 24 © Amy Alexandra Wilson
Chapter 25 © Lalitha Vasudevan and Tiffany DeJaynes
Chapter 26 © Joyce S.R. Yee
Chapter 27 © Ralf Nuhn

First published 2012

SAGE Publications Ltd
1 Oliver's Yard
55 City Road
London EC1Y 1SP

SAGE Publications Inc.
2455 Teller Road
Thousand Oaks, California 91320

SAGE Publications India Pvt Ltd
B 1/I 1 Mohan Cooperative Industrial Area
Mathura Road
New Delhi 110 044

SAGE Publications Asia-Pacific Pte Ltd
33 Pekin Street #02-01
Far East Square
Singapore 048763

Library of Congress Control Number: 2011936227

British Library Cataloguing in Publication data

A catalogue record for this book is available from the British Library

ISBN 978-0-85702-739-9

Typeset by Cenveo Publisher Services, Bangalore, India
Printed in India at Replika Press Pvt Ltd
Printed on paper from sustainable resources

Contents

About the Editors

Richard Andrews is Professor in English and Dean of the Faculty of Children and Learning at the Institute of Education, University of London. He has edited and written two books for Sage, both with Caroline Haythornthwaite: *The SAGE Handbook of E-learning Research* (2007) and *E-learning Theory and Practice* (2011). He was co-director of the ESRC seminar series, 'The nature and format of the doctoral thesis in the digital and multimodal age' from 2008 to 2010 with Erik Borg, Stephen Boyd Davis and Jude England; and has worked with Myrrh Domingo at both New York University and in London.

Erik Borg is a Senior Lecturer at Coventry University's Centre for Academic Writing, where he teaches undergraduate and Masters level modules on writing and research. His research focuses on intertextuality and multimodal communication, particularly in Fine Arts and Design, and it might be characterised as research into the nature of writing in a rapidly changing communication environment. He has published widely, including recent articles in *Assessment and Evaluation in Higher Education*, *The Journal of Writing in Creative Practice* and *Teaching in Higher Education*.

Stephen Boyd Davis is Research Leader in the School of Design, Royal College of Art. He has worked and taught in art and design, mainly in digital media, for many years. Until 2011, he ran the Art and Design Research Institute at Middlesex University where staff use a wide range of forms of research including theoretical and historical texts, studio practice and materials science. He was also Head of the Lansdown Centre for Electronic Arts, a research centre dedicated to interdisciplinary work in digital media. Stephen is a member of the Peer Review College for the UK Arts and Humanities Research Council, a reviewer for many conferences and journals and advisor to companies and government organisations. His personal research interest is the visualisation of historic time.

Myrrh Domingo is Visiting Assistant Professor in English Education and Literacy Education at New York University. Her work explores literacy development and multimodal textual production in the context of digital technologies and global migration. She was the recipient of the National Academy of Education Pre-doctoral Adolescent Literacy Fellowship from the Carnegie Corporation of New York. Her most recent work appears in *The International Journal of Social Research Methodology*.

Jude England is Head of Social Sciences at the British Library, responsible for developing and implementing the Library's strategy for the commissioners, users and producers of social science research. She is a member of the ESRC's Methods and Infrastructure Committee, and part of the team that produced the ESRC seminar series, 'The nature and format of the doctoral thesis in the digital and multimodal age' from 2008 to 2010.

Notes on Contributors

After completing her BA in English Literature at Durham University, **Zoë Beardshaw Andrews** went on to gain a Masters degree in Text and Performance Studies at King's College London and the Royal Academy of Dramatic Art in 2010. Internships in the education departments of the Metropolitan Opera, the Royal Shakespeare Company and the National Theatre inspired her interest in the changing landscape of arts education. Zoë currently works as Creative Learning Officer for the Ambassador Theatre Group in London's West End.

Denise Beale taught English and languages in schools in the state of Victoria, Australia, for many years before completing a prize-winning PhD thesis in 2009 which examined federal government policy to promote computers in Australian schools. She has since completed a number of literature reviews and is currently working on two ongoing research projects in the Faculty of Education, Monash University, which explore the challenges of social media to schools and the role of doctoral education in the knowledge economy.

Helen Beetham is an independent consultant, researcher and author in the field of e-learning. Since 2004, she has been an adviser to the UK JISC e-learning programme and she currently specialises in digital literacy and digital scholarship. She was Principal Investigator for the 'Learning Literacies for a Digital Age' study (2009), and joint holder of an ESRC seminar series on Literacies in the Digital University (2009–2010). Helen co-edited *Rethinking Pedagogy for the Digital Age* (Routledge, 2007) and *Rethinking Learning for the Digital Age* (Routledge, 2010), both of which are regular set texts on Masters programmes.

Mary Brydon-Miller directs the University of Cincinnati's Action Research Center and is Professor of Educational Studies and Urban Educational Leadership in the College of Education, Criminal Justice and Human Services. She is a participatory action researcher who engages in both community-based and educational action research. Her current scholarship focuses on ethics and action research.

Pauline Hope Cheong is Associate Professor of Communication, at the Hugh Downs School of Human Communication at Arizona State University. She is the lead editor of two volumes: *New Media and Intercultural Communication: Identity, Community and Politics and Digital Religion, Social Media and Culture: Perspectives, Practices and Futures*, and is co-author of *Explosive Narratives*.

Tiffany DeJaynes recently completed her doctorate at Teachers College, Columbia University, in the Program in Communication, Computing, and Technology in Education. She is currently a high school English Language Arts teacher in New York City invested in practitioner inquiry work. Her research explores the evolving landscape of adolescents' digital literacy practices across the multiple contexts of their lives as well as pedagogies that engage multiple modalities.

Mine Doğantan-Dack is a professional concert pianist and music theorist. She is a Research Fellow in Music at Middlesex University, and an Associate of the AHRC-funded research centre CMPCP. Mine studied at the Juilliard School (BM, MM) and received her PhD in music theory from Columbia University. She also holds a BA in Philosophy. Mine published articles on the history of music theory, affective responses to music, practice of chamber music and phenomenology of piano performance. Her book titled *Mathis Lussy: A Pioneer in Studies of Expressive Performance* was published in 2002 by Peter Lang. Her recent volume *Recorded Music: Philosophical and Critical Reflections* (Middlesex University Press, 2008) was a finalist for the annual Excellence in Research Award given by the Association for Recorded Sound Collections. Mine is currently contracted to edit a volume titled 'Artistic Practice as Research in Music' for Ashgate, and co-edit a volume titled 'Music and Value Judgment' for Indiana University Press.

Brian Fitzgerald studied law at the Queensland University of Technology, graduating as University Medallist in Law, and holds postgraduate degrees in law from Oxford University and Harvard University. He is well known in the areas of intellectual property and internet law and has worked closely with Australian governments on facilitating access to public sector information. From 1998 to 2002, he was Head of the School of Law and Justice at Southern Cross University in New South Wales, Australia, and from January 2002 to January 2007 was appointed as Head of the School of Law at QUT in Brisbane, Australia. Brian is currently a specialist Research Professor in Intellectual Property and Innovation at QUT and a Chief Investigator in the ARC Centre of Excellence for Creative Industries and Innovation. In 2009, Brian was appointed to the Australia Government's 'Government 2.0 Taskforce' and to the Advisory Council on Intellectual Property (ACIP).

Jude Fransman is a Research/Policy Officer and Teaching Associate at the Institute of Education, University of London. Her research focuses on community studies (multimodal practices of representation in community activism and community-based research); communication studies (social semiotics, New Literacy Studies and visual methods); and academic practice (academic identity, digital scholarship and the politics of method). She has conducted research for a variety of international organisations (including UNESCO, the OECD Development Centre and Action Aid International) and in a number of countries (including South Africa, Tanzania, Vietnam and Thailand).

Richard Freeman is a psychologist who supports the development of generic skills in early-career researchers. Based in the Doctoral School of the Institute of Education, he is the author, together with the late Tony Stone, of *Study Skills for Psychology*. From 2001 to 2009, he was the Secretary General and Senior Vice-President of the European Federation of Psychologists' Associations.

Lesley Gourlay is a Senior Lecturer in Contemporary Literacies in the Department of Culture, Communication and Media, and Director of the Academic Writing Centre. Her background is in applied linguistics, with her doctoral study focussing on emergent norms in adult language classroom discourse. She has worked at Edinburgh University, Edinburgh Napier University and King's College London. Her research work focusses on aspects of meaning-making, digital literacies, multimodality and post-human theory in higher education. She also works in the area of boundaries, transitions, trajectories and 'liminal spaces' in the academy, looking at issues such has internationalisation, support staff, practitioner-lecturers and 'non-traditional' staff and students.

Gunther Kress is Professor of Semiotics and Education at the Institute of Education, University of London. He is interested in the ongoing development of social semiotic theory, with multimodal representation and communication constituting the frame of application. Related publications are *Social Semiotics* (1988, with R. Hodge); *Before Writing: Rethinking the Paths to Literacy* (1996); *Reading Images: the Grammar of Graphic Design* (1996/2006, with T. van Leeuwen); *Literacy in the New Media Age* (2003) and *Multimodality: A Social Semiotic Approach to Contemporary Communication* (2010). Recent research projects are 'Museums, exhibitions and the visitor' and 'Gains and losses: changes in teaching materials 1935–2005' (funders: Swedish National Research Foundation, and Economic and Social Science Research Council, UK).

Allison Littlejohn is Director of the Caledonian Academy, a centre exploring technology enhanced professional learning in the public and private sectors. She is Chair of Learning Technology at Glasgow Caledonian University, UK.

Through her research in sustainable e-learning, professional learning and transformational change, Allison has led research with a range of academic and industry partners around the world, most notably Royal Dutch Shell, for whom she was Senior Researcher 2008–2010. Her research has been funded by the UK Joint Information Systems Committees (JISC), the UK Higher Education Academy (HEA), the Scottish Funding Council (SFC) and academic–industry sponsors, including the UK Energy Institute and BP and has been a senior scientist on projects funded by the Australian Research Council, the US National Science Foundation (NSF) and the UK Economic and Social Research Council (ESRC) the European Union (EU). Professor Littlejohn has around 100 academic publications and is a Series Editor for Routledge. She is a Fellow and former Scholar of the Higher Education Academy and has received international travelling fellowships from ASCILITE (Australasia) and the Churchill Trust (UK).

Juliet MacDonald is an artist and researcher based in the UK whose solo projects include: 'De-skill Re-skill', 2008, at Drawing Spaces, Lisbon and 'Inverted Garden' in *The Drawing Shed*, 2010, at Project Space Leeds. She is a finalist in INDA6, published by Manifest, 2012. MacDonald's practice-based PhD, *Drawing Around the Body: the Manual and Visual Practice of Drawing and the Embodiment of Knowledge*, was completed in 2010 at Leeds Metropolitan University. She has published in *TRACEY*, 'Out of Hand', 2004, and presented at conferences: *Creative Practice Creative Research*, York St. John, 2009, and *Observation: Mapping: Dialogue*, Brighton, 2010. She is currently Research Assistant in Art at the University of Huddersfield.

Susan Melrose is currently Associate Dean for Research in the School of Arts and Education, Middlesex University. Widely published in the field of performing arts and Practice as Research, she has argued, over the past decade, for the recognition of discipline-specific knowledge in the creative and performing arts; for the systematic identification of the 'knowledge status' of expertise in the performing arts and for an ongoing epistemic enquiry into expert/professional practices in the performing arts.

Anna-Marjatta Milsom is a Senior Lecturer in Applied Translation Studies at London Metropolitan University. Her research interests relate primarily to the ways in which translation practice and theory can benefit from an interdisciplinary approach, a focus which stems from her background in visual arts. She is especially interested in the role of creativity in translation and in exploring the potential for texts to gain, as opposed to lose, in translation. A literary translator as well as academic, she recently became a member of the Translators Association of the Society of Authors.

Colin Milligan is a Research Fellow with the Caledonian Academy at Glasgow Caledonian University, and has worked in the area of educational development and learning research for around eighteen years performing roles in further and higher education, and in the private sector. His research interests centre on learning in and for the workplace and the role of technology in mediating this learning. He is currently supervising a PhD researcher examining perceptions of employability and development of employability skills among doctoral students.

Joanna Newman is Director of the UK Higher Education International and Europe Unit, which is an observatory and intelligence unit for the UK HE sector. She was formerly Head of Higher Education at the British Library. She is an Honorary Fellow at the University of Southampton and a Fellow of the Royal Society of Arts, Manufactures and Commerce. She was the recipient of a Parkes PhD studentship at the University of Southampton and an Institute of Commonwealth Studies Fellowship at the University of London. She has taught history at the University of Warwick and University of Southampton. Her PhD (1998), *Nearly the New World: Refugees and the British West Indies 1933–1947*, was turned into 'A Caribbean Jerusalem' which she presented for BBC Radio 4's *The Archive Hour*.

Ralf Nuhn was born in 1971 near Kassel (Germany) and now lives between London and Roubaix (France). He is currently a Research Fellow at the Lansdown Centre for Electronic Arts in London where he obtained a PhD in 2007. Since 2003, Nuhn has developed a shared artistic practice with Cécile Colle. Their work revolves around the human experience of a world saturated with technology and has been shown internationally, including the National Museum of Fine Arts (Taiwan), ZKM – Center for Art and Media (Germany), V&A – National Museum of Childhood (London), CASO Gallery (Japan) and Haus am Lützowplatz (Berlin).

Damien O'Brien holds a Bachelor of Laws from Queensland University of Technology, a Graduate Certificate in International Studies (International Relations) from the University of Queensland, a Graduate Diploma in Legal Practice from the Queensland University of Technology, a Master of Laws (Intellectual Property and Technology Law) from the National University of Singapore and is admitted as a Solicitor of the Supreme Court of Queensland. He has published articles and book chapters on topics such as blogs and the law, search engine liability for copyright infringement, digital music law and digital copyright law.

June E. Parnell is a PhD student at the Institute of Education, University of London. Her research explores the usefulness of complexity theory in understanding the transformative effects of e-learning in higher education. Her academic interests include how students in higher education develop and adapt to new learning technologies and how computer-mediated interaction supports and affects their learning. However, her central curiosity revolves around new possibilities for researching e-learning and she is inspired through the process of challenging the discourses surrounding technology and education. June is a lecturer in health sciences in British Columbia, Canada, where she teaches in both class and on-line forums.

Martin Rieser has delivered papers on interactive narrative and exhibited at many major conferences in the field including ISEA: Montreal 1995, Rotterdam 1996, Chicago 1997, Nagoya 2002, Belfast 2009, University of Oslo 2004, Siggraph 2005, Refresh Banff Arts Centre 2005, Digital Matchmakers Trondheim 2005, Plan ICA 2005, NAI Rotterdam 2008, Intelligent Environments Seattle 2008, Barcelona 2009, Locunet University of Athens 2008, ISEA 2009 and at many other conference venues across the UK and mainland Europe. He has published numerous essays and books on digital art including *New Screen Media: Cinema/Art/Narrative* (BFI/ZKM, 2002), which combines a DVD of current research and practice in this area together with critical essays. He has recently edited *The Mobile Audience*, a book on locative technology and art which will be published during 2011 from Rodopi, also logged in a blog: www.mobile audi-ence.blogspot.com. He has also acted as consultant to bodies such as Cardiff Bay Arts Trust and the Photographer's Gallery London, Arkive in Bristol, The Soros Media Institute in Prague and UIAH in Helsinki.

Michael Schwab is an artist and artistic researcher who interrogates post-conceptual uses of technology in a variety of media including photography, drawing, printmaking and installation art. He is a tutor at the Royal College of Art, London, research associate at the Berne University of the Arts, Switzerland and research fellow at the Orpheus Institute, Ghent. Since 2003, his exhibitions and associated events have increasingly focused on artistic research. He is co-initiator and inaugural Editor-in-Chief of *JAR*, the *Journal for Artistic Research*, and joint project leader of the Artistic Research Catalogue (ARC), funded by the Dutch government.

Ilana Snyder is a Professor in the Faculty of Education, Monash University, Australia. Her diverse interests are represented in many publications on issues ranging through hypertext and technoliteracies, to equity in educational outcomes in the global south, to her retort to populist debates in *The Literacy Wars*. Books that explore these themes include: *Hypertext* (1996), *Page to Screen* (1997), *Teachers and Technoliteracy* (2000), co-authored with Colin Lankshear and Bill Green, *Silicon Literacies* (2002) and *Closing the Gap in Education?*

(2010), co-edited with John Nieuwenhuysen. *A Home Away From Home?* (2011), also co-edited with John Nieuwenhuysen, focuses on international students in Australia and South Africa.

Lisa Stansbie is Head of The Department of Art and Communication me at The University of Huddersfield, U.K. She completed her PhD, *Zeppelinbend: Multiplicity, Encyclopaedic Strategies and Nonlinear Methodologies for A Visual Practice*, in 2010 at Leeds Metropolitan University. The thesis exists only as a website submission (www.zeppelinbend.com). As an artist her work crosses the disciplines of film, sculpture, installation, photography and digital practices. She has exhibited work internationally and continues to show artwork online. Stansbie is also the co-founder and joint editor (with Derek Horton) of www.soanyway. org.uk an experimental online magazine project centred on notions of narrative and storytelling.

Andrew Tolmie is a developmental psychologist with longstanding interests in doctoral training and institutional provision to support doctoral students. He was formerly Head of the Department of Psychology and Human Development at the Institute of Education, and is currently Dean of the Doctoral School there. He is also Deputy Director of the IOE/Birkbeck/UCL Centre for Educational Neuroscience, and editor of the *British Journal of Educational Psychology*.

Lalitha Vasudevan is Associate Professor of Technology and Education at Teachers College, Columbia University. She is interested in how youth craft stories to represent themselves and enact ways of knowing through their engagement with literacies, technologies and media. Her recent publications have appeared in *Digital Culture and Education*, *Written Communication*, *Teachers College Record* and *Review of Research in Education*, and she is editor of a forthcoming volume on the use of digital media and arts-based literacy pedagogies to cultivate inquiry among court-involved youth.

Bronwyn T. Williams is a Professor of English at the University of Louisville. He writes and teaches about issues of literacy, popular culture, digital media and identity. His books include: *Tuned In: Television and the Teaching of Writing*, *Identity Papers: Literacy and Power in Higher Education*, *Popular Culture and Representations of Literacy* (with Amy A. Zenger) and *Shimmering Literacies: Popular Culture and Reading and Writing Online*.

Amy Alexandra Wilson is a doctoral student in the Department of Language and Literacy Education at the University of Georgia and a National Academy of

Education Adolescent Literacy Pre-doctoral Fellow. Her work addresses the intersections between adolescent literacy and social semiotics, and has appeared in journals such as *Research in the Teaching of English* and *Journal of Adolescent & Adult Literacy*.

Dylan Yamada-Rice is an Economic and Social Research Council (ESRC) funded PhD candidate at the School of Education, University of Sheffield, UK. Previously she worked and studied for more than a decade in Japan; first, in the faculty of Japanese Art History at Kyoto University and then as an Assistant Director of an international preschool in Tokyo. Her current doctoral research focuses on young children's interaction and comprehension of the visual mode as one aspect of contemporary multimodality. Her wider research interests lie in Japanese semiotics and early childhood education. Her previous postgraduate work (which is described in this book) was awarded the United Kingdom Literacy Association (UKLA) Postgraduate Research Award (2010).

Joyce Yee is a Senior Lecturer at Northumbria University's School of Design, teaching across undergraduate and postgraduate levels. Formally trained in visual communication, she has over 10 years working experience in wide range of academic and professional environments. Joyce has published regularly since 2003 and her research is bound by a common theme of exploring and identifying how designers develop and improve their own practice. Joyce's current research is concerned with understanding how designers research and gain new knowledge, particularly in the area of designerly 'enquiring' and its resultant processes and methods. A simple way of describing the research area is 'research on design research'.

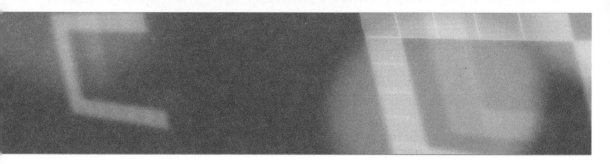

Introduction

Richard Andrews, Erik Borg,
Stephen Boyd Davis, Myrrh Domingo
and Jude England

The SAGE Handbook of Digital Dissertations and Theses is published at a time when increasing numbers of students at undergraduate, Masters and doctoral levels are questioning why they have to submit their research in conventional printed formats, and why the digital version is an *accompaniment* to these printed copies, rather than the main submission. At the same time, other aspects of postgraduate dissertation or thesis work are being questioned. These include the interest in practice-led or practice-based research; the relationship between the creative and critical in dissertations and increasing questioning of the relationship between a fast-moving knowledge landscape on the one hand, characterised by provisionality and uncertainty, and reluctance on the part of some universities to 'get up to speed' with current developments and adapt their regulations and guidance accordingly. These aspects interact with a philo-sophical debate about the primacy of the word and contestation of the assump-tion that words are essential to the validation of an activity as research. These and other issues regarding the place of the dissertation or thesis in the contemporary university, and within society, are the subject of this handbook.

As far as the first set of questions is concerned, universities around the world have, for some years, required students to submit their work in hard copy, accom-panied by a digital version. It is not always clear how these different formats are managed, or what function they fulfil. Our guess is that lecturers and examiners still prefer to receive a printed copy (and that even if they receive a digital version, they often print it out to read and assess) and that the digital copy is kept on administrators' and institutional hard drives as back-up.

Recently, however, some universities are requiring a digital-only submission. This shift in practice has implications, not only for the students who are submitting the work, but also for supervisors, markers, examiners and administrators. It also has profound implications for storage, archiving and access to these dissertations once they are approved and completed. The present handbook addresses the problems and opportunities afforded by a shift to digital submission.

THE WIDER CONTEXT

Writing has always had a material instantiation in addition to its ideational component; consider the limitations on the dissemination of knowledge when hand copying provided the only means to reproduce texts. The development of the printing press led to a bifurcation of writing: texts meant for individual use were handwritten by their authors, while texts for a wider audience were handwritten by individuals, but then prepared by experts (printers) who considered the visual presentation of text and supporting visual data, such as charts and illustrations. However, the technologies of the late nineteenth and twentieth centuries, allowed the production of very small run texts that were not intended solely for individuals. The dissertation, which developed from the doctorate by research and reported new knowledge, was closely linked to the new technologies. Among these technologies were inexpensive manufactured paper, the typewriter and carbon paper, which offered dissertation readers and writers both material possibilities and constraints. Yale University's first doctoral dissertation in 1861 was handwritten on six sheets of paper (Weeks, 2002). Inexpensive paper allowed dissertations to grow to hundreds of sheets in length, altering expectations of a 'proper' dissertation. Typewriters and carbon paper allowed texts to be read more easily than handwritten manuscripts, and the few required copies to be more easily disseminated. At the same time, the typewriter with its single font obscured possibilities of design. Visual material such as charts and graphs had to be laboriously redrawn to be included, while photographs had to be reprinted to the number of copies needed for submission, and then pasted into the volume, generally in an appendix. Material constraints and the expectations of audience and writers of the functions that written texts should fulfil (e.g. that complex concepts should be represented in syntactically complex sentences; Kress, 2003) conspired to focus largely on the possibilities of the written word.

The advent of the personal computer and word processing in the 1980s marked a significant change in the production of dissertations. Whereas, in the era of the typewriter, the dissertation was written by hand and then typed (either by the author or a hired typist), the personal computer firmly put the responsibility for authorship and production into the hands of a single person. With the responsibility for production as well as composing came a host of specific tasks: design, layout, type size, headings, pagination and line spacing, to list but some. These skills had been previously the domain of book designers and typesetters, a tradition going back to Gutenberg, Plantin, Caxton and others. Now they were in the hands of students who, in preparing their work for submission, often under-estimated the time needed for good presentation of this kind. A decade later, in the 1990s, the ability to include images embedded in written text, and the widening presence of the Internet, added two new dimensions to dissertation production.

The first of these – the addition of still images – allowed the presentation of dissertations with high quality colour and black-and-white illustration. Technically, once the skill had been gained, the inclusion of images in a dissertation involved issues of copyright and argumentation rather than of the simple act of saving and inserting such images into the text. The second dimension – that of the advent of the Internet – had much wider influence, in that not only was searching for existing research transformed (via electronic databases, the Net) but the very nature of the format of dissertations began to be called into question. In the early days, digital copy was often appended to the dissertation and saved on a CD Rom. However, the present handbook explores how current practices allow for 'bringing the appendices into the main body of the text' where they are relevant and where they contribute to the argument.

The 2000s have seen further development of these trends, with dissertations more readily available in digital format for easy and quick access by fellow students and other researchers; libraries working out how to preserve and store digital copies alongside hard copies; distribution networks opening up so that more research is available more readily (e.g. via Creative Commons licences); dialogic exchanges regarding research; crowdsourcing and communities of research operating to explore research issues collectively and the induction of the research student into a richer and more varied context for discussion and dissemination (see Haythornthwaite and Andrews, 2011).

The above suggests that when we address the issue of digital dissertations and theses, we are talking about more than composition and production. As a dimension of production, design is central to the activity of 'writing' a dissertation. In the production phase, students have to address issues of transduction from one mode to another (e.g. in the transcribing of an oral interview to a written record); and also the relative positioning of one mode alongside another (see Kress, 2003). There are also the issues of archiving, storage and dissemination, once the dissertation is complete and approved.

DIGITAL DISSERTATIONS AND THESES

What do we mean by *digital* dissertations and theses? First, we should say that we use the terms 'dissertation' and 'thesis' almost synonymously. If there is a distinction in the UK, 'dissertation' is reserved for the longest piece of assessed composition in a taught programme or course – like an undergraduate or Masters programme. 'Thesis' tends to be reserved for longer and research-based works at Masters and doctoral level. In the present handbook, most of what we discuss refers to both dissertations and theses, so we use the terms interchangeably.

But 'digital' requires some definition. We think of the term digital as (potentially) referring to the whole process of dissertation development, from conception through planning, composition, supervision and examination through to storage, archiving and dissemination. Basically it means embodying information in a form that may include written text, but may also include other modes and formats that may not be sequential, but which may offer other possibilities and limitations. Each mode may offer its distinct possibilities, with the lamination of the combined modes needing to be assessed as a whole.

Jakobson (1959; see also Kress, 2003), theorising translation, described three types of translation: *rewording*; *translation proper*, or interpreting verbal signs in another language and *transmutation*. Transmutation is intersemiotic translation, the interpretation of verbal signs in a non-verbal sign system (and presumably the movement of meaning from non-verbal systems into words). However, as the Italians remind us, *tradurre è tradire*, 'to translate is to betray'. To what extent can written words convey the meaning of visual or other modes? Conversely, to what extent can visual or other modes carry the burden of argumentation, which, with the claim of new knowledge, has been one of the expected components of the dissertation?

A digital research project would be conceived *ab initio* as using digitisation to explore either the nature and substance of digital matters, or use it as a means to end to explore any topic. We need to make this distinction early in the handbook, as we are interested in the use of digitisation to explore any topic, not in the nature of digitisation itself (in other words, this is a not a handbook about computer science, but about its application in the broad disciplines of the arts, humanities and social sciences). Early considerations of the digital, therefore, would be concerned with the means and scope of recording data (via film, video, sound recording, etc.); with the interface of the digital and the physical (e.g. in theatre productions that combine both) and with 'purely digital' areas of research, such as the analysis of websites and systems, that depend on digitisation[1].

Once the topic and focus of the research are established, the development and supervision of the project can take place digitally. There are many circumstances now where supervision of an undergraduate, Masters or even doctoral project can take place without the supervisor meeting the student. Skype, e-mail, telephone calls and other means of communication have made this possible. Supervisors, students and institutions who claim that exclusive use of digital media for supervision and completion of a dissertation is not feasible are perhaps not aware of the many successful instances of such work. This range of possibilities allows for trans-national exchanges that might otherwise not have been possible, enabling both researchers and their work to grow communally. Thus, the integration of the digital in the dissertation process not only enables new forms of text to circulate but also enables the cross-cultural exchange of ideas among researchers.

Upgrading of registration from MPhil to PhD, for example, and fully fledged examination of finally submitted theses and dissertations – in other words, issues of assessment – also pose challenges for academics if the work is submitted digitally. Many academics find they cannot read long works on-screen. The issue of whether a verbal work is sent to examiners in printed form or electronically is not the main issue here (etiquette might, for the moment, require a hard copy); the more important issue is whether there are intrinsic elements of the thesis that need digital formatting and which could not be properly assessed in printed form. Let us take the simple example of a doctoral research project which involves the design and creation of a website as a key component. The simplest and best way to relay the work to the examiner is via a URL address, so that he/she can look it up and explore it. The challenge for the examiner is to navigate their way around the site in whichever order they wish, gauging the quality of material, the range and layout of the material and the overall design (both in terms of aesthetics and use). Issues of argumentation will be at stake, because the conventional printed and written argument, so essential to a successful thesis or dissertation, is sequential in its logic and narrative. In a web-based submission, such sequentiality may exist within sections and sub-sections of the site, but overall the structure is not sequential or time-based, though it may be logical. What we can say here is that a website, because of its collage-like structure, operates via a different logic. It is important for examiners to understand that logic/paradigm, and not to impose logics from other formats and genres on to the student's work if it is not appropriate. Imposing a linear structure alters not only the representation but impacts the meaning making possibilities. For example, relying only on the written word to convey a range of thoughts and ideas that may not lend itself to linear forms, will invariably shift the overall design of argumentation on the page.

The final stage in the process of submission and success of a thesis concerns questions of storage, archiving, dissemination and accessibility. In all these aspects of the final stage, digital works would seem to have the edge (with the caveat that books have a proven accessibility of 500 and more years, while digital formats may be inaccessible for hardware or software reasons in less than ten). They do not take up shelf-space; they can be archived easily and saved in a number of places for security's sake. They can even be printed out if required in that format. In terms of access and dissemination, they can be lodged on an institutional e-repository for access by other students, academics and the general public. This wider circulation also has implications for the sharing of knowledge. Rather than narrowly defining the communal reach of research via physical migration, the more porous boundaries of the digital world permits the exchange of ideas and large bodies of work across communities and cultures. Recent anecdotal evidence suggests that when university libraries and doctoral schools require digital-only submission, and thus make the digital process and product the main focus of storage and dissemination, then readership increases ten-fold, even over a short period of time. Such readership is mostly by other students who are interested in accessing new work, and also in examining successful examples of such work. Such sharing often happens globally and opens the channels for transcultural exchanges of theoretical, conceptual and pedagogical approaches in research. Further, the ways in which the works are archived by keywords may lead scholars to bodies of work outside their discipline which nonetheless are relevant to their research. Hence, digital sharing not only increases readership but also opens new communities of sharing and new ways of publicly sharing knowledge.

THE STRUCTURE OF THE HANDBOOK

Conventionally, a final section of an Introduction to a handbook or edited collection would go through the chapters, providing a summary of each. As that function is provided by the section introductions elsewhere in the handbook, here we limit ourselves to justifying the overall structure of the handbook in its constituent sections.

First, we wished to situate the handbook in a historical and institutional context. The history of the thesis and dissertation is an important one to outline, and we do not pretend that we have the space here to provide a full history of the form. That indeed could be the subject of a separate book or thesis! What we wanted to do, however, is situate the digital thesis within its historical context so that readers can be aware of the distinctive nature and affordances of printed as opposed to digital theses. We also wish to record that the present handbook grew from an Economic and Research Council seminar series in 2008–2010, coordinated by four of the five editors of the handbook and taking place in their respective institutions: The Institute of Education, University of London; Middlesex University; Coventry University and the British Library. Each of these institutions provided their own history and specialisms, and each contributed to the overall picture we have tried to draw in the handbook. Furthermore, in the section on institutional perspectives, there is a chapter on the role of the graduate or doctoral school in setting the parameters for the research, composition and production of theses and dissertations.

Second, the handbook includes a section on student perspectives. This is important, not only to include the student voice, but because it is undergraduate, Masters and especially doctoral students who are setting the pace in change in the nature and format of the dissertation. We thus include chapters by graduate students, all of whom record the challenges and pleasures of working in this mode.

Ethical and intercultural issues are the subject of the third section. We have put these two dimensions together in order to explore synergies between them. Our first consideration was to think about the changing ethical considerations of digital research. Much of this centres on issue of copyright and reproduction, but the classic issues in education and social science research of consent, propriety and the wish to do no harm to respondents are still at play. As research and research students are increasingly global in their reach, intercultural issues need to be addressed as there may be implications for methodology and methods, translation, cultural difference and etiquette.

The fourth section focuses on multimodality. Digitisation and the rise of information and communication technologies have been largely concurrent with the establishment of multimodality as a lens through which to create and assess contemporary communication. The reason we devote a separate section to multimodality is that we need to keep digitisation and multimodality apart for conceptual and categorical reasons. Multimodality existed long before digitisation, and has been a part of social and aesthetic communication for millennia. It is the case, however, that digitisation has brought to the fore, again, issues of multimodal communication, largely, but not entirely, through the computer screen.

Archiving, storage and accessibility provide the theme for the penultimate section. This section is not only about the expanded archive, but also about the changing role of libraries in storing, archiving and disseminating research. Effective and comprehensive guidelines for data management are essential, especially where personal and confidential data is attached to the digital output, but also for re-use and citation. Furthermore, the diversity of digital outputs and continuing development of technology present major challenges for preservation and access in the long term. Getting this right is critical as early results from services such as the Electronic Thesis Online Service (EThOS) suggest that demand for hitherto hard to find and access resources is high.

Finally, we turn our attention to research methodologies and methods in a digital age. In many ways, this section is at the core of what we intend the handbook to provide: advice on the process of undertaking a digital dissertation or thesis, from initial conception right through to the final production and submission. At the core of the process are students and their supervisors, who need to work out, in collaboration, how to address a particular research problem. We hope the handbook as a whole meets some of those needs.

NOTE

1. By 'digitisation' in the present handbook, we refer to the wider sense of that term as referring to processes of managing, using and re-making 'information' in ways that are afforded by digital encoding. In one of its more specific senses, it can mean taking existing non-digital artefacts and making digital representations of them. The handbook certainly includes that specific sense, but in general uses the term in its broader sense(s).

REFERENCES

Haythornthwaite, C. and Andrews, R. (2011). *E-learning Theory and Practice*. London: Sage.
Jakobson, R. (1959). On linguistic aspects of translation. In R. A. Brower (Ed.), *On Translation* (pp. 232–239). Cambridge, MA: Harvard University Press.
Kress, G. (2003). *Literacy in the New Media Age*. London & New York: Routledge.
Weeks, L. (2002). You're the Dr. *Washington Post*, 18 March, p. C01.

Institutional Perspectives

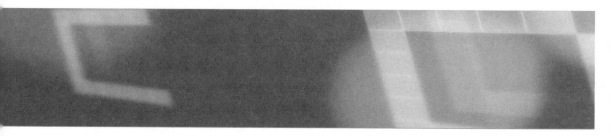

The turn to digital in the conception, design, supervision, production and examination of dissertations and theses might be said to have significant implications for institutions: graduate schools, doctoral schools, senior academic bodies and their administrators. It is the institutions who set the parameters for study and who award the degrees. In many ways, they are the gatekeepers of how knowledge is presented; and certainly they control how research is presented for academic awards. It is thus appropriate that the first section of the present handbook is devoted to institutional perspectives.

In the opening chapter, Erik Borg and Stephen Boyd Davis take a historical perspective, looking in particular at the relationship between the means of production and the nature of the thesis that is produced. One of the key moments that they examine is the establishment of the written doctorate by research in the early nineteenth century, emerging from von Humboldt's reform of the German higher education system. This move from the oral to the written form as the principal qualification for teaching at university level was significant as it reinforced the centrality of words in the expression of knowledge. Whereas in disputation or other forms of oral delivery there were always the accompanying modes and modalities of gesture, physical presence, voice; in the written form, the message depended more heavily on words themselves (albeit as arranged visually on a page). This close association of written language and research-based knowledge has remained with us, sometimes to the extent that those of a classical bent cannot see that a thesis or dissertation can be composed by any other means than the written word. Related to the emergence and dominance of the written word in the doctoral thesis, Borg and Boyd Davis identify the invention of the typewriter in the late nineteenth century as crucial to the arrangement and presentation of advanced knowledge. As they say, the typewriter, with its affordances of being able to produce writing quickly, to reproduce it via carbon copies and thus to begin to disseminate research more widely was part of the toolkit – social, institutional and material – that enabled the expansion of doctoral study during this period.

Andrews and England, in their chapter on the seminar series that gave rise to the present handbook, first describe the series itself. It was funded by the UK's Economic and Social Research Council between 2008 and 2010, and consisted of six-day long seminars, culminating in a conference at the British Library in London. The series was entitled 'The nature and format of the doctoral thesis in the digital and multimodal age', and attracted researchers, students, academics and administrators from across the UK and internationally. The patchy nature of provision for the digital thesis or dissertation in the UK universities became clear during the series, as did the wide spectrum of practices in the actual production and examination of student submissions. One of the significant angles that is reported in this chapter is the influence of arts- and practice-based degrees upon what is possible in the humanities and social sciences. Through studio- and exhibition-based doctoral submissions in the arts (usually accompanied by words to some extent), the possibilities of non-verbal forms of thesis and dissertation have been practised in the arts for several decades. Andrews and England's chapter concludes by providing suggestions for universities as to how they might frame their regulations and guidance to graduate students who are thinking about, or are in the process of submitting a multimodal and/or digital work.

The third chapter in this opening section is by Richard Freeman and Andrew Tolmie, psychologists who work in a leadership role in the Doctoral School of the Institute of Education, University of London. First, they consider the nature of doctoral schools in European universities, then go on to discuss the range of doctorate degrees that is available. While the focus of the seminar series that was the basis for the present handbook was originally conceived to be the Doctor of Philosophy degree (PhD), Freeman and Tolmie indicate the range of professional and/or practice-based doctorates available in a social science institution such as the Institute of Education. They then go on to consider the implications for examiners in reading theses and dissertations via electronic media (e.g. the iPad), and also of making theses available online. In the latter case, they suggest that graduate or doctoral schools need to work closely with libraries to make sure the formats in which work is finally presented is conducive to storage and access. They set the debate about the nature and format of the thesis within a wider shift from the thesis as product to an emphasis on the process of the doctoral experience for students; this process appears to coincide with increasingly provisionality in the nature of knowledge in it social context, a theme developed later in the handbook by Gunther Kress in the section on multimodality.

In the final chapter of this section, Helen Beetham, Allison Littlejohn and Colin Milligan explore the nature of digital literacies and their implications for researcher development. First, they depict a world in which skills in information and communication technologies (ICTs) are essential in about 90% of employment, and in which graduate students are expected to bring a high degree of capability. Such demands have implications for the pursuit of knowledge through postgraduate study, and especially for the modes and media of research, research presentation and access to reliable information. The institutional imperative is for supervisors, examiners and graduate schools to be aware of these demands and to devise strategies for supporting postgraduate and research students. While it is acknowledged that university infrastructure may not support – in some cases inhibit – such exploration and innovation, it is beholden upon universities to provide the conditions within which such students can thrive. The implications are that research training programmes need to be well thought out, comprehensive and fit for purpose.

We can already see that such institutional demands, driven by the turn to the multimodal and digital in the production and examination of theses and dissertations, are considerable; and we can see why governments are increasingly funding large-scale consortia of universities to provide doctoral training, better support services and a richer context for postgraduate work.

The Thesis: Texts and Machines

Erik Borg and Stephen Boyd Davis

INTRODUCTION

In order to provide a context in which to think about the dissertation now, this chapter looks both to the past and future. We deal with earlier forms of the dissertation in the nineteenth and twentieth centuries and with the forms that the dissertation might take in the twenty-first. What unites these approaches is the conviction that the dissertation is contingent, changing and changeable. While supervisors may expect their students to produce a dissertation that resembles the one they wrote themselves, changes both in the available technologies and in the kinds of knowledge the dissertation is expected to represent are having a significant effect on its form as well as its content.

This chapter makes no claims to be a general survey of the media technologies relevant to the dissertation; instead it highlights some of the key issues arising from the interaction between media technologies and scholarly practice. We are engaged in a process that Haas (1996, p. 221) called *historicising technology*, that is, looking at the historical development of current technologies. In this case, we consider the knowledge dissemination device of the dissertation, and the material technologies that have and might in the future support it. In her discussion of Ong (1982/2002), Haas describes how writing 'transforms sound into space' (p. 9). The representation of sound by graphic symbols, that is, the spatialisation of language, was for Ong as well as other theorists of literacy such as Goody (1987), and Havelock (1986), a fundamental shift in human history.

Haas, however, draws on other scholars (Scribner & Cole, 1981; Lave & Wenger, 1991) to argue that literacy does not represent a 'great divide', but that it is a material technology that is value-laden, and 'that to treat written language as if it were neutral or transparent has severe political, theoretical, and practical consequences' (p. 21). As dissertations increasingly allow for the possibility of de-spatialising language, as well as inscribing in context still images, sounds and other time-based data, the values and opportunities of the written text become apparent and disputable.

We first consider how the doctorate moved from a largely oral tradition, in which texts played the supporting role of framing public disputations, to the doctorate's own 'great divide' with the emergence of the doctorate by research from Wilhelm von Humboldt's reform of the German higher education system at the beginning of the nineteenth century. Instead of representing a mastery of all knowledge, the doctorate by research demonstrated the candidate's ability to carry out a research project that generated new knowledge and to disseminate that in a written text. Alongside the development of this form of doctorate, sharing in wider social trends of systematisation and industrialisation, we look back on the role of one particular technology – the typewriter – developed from various attempts to create a machine that would replicate Gutenberg's reproductive technology in text production. The typewriter functioned synergistically in the period from the 1880s to create dissertations that were linear, objective and often gendered (dictated or handwritten by men, to be typed by women). 'Our writing tools are also working on our thoughts', as Nietzsche wrote (Kittler, 1999, p. 200).

We then discuss the purposes of the dissertation and the many affordances that the written text offers, possibilities that are enlarged rather than obviated by moving from the typewriter to the computer. Supplemented but not replaced by images, sound and other time-based data, texts, we argue, allow an important interplay between external representation and internal conceptualisation. With the enhancement of computer technology, texts become easily searchable in ways that other forms of representation, unless provided with metadata in the form of text, are not. Meanwhile, the dissertation on paper retains its simple accessibility and known longevity. We conclude by proposing a seven-fold heuristic which might guide our consideration of competing technologies for the dissertation. Most of these are also relevant to Masters theses and undergraduate final papers.

Although the doctorate is an ancient qualification, the modern doctorate by research is, against this antiquity, quite recent in development. As now, it existed in the past in a complex network of tools and technologies, institutions and the societies that produced it. We will briefly discuss the development of the doctorate (Doctor of Philosophy; PhD, DPhil) and the tools that have supported it. Tools here refer both to the cognitive tools of language and to the material tools (e.g. pens, paper, typewriters, computers and software) that enable and shape written texts and the doctorate (Haas, 1996). Until recently, the doctorate has been the qualification for teaching in universities, and so the nature of that teaching will be considered. Combining the development of the doctorate with a consideration of these tools, and, in particular, the typewriter as the tool for the production of the modern research-based doctorate helps to historicise the doctorate (Haas, 1996) and suggest the linkages between the doctorate and writing technology.

ORIGINS

The doctorate is as old as the European university; contributors to Powell and Green (2007) write that the doctorate has been awarded for 700 years in Britain and a thousand in France. It entitled the holder to teach at university[1], and demonstrated that the holder had mastered the liberal arts of the *trivium* and *quadrivium* (Simpson, 1983). However, in comparison with modern society, the early doctorate emerged in a society with very limited access to books and other textual material, and the role of the holder of the doctorate was to expound their interpretations of texts. Teaching and learning in the medieval universities was primarily oral, with written texts playing a supporting role (Kruse, 2006). Lectures in which a teacher would comment on passages from an authoritative text comprised the main form of teaching. These lectures were complemented by formal disputations in which participants would address set questions. Both teachers and students would engage in public disputations, which established the reputation of a university in a way similar to that of today's published research (Kruse, 2006).

In public disputations, the participants would address a thesis or *dissertatio*. The disputation was rooted in the epistemology of the university; 'knowledge had to be deduced interpretively from the old, authoritative writings. These were the primary sources of knowledge ...' (Kruse, 2006, p. 336). According to Kruse (2006), the thesis was initially laid out orally, but later took the form of a written poster. Students would defend or oppose the thesis, and an arbiter would decide the outcome. By the sixteenth and seventeenth centuries, the thesis was disseminated in a pamphlet that participants and audience would read in advance. Russell argues that the tradition that texts were primarily used as the starting point for oral discussion continued into the nineteenth century. This tradition prepared students for 'the pulpit, the senate, the bar' (Russell, 2002, p. 36). These professions, like teaching at university, involved oratory. The tradition of disputation continues in the oral examination (*viva voce*) for the doctorate; however, the doctorate by research, the modern doctorate, is different in terms of the knowledge it represents and the means by which that knowledge is presented[2].

In the eighteenth century, the nature of the university and its students began to change, a trend that accelerated strongly after the Napoleonic wars. At the beginning of the nineteenth century, a revolution in higher education occurred. 'The stimulus for this development stemmed from Napoleon's military defeat of

Prussia in 1806. Smarting over the loss of the university at Halle, which was situated in territory forfeited to Napoleon, a new system of higher education was formulated to assist the rebuilding of the demoralised Prussian state' (Noble, 1994, p. 6). The Prussians founded the Friedrich-Wilhelm University in Berlin, incorporating innovations that had been pioneered in Göttingen and Halle. It was there that the Humboldt model of the university emerged. Wilhelm von Humboldt (1767–1835) reoriented the university away from the analysis and debate of authoritative texts. Instead, the goal of university teaching became that of modelling and instilling the means for the discovery of scientific knowledge (Rüegg, 2004). The university was to become a factory for the creation of new knowledge. In the process, '… the university gradually replaced the church as the central cultural and intellectual institution of the modern nation state …', and '… its indispensable economic power house …' (Nybom, 2003, p. 147).

The shift that established research as the primary goal of the university built on changes that had occurred outside the university, primarily in academies and scholarly societies. The most notable of these was the Royal Society (founded in 1660) in which members, for the most part outside universities and unsupported by them, investigated the natural world through experimentation and observation. Knowledge creation through experimentation broke with the university's tradition of disputation and with alchemy, the secret investigation of the natural world (Shapin, 1984). Instead of disputation or secret investigation, experiments would be witnessed, and the knowledge would be disseminated through letters to members who could not attend and directly observe the experiments.

Humboldt's reorientation of the university along the line of the scientific societies brought public research into universities on the continent. Quoting Frederich Schleiermacher, Rüegg writes that the goal of the university was to 'demonstrate how this [scientific] knowledge is discovered, "to stimulate the idea of science in the minds of the students, to encourage them to take account of the fundamental laws of science in all their thinking"' (2004, p. 5). Friedrich-Wilhelm University was founded in 1810; by 1815, German universities were attracting ambitious graduate students from Britain and the US who could not pursue their studies in their own countries (Park, 2005). The Humboldt University continued to prepare students for the learned professions, but its mission focused on training students in science and the scientific approach to fields such as history and linguistics. The Doctor of Philosophy degree reflected the student's embrace of the idea of science. Because of these changes the modern PhD 'had no equivalent in the mediaeval university' (Simpson, 1983, p. 5).

The development of the research university marked a shift in the mode through which knowledge would be disseminated, as well as a shift in epistemology. Knowledge would be explicated through written texts rather than through oral disputation. The form of the written text for the dissemination of knowledge had been in gradual development since the seventeenth century. The research article emerged from the letters of the Royal Society, and was a 'virtual technology' that was 'designed to enable readers of the text to create a mental image of an experimental scene they did not directly witness' (Shapin, 1984, p. 481). The virtual technology of the text complemented the mechanical technology of the instruments used to conduct the experiment. Initially observed by eyewitnesses, an experiment was transformed into an inscription through the medium of the letter; the letter evolved into the journal article. Its tone was to be neutral and straightforward, a mirror of nature. Shapin (1984) argues that the technology of the experiment – both in its material tools, such as the air pump, and its literary tools in the form of the experimental report – were designed to present the knowledge created by the experiment as a matter of fact, a feature of natural reality and not a human artefact. This written text, with its rhetoric of neutral description, became the model for the dissertation. Knowledge would be created by empirical investigation and reported in a form and manner that was honed to obscure its constructed nature.

Knowledge of research practices within the university was transmitted through the intensely human interaction represented by the 'master' and 'apprentice' model of doctoral education. Doctoral candidates would learn the procedures for discovering knowledge under the guidance of an experienced researcher. The doctorate would be evidence not of candidates' mastery of all knowledge, but research procedures and the successful completion of a research project. The model of the university based on Humboldt's concept of graduate training in research rather than undergraduate education (Russell, 2002) spread, with Yale University presenting its first PhD in 1861 and, in 1876, with the founding of Johns Hopkins University, which was a graduate institution explicitly created along the lines of the German universities. British universities did not follow until the end of the century, when, first, Cambridge approved ScD and LittD (Doctorates of Science and Literature) in 1882, followed by Oxford founding a DPhil programme in 1917. By 1921, all universities in Britain offered PhD programmes (Simpson, 1983). The PhD that these universities offered embodied training in research and the representation of this research in a scholarly text. This is the modern doctorate and barely more than the title links it to its ancient ancestor. The first requirement of a modern doctorate is, in the words of the British Quality Assurance Agency, 'the creation and interpretation of new knowledge, through original research or other advanced scholarship, of a quality to satisfy peer review, extend the forefront of the discipline, and merit publication' (QAA, 2001).

WRITING MACHINES

As the doctorate developed over the nineteenth century, and more candidates pursued the qualification, the dissertation became increasingly formalised and bureaucratised. This is consistent with changes in the wider western society, in which both businesses and governments became departmentalised and rationalised (Yates, 1989). As Yates describes, businesses in the nineteenth century adopted communication and management systems that enabled growth and continental expansion, including the filing system, the typewriter and carbon paper. Universities also adopted these tools, which contributed to the expansion of higher education, including the doctorate by research. One of the key innovations in the production of documents in the last quarter of the nineteenth century was the typewriter. It speeded up the production of documents and replaced laborious hand copying with clear machined texts. The new inscription system facilitated the production of an important but not widely read text in a cheaper and more accessible form that was also more similar to the scholar's traditional book. Fundamentally, the typewriter was, as Kittler writes (1999, p. 228) 'nothing but a miniature printing press'.

The typewriter achieved a form sufficiently stable to be incrementally improved with the 'Sholes and Glidden Type Writer' of 1876, which was built by the Remington company. At the time, Remington manufactured guns and sewing machines; the typewriter would facilitate the rapid production of text in a way similar to the advances of the sewing machine. This typewriter included the QWERTY keyboard and the roller that both held and advanced the paper (Adler, 1973; Yates, 1989). Although early dissertations were hand written and could have been published (the QAA text above alludes to research meriting publication), many were not. For example, Karl Marx's dissertation, which was submitted to the University of Jena in 1841, was not published until 1902, long after his death (Kamenka, 1983). Yale University's first dissertation was handwritten in Latin and six pages long (Weeks, 2002, 18 March). However, the typewriter allowed the production of a text that in many ways resembled a book, with machine-formed letters that ran in parallel lines across the page. (In some countries, for example Switzerland, all dissertations were published in typeset form; however, this requirement did not emerge in the US or UK, where theses had to satisfy at least the commercial needs of the academic publishing houses.) It introduced 'Gutenberg's reproductive technology into textual production' (Kittler, 1999, p. 187). The typewriter allowed text to be written at more than three times the speed of handwriting, and, with the introduction of carbon paper, it allowed the production of multiple copies of the text. This allowed the dissemination of research, which was one of the primary aims of the doctorate, a key aspect to which we return below.

Famous early adopters of the typewriter included Mark Twain (Samuel Clemens), who claimed to be the first author to deliver a typed manuscript for a book, and Friedrich Nietzsche, who, suffering from loss of sight, renounced his professorship at the University of Basel. He subsequently learned to write on an early typewriter and reflected in a letter that 'our writing tools are also working on our thoughts' (Kittler, 1999, p. 200). The use of the typewriter impelled him to write in a telegraphic style, which he felt responded to his new writing machine. Later, the most academic of great writers, T. S. Eliot, composed *The Waste Land* on a typewriter. Like Nietzsche, he found that in 'composing on the typewriter' he 'sloughed off all the long sentences [he] used to dote on'; the typewriter 'makes for lucidity', if not for subtlety (Eliot, 1971, p. x).

The use of a typewriter, however, did not always lead to a staccato writing style. Henry James began to dictate his novels to young women who would type them and came to depend on Theodora Bosanquet and her Remington typewriter. She typed for him from 1907 to his death in 1916. She wrote that dictating to the typewriter invariably led to longer texts; he wrote by hand only for shorter works such as short stories. The sound of the Remington typewriter soothed him, and he asked her to take his dictation after suffering the series of strokes that eventually killed him (Kittler, 1999; Wershler-Henry, 2005).

Rather than seeing the technology of the typewriter as impelling a writing style, it might be better to think of typewriters supporting and reinforcing social roles. Bosanquet was a famous and articulate model of the typewriter, a word initially synonymous for the machine and its operator. Although men initially took up the new profession of typewriting – moving from clerk in the style of Bob Cratchit to typist – women quickly came to dominate the profession, increasing from 40% of stenographers and typists in the US in 1880 to 95.6% in 1930 (Kittler, 1999, p. 184). The proportion of women in commercial schools that taught typing and shorthand increased from 10% in 1880 to 36% in 1900 (Yates, 1989). Kittler describes how, after his typewriter failed as the ribbon became sticky in the humidity of the Italian seaside to which he had retired, Nietzsche hired young students to replace the machine. Nietzsche's sister wrote that 'professors at the University of Zurich "very much appreciated having emancipated women of the time at universities and libraries as secretaries and assistants"' (Kittler, 1999, p. 208). Bosanquet and Neitzsche's secretaries were followed by countless others who typed their partners' dissertations and theses.

Universities changed as well; Andrew Carnegie gave an address at Pierce College of Business and Shorthand in Philadelphia to a graduating class consisting of both men and women in 1891, in which he said:

> I rejoice to know that your time has not been wasted upon dead languages, but has been fully occupied in obtaining a knowledge of shorthand and typewriting … and that you are fully equipped to sail upon the element upon which you must live your lives and earn your living. (Donoghue, 2008, p. 4)

The founding of the land grant universities in the US and the civic universities of Britain represented social change, a widening of the possibilities of university attendance as well as a shift in the areas studied from 'dead languages' to scientific study, whether of linguistics, history, physics or other modern subjects. In the period from roughly the 1870s, when Sholes received his patent for a typewriter and Johns Hopkins University was founded, to the period between the two world wars, textual production became industrialised.

> It became a process with definite steps, a process that could be reproduced on the assembly line. And, for the first time, the representation of work in writing, and all of the attendant filing, sorting, processing, and publishing, became an equally important part of the work itself. (Wershler-Henry, 2005, pp. 137–138)

This was nowhere more true than in the production of dissertations and doctoral students. Although PhD degrees remained relatively less common in the humanities, by 1903 William James could publish 'The PhD Octopus' in *Harvard Monthly* decrying the increasing demand that academics have doctorates (James, 1903).

After an initial period in which typewritten texts were considered inferior or socially unacceptable (Kittler, 1999), typewritten texts came to be seen as superior. Heidegger, quoted in Kittler, wrote that 'mechanical writing provides this "advantage", that it conceals the handwriting and thereby the character. The typewriter makes everyone look the same ...' (1999, p. 199). This neutrality, evoking the objective qualities of scientific reporting, may have been behind Margaret Mead's use of still and motion picture cameras and the typewriter, as reported by Blake and Harbord (2008). Tools such as cameras and typewriters conferred authority and methodological precision. In Bali, Mead handwrote her personal correspondence, but had her field notes typed. 'But despite the transformative qualities of the device (for why bother with the labour of typing unless it has an effect), Mead chose to regard the machine as a neutral vehicle, incapable of affecting that which is produced' (Blake & Harbord, 2008, p. 220). However, as Heidegger wrote, 'technology is entrenched in our history' (Kittler, 1999, p. 201).

The typewriter was part of the toolkit – social, institutional and material – that enabled the expansion of doctoral study during this period. As Haas (1996) indicates, the tools that we use are not neutral. They create possibilities, but also carry their own limitations, which may not be immediately apparent. Compared with handwriting, the typewriter produced texts that were neater and more easily readable and, with carbon paper, more easily multiplied. Typewriting favours written information design and transmission over, for example, graphical information design. Typescripts reproduced well with microfilm, and were much cheaper than typesetting extremely limited distribution books. Typewriting was also consonant with hierarchies of gender and power in this period.

On the other hand, typewriters do not easily support other ways of providing information. Mathematical symbols, graphs and charts, and images such as photographs must be laboriously copied to each text. Colour, and of course sound and moving images are not accommodated at all. These limitations were either invisible or, in the case of mathematical symbols, graphs and photographs were considered marginal issues, which could be moved to appendices to the text.

WHAT IS THE DISSERTATION FOR?

In the 1790s, Gauss investigated the concept of imaginary numbers, opening up new territory in mathematics. In doing so he made extensive use of diagrams – but only in his private notebooks, not in his 1799 doctoral dissertation. At that time and place, any format other than numbers and words was frowned on (du Sautoy, 2003, p. 70). Yet it is far easier to grasp the concept of imaginary numbers using diagrams than text, as Gauss must have been aware. The conventions of the doctoral dissertation at that historical moment militated against the use of the very form which would have most effectively communicated the idea.

As this example suggests, technologies have particular affordances: they facilitate particular kinds of knowledge production. If each modality has its own special properties, how well do these match the objectives of the dissertation? In order to think about this we must first decide what the dissertation, in whatever form, is for.

For obvious reasons, advisory texts for students on dissertation-writing – of which there are an ever-increasing number – tend to concentrate on the document as a form of transaction between the student and the examiners. This is after all the immediately pressing need from the student's point of view. But there is another requirement, especially but not exclusively at doctoral level. The dissertation is a contribution to knowledge – to a body of knowledge shared with a potentially worldwide community. The dissertation must enable the research to be known about, acting as a public document that allows the research to be understood by others. This has an important bearing on the technologies adopted, as we shall show.

The dissertation is part of the means by which the candidate claims an academic award, validating its author's claim to be a researcher at the appropriate level. A doctoral dissertation provides a basis for an in-depth verbal examination, the viva. Indeed, in many countries the viva is a public occasion, uniting in a single event the transaction between the student and examiners on the one hand and the beginnings of the process of dissemination to the wider community on the other.

We assume here that whether it is considered primarily in terms of examination or dissemination, the dissertation is intended to *communicate*. We note in passing that this has implications for practice-based research – discussed elsewhere in this volume – since many forms of practice are not intended as communication but have quite other motivations. The dissertation is expected to communicate in rather distinctive ways. It needs to make explicit things which would simply be implied or skated over in a more casual document. Vagueness, implicitness, allusiveness, ambiguity, multiple meanings are not benefits in the dissertation. Hence, the need to do those things that some dissertation-authors find repellent, such as defining terms, making clear the original contribution to knowledge or clarifying the domain to which the dissertation is relevant. Most uncomfortably perhaps, the dissertation should reveal its own weaknesses. A medium that enables significant failings to be glossed over or concealed cannot serve the needs of a publicly validated examination process.

A dissertation is called upon to convey both the ideas of the author and of others. This is important, since in choosing media according to their appropriateness to the task, we need to distinguish between those which are most appropriate for re-presenting artefacts already existent in a range of media, and those most appropriate to the presentation of the dissertation as such. Let us take the case of a dissertation in field geology. It is very likely that photographic images will be helpful – perhaps essential – in representing geological features. If the dissertation is at least in part about visual evidence, the author must be free to bring that evidence to the eyes of the reader. It is normal in dissertation regulations for such pictorial and diagrammatic material to be admitted into the document. Whereas at one time the regulations might have stipulated that such graphics be placed separately at the end of the dissertation text, now, quite rightly, it is normal for the opposite to be stipulated: that the illustrations should appear at the point in the text where they are most pertinent.

Take now the slightly more complex case of a dissertation about the oral dialects of geographical regions. It can be convincingly argued that the author should be allowed to make use of non-text, time-based media. Audio recordings of the regional speech in question are almost certain to be a good means to capture and communicate as directly as possible nuances that would be lost in another representational form. However, formal, textual means of representing dialectal variation will probably have their own advantages for some purposes. For maximum effectiveness it is likely that we would want to use more than one form of representation for different purposes within a single dissertation, always attempting to select the one that is most appropriate to the needs of the moment. The decision needs to be based on a pragmatic concern for purpose, not on an assumption that one medium is somehow inherently better than another.

The photographs in the geological dissertation and the auditory material in that on dialects serve similar purposes. In both cases, these media seem likely to be the most appropriate for presenting particular kinds of evidence. If in these cases the dissertation were limited to text alone it would almost certainly be less effective in conveying important information to the reader. However, the main argument of the dissertation is still developed through words. What would it be like if the dissertation consisted only of photographs taken in the field, or only of primary oral recordings? Then these other media would be doing two kinds of work: they would be both acting as evidence, and carrying the burden of the argument. If the material being studied comprises films, there is a strong argument (leaving aside issues of intellectual property) for presenting pertinent examples of those films within the dissertation so that what is discussed and what the dissertation author says about it are in the closest possible proximity. This is a different issue from the question of whether the dissertation itself should be a film.

Finally, the dissertation is not simply presentation: its development should clarify and perhaps transform the author's thinking. The dissertation is thus not just a report, but a construction. Creating the dissertation is (or should be) an iterative, reflective process giving its maker insights that were not otherwise achievable. Scaife and Rogers (1996) coined the term *external cognition* for representations (they were interested primarily in diagrams) that we use to assist our own thinking, building on the concept of a *cognitive artefact* discussed by Norman (1991). Crucial to this concept is the idea that there is a reflexive relationship between knowledge-in-the-head and knowledge expressed in some

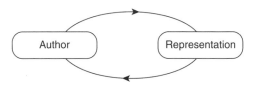

Figure 1.1   An external representation as a point on an arc of interaction, from author to representation and back again

external form. In this model, rather than an external representation being the end-point of a process, it becomes a point on an arc of interaction, from author to representation and back again (Figure 1.1). Maglio, Matlock, Raphaely, Chernicky, and Kirsh (1999) showed how in playing Scrabble the player performs better if allowed to physically rearrange the letters: while trying to generate as many words as possible from the available seven-letter set, more words are generated when players are allowed to manipulate the tiles than when they were not. The player manipulates the representation, and this in return helps generate new ideas which might otherwise have been missed – a nice demonstration of ongoing interaction between an external representation and processes in the mind.

AFFORDANCES OF DIFFERENT MEDIA

We noted above how diagrams seemed to be more productive than letters and numbers as a way to understand a particular aspect of number theory. Each medium has its own affordances, making available certain kinds of knowledge in distinctive ways. Diderot in the mid-eighteenth century was one of the first to make the case, based on his conversations with a single blind man, that the channels of communication we use influence in a fundamental way the concepts we are able to form (Diderot, 1749). Much twentieth century thinking on media has amplified this notion, summarised in McLuhan's quip that the medium is the message. At a more technical level, Larkin and Simon (1987) influentially distinguished between information equivalence and computational equivalence. Two representations are informationally equivalent when in theory the same information can be extracted from them both; they are only computationally equivalent when in reality the human viewer, reader or listener can and does – with equal facility – indeed extract the same information. For all practical purposes connected with a document as complex as the dissertation, we suggest, such equivalence cannot exist. The choice of media will be crucial to what can be conveyed.

It may be tempting to hope that there is some perfect representation. Students may sometimes suggest that a recording of a piece of music is more faithful to its original than a score, that a photograph is more faithful than a drawing or that almost any medium is more faithful than verbal text. This touches on a debate which there is no space to investigate here: suffice to say that the argument here does not concern the faithfulness of a particular representation, but its utility. Our discussion prioritises the *effectiveness* of a medium or mode of communication in the context of the purposes that the dissertation serves.

RECLAIMING THE VALUE OF TEXT

Perhaps the commonest objection to verbal text is that it is too abstract, too remote from lived reality. If the world being studied is visual, aural, tactile, multimodal, multidimensional, polysemic, is it not unreasonable to squeeze this richness into a single channel of communication? Given the growing range of other options such as sound recording, film-making and the construction of websites or other interactive media, it might seem that the textual dissertation is increasingly irrelevant. However, if we consider its properties, text turns out still to have some remarkable strengths. In the remainder of this chapter, we shall concentrate on just two: the visual properties of text, and its usefulness as part of a worldwide information resource.

TEXT AS A VISUAL MEDIUM

Text offers powerful generic structures such as the sentence and paragraph as well as more specialised forms associated with the conventional dissertation such as the table of contents, footnote, index, bibliography and so forth. The familiarity of these structures means that we tend to take these visual forms for granted. However, it is only necessary to glance at a dissertation or any similar structured document to see that it conveys much of its meaning through visual form. Because the forms of conventional writing are just that – conventional – a delicate balance within its characteristic structures is easily overlooked. If we look for a moment at a misguided attempt to introduce a new visual form for text, the merits of the conventional forms stand out more clearly. Tonfoni and Richardson (2000) proposed that the components of texts should be boxed up within differently shaped outlines representing the function of each paragraph, so that, for example a concept would appear in a semi-circle, a comment in a triangle. Such devices would fatally restrict the role of each component in all but the simplest documents. By contrast, the visual structure of conventional writing, typing or printing strikes a balance between allowing the words themselves to speak and enabling the reader to see at a glance the purpose they serve within the larger text and how to read them. Every such device of the conventional dissertation is an invention which should of course be questioned – but it may prove worth retaining, at least for the time being.

Even within the apparently conventional domain of text, variables now used to affect meaning may previously have been used quite differently. For example, in the title pages of books from the sixteenth and seventeenth centuries, the choice of type size was made with 'singular disregard for the content of the message' (Twyman, 1986, p. 201) in a way that we now find strange. This has important implications for digital technology: if the meanings of such spatial variables have been different in the past, it is safe to assume that they will change again.

Two theorists who have given extensive consideration to the effects of making words spatial and visual in the transition from speaking to writing are Goody and Ong, cited earlier. Their work predates most digital texts. Ong claims that, 'more than any other single invention, writing has transformed human consciousness' (Ong 1982/2002, p. 77). The word 'invention' captures an important idea: that writing is a technology, artificial by contrast with the naturalness of oral speech. Goody (1987) identifies two main functions of writing. One is the familiar storage function, allowing communication over time and space. The second, shifting from the aural to the visual, makes possible a different kind of inspection at all levels down to that of individual words. The spatial relationships between words take on new meanings for the very reason that they are abstracted from the linear oral flow. Twyman (1986) remarked that 'graphic language is very different from spoken language. The one is not an interpretation of the other', while Ong (1982/2002, p. 152) argued that text 'styles what we know in ways which make it quite inaccessible and indeed unthinkable in an oral culture'. Goody (1987, p. 187) suggested, 'writing permits not only the recording but the reorganisation of information. One can operate on these representations'. Just as in Scaife and Rogers' example of diagrams as tools for external cognition, the emerging dissertation acts as a stimulus to the mind, even when it is wholly textual. We may be used to thinking this way of diagrams, less so of text.

TEXT AS PART OF A WORLDWIDE INFORMATION RESOURCE

Thanks to digital technologies, the dissertation has progressed from the often unread volume on a dusty shelf to internationally accessible resource. Previously, the bound paper dissertation would be filed in the examining institution's library as the primary record of the candidate's achievement. In most cases from then on it was rarely if ever consulted. It was not easy to find, nor were its contents easily explored. Though the title and abstract might be recorded and made available in some public form, the majority of the text could only be used by someone having physical access to the volume and turning the pages. The case is altered now, thanks to the Web. Institutions increasingly put theses, especially doctoral theses, into institutional repositories, or post them to some other location accessible to Web users. Once the document is present on the Web, it takes only a matter of days before the indexing engines of the major browsers discover its existence. When they do, they trawl through the entire text. As a result, every part of the document can be discovered. In addition, someone using the Web – whether in an adjoining room or on the other side of the world – can get access to the document at the particular point that interests them. There are two interrelated but distinct issues here: whether the contents of a document are discoverable, and whether they are addressable. After assessing how text performs in this respect we shall need to compare the current performance of other media.

DISCOVERABLE AND ADDRESSABLE

In an article in 1945, Vannevar Bush, science advisor to the Roosevelt government, complained that 'our methods of transmitting and reviewing the results of research are generations old and by now are totally inadequate for their purposes' (Bush, 1945, p. 101). He proposed the Memex, a microfilm-based system that would allow not only the compact storage of large quantities of documents, but the meaningful interlinking of each text to many others. Though the system was never built, Bush's article influenced the pioneers of the Web. With the aid of the Internet, what we can now do with text is better than Bush envisaged, since his system relied on photographs of pages: there was no access at the level of individual words except where these had been explicitly identified and marked up with codes by a human reader. Now every word is seen by search engines, however deep within the document. Users can discover a dissertation that is useful to them, even if neither the title nor the abstract gives sufficient clue to the contents.

Not only is text discoverable down to the level of individual words, the user can normally navigate easily to any part of a text document, whether it is a web page, a PDF or a word-processing file. The text is addressable with a high degree of granularity.

It should be noted that computer software currently does not generally determine what a text is *about* – this is the subject of work in semantic search and lies at the heart of proposals for the 'semantic web' (Shadbolt, Hall, & Berners-Lee, 2006) – but the words in a text are usually a very good clue to the concepts it discusses.

What we have said about the discoverability and addressability of text may appear unremarkable until we contrast text with other media. In considering the strengths and weaknesses of particular media technologies as a means to share research knowledge, the current weaknesses of other media in this respect need to be acknowledged. If our means of dealing with images were similar to those available for text, we would be able to discover at a distance everything depicted in an image – and would be able to navigate to the exact place in the image where the object of interest appears. If images were as discoverable and addressable as words, we would be able to rapidly identify all the images on the web containing, for example, a particular species of tree. We would be able to do this whether the tree appeared in botanical drawings, religious allegorical paintings, holiday photographs or any other kind of image. In addition, having retrieved one of these images we would be able to navigate rapidly and assuredly to the place or places in the image where this particular tree appears. Currently, none of this is a practical proposition. In recent years when searching the web for images, users have been obliged to use text as the means of finding images. The user types in a word or phrase and the search engine seems to find images of what was named. What in fact the search engine does is to search the text of the web pages that contain those images and infer – correctly or not – the subject of the images from the surrounding words. Unfortunately, using this method, many of the results returned are irrelevant to the user's needs. Clearly, this is still far from the scenario described above where individual elements of pictures would be easily discovered and accessed. Currently, search engines do not look at what is contained within an image in the way that a human viewer does. Some early steps have been taken towards visual comparison between images, so that the form of the image is used in addition to the surrounding text. Such approaches are based on the idea that related images typically look similar while unrelated images typically look different (Fergus, Perona, & Zisserman 2004). However, this is still not much like the processes that humans use for grouping and choosing images. Humans segment an image into identifiable components. Asked to find images of figures in a landscape, a human looks in every image for figures and for landscape backgrounds, selecting only images with both. A machine search on the other hand is likely to produce images of landscape with no figures and vice versa, together with many other even less relevant images. As often with computers, within limited domains things work better. For example, the FABRIC system (Jia, McKenna, & Ward, 2009) can find shapes within textile patterns; but for general image searching we are still heavily dependent on words.

In recognition of the power of words as a means to access images, an important approach widely used for the large image databases held by picture libraries and other large media collections, is for a team of humans to 'tag' every image: to enter a set of terms that denote the things the image depicts, together perhaps with qualitative descriptions. Whereas the image itself is *data*, such information about the images is *metadata*. This approach has its own problems. One is that images tend to contain a very large number of components, so an exhaustive list of all the things in an image is not possible. In addition, tagging is biased to the needs and preconceptions of the organisation: thus, images owned by a particular organisation, such as a transport museum, will tend to be tagged in relation to the dominant subject matter, whereas the researcher may have completely different interests, such as the clothing of the travellers or the typography of the posters in railway stations. It is less likely that these aspects will have been captured by the tagging process. The other very significant problem for tagging is the cost. Since it requires skilled human intervention, and the number of images is typically very large, the costs can be prohibitive. A way round this problem is to incentivise either the makers or the users of images to create tags, a form of crowdsourcing (Howe, 2006), but this has had limited success. We are not aware of any university that currently asks its students to tag the images in their dissertations.

Time-based data such as moving images and sounds present problems analogous to those relating to images. Large media-owners such as film libraries and broadcasters invest significantly in the creation of metadata. Nevertheless, it will be readily understood that the occurrence of a particular, apparently insignificant, sound in an audio file, or a detail in a moving image – either of them perhaps of great significance to the researcher – is not likely to be captured by such a process. Again, when such media are submitted as part of, or appendices to, dissertations, there is no requirement that significant metadata be provided.

We cannot leave the subject of media technologies and the dissertation without mentioning the problem of longevity: in a scholarly library one can rather easily access every part of an early seventeenth century book, but it is hard to imagine that a digital multimedia dissertation will be accessible four hundred years from now. The dissertation regulations of MIT (presumably more optimistic about new technologies than some universities) permit the use, at least as a supplement to the dissertation, of 'digital or magnetic materials' but warn that 'students should recognise […] that rapid changes in technology make these formats obsolete quickly' (MIT, 2010). Once again, words tend to fare better than other media: the text of digitised books is often recoverable to a far higher standard than the graphics.

REASSESSING THE TECHNOLOGIES OF THE DISSERTATION

It should be clear that there are few easy answers when choosing technologies for the dissertation (or, for that matter, other scholarly documents such as the Masters thesis) today. Any simple notion that non-text is somehow more truthful or faithful than words should be discarded. What matters is how different media technologies measure up to the criteria we have discussed. This requires asking:

1. To what extent do the chosen technologies support an iterative, reflexive form of development as cognitive artefacts?
2. How well are they suited to the particular domains and communication tasks to which they are applied: what conceptual operations do they afford?
3. Can they be used effectively in the transaction between the student and the examiners: can they convey information explicitly and unambiguously, including making any weaknesses apparent?
4. How well can disparate technologies be integrated, so that – once each technology has been chosen for its fitness for purpose – the dissertation functions as a whole?
5. What are the requirements arising from, on the one hand, presenting evidence and, on the other, making the dissertation argument: how are these different demands served?
6. Do the technologies adopted enable the new knowledge created by the researcher to become known, and made easily accessible, to the world wide community?
7. What are the implications for longevity: will the dissertation still be accessible in five, fifty or five hundred years?

NOTES

1. According to Simpson (1983, p. 5), the doctorate developed in the universities influenced by the University of Bologna, while the Masters degree developed in those influenced by the University of Paris (Thomas Aquinas at Paris and Roger Bacon at Oxford held Masters). Both qualifications indicated that the holder was entitled to teach in universities. The undergraduate degree evolved much later.

2. In Australia, oral defences are rarely part of the examination process; candidates are generally assessed solely on their texts (Evans, 2007, p. 117).

REFERENCES

Adler, M. H. (1973). *The Writing Machine*. London: Allen & Unwin.

Blake, T. & Harbord, J. (2008). Typewriters, cameras and love affairs: The fateful haunting of Margaret Mead. *Journal of Media Practice*, *9*, 215–227.

Bush, V. (1945). As we may think. *Atlantic Monthly*, *176(July)*, 101–108. Reprinted in Wardrip-Fruin, N. & Montfort, N. (Eds.), *The New Media Reader* (pp. 37–48). Cambridge, MA: The MIT Press.

Diderot, D. (1749). Letter on the blind, for the use of those who can see (translation 1916 by Margaret Jourdain of Lettre sur les Aveugles, a l'Usage de Ceux qui Voyent). In Diderot, D. (1999). *Thoughts on the Interpretation of Nature and other Philosophical Works*, D. J. Adams (Ed.), (pp. 149–150). Manchester: Clinamen Press.

Donoghue, F. (2008). *The Last Professor: The Corporate University and the Fate of the Humanities*. New York: Fordham University Press.

du Sautoy, M. (2003). *The Music of the Primes*. Fourth Estate.

Eliot, T. S. (1971). *The Waste Land: A Facsimile and Transcript of the Original Drafts Including the Annotations of Ezra Pound*. V. Eliot (Ed.). San Diego, CA, New York & London: Harvest.

Evans, B. (2007). Doctoral education in Australia. In S. Powell & H. Green (Eds.), *The Doctorate Worldwide* (pp. 105–119). Maidenhead, UK: SRHE & Open University Press.

Fergus, R., Perona, P., & Zisserman, A. (2004). A Visual Category Filter for Google Images. *Proceedings of the 8th European Conference on Computer Vision*, Prague, Czech Republic, May 11–14, 2004. Part I (pp. 242–256). Springer: Germany. ISSN 0302-9743.

Goody, J. (1987). *The Interface Between the Written and the Oral*. Cambridge, UK: Cambridge University Press.

Haas, C. (1996). *Writing Technology: Studies on the Materiality of Literacy*. Mahwah, NJ: Lawrence Erlbaum Associates.

Havelock, E. A. (1986). *The Muse Learns to Write*. New Haven, CT: Yale University Press.

Howe, J. (2006). The Rise of Crowdsourcing. *Wired Magazine*, Issue 14.06.

James, W. (1903). The PhD octopus. *Harvard Monthly*, *XXXVI*, 7.

Jia, W., McKenna, S. J., & Ward, A. A. (2009). Extracting Printed Designs and Woven Patterns from Textile Images. VISAPP 2009 – *Proceedings of the 4th International Conference on Computer Vision Theory and Applications*, Lisbon, Portugal, February 5–8, 2009 – Volume 1. pp. 201–208.

Kamenka, E. (1983). *The Portable Karl Marx*. New York and London: Penguin.

Kittler, F. A. (1999) *Gramophone, Film, Typewriter* (translated by G. Winthrop-Young & M. Wutz). Stanford, CA: Stanford University Press.

Kruse, O. (2006). The origins of writing in the disciplines. *Written Communication*, *23*, 331–352.

Lang, J. & Wenger, 4. (1991). *Situated Learning: Legitimate Peripheral Participation*. Cambridge, UK: Cambridge University Press.

Larkin, J. H. & Simon, H. A. (1987). Why a diagram is (sometimes) worth ten thousand words. *Cognitive Science*, *11*, 65–100.

Maglio, P. P., Matlock, T., Raphaely, D., Chernicky, B., & Kirsh, D. (1999). Interactive Skill in Scrabble. *Proceedings of the Twenty-first Annual Conference of the Cognitive Science Society*. M. Hahn & S. C. Stoness (Eds.), Routledge.

Massachusetts Institute of Technology. (2010). *Specifications for Thesis Preparation 2008–2009*. Retrieved December 7, 2010, from http://libraries.mit.edu/archives/thesis-specs/

Noble, K. A. (1994). *Changing Doctoral Degrees: An International Perspective*. Buckingham, UK: SRHE & Open University Press.

Norman, D. A. (1991). Cognitive Artifacts. In J. M. Carroll (Ed.), *Designing Interaction: Psychology at the Human–Computer Interface* (pp. 17–38). Cambridge, UK: Cambridge University Press.

Nybom, T. (2003). The Humboldt legacy: Reflections on the past, present, and future of the European university. *Higher Education Policy, 16*, 141–159.

Ong, W. J. (1982/2002). *Orality and Literacy – The Technologizing of the Word*. New York: Routledge.

Park, C. (2005). New variant PhD: The changing nature of the doctorate in the UK. *Journal of Higher Education Policy and Management, 27*, 189–207.

Powell, S. & Green, H. (Eds.). (2007). *The Doctorate Worldwide*. Maidenhead, England: SRHE and Open University.

Quality Assurance Agency for Higher Education. (2001). *The Framework for Higher Education Qualifications in England, Wales and Northern Ireland – January 2001*. Retrieved September 3, 2007, from http://www.qaa.ac.uk/academicinfrastructure/FHEQ/EWNI/default.asp

Rüegg, W. (2004). Themes. In W. Rüegg (Ed.), *A History of the University in Europe: Universities in the Nineteenth and Early Twentieth Centuries*, Vol. III (pp. 3–31). Cambridge, UK: Cambridge University Press.

Russell, D. R. (2002). *Writing in the Academic Disciplines: A Curricular History*. 2nd edn. Carbondale & Edwardsville, IL: Southern Illinois University Press.

Scaife, M. & Rogers, Y. (1996). External cognition: How do graphical representations work? *International Journal of Human–Computer Studies, 45*, 185–213.

Scribner, S. & Cole, M. (1981). *The Psychology of Literacy*. Cambridge, MA: Harvard University Press.

Shadbolt, N., Hall, W., & Berners-Lee, T. (2006). The Semantic Web Revisited. *IEEE Intelligent Systems 21*, 96–101.

Shapin, S. (1984). Pump and circumstance: Robert Boyle's literary technology. *Social Studies of Science, 14*, 481–520.

Simpson, R. (1983). *How the PhD Came to Britain: A Century of Struggle for Postgraduate Education*. Guildford, UK: Society for Research into Higher Education.

Tonfoni, G. & Richardson, J. (2000). *Writing as a Visual Art*. Intellect Books.

Twyman, M. (1986). Articulating graphic language: A historical perspective. In M. E. Wrolstad & D. F. Fisher (Eds.), *Towards a New Understanding of Literacy* (pp. 188–251). New York: Praeger.

Weeks, L. (2002). You're the Dr. *The Washington Post and Times Herald, 18 March*, p. C1.

Wershler-Henry, D. (2005). *The Iron Whim*. Ithaca, NY & London: Cornell University Press.

Yates, J. (1989). *Control Through Communication: The Rise of System in American Management*. Baltimore, MD: Johns Hopkins University Press.

2

New Forms of Dissertation

Richard Andrews and Jude England

INTRODUCTION

In 2008, in collaboration with Stephen Boyd Davis (Middlesex University) and Erik Borg (Coventry University) we won a grant from the UK's Economic and Social Research Council for a seminar series entitled 'New forms of doctorate: the influence of multimodality and e-learning on the nature and format of doctoral theses in Education and the social sciences'. This chapter presents the case for the series, summarises its achievements and discusses in particular its proposed guidance for universities and other degree-awarding institutions. Initially, the focus was on the doctorate in all its forms, but the aperture widened to include all dissertations and theses – from final year undergraduate to Masters and doctorates. Consequently, our attention in the present handbook is on the dissertation and thesis in the arts, humanities and social sciences, not on any one particular level of award in the education system. Furthermore, although the title of the series included consideration of multimodality and e-learning, a shift in our thinking since the start of the series, and for the purposes of the present handbook, has been to embrace these categories under the umbrella term 'digital'. We are aware of the complexity and range of the term 'digital' (discussed already in the Introduction) and that multimodality, although brought to the fore again by digitisation, is not synonymous with it.

THE PROBLEM OF THE CONVENTIONAL PRINTED THESIS

The problem that the conventional printed thesis presents for students who are exploring the implications, nature and (potential) formats of digitisation, e-publication and digital methodologies, especially where multimodality is fore-grounded, is that it necessitates a linear, largely monomodal (i.e. verbal) medium for the presentation of the research. In much contemporary research, this format is not problematic; even where screen shots and other images need to be included, they can be incorporated into the print medium of the conventional thesis. Often such material, including any moving images and sound, are appended in a CD and bound into the back cover of the thesis.

The speed of technological development indicates, however, that such solutions are partial and transitional. Even CDs have problems of preservation and, more profoundly, a linear print-based format may not be suitable for the subject-matter of the thesis, which may require a different logic and a different rhetorical shape. For example, a research study on complexity theory or on a problem with many variables may require *different points of entry*, allowing the reader/user to choose which point of entry, and which navigational route through the material, best suits their ends. Furthermore, in terms of curation, dissemination and speed of access, electronic formats for the thesis will make it more readily available to other researchers and users. A 2007 survey of policies relating to electronic theses by the Consortium of Research Libraries in the UK (now Research Libraries UK) found considerable variations in practice (eleven institutions were considering the matter, two had voluntary schemes, eight had mandatory depositing of electronic versions of theses). In 2011, things had moved on, and it would be informative to update this research. However, it will still be important to bear in mind such variations, and to ensure that readers/examiners are fully apprised of the need to read such theses differently from – though still as carefully as – the conventional format.

The problem is set out and explored more fully in Andrews and Haythornthwaite (2007), with some solutions offered. This *Handbook of E-learning Research* emerged from a previous ESRC seminar series on dialogue and communities of enquiry in e-learning in higher education. That handbook contains sections on the content for researching e-learning, theory, policy, language and literacy, and design issues. However, it does not address specifically the question of the format of dissertations in the social sciences, nor the questions of multimodality and/or digitisation. Such questions are central to the concerns of research students in this increasingly popular field for research; and for supervisors and users of the research. The problem is compounded by the fact there is little or no research literature on the topic. The information on the degree to which electronic and digital formats are allowed is buried in diverse regulations and practices of the UK universities. Part of the aim of the seminar series was to bring these practices to light, and to see where and how arts- and computer science-based practice could inform new developments in the humanities and social sciences.

CONTEXT

All universities in the UK have print-based requirements for the submission of dissertations in humanities and social sciences. Such formats will remain excellent in terms of suitability for most topics, and for archiving and dissemination. However, the format may not be the most appropriate vehicle for research that addresses e-learning, digitisation and/or multimodality, nor may it be the best way to archive and disseminate the research. The issue is more complex and more urgent than it may at first appear. It is not only a matter of the relationship between the content of the research and its presentation; it is also a matter of the arrangement (in classical rhetoric, *dispositio*) of the research. The print-based thesis or dissertation assumes a linear sequence: chapter 1 is followed by chapter 2, and so on. The conventional shape of the thesis is to set out an introduction followed by chapters on the literature, on context, on methodology, on results and thus on to the conclusion in the social sciences (with some variation in the humanities where the methodology section often comes nearer the front of the dissertation). There is thus an implied logic to the arrangement, and a framework for argumentation.

Research into e-learning (by which we mean any learning mediated by digitally informed electronic media), for example, looks at two dimensions which have implications for the presentation and format of theses. First, *electronic media* on handheld and desktop computers and software such as Word, data processing programs, etc. provide a fluid, revisable approach to verbal language. Increasingly, users of these media are encouraged not to print their texts for reasons of sustainability and ecology. Second, the convergence of these new media with an increased attention to *multimodal* communication (the combination of verbal, visual, aural and other modes of communication) brings about a need to address research both *about* and *through* multimodality. Bringing e-learning together with multimodality (as evident on the computer screen, however large or small, desk-based or portable) provides a rich field for research and particularly the consideration of formats for research presentation and dissemination.

These two dimensions have been considered in the regulations and guidelines for arts-based, computer-science-based and some practice-based doctorates (though not, on the whole, professional doctorates) at some universities, but they do not form part of conventional practice at most universities. Research students are therefore forced to compromise the intellectual momentum of their research by using a print-based, linear format that is not always entirely suitable to their needs, or to the needs of the wider research and research transfer communities. Most literature to date (very little of it is research) is about the archiving of electronic theses. Copeland, Siddhartha and McMillan (2007); JISC (2009); MacColl (2002); Key Services Ltd and UCL Library Services (2006) and UNESCO (2002), all discuss the matter and propose solutions, the latter most comprehensively; but the UK response has been patchy to date, and the humanities and social sciences have not addressed the key issue in the present handbook: the creation, supervision and administration of theses in and about electronic/digital multimodality, as well as the archiving of and access to them.

ARGUMENTATION IN MULTIMODAL AND/OR DIGITAL DISSERTATIONS AND THESES

One of the seemingly intractable problems in considering the nature and format of dissertations and theses in the digital and/or multimodal age is that of argumentation. Conventionally, argument – an essential ingredient in a thesis – is seen to be best couched in words. Indeed, some academics cannot conceive of an argument in any other mode. The questions, then, are (a) whether argument can take other modal forms than the verbal; and (b), if the answer to (a) is positive, what multimodal argument might look like. As such, these considerations are more to do with modal issues than with whether the thesis is digitally conceived and produced, or not.

There is no doubt for us that a single image can contain an argument if there is tension and contrast within it. The contrast and tension must be more than merely visual (e.g. the differences between light and shade, foreground and back-ground). Rather the difference must be conceptual. We are firmly of the belief that a single image can contain such conceptual tension. Notable examples are of a child burning with napalm from the Vietnam war; or the image of a fashion model in contemporary 1960s London mini-skirt at the more soberly (and more 1950s style) dressed crowd at the Melbourne Cup races in 1965. Each image, in its very different way, makes a point and provides evidence to drive home that point. The difference between the points made in verbal argument and those made in visual argument are fundamentally that although the visual images are more direct and more visceral, their impact is less explicitly stated. The 'point' is not spelled out to the reader/viewer; it is implied.

When forms of representation take sequential form, the analogy with argumentation is that much more obvious. A photo-essay, a film and a piece of music all operate sequentially. With sequence comes the assumption of *post hoc ergo propter hoc* – 'after this therefore because of this'. Causality and logic are invoked, and argumentation is more obviously presented.

What happens when more than one mode is at play? There may be different logics of interpretation that are operating, but if the modes are included in an overall sequential array (e.g. a series of chapters numbered 1 to 10) then the argument is deemed to exist in the structural sequence. If, however, the constitu-ent parts of the thesis or dissertation are arrayed in a non-sequential manner (e.g. in a website format), the constructed argument(s) may be more in the hands of the reader than the writer/composer of the work. It does not mean to say there is *no* argument, as the construction of the non-sequential website may be highly conceptualised and thus logical and deliberate. One question, then, that comes to mind for theses and dissertations that take non-sequential format, is whether the university asks for a rationale for the presentation, or leaves it to the examiner to work that out for him- or herself.

THE RESEARCH SERIES

The main aims of the ESRC research seminar series on new forms of dissertation were to:

- Explore the intellectual and practical opportunities, problems and risks concerning the rise in digital and multimodal research presentation – particularly that of the PhD thesis
- Provide a forum for the exchange of practice in this area
- Inform thinking, including that on regulations and guidance, regarding new formats for the PhD in education and the social sciences
- Provide better commerce between the creation of knowledge in the field and its dissemination to users

The objectives deriving from the aims and the problems were:

- The creation of generic regulations and guidance for new formats for the PhD in education and the social sciences
- To see what education and the social sciences could learn from arts-based theses and computer science practice
- The distillation of the debates about new formats into articles, a book and a website
- The identification and possible creation of a sustainable community of scholars to take forward thinking in the field

Overview of the series

In order to explore issues arising from the topic, 'New Forms of Doctorate: the influence of multimodality and e-learning on the nature and format of doctoral theses in education and the social sciences', five seminars and a large one-day conference were held between October 2008 and May 2010. Two seminars were organised by the Institute of Education; two by Middlesex University; one by Coventry University and the large-scale final conference by the British Library. Attendance built up from fifteen attendees at the first seminar to 200 at the final conference. A full record of the series is held at www.newdoctorates.blogspot. com. Many of the contributors to the series appear in separate chapters in the present handbook. Here, we summarise a selection of those papers that are of relevance to the question of how best to prepare for digital dissertations and theses … and which do not appear elsewhere in the present volume.

Benford (2010), head of the Department of Computer Science and Information Technology at Nottingham, discussed interdisciplinary research in mixed reality performance. For over ten years, he has been working with artists to create, tour and study mixed reality performances that combined real and virtual stages and also interaction with computers with live performance by humans. Such work had driven the evolution of an interdisciplinary approach to research that drew on Computer Science, Ethnography and increasingly the Humanities in an attempt to bridge practice- and theory-based approaches. In his presentation, Benford considered the challenges that such work raises for PhD students working in the field and explained some of the ways in which the Horizon Doctoral Training Centre at The University of Nottingham were trying to address these (www. horizon.ac.uk).

Andrew Brown (2010), then Director of the Doctoral School at the Institute of Education, London, examined professional doctorates and electronic theses. The key criterion that has to be met for a candidate's work to warrant the award of doctorate is that it makes an original contribution to knowledge in the field of research. Over the past decade, Brown noted a marked diversification in both the form taken by doctoral programmes and the means available for the (re)presentation of research. Professional doctorates have brought together academic research and professional practice in new ways. Performance and practice based doctorates have placed non(-verbal) textual elements as the heart of the thesis. Electronic theses bring the potential of hypertext and multimodality to the presentation of the process and outcomes of research. Digital technologies create new opportunities for the creation of communities of researchers and for more flexible modes of doctoral study. Along with these developments comes diversification in the community of postgraduate researchers, and changing expectations about what is gained from studying for a doctorate.

Nuhn (2009), in a paper on his mixed-mode PhD in Media Arts (an expanded version of which *is* included in this volume), commenced with a video recording of the key practical project for his thesis, UNCAGED, which is a series of six interactive installations aiming to bridge the gap between the screen-based worlds of computers and their immediate physical surroundings (see www. telesymbiosis.com). This was followed by a discussion of UNCAGED's contextualisation within a broader theoretical framework ranging from aesthetic considerations, scientific and philosophical concepts, the particular role of sound to human computer interaction (HCI). He then described how his critical engagement with the work, largely informed by Jean Baudrillard's conception of the 'real' and the 'virtual', resulted in a heightened sensitivity to the role of digital technology in his artistic practice and how it had strongly influenced his subsequent artistic creations. The presentation problematised two related notions regarding his sentiments about his own PhD as well as mixed-mode PhDs more generally. First, he (simply) questioned the adequacy of academic regulations concerning the actual format of mixed-mode PhDs, in particular the requirement for the thesis to fit on a library shelf, which inevitably seems to obscure the practical dimension of the work. Second, he discussed the relationship between the written and the practical part of the thesis from a more theoretical perspective arguing that, at least in some cases, the former might just be an unnecessary 'interface' narrowing the richness of the practical work within very clearly defined limits and, thus, becoming a mere academic exercise.

Finally, Jewitt (2008) in 'New multimodal and visual forms: what counts as knowledge in the doctoral thesis?' explored the dynamic between visual and verbal modes in the contemporary thesis. Until relatively recently, the thesis has been a written form sometimes quietly 'illustrated' with visual evidence. The noise of audio files and multimodal media has been allowed to live in the appendix of the thesis. This separation of writing, image and multimodal forms is, however, challenged by the rise in research on and through digital media. Visual and multimodal perspectives, technologies and the data these generate in combination, put writing, image and the multimodal into new relationships. Furthermore, this multimodality has led to new forms of transcription and representation of data and findings and the re-thinking of what counts as knowledge. Contemporary multimodal texts were used to explore the opportunities and problems of rethinking the relationship between writing, image and other modes in order to comment on the possible futures for the thesis. The paper explored how image and writing might be put into more dynamic conversations within a thesis to move beyond the written comment on the visual or multimodal; and considered what visual and multimodal dialogues and arguments might look like. In short, consideration focused on how the multimodal might move 'out of the appendix' and into the main body of the dissertation.

In general, the series found that arts-based practice in the nature and format of the PhD (and other Masters and doctoral dissertations) had much to teach the social sciences. A spectrum was defined from the submission of a conventional soft- or hard-bound thesis/dissertation at one end, to non-verbal art installations, films and other media at the other. However, the full non-verbal submission was unusual. Most universities required some degree of verbal mediation of the submitted artefact for the award of a higher degree. The series enabled us to draw a table of different practices (see later in this chapter), and to present and discuss the advantages and disadvantages of the range of types of thesis/dissertation.

We also found that provision for digital submission of dissertations and theses in the UK universities is patchy. Few universities appear to have thought the issue through from the beginnings of the research project through supervision, upgrade (where appropriate) to examination, dissemination, archiving and preservation. Libraries and students seem most well prepared, with supervisors, examiners and staff development trainers least well prepared. Doctoral and graduate schools were all addressing the issue through regulations and guidance in one way or another, but there was no consistency across the sector. The only university worldwide to have moved to the requirement of a digital-only submission of the doctoral thesis at the time of writing is the University of Illinois at Urbana-Champaign.

DRAFT GUIDANCE FOR UNIVERSITIES

One of our objectives in and beyond the seminar series was to prepare draft guidance for universities on how to develop a strategy for dealing with digital dissertations and theses. What follows are extracts from that draft guidance, with interspersed commentary. The eight-page brochure was designed to be of interest to: undergraduate, Masters and doctoral students; dissertation supervisors; examiners; doctoral schools and other departments responsible for the regulations and guidance of under- and postgraduate dissertation work; librarians and the wider arts, humanities and social science community.

The first section shows the cover and a table depicting a spectrum of possibilities in dissertations and theses in the digital age, from the conventional print-led dissemination to the fully fledged multimodal product.

Our aim is to depict a range of possibilities to enable universities to decide where they are on this spectrum (see Table 2.1). Not only does such a table help to categorise *existing practices*; it may also help to project into *possible submissions* at undergraduate, Masters or doctoral levels. Usually, criteria for the marking of dissertations and theses are general enough to accommodate all types of format. However, it might be helpful for specific criteria to be added by institutions for the guidance of students, supervisors, markers and examiners. For example, a thesis that fully exploits multimodality and media might move away from the conventional sequential structure. If it does, questions of logic and argumentation arise, for example, what counts as an argument (assuming one still needs an argument) in a fundamentally non-sequential form like a website? Are the markers and examiners free to read the material in any order they wish, or is there an implied sequence? Are correspondences and links between sections of the material made explicit or left implicit? The next section considers the question of digitisation and digital methodologies more directly.

DISSERTATIONS IN THE DIGITAL AGE

All dissertations in the twenty-first century are digital in one sense, in that even the conventional ones are mostly composed on word processors. But others are digitally born in that they are conceived, researched and presented via digital, electronic formats. There is the likelihood that dissertations of the future may never be transposed into print: that they will be created, presented and stored digitally. Indeed, the digital storage of dissertations makes them (potentially) more accessible and easier to distribute. However, there are implications for indexing and searching if the potential is to be exploited.

Conceiving a research project digitally

Digitally born research imagines the problem, before any research begins, in terms of its resources and the possibilities of transduction or movement between different modes. The topic of the research may be one that *concerns digitisation directly*, like the creation and storing of artworks or film or sound archives. But it may also *use* digitisation, consciously or unconsciously, to transpose one text

Table 2.1 Dissertations in the digital and multimodal age: modes and methods, archiving and access

	Conventional dissertations	Some typographic variation and/or awareness	Illustrated dissertations	A more equitable distribution of visual and verbal modes	Use of other modes beyond the visual and verbal	Fully fledged multimodal dissertations in different media
Type of dissertation	These dissertations are mostly in words. They might include data and tables, which are structural in format, yet still consist of words and/or numbers	Dissertations are typographically inventive, introducing book design standards, use of spacing, typographic codes, etc.	Dissertations are still print-based but include illustrations as well as, or instead of, tables. Usually produced to a high standard	Dissertations move beyond the tipping point to a position where the visual plays an equal or more substantial part than words in the presentation	Presentation includes three-dimensional, tactile and other modes of communication used within a conventional printed format, e.g. examples of material Dissertations might include CDs as appendices	Portfolio, web-based, film-based or other kind of non-print based installation or medium/media submitted for final examination This type of submission *replaces* the dissertation rather than being the 'practical' and/or 'creative' part
Examples	Any number of examples from the arts, humanities and social sciences	Norden Barbara, Royal Holloway, University of London *How to write a play* Includes the text of two plays and photographs, and recorded speech from the author written as a play Savage, R.W.H University of Sussex *Structure and Sorcery: the aesthetics of post-war serial composition and indeterminacy* Includes musical notation, linked to letter and number sequences	Ellis, K. (2007) *The emergence of study manga: a historical and semiotic approach* York: University of York unpublished PhD thesis	See chapters by Juliet Macdonald; Lisa Stansbie and others	Beardshaw, D. (1977) *An introduction to papermaking by hand* Leeds: University of Leeds, unpublished MA dissertation	Milsom, A-M. (2008) 'Picturing Voices, Writing Thickness: A Multimodal Approach to Translating the Afro-Cuban Tales of Lydia Cabrera'. PhD dissertation, Middlesex University, London
Archiving, access and presentation	Archived in libraries in bound, printed form; conventionally transposed to microfiche or possibly scanned as a pdf ... thus making electronic access possible	Microfiche is not possible for colour and other features of book design standard. Pdfs are a more suitable format	Microfiche is not possible for colour and other features of book design standard. Pdfs are a more suitable format	Pdf is possible	This is where archiving and dissemination might become more problematic. Three-dimensional artefacts need to be preserved – or photographed and conveyed in two dimensions	The preservation of websites and other 'non-material' formats. Important to check and ensure persistent of urls and links for dissemination and preservation in the long term

into another, one mode into another. Characteristic of this approach would be a researcher who sees verbal texts as digitally realised, with the possibility of fluid transformation into other forms. A study of e-learning, for example, would assume that text is embodied digitally. The nature of research questions for work that is conceived digitally is an important issue to explore. A 'digital native' would probably conceive of a research problem *ab initio* as one that involved transduction (the movement from one mode to another) and the movement between media.

Researching digitally/electronically

E-research has been around for at least twenty years. It involves the electronic searching for material via databases, e-libraries, e-journals and other digitally stored resources; via search engines; and using the device of keywords to locate and retrieve material. There are implications for training of undergraduate, Masters and research students: what makes a good researcher in the Google/ Facebook generation? What systems and approaches are necessary when researching digitally/electronically? Most search terms are words – is there scope for a search vocabulary that is visual or in some other mode?

Additionally, the use of digital tape recorders, computer-assisted telephone and personal interviewing, easily accessible survey design methodologies, digital cameras, quantitative and qualitative software analysis packages, have all revolutionised the process of research, making it quicker, possibly cheaper, and more data-rich. Researchers will increasingly want to show off the range and potential of their tools and content.

Developing the work multimodally and digitally

There are at least four issues in the development of research with new dissertations: (a) what material will be sourced; (b) what are the possibilities of structuring the work; (c) what methodologies and methods are best employed and (d) what are the best filing and storage routes to take during the course of the project. In detail:

1. *Sourcing material*: if the material is in different modes, is it in separate modes (unlikely) or is it in multimodal combinations (more likely). How will it be gathered and stored prior to methodological and analytical processing?
2. *Structuring*: does the nature of the research question(s) require a particular type of structure to the intellectual shape of the dissertation in order to answer it? Is the conventional structure of an academic dissertation, with literature review preceding pilot study, and results of the main study preceding the conclusion, the best structure for the work in hand? Does the final medium of communication (e.g. a website) follow a different structure? Will there be a combination of both/ is the data to be used primary source material or provided via existing data facilities?
3. *Methodology and method*: does the subject matter and/or the question require a particular methodological approach? Can existing methods be used, or are new methods needed? For example, is transcription necessary? If the study includes video material and video data

analysis, how is that problem best approached? What about ethical issues? What about permissions for use and re-use? Confidentiality assurances?

4. *Filing and organizing material:* what is the relationship between research material that is digitally stored and that which is stored and filed in print? Are there other forms of filing that need to be used? How are different emerging versions of the dissertation stored?

These four points are in many ways at the heart of the problem the present handbook tries to address. It is suggested that in the inception of a research project that will lead to a dissertation or thesis, however large or small, consideration must be given to the nature of the source material (both from published sources and from empirical data gathering). In other words, even if the research project is not 'digitally born', the researcher and his/her supervisor must take into account issues of sourcing and storage during the project, and dissemination at the end (and/or during it). Such considerations are not merely issues of formatting; they are fundamental to the nature of knowledge itself – which draws us on to the changing nature of knowledge creation and storage.

THE CHANGING NATURE OF KNOWLEDGE CREATION AND STORAGE

Archiving and storage of digitally conceived research, or of completed work that is converted to digital format, presents problems to libraries and university repositories, though recent research by RIN and RLUK (2011) suggests that a healthy repository raises the visibility and credibility of an institution. In addition:

- The nature of research and the type of data, and the creation of knowledge has changed radically with innovative digital technologies; expanded methodologies are available to researchers, changing the practice of research; researchers are increasingly exploiting computational capacity and capability for collaborative, experimental and observational research in all disciplines.
- The growing 'data deluge', the simple fact that there is more and more of it as digital technologies make it easier (and often cheaper) to create and collect information. There is an increasing need to integrate traditional and digital formats. Additionally, the value of data as a national asset is recognised with growing emphasis placed on the re-use and sharing of material. The latter in turn raise a range of issues on data storage, preservation and access, as well as permissions and acknowledgments.
- The definition of data has expanded to anything that is machine readable, not just quantitative or qualitative databases, but text, images (still and moving), websites, podcasts, blogs, CCTV and social media from Facebook to Twitter all present a range of issues on preservation and access.
- Research funding conditions now require plans for the long-term preservation of and access to data and place obligations on researchers to ensure is data stored to a high standard. However, researchers have a tendency to neglect this aspect of their work as their primary concerns may be with the research issues and on enhancing their (their institution's) academic reputation – looking to peer-reviewed publication. The Research Excellence Framework criteria in the UK place weight on dissemination and impact, and will have implications for availability and accessibility of data. ESRC, NERC, BA, for example, contractually require researchers to offer all

research data resulting from their grants to designated data centres; many data centres are looking at the creation of persistent identifiers (DOIs – digital object identifiers) to secure the preservation and citation of data, as well as facilitate access.

- Sustainability is a key issue, with some repositories working on the principle of LOCKSS: *lots of copies keeps stuff safe*, but this approach does not operate in a cost-neutral environment and researchers are well-advised to include some sort of assessment of the costs of storage in their initial workplans. Digital outputs also require explicit metadata, that is, description and definition of data, setting out access conditions, data use permissions, confidentiality conditions, embargos, IPR and any ethical issues, all facilitate resource discovery and even the replication of the research, as well as bibliographic records. Interestingly, different disciplines can have very different standards and requirements so explicit, simple to understand metadata are essential.

A number of organisations are working in this field, including: the UK Data Archive, the Economic and Social Data Service, the Secure Data Service, ESDS Qualidata; LIST; Digital Social Research. All include work, for example, on data management; development of new methods for analysis of heterogeneous data and ethical, legal and institutional issues of collaborative working facilitated by digital technologies. The Digital Preservation Coalition: a not-for-profit membership organisation whose primary objective is to raise awareness of the importance of the preservation of digital material and the attendant strategic, cultural and technological issues; the Digital Curation Centre, which exists to provide a national focus for research and development into curation issues and to promote expertise and good practice, both national and international, for the management of all research outputs in digital format and DataCite, an international collaborative initiative on DOIs.

The next section of the draft guidance is focused on regulations and guidance. There is not always a clear distinction between regulations and guidance in universities' documentation. Here we have tended to propose *guidance* so that universities and other bodies can adapt their own documentation as necessary. Basically, regulations specify what *has to be done* for the award of a particular degree; guidance takes the form of *interpretation or explication* of those regulations.

PROPOSED GUIDANCE FOR INSTITUTIONS: UNIVERSITIES

CNAA guidance informed arts-based practice for many years:

> A candidate may undertake a programme of research in which the candidate's own creative work forms, as a point of origin or reference, a significant part of the intellectual enquiry. Such creative work may be in any field (for instance, fine art, design, engineering and technology, architecture, creative writing, musical composition, film, dance and performance), but shall have been undertaken as part of the registered research programme. In such cases, the presentation and submission may be partly in other than written form. The creative work shall be clearly presented in relation to the argument of a written thesis and set in its relevant theoretical, historical, critical or design context. The thesis itself shall conform to the usual scholarly requirements and be of an appropriate length. The final submission shall be accompanied by some permanent record (for instance, video, photographic record, musical

score, and diagrammatic representation) of the creative work, where practicable, bound with the thesis.

We see the CNAA guidance as a precursor and template for what might be adapted by a wider range of disciplines (e.g. humanities, social sciences).

The following wording is *proposed* as guidance for universities which do not have, or wish to review their existing regulations and guidance for the submission of undergraduate, Masters and/or doctoral dissertations. There are two models presented: the 50/50 model, and one in which the main part of the submission is not in words. The advantage of specific examples is that they can serve as palimpsests for other institutions to adapt as they see fit. The Institute of Education at The University of London, for example, has adopted the following wording which embraces and requires both the 'creative' element and words which provide a critical commentary. This example is adapted from a set of regulations for a doctorate:

> If appropriate to the field of study, and subject to approval by the Head of Department at the start of the programme, a candidate may submit, partly in lieu of a dissertation, a *portfolio of original artistic, design and/or technological work* undertaken during his/her period of registration. The work may take the form of, for example, *objects, images, films, performances, musical compositions, webpages or software,* but must be documented or recorded in the portfolio by means appropriate for the purposes of examination and eventual deposit in the [institution] library. The portfolio must include *written commentary on each item of artistic or technological work* and either an extended analysis of one item or a dissertation on a related theme. The written commentaries and extended analysis or dissertation must together be *no more than 40,000 words.* (adapted from Institute of Education regulations and guidance, 2008)

It is also possible to conceive of a dissertation in which there are no words, but 100% 'original artistic or technological work' in modes other than the verbal, and media other than printed 'book' form; or a fully multimodal and/or digital submission. Examples can be imagined in which, rather than a portfolio with accompanying words, an art/design work, piece of software or installation is submitted. But we recommend the retention of a certain number of words in a dissertation submission. The proportion of words to other material might be anything from 49% to 5%. For example:

> A candidate may submit, in lieu of a principally written dissertation, a multimodal work in a range of media. The work must be original in nature, be designed, and be assessable within the terms of the modes and media in which it is cast. It may take the form, for example, of *objects, images, films, performances, musical compositions, fine art, design, engineering and technology, architecture, creative writing, dance and performance, webpages or software.* A full version of the submission must be made available for deposit in the institution library. There must be a cogent written rationale for the submission. The criteria for the award of the degree will include (a) an original contribution to public knowledge, (b) a coherent rationale, (c) scholarship or craft/artistry in execution and (d) sufficient scale to be comparable to work that might be expected of three years' advanced study and (e) of publishable quality.

In other words, what we are recommending does not abandon words. Rather, it uses words where they are appropriate and where the particular affordances of verbal language help to communicate the research – and the intention of the research. These affordances of the verbal (by which we mean oral and written verbal language – not just the oral as is sometimes implied by the term 'verbal') are its sequentiality; its ability to generate and maintain hierarchies of concept and reference; its range of tone; its translatability and its relative economy in terms of the meaning it can carry.

Finally, we propose guidance and questions for students, their supervisors and libraries.

PROPOSED GUIDANCE AND QUESTIONS FOR STUDENTS, THEIR SUPERVISORS AND LIBRARIES

Anyone thinking of undertaking an undergraduate, Masters or doctoral dissertation, or in the early stages of their research, should consider a number of questions. These include:

1. Is the final output of the proposed work 'digitally conceived' or taking a more conventional route? On the spectrum from a conventional dissertation at one end, to a fully fledged multimodal and digital format the other, where does it sit?
2. Is the university or higher education institution open to dissertations in a multimodal and/or digital formats? Is there easily findable and understandable guidance on practice and requirements at the institution? What are the rules by discipline, if different?
3. What are the library facilities with regard to the archiving and dissemination of undergraduate, Masters and doctoral dissertations? Are there digital/electronically accessible repositories of past work? What is the general approach to the e-dimension of searching for material online or via digital databases?
4. How do supervisors or supervisory teams with experience of work using digital and multimodal facilities make themselves known? Are other teams willing to supervise such work?
5. Does the research training programme offered at undergraduate, Masters or doctoral level include methodological or methods sessions on how to research in a multimodal, e-learning and/or unconventional dissertation context? If not, how can students access such help?
6. Is there any experience among the staff of upgrading or of examination at doctoral level?
7. What happen to dissertations after it has been passed by the university? What about support with plans to publish wider?

CONCLUSION

It is hard – perhaps impossible and unwise – to try to come to conclusions in a fast-moving field. Instead, we offer here some final thoughts by way of summary and looking forward to future developments.

It seems likely that the submission of hard- or soft-bound copies of dissertations will soon cease to exist. Instead, we anticipate that students, supervisors, examiners and university libraries will require – or be required to produce – digital copies of completed work, with the option to print out (if possible). We have suggested in the present chapter and elsewhere in the handbook that such changes are about more than mere format. They have implications for the conception, production, storage, access and dissemination of advanced research.

In particular, in the present chapter, we have addressed the problem of argumentation. It is not likely that the basic criteria for the award of a doctoral thesis will change much. Conventionally, these include originality, structural and thematic coherence, 'a contribution to the field', scholarship, accuracy/fluency and the rather vague notion that the work must be 'publishable' in part or in whole, perhaps after revision. The desire for a well-argued thesis is taken for granted, though not always stated. We have suggested in this chapter that as well as issues of storage and archiving, the problem of digital and multimodal argumentation remains one of the most pressing to solve.

Assuming these problems can be solved, we can look forward to a position where undergraduate, Masters and doctoral levels theses/dissertations will be well preserved, readily accessible and accompanied by – say – twenty-page summaries for those, like fellow researchers, who are interested in a fairly technical and full summary report; two- to four-page summaries for the busy practitioner or policy-maker who is more interested in the application of the research; and the conventional half-page abstract for searching, indexing and access.

REFERENCES

Andrews, R. & Haythornthwaite, C. (2007). (Eds.). *The Handbook of E-learning Research.* London: Sage.

Benford, S. (2010). Interdisciplinary research in mixed reality performance – implications for the doctorate, keynote address given at 6th seminar, ESRC seminar series on New forms of doctorate: The influence of multimodality and e-learning on the nature and format of doctoral theses in Education and the social sciences, British Library, May 18, 2010.

Brown, A. (2010.) Professional doctorates, electronic theses and other challenges and opportunities in the evaluation of 'a contribution to knowledge in the field', paper given at 6th seminar, ESRC seminar series on New forms of doctorate: The influence of multimodality and e-learning on the nature and format of doctoral theses in Education and the Social Sciences, British Library, May 18, 2010.

Copeland, S., Siddhartha, S., & and McMillan, G. (2007). *Electronic Theses and Dissertations: Pragmatic Issues and Practical Solutions.* Oxford: Chandos.

Jewitt, C. (2008). New multimodal and visual forms: What counts as knowledge in the doctoral thesis. Paper given at 1st seminar, ESRC seminar series on 'New forms of doctorate: The influence of multimodality and e-learning on the nature and format of doctoral theses in Education and the social sciences', London Knowledge Lab, December 10, 2008.

JISC (2009). *Electronic Theses.* Retrieved November 10, 2009, from http://www.jisc.ac.uk/whatwedo/programmes/programme_fair/project_rgu_etd.aspx

Key Services Ltd and UCL Library Services (2006). *Evaluation of Options for a UK Electronic Thesis Service: Findings from a Study of EthOS.* London: University College London Library Services.

MacColl, J. (2002). *Electronic Theses and Dissertations: A strategy for the UK, Ariadne,* issue 32(July).

Nuhn, R. (2009). Theory and practice in the PhD: A personal reflection. Paper given at 3rd seminar, ESRC seminar series on 'New forms of doctorate: The influence of multimodality and e-learning on the nature and format of doctoral theses in Education and the social sciences', London Knowledge Lab, May 19, 2009.

RLUK RIN (2011). The value of libraries for research and researchers, March.

UNESCO (2002). *The Guide to Electronic Theses and Dissertations.* Retrieved November 3, 2009, from http://www.etdguide.org/

BIBLIOGRAPHY

Bougourd, J., Evans, S., & Gronberg, T. (Eds.). (1989). *The Matrix of Research in Art and Design Education,* London: Central Saint Martins College of Art and Design.

Index to Theses (2009). Retrieved November 3, 2009, from www.theses.com

Networked Digital Library of Theses and Dissertations (2009). Retrieved November 3, 2009, from www.ntltd.org

RELU (2009). Rural Economy and Land Use Programme Data Management Plans. Retrieved November 10, 2009, from http://www.relu.ac.uk/about/Data%20Management%20Plan.pdf

UK Council for Graduate Education (1997). *Practice-based Doctorates in the Creative and Performing Arts and Design.* Retrieved April 8, 2004, from http://www.ukcge.ac.uk/Resources/UKCGE/Documents/PDF/PracticebaseddoctoratesArts%201997.pdf

Van den Eynden, V., Corti, L., Woolland, M., & and Bishop, L. (2009). *Managing and Sharing Data.* Colchester: University of Essex, UK Data Archive and JISC.

Wellcome Trust (2009). Policies on data management and sharing; consent and revenue sharing agreement; good research practice. Retrieved November 10, 2009, from http://www.wellcome.ac.uk/About-us/Policy/Policy-and-position-statements/WTX035043.htm

3

The Role of Doctoral and Graduate Schools

Richard P.J. Freeman and
Andrew Tolmie

INTRODUCTION

While we are all aware of the rapid changes in electronic devices and electronic communication, it is important to be aware of the changes that have also occurred in recent years in both the form of the doctorate and the expectations of what *doing* a doctorate is intended to achieve. Central to managing and leading such change within an academic institution is its Doctoral or Graduate School. In this chapter, we consider the role of the Doctoral or Graduate School, different forms of doctorate, and the shift in emphasis within doctoral programmes from focussing on assessment alone to inclusion of the development of the researcher and their contribution to academic practice and knowledge. Then, we consider the role of the Doctoral or Graduate School in facilitating the provision of theses online and how it will need to support doctoral candidates as part of this process. Finally, we consider its role in the future of the digital thesis.

DOCTORAL AND GRADUATE SCHOOLS

While there is still much diversity across Europe in the provision of doctoral education there are two main models of organisation:

Graduate Schools – an organisational structure that includes doctoral candidates and often master students. It provides administrative, development and transferable skills support, organises admissions, courses and seminars, and takes responsibility for quality assurance.

Doctoral/Research Schools – an organisational structure that only includes doctoral students. It may be organised around a particular discipline, research theme or cross-disciplinary research area and/or it is focussed on creating a research group/network and is project driven. It may involve one institution only or several institutions in a network. (EUA, 2007a, p. 10)

In 2010, 49% of institutions (up from 29% in 2007) across Europe had Doctoral Schools that included only doctoral students while 16% had Graduate Schools that included both doctoral and Masters students (EUA, 2010). These structures support the creation of a stimulating research environment, promote multidisciplinary work, facilitate the maintenance of quality standards and have enabled the provision of transferable skills training. Indeed, one of the ten 'Salzburg Principles' (Christensen, 2005) is that:

Doctoral programmes should seek to achieve critical mass and should draw on different types of innovative practice being introduced in universities across Europe, bearing in mind that different solutions may be appropriate to different contexts and in particular across larger and smaller European countries. These range from graduate schools in major universities to international, national and regional collaboration between universities.

Since Doctoral Schools are over three times more common than Graduate Schools in Europe, throughout this chapter the term 'Doctoral School' is used as a generic term to include Graduate and Research Schools. The Institute of Education (IOE), University of London, operates a Doctoral School model and we will draw on our experiences in this chapter.

THE CHANGING NATURE OF DOCTORAL DEGREES AND THESES

It is easy to treat the doctoral thesis (called dissertation in North America) as completely synonymous with a PhD thesis, where the student undertakes a supervised research project and consequently produces a substantial piece of writing of 80,000–100,000 words that is then examined. However, in the UK and some other countries there are now other possible routes to achieving a doctorate. The UK Council for Graduate Education (UKCGE) found that professional and practice-based doctorates have become increasingly popular in the UK with the number of professional doctorate programmes increasing steadily from one hundred and nine in 1998 to three hundred and eight in 2009 (UKCGE, 2010a). Professional doctorates normally have an assessed taught component that is delivered to cohorts of students. However, there is still a supervised research project that is assessed as a thesis (although usually smaller, more applied and work-based compared with a PhD). Practice-based doctorates are found in the performing arts, where they may involve production of a written commentary (shorter, reflective and contextual) and one of more pieces of 'work', for example, a novel, portfolio of work or performance pieces.

Practice-based doctorates are also found in clinical contexts where they focus on reporting work such as clinical trials. Similar in some ways is the 'New route PhD' or 'Integrated PhD' that combines a structured programme of research with assessed, taught components and a supervised research project that again is assessed as a thesis (although of the same form and length as a traditional PhD). Many institutions also offer a 'PhD by publication' that consists of a number of peer-reviewed published/in-press articles with a substantial commentary linking the work and highlighting its significance and coherence, which is then examined in the usual way (Park, 2005). However, for all these doctorates the focus remains on a contribution to knowledge in the discipline, usually through original research or the application of existing knowledge in an original manner.

One of the roles of the Doctoral School is to support the production and examination of the 'product' of doctoral/Masters study, that is, the dissertation or thesis, whatever form this takes. Institutional instructions or regulations on the production and form of theses have been formed over the past hundred years or so and can easily be seen as set in stone, especially for the PhD, which is commonly regarded as the 'gold standard' academic qualification. Indeed, it is not uncommon to hear academics referring to the acquisition of PhD status as a rite of passage with three years [sic] of lonely work being distilled into a thesis that is then the focus of a terrifying oral examination. This 'need' for a PhD as the most advanced academic qualification is seen as more important than having expertise and experience and experienced researchers who move into an academic environment are often under pressure to obtain this qualification.

However, as the doctorate begins to take on many different forms there is a danger that an institutional reluctance to change could mean that the real learning needs of contemporary postgraduate students are left unmet. In particular, as forms of accepted writing, dissemination and publication practices develop among established academics working in the different areas of research there is a risk that the traditional thesis could become an anachronism. This tension between the new models of writing practice and older traditions will only grow as the former become more ubiquitous. The task of the Doctoral School is to ensure that the 'thesis' is still appropriate for examination, while making use of its closeness to individual departments to ensure that its form retains relevance in the different academic fields. This entails balancing the necessary regulatory requirements for the award of degrees with incremental change in the practices surrounding the production of theses. So, for instance, Wilson (2002) stated that the thesis 'only rarely, and certainly not compulsorily, contains published work based on the candidate's approved research programme'. However, some Doctoral Schools and some disciplines now encourage doctoral students to publish their research during their studies. In part, doing so indicates that the research is making a contribution as it is of a publishable standard, but it also helps the student improve their career prospects. Of course, the 'PhD by publication' – a relatively new innovation in many institutions – by definition contains published work.

Another example is the shift in the specification of the form of theses, though keeping pace with changing demands is not without its problems. The Doctoral School at the IOE has specific 'Instructions and notes on submission, format and binding of theses submitted for the degrees of MPhil and PhD'. Here we will consider a recent version (IOE, 2008) that begins:

> Theses have to be robust enough to endure the examination process and also have to be easily identified: while they are in the Doctoral School, Room 522, Institute of Education, they are stored on bookshelves and need to have the candidate's name on the spine to distinguish them.
>
> Once the examination is successfully completed, copies of the thesis are deposited in the library so that the research undertaken can be publicly available: one hard-bound copy will be deposited in the Institute Library (or the University library if you are examined under University of London regulations). This will be the archival copy. One soft-bound copy will be held in the Institute library and may be used to make a microfilm or digital copy if requested.

Subsequently, instructions are given specifying: presentation; paper; layout; pagination; title page; abstract; table of contents; illustrative material and binding. For the illustrative material, the instructions are:

> Illustrative material may be submitted in the following forms:
>
> (a) Audio recordings: compact cassette tape C60 or C90.
> (b) Photographic slides: 35 mm in 2″ × 2″ frame.
> (c) Illustrative material in other forms (including videotapes) may be submitted at the discretion of the Academic Registrar. Enquiries should be made well in advance of the submission of the thesis to the Research Degree Examinations Officer.

Each copy of the thesis submitted must be accompanied by a full set of this material.

During the examination process, the concern is that the thesis is a single, unitary work that is identifiable and sufficiently robust to survive transport and use. Illustrative material considered here is of three forms: audio; visual and audio-visual. Although these instructions are relatively recent, the three forms of media are already rather archaic. Audio recordings on compact cassette are still available, but audio recording devices provided to students are now exclusively digital. Indeed, it is already difficult to buy devices that are capable of playing compact cassettes. Visual material is now commonly included as a regular part of the word-processed thesis, printed using a colour laser printer if necessary. If a particularly high-quality image is required, it is printed separately on a page. Like the compact cassette, the photographic slide is fast disappearing, apart from some fine art practice. Audio-visual material was once ubiquitous in the form of VHS videotapes (having usurped the Betamax format in the 1980s) and VHS videotapes are still found in many homes. However, the players are increasingly rare with the creator of VHS, JVC, halting production of stand-alone units in 2008. So these three data storage methods – common in every home in the 1990s/2000s – are already problematic for data access.

It is instructive to consider a similar example. The BBC Domesday Project was a pair of interactive videodiscs created to celebrate the 900th anniversary of the original Domesday Book that was completed in 1086. The resource was intended to be widely available for educational purposes and would, like the Domesday Book, be available for future generations to view. However, as little as fifteen years later, it was inaccessible while its predecessor was still completely readable (McKie & Thorpe, 2002).

Although the description of the thesis format contains some anachronisms, there have nevertheless been various efforts to update requirements, though not always in fully joined up fashion. As noted earlier, the current 'archival copy' of the thesis is the hard-bound version that is deposited in the IOE Library. The soft-bound copy was previously used to create a microfilm by the British Library if the thesis was requested as an Inter-Library Loan, but is now being used to create an electronic version upon receipt of a request (and payment) via the British Library's Electronic Theses Online Service (EThOS). The electronic version is in the form of Adobe Systems open standard Portable Document Format (PDF) with each page presented as a scanned graphical image overlaid on text that is produced using an optical character recognition process.

Similarly, the IOE's *Regulations for the Degrees of MPhil and PhD* (IOE, 2008) now contain regulations on requirements for the thesis that necessitate the submission of an electronic copy as well as two paper copies for the examiners and a printed copy for the candidate's use in the oral examination. The Regulations also allow for the 'PhD by publication' model described earlier requiring that the 'published papers themselves may not be included in the body of the thesis, but may be adapted to form an integral part of the thesis. Publications derived from the work in the thesis may be bound as supplementary material at the back'.

In addition, there is provision in the Regulations for the practice-based doctorates described earlier where a portfolio of work may be submitted taking the form of 'objects, images, films, performances, musical compositions, webpages or software, but must be documented or recorded in the portfolio by means appropriate for the purposes of examination and eventual deposit in the Institute library'. It is important to note this last point, and the tensions it reveals. These institutional Regulations focus on the perceived historical requirements of a thesis examination and storage of the thesis in the library, but *not* on wider, online, dissemination. Currently, materials stored in the library include bulky items such as VHS videocassettes and some physical objects that are the product of the doctoral work. These materials are shelved alongside the hard-bound thesis creating storage issues for the library, which can only worsen as the number of doctoral theses examined steadily increases. It is also questionable how well these requirements meet the needs of the examiners and we will consider this later.

WHY SHOULD A THESIS BE MADE AVAILABLE?

So far, we have focused on the submission requirements and the subsequent storage of the examined thesis or portfolio. Although it is usually stored, it is not normal for work examined as part of a university award to be made publicly available. For example, an institution retains examination scripts for a number of years post-examination, but only in case of student appeals and for quality control audits. Why should a doctoral – or Masters – thesis be different?

In the UK, the recent focus has been on the development of the researcher, with the Joint Skills Statement (2001) setting out seven areas that doctoral research students funded by the UK Research Councils would be expected to develop during their research training. In 2010, all the skills and attributes of the Joint Skills Statement were incorporated within the Researcher Development Statement (RDS) that sets out the knowledge, behaviours and attributes of effective and highly skilled researchers appropriate for a wide range of careers – making explicit the continuity expected between doctoral training and subsequent career development. Across Europe from 2007 to 2010 the number of institutions offering additional taught courses rose from 49% to 72% (EUA, 2010b).

The main driver for this focus on researcher development was Sir Gareth Roberts' *SET for success: The supply of people with science, technology, engineering and mathematics skills* (Roberts, 2002). Roberts himself said that 'The product that the PhD researcher creates is not the thesis – vital though that is to their subject area through the creation of original knowledge – no, the product of their study is the development of themselves'. In this famous statement, Roberts was noting the two key goals of doctoral study: the creation of original knowledge and the development of the appropriate academic skills set.

Roberts reminds us that the creation of original knowledge is vital to the subject area. This requirement is arguably what distinguishes the doctorate from other lower levels of academic qualification. However, if original knowledge has been created, then it should be of interest to the wider academic community. One approach to the doctoral thesis is that it should be thought of as an 'apprentice piece', akin to the carpenter producing a scaled-down piece of furniture to demonstrate their skills and knowledge (cf. a 'masterpiece' that was required to become a master craftsman). In this view, a thesis might (and hopefully does) contain research of wider interest, but that research has typically been seen as best produced separately as publications (i.e. journal articles, books) and/or presentations, often after the thesis has been completed. Indeed, the necessity of reworking the thesis to make it suitable for 'real' academic usage highlights the fact that the traditional thesis is not really well adapted to the professional needs of doctoral students. However, Vitae (2010) reported that six months after graduation just 26% of doctoral graduate respondents were working in higher education research roles (with another 17% in teaching and lecturing roles) and that fell to 19% of respondents (with another 22% in teaching and learning roles) three and half years after graduation. Even for those choosing careers in higher education, time to produce publications from the thesis is often limited, especially at the start of their careers. This is particularly problematic for those in

Arts and Humanities who might wish to produce a book building on the work presented in their thesis. For those in research posts, there is usually no time available within their research contract for their own work so that must be completed in their spare time.

Given the difficulties of subsequent publication of the thesis or material from it, it is valuable for the research to be made available as a thesis. The research might have been presented as an oral or poster presentation at a conference, but it is more useful to the consumer of the research if it is available in more detailed form such as a thesis. Since the thesis makes an original contribution, other researchers may wish to cite the thesis itself. Such citation benefits the student in terms of their academic career progression and can even produce a demand for the material to be published elsewhere, for example, as a monograph. There is also a benefit to the institution as citation of theses is a marker of prestige. Awareness that the thesis will be made available encourages students to remember that their work is not a mere examination script, but a valued contribution to knowledge. With their focus on both the doctoral process and the development of doctoral students, the Doctoral School is well placed to institute a policy that theses are made available in a digital archive as part of normal practice. Then, students can be made aware from the start of their doctoral studies that the audience for their thesis will be greater than their supervisor and examiners – and can write accordingly, with appropriate training support from the Doctoral School.

THE EXAMINATION PROCESS

We have focused on the digital thesis as something that is produced post-examination. However, it seems rather wasteful to produce another version of the thesis. Instead, there is the possibility of producing a digital thesis as the only form of the thesis. This carries a number of potential advantages for the examination process itself. For instance, with the increasing focus on developing skills as part of the doctorate, Doctoral Schools often provide support not only for preparation for the thesis examination, but also for the production of the thesis itself. If a digital thesis were introduced, it is likely that the Doctoral School would then move to extend support to enable inclusion of non-traditional content such as audio and video material, making this a more seamless part of what examiners see.

Similarly, part of the examination process requires that the examiners are satisfied that the thesis is the work of the candidate. An advantage of electronic submission is that it facilitates use of plagiarism detection software and compliance with requirements such as maximum word length. Such initial screening is usually carried out within the Doctoral School, as happens at IOE. Routine use of plagiarism detection software also protects the author of a thesis from subsequent plagiarism as their thesis will have been added to the archive of documents.

A common complaint of thesis examiners, particularly in the Arts and Humanities and Social Sciences is the sheer bulk of a bound thesis. Even if the examiner reads the thesis in their office, the examiner still has to carry the thesis to the examination. For an external examiner, that may mean carrying the thesis some distance including on a flight. Electronic submission makes possible the use of highly portable electronic devices, such as laptops, netbooks and, more recently, Amazon's Kindle or Apple's iPad. These do not simply facilitate reading of the thesis, but enable two other activities: annotation and searching. Examiners often make annotations to a thesis they are examining, either in the form of numerous post-its or scribbled notes in margins. An electronic device (handheld, laptop or a desktop computer) allows notes of unlimited length to be added at any point, which can then be easily shared with the doctoral candidate if the examiner wishes to do so. The other activity – searching – is very difficult with a printed thesis. An examiner might dimly remember reading something similar earlier in a thesis (or the exact opposite point having been made), but visually searching for material is time-consuming and difficult. With a digital thesis, the task becomes trivial, easing the demands on the examiners.

Compared with a bound thesis these portable electronic devices are very small, lightweight and may already be owned and used by the examiners. Unfortunately, such devices are a recent consumer innovation with a wide variety currently available with other versions in developments by a number of manufacturers. This creates a dilemma for the Doctoral School, which is responsible for managing the examination process. The Doctoral School might decide to adopt a particular standard, for example the iPad, and provide guidance in the preparation of a suitable electronic thesis as well as access to suitable iPads for examiners. An additional problem might be that the examiners have not previously used an iPad and might require training, which would require resources from the Doctoral School and demand time and effort from the examiner. These difficulties notwithstanding, the best agent for managing these changes remains the Doctoral School, as it possesses the right level of focus and coordination within the institution.

In the short term, it seems likely that the digital thesis would be an option for the examination process, but with a standard printed thesis required in addition. Over time, it is likely that such content readers will become more ubiquitous and standardised, facilitating their use by examiners. Moves towards multimodal content in theses can only accelerate this shift. Another advantage of the use of a digital thesis for the examination is the saving of the resources required, that is, high quality paper, high quality printing and binding, which can be a substantial cost when doctoral funding might have finished. Since most theses require modification post-examination, examination copies of the thesis are usually soft bound, with hard bound versions produced once the examiners have passed the thesis. Indeed, where modifications are required it is usual for candidates to have these changes approved via email, perhaps even using the 'track changes' function in software such as Microsoft Word. The digital thesis avoids the production of multiple physical copies with the time and cost these involve.

WHY SHOULD A THESIS BE MADE AVAILABLE ONLINE?

Since July 1980, every thesis produced in the UK has included an abstract of up to 350 words produced by the author, which has been stored electronically (and, since 1988, 150-word abstracts have been similarly produced). Over the period 1970–1985, the abstracts were available on microfiche, but the 44,000 are now available in PDF format. From 1986, the abstracts were searchable electronically and are now available over the internet (www. theses.com). Where a thesis is not available electronically, it is possible in the UK to request a copy via the Inter-Library Loan system for a modest fee. Previously, the thesis would be sent to the British Library where a copy would be made onto microfilm and the thesis returned to the original library. However, in January 2009, the British Library launched EThOS – Electronic Theses Online Service – (http://ethos.bl.uk/), which enables free searching of more than 250,000 theses with digitisation of non-electronic theses within thirty days.

The decision as to whether electronic submission is simply encouraged or is mandatory is usually made within the Doctoral School. It is typical to begin by making electronic submission optional, but institutions can be expected to make it mandatory once they are assured that there will be no subsequent problems. Increasingly, theses are being submitted electronically and post-examination stored in electronic archives. Table 3.1 shows how the majority of sampled institutions in the UK, across all sectors, are making electronic submission mandatory. In addition, Table 3.1 demonstrates the existence of electronic repositories for theses, although these are predominantly for access only within the institution.

A measure of the ubiquity of general e-repositories can be seen at OpenDOAR (Directory of Open Access Repositories http://www.opendoar.org) who state 'OpenDOAR maintains a comprehensive and authoritative list of institutional and subject-based repositories ... sites where any form of access control prevents immediate access are not included: likewise sites that consist of metadata records only are also declined'. Of the 1915 repositories in their directory (as of April 2011), the majority are in Europe (878, 46%) or North America (460, 24%). However, there are repositories across the world: Asia (318); South America (112); Australasia (80); Africa (47); Caribbean (12); Central America (8). Importantly, since these general e-repositories are accessible online, they are freely *available* anywhere in the world that has internet access. The overwhelming majority of these repositories are institutional (82%) or cross-institutional (11%). The most common content type for these repositories are journal articles (65%), followed by theses and dissertations (52%). Interestingly, 23%

Table 3.1 Trends in electronic submission and storage of theses. Taken from UKCGE (2010b)

Institutional group	Sample size	E-submission		Sample size	Repository for E-theses	
		Encouraged	Mandatory		Internal	External
Russell group[1]	9	4	6	10	9	3
1994 group[2]	9	3	7	9	9	4
Post-1992 group[3]	25	7	19	30	28	7
Other	8	2	6	8	7	2
Percentage of total survey sample	65	20	48	72	67	20

[1] The Russell group is an association of 20 UK universities that account for approximately two-thirds of the UK universities' research grant and contract funding in the UK.
[2] The 1994 group is an association of 19 smaller, research-intensive universities in the UK.
[3] The post-1992 group is an umbrella term for those institutions given university status through (and since) the Further and Higher Education Act 1992.

have multimedia and audio-visual materials. So while most of these institutional e-repositories are focused on provision of journal articles more than half also make available theses and dissertations and it seems likely that this proportion will steadily increase.

Theses are increasingly available online, but what are the benefits, and to whom? Universities worldwide are competing for students and that competition is not simply on a national basis, but is increasingly focused on international students especially at the postgraduate level. To attract the best students, a Doctoral School needs to ensure that its research outputs (i.e. theses and dissertations) are as widely available as possible. The Joint Information Systems Committee (JISC) noted in a briefing paper (JISC, 2008) that 'there has never been a more important time for universities to secure the highest possible visibility for their research publications and outputs. One of the ways in which universities can make their research more visible is to encourage their researchers to deposit their research papers into an Open Access repository'. What is true for research papers is even more true of research theses. A doctoral thesis on a single library shelf is accessible only to those visiting that library in person. Once digitised, and made available in an open access repository, it can be a resource accessible worldwide and returned as a search result using applications such as Google Scholar. This may be a benefit for the institution, but it is also valuable for the doctoral graduate as it increases their visibility. With the increase in availability of resources such as Zotero, Mendeley and EndNote as well as their social networking aspects, researchers are likely to become increasingly comfortable using digital versions of research.

Another advantage of making material freely available online is that it then becomes accessible to researchers in other countries, especially those with more limited resources. For example, Ghosh (2009) notes how online repositories are increasing accessibility in India. Finally, it is worth noting that readers with accessibility problems, for example, visual impairment, are able to more easily access printed text when theses are made available electronically. In particular, when the theses are available online, it facilitates access by the reader's own device that they will have had configured for optimal use by them. Ensuring all students are able to access materials is a key concern for a Doctoral School.

ISSUES WITH ELECTRONIC PROVISION OF THESES

While the momentum for theses to be made available online appears unstoppable, there are issues with making theses available electronically. In particular, there are issues of copyright, confidentiality, student support for electronic production and reputational risks for the institution.

The essence of the doctorate is the 'creation of original knowledge' so it seems somewhat perverse that one of the biggest issues with the digital thesis is making it widely available. Copyright owners have traditionally been very generous to doctoral researchers in allowing use of copyrighted material (such as text and images) without payment of a copyright fee. However, this generosity is conditional on the thesis not being published, but it has been acceptable for the thesis to be made available in a university library. If the thesis is digitised and made more widely available, some copyright holders might be reluctant to make their materials available. Some archives, for example, collections of an author's personal correspondence, make it a condition of access that those letters are not published. Similarly, images of artworks are made available at no cost on condition that those images are not 'published'. Inclusion of such material in the thesis might be essential for the examination process, but unacceptable if the thesis was made widely available. By contrast, some STEM funding is conditional on the results being made freely available, as well as the raw data. Of course, the 'PhD by publication' by definition contains published work and most journal and book publishers require the transfer of copyright as a condition of publication.

Another problem results from universities being encouraged by government to work with industrial partners. With funding from other sources being reduced, industry is an alternative funding source for doctoral study (Crespo & Dridi, 2007), but relationships between academia and business can lead to tensions (Dooley & Kirk, 2007). Academia operates by sharing with the academic community; peer-review of results and ideas is central to academic work. By contrast, business seeks a competitive advantage and tries to keep its knowledge as secret as possible (i.e. trade secrets) or available under licence (i.e. patents and copyright). All of these are already threatened in the digital age via illegal activities such as hacking and anonymous file-sharing, but the Doctoral School must ensure that procedures are in place that protect the interest of copyright holders and commercial funders of research while also protecting the interests of academia, including the interests of the doctoral candidate.

In 2010, UKCGE sent out a survey on confidentiality of theses to all one hundred and twenty-three of its member institutions with 67% responding. Respondents were asked whether their regulations permit theses submitted for the degree of PhD to be kept confidential after the examination period, whether the regulations stated an upper limit on length of time that theses can be kept confidential and the usual reasons given for theses to be kept confidential (among other questions). The maximum time period varied across institutions from just one year to five years. In Table 3.2, the cited reasons for requesting restricted access to theses across a variety of universities in the UK are given. Strikingly, commercial reasons are the most common reason for restricting access for all types of universities and these are typically found for Science, Technology, Engineering and Mathematics (STEM) subjects. With pressure on universities to seek more industrial funding for research studentships, it is important that the Doctoral School monitor these requests for restricting access to theses and explore ways in which they might be reduced. For example, confidential information might be included as an annex to the thesis to enable easy removal before the thesis is made available online. In Arts and Humanities, Social Sciences and Medicine, the concerns are more usually related to protection of individuals – the participants in research or the researcher themselves. For participants, the main concern is that they might be identifiable from the research and could suffer from this loss of privacy. For researchers, the main concern is that they might be vulnerable to reprisals due to the nature of the work.

The Doctoral School is able to provide support and guidance to students to address these problems. For copyrighted images, the image can be removed by the author from a thesis that is to be made available via an online archive with an explicit reference to the image concerned. For example, if the work of art were available in a museum's permanent collection then a link to the museum's web site would be sufficient. Alternatively, it might be possible to use a lower resolution version of the artwork or a black and white image rather than colour that

Table 3.2 Cited reasons for requesting restricted access to theses. Taken from UKCGE (2010b)

Reasons for requesting restricting access to theses	Russell group	1994 group	Post-1992 group	Other
Commercial reasons	12	12	34	8
Protection of individuals	5	5	6	4
Protection of priority in publication	5	5	4	4
Third party confidentiality	3	4	0	2
Politically or religiously contentious material	2	2	10	2
National security	1	0	2	1

would be sufficient for its use within the context of the thesis, but not problematic for the copyright holder (as Wikipedia does with 'fair use' of images). Where the concern is to protect individuals, it is usually possible to remove the material that identifies those individuals. For example, information necessary in describing individuals for the purposes of the thesis examination might be removed when the thesis is made more widely available. As theses become more multi-modal, the Doctoral School is well-placed to act swiftly to develop a similar procedure that might become necessary for audio and video material. Such material might be invaluable for the examiners of the thesis but could be replaced with a transcript or a description of the behaviour seen or whatever is most appropriate for academics working in that field.

Although copyright is assigned to a publisher when research is accepted for publication, there has been increasing pressure on publishers to allow a version of the material to be made accessible in institutional archives (e.g. for the IOE, it is the e-prints system http://eprints.ioe.ac.uk/). Some publishers have introduced either an embargo period (e.g. twelve months after publication) and/or require the published work to be made available in a word-processed form (i.e. the 'author version') rather than the final version seen in the journal article or book (i.e. the 'print ready' version). For those students taking the 'PhD by publication' route, these procedures should allow their 'thesis' to be made available online in some form. Similarly, most institutions have regulations that restrict access to post-examination versions of theses. UKCGE (2010b) found that just ten institutions, from seventy-nine who responded, did not currently have such specific regulations. Of the total sample, sixty-six (86%) stated a maximum time for which access to theses could be restricted, with that ranging from one to five years. This delay in making the thesis available allows the patent process to be completed. A delay is usually acceptable to both the industrial partner and the university and is often explicitly specified in the funding agreement that is drawn up in conjunction with the Doctoral School. The other approach is to simply remove particular components of the thesis in line with direction from the industrial partner.

The actual mechanics of making material available online in an institutional repository is normally the responsibility of the institution's library, but the Doctoral School is usually responsible for ensuring that the material is in a suitable format and supporting the student in achieving that. If a student is aware at the start of their studies that their thesis was expected to be made freely available and searchable online then recognition of that wider audience might affect the form of the student's final thesis. Indeed, there may be pressure from some students for them to be allowed an examination version of thesis and an archive version and the Doctoral School would be best placed to provide leadership within the institution on this matter.

Similarly, such openness may have consequences for the institutional reputation. Currently, the quality control of an institution's doctorate is controlled by the institution, which selects the supervisor, internal and external examiners.

When theses were simply shelved in institutional libraries, they were largely forgotten. If all theses are online, their quality is subject to question. For example, in 2011 the then German Defence Minister, Karl-Theodor zu Guttenberg, was forced to stand down after he was found to have plagiarised substantial parts of his PhD thesis (BBC News, 2011a) and Saif Gaddafi's PhD thesis authenticity was called into question with claims of plagiarism and ghost-writing (BBC News, 2011b). With theses readily available it is easy for interested individuals to explore and debate issues of quality control relating to the thesis. In both these cases, there has been substantial reputational damage to the institutions concerned, University of Bayreuth and London School of Economics and Political Science, who have had their academic integrity and competence questioned. Here again there is an important role for the Doctoral School as it is able to ensure that there is consistency in the process of appointment of examiners across the institution by monitoring the process across departments or overseeing the appointments in a central committee. In addition, some Doctoral Schools such as the IOE, have introduced independent chairs for the oral examination. The United Kingdom's Quality Assurance Agency for Higher Education (QAA) states:

> Institutions will wish to satisfy themselves that processes enable the viva to meet agreed criteria for fairness and consistency. Some institutions now appoint an independent, non-examining chair: this is thought to be good practice, not least in ensuring consistency between different vivas and in providing an additional viewpoint if the conduct of the viva should become the subject of a student appeal. (QAA, 2004)

The independent chair does not read the thesis so may be from a completely different discipline to that of the thesis. Instead, the independent chair is responsible for ensuring that regulations are followed appropriately and monitoring the conduct of the oral examination. For this reason, the Doctoral School usually coordinates their appointment across the institution, balancing out the burden across disciplines and individuals.

THE FUTURE OF THE DIGITISED THESIS/DISSERTATION

With the focus having shifted from the 'product' of the doctorate (the thesis) to the 'process' and an internet era notable for its provisionality, it seems almost certain that the doctoral thesis will continue to change. Already, the doctorate takes a number of different forms, with an increase in portfolio models. Researchers are increasingly using social networking as part of their research process using blogs and microblogging (e.g. Twitter) to engage with communities, providing a running commentary on their progress and their results. In this chapter, we have considered the thesis as a static summation of the doctorate that might be reworked once the doctorate is completed. When we were growing up, most 'educated families' either had or aspired to have a set of encyclopaedia such as the *Encyclopaedia Britannica*. Today, Wikipedia has largely replaced these static tomes, updated in seconds in the light of current events. It is possible that the thesis could become something similar – a resource for the academic community that either continues to develop or is largely ignored in the manner of Lakatos' research programmes (Lakatos & Musgrove, 1970).

CONCLUSIONS

We have shown how the doctorate continues to change from a largely institution-only activity to a focus on the genuine contribution to knowledge and the development of the researcher themselves. As the doctorate continues to change its form to match the publication standards of different disciplines, the Doctoral School is well-placed to ensure that the institutional standards keep pace with these changes and that the researcher is properly supported in developing the necessary awareness and skills required. The Doctoral School will need to ensure that it is proactive rather than reactive to such events and to avoid a conservative retreat to a mythical gold standard. Indeed, it is essential that the Doctoral School take the lead within the institution in making the arguments for change. There should be a focus on the key aspect of the doctorate – the original contribution to knowledge – and an engagement with a truly digital future.

REFERENCES

BBC News (2011a). German Defence Minister Guttenberg resigns over thesis. Retrieved from http://www.bbc.co.uk/news/world-europe-12608083

BBC News (2011b). LSE investigates Gaddafi's son plagiarism claims. Retrieved from http://www.bbc.co.uk/news/education-12608869

Christensen, K. K. (2005). *Bologna Seminar: Doctoral Programmes for the European Knowledge Society*. Retrieved from http://www.eua.be/eua/jsp/en/upload/Salzburg_Report_final.1129817011146.pdf

Crespo, M. & Dridi, H. (2007). Intensification of university–industry relationships and its impact on academic research. *Higher Education, 54*, 61–84.

Dooley, L. & Kirk, D. (2007). University–industry collaborations: Grafting the entrepreneurial paradigm onto academic structures. *European Journal of Innovation Management, 10*, 316–332.

EUA (2007a). *Doctoral Programmes in Europe's Universities: Achievements and Challenges*. Retrieved from http://www.eua.be

EUA (2007b). *Trends V: Universities shaping the European Higher Education Area*. Retrieved from http://www.eua.be

EUA (2010). *Trends 2010: A decade of change in European Higher Education*. Retrieved from http://www.eua.be

EUA Council for Doctoral Education (2010). *Salzburg II Recommendations: European universities' achievements since 2005 in implementing the Salzburg Principles*. Retrieved from http://www.eua.be/Libraries/Publications_homepage_list/Salzburg_II_Recommendations.sflb.ashx

Ghosh, M. (2009). E-theses and Indian academia: A case study of nine ETD digital libraries and formulation of policies for a national service. *The International Information & Library Review, 41*, 21–33.

Institute of Education (IOE) (2008). Regulations for the Degrees of MPhil and PhD.

Joint Information Systems Committee (JISC) (2008). Managing and sharing research resources: How Open Access repositories can help. Briefing paper.

Lakatos, I. & Musgrove, A. (Eds.) (1970). *Criticism and the Growth of Knowledge.* Cambridge: Cambridge University Press.

McKie, R. & Thorpe, V. (2002). Digital Domesday Book lasts 15 years not 1000. *The Observer,* 3 March. Retrieved from http://www.guardian.co.uk/uk/2002/mar/03/research.elearning

Park, C. (2005). New variant PhD: The changing nature of the doctorate in the UK. *Journal of Higher Education Policy and Management, 27,* 189–207.

QAA (2004). *Code of Practice for the Assurance of Academic Quality and Standards in Higher Education.*

Roberts, G. (2002). *SET for Success: The Supply of People with Science, Technology, Engineering and Mathematic Skills* – The Report of Sir Gareth Roberts' Review. London: HM Treasury.

United Kingdom Council for Graduate Education (UKCGE) (2010a). *Professional Doctorate Awards in the UK.*

United Kingdom Council for Graduate Education (UKCGE) (2010b). *Confidentiality of PhD Theses in the UK.*

United Kingdom Council for Graduate Education (UKCGE) (2010c). *A Review of Graduate Schools in the UK.* http://www2.le.ac.uk/departments/gradschool/about/role/external/publications/graduate-schools.pdf

Vitae (2010). *What Do Researchers Do? Doctoral Graduate Destinations and Impact Three Years On.* Retrieved from http://www.vitae.ac.uk/policy-practice/107611/What-do-researchers-do-.html

Wilson, K. (2002). Quality assurance issues for a PhD by published work: A case study. *Quality Assurance in Education, 10,* 71–78.

4

Digital Literacies for the Research Institution

Helen Beetham, Allison Littlejohn
and Colin Milligan

DIGITAL LITERACY AND KNOWLEDGE WORK

The academic community has a complex relationship with digital technology, driving innovation and often spearheading adoption, but troubled by the impact that socio-technical change is having on long-established norms. No core university processes are untouched by the digital revolution. In this chapter, we describe how research and writing at university level demand a set of capabilities at the interface of traditional scholarship and technology use, which we call 'digital literacy'. We set out some of the challenges this represents to students, focusing on postgraduates. We also introduce a framework for describing digital literacy and for supporting students as they bring digital tools to bear on the work of knowledge creation.

Digital literacy is now an essential capability for researchers. Its importance is due to broader socio-political and technological changes (Jakupec & Garrick, 2000) that include new working practices and employment patterns, changes in the nature of knowledge and the ways it is circulated, and new kinds of knowledge exchange across disciplinary and sectoral boundaries. Professional roles now require the capacity to work productively with digital knowledge, and to participate in digital networks of collaboration and co-creation. Professionals also have to take responsibility for their own learning (Rychen, 2003) not only through formal postgraduate study and professional development opportunities but across their working lives. Digital practices evolve with extraordinary speed, demanding individuals who can respond with resilience and flexibility (Candy, 2004; Hiemstra & Brockett, 1994).

Global digital networks are having a pragmatic impact on employment patterns and the ways organisations recruit the expertise they need. For example, in the UK over 90% of graduate jobs demand some form of ICT competence, and around 70% involve 'knowledge intensive' roles (Levy & Hopkins, 2010), requiring constant updating of capabilities as technology evolves (HESA, 2010). Postgraduates, who were traditionally expected to take up academic position, are now largely employed in sectors outside academia (Kaplan, 2010). This trend was reflected in a UK study that identified 53% of PhD graduates are now employed outwith academia six months after graduation (The Royal Society, 2010).

This trend reflects the connection between university research and development and the rest of the knowledge economy, embodied in the growth of industrial partnerships and knowledge transfer centres between academia and industry. International policies and programmes, for example those in the EU, have promoted public–private collaborations. At a national level, EU member states have placed priority on establishing transfer or competence centres that bridge academia and industry. At the same time, universities are being encouraged to seek funding from the private sector, as large corporations establish industry–academia research collaborations. This trend signals that the separation between academia and industry is eroding as research and development become intricate parts of a knowledge economy based on innovation.

Arguably, as industry and academia come closer together, organisational practices are coming to resemble those of research and scholarly communities more closely. However, the practices of scholarly communities are also changing in sometimes radical ways. What counts as useful knowledge is increasingly biased towards what can be represented and made available for analysis in digital forms. Scientific and research projects now depend on data being shared in the almost instantaneous fashion enabled by the Internet, while the sheer processing power available to researchers is ushering in new methods of investigation, and in some areas whole new disciplines and genres of knowledge. The processes of writing, collaborating, reviewing, sharing, commenting on and publishing research are in revolution.

As the knowledge economy has developed, knowledge-based work practices have migrated from specialist sectors such as digital media and ICT into the mainstream. In the developed world at least, economically productive work involves – centrally or incidentally – generating immaterial products such as information, knowledge and networks (Hardt & Negri, 2008, p. 65). Production units are typically becoming smaller, more flexible and dynamic, geographically distributed and technologically mediated. Not only do these new modes of production depend on networked technologies, but they also adopt technologies such as a model for organisational structures (ibid., p. 82). Examples of emerging work practices include *bricolage* – the aggregation of disparate resources to create novel representations; *localisation* – the use of globally sourced information and networks to solve local problems (Fiedler & Pata, 2009); *crowd-sourcing* – posing problems or questions to a diffuse network of experts to generate a range of novel solutions and *open knowledge* – making intellectual property publicly or semi-publicly available, perhaps as a solution in search of a problem.

'Taylorism' is a term that has been used for decades to describe the breaking down of job roles into small and simple segments to increase efficiency. 'Digital taylorism' is a term used to describe a related trend towards division of labour in the service and intellectual industries, dissecting previously coherent professional roles into discrete projects or even tasks. One consequence can be seen in the trend towards self-employment among professionals. Another can be seen in the stratification of so-called 'middle-class jobs', with 'permission to think' and to make decisions being reserved to a small proportion of senior employees, and a large majority undertaking technical, managerial and professional tasks with little of the autonomy previously associated with this level of work.

'Middle class labour' is becoming less secure as digital networks make it easier for tasks to be contracted out on a piece-meal basis, extending consultancy-based work, and loosening the ties between individuals and employers. Moreover, postgraduates from developed countries are competing for high skills, high value jobs on a global stage, and graduates from emerging economies have a growing advantage. As the performance gap narrows rapidly, differences in labour costs are narrowing far more slowly, giving companies greater scope to extract value from highly skilled people in different locations. '*Colleges and Universities in emerging economies are expanding faster than those in the UK and arguably expanding smarter, learning lessons from other education systems without the same brakes on organisational and cultural innovation*'.

Postgraduate study is increasingly viewed as necessary for entry to the knowledge middle class. It provides an opportunity for individuals to develop not only expertise and specialist knowledge, but the more general capabilities they will need to thrive. Digital tools are fundamentally changing what it means to research, communicate, make meaning, think, work and learn. The implications for graduate courses of study are that 'employability' and scholarship both need to be rethought in ways that begin from the changing knowledge practices of the subject under study.

Individual working lives are, as a result more complex, unpredictable and inter-woven (Bandura, 1997). There is a greater requirement for workers to be independently self-motivated, as well as a tendency for individuals to move jobs and careers more frequently and to be in fixed-term or flexible contracts (Naswall, Hellgren & Sverke, 2008). The ability to manage and regulate one's own learning is an increasingly critical disposition of postgraduate students, given their strong connection with and reliance on knowledge. The ability to pursue and persist in learning can be enhanced through positive experiences of study. However, there is some evidence that exposure to successful habits, or explicit prompts to reflect, self-diagnose, analyse and plan, may help postgraduate students to develop their own strategies of study (Lindblom-Ylanne, 2004).

DIGITAL LITERACY AND NEW MODES OF STUDY

Knowledge-based industries are characterised by a continuous redefinition of organisational goals along with radical and discontinuous change. Employees must be capable of getting up to speed quickly. They should be able to discover and integrate knowledge from many different sources as they gain key competencies within the organisation. They must be able to draw on the knowledge of experts and peers in groups or networks, using relevant technologies. Therefore, ability to source, access and use digital information is an essential capability for postgraduate students.

For decades higher education institutions have been using technology to enhance teaching methods, and libraries have been supporting students to use digital resources alongside print. In the last five years, the impetus for change has moved from institutional systems such as library catalogues and virtual learning environments, to technologies in the hands of students. Although these enhancements have potential to improve research and study, they also present confusing choices for tutors who may lack the expertise to guide students in using digital technologies successfully.

Networked tools (such as mobile phones, cameras, laptops) and services (such as Facebook, Twitter, Skype, YouTube, Flickr, multi-player games, immersive environments and location-aware services) allow students to access multiple data streams (such as newsfeeds, RSS feeds, Twitter hash tags, realtime datasets and so on), and enhance the potential for learning (Siemens, 2010).

Arguably they also represent a paradigm shift in the relationship between students and universities. Universities should no longer seek to provide a digital learning environment with all the technology tools a student requires, but should instead focus on providing an environment which integrates with the various tools and the mode of engagement which the student adopts. Third party services are overtaking campus-based facilities in the choices students make. High quality educational and research content can be accessed from other universities where the same subjects are studied as well as from a range of high quality public and private sector sources, such as museums, multinational companies and non-governmental organisations. Particularly for postgraduate students, online social networks (via Facebook, Twitter or other Web2.0 environments) are likely to be at least as significant as local peer groups and mentors when it comes to seeking support. All of these socio-technical changes trouble the relationship between the student and his or her institutional context.

Trends in technology enhanced learning include:

- Large-scale, stable applications being replaced by small–scale services, some in constant beta mode

- Institutional technologies giving way to learners' personal technologies and personal access to third party (or 'public') services
- Restricted online learning environments giving way to networked, learner-owned or -shared spaces for collaboration and knowledge building
- Content created by tutors being mixed with learner-generated resources.
- Data capture devices such as cameras, video cameras, audio microphones, etc. being extensively used to capture research evidence and evidence of learning
- Content sources being superseded by dynamic, constantly changing resources and datastreams accessed via online, personal aggregators
- Tutor-selected content being replaced by constant datastreams, selected, spliced and reassembled by learners
- Changing assessment practices, where personalised outcomes are negotiated and evidenced via e-portfolios, blogs and other personal virtual spaces
- Well-developed ideas being replaced by evolving knowledge. Cutting-edge research may well be reported online long before it is in print; online articles being supplemented with comments, blog entries and tweets
- Expert knowledge being opened up and filtered through social bookmarking.

All this places much greater responsibility on students to select, use and manage their own technologies, develop their own working spaces and practices, and find their own learning communities (Väljataga and Fiedler, 2009). It also puts strain on institutional ICT support and ICT skills provision. Graduate students, with their more specialist interests, cannot expect to find all the technologies and applications they might need being supported by generic ICT services. Once they have functional access to a networked computer and relevant applications, students will look to their supervisors, mentors and tutors for guidance on how technology use is shaping their subject area. This makes the digital literacy of tutors and research supervisors a critical issue, one which has been shown to have an impact on the learner (Margaryan, Littlejohn, & Vojt, 2011). Bullen, Morgan, Belfer, and Qayyum (2008), reported a major influencing factor of technology use was 'the student and instructor dynamic' within a course. However, student peers can be equally if not more important guides to successful digital strategies (McGill, Nicol, Littlejohn, & Grierson, 2005; Nicol, Littlejohn, & Grierson, 2005). Formal or informal mentoring schemes have proved successful at many institutions.

Once they have tried a range of strategies and applications, students will begin to make choices of their own (Väljataga & Laanpere, 2010). Indeed, choice and consumption are key frames through which students view the technology-mediated world. Just as we find some students prefer social situations and others prefer quiet, solo environments for study, so researchers and students in the same field will differ in their technology choices. There is even evidence of some learners making active choices to avoid the use of technology tools for learning (Kennedy, Judd, Churchward, Gray, & Krause, 2008; Margaryan et al., 2011), adding to the challenge of supporting students. Students do best where they are shown a variety of successful strategies and where it is made explicit which technologies are central to effective practice in their subject, and which are an aspect of personal choice or style.

Ubiquity, accessibility, rapid feedback and ease of use of digital technology tools are all features of individuals' daily experience which are changing societal expectations. However, in some contexts there is little evidence of learners exhibiting digital literacy, connectedness, a need for immediacy and a preference for experiential learning (Bullen et al., 2008). A number of studies have found that educators tend to overestimate students' facility with technology (Kennedy et al., 2008; Bullen et al., 2008; Hargittai, 2010). For example:

- Active engagement with web 2.0 technologies such as the creation of study-oriented blogs and wikis, tagging, meme-ing, commenting and reviewing of others' academic work remain minority activities to which most students have to be introduced by educators.
- Even confident internet researchers often lack appropriate evaluative and critical skills.
- Students with multiple personal devices may have little idea how to use them to support their study, or how to obtain support for using them on campus.

There may be considerable variation in the abilities of postgraduate students to use technologies for learning. Some of these differences have been linked to socioeconomic status. Hargittai suggests that the variations may be explained by 'differentiated contexts of uses and experiences' (p. 108).

There are similar variations in individuals' abilities to apply digital technology tools to research practices. A study by the British Library into research practice also found that the context of study was more significant in determining technology use than the age of the student (CIBER, 2008). What is clear is that the same devices and applications take on different meanings in different contexts. We should beware of assuming that proficient personal use translates directly into use of technology for research and study purposes. Graduate students need contextualised support, that is they need guidance in the use of digital technologies for authentic research and study tasks, and enculturation to the ways digital knowledge practices are changing their subject area.

DIGITAL LITERACY AND KNOWLEDGE SHARING IN NETWORKS

Existing conceptions of information literacy have been criticised for focusing too strongly on individual use of information in the context of a specific task or problem, and for failing to recognise different cultures of information use. A UK national study of Learning Literacies in the Digital Age (LLiDA) argued the case for extending the idea of information literacy to acknowledge that many informational tasks are carried out collaboratively, to include sharing of information as a central competence, and to accommodate cultural, ethical, safety and citizenship dimensions. At the same time, research is becoming increasingly collaborative and inter-disciplinary.

Communication in the academic world is changing profoundly and rapidly. While print retains the imprimatur of quality and credibility – and is still mandated in some academic processes such as submission of theses and validation of programmes – research findings are regularly communicated in digital media. Mathematical and scientific notation systems, data sets, spatial representations, narrative and hyper-narrative accounts, graphics and audio files, video clips and simulations all have different affordances for conveying complex ideas. To some extent these different formats were available in pre-digital forms, but digital media are far easier to search and to share, to combine, to repurpose and to translate as barriers to production have been lowered.

In this space, the idea of multimodal literacy has emerged. This is understood as a complex set of capabilities, supporting critical engagement with ideas in different media and the apprehension of new meanings that emerge when modes of communication collide. Once an aspect of specialist courses, such as media studies, media literacy is becoming understood as an essential skill for navigating the information age and for communicating understanding. Open communication of ideas to different audiences is escalating the breakdown of sectoral boundaries, contributing to the emergence of interdisciplinary research with a range of different audiences. As well as critically evaluating information, students need practice in producing representations, making arguments and sharing ideas in a variety of forms. Writing has moved from a paper-based to a largely screen-based medium and associated searching and editing software have profoundly changed the way in which academic writing is typically constructed even if these changes are not always acknowledged. Referencing practices, for example, rely heavily on searchable public and private databases, and rarely on a close engagement with prior texts. Images and video are also increasingly embedded in academic texts, and data sets can be directly linked into the documents reporting on their analysis (CIBER, 2008).

None of these changes in knowledge sharing is universal in its effect. Knowledge practices and the influence of digital technologies on them remain situated in disciplines of study. In some subject areas, such profoundly novel means of collecting and analysing data are emerging that whole new branches of the subject are being instituted. Examples would include the impact of Geospatial Information Systems on the use of large datasets in the geographical sciences, the streaming of realtime datasets in chemistry and astronomy, the analysis of large corpus texts in linguistics, healthcare informatics and future markets analysis. In other subjects, professional codes of conduct are being rewritten to account for previously unforeseen aspects of public and private behaviour. Graduate students are at the cutting edge of these changes, and postgraduate education should not only be responding to them, but should be aspiring to shape them.

Whatever their subject area, however, students and researchers need skills in collaborating with people who are not co-located with them. Research teams share data across continents and time-zones. Project teams use valuable face-to-face time only for interactions that cannot be done virtually. Even individual researchers are likely to find themselves being mentored or advised by experts from other institutions. Work placements and fieldwork are extensively supported by collaborative technologies, and students are expected to keep in constant touch with their tutors and programmes of study, whether they have gone home for the evening or across the world for a year-long exchange.

These pragmatic arrangements, made possible by digital networks, are creating a paradigm shift in the nature of knowledge. Ideas can no longer be said to be privately produced and published, so much as they are in a state of constant repurposing, refinement and recirculation. Much of the knowledge available on the internet is collectively authored as is the case most famously with Wikipedia – and depends on collective action rather than structures of authority and quality control to remain in use. Such knowledge tends to have a shorter lifespan that some of the knowledge in print media. It evolves dynamically, changing rapidly. These considerations take us beyond knowledge sharing in bounded networks to the phenomenon of completely open scholarship.

DIGITAL LITERACY AND OPEN SCHOLARSHIP

The open science and open data movements have been driven forward by changes in research funding, which requires data to be made openly available within an agreed timeframe. These changes in funding are a necessary response to the increasing complexity of knowledge work. For example, data on climate change are shared across interdisciplinary teams to improve analysis and interpretation of findings. Open release of the data sets on which conclusions have been based allows peer review of the entire process end-to-end. And just as open source software benefits from the attention of many developers – fixing bugs that would not have been spotted by a small team – so the idea behind much of the open scholarship movement is that many minds make light (more accurate, robust and credible) work of a knotty problem. Although peer review and collaboration are founding principles of the academic tradition, traditionally this has been within closed communities of practice where the rules, roles and divisions of labour were understood and where participants were often on first name terms. Open scholarship demands a more radical kind of collaboration, in which work is never finalised and sent to print but continually open to critique, extension, subversion and reinterpretation by people who may never be known to the earlier authors.

Underpinning the idea of open scholarship is the notion that people are progressively more connected through pervasive social systems, affording opportunities for open access to the collective knowledge that resides in materials, people, networks and machines. These networked technologies enable individuals to work as an inseparable part of 'the Many' – the range of distinct groups, networks, communities or collectives that are part of everyday life (Dron & Anderson, 2007). Increasingly, these resources are openly available, opening up opportunities for new conceptualisations of learning.

Through social networks individuals can connect with and tap into groups, networks, communities or collectives to consume, filter and create new knowledge. Collective knowledge is available through the open formation of tag clouds, recommendations or navigation in social systems based on prior use, evaluation or other indicators (ibid., 2007). Generation of collective knowledge enables spontaneous and serendipitous learning and knowledge sharing (Sunstein, 2001). In this new conceptualisation, learning and scholarship can be viewed as a process of creating networks that connect people, organisations and resources (Siemens, 2006). In this new conceptualisation, individuals can learn by drawing on and at the same time contributing to the collective knowledge (Paavola, Lipponen, & Hakkarainen, 2004; 'Littlejohn, Milligan & Margaryan, 2012).

The academy is also taking on board the new working practices outlined in the first section: indeed, like the internet itself, social networking sites and practices can be said to have spread from the academy outwards. One manifestation of this trend is the online celebrity academic, known through blogging or podcasting to a much wider audience than any lecture theatre could accommodate. While not all researchers aspire to be public figures on such a scale, there is no doubt that managing reputation – professional, personal or academic – is a quintessential skill for the digital age. Arguably, reputation is a more marketable asset even than qualification. Even for students who cringe at the idea of marketing themselves, being personally and publicly identified with their research interests is an essential aspect of academic communication.

Associated with these changes in the ways knowledge is generated is the relationship between research, publication and reputation. Academic reputation, while still founded on print publication of original research, is increasingly being developed and managed in virtual ways. Impact ratings include evidence of non-print citations; some subject areas now publish predominantly online (e.g. Medicine); content, including original research, is increasingly made available on the internet simultaneously with or very shortly after print publication; grey literature and pre-proof versions of print-published literature abound. As in the days of the old university presses, universities are waking up to the fact that the research outputs of their staff and students are important capital, but instead of keeping it under copyright lock and key, many are taking the opposite approach. Open access to locally produced content, for example in an open institutional repository, has many advantages, not least in being much easier to administer. Content is accessed by those who need it, not pushed to those who can pay. Universities such as Nottingham and the Open University in the UK have used open educational content to recruit new students to fee-paying courses; research staff are increasingly encouraged to make their outputs openly available as a sign of departmental quality and commitment to research.

CURRENT PROVISION FOR GRADUATE DIGITAL LITERACY DEVELOPMENT

In this landscape it is clear that digital literacy involves a complex range of capabilities, generic and subject-related, technology-focused as well as oriented on the processes of research and study. How can institutions assist their postgraduate students in acquiring these capabilities in the course of their study? The study on Learning Literacies for the Digital Age (Beetham, McGill, & Littlejohn, 2009) found that there were some barriers to students – at all levels of post-compulsory study – accessing the support they need. It must be emphasised that the evidence is not detailed enough to warrant any conclusions about the outcomes of different kinds or levels of provision. The following points of actual or potential stress are particularly relevant to graduate students. The study found:

- Strong and credible evidence that students require support for online research skills and critical/ evaluative approaches to information; also that they over-estimate their own capabilities and are naïve about the provenance and purpose of messages in digital media.
- Strong evidence from UK-based programmes that students require support in migrating to more ICT-based study practices, and in using subject-appropriate technologies for deep learning. There is also evidence that learners benefit from being able to use their own technologies for learning, including software and services, and that in some institutions this is still problematic. There are indications that support for ICT skills should migrate from 'training' on institutionally provided technologies to more tailored support for the technologies students choose, which can be peer-led (e.g. student help desks, study 'buddies').
- Evidence that technologies can be used to extend the process and period of induction well before students actually arrive on course, and that they help to ease social transition. This is also a critical window in which expectations about study practice can be communicated.
- Evidence from the US but borne out in the UK studies that students lack general research skills, that moving to third year and postgraduate study can be a source of difficulty, and that 'digital scholarship' should continue to be an element of the curriculum throughout study with a focus on changing knowledge practice in the subject area. There may be a clash between academic norms and everyday social practices with digital media, which is particularly evident around issues of plagiarism and originality in student writing.
- Evidence that students are still strongly led by tutors in choosing and using technologies for study. Tutors skills and confidence with technology are therefore critical to students' development.
- Evidence that despite an apparent facility with technology, most students use only basic functions of their personal devices and are reluctant to explore the capabilities of technology to support their study.

The research review was followed by an audit of current provision in the UK HE institutions. This audit concluded that the development of digital literacy is typically fragmented across universities. Information literacy will be supported by library services, technical literacy by the ICT support desk, study skills by learning development, employability by careers. While these individual services may do a good job of responding to students' needs, where these are identified, their expertise is not typically used to reframe programmes of study nor to embed opportunities for developing digital capabilities on task. Students do best when they have access to ongoing diagnosis and support, in the context of their chosen field of study, and in relation to tasks that are intrinsically meaningful to their study goals.

THE RESEARCHER DEVELOPMENT FRAMEWORK

One key competence framework which highlights the importance of digital literacy is the Researcher Development Framework (RDF). The RDF is a recent attempt to map and inter-relate the knowledge, behaviours and attitudes of researchers (Vitae, 2010). The framework was developed from empirical data and represents a comprehensive competence map of skills for new and established researchers. The RDF covers a broad spectrum of competencies which are of relevance to researchers, organised under four domains: Knowledge and Intellectual Abilities; Personal Effectiveness; Research Governance and Organisation and Engagement, Influence and Impact. Each domain contains three sub-domains, each represented by a number of key descriptors expressed as a range of experience phases. Digital literacy competences are represented under each domain as follows:

- *Domain A: Knowledge and Intellectual Abilities.* This domain focuses on the core knowledge skills which an individual researcher should possess. The descriptors indicate that researchers should have knowledge of *'sources of information bibliographic software and other information technologies'* and *'Literacy and numeracy skills and language abilities appropriate for research'* and should be able to *'Conduct effective and comprehensive information searches'* as well as *'Record, manage and handle information/data using appropriate bibliographic software and other information technologies'*. These statements represent the most explicit references to digital literacies contained within the RDF, focusing on the identification, management and retrieval of knowledge.
- *Domain B: Personal Effectiveness.* This domain defines the personal qualities and skills required of effective researchers. An individual researcher would be expected to 'Actively network for professional and career purposes and seeks to enhance research reputation and esteem'. In the modern research context, networking goes beyond behaviour at conferences, and includes participation in general social networks such as Twitter and Facebook as well as specialised research communities. The RDF also highlights the importance of *'recording and maintaining a record of achievement and experience'*, an activity which is often conducted online and which demands an awareness of the most effective and rewarding way to do this.
- *Domain C: Research Governance and Organisation.* This domain is concerned with the standards of professional conduct necessary for effective research administration and management. Researchers are expected to have knowledge of the *'principles of Intellectual Property Rights (IPR) and copyright issues'*. Again, this competence inherently implies an awareness of the copyright and IPR issues relevant to operating in a networked world.
- *Domain D: Engagement Influence and Impact.* This domain relates to the broader context within which a researcher operates, including working collaboratively. The framework indicates that researchers are expected to *'build and sustain collaborative relationships'* have knowledge of *the appropriate communication and dissemination mechanisms for different audiences'* and the *'importance of engaging in the process of dissemination of research results'*.

The RDF is a high profile competency framework adopted by key organisations in the UK. The framework is supported well by interpretative documents which make it easy to use for both researchers and researcher developers. It builds on previous work and is based on empirical data and is therefore robust and relevant. As a general framework, however, the RDF does not always acknowledge how researcher development can be supported by digital practices. For example, reputation management may involve the use of tools such as blogs and e-portfolios, or the participation in digital networks and communities of practice. Since the LLiDA project reported its findings, Vitae has begun updating the RDF to acknowledge the speed with which digital developments are changing practice in research areas, and the role of digital capability in allowing students to keep abreast of these changes.

A FRAMEWORK FOR DIGITAL LITERACY

In addition to reporting on current provision, the LLiDA project proposed a new digital literacies framework (Table 4.1). The framework was drawn from an analysis of more than 30 competence frameworks relevant to digital literacy from across the UK and Europe. The outcome was a summative framework for understanding components of digital literacy, and to some extent how they are supported and developed in a typical institution. The digital literacy framework applies to all post-compulsory learning contexts and has not been specifically tailored for postgraduate study.

Because the components of digital literacy have to date been addressed by separate competence frameworks, owned by and located in different departments, the framework appears atomised. In practice, students need to encounter digital practices in the context of authentic research tasks and study goals, and not as separate skills to be mastered in isolation. Therefore, the framework can be used as a checklist for those involved in supporting postgraduate students, to ensure that provision includes these elements, without advocating that they be offered separately from other aspects of academic development. Taken together with the RDF, the LLiDA Framework can ensure appropriate attention is given to the changing practices of academic research and writing, and that the next generation of researchers uses digital opportunities in critical, creative and productive ways.

BECOMING DIGITALLY LITERATE: DEVELOPING THE RESEARCHERS OF THE FUTURE

There is evidence that students become more critical, evaluative, self-aware, self-confident, skilled and capable in the use of technologies as they progress in their studies (Sharpe & Beetham, 2010; Hardy & Jefferies, 2010). They also develop a wider and more effective range of strategies for their own learning. However, support for this progress is not well integrated or understood. Although some of these capabilities may be 'generic', the consensus is that they are best supported in communities of practice or inquiry, which is in research or study groups focused on tasks of value and interest to the student. This finding may indicate

Table 4.1 A framework for digital literacy

High-level term, framing idea	Example component capabilities	Comments
Learning to learn, lifelong learning *Attitude: I can manage my learning and personal development*	Reflection Strategic planning Self-evaluation, self-analysis Organisation (time, etc.)	Owned/defined by: the student; learning support Students addressed as: self-directed learners, lifelong learners, potential professionals Changing due to: different needs of arriving students; different expectations of study; availability of online and open learning opportunities; technology-supported study and CPD practices
Academic practice, study skills *Attitude: I can make and interpret meanings in this field of knowledge*	Comprehension Reading/apprehension Organisation (knowledge) Synthesis Argumentation Problem-solving Research skills Academic writing	Owned/defined by: the academy, especially academic development, research/study skills unit Students addressed as: academics/researchers in training, prospective graduates in specific subjects Slow changing due to cultural values being embedded in institutional, disciplinary/professional/ vocational and wider social practices and expectations. But changing due to: changing knowledge practices; changing research cultures
Information literacy *Attitude: I can find and use information in a meaningful way*	Identification Accession Organisation Evaluation Interpretation Analysis Synthesis Application (Based on the SCONUL 7 Pillars of Information Literacy)	Owned/defined by: the library Students addressed as: researchers, information users Information literacy has evolved rapidly to meet demands of rapidly changing information environment. At the same time, it is a place where lasting values are asserted (evaluation, reflection and judgement, critical awareness, provenance of sources, evidence, method). Established information literacy models are being challenged by widespread sharing of content and blurring of boundaries between information and communication
Communication and collaboration skills *Attitude: I can work with others to produce shared meanings*	Teamwork Networking Effective communication in a range of different media Awareness of audience Openness/sharing Repurposing, re-aggregation, re-editing	Owned/defined by: unclear. Most institutions and programmes claim that this is a key graduate attribute but there are few examples of it being consistently developed or assessed. Some professions require particular forms of communication; in practice there is overlap with use of digital tools (below) Students addressed as: communicators, social participants Fairly rapidly changing to keep pace with emerging new technologies, networks, devices and forms of tele-presence. However, common values are asserted across communicational media, e.g. in acceptable use policies, netiquette, etc. listening, turn-taking, facilitation, mediation, respect; also practices of acknowledging particular contributions. Challenged by some features of informal communication including flaming, dissing, etc. Also challenged by proliferation of communication channels – making it difficult for institutions/tutors to control communications around research and study

Cont'd

Table 4.1 Cont'd

High-level term, framing idea	Example component capabilities	Comments
Media literacy (also 'visual' and 'audio' and 'video' literacies) *Attitude: I can make and interpret meanings in different media*	Critical 'reading' Creative production	Owned/defined by: generally unclear, though some media literacies are well defined in specialist subject areas, e.g. film, photography, media studies. Students addressed as: consumers and producers of messages in a range of media. Area of focus for European and UK government, which assert value of some traditional academic practices, e.g. critique, review, scepticism, originality and creativity. Moderately fast-changing to keep pace with emergence of new media, e.g. gaming, media sharing sites and some new values – currency, cool, reputation, etc. Changing due to new availability of capture, editing and production technologies; spread of intellectual ideas in multiple media and to mass practices of shared production and reproduction
ICT/digital/computer literacy *Attitude: I can use and explore the affordances of different digital tools*	Keyboard skills Use of capture technologies Use of analysis tools Use of presentation tools General navigation/UI skills Personalisation of technologies Critical choice in ICT adoption and use Confidence to explore new devices and applications	Owned/defined by: technology developers, designers and support staff. Students addressed as: technology users (and consumers?). Very rapidly changing skill-set, requiring constant updating. Skills often acquired informally, e.g. from more competent peers, but very significantly also through direct instruction. Agile adopters will use help menus, online discussion forums and user groups, trial and error, etc. but others need active support. Some capacities remain relevant, e.g. risk-taking, innovation, the capacity to evaluate and be an informed consumer, increasingly involvement in development, criticise the ends for which technologies are offered as the means ... Changing in response to technical development and consumerism, learner expectations, open source/constant beta, personalisation of ICT services and environments and rapid obsolescence of existing skills
Employability *Attitude: I contribute to the economic life of my community*	Self-management (time, task, etc.) Teamwork Problem-solving Business and customer awareness Innovation/enterprise	Employability encompasses all or many of the other skills but is included here as a distinctive framework for theorising about and organising these skills, i.e. the production of the learner as a competent worker/employee. Component skills are those distinctive to this framework. The UK government and bodies such as the CBI and sector skills councils take a close interest in how this area of competence is changing
Citizenship *Attitude: I contribute to the social life of my community*	Digital citizenship (Managing) digital identity Participation and engagement Social enterprise Ethical awareness Political, social, personal responsibility	Like employability, citizenship encompasses many other skills but is included as a distinctive framework for theorising about and organising these skills, i.e. the production of the researcher/student as a competent citizen or member of wider society. The European Commission takes a particular interest in this aspect of digital literacy, which it treats in terms of cultural and political inclusion

that students sometimes fail to see that the skills they gain in authentic tasks are transferable.

As we have argued, use of digital technologies to support knowledge work is best considered as a set of integrated, life-wide practices rather than a bundle of separate skills (see Table 4.1). Such practices cannot be acquired through one-off induction sessions or skills training, though these can help orient students to what will be required of them in postgraduate study, and are essential to students whose prior experience has not equipped them with basic ICT and information skills. Capable researchers and students have a range of meaning-making practices available to them, including digitally supported practices that make use of different media. They make active choices about which strategies to deploy and they manage any tensions and contradictions inherent in their participation in different contexts, a capability which is sometimes termed 'rhetorical competence'. This capability relates to the management of different communicative identities, so for example a graduate student should be aware that different rules govern communication in research networks from communication in social networks, even though the same digital environments may be used for both.

Students require opportunities for ongoing practice, embedded in their area of research or study, and in tasks of real relevance to their study goals. Practices of knowledge creation and sharing in subject areas must be made clear to students as part of their ongoing development. These approaches require that tutors with subject knowledge are themselves digitally literate and confident in modelling digitally supported approaches alongside other approaches to research and study. However, other professionals can play an important role in students' development, including subject specialist librarians and research skills professionals. Particularly among graduate students, the capacity to find and ask for help should be cultivated. Peers are at least as valuable as tutors when it comes to acquiring specific digital habits of study.

The DigEULit (European Framework for Digital Literacy) and CEDEFOP (European Centre for the Development of Vocational Training) initiatives found evidence of HE institutions taking a functionalist approach to digital skills, under the assumption that skills are highly transferable across different contexts (Martin, 2005). This assumption has not been borne out by research, which shows instead that digital capability is very highly context dependent. Instead, these projects advocate either a more behavioural/professional approach, which focuses on the development capability in specific task contexts, or an interpretive approach, which focuses on how individuals understand tasks and how social contexts support that understanding. These approaches are particularly likely to be effective at postgraduate level.

The LLiDA study summarised what we know about developing digital literacy as follows. Learner development requires:

- *Authentic contexts* for practice, including digitally mediated contexts as appropriate
- Subject/research community practices being made explicit, and *practices being explicitly modelled* to them

- *Exposure to a range of practices* where this is appropriate
- Help in *understanding and managing conflict between different practice contexts*, such as social, professional and academic contexts
- *Individualised support* for skills development.

While support should encompass a generic entitlement to digital skills and access, at postgraduate level particularly, technology practice is necessarily diverse and constitutive of personal/professional/academic identities.

Looking at the wider impacts of digital technology on society and the economy, programmes of postgraduate study should support graduates to deal with:

- Economic uncertainty and high competition for employment in the global knowledge economy
- Increased levels of alternative, contract-based and self-employment
- The rise of inter-disciplinary and multi-disciplinary teams
- A networked society and communities
- Multi-cultural working and living environments
- Blurring boundaries of real and virtual, public and private, work and leisure
- Increasingly ubiquitous and embedded digital technologies
- Distribution of cognitive work into (human and non-human) networks of expertise
- Rapid social and techno-social change.

CONCLUSIONS

Looking to the future, how do we recognise the changing contexts for study and research, bring them into programmes of study in ways that are accessible to students, change our teaching and support practices and help students transform their own practices to become more effective researchers and citizens of a knowledge society? A new paradigm may be required, in which staff and students bring diverse personal resources to bear on the problems of digital research and study, and in which more flexible structures support collaborations within and beyond the boundaries of the institution.

REFERENCES

Bandura, A. (1997). *Self-Efficacy in Changing Societies.* Cambridge: Cambridge University Press.
Beetham, H., McGill, L., & Littlejohn, A. (2009). Thriving in the 21st Century: Learning Literacies for the Digital Age (LLiDA), Final Project Report. Retrieved from http://www.jisc.ac.uk/media/documents/projects/llidareportjune2009.pdf
Bullen, M., Morgan, T., Belfer, K., & Qayyum, A. (2008). The digital learner at BCIT and implications for an e-strategy. In Proceedings of the 2008 Research Workshop of the European Distance Education Network (EDEN) 'Researching and promoting access to education and training: The role of distance education and e-learning in technology enhanced environments', Paris, France, October 20–22.
Candy, P. (2004). Linking thinking: Self-directed learning in the digital age. Retrieved from http://www.dest.gov.au/sectors/training_skills/publications_resources/profiles/ documents/report_x7_pdf.htm
CIBER for JISC and the British Library (2008). Information Behaviour of the Researcher of the Future. Retrieved from http://www.jisc.ac.uk/media/documents/programmes/reppres/gg_final_keynote_11012008.pdf

Dron, J. & Anderson, T. (2007). Collectives, networks and groups in social software for e-learning. In T. Bastiaens & S. Carliner (Eds.), *Proceedings of World Conference on E-Learning in Corporate, Government, Healthcare, and Higher Education 2007* (pp. 2460–2467). Chesapeake, VA: AACE.

Fiedler, S. & Pata, K. (2009). Distributed learning environments and social software: In search for a framework of design. In S. Hatzipanagos & S. Warburton (Eds.). *Social Software and Developing Community Ontologies* (pp. 145–158). Hershey, PA, USA: IGI Global.

Hardt, M. & Negri, A. (2008). *Multitude* (p. 82). London: Penguin.

Hardy, J. & Jefferies, A. (2010). How learners change: Critical moments, changing lives. In R. Sharpe, H. Beetham, & S. de Freitas (Eds.), *Rethinking Learning for a Digital Age* (pp. 114–127). London: Routledge.

Hargittai, E. (2010). Digital Na(t)ives? Variation in internet skills and uses among members of the 'Net Generation'. *Sociological Inquiry, 80*, 92–113.

HESA (2010). Destinations of Leavers from Higher Education Institutions, Higher Education Statistics Agency. Retrieved from http://www.hesa.ac.uk/index.php?option=com_pubs&task=show_pub_detail&pubid=1708&Itemid=286

Hiemstra, R. & Brockett, R. G. (1994). *Overcoming Resistance to Self-Direction in Adult Learning.* San Francisco, CA: Jossey–Bass Inc.

Jakupec, V. & Garrick, J. (Eds.) (2000). *Flexible Learning, Human Resource and Organisational Development: Putting Theory to Work.* London: Routledge.

Kaplan, K. (2010) The changing face of tenure, *Nature, 468*, 123–125.

Kennedy, G., Judd, T., Churchward, A., Gray, K., & Krause, K.-L. (2008). First year students' experiences with technology: Are they digital natives? *Australasian Journal of Educational Technology, 24*, 108–122.

Levy, C., & Hopkins, L. (2010). Shaping up for Innovation: Are we delivering the right skills for the 2020 knowledge economy? The Work Foundation.

Lindblom-Ylanne, S. (2004). Raising students' awareness of their approaches to study. *Innovations in Education and Teaching International, 41*, 405–422.

Littlejohn, A., Milligan, C. & Margaryan, A. (2012). Charting Collective Knowledge: Supporting Self-regulated Learning in the Workplace, *Journal of Workplace Learning 23*.

McGill, L., Nicol, D.J., Littlejohn, A., & Greirson, H. (2005). Creating an information-rich learning environment to enhance design student learning: challenges and approaches. *British Journal of Educational Technology, 36*, 629–642.

Margaryan, A., Littlejohn, A., & Vojt. G. (2011). Are digital natives a myth or reality? University students' use of digital technologies. *Computers and Education, 56*, 429–440.

Martin, A. (2005). DigEULit – a European framework for digital literacy: A progress report. *JeLit, 2*.

Naswall, K., Hellgren, J., & Sverke, M. (2008). *The Individual in the Changing Working Life.* Cambridge: Cambridge University Press.

Nicol, D.J., Littlejohn A., & Grierson, H. (2005). The importance of structuring information and resources within shared workspaces during collaborative design learning, Open Learning: *The Journal of Open and Distance Learning, 20*, 31–49.

Paavola, S., Lipponen, L., & Hakkarainen, K. (2004). Models of innovative knowledge communities and three metaphors of learning. *Review of Educational Research, 74*, 557–576.

The Royal Society (2010). The Scientific Century: Securing Our Future Prosperity. Retrieved October 10, 2010, from http://royalsociety.org/the-scientific-century/

Rychen, D. S. (2003). Key competencies: Meeting important challenges in life. In D. S. Rychen & L. H. Salganik (Eds.), *Key Competencies* (pp. 63–108). Göttingen: Hogrefe and Huber.

Sharpe, R. & Beetham, H. (2010). Understanding students' uses of technology for learning. In R. Sharpe, H. Beetham, & S. de Freitas (Eds.), *Rethinking Learning for a Digital Age* (pp. 85–99). London: Routledge.

Siemens, G. (2006). Knowing Knowledge. Retrieved from http://www.knowingknowledge.com/book.php

Siemens, G. (2010). Connections, clouds, things and analytics, presentation at the UK Technology Enhanced Professional Learning Special interest Group, Glasgow, UK December 2010. Retrieved from http://gcal.emea.acrobat.com/p94698893/

Sunstein, C. (2001). *Republic.com*. Princeton, NJ: Princeton University Press. Retrieved from http://press.princeton.edu/chapters/s7014.html

Väljataga, T. & Fiedler, S. (2009). Supporting students to self-direct intentional learning projects with social media. *Journal of Educational Technology and Society, 12*, 58–69.

Väljataga, T. & Laanpere, M. (2010). Learner control and personal learning environment: A challengefor instructional design. *Interactive Learning Environments 18,* 277–291.

Vitae (2010). Researcher development framework, Retrieved January 16, 2011, from http://www.vitae.ac.uk/rdf/

APPENDIX: A CHECKLIST FOR SUPPORTING GRADUATE ATTRIBUTES FOR THE DIGITAL AGE

- Design flexible opportunities for research and study
- Situate those opportunities, where possible and appropriate, in authentic contexts (workplace, community, placement)
- Design tasks suitable for highly interconnected individuals, operating in distributed networks of expertise
- Continually review how technologies are integrated into study tasks
- Assess students' own techno-social practices and the practices of professional and scholarly communities, anticipating that these will be different and that helping students negotiate the differences will become part of the pedagogic agenda
- Support students to use their own preferred technologies, and to develop effective strategies for studying and collaborating
- Use feedback to encourage innovation in approaches to study, rewarding exploration as a process: current assessment regimes often reward conservatism
- Articulate the benefits and importance of digital literacies
- Model the development and management of an academic identity through digital means
- Recognise and reward the expertise that digitally proficient students can offer to others in the learning community
- Support portfolio-building, blogging and other forms of personal reflection on developing practice
- Enable students to record their study experience in diverse ways, and present rich accounts of their study and research history to different audiences.

Student Perspectives

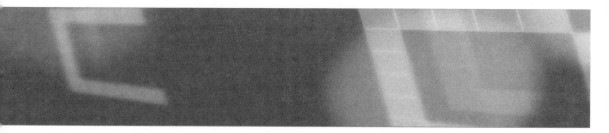

Whereas the traditional dissertation and thesis format privileges written language to convey knowledge, the chapters in this section lend student perspectives that explore how inscribed documentation combined with sound, image among other modes provide students with a range of rhetorical, symbolic and linguistic tools to more aptly prove, theorise and present arguments to a wider public audience. Thus, the chapters comprise student insights that record both the inherent challenges and intrinsic rewards of working within and across communicative modes in our increasingly global and digital world.

As previously stated in the Introduction to this handbook, student perspectives are included not only to incorporate the student voice, but also because it is often the collective work of undergraduate, Masters and especially doctoral students that are at the forefront of the shifting nature of dissertations and theses. To this end, the student perspectives in this handbook paint a picture of integrating the digital in dissertations and theses as a process by which new meanings can be made, analysed, represented and shared. For example, student research experiences, case studies and historical examples are used to illustrate how modes beyond writing in digital dissertations and theses offer a more integrative medium for documenting expertise about a research topic, while also opening new learning spaces where ideas, thoughts and texts can evolve through design. As expressed by the five authors in this section, this multimodal learning process often spans the duration of the study rather than focusing on a finalised product.

Lesley Gourlay's examination of the inter-relationship among *media systems*, educational practices and university orientation, points to shifts in pedagogical patterns that increasingly integrate intertextuality, multimodality and digitisation of knowledge. She begins by focusing on the ways in which the written word no longer solely conveys meanings as more technological tools are invited into institutional settings. However, she also notes that despite the prolific use of media systems across learning spaces, the printed word still remains the dominant mode for university assessment. Given this observation, Gourlay sets out to investigate what non-textual elements (or modes beyond written language) might afford students in the context of the dissertation. What emerges from this chapter is the notion that while a vast majority of final dissertations and theses remain largely an 'analogue print text', the process leading to this end result integrates multimodal, digital and 'posthuman' practices that in fact reflect a co-evolutionary meaning-making relationship between the writer/learner and the text (writing produced) in digital contexts. She concludes that while multimodal representation is becoming a prevalent design feature in academic works, written language remains a necessary – although not exclusive – medium for clearly constructing arguments that carry complex and abstract ideas.

In a chapter about the performing arts, Beardshaw Andrews departs from Gourlay's perspective of the co-evolutionary relationship between student learning and media systems to explore a more causal approach. Specifically, she attends to the progression of arts education in the UK and the USA as a 'consequence of the inclusion of digital technology in everyday practice'. Beardshaw Andrews' investigation of the topic is supported by both empirical evidence and reflective insight regarding the use of digital technology to better attend to issues of access, offer aid in the analytic process, and provide new environs that fuse play and creativity with academic practices. She asserts that the proactive integration of digital technology is a necessity for arts education to 'gain a place as a vital component of twenty-first century culture', and that such inclusion must be supported both by pedagogical and policy-oriented practices.

The third chapter by June Elizabeth Parnell introduces complexity theory as a framework for comprehending 'emergent and self-organising behaviours' and its relevance to concepts of non-linear dynamics in educational contexts. This chapter is particularly useful for students, examiners and educators involved in multimodal and digital studies as Parnell delves into the challenge of finding a theory that can flexibly accommodate the 'unbordered' dimensions of the digital domain, while at the same time adequately providing academic structure. Further, Parnell relates issues discussed regarding student participation in digital domains as bearing relevant implications to e-learning and to that of educational research.

In the remainder of this section, emphasis moves away from conceptual frameworks to more readily explore the shifting nature of dissertations and theses by referencing personalised field experiences. Lalitha Vasudevan with Tiffany DeJaynes, and Dylan Yamada-Rice discuss, from their own research perspectives, the tensions in navigating the demands of the university and the evolving nature of their work as straddling traditional dissertation formats and non-linear forms of knowledge production. Vasudevan and DeJaynes draw from their studies of adolescent literacies, conducted six years apart, to reflect about their respective dissertation processes and the methodological implications of conducting research about participants whose technological practices span 'digitally mediated contexts'. The authors set out to visibly display how researchers might enact methodological and pedagogical considerations of sociocultural theories of multimodality that respond to the changing social literacies and digital practices of adolescents. They reference their past experiences as students conducting ethnographic research and their engagement of modes as a means to investigate, interpret and represent their learning. Their approach calls forth an ethical response to including student and participant multimodal meaning-making that might otherwise be silenced in traditional research approaches.

Yamada-Rice, in the final chapter in this section, also raises ethical concerns as a component of maintaining traditional dissertation formats despite the prolific integration of digital technologies in contemporary communication. She begins by investigating the shift in the communication landscape from a primarily written mode to that of multiple modes such as image, writing, music, gesture and speech. She applies her review of literature to reflect on her own postgraduate case study research about young children's communication practices in Japan as primarily using visually based media. In her research, Yamada-Rice uses *Google Street View* to comparatively explore variance and quantity of visual types and their relationship to the written mode in the urban landscapes of Tokyo and London. Among the challenges she identifies is how she had to adapt representing 360° resources to fit two-dimensional page restrictions.

As each of the chapters identify, the communicational tools afforded in our increasingly global and digital world present new ways for making meaning. The range of subjects and specialties discussed by the five authors in this chapter are a sampling of the ways in which students are addressing issues of submitting dissertations and theses that privilege the written word over other modes. Where spoken or written words once sufficed to convey ideas, technological advances and its vast integration across social contexts permits new ways for organising thoughts that no longer exist in mono-modal forms. Thus, each author in this section offers insight into this shift and how their respective research and experiences shaped and were shaped by these social and semiotic changes.

5

Media Systems, Multimodality and Posthumanism

Lesley Gourlay

INTRODUCTION

Various accounts can be made about the origins, nature and purposes of the dissertation (used in this chapter to refer to all levels, from undergraduate to PhD) as a text, process, qualification and set of social practices. Its status is in many ways iconic; seen as the centrepiece and crowning achievement of the degree, and a key opportunity for the student to produce an in-depth and to some degree original piece of work. In that regard, it is both a symbolic carrier of academic tradition, but also arguably a crucible within which new forms of academic expression may be forged. In the early twenty-first century social and academic context, ubiquitous digital networks increasingly permeate our day-to-day lives, work practices and ways of learning and expressing ourselves. Communication practices are increasingly multimodal, interconnected, performed on the move and dispersed across a range of communities. However, the mainstream academic dissertation – at least as a finished product – has remained largely an artefact of the press-digital, pre-networked era dominated by print literacies. The theme of this volume is clearly to explore new possibilities in this area, and how the features of new technologies might change and enhance the potential of the dissertation to provide a space for academic argument and knowledge construction for students across a range of levels.

This chapter will attempt to examine it drawing on media theory, concepts of multimodality and posthuman theory.

This chapter will seek to explore this theme in three sections. The first will attempt to situate the dissertation historically as part of an evolving 'media system' drawing on media theory and the history of media systems in universities through the ages, looking at how they have evolved and responded to new technologies over centuries in a close symbiotic relationship, positioning social actors such as students and lecturers in various ways alongside the texts they have interacted with. The next section will explore the current and potential uses of multimodal meaning-making practices in academic writing, looking at examples of attempts to situate academic argumentation in non-textual, visual formats. It will argue that verbal text is characterised by a range of affordances for the expression of complex propositional arguments that visual images *alone* are less equipped to achieve due to their allusive and metaphorical nature, which arguably demands greater interpretation on the part of the viewer/reader, rendering them more unstable than language in terms of amenability to critique. The final section will propose some of the key ideas from posthuman theory – a field of thought which considers the human interrelationship to technologies – as a potential means by which to understand meaning-making in a digitally mediated age. In particular, it will be focusing on how these ideas from posthuman theory may allow us to see the writer and the technologies of inscription as an interrelated and inseparable whole – thus challenging long-cherished notions of the author as a stable and autonomous individual acting/writing independently in the world. The chapter will conclude with a discussion of how these perspectives might help us to conceptualise new digital forms of the dissertation.

THE DISSERTATION AS PART OF A MEDIA SYSTEM

This discussion of the dissertation foregrounds the close contingent relationship between media, meaning-making and educational practices, and draws closely on Friesen and Cresswell's (2010) discussion of Kittler's notion of the university as a *media system*. Friesen and Cresswell provide a fascinating overview of Kittler's notion of the co-evolution of media and the university, pointing out that 'The history of the university... is impossible to consider without recognising the intimate relationship that this institution has with changing media technologies for storing, producing and disseminating information' (2010, p. 2).

Kittler (2004) presents a history of the university understood in terms of contemporary media, beginning with 'The Manuscript Era' of 1100–1500. During this period, he argues, the university was characterised by a complete and self-contained media system of oral and handwriting practices. Dictation was used at this time in lectures as a means of reproducing texts when manuscripts were scarce. This led to 'a central pedagogic process as simultaneously a form of recording, processing and of mediatic production' (Friesen & Cresswell 2010, p. 10). As Friesen and Cresswell point out, the invention of the printing press transformed the nature of the pedagogic encounter as books began to displace the central authority of the teacher. Additionally, the printing press rendered possible the accurate mass reproduction of diagrammatic visual representation – an aspect of what we now call multimodality.

Friesen and Cresswell go on to discuss the influence of the Humboldtian hermeneutic model of education on media practices, in particular the increased emphasis on the importance of interpretation in higher education via the student essay or research paper, in contrast to previous emphasis on recitation and reproduction via lecture notes. The next historical period focused on by Kittler is 1900 onwards, which is characterised by the turn-of-the-century preoccupation with psychology, innate biological capabilities and the beginnings of behaviourism. This period coincided with the introduction of technologies such as the typewriter and the telegraph, which '... have the ultimate effect of marginalizing or eliminating semantic elements constitutive of the subject and its inwardness – specifically as the writing hand and the feeling body' (Friesen & Cresswell, 2010, p. 26), replacing them with arbitrary components which themselves do not convey meaning. Friesen and Cresswell also refer to McLuhan's analysis of the typewriter, a device which 'fuses composition and publication' (1964, p. 260). With these technologies, they argue that the student, '... is re-installed as a producer and transmitter in a media system' (2010, p. 29), as in the pre-printing era. They make the crucial point that the present-day student is also a generator and processor of content via the internet.

Such history underscores the overwhelming degree of interdependence between media affordances, epistemologies and pedagogies in the university. The point about such interdependence has also been made within philosophy of education by Stables (2005), who argues for a semiotic understanding of educational process, seeing 'classrooms as texts' (p. 185), with communication and semiosis at the heart of the educational enterprise. This interrelationship brings with it profound implications for the dissertation in the current context of digital mediation and the related rise of multimodal semiosis. The next section will look at the current position of the dissertation in terms of accepted conventions surrounding the use of print text as opposed to non-textual elements such as visual images. It will also speculate on the extent to which argument might be carried by non-textual elements within the dissertation.

MULTIMODALITY AND THE DISSERTATION

It has been argued that the current rise of multimodal and digital media has disrupted and questioned our assumptions around the primacy of text as the dominant mode of meaning-making in digitally mediated society. As Kress and van Leeuwen (2001) have argued, the text has become increasingly superseded by the screen in popular media, and as a result text rarely appears in isolation from visual or graphic features. This is a powerfully generative observation, drawing attention to a wide range of practices. Such a move towards the screen as a dominant multimodal interface for communication can be exemplified in the widespread use of multimodal social networking websites such as Facebook which give the user potential to deploy text combined with photos and other multimodal elements; or a microblogging site such as Twitter which displays a highly degree of intertextuality with tweets often embedding links to other websites, images, videos or music. The move towards using the non-textual for communication can also be observed in the popularity of photosharing websites such as Flickr and video sites such as YouTube. These sites, often used on the move via hand-held devices, allow complex new social practices for meaning-making and the construction of subjectivities to arise; practices which mobilise a range of multimodal semiotic resources. Communication in general becomes more multimodal, as users participate in '... visual events in which the user seeks information, meaning or pleasure in an interface with visual technology' (Mirzoeff, 2002, p. 5).

Such widespread use of digitally mediated and multimodal communication in wider society raises questions regarding whether similar changes might be taking place in the university, and by implication in the context of the dissertation in particular. In fact, the shift towards multimodality in society as a whole can already be observed in the practices of higher education, as digital technologies and visual modes become more mainstream in pedagogic process. An example of such mainstreaming can be observed in the (now ubiquitous) use of PowerPoint for classroom teaching, an application which sets text out in a graphic fashion, and is likely to encourage the inclusion of video or images. Virtual learning environments (VLEs) and contemporary student textbooks also utilise more visual resources than traditional textbooks of the past. Perhaps most significantly however, is the fact that the internet is arguably now the primary site of research for the majority of students, who therefore spend substantial amounts of study time engaged with text which is surrounded by interlinked, interactive and multimodal elements such as image, video and sound.

However, despite the rise in the prominence of multimodal representation in popular media within university pedagogy and for desk research, text (used to mean here the written or printed word) has arguably remained the dominant means of carrying meaning and argument for university assessment, and as a result remains at heart of the process of dissertation writing as the dominant carrier of narrative or propositional knowledge or argument, although other non-textual elements are also deployed for meaning-making. One of the key goals of this chapter is to explore what the non-textual might offer meaning-making in the context of the dissertation. In order to investigate this topic, it seems useful to begin by considering the current uses of non-textual elements. The following sections will seek to explore how the functions and positions of non-textual semiotic elements are already mobilised in academic work and in the dissertation. Five categories of function are suggested: information, illustration, visual methodology, object of analysis or creative practice (building on Gourlay, 2010).

Information

The informative function is perhaps the most familiar use of the non-textual (particularly visual) element in extended academic texts such as dissertations – for example, charts, tables of figures or diagrams. These elements are likely to be deployed as they provide an easier or more efficient means to depict certain types of meaning in a non-textual format. Examples of such efficiency include tables of figures, which would be laborious and difficult to process in textual format, and diagrams which illustrate concepts in spatial relation to each other such as flow charts. These are widely used in scientific disciplines and are an accepted part of meaning-making practice in academic writing where quantitative empirical data are depicted and analysed, and pass unremarked as an accepted part of meaning-making in a range of disciplines.

Illustration

Illustrative uses of non-textual elements may also be used in 'conventional' academic work and dissertations. These might include the use of images to illustrate topics focused on in the text using photographs, drawings or other forms of visual representation to augment the reader's understanding of phenomena under discussion. However, the inclusion of this type of visual image is perhaps less commonly used across a range of disciplines than the use of tables and diagrams. It might be speculated that this use of images is often viewed within academic writing as surplus to requirements, as perhaps the image is not seen as carrying meaning otherwise absence in the text (unlike a table of figures). The increased use of PowerPoint has allowed the inclusion of the visual images to become mainstream in academic presentations, but interestingly the ability to include visual images in written academic texts has not lead to a wholesale deployment of them alongside verbal print text, in published work or in the dissertation. This may be seen as a reflection of certain dominant values surrounding what counts for legitimate and appropriate academic expression, which is still largely expected to be enacted via verbal text.

Multimodal methodologies

Non-textual artefacts such as photographs, videos and drawings might be included in the thesis as they were created or were assembled as part of the research methodology (Gourlay, 2009). Visuals are perhaps best established in qualitative research as an element of ethnographic fieldwork. Pink (2007) provides examples of video, photography and digital media are incorporated into ethnography, tracing this tendency back to the 'new ethnography' of the 1980s, the related critique of positivism/realism. Images are seen here as part of a richer approach to documenting social practice on the part of the ethnographer. Research participants can also be asked to produce non-textual artefacts such as photos and drawings as part of the data collection methodology, arguably providing an alternative means to express meanings which may be difficult to articulate in words. Another feature of the image is its potential for the expression of metaphor, and how images can be put to work to represent a subtle or difficult-to-express aspect of experience. An example of this can be seen in Gourlay (2009), which reports on a study in which students kept a multimodal journal reflecting on their experiences of the transition into the first year of higher education. Figure 5.1 (along with five similar images) was produced by a student who seemed to struggle to express herself in interviews. However, she produces a series of detailed images and brief accompanying notes to explore her experience of first year at university (Figure 5.1).

In addition to visual images, physical artefacts may also be deployed as part of the research process, as Archer (2008) shows us in her investigation of student experiences via an exploration of culturally significant *symbolic objects* such as wood in the South African context, referring to Kress and van Leeuwen's (2006) notion of the multimodal 'semiotic landscape'. However, these approaches to research methodology remain rather marginal and as such perhaps less 'regulated' in terms of accepted approaches and precedents to draw on. For these reasons, they may be seen by supervisors and students as 'high-risk' options when approaching the dissertation – which remains primarily a form of assessment for students to gain a qualification.

Objects of analysis

In the case of objects of analysis, the non-textual elements may be presented in the thesis because they constitute the object of analysis as separate, pre-existing phenomena in the world of social and cultural practice. An example of this type of analysis in published work can be seen in Bayne (2008), who explicitly addresses higher education as a visual practice in her analysis of the uses of iconography in the VLE, including a critique of the WebCT logo. This logo shows a white male cartoon figure dressed in an academic gown and mortar board, holding what appears to be a degree certificate, which in Bayne's analysis is representative of a stereotyped vision elitist higher education.

Although the visual and multimodal does receive a great deal of attention in some approaches to interaction and discourse analysis within Applied Linguistics, such as in the work of Goodwin (2007), approaches which explicitly look at the visual or multimodal *as objects of analysis* are relatively marginal in social research. Even studies focusing on overwhelmingly visual phenomena tend not to look directly at the visual elements of practice in the methodology; but prefer to restrict themselves to traditional textual methodologies such as surveys and interviews to generate participant accounts of experiences of visual or multimodal phenomena. An example of this is the special issue of the journal of the Association for Learning Technology on 'Learning and Teaching in Immersive Virtual Worlds' (ALT-J 2008), in which only two out of nine papers include visual images, with these used for illustrative purposes. This is particularly noteworthy

Figure 5.1 Louise's image and notes
Main image: Sometimes life is a bit of a blur to me. I'm not sure what will happen to me after I graduate, whether I'll stay within the publishing industry or whatever.
Picture of silly sandwiches: I'm laughing a lot more now. =D
Picture next to silly sandwiches: Now that I'm older I feel that I can see myself more clearly than when I was in high school. I notice more of my strengths and weaknesses.
Umbrella: One of my weaknesses is that I need someone to be a 'protector' for me, who is around my age and won't be judgemental. Feeling isolated still exists.
Chair: I feel lazy and tired sometimes which affects my learning.
Bus sign: I feel more independent.

as this issue is looking at a field of practice which is defined by its multimodal and visual nature, and illustrates the continued dominance of text-only as a mode of representation in research and resultant published academic work. Again, this is a relatively niche form of analysis, with the vast majority of qualitative research taking place in a paradigm which revolves around verbalisation and the analysis of account data – such as interviews – as texts. Approaches to multimodal data analysis are still relatively new, and again this may be viewed as a 'high-risk' choice when compared with more established forms of analysis.

Creative practice

This broad category is intended to cover the inclusion of non-textual elements in a thesis which focuses on creative practice such as fine art, dance or music. As discussed elsewhere in this volume, provision is already made for candidates to present a dissertation partly in visual or auditory formats for this reason, although a text-based commentary is still required. Within these disciplines, the convention is often to present the creative work itself using non-textual means – such as a video or sound recording of a performance, or the presentation for examination of a visual image or a three-dimensional artefact. However, the student is still required to write a substantial text to accompany the creative element of the thesis (about 40,000 words). This verbal text acts as a commentary which expresses the theoretical background for the creative element, which raises interesting questions: is such an exposition in text necessary? To what extent can the key meanings in the dissertation be expressed by non-textual means? The next section seeks to explore this latter theme in more detail.

As carrier of academic argument?

This final category is speculative as opposed to descriptive. Although it is widely recognised that visual modes of expression in the arts can carry argument, this section seeks to explore the question of whether and to what extent academic argument *which has conventionally been expressed in verbal textual format* might also be carried by non-textual means. Such academic argument is taken to include narrative and propositional content which is not conventionally expressed in non-textual formats in academic settings, and therefore does not fit into one of the categories proposed above.

One example of innovative practice in this area can be seen in the context of a Masters programme at a UK university focusing on e-learning. Bayne and Ross (2010) required students to produce a 'digital essay' in non-textual formats as the object of assessment on one of their modules. This resulted in a broad range of digital artefacts, in one case the creation of a visual space in the immersive virtual of Second Life to explore the work of Donna Haraway. The student had created a virtual three-dimensional chamber, in which images and quotations associated with Haraway's (1991) work on the cyborg were presented.

Through the presentation of this work, Bayne and Ross raised the question of the extent to which the affordances of this predominantly non-textual world are suitable for the communication of an investigation of Haraway's complex and highly conceptual work. As this assessment was taking place at Masters level, the related question was raised as to whether the largely non-textual semiotic resources of the immersive virtual world were adequate to the demands of demonstrating postgraduate level analysis. This example brings forward a host of issues which are also of close relevance to the question of non-textual argumentation in the dissertation.

Arguably, the first limitation of a non-textual representation of this type of abstract meaning is that clarity of argumentation may be lost or compromised by the use of images, which tend by their nature to be symbolic, metaphorical or allusive. By contrast, comparatively unambiguous shared meaning is made available through the lexical and syntactic resources of language; which are relatively stable in terms of their agreed referents, particularly in the rule-governed genre of academic writing within a given discipline. Particular words can be used to denote concepts and their referents which can be assumed to be broadly shared by the readers – this need for clarity is often reinforced in academic writing by the explicit use of definitions to pinpoint exact intended referents for the purposes of the text. Similarly, grammatical structures can be deployed to convey precise relationships between these referents. Tenses are deployed to demote narrative, chronology or sequence, and a range of devices can be used to denote relationships such as causality, contrast or opposition. Language is composed of thousands of lexical items which have evolved over time through situated social practice to be used in infinite combination to express fine shades of meaning, in a system which is clearly dynamic and in a contact state of flux, but still remains sufficiently shared as to be able to convey meaning across time and space in the form of a print text as a stand-alone semiotic artefact. By contrast, an image of a cyborg combined with quotations from Haraway's work arguably cannot begin to accurately represent in detail the arguments deployed by Haraway in her textual work.

Although it may be claimed that visual design has a 'grammar' (Kress & van Leeuwen, 2006) – a set of shared conventions to combine elements in order to structure and convey meaning – two objections may be raised to applying a strong version of this notion of visual imagery in academic argumentation. First, it can be argued that these elements may not be recognised and shared to the same degree of precision as lexical items. For example, the word 'cyborg' refers to multiple concepts, but at least in textual format may appear unambiguously and constantly as the same word, whereas multiple images (and therefore interpretations) of a cyborg exist. As a print word, it can be introduced, contextualised and defined in the text. If still in doubt, the reader has recourse to definition via shared resources such as dictionaries. By contrast, a visual image of a cyborg arguably must appear in isolation without the same supporting context of preamble, definition or 'unpacking' or discussion available in print.

Precise propositions about the relationships between the cyborg and other cultural practices and concepts cannot be clearly expressed readily in a visual format, except perhaps via sequence, placement and proximity – which seem rather rude instruments of meaning-making in comparison with the vast range of lexical and grammatical resources available to a writer. Language constitutes a rich store of shared meaning and subtle interplay and reference which has developed over centuries in textual practices to suit the needs of various argument-based disciplines. By contrast, as images tend often to be associative as opposed to strictly denotive, the use of images places a heavier burden of interpretation on the reader, and the resultant assumed meaning is highly unpredictable and reliant on the reader's individual and unknowable set of personal associations.

Additionally, it can be argued that the use of an assemblage such as pictures plus brief quotations can only really be used effectively with a 'knowing' audience. Such grouping of elements relies heavily for effective communication on the assumption of already-established shared meanings on the part of the audience, likely to have been garnered from previously read verbal texts. In this regard, it is undoubtedly illustrative and intertextual, but does not seem to afford a clear space for the construction of *new* meaning in any degree of academic complexity. Further to this point, the use of linguistic realisations of conceptual ideas in the form of text also offers the advantage of being more able to express and also invite critique – crucial to any definition of advanced academic achievement. Critique and discussion of ideas in texts rely heavily on linguistic elements to allow the writer to refer to other concepts expressed and published elsewhere, in order to interpret and deconstruct them explicitly. Visual elements may of course convey powerful critique through devices such as juxtaposition, pastiche and irony; but arguably remain less well-endowed than verbal text with the means with which to provide sustained, closely argued and unambiguous critical examination of complex propositions. In a related point, it can also be argued that while images are clearly capable of carrying intertextual meaning, they are less able to be deployed for the complex and precise orchestration of a range of voices from academic literature via references and quotations.

Ingraham explores this issue in detail, in particular '... what constitutes a "valid" scholarly argument and to what degree the rhetorical affordances and constraints of its mediation play a role in that valorisation' (2005, p. 46). His chapter focuses in particular on the extent to which scholarly argument can be conducted in non-print media. He proposes the BBC programme about prehistoric wildlife 'Walking with Beasts' as '... a model of what an interactive scholarly article might look like' (2005, p. 49). He bases his argument on two main points: that online fact files about the animals were available alongside the programme, and that the programme used a narrative structure about the lives of the animals to frame the argument. However, it is noteworthy that the associated fact files – although multimodal – largely rely on print text on convey propositional meaning. The images available are mostly illustrative, such as a picture of a mammoth appearing alongside blocks of text giving information about the animal.

Ingraham also argues that argument is carried by the narrative by the film itself, which is composed of computer-generated images of prehistoric animals, with a voiceover. The following is proposed by Ingraham as an example of this. In a section of the programme a mammoth is trapped. The rest of the herd gather nearby and are distressed:

> At this point the voiceover continues. 'Before long the scavengers start to gather'. An image of a human observing the scene appears, followed by the image of a wolf. The rhetorical force of this passage, which is setting the scene for the whole programme, is to humanise the mammoths and bestialise the humans. (Ingraham, 2005, p. 51)

However, a viewing of the section of the programme under discussion (BBC, 2001) reveals that the rhetorical devices used by the programme-makers are not those of proposition and evidence. Instead, their rhetorical claims for persuasiveness are various tropes more associated with wildlife films such as a focus on appealing baby animals, narratives constructing the animals as 'plucky' victims under attack, and as a result arguably an anthropomorphising of the computer-generated animals in the programme. Using these devices, various meanings are conveyed, but Ingraham's claim that this visual narrative carries an argument which will '... humanise the mammoths and bestialise the humans' (2005, p. 51) is not entirely convincing. If these meanings are present, it seems that they are presented in a rather implicit manner which depends to a large extent on the individual viewer's interpretation, and also the viewer's prior familiarity with the generic mores of the wildlife documentary (whose conventions the programme follows, although the scenes are clearly created using computer imagery) and the established values underpinning these documentaries. In this regard, the programme is profoundly intertextual, relying for the conveyance of the key point in this argument on viewers' previous experience with documentaries in which animal scavengers gather. Additionally, the moving images are accompanied throughout by a voiceover which conveys narrative and propositional information in a formal, pseudo-scientific style, using a high-status male English-accented voice throughout – arguably indexing notions of scientific authority and power – and in that sense deeply conventional. As such, although interesting, in this regard Ingraham's analysis does not seem to constitute a wholly persuasive example of a groundbreaking, non-textual, multimodal set of resources conveying complex argument.

Additionally, it is worth noting that this argument is a relatively simple one, and yet it is not unambiguously conveyed here – and also that the means by which it was presented were largely verbal. This raises doubts concerning the utility of non-verbal semiotic assemblages such as this to convey unambiguously complex, abstract, multi-stranded and novel arguments – which would be less-easily indexed by established generic conventions. This seems to underscore the point that visual resources are perhaps more allusive than denotive – in the sense that the TV viewer as 'reader' of the visual text about the mammoths is assumed to be able to recognise elements which Ingraham interprets as constructing the meaning that the animals are 'humanised' and the humans 'bestialised' in this scene, through a combination of images and verbal commentary. Leaving aside the rather problematic connotations of the terms 'humanised' and 'bestialised', this emotive depiction of the prehistoric humans gathering to hunt a mammoth stuck in the ice is highly culturally specific and could be read quite differently by a viewer from a different context, for example, a modern-day hunter-gatherer who may not share our squeamishness. In this regard, it is laden with unexamined and unexpressed ideological content which is not made explicit. Arguably, a clearer linguistic statement would have anchored this argument in a format more amenable to critique of this kind; an openness to contestation, which is a cornerstone of advanced academic argument. This is perhaps one of the paradoxes of using visual assemblages to carry argument; that the images open up a greater interpretive space for the reader/viewer to occupy. This allows for subtlety and multiplicity of interpretation – which may enhance and open up meaning in creative or illustrative uses, but may be less effective if the presentation of (relatively) precise, shared, complex propositional argument is the aim.

This section has attempted to show that there exists a range of uses for non-textual elements for meaning-making in the construction of argument, but has also argued that verbal text remains a vital element for the construction of complex argumentation. However, this does not obviate Kress and van Leeuwen's (2001) point about the increased dominance of the screen over the page in our digitally mediated society, and the implications of this change for the academy and for academic writing. The next section will explore posthuman theory as a potentially generative lens through which to consider this issue.

POSTHUMAN PERSPECTIVES

The first point to be made is that the notion the 'posthuman' is in no sense unitary, but is in fact a loosely associated group of perspectives which seek to interrogate the dominant assumptions of liberal humanism from a range of angles (an up-to-date overview is provided by Wolfe, 2010). These have generated a series of compelling challenges to dominant and seldom-questioned notions of the human as a central and entirely separate category of being distinct from the environment, animals and information technology. This section will focus on the latter interface and its implications for the dissertation in a digitally mediated academy.

This questioning of assumptions around categories of human being was prompted in part by Donna Haraway's now iconic text 'The Manifesto for Cyborgs' (1991). In a complex, ironic and iconoclastic text, Haraway proposes a blurring of boundaries between a range of categories, in particular the supposedly

clear distinction between the technological and the biological, inspiring a generation of theorists to consider the notion of the cyborg in terms of literal interfaces
of technology and biology in the body, but also the intertwining of machine and
human in social practice. Building on the latter strand, this section will draw
on Katherine Hayles's 'How we Became Posthuman' (1999), and her notion of
flickering signification in a digital age. She defines the posthuman as follows:

> In the posthuman, there is no essential difference or absolute demarcations between bodily
> existence and computer simulation, cybernetic mechanism and biological organism, robot
> teleology and human goals. (Hayles, 1999, p. 3)

She describes the posthuman subject as:

> ... an amalgam, a collection of heterogenous components, a material-informational
> entity whose boundaries undergo continuous construction and reconstruction. (Hayles,
> 1999, p. 3)

Importantly, Hayles is not proposing a literal cyborg – a mixture of biological
being and technological implants – but instead is examining the interweaving
of the biological and the technological at the level of social practices and
subjectivities. As she says of posthumanism, '... the defining characteristics
involve the construction of subjectivity, not the presence of nonbiological
components' (1999, p. 4). Our close relationship with technology and the notion
of the computer being an intrinsic part of our lives both socially and psychologi-
cally has also been explored in depth by Turkle (2005), a perspective which
Hayles explicitly builds on. Hayles's book is a wide-ranging work, interrogating
the cultural meanings produced by postwar cybernetics, and the implications
for notions of embodiment and virtuality, an analysis she extends in her more
recent work on the notion of the cognisphere (2006). For the purposes of
this chapter, I will focus on one particular area of her work, the notion of *flickering signification*, as it seems to offer a helpful perspective on the future of the
dissertation.

Flickering signification

Hayles (1999) examines various mediating technologies of inscription, also
drawing on Kittler's (1990) work, in particular his comparison of the handwritten
word as flowing image, compared with the geometrically arranged letters on a
typewritten page in which the signified and signifier hold a one-to-one relationship – one key to one letter. Hayles takes this notion forward and explores the
difference between writing on a typewriter and writing on a computer, arguing
that digital mediation disrupts the one-to-one relationship between the signifier
and signified provided by the typewriter as physical machine. As she puts it,
'Carrying the instabilities implicit in Lacanian floating signifiers one step
further, information technologies create what I will call *flickering signifiers*,
characterised by their tendency towards unexpected metamorphoses, attenuations,

and dispersions' (Hayles, 1999, p. 30). For Hayles, in digital mediation the signifier is no longer a single marker like the ink mark left by the typewriter key, but is a flexible chain of markers. As she argues, 'When narrative functionalities change, a new kind of reader is produced by the text. The material effects of flickering signification ripple outwards because readers are trained to read through different functionalities which can affect how they interpret any text' (1999, pp. 47–48).

Hayles' notion of digital text as *flickering signifier* may be of particular relevance in seeking to understand the position of the author of the current-day dissertation (and in academic writing in general). As the relationship between signifier and signified is further decoupled in this way, then arguably the notion of the stable and singular human author is brought into question. The 'writer' of the text arguably cannot be identified as solely the embodied human subject. Instead, the dissertation is produced by a hybrid biological-informational entity which is looped into wider networks of online information throughout the research and writing process. In this regard, it might be argued that all dissertations or theses are fundamentally hybrid in terms of a blurring of the apparent divide between analogue and digital in terms of writing process, if not actual product. In this respect, all dissertations are now digital, but are still forced to masquerade as an analogue print text, the final stage of the thesis production being the printing and binding of the digital document into a paper book.

CONCLUSIONS

This chapter has attempted to explore the status of the dissertation from the point of view of media theory, multimodality and posthuman notions of the relationship between the writer and the text in a digitally mediated environment. It has sought to emphasise first the close relationship between technologies of inscription from a historical point of view; looking at their features and the resultant epistemologies and pedagogies which the academy has come to value. Looking at the present day, an overview of the various ways in which print text and visual elements are deployed in the dissertation in multimodal combinations for a range of purposes was proposed. In examining this area, I made the argument that although multimodal representation may be becoming more prevalent in academic dissertations, linguistic realisation via print texts remains a necessary (though not exclusive) medium for the clear and precise construction of complex abstract argument, discussion of other texts and critical engagement with propositional content – due to the features of language as opposed to visual media in particular. I looked at an example from the literature (Ingraham, 2005) which proposes a TV programme as an example of an argument carried by a multimodal set of non-verbal semiotic resources, concluding that the excerpt from the programme under discussion relied on the verbal voiceover, and the viewers' familiarity with a culturally situated set of values and conventions, and that in these respects it did not represent a clearly successful example of a complex argument carried by non-verbal means.

The chapter then went on to consider the thesis in today's context of digital mediation, drawing on Hayles's (1999) notion of posthumanism. The key point here is that the biological human subject and information technologies are strongly intertwined in terms of social practices and ways of communicating, to the point where it becomes impossible to meaningfully separate biological human beings and the technologies that sustain their communication. Particular focus was given to Hayles's notion of *flickering signification* and the implications of this notion for our conceptions of the dissertation in terms of writing process, and the resultant status of the writer and text.

Perhaps the central conclusion which can be reached from these interrelated analyses of the dissertation is that the vast majority of texts produced within the academy are now multimodal, digitally mediated and posthuman in terms of process, even if the end result might still closely resemble an analogue print text. So what are the implications for the future? Arguably, the current system requires the dissertation to pose as an analogue, pre-digital text, when in reality it is the result of a complex multimodal and digitally mediated process involving a biological being in complex interplay with 'flickering' technologies of inscription. This complex digital artefact is then squeezed into a paper book format at the final stage of the process – with non-textual elements admitted rather grudgingly, if at all. The question presents itself as to how the dissertation might be allowed to expand beyond this format to take advantage of the additional features for meaning offered by multimodal semiotic resources beyond print text, while also maintaining the qualities of the dissertation which seem to carry the essence of advanced academic engagement; such as complex, high-level critical argument and engagement with theory.

This is an important issue for dissertations at all levels, but is perhaps particularly pertinent in any discussion of the future of the doctorate in particular, whose definition invariably includes a degree of originality of argument, theory and critique. It seems that language remains a relatively stable and shared means by which this type of argumentation can be expressed in a format which allows for clear inclusion of a range of viewpoints, incorporating nuanced, precise discussion of complex propositions which can be critiqued. However, this is not to advocate a rejection of future experimentation and the expansion of our semiotic repertoires in academic expression, both in the dissertation and in published work. In pushing back the boundaries of what constitutes a dissertation, we can allow a more complex range of meaning-making practices to be orchestrated alongside print text in a more multimodal/digitally mediated assemblage as product, reflecting the multimodal and hybrid nature of the process. In doing so, we can also perhaps not only maintain the essence of scholarship developed in context over the centuries, but also extend and renew it in the dissertations of the future.

REFERENCES

Archer, A. (2008). Cultural studies meets academic literacies: Exploring student sources through symbolic objects. *Teaching in Higher Education, 13*, 383–394.

Bayne, S. (2008). Higher education as a visual practice: Seeing through the virtual learning environment. *Teaching in Higher Education, 13*, 395–410.

Bayne, S. & Ross, J. (2010). It's alive! Digital literacy events in (and out of) context, paper presented at Literacy in the Digital University ESRC seminar series, Open University, Milton Keynes, October 14–15.

BBC (2001). *Walking with Beasts: Episode 6 Mammoth Journey* Retrieved June 26, 2011, from http://www.youtube.com/watch?v=cHp9yY785Ds

Friesen, N. & Cressman, D. (2010). Media theory, education and the university: A response to Kittler's history of the university as a media system. *Canadian Journal of Media Studies 7.*

Goodwin, C. (2007). Participation, stance and affect in the organisation of activities. *Discourse and Society, 18*, 53–73.

Gourlay, L. (2009). Threshold practices: Becoming a student through academic literacies. *London Review of Education, 7*, 181–192.

Gourlay, L. (2010). Multimodality, visual methodologies and higher education. In M. Savin-Baden & C. Howell-Major (Eds.), *New Approaches to Qualitative Research: Wisdom and Uncertainty* (pp. 80–89). London: Routledge.

Haraway, D. (1991). *Simians, Cyborgs and Women: The Reinvention of Nature.* London: Routledge.

Hayles, N. K. (1999). *How We Became Posthuman: Virtual Bodies in Cybernetics, Literature and Informatics.* London: University of Chicago Press.

Hayles, N. K. (2006). Unfinished work: From cyborg to cognisphere. *Theory, Culture, Society, 23*, 159–166.

Ingraham, B. (2005). Ambulating with mega-fauna. In R. Land & S. Bayne (Eds.), *Education in Cyberspace* (pp. 45–54). Abingdon: Routledge Falmer.

Kittler, F. (1990). *Discourse Networks 1800/1900.* Trans. M. Metteer. Stanford, CA: Stanford University Press.

Kittler, F. (2004). Universities: Wet, hard, soft and harder. *Critical Inquiry, 31*, 244–256.

Kress, G. (2003). *Literacy in the New Media Age.* London: Routledge.

Kress, G. & van Leeuwen, T. (2001). *Multimodal Discourse: The Modes and Media of Contemporary Communication.* London: Routledge.

Kress, G. & van Leeuwen, T. (2006). *Reading Images: The Grammar of Visual Design.* 2nd edn. London: Routledge.

McLuhan, M. (1964). *Understanding Media: The Extensions of Man.* New York: New American Library.

Mirzoeff, N. (Ed.) (2002). *The Visual Culture Reader.* 2nd edn. London: Routledge.

Pink, S. (2007). *Doing Visual Ethnography.* 2nd edn. London: Sage.

Stables, A. (2005). *Living and Learning as Semiotic Engagement: A New Theory of Education.* Lampeter: Edwin Mellen.

Turkle, S. (2005). *The Second Self: Computers and the Human Spirit.* Cambridge, MA: The MIT Press.

Wolfe, C. (2010). *What is Posthumanism?* Minneapolis, MN: University of Minnesota Press.

6

Reframing the Performing Arts

Zoë Beardshaw Andrews

INTRODUCTION

In this chapter, I set out the main body of my Masters dissertation for the MA in Text and Performance Studies at King's College, London, and the Royal Academy of Dramatic Art (September 2009 to November 2010). The dissertation is not digitally conceived; rather, it is *about* the incorporation of the digital into arts education. It took a conventional format: the submission of a soft-bound print dissertation. At the end of the chapter, I reflect on the process of undertaking a dissertation with a digital dimension in mind.

In the dissertation I set out to examine some examples of projects devised by performing arts organizations and to explore how far arts education in the UK and USA has progressed as a result of the inclusion of digital technology in regular practice. In the absence of comprehensive and sustained critical debate on the impact of the digital on arts education projects, I decided to investigate the practical and pedagogic advances occurring within this field as a result of the rapid technological progress of the last quarter-century. I found that existing academic study of the digital in arts education neglected analysis of the current practical projects initiated and developed by education departments within performing arts institutions, instead providing general analysis of the evolving field and including detailed accounts of authors' own academic experiments in performance and technology. I do not claim to provide comprehensive evaluation of all instances of the digital in arts education, but rather seek to examine in detail current arts education projects that depend on the digital to succeed, while grounding my research in more general analysis of the field and the changes that are occurring.

RESEARCH METHODOLOGY

The research for this dissertation consisted of a combination of reflective and empirical pathways, the emergent nature of the field requiring an investigative, pre-paradigmatic approach. Considering the lack of any statistical evidence of the impact of digital technology on arts education, I chose to supplement my literature review with in-depth interviews with professional experts in the field, each of whom shed light on my inquiry with examples of the practice of their respective companies and organizations. I gathered specialist opinions and anecdotal evidence and asked about particular projects as well as questioning rationales. I quizzed interviewees about their personal views on the reasons for digital inclusion in the arts, and encouraged them each to communicate a sense of their organisation's outlook in the field. I challenged their responses and pushed for detailed examples of their project work to illustrate their principles.

I conducted eight interviews in London and New York. Rebecca Meitlis, co-founder of ENO Baylis, the education department at the English National Opera, spoke of ENO's drive to embrace technology and the importance of linking use of the digital to an already existing human interaction as part of a project. Jesse Cohen, Director of Development, and Maggie Koozer, School Programs Manager, from the Metropolitan Opera Guild, New York, both discussed the Guild's use of the digital to document and evaluate their opera education programs, outlining the need to share best practice within arts education models and claiming the digital as the best tool for fulfilling this need. Maya Gabrielle, Digital Content Producer at the National Theatre, who has a specific remit to work with the Discover department on education projects, identified the specialized and developing field of professional work in the digital in arts education, and brought up the problem of the arts being very London-centric in the UK. Terry Braun, co-founder of Braunarts, an independent community arts initiative, described past projects which exploited the digital for artistic gain. Hannah Elder, Orchestra Education Manager at the Royal Opera House, highlighted the challenge for arts institutions to remain true to their core audiences and their identities while endeavoring to keep up with fast-moving media trends. Tom Shaw, Production and Development Director, and Fiona Lindsay, Education Consultant, from Digital Theatre both described the huge potential of their work – capturing live performance on film for archiving and access purposes – in a school environment.

As well as recording and evaluating my interviews, I accessed documentary resources from specific projects devised and developed by these experts and their departments, in order to explore particular case studies. Hannah Elder provided me with publicity materials, complementary teachers' resources and departmental documentation (including specifications and teachers' and students' feedback) relating to the Royal Opera House's annual composition competition, *Fanfare*. Terry Braun led me to websites and a CD Rom providing access to information about Braunarts' digital audio work, *The DARK*, enabling me to listen to the production and gain a sense of the rationale behind the project. Rebecca Meitlis described the English National Opera's iPhone application 'Play Ligeti', which I downloaded to explore as a consumer and learner. I was particularly interested in Digital Theatre's plans for a specific education site, DT Plus, but since its launch was in January 2011, my investigation consisted of hearing accounts of its progress from Fiona Lindsay and Tom Shaw.

These two methods for eliciting empirical data from the publicly operating field of arts education allowed me to cultivate a sense of the presence of the digital within examples of real work. Replayed recordings of the interviews and careful note-taking encouraged comparisons and analysis of my findings, cross-referencing between anecdotal evidence from the interviews and the more tangible evidence from the project documentation.

I investigated published work on the topics of the arts, education and digital technology, including systematic research reviews on the benefits of the arts in the classroom. Most useful here were Anderson, Carroll and Cameron's work *Drama Education with Digital Technology* (2009) and Chapple and Kattenbelt's *Intermediality in Theatre and Performance* (2006). Contextualizing my empirical discoveries in academic research, I built up an understanding of the wider field of study and gained a grasp of the rapidly broadening impact of the digital in arts education practice.

CONTEXT: OUR MEDIATIZED WORLD AND ITS PARTICIPANTS

It's a completely changing landscape, and I do think that [the arts] will be slow to catch up. (Maya Gabrielle, National Theatre)

The developed world – and with it the field of the performing arts – has been altered by rapid progression in technology in the last half-century. The terms used to describe the agents of these changes vary from 'technological advances' to 'digital progress', the 'digital revolution' and Auslander's 'mediatization' (1999). Dixon helpfully points out that "digital" has become a loose and generic term applied to any and all applications that incorporate a silicon chip' (Dixon & Smith, 2007, p. x) and I use the term broadly in this chapter. Dixon reflects on Auslander's 'increasingly undifferentiated ontologies of live and mediatized forms' (2007, p. 123) as the digital creeps into our lifestyles and into performance, becoming a dominant force in culture. Now, in the twenty-first century, the digital is not only a force external to an artwork, changing it from the outside or changing the way it is presented, but has become part of the way humans approach art, changing the artist's and audience's attitudes from conception through creation and onwards. Jensen summarizes these shifts in attitude in relation to theatre when she states that 'mediatization [is] acting as an internal mechanism or influence on the cultural language and structures of theatre' (Jensen, 2007, p. 2). A major catalyst of the digital take-over of culture was the birth of the Internet, eventually allowing extended downloads, sharing, streaming – 'an immense interactive database … a performance collaboration and distribution medium' (Dixon, 2007, p. 3).

All art forms have been revolutionized by the digital in recent decades, from digital photography in online galleries to films on YouTube to David Hockney's innovative visual artworks created on Apple's iPad. Even dance, which focuses on the human body, has been infiltrated by the digital as a special relationship between moving image and dance has emerged: in ZooNation's *Into the Hoods* at the Southbank Centre in 2010, each dancer had an onscreen cyber-version of themselves, and one merged into the other seamlessly, with the dancer entering the stage through a slit in the backdrop, onto which the digital cyber-character had been projected. Music, however, 'has arguably been more radically revolutionized by the "digital revolution" than the other performance arts' (Dixon, 2007, p. x). It is common practice now to compose digitally, using sequencing and editing software and music notation software; equally, music has embraced technology in terms of its commercial distribution, via iTunes and other sites (both legally and illegally). This progress was harnessed by the Royal Opera House education department in their *Fanfare* project, a competition that encouraged young people to compose and submit compositions digitally. Technology has become a musical instrument and a tool that 'mediate[s] in the reception and consumption of music' (Finney & Burnard, 2007, p. 2). It is within the field of music that technology has made the furthest inroads into arts education so far, with teachers recognizing students' expertise in digital composition and established national exams and degrees in Music Technology. Finney claims that these advances in music technology offer 'music teachers and the young people they are teaching unprecedented scope for democratic engagement in making music' (2007, p. 2). An unlikely but fascinating tangent here is the link made by young people between musical sounds and digital imagery: a link created by the culture of music videos and the 'visualizers' installed in most music library and DJ programs, that create firework-like computer-generated moving images with the animation dictated by the sounds and rhythms of the music playing. Finney insists that young people's 'musical thinking is infused with digital imagery' (2007, p. 10) – further proof that music is the art form most deeply integrated into the digital.

As we begin to trace the effect of the digital revolution on education we come across two more examples of its impact: on participation and on generations. To participate can mean a very different kind of action when combined with the use of technology. It excludes the necessity of being present which in turn excludes the need to speak or make eye contact with others and it puts onus on the contribution one makes rather than the way in which one makes it. Goodfellow writes

that 'developments in the technologies of e-learning are not tied to the proliferation of interaction-based models of participation' (Lockard & Pegrum, 2007,
p. 69) – but I suggest that even e-learning forums still demand participation,
where the interaction may not be human to human, but would be human to technology, or human to human through technology. The digital has widened
the generational gap between young and old, not only through differences in
capacity for understanding and using technology, but also though differing attitudes to it: 'the modern inclination is to view technology as either neutral or
unambiguously beneficial ... our public culture predisposes us toward recognizing technology primarily as an opportunity' (Barney in Lockard & Pegrum, 2007,
p. 271) whereas previous generations regard it with fear or apprehension.
Furthermore, generational attributes have shifted due to familiarity with
and dependence on the digital, which Krause identifies as the 'attributes of the
"information age mindset": multitasking as a way of life; emphasis on doing
rather than knowing; greater familiarity with typing rather than handwriting; the
importance of staying connected; zero tolerance for delay, along with a 24/7
mentality; and reliance on the web as the primary source of information' (Krause
in Lockard & Pegrum, 2007, p. 126). The tangible digital impact on generation
and participation sparks an inevitable shift in society's approach to culture – our
access, interpretation and participation in art, theatre and music has begun to
change.

With the effect on art forms, identity, participation and generation comes an
inevitable impact of the digital on learning. Schools are perhaps the locations
within culture that have most responsibility to advance with the technology,
since they must support and challenge our most advanced generation. Booth
acknowledges the problem: 'so swift has been the cultural flood that educators
are struggling to accommodate digital connections inside (and outside) school
walls' (in Anderson, Carroll & Cameron 2009, p. 222), while Kibby champions
a hybrid teaching mode of the personable and the digital:

> Using a hybrid mode to deliver learning activities enhances student learning in a number
> of ways, including making study more convenient, by allowing time shifting; improving
> interaction, by enabling considered responses to discussions; increasing individualized
> learning opportunities, through the ability to provide a menu of learning activities; providing
> a student-focused environment, where passive tasks such as note-taking are replaced
> by active experiences; developing core skills, including an ability to self- and peer-evaluate,
> and to apply logical, critical and creative thinking to information; and enabling support
> networks, from peer study groups to mentoring programs. (Kibby, in Lockard & Pegrum,
> 2007, p. 88)

Despite this comprehensive argument in support of changes in pedagogy, it is
possible to suggest that teachers' aims should stay in line with their perpetual
mission to impart information, hone skills and develop understanding in young
people using available resources and to do this in a way that excites and engages
the students. Returning to drama education, Cameron and Anderson insist that
nothing has changed apart from the tools obtainable: 'the teacher's role in the

drama classroom of today infused (or not) with technology is the same as it always has been: to provide students with access to the tools of creation and support their growing control of those tools to create meaning' (2009, p. 14).

The effect of the digital on all these aspects of life and art is not discrete, but ongoing without pause as the rate of advance in technology outstrips capacity for change in culture. Nevertheless, present practices in education or art are re-evaluated in the light of technology, even recontextualized, which allows a 're-envisioning of the future [to] take place' (Finney & Burnard, 2007, p. 1). Arguably, it is the digital that is establishing a place for the arts in the twenty-first century world; Chapple calls it 'the language of the new media ... the new medium appropriate to engage with interculturalism and globalization' (2006, p. 89). To further champion this claim, and to dissect the generational contrasts in approach to the digital in culture, we must examine those exposed to the digital in cultural and educational activity.

'DIGITAL NATIVES' AND 'DIGITAL IMMIGRANTS'

The present study demands investigation into the body of learners that come into most contact with the digital in their artistic learning and practice. I refer here to the younger generation of today – those born from circa 1985 onwards, who have been exposed to information and communication technology for all of their lives, and particularly who have experienced formal education in a world that is already saturated with the digital. Prensky (2001) termed this generation 'digital natives', in contrast to the older 'digital immigrant' generation, those who have gradually 'migrated' (Krause in Lockard & Pegrum, 2007, p. 126) to technology use through necessity or interest. People in many developed societies and economies are now 'bombarded with greater access to information, communication and expression through technological innovations' (Finney & Burnard, 2007, p. 197) but it is the digital native generation which fosters the skills and experience to capitalize on digital opportunities, building on an instinctive dexterity with technology. For these young people, many educational and social opportunities occur through technology in parallel to those occurring in the 'real' world, and for some the self is moulded and established through the digital – for example, 'young people's online authorship of blogs and home pages ... can provide important opportunities for self-reflection and self-realization' (Buckingham, 2008, p. 3). Much published criticism and analysis seems to take a stance in awe of digital natives – probably in part due to the digital immigrant status of the authors – but Buckingham reminds us of the banality of many young people's media use: 'most young people's everyday uses of the Internet are characterized not by spectacular forms of innovation and creativity, but by relatively mundane forms of communication and information retrieval' (2008, p. 14). Despite this, we can expect those who are familiar with the digital to gain most profitably from its inclusion in arts education, due to their willingness to accept the digital as a beneficial addition to learning. Further, we must acknowledge the altered learning and thought processes of digital natives, complimented by the multi-representational mode of the digital in art.

The current generational divide determined by technology provides specific challenges for teaching, a field in which the younger learners are stimulated by uses of technology with which the older teachers may not be confident. Online learning can be especially testing: 'the recent and ubiquitous dissemination of online technologies into the home and the classroom has provided great challenges for those "digital immigrant" educators striving to make pedagogy and technology complement each other' (Anderson et al., 2009, p. 11). I suggest that as a result of this dissemination, the pedagogy, not the technology, needs to change – technological advance is already rapid, and teaching practice must be flexible enough to keep up. Krause reiterates this necessity: 'academics, institutional leaders and policy-makers alike have a responsibility to develop proactive strategies for keeping students connected to learning communities, whether through virtual or real learning settings' (in Lockard & Pegrum, 2007, p. 139) – this now includes a responsibility to embrace the digital. Digital natives learn differently, and teaching practices must adapt to this; similarly, arts organizations ought to recognize these changes in their market audiences when developing their education programs.

The use of computers in learning environments both helps to facilitate learning and affects young people's approach to a task. 'Young people growing up in performative societies inevitably absorb the imagery they see' (Nicholson, 2009, p. 45) and thus their imagination is highly influenced by a mediatized and commodified culture industry – even approaches to classwork that don't utilize technology will be influenced by it via a young person's interpretation of the world around them. Seddon champions the digital as a social tool in the classroom, and proposes that 'certain personality types, such as very introverted students, find it easier to engage in collaborative computer-based composition in e-learning environments than face-to-face environments' (in Finney & Burnard, 2007, p. 113). Though this would stand to reason considering digital natives' familiarity with technology, it is an assertion to be treated with caution, as it would be easy to imagine the digital – if relied upon too fully – robbing young people of their social skills, personal voices and the ability to relate humanly to peers and others. Of course, honing these skills in young people is one of the essential aims of education. However it is, interaction in digital form is beyond an additive process for digital natives – an already internalized way of thinking.

The digital native generation has developed a nuanced relationship to the arts, with their social aspirations, skills set and attitudes to culture affecting approaches and opinions relating to artworks. Nicholson credits young people's ability to create 'theatre as they would like life to be rather than simply reproducing the theatre as it already exists' (2009, p. 80) – the relationship between art and life is affected by the digital only in that technology is now a fundamental part of life, so it duly impacts on artwork and practice. The performing arts can give 'shape and form to the circumstances and difficulties faced by young people in the here-and-now' (2009, p. 43) and arts education practitioners should be particularly aware of encouraging young people to represent their lives rather than departing from them in their work. This challenge is partly due to freedom of theatrical language – young people need to find 'a place to develop with professional theatre-makers theatrical languages and performance vocabularies that reflect their identities and represent their experiences in an increasingly globalized and mediatized world' (2009, p. 46). Nicholson cites the wide range of terms used to describe arts education practice as evidence of the erosion of divisions between theatre as art and theatre as a learning medium (2009, p. 47) – digital natives tend not to need to distinguish so clearly between the two.

For digital natives, technology has become a contributor to identity and to citizenship as well as an agent of learning, communication and play. A young person's demeanor now is not only categorized via their external appearance, their manner and their behavior toward others, but also via their online versions of these traits. Possession of technology also represents status and wealth, reiterating technology's role as an instrument of identity. Ultimately, a person's engagement with culture via the digital may shape and correspond to who they are. Barney goes further to propose that digital technology is also an object of citizenship: 'it is intimately bound up in the establishment and enforcement of prohibitions and permissions, the distribution of power and resources, and the structure of human practices and relationships' (Barney in Lockard & Pegrum, 2007, p. 274). Education and culture also contribute to citizenship, so the combination of the three agents simultaneously creates a potentially powerful trio in the make-up of a community. When analyzing digital natives, Buckingham reminds us that 'the emergence of a so-called 'digital generation' can only be adequately understood in the light of other changes – for example, in the political economy of youth culture, the social and cultural policies and practices that regulate and define young people's lives, and the realities of their everyday social environments' (2008, p. 15). Nevertheless, digital natives are a generation now embedded in society, and they hold the power to change cultural and artistic methodology in the years to come.

DISCOVERY: ARTS EDUCATION AND THE DIGITAL IN PRACTICE

When I asked Fiona Lindsay where she thought the niche for the digital lies in arts education, she recoiled from the idea that the potential connection was solely a 'niche' and insisted that it is absolutely *necessary* for arts education to embrace the digital. Broadly, it is our global cultural economy that necessitates this connection – the digital is now so deeply embedded into urban culture that there will soon come a point where arts education *must* utilize the digital in order to be understood, recognized and valued. When Dixon writes of 'a newly global connectivity creat[ing] new arenas for interaction between science, art and technology' (2007, p. vii), he describes an environment that is increasingly dependent on E. M. Forster's maxim, so applicable to culture, learning and technology: 'Only connect'. McMaster, in his 2008 report to the UK's Department for Culture, Media and Sport on excellence in the arts, states that 'harnessing the possibilities offered by the exponential growth and development in new technologies is an important part of enabling risk and innovation' (2008, p. 18). This is true in arts education as in performance and production. When McMaster asks, 'Why is it that we see cultural organizations, with some notable exceptions, following behind the demand for technological advances rather than driving it?' (2008, p. 18), he identifies the gap within our cultural economy that needs to be filled: between advancing technologies and the traditional arts. Most of the professional experts I interviewed for the dissertation spoke of the attempt to balance a commitment to the traditions of their art form, and to their core audiences, with a responsibility to advancing culture in line with communicative media forms. Education departments can promote their commitment to younger generations in order to further justify exploitation of digital technology in their work. Nicholson points out the counter-argument that 'theatre is, by its very nature, live, local and public, and therefore has the potential to disrupt the homogenizing tendencies associated with globalization' (2009, p. 44); without denying these characteristics of live theatre, a connection between arts education and digital technology can tap into the global-reaching – yet often privately experienced – traits of art forms, while contradicting homogenization by maintaining focus on the art form itself and the extensive range of artworks that exists within any form.

The digital is now established as a strong feature of the performing arts – it is often employed within theatre, opera and dance productions as a visual or aural element, either on or alongside the stage. Chapple describes these multimodal productions as part of 'a non-hierarchical, multi-layered mode of performance, where all the elements of media text and performance styles come together into an intermedial texture awaiting the organizing mind and body of the audience' (2006, p. 99). It is the ease with which we now understand and receive multimodal expression that has channeled and promoted artistic evolution toward the digital. Chapple and Kattenbelt's term, 'intermedial', sums up the new hybridity of the performing arts, representing the 'blurring of generic boundaries' (2006, p. 11). They insist that intermediality and the presence of digital technology in performance 'is creating new modes of representation; new dramaturgical strategies; new ways of structuring and staging words, images and sounds; new ways of positioning bodies in time and space; new ways of creating temporal and spatial interrelations' (2006, p. 11). Furthermore, an intermedial artwork does not have to rest within the original framework of the art form – for example, a production is intermedial when it is performed live in a theatre and simultaneously broadcast to cinemas. For the cinema audiences here, the essence of the artistic experience lies *between* the stage and the screen. Digital technology is now regularly used within the arts to support, enhance or communicate the live, whether as an artistic feature in its own right such as a video screening alongside choreographed dance, or as technical support such as an amplifying and balancing sound system at a music concert. This integration of technology and art calls for a parallel integration in arts education; 'the Academy must respond and change curriculum and research practices to put intermediality at the centre (not the side) of theatre and education research' (2006, p. 83).

Technology has not only become a vital component of our global economy in the developed world; it has infiltrated our everyday lives, routines and livelihoods. Dixon's joke about 'the proscenium arch of the computer monitor' (2007, p. 4) is not far from the truth due to the widespread practice of viewing television programs, films, photographs, visual art and recorded performing arts on one's computer. Where technology functions solely as a tool for an older generation, it is integral to the habits and social lives of the younger generation of today. Environments, both personal and public, often rely on digital technology to maintain their purpose or atmosphere. Furthermore, the arts cannot choose but to embrace digital technology, if they are to succeed in representing our lived world. The presence of technology also changes our demands on learning and entertainment – most significantly, 'young people in our classrooms...are seeking, expecting and creating new ways of utilizing the technologies of now to more accurately describe and communicate their lived experiences and responses to the world' (Neelands in Anderson, Carroll & Cameron, 2009, p. xiv). Auslander traces the battle between the live and the mediatized in his argument on 'liveness' (1999), emphasizing the altered attitudes to the live in environments infused in media. Booth writes of a 'need to create our drama events in terms of the multimodal digital nature of what students now accept as necessities' (in Anderson, Carroll & Cameron, 2009, p. 224) – it is clear that arts education policies and projects must adapt to the different demands of the younger generation, not least because of future audience development.

The most significant impact that digital technology is having on the arts and education is via affecting access. Through the Internet, teachers can access resources and the art forms themselves without needing to leave the classroom. This is the premise upon which Digital Theatre has founded its principles: their mission to create universally downloadable videos of live performance is giving their subscribers access to top quality British theatre all over the world; their education mini-site will provide a one-stop access point for videos of productions and behind-the-scenes interviews, teaching and learning resources and downloadable interactive information packs. This type of work could revolutionize a school's curriculum for the arts, especially through providing inexpensive access to the performing arts without the extra effort associated with taking students out of school. Finney also notes the access route created by technology between school and home: 'the school can now be accessed from home, home accessed from school, and the rest of the world from both' (2007, p. 1) making learning a constant, active process.

With technological progression comes the responsibility of educational and artistic institutions to keep up with the resources and equipment available and to match young people's interest and skill within the digital realm in order to tap into the way they are stimulated. Technological advances necessitate a parallel drive in pedagogy. Where arts organizations aim to inspire young people, the familiar media of digital technology can serve as a motivating hook, and in some cases can even make the art form more attractive to young people when framed through a project working with digital technology.

DRAMA EDUCATION AND THE BODY

Drama education, at best taking place in either a spacious classroom or a studio, explores the dramatic canon and encourages young people to use their bodies and voices in performance in order to inform, explore or entertain. Jensen suggests that the inclusion of the digital in this sector of education reduces young people's understanding of their physicality and marginalizes the body in performance (2007, p. 167). Many dance companies have explored engagement with the digital via sensors which can map dancers' movements and model them digitally; virtual performance games have players guide a virtual version of themselves. The body and the physical self are re-imagined by the digital: 'mediatized interactions become dramatic, theatrical performances where participants see their own bodies, and their virtual extension, as the sites of interpretation or reinvention' (Jensen, 2007, p. 169). Most interactions with the digital are visual, stimulating the brain but not the body, but lack of physical involvement does not mean that the body is not represented in the encounter: in virtual reality encounters, a projection of a second self is represented onscreen; or when watching a 'National Theatre Live' or 'Met Opera Live in HD' cinema broadcast, the viewer imagines their body in a seat in the Olivier or Lincoln Center auditorium. The digital does not undermine the body, but reinvents it in new spheres of interaction.

PLAY

A strong feature of any project that includes creative input and interaction is a sense of play. The back-and-forthness of interaction (whether it is between two people or between a person and a computer), the creative interplay, and the sense of the unknown in every new exchange are all part of playfulness, an element of interactive learning that stimulates and excites both the teacher and the learner. Dixon defines four patterns of interaction: navigation, participation, conversation and collaboration, and insists that 'play pervades and unites all four interactive paradigms' (2007, p. 597). The success of play within educational models gives rise to the potential for artists to design games and playful encounters that lead to deliberate learning objectives, and more control could be gained by designing digital play. 'A core design tenet for facilitators of drama and architects of games [is] to encourage engagement by providing scaffolded but open-ended experiences for the participants' (Dunn & O'Toole in Anderson, Carroll & Cameron, 2007, p. 22) – these demand skilled writers and careful testing to strike a balance of freedom of experience while maintaining a structured learning curve.

Rebecca Meitlis explained to me that digital play worked best, in her experience, when based on a project that firstly worked with interaction between young people and artists on a human level. She showed me a very successful recent foray into the digital as part of an ENO Baylis project on Ligeti's opera *Le Grand Macabre*. Following a summer workshop studying percussion in the context of the opera, out of which a short filmed documentary was created, ENO Baylis commissioned an iPhone application to explore the overture to *Le Grand Macabre*, scored for tuned car horns. 'Play Ligeti' is a stunning arena for handheld digital play which ventures into the realms of research, composition, ensemble and performance. It offers a recording of the overture itself; a 'play' section in which twelve car horn icons are arranged onscreen as they are in the orchestra pit to be sounded by a touch; ideas for composition and technique; a pdf of the score itself in staff notation and with numerical notation to be performed on the iPhone or in an iPhone ensemble; an information page about Ligeti, *Le Grand Macabre* and ENO and links to relevant websites. Such opportunity for interactive digital play is becoming more common with various applications and computer programs, but this one is quite unique in the field of opera and makes attractive an otherwise potentially intimidating work.

ENVIRONMENTS AND FRAMING

Artworks are contextualized by framing, and this act of framing can help to hold up a theatre work or piece of music in educational study. The digital transmits or recommunicates an artwork, reframes it and places it in a new context, inevitably refocusing audience reaction to the work. In the classroom, in the case of Digital Theatre's education initiatives, an electronic whiteboard, its position at the front of a classroom, and the students' formation in relation to it could form the frame that holds a film of a theatrical production, doubling the frame of the original stage space. 'Theatrical frame could then be said to consist of the boundary line, visible or invisible, that theatre artists deliberately draw around the piece of experience that they wish to highlight or examine' (Jackson, 2007, p. 161). Equally, this line is drawn by teachers, by students and by the technology utilized to gain access to the work. Frames constitute the boundaries of the environment of the artwork – and, particularly in interactive arts – the crafted environment is key. The integration of the digital in the arts massively expands the potential of environments to move beyond the real and greatly affect the artistic experience. Goodman (2007) recognizes 'the many and varied ways in which new technologies call us out of ourselves and our moments of being in shared time-space with others, and beckon us through the screen to other places' (Vol 3, Numbers 2 & 3, p. 104) – just as a novel leads us through our imagination to other worlds, so a digitally constructed environment can lead us visually to another space. The framing of a piece of theatre also relies upon the delicate relationship between performer and audience, which is simulated in a filmed version of a theatrical event: where in the theatre building, the fictional environment is kept at a distance from the audience, a film of the production might bring the viewer far closer to the characters, allowing them access to the created environment.

Virtual reality games take this concept further, immersing the player in a virtual environment and giving them autonomy to interact and function digitally within it, controlling a second virtual self. Dunn and O'Toole note the 'immediate sense of connection and shared enthusiasm for the notion of creating "other worlds"…a shared desire for engagement and playfulness' (in Anderson, Carroll, & Cameron, 2007, p. 21) that exists in this field. There is potential here for use of online simulations in the educational sphere, worth exploring: 'online simulations have in recent times become very popular for learning contexts, where in fact they merge with role playing games to provide easily controllable virtual environments whose outcomes can be circumscribed and designed to fulfill pedagogical objectives' (Dunn and O'Toole in Anderson, Carrol & Cameron, 2007, p. 28). The danger, which nevertheless stimulates the player, is the risk of losing a sense of the boundaries between the virtual and the real. Speaking at the British Library on 18 May 2010 at a conference exploring 'The Doctoral Thesis in the Digital and Multimodal Age', Steve Benford described many emerging performance works in which audience members are required to journey through real landscapes while following an aurally or visually dictated path, meeting other players and actors (but being unable to distinguish between the real and the performed) and often also operating in the virtual sphere via a handheld device. Here, audience members or players tend to lose all track of the divisions between real, performed and virtual, and thus a narrative or course of challenge can be devised by the creators. In this way, educators could devise a learning journey to be undertaken similarly.

A project conceived by Terry and Gabi Braun at Braunarts provides a fascinating case study here. *The DARK* was a dramatic work consisting of a pre-recorded, surround-sound storytelling piece, played in a custom-made space in total darkness. It conjured up the three-dimensional environment of the bowels of a slave ship, revealing the stories and fates of its inhabitants. Audiences entered the space to be aurally bombarded by soundscapes and narratives while losing all capacities of sight and touch; each experience was unique as the story was heard from different angles and aural perspectives. Created as an artwork and consequently an educative piece about slavery, *The DARK* toured schools and arts centers nationwide, and Braunarts devised special educational activities to supplement the experience itself. During the 2007 tour of *The DARK*, called

Dark Heritage, they offered workshops in which school children created their own surround sound version of the story, which was recorded and played back through the same surround sound installation in which they had previously experienced *The DARK* sonic installation. These children were engaged in a participative learning experience on the same stage that housed the performance that inspired them in the first place. Like the parallel between the conventional theatrical experience and Digital Theatre's solitary viewings, the soundscape of *The DARK* could also be downloaded from Braunarts' website to be experienced alone, leaving the consumer to create their own restrictions on the other senses, with a dark computer screen. This is an example of a wholly digitized sound-scape creating compelling drama – a new kind of theatre where the digital inspired human emotional reactions. The environment created and the framework held up by the darkness were both vital to the artistic and educative success of the piece.

MUSIC EDUCATION AND DIGITAL TECHNOLOGY

Just as theatre companies and drama teachers are gradually embracing tech-nology in their practice and pedagogy, opera companies and music teachers are joining the progress toward the digital. In fact, with regular live radio broadcasts and HD simulcasts to cinemas worldwide, opera companies are leading the way with using the digital to expand their audiences. My interviews with experts from the English National Opera, the Royal Opera House and the Metropolitan Opera all led me to analyze projects and professional practice within opera education departments specifically, focusing on an art form with unique capacity for educa-tion across the arts, encompassing theatrical, musical, physical and visual arts learning. The digital is used within opera productions as an artistic visual feature of a work, and also as a transmitter of opera, hugely improving access to high quality, professional opera. As viewers we are asked to 're-perceive the opera stage as an integration of the live with the mediatized in a non-hierarchical intermedial world' (Chapple & Kattenbelt, 2006, p. 88).

In the music classroom, technology has greatly altered compositional tech-nique, ensemble work and appreciation of instruments: although orchestral instruments are still learned and studied, sequencers, mixing and editing suites, and synthesizers also feature in young people's musical consciousness. 'While, on the one hand, technologically mediated music making can challenge the most cherished practices of classroom music teachers, on the other hand, it can generate the desire to (and ways in which to) diversify existing pedagogical prac-tice' (Finney & Burnard, 2007, p. 200) – for the most part, the digital serves to encourage young people to further engage with music and composition. Hannah Elder used the example of the Royal Opera House's composition competition, *Fanfare*, to showcase the success of a digitally integrated project in their depart-ment. Eleven to fourteen year olds were invited to submit compositions to be considered for use as a fanfare to alert audience members to take their seats at the start of a performance and after the interval. Students submitted their work digitally, via the NUMU website, 'a safe community for young people to show-case their music, collaborate, compete and develop their talent' (www.numu.org. uk), and the submissions were judged aurally before the selected winners were invited to record their fanfare with the Orchestra of the Royal Opera House and in the ROH editing suite. The majority of the project was marketed, dis-seminated and accomplished digitally before students came to the Royal Opera House for face-to-face musical interaction with the artists. The immense success of *Fanfare* proves that accessing already existing online platforms and communi-ties (such as NUMU and www.teachingmusic.org.uk) to publicize and distribute a project is vital. The Royal Opera House's *Fanfare* competition model could be successfully adapted for other arts projects that include submissions, using online communities that facilitate global geographical outreach.

CONCLUSIONS

The arts, as twenty-first century agents and subjects of education, will increas-ingly rely on digital technology for communication and representation within the cultural sphere. As technology continues to advance, so must artistic practice, in order to maintain its established position in the global cultural economy. The case studies I have explored signify the best practice in arts education with the digital, using technology to improve access, aid analysis, set up new environ-ments for play and creativity and challenge the senses. One possibility is that digital forums be set up to disseminate this practice amongst other arts organiza-tions. These studies have shown the benefits of harnessing changes in the market audience of young people, especially as culture develops in an increasingly mediatized world. Throughout the dissertation, my research showed that the most significant potential of the digital is its capability to improve access to the arts, a function championed by the professional experts I interviewed as fundamental to the field.

In order for arts education to gain a place as a vital component of twenty-first century culture, the success of these few case studies proves that it is necessary for change to continue in pedagogy and policy, toward proactive integration with digital technology.

I was driven to write about the digital in arts education by an ambition to reflect the immediacy of the digital, its relevance and demands on the arts *now* and an instinct that the significance of the digital in the arts will only increase. The digital demands exploration, and criticism in performance studies lacks comprehensive study in this field. A dissertation with a digital dimension pres-ents particular challenges. I was conscious that even as I wrote, my conclusions and observations were going out of date – any reader of analysis of the digital within culture must acknowledge its time frame, as technological advances outstrip the pace of academic study. Sociological context was imperative to the study, though it was important to find a balance between specificity and general grounding. I felt compelled to admit my constraints – lack of statistical data, relatively narrow range of anecdotal research – to frame my work's specific remit in such a wide field. Another challenge was to be as focused as possible in my use of terminology when referring to the wider use of the digital.

I chose not to present my work digitally as the academic remit of my course offered no precedent in non-traditional presentation. To maintain comparison with the work of my peers, and to fulfill the marking scheme for the course, I felt restricted to written analysis. My digital audio records of the interviews conducted are archived alongside the digital records of my research, but were not submitted with the work.

REFERENCES

Anderson, M., Carroll, J., & Cameron, D. (Eds.). (2009). *Drama Education with Digital Technology.* London: Continuum International Publishing Group.

Auslander, P. (1999). *Liveness: Performance in a Mediatized Culture.* London: Routledge.

Barney, D. (2007). The question of education in technological society. In J. Lockard & M. Pegrum (Eds.), *Brave New Classrooms: Democratic Education & the Internet.* New York: Peter Lang Publishing Incorporation.

Booth, D. (2007). Afterword. In M. Anderson, J. Carroll, & D. Cameron (Eds.), *Drama Education with Digital Technology.* London: Continuum International Publishing Group.

Braun, T. (2010). Interview on 27th August. Retrieved from http://www.braunarts.com. *The DARK* information CD Rom. Retrieved from http://www.braunarts.com

Buckingham, D. (Ed.). (2008). *Youth, Identity and Digital Media.* Boston, MA: The MIT Press.

Chapple, F. (2006). Digital opera: Intermediality, remediation and education. In F. Chapple & C. Kattenbelt (Eds.), *Intermediality in Theatre and Performance.* Amsterdam/New York: International Federation for Theatre Research.

Chapple, F. & Kattenbelt, C. (Eds.). (2006). *Intermediality in Theatre and Performance.* Amsterdam/New York: International Federation for Theatre Research.

Cohen, J. (2010). The Metropolitan Opera Guild. Interview on 21st July.

Dixon, S. with Smith, B. (2007). *Digital Performance: A History of New Media in Theater, Dance, Performance Art and Installation.* Cambridge, MA: Massachusetts Institute of Technology Press.

Dunn, J. & O'Toole, J. (2007). When worlds collude: Exploring the relationship between the actual, the dramatic and the virtual. In M. Anderson, J. Carroll & D. Cameron (Eds.), *Drama Education with Digital Technology.* London: Continuum International Publishing Group.

Elder, H. (2010). The Royal Opera House. Interview on 2nd September.

Finney, J. (2007). Music education as identity project in a world of electronic desires. In J. Finney & P. Burnard (Eds.), *Music Education with Digital Technology.* London: Continuum International Publishing Group.

Finney, J. & Burnard, P. (Eds.). (2007). *Music Education with Digital Technology.* London: Continuum International Publishing Group.

Goodfellow, R. (2007). From 'equal access' to 'widening participation': The discourse of equity in the age of e-learning. In J. Lockard & M. Pegrum (Eds.), *Brave New Classrooms: Democratic Education & the Internet.* New York: Peter Lang Publishing Incorporation.

Goodman, L. (2007). Performing self beyond the body: Replay culture replayed. *International Journal of Performance Arts and Digital Media, 3,*(2 & 3) 103–121.

Hiscock, C. The Royal Opera House. *Fanfare* publicity materials, development document and KS3 Curriculum Unit Resource.

Jackson, A. (2007). *Theatre, Education and the Making of Meanings: Art or Instrument?* Manchester: Manchester University Press.

Jensen, A. P. (2007). *Theatre in a Media Culture: Production, Performance and Perception Since 1970.* Jefferson, NC: McFarland & Company Inc.

Kibby, M. D. (2007). Hybrid teaching and learning: Pedagogy vs. pragmatism. In J. Lockard & M. Pegrum (Eds.), *Brave New Classrooms: Democratic Education & the Internet.* New York: Peter Lang Publishing Incorporation.

Koozer, M. (2010). The Metropolitan Opera Guild. Interview on 21st July.

Krause, K.-L. (2007). Who is the e-generation and how are they faring in higher education? In J. Lockard & M. Pegrum (Eds.), *Brave New Classrooms: Democratic Education & the Internet.* New York: Peter Lang Publishing Incorporation.

Lindsay, F. (2010). Digital Theatre. Interview on 21st September.

Lockard, J. (2007). Manifesto for democratic education and the Internet. In J. Lockard & M. Pegrum (Eds.), *Brave New Classrooms: Democratic Education & the Internet.* New York: Peter Lang Publishing Incorporation.

Lockard, J. & Pegrum, M. (Eds.). (2007). *Brave New Classrooms: Democratic Education & the Internet.* New York: Peter Lang Publishing Incorporation.

McMaster, B. (2008). *Supporting Excellence in the Arts: From Measurement to Judgement.* London: Department for Culture, Media and Sport.

Meitlis, R. (2010). Co-Founder of English National Opera Baylis Programme. Interview on 8th June.

The Metropolitan Opera Guild (2010). Resource materials from the Opera Institute Network Summer 2010.

Neelands, J. (2009). Foreword. In M. Anderson, J. Carroll & D. Cameron (Eds.), *Drama Education with Digital Technology.* London: Continuum International Publishing Group.

Nicholson, H. (2009). *Theatre & Education.* Basingstoke: Palgrave Macmillan.

Prensky, M. (2001). Digital Natives, Digital Immigrants. From *On the Horizon*, MCB University Press, Vol. 9, No. 5. Retrieved from http:// www.marcprensky.com

Seddon, F. A. (2007). Music e-learning experiments: Young people, composing and the Internet. In J. Finney & P. Burnard (Eds.), *Music Education with Digital Technology.* London: Continuum International Publishing Group.

Shaw, T. (2010). Digital Theatre. Interview on 24th August.

www.braunarts.com

www.digitalperformance.org

www.digitaltheatre.com

www.eno.org.uk

www.music-in-education.org

www.numu.org.uk

www.roh.org.uk

www.teachingmusic.org.uk

www.thedark.net

BIBLIOGRAPHY

Appleyard, B. (2011). Restlessly inventive: David Hockney is funny, cranky and, with his drawings created on the iPad, still brilliantly showing how art can exploit technology. *The Sunday Times*, 30 January.

Baïdak, N. (coordination), Horvath, A., & Delhaxhe, A. (Eds.). (2009). *Arts and Cultural Education at School in Europe.* European Commission.

Bailey, H. Ersatz dancing: Negotiating the live and mediated in digital performance practice. *International Journal of Performance Arts and Digital Media, 3,*(2 & 3), 151–165.

Bakhshi, H., Mateos-Garcia, J., & Throsby, D. (2010). *Beyond Live: Digital interaction in the performing arts.* National Endowment for Science, Technology and the Arts.

Best, A. L. (Ed.). (2007). *Representing Youth: Methodological Issues in Critical Youth Studies.* New York: New York University Press.

Bodilly, S. J., Augustine, C. H., & Zakaras L. (2008). *Revitalizing Arts Education Through Community-Wide Coordination.* The Wallace Foundation.

Burnard, P. (2007). Creativity and technology: Critical agents of change in the work and lives of music teachers. In J. Finney & P. Burnard (Eds.), *Music Education with Digital Technology.* London: Continuum International Publishing Group.

Cameron, D. (2007). Mashups: Digital media and drama conventions. In M. Anderson, J. Carroll, & D. Cameron (Eds.), *Drama Education with Digital Technology.* London: Continuum International Publishing Group.

Carey, J. (2005). *What Good Are The Arts?* London: Faber & Faber.

Carlson, M. (2001). *The Haunted Stage: The Theatre as Memory Machine.* Michigan: The University of Michigan.

Carroll, J., Anderson, M., & Cameron, D. (2006). *Real Players?: Drama, Technology and Education.* Stoke on Trent: Trentham Books.

Chatzichristodoulou (Ed.). (2009). *Interfaces of Performance.* Farnham: Ashgate Publications.

Davidson, J. (1998). Are You Ready for Digital Opera? *Los Angeles Times,* 12 April.

Downing, D., Ashworth, M., Stott, A. (2002). *Acting with Intent.* London: National Federation of Educational Research.

Drotner, K. (2008). Leisure is hard work: Digital practices and future competencies. In D. Buckingham (Ed.), *Youth, Identity and Digital Media.* Boston, MA: The MIT Press.

Eames, A., Benton, T., Sharp, C., & Kendall, L. (2006). *The Impact of Creative Partnerships on the Attainment of Young People.* National Federation of Educational Research.

Elleridge Woodson, S. (2007). Performing youth: Youth agency and the production of knowledge in community-based theatre. In A. L. Best (Ed.), *Representing Youth: Methodological Issues in Critical Youth Studies.* New York: New York University Press.

Fortier, M. (1997). *Theatre/Theory: An Introduction.* London: Routledge.

Gabrielle, M. (2010). National Theatre. Interview on 26 August.

Goodman, L. Performing and being (there), live and online. *International Journal of Performance Arts and Digital Media, 3,*(2 & 3) 97–99.

Goodman, L. First, second and third spaces: Digital Narratives and the spaces of performance. *International Journal of Performance Arts and Digital Media, 3,*(2 & 3) 167–168.

Graham, A. & Davies, G. (1997). *Broadcasting, Society and Policy in the Multimedia Age.* Luton: John Libbey Media.

Grindley, N. (2007). *Digital Tools for Performance.* Arts and Humantities Research Council ICT Methods Network.

Higgs, P., Cunningham, S., & Bakhshi, H. (2008). *Beyond the Creative Industries: Mapping the Creative Economy in the United Kingdom.* National Endowment for Science, Technology and the Arts.

Hiscock, C. The Royal Opera House. *Fanfare* publicity materials, development document and KS3 Curriculum Unit Resource.

Jackson, A. Positioning the audience: Inter-active strategies and the aesthetic in educational theatre. *Theatre Research International, 22.1,* 48–60.

Jackson, T. (Ed.). (1993). *Learning Through Theatre: New Perspectives on Theatre in Education.* London and New York: Routledge.

Kendall, L., Sharp, C., Morrison, J., & Yeshanew, T. (2008). *The Impact of Creative Partnerships on Pupil Behaviour.* National Federation of Educational Research.

Kendall, L., Sharp, C., Morrison, J., & Yeshanew, T. (2008). *The Longer Term Impact of Creative Partnerships on The Attainment of Young People: Results From 2004 & 2006*. National Federation of Educational Research.

Mackey, T. & Ullman, A. (2006). Creative partnerships: Survey of headteachers'. British market research bureau: Social research. Commissioned by Arts Council England.

Matthews Millman Ltd. (2006). Impact of Artsmark on schools in England. Commissioned by Arts Council England.

National Advisory Committee on Creative and Cultural Education (1999). All Our Futures: Creativity, Culture and Education. DfES.

Phelan, P. (1993). *Unmarked: The Politics of Performance*. Oxon: Routledge.

Remer, J. (2010). From lessons learned to local action: Building your own policies for effective arts education. *Arts Education Policy Review*, *111*, 81–96.

Roberts, P. (2006). Nurturing creativity in young people: A report to government to inform future policy. Department for Culture, Media and Sport.

Savage, J. (2007). Pedagogical strategies for change. In J. Finney & P. Burnard (Eds.), *Music Education with Digital Technology*. London: Continuum International Publishing Group.

Saxton, J. & Miller, C. (Eds.). (1998). *Drama and Theatre in Education: The Research of Practice, the Practice of Research*. Brisbane: IDEA Publications.

Schechner, R. Theatre in the 21st Century. *The Drama Review*, *41*, 5–6.

Sharp, C. (2006). National Evaluation of Creative Partnerships – Final Report, National Federation of Educational Research.

SQW Consulting (2009). Evaluation of 'Find Your Talent' Programme. Commissioned by DCSF and DCMS.

Travers, T., Eleanor Stoker E., & Kleinman, M, with Hazel Johnstone, H. The Arts and Cultural Industries in the London Economy. Commissioned by London Arts Board, compiled by LSE.

Winterson, J. M. (1998). The community education work of orchestras and opera companies: Principles, practices and problems. PhD thesis, University of York.

7

Complexity Theory

June Elizabeth Parnell

INTRODUCTION

The advancement of technology in the twenty-first century has caused many students in the field of social sciences to take creative, unconventional and innovative approaches toward their research. Interacting and working on and with the Internet is, for many students in higher education, not just a novel use of a technological means, but a deliberate practice highlighting their engagement with the social, cultural and academic world. As networked information continues to proliferate, research students are led to re-examine many of the assumptions underlying the accepted mode of presenting their academic research and there is a break with the conventional methods of doing and reporting research. Many students from undergraduate to doctoral level of study, have encountered conflict at some point in regard to the design and delivery method of their research, and have found the dominant and stipulated requirements of some higher educational institutions, have caused them to change the style and presentation of their research ideas (Dadds & Hart, 2001). Though many of us, as aspiring academic students, appreciate the traditional guidelines and frameworks set up by our academic institutions as generally helpful, such as the linear format of a text-based thesis, there is however, a need to sometimes split from 'official academic genres' (Ely, Downing, & Anzul, 1997, p. 11) in order to break new ground in terms of how we design and present our research while balancing the criteria set out by higher education establishments.

In considering how to incorporate digital dissertations or theses as Net-based research or projects, it is important to note that the nature of them is not usually about the Net, its obvious form, but much more about generating practice and engaging with or about networks. To refer to the digital encompasses more than a technical term to illustrate systems and media that are dependent on electronic computation. Digital words and images, in contrast to physical texts, embody semiotic codes which as Landow (1999) describes as 'the defining qualities of digital infotech: (a) virtuality, (b) fluidity, (c) adaptability, (d) openness (or existing without borders), (e) processability, (f) infinite duplicability, (g) capacity for being moved about rapidly, and (h) networkability' (1999, p. 166). Digital textuality facilitates various Net-based texts to connect together through the means of electronic linking thus the digital text is fluid in nature and the form of codes can be refigured, reformatted and rewritten (Landow, 1999). 'Digital text hence is infinitely adaptable to different needs and uses, and since it consists of codes that other codes can search, rearrange, and otherwise manipulate, digital text is always open, unbordered, unfinished, and unfinishable, capable of infinite extension' (Landow, 1999, p. 166).

Finding a theory to 'fit' a digital thesis or project that by nature is open and unbordered, can be challenging in the academic domain. As a doctoral student, I have explored the relevance of complexity theory as a research framework for educational practice and in particular e-learning research. E-learning is a case in point of a field of digital communicative practice that is still emerging and evolving nearly thirty years after its earliest appearance. Since communication is central to the heart of educational interaction, its impact on education systems, individual teachers and learners is significant. However, due to technological advances in the rapidly changing world of the Internet and the Web, theory and research frequently grapple to keep up with the developments and 'it becomes a significant challenge to interpret, differentiate, and disentangle hype and backlash, design and accident, as well as past certainties and future possibilities' (Friensen, 2009, p. 1).

Although e-learning has the ability to transform education as the new era of learning, research in this field has generally been more inclined toward many of the same methods and philosophical frameworks used to investigate out dated instructional technologies and practices. These assumptions about the nature of technology and of human interaction with technology are no longer valid for today. There is no 'grand theory' of e-learning yet mainly due to the fact that e-learning is a relatively immature field within education. Andrews and Haythornthwaite state that, '[i]n defining and building a research agenda for e-learning, it is necessary to find the theoretical base that informs evolving processes in a rapidly advancing technological environment, yet also addresses the kind of transformative activity that is entailed in e-learning and e-learning communities' (2007, p. 23).

COMPLEXITY THEORY

'Complexity theory has emerged in the sciences as a way of explaining the patterning in nature, which cannot be readily explained through traditional notions of cause and effect' (Edwards, 2010, p. 69). Complexity theory/thinking has evolved over the last thirty years or so and has frequently been branded the 'new science'. Although its beginnings can be traced back to physics, chemistry, cybernetics, information science and systems theory (among other fields), its insights have reached a broad area of the social sciences such as health, psychology, economics, business management and politics to name a few. More recently, complexity thinking has been embraced by an ever-increasing amount of educationists whose broad range of research interests span from topics such as subjective understanding, interpersonal dynamics, cultural evolution, neurological processes, curriculum development and the politics of education (Doll, 1993; Davis & Sumara, 2006; Mason, 2008; Osberg & Biesta, 2010).

Complexity is concerned with the concepts of non-linear dynamics, emergence and self-organization. Nigel Thrift describes complexity in his article *The Place of Complexity* as '… a structure of feeling in Euro-American societies which frames the world as complex, irreducible, anti-closural … producing a much greater sense of openness and possibility about the future' (1999, p. 34). New possibilities for science have emerged due to the advancing power of technology and relying on one of science's analytical methods to understand, by taking the whole and dividing them into manageable parts, has proven to be challenging (Mitchell, 2009). This is because a 'complex system is not constituted merely by the sum of its components, but also by the intricate relationships among these components. In "cutting" up a system, the analytical method destroys what it seeks to understand (Cilliers, 1998, p. 2). Therefore, it is not surprising to find an increased interest over the last decade in complexity as a theory (Cilliers, 1998; Byrne, 1998; Johnson, 2007), a way of thinking (Morin, 2008; Davis & Sumara, 2006; Kuhn, 2008), a science (Waldrop, 1992; Mitchell, 2009), a dynamic system theory (Fogel, Lyra, & Valsiner, 1997; Valsiner, 1998) or as theories of emergence (Goldstein, 2000; Johnson, 2001).

DEFINING COMPLEXITY THEORY

Many authors and researchers step away from trying to clarify the term but rather attempt to explore the notions of complexity and complex systems. Instead of trying analyze complex phenomena within social and scientific research, many authors take the approach that it is not possible to explain an exclusive story about something that is really complex (Cilliers, 1998; Byrne, 1998; Mitchell, 2009; Davis & Sumara, 2006). 'It should not be forgotten that these are "ideas" … a collection of mappings for an already and always changing world' (Stanley, 2005, p. 149).

The concept of complexity is not universal (Cilliers, 1998; Davis & Sumara, 2006) therefore it requires the distinction between the notion of 'complex' and 'complicated'. Cilliers explains the dissimilarity of these concepts and states:

> If a system – despite the fact that it may consist of a huge number of components – can be given a complete description in terms of its individual constituents, such a system is merely complicated. Things like jumbo jets or computers are complicated. In a complex system, on

the other hand, the interaction among constituents of the system, and the interaction between the system and its environment are of such a nature that the system as a whole cannot be fully understood simply by analyzing its components. Moreover, these relationships are not fixed, but shift and change, often as a result of self-organization. (1998, pp. 3–4)

Davis and Sumara 'position complexity thinking somewhere between a belief in a fixed and fully knowable universe and a fear that meaning and reality are so dynamic that attempts to explicate are little more than self-delusions' (2006, p. 4). The authors make the distinction that complexity thinking is not defined in terms of its methods of inquiry as there is no complexity scientific model and there are no gold standards for complexity research; but it is, however appropriately, typified in its objects of study. Waldrop (1992) in his book *Complexity* defines complexity as the realm between linearly determined order and unfixed chaos. Davis and Sumara (2006) state that there is a transdisciplinary quality to complexity thinking; however, the authors wonder whether it should be called a research attitude, a field, a domain or a system of interpretation. They do hold a pragmatic belief toward the use of the term complexity thinking as a research attitude rather than a science and feel this attitude is important to educational researchers. Their research is centered on the presentation and development of an emergent vocabulary surrounding the complexities of educational inquiry.

Many authors believe that complexity focuses on emergent behaviors that come about from interactions within and among self-organizing and adaptive systems (Barlow & Waldrop, 1994; Richardson, 2005; Horn, 2008). Therefore, an overarching goal of complexity science is to understand and clarify general laws of pattern formation that indicate certain transitions within independent and self-sufficient open systems (Waldrop, 1992). The study of complexity 'is bounded by the capacity of self-sustaining systems to interact and adapt autonomously within the self defining boundaries that sustain the agent intra-actions and inter-actions' (Horn & Wilburn, 2005, p. 3).

Kuhn (1962) in *The Structure of Scientific Revolutions*, recognized that phenomena that are not predictable and do not follow the rules of a particular theoretical paradigm tend to be marginalized by the rigid theories until these subsidiary or marginal studies gather sufficient momentum to cause a paradigmatic shift. Complexity's impetus began under the umbrella of the postmodern New Sciences, which also included Chaos, and emerged over the last thirty years of the twentieth century (Bertalanffy, 1968, 1975; Nicolis & Prigogine, 1989; Waldrop, 1992; Gleick, 1987; Lewin, 1995; Capra, 1996).

LINKS TO CHAOS THEORY

Chaos mainly reflects phenomena in mathematics and concerns itself with the notion that small differences in the way things are now have huge consequences in the way things will be in the future. The 'butterfly effect' became a trendy catchphrase for chaos and chaos dynamics concerns itself with recurring patterns across layers of complexity. Complexity concerns itself within science and with the concept of understanding nature rather than the idea of control. The origins of chaos[1] and complexity can be traced back to the general systems theory and Bertalanffy (1968, 1975) was among the first to explore this approach to try and understand evolving complex phenomena. Capra (1996)[2] states that systems thinking/theory rejects the mechanistic and reductionistic thinking of modern science and emphasizes a more holistic approach toward the phenomena of emergence and patterns of organization. Multiple perspectives and distinct domains of inquiry were established with James Gleick (1987) focusing on chaos theory as a quintessential 'New Science', Mitchell Waldrop (1992) emphasizing studies and methods involving 'Complex Adaptive Systems', David Bohm (1980) focusing on dissipative structures highlighting the shift from explicit to implicit relationships and emergence, and Prigogine and Stengers (1984, 1997) initiating the field of non-equilibrium physics related to thermodynamic interactions to name a few.

The study of both complex systems and deterministic systems exhibit random behaviors and are connected in various ways. Both fall under the contemporary process of reconsidering classical dynamics, acknowledging novel kinds of dynamical systems and finding new relationships between determinism and predictability (Lorenz, 1963). They both also rely heavily on computer models for research purposes and robustness is central to both fields since research in chaos theory is very much concerned with stability and structure as with instability and disintegration and most importantly the transitions that take place between these systems (Marcus, 1985).

AN OPENING FOR COMPLEXITY SCIENCE

An ensemble of complexity scientists from divergent backgrounds gathered themselves in New Mexico at the Santa Fe Institute in 1984 and created the center for the study of complex systems[3]. 'Their goal was to plot out the founding of a new research institute that would pursue research on a large number of highly complex and interactive systems which can be properly studied only in an interdisciplinary environment and promote a unity of knowledge' (Mitchell, 2009, p. 5). As with any promising, expanding and vital area of science and education, scholars' opinions will vary about what the core ideas are all about, their significance and answers they might elicit. This can be seen in the growing number of various disciplines and interdisciplinary realms that have embraced a complexity perspective. These disciplines range across most of the sciences, including neurosciences, psychology (Butz, Chamberlain, & McCown, 1997; Eenwyk, 1997), physiology, biology, ecology, geology, mathematics, computer science and presently emerging technologies. The complexity approach also appears within the social sciences, sociology (Eve, Horsfall, & Lee, 1997), education (Morin, 2001), economics (Hawken, 1994), urban studies, architecture (Sakai, 2001), healthcare, organizational studies, politics and the military. This list is of course indicative rather than comprehensive.

DIFFERENT APPROACHES TO COMPLEXITY

Complexity is an emerging field where scientists and scholars are concerned with patterns and relationships within systems. One way of understanding the disparity throughout complexity studies is to examine some of the different approaches taken. Richardson and Cilliers (2001)[4] sum up three variations of classes within complexity studies that are represented across complexity research, these being:

- *Reductionist or hard complexity science*, which is an approach predominately taken by physicists where they basically take the same stance as analytic science to expose and *understand the nature of reality*, under the hypothesis that such a reality is determined and therefore determinable.
- *Soft complexity science*, which is a more common approach within the social sciences and biological fields of study that generally draw on principals and metaphors developed from hard complexity science to illustrate social systems and living organisms. This interpretative method is concerned more about *a way of understanding the world* rather than a representation of reality.
- *Complexity thinking*, which is positioned in the space between the hard and soft approach, is more an attitude or notion related to the philosophical and pragmatic associations of the taken for granted complex world and can be expressed as signifying *a way of thinking*.

As its name might imply, reviewing complexity has been less than a straight-forward task due its evolving nature and lack of tidy clear descriptions and unambiguous meanings and classifications. An overwhelming challenge remains surrounding its definition and purpose. As Melanie Mitchell asks, 'how can there be a science of complexity when there is no agreed-on quantitative definition of complexity?' (2009, p. 13). Mitchell, a leading complex systems scientist[5] answers this question with a statement where she believes neither a single *science of complexity* nor a single *complexity theory* exists yet, despite the numerous articles and books from researchers using these terms because of the 'struggle to define its central terms' (2009, p. 14). Johnson defines complexity as a fledgling science – and hence of a complex system – which 'is the study of the phenomena which emerge from a collection of interacting objects – and a crowd is a perfect example of such an emergent phenomenon, since it is a phenomenon which emerges from a collection of interacting people' (2007, pp. 3–4). Johnson[6] gives examples of such crowds as human cells, the financial market, traffic jams, guerilla wars, and even extreme weather conditions. Other examples show up throughout the literature with an overarching commonality in the interest of emergent phenomena where a collection of objects, be it cells, people, ants or the internet, is able to self-organize in such a manner that the phenomenon develops all by itself.

EMERGING FIELD OF COMPLEXITY

Waldrop (1992) gives an interesting account of the emerging field in his book, *Complexity: The emerging science on the edge of order and chaos*. Well before the buzz words or phrases such as complexity theory/science or thinking came to the stage early research studies of complex phenomena were undertaken. Mainly, this work was largely unconnected and incongruent research of specific phenomena. Examples include Friedrich Engles (1987) research of the emergence of social structures in the free market world, Deborah Gordan's (1999) multi-year observations concerning the life cycles of anthills, Rachel Carson's (1962) assessment of the ecological implications of industrialized societies, Jane Jacobs' (1961) investigation of the rise and fall of cities and Humberto Maturana's (1980) study into self-producing and self-maintaining biological unities to name a few of many other similar research studies. Although the methods used in these studies were mainly observational and descriptive, there remains a common theme that links their diversity. Whether ants and anthills or cultures and cities, the investigators all wanted to capture a rich account of specific phenomena that concerned levels of emergence and not in terms of sub-parts, components or particles or universal laws.

Complexity studies moved forward with an emphasis that was less concerned with detailed descriptions of specific instances but rather focused on more generalized characterizations (Lewin, 1992; Waldrop, 1992) and identified certain markers that distinguished complex systems from complicated mechanical systems. Complexity research came together in the late 1970s and early 1980s as researchers began using computer technology to design computer simulations rooted in mathematics of growing cities, flocking birds, anthills and other complex phenomena which became popular software, video games and interactive websites[7] in the late 1980s and 1990s. Institutes and conferences were set up by the 1990s to bring together cross disciplinary researchers to share a forum for their studies along with the publication of several popular books on the promising and emerging field (Lewin, 1992; Waldrop, 1992). With the vast accumulation of inter-case studies and comparisons, complexity research began to turn its focus toward the prompting and manipulation of complex systems from a variety of phenomena such as immune systems, ecosystems, interneuronal networks to social groupings. Researchers began asking such questions as, could one cause a complex unity to emerge? If so, how? Once emergent, could a complex phenomena be intentionally manipulated? If so, how and to what extent?[8] Such questions continue to be asked today through a variety of methods, most increasingly through sophisticated computer technology. Computer simulations continue to develop and expand in order to replicate the complex relationships among neurons in the brain (Mitchell, 2009), species in an ecosystem (Johnson, 2007) or people in the workplace (Lewin & Regine, 2000). These computer simulations grounded in mathematics that hard or science-based complexivists argue that this method enhances the phenomena being studied (Holland, 1998;

Kauffman, 1995). However, Osberg (2005) argues that although mathematics is useful in generating bottom-up computer simulations that are reasonably convincing of complex phenomena, she doubts that a rule-based approach is adequate to comprehend the diversity of complexity and believes that it can thwart the sought after knowledge. Osberg's case in hand is that a computer is primarily a complicated tool and is used to replicate a complex phenomenon and can be limited or limiting. Other authors believe that simulation acts alongside of analogy where it can make important aspects of complex behavior difficult to understand (Auyang, 2000). Overall, many researchers have applied these complexity principles to restructure major companies and workplaces (Lewin & Regine, 2000) or to rethink taken for granted medical orthodoxies (Maturana & Varela, 1980). It is through the evolution of these various research studies that Davis and Sumara (2006) surmise that complexity research has transformed to a complexity science:

> This emergence of a pragmatics of transformation within complexity research is associated with the change in title of complexity research, from complexity theory to complexity science. This shift was a deliberate one made by complexivists to flag the fact that research had achieved a certain rigor and respectability, if not the requirements of replication that are better suited to studies of mechanical phenomena. In our view, the shift toward considerations of pragmatics of transformation has also rendered the discourse much better fitted to the particular concerns of educators and educational researchers, given educationists' societal responsibilities for deliberately affecting learners and communities. (p. 21)

Davis and Sumara (2006) argue that although a hard approach to complexity science is relevant and appropriate for some emergent phenomena such as the study of insects or neurons, it is of little worth to educators and educational researchers. This is because the conditions and purposes of educational establishments are constantly shifting and evolving and taking a hard approach by assuming a certain stability in the phenomena being studied becomes problematic particularly when the investigators ignore their own presence contributing to the on going evolutions or emerging phenomena.

As previously mentioned, soft complexity is utilized more by the social sciences with the use of metaphors and images to draw attention to obscure links of certain complex phenomena. Rucker (1987) studied personal memories as a fractual structure where recollections became a web of associations when closely examined. Other similar studies carried out by sociologists and neurologists drew upon a subdivision of complexity science-namely network theory – to redevelop interneuronal structures and interpersonal relationships in terms of 'scale-free networks' (Watts, 2003). These efforts to re-describe certain phenomena have been predominantly carried out by psychologists, sociologists and neurologists with less significance within educational research. However, there has been some noteworthy studies concerning the nature of teaching (Davis & Simmt, 2003), learning (Barab & Cherkes-Julkowski, 1999; Ennis, 1993) and educational research (Middleton, Sawada, Judson, Bloom, & Turley, 2002) in terms of their practical suggestions for educationists. For example, Sawada and Caley (1985) expand on the idea of *dissipative structures* (a term created by Nobel Laureate Ilya Prigogine, 1997) to describe learners and classrooms as complex unities. Capra states that Prigogine used the term 'dissipative structure' 'to emphasize the close interplay between structure on the one hand and change (or dissipation) on the other' (200, p. 13). The educational research by Davis and Sumara (1997, 2002, 2005) lean more toward a soft complexity science where they describe learning, classrooms, schools, curriculum and administration structures as open, nested and self-organizing systems far from a state of stability.

The third classification given by Richardson and Cilliers (2001) is complexity thinking which can be described more as a way of thinking and acting. It seeks to ask, 'how should we act?' rather than the hard and soft complexity questions that seek to know 'what is?' and 'what might be?' (Davis & Sumara, 2006). Kuhn states that 'complexity offers principles; it does not substitute for thoughtfulness. Complexity presents preferred ways of thinking about the organization of the world, while simultaneously pointing to the impossibility of accuracy in knowledge and prediction' (2008, p. 185).

Davis and Sumara (2006) continue this frame of thought by stating:

> Complexity thinking is fully consistent with a science that is understood in terms of a disciplined, open-minded, evidenced-based attitude toward the production of new, more useful interpretive possibilities. On this count, complexity thinking is compatible with pragmatist philosophy, in which truth is understood in terms of adequacy, not optimality. A claim is deemed truthful if it enables knowers to maintain their fitness- and so, in contrast to the demands for validity, reliability, rigor, and generalizability, complexity thinking is more oriented truths that are viable, reasonable, relevant, and contingent. Once again, this attitude foregrounds the role of the knower in the known, in contrast to the efforts of analytic science to erase any trace of the observer from the observation. (p. 26)

DISTINCTIONS BETWEEN SIMPLE-AND-COMPLEX AND COMPLICATED-AND-COMPLEX

Before naming the characteristics or components that are evident in a phenomenon before it is classed as complex, two important distinctions need to be made. The first is between 'simple' and 'complex' (Nicolis & Prigogine, 1989). 'Many systems appear simple, but reveal remarkable complexity when examined closely (e.g. a leaf). Others appear complex, but can be described simply, for example, some machines, such as the internal combustion engine. To compound matters, complexity is not located at a specific, identifiable site in a system. Because complexity results from the interaction between the components of a system, complexity is manifested at the level of the system itself' (Cilliers, 1998, p. 2). Complex systems do have characteristics that are not just determined by the point of view of the observer. Cilliers (1998) gives the example of a small aquarium portrayed as a simple ornament in a room (seen from afar) but as a system (seen from close by) is quite complex. The simple and the complex can often mask each other.

The second distinction is between complicated and complex. A complicated system is one that may have a large number of components to it and perform sophisticated tasks but it can be analyzed accurately for example the jumbo plane. A complex system which is usually associated with living matter such as a brain, a cell or a social system are composed of an intricate set of 'non-linear relationships and feedback loops that only certain aspects of them can be analyzed at a time' (Cilliers, 1998, p. 3).

CHARACTERISTICS OF A COMPLEX SYSTEM

Researchers have identified many key elements for certain phenomena to be categorized as complex or as an open system. The following characteristics concerning complex systems have consistently shown up throughout the literature with slight variations in the terms used:

- *Open system.* Complex systems are dynamic open systems, which mean they have the ability to interact and be influenced by their environment. They are ambiguously bounded[9]. They constantly exchange information and energy with their surroundings causing behavioural pattern formations. They are dynamic because they are constantly changing. Closed systems are usually merely complicated. These interactions have their own characteristics. One such important quality is that they are non-linear which means small causes that can have large results and vise versa versus a linear system which can be broken down into smaller parts.
- *Self-organization.* The most commonly cited quality of a complex system. Complex systems/ unities spontaneously arise as the actions of autonomous agents come to be interlinked and co-dependent. Self-organization is also known as emergence and somehow, these sorts of collectives develop the ability to exceed the possibilities of the same group of agents if they were made to work independently and seem to have clear purposes. Patterns emerge which cannot be predicted.
- *Large network of individual components* – (ants, cells, neurons, stock market) each typically following relatively simple rules with no leader or central controller. It is the collective actions from this large network of components that give rise to complex phenomena. 'A large number of elements are necessary, but not sufficient. The grains of sand on a beach do not interest us as a complex system. In order to constitute a complex system, the elements have to interact, and this interaction must be dynamic' (Cilliers, 1998, p. 3).
- Complex systems maneuver under conditions that are far from equilibrium and not in balance. 'There has to be a constant flow of energy to maintain the organization of the system and to ensure its survival. Equilibrium is another word for death' (Cilliers, 1998, p. 4).
- Complex systems are adaptive – they embody their histories, and they learn and adapt. Their behaviors change to advance their chances of survival which can be understood from a Darwinian point of view rather than Newtonian mechanics. 'Not only do they evolve through time, but their past is co-responsible for their present behavior' (Cilliers, 1998, p. 4)[10].
- Complex systems have short range relationships – which means that information is exchanged from local neighbors meaning that the 'system's coherence depends mostly on agent's immediate interdependencies, not on centralized control or top-down administration' (Davis & Sumara, 2006, p. 5)[11]. Complexity emerges through the patterns of interactions when the complex system is viewed as a whole, rather than through the individual elements.

WHAT COMPLEXITY IS NOT

Many authors feel strongly that complexity theory or thinking is not an explanatory system, meaning it does not make available all-encompassing enlightenment. Davis and Sumara (2006) sum this thought up by stating that:

> One of the most condemning accusations that can be made in the current academic context is that a given theory seems to be striving toward the status of a metadiscourse – that is, an explanatory system that somehow stands over or exceeds all others, a theory that claims to subsume prior or lesser perspectives, a discourse that somehow overcomes the blind spots of other discourses. The most frequent target of this sort of criticism has been leveled against religions, mathematics, and other attitudes that have presented themselves superior and totalizing. (p. 7)

Complexity does not in any way endeavor to replace or encompass analytic science or any other discourse. 'Complexity thinking is not omniscient thinking. It is, on the contrary, a thinking which knows it is always local, situated in a given time and place. Neither is it a complete thinking, for it knows in advance that there is always uncertainty. By the same token, it avoids the arrogant dogmatism which rules non-complex forms of thinking' (Morin, 2008, p. 97). So while complexity does not search for all the answers, it does seek to observe similarities among seemingly incongruent phenomena. 'Complexity does not rise over, but rises among other discourses' (Davis & Sumara, 2006, p. 8). In keeping with the essence of complexity the authors give caution to refraining from importing or imposing a ready-made discourse (because that is not what complexity represents) into or onto educational research and practice. Rather, educational researchers and educationists interested in this field are encouraged to simultaneously ask reflexive questions such as, 'how might complexity thinking lend itself to educational research?' and 'how might educational research contribute to the field of complexity?' Morin states that complexity thinking 'does not lead to a resigned skepticism, since, by completely breaking with the dogmatism of certainty, it throws itself courageously into the adventure upon which, from its birth, humanity has been embarked' (2008, p. 97). Osberg and Biesta also state that many educationalists have found complexity theory useful 'for describing, characterizing and understanding and the dynamics of education differently, not in the least because the language of complexity makes it possible to see the non-linear, unpredictable and generative character of educational processes and practices in a positive light, focusing on the emergence of meaning, knowledge, understanding, the world and the self in and through education' (2010, p. 2).

COMPLEXITY AND EDUCATION

Education is complicated but it is also complex as it continues to emerge and evolve. St. Julien states:

It is a recursive, open system characterized by emerging entities, the evolution of new capacities, and by developmental growth. Most importantly, complex systems are systems for which history matters. Something that was done yesterday, in yesterday's circumstances, with yesterday's students, does not have the same effect when repeated today. The situation is not stable. The seasoned teacher knows how to shift methods, content, and even the lesson's very purpose with the time of day, or the day of the week, or the mood of the students. The teacher recognizes the relevant pattern, makes sense of the poetics of the classroom. (2005, p. 101)

The nature surrounding the answers teachers find to the variety of challenges within the classroom or the e-learning environment are scarcely observable to researchers who come from a more traditional analytic approach. Such phenomenon are not studied because the traditional method to elucidate such problems are based on finding universal and firm answers and uses a logic that tends to be more of a reductive first glance approach that is a simple understanding to the problems (St. Julien, 2005; Haggis, 2008; Mitchell, 2009). Such phenomena have thwarted the dominant approach of reductionism, which has been around since Descartes and Newton and other founders of the modern scientific method since the 1600s and 'in spite of its great successes explaining the very large and the very small, fundamental physics, and more generally, scientific reductionism, have been notable mute in explaining the complex phenomena closest to our human-scale concerns' (Mitchell, 2009, p. 5). Educators and educational researchers are encouraged to look at the emerging bigger pattern because the new sciences and emerging technologies in the social sciences constitute something more than the standard sporadic, irregular progress of human endeavor and as Kuhn (1957) states, something other than the advance of normal science.

So what strides has complexity research made in the domain of education and educational research? A double issue was devoted to complexity theory and philosophy of education in the fortieth volume of *Educational Philosophy and Theory* in 2008. Academic papers were gathered from a distinguished group of international scholars who have devoted their thinking and writing to complexity theory and its relationship to educational discourses. Two papers address the issue of complexity theory and philosophy of education (Morrison, 2008; Mason, 2008). Morrison believes that complexity theory challenges educational philosophy to re-evaluate the accepted norms of teaching, learning and educational research and although its appeal lies in its critique of positivism, its similarity to Dewey and Habermas, and its strong arguments for diversity, openness, relationships and creativity, Morrison states the theory is not without difficulties. These difficulties concern the theory's nature, status, methodology and utility because it is a descriptive theory that can be easily misunderstood as a prescriptive theory and it fails to address issues of value and ethics which are important concepts within educational philosophy. The author also believes that the theory is too ambiguous concerning the boundaries of systems and although the theory advocates wholism, Morrison begs the question as to what constitutes the 'whole' when one asks, what is the whole realm of a class, and of an individual?

Mason (2008) in the same topic raises issues and questions for the challenge of complexity theory for the philosophy of education and conversely, the challenge for complexity theory from educational philosophy. He reiterates Morrison's concerns regarding the theory's challenges and feels that complexity theory has not made much headway in the realm of education. 'Engaging complexity in educational research and practice thus involves educational philosophers, practitioners and researchers in a complex process of meshing the perspectives of complexity with a range of normative commitments. On those commitments and on their integration into research and theorizing in this paradigm, complexity theory has been largely silent' (2008, p. 17).

Six further papers from notable scholars within this volume of *Educational Philosophy and Theory* concern their attentions to discussing the implications and appropriateness of a complexity approach to educational research. Kuhn suggests that, 'like all human encounters, approaches to research emerge out of discursive communities and can be understood as self-organizing, dynamic and emergent over time' (2008, p. 177). The author uses a complexity approach to social inquiry and highlights the importance in partaking in critical and reflective discourse about the nature of education and conceptual frameworks so as to influence the ongoing emergence of research approaches. As an active leader in the development of complexity informed ethnographic research approaches, Lesley Kuhn states, that '[e]ngaging complexity in educational research involves researchers in a complex process of marrying complexity habits of thought with a range of aims. It means recognizing that complexity *per se* does not have an ethical intent. It is the researcher who is committed to human betterment' (2008, p. 187).

Haggis continues along this thread in exploring complexity as an ontology in providing 'a way of thinking about institutions, cultures, groups and individuals as systems of interactions which are, in some important ways, always unique. This uniquely presenting system of interactions, however, is partially constituted by the interactions of other, larger systems; system of governance, for example, of culture, language, policy, or of funding' (2008, p. 169). Haggis makes the point that whilst a more conventional way of tracing the workings of these interactions among larger systems in relation to the idea of 'underpinning structures' which cut across individual examples (such as gender), a complexity framing might propose the ways in which aspects of these larger system interactions work within particular, smaller cases (e.g. how is this woman 'gendered' compared with this one?). 'The first approach privileges the similarities observable by comparison (leading to the ability to formulate a category such as 'gender' in the first place), while the complexity approach is as likely to find difference as it is to find similarity. When it does find patterns of similarity, these will relate to quite different aspects of the focus of the study' (Haggis, 2008, p. 169). With respect to the issues raised above by Haggis[12], the author also believes that taking a complexity approach helps in the conceptualization of the context. 'Thinking of people and social/institutional/cultural contexts as complex, dynamic systems allows for the separation of these two distinct types of context, even though (and perhaps crucially because) they made be embedded in each other' (2008, p. 169). Byrne (2005) agrees with this thought and states that complexity theory challenges the nominal program of universally applicable knowledge at its core and it emphasizes that knowledge must be contextual.

Davis (2008) puts forward a case for educators and educational researchers to embrace complexity science as 'a properly "educational" discourse' (p. 50) and suggests that educational research has a history of adopting interpretive frames from other domains with little adaptation. As he states 'Complexity science is argued to compel a different sort of positioning, one that requires accommodation and participation rather than unproblematized assimilation and application' (p. 50). Davis addresses the issue of how complexity science might be understood as appropriate to the concerns of educators and educational researchers by exploring several simultaneities offered by complexity thinking. The word *simultaneity* is used to describe phenomena or actions that exist or operate at the same time. In the author's paper, it is used as a contrast to the modern and Western habit of thinking in terms 'of *discontinuities* around such matters as theory and practice, knowers and knowledge, self and other, mind and body, art and science, and child and curriculum. In the context of popular debate, the terms of these sorts of dyads tend to be understood as necessarily distinct, opposed, and unconnected, even though they always seem to occur at the same time. In other words, such simultaneities tend to be seen as coincidental, but not complicated' (2008, p. 51). Complexity thinking offers concern toward this type of interpretation and as the author believes, it presents important alternatives and advice to the concern of education and educational research.

Many authors in this volume of scholarly papers agree that one of the downfalls of classical inquiry has been the confirmation of the theoretical, descriptive and/or experimental to give results that are secure and firm knowledge. Using a complexity approach helps to avoid such error mainly because certain phenomena related to learning cannot be pinned down easily or with any certainty. From an ethical stance, one major issue surrounding the classical inquiry is the tendency for the researcher/observer/experimenter or theorist to write herself or himself out of the research result (Haggis, 2008; Kuhn, 2008; Horn, 2008; Davis, 2008; Radford, 2008). 'The complexity researcher has an obligation – an ethical imperative, I would argue – to be attentive to how she or he is implicated in the phenomenon studied' (Davis, 2008, p. 63).

There is no doubt that the education system is one of the most complex and challenging systems for research. Many researchers believe that complexity offers a way toward a new research agenda. Despite what is known about the cognitive aspects of learning or pedagogical approaches thus far, 'we currently lack the modeling capability needed to help practitioners and policy makers explore the potential impact of proposed interventions, since efforts in this area are still at a very preliminary stage of development' (Lemke & Sabelli, 2008, p. 128).

The authors also feel that what is needed is a change in the paradigms of our thinking about research regarding education. What is required is a switch away 'from input–output "black-box" casual models to modeling the specific, local linkages that actually interconnect actors, practices, and events across multiple levels of organization' (Lemke & Sabelli, 2008, p. 128).

CONCLUSIONS

The allure of complexity, whether it is a theory, a science or a way of thinking, has no doubt opened a significantly different view of the various diverse world phenomena. There seems to be an increasing proportion of the research community embracing the notion or idea of complexity to bring about a better understanding in human medicine, education, sociology or economics to name a few. While it is agreed that complexity is still in its early stages, that is, it is still evolving, one thing is clear as Mitchell states, 'pursuing these goals will require, as great science always does, an adventurous intellectual spirit and a willingness to risk failure and reproach by going beyond mainstream science into ill-defined and uncharted territory' (2009, p. 303). For education and educational researchers, complexity offers the insight that the study of human systems is best done where it is happening with students and teachers, and where they 'consider their own practice as a learning process that does not require the reduction of the antagonisms and the complementarities that shape its own complexity' (Alhadeff-Jones, 2008, p. 66). The issues that seem to be important for educational researchers, and academic students working on dissertations is not how to control what occurs, but how to participate and embrace in the unfolding of possibilities.

NOTES

1. Howard Eves (1990) points out in his book, *An Introduction to the History of Mathematics,* that the French mathematician, Henri Poincaré (1854–1912) was one of the early pioneers who rebelled against Newtonian determinism and in his 1879 doctoral dissertation paved the way for thinking about non-linear solutions to particular systems of differential equations.

2. As Capra (1996) states, 'The basic tension is one between the parts and the whole. The emphasis on the parts has been called mechanistic, reductionistic, or atomistic; the emphasis on the whole holistic, organismic, or ecological. In twentieth-century science the holistic perspective has become known as "systemic" and the way of thinking it implies as "systems thinking"' (p. 17).

3. Waldrop (1992) gives a thorough historical review of many of the scientists associated with the Santa Fe Institute and highlights the studies generated as a result of their interactions in his book, Complexity: The Emerging Science at the Edge of Order and Chaos.

4. Richardson and Cilliers take a complexivist attitude where they acknowledge an artificial and misleading tidiness of this classification. The diverse attitudes toward complexity are highly intertwined and sometimes simultaneously apparent. The authors state that it is not about aligning or committing to a category but rather to provide a useful tool for understanding some of the inevitable inconsistencies within complexity research.

5. Professor of Computer Science at Portland State University and external Professor at the Santa Fe Institute, New Mexico.

6. Neil Johnson is head of a new inter-disciplinary research group in Complexity at the University of Miami, Florida and was previously Professor of Physics at Oxford University.

7. Sims' website, <http//thesims.ea.com/>, or the 'interactive and visual representations link at the website of the New England Complex Systems Institute' (http://necsi.org/).

8. To study these surveys and research projects read K. Kelly, *Out of control: the new biology of machines, social systems, and the economic world*. Cambridge, MA: Perseus, 1994.

9. Cilliers (1998) states that it is often difficult to define the border of a complex system. 'Instead of being a characteristic of the system itself, the scope of the system is usually determined by the purpose of the *description* of the system, and is thus often influenced by the position of the observer. This process is called *framing*' (p. 4).

10. Any study that ignores the dimension of time within a complex system is deficient or as Cilliers (1998) states is 'at most a synchronic snapshot of a diachronic process' (p. 4).

11. Cilliers (1998) believes this is an extremely important point because if each agent knew what was going on with the whole system all of what is complexity would have to be entailed in that one agent or element. This would either be a physical impossibility because of the needed capacity of the element to contain all complexity or 'constitute a metaphysical move in the sense that "consciousness" of the whole is contained in one particular unit' (p. 5).

12. Haggis makes the point that although complexity theory may be seen by some as providing a way of discussing about random, intuitive, even 'spiritual' phenomena, her research article is not arguing those points. The causalities involved in the interactions may be untrackable, but what emerges from them is not 'mysterious'. In this sense, it is consistent with the nature and histories of the interactions involved.

REFERENCES

Alhadeff-Jones, M. (2008). Three generations of complexity theories: Nuances and ambiguities. *Educational Philosophy and Theory, 40*, 66–82.

Andrews, R. & Haythornthwaite, C. (Eds.). (2007). *The Handbook of E-Learning Research*. London: Sage.

Auyang, S. Y. (2000). *Foundations of Complex-System Theories in Economics, Evolutionary Biology, and Statistical Physics*. Cambridge: Cambridge University Press.

Barlow, C. & Waldrop, M. (1994). Worldview extensions of complexity theory. In C. Barlow (Ed.), *Evolution Extended: Biological Debates on the Meaning of Life*. Cambridge, MA: The MIT Press.

Bertalanffy, L. (1968). *General Systems Theory: Foundations, Development, Applications*. New York: Braziller.

Bertalanffy, L. (1975). The history and development of general systems theory. In E. Taschdjian (Ed.), *Perspectives on General Systems Theory: Scientific-Philosophical Studies*. New York: Braziller.

Barab, S. A. & Cherkes-Julkowski, M. (1999). Principles of self-organisation: Learning as participation in autocakakinetic systems. *The Journal of the Learning Sciences, 8*, 349–390.

Bohm, D. (1980). *Wholeness and the Implicit Order*. New York: Routledge.

Butz, M., Chamberlain, L. & McCown, W. (1997). *Strange Attractors: Chaos, Complexity and the Art of Family Therapy*. New York: J. Wiley & Sons.

Byrne, D. (1998). *Complexity Theory and the Social Sciences*. London: Routledge.

Byrne, D. (2005). Complexity, configurations and cases. *Theory, Culture and Society, 22*, 95–111.

Capra, F. (1996). *The Web of Life: A New Scientific Understanding of Living Systems*. New York: Anchor Doubleday.

Capra, F. (2002). *The Hidden Connections: Intergrating the Biological, Cognitive, and Social Dimensions of Life into a Science of Sustainability*. New York: Doubleday.

Carson, R. (1962). *Silent Spring*. New York: Houghton Mifflin Company.

Cilliers, P. (1998). *Complexity and Postmodernism*. London: Routledge.

Dadds, M. & Hart, S. (2001). *Doing Practitioner Research Differently*. London: Routledge.

Davis, B. & Simmt, E. (2003). Understanding learning systems: Mathematics teaching and complexity science. *Journal for Research in Mathematics Education, 34*, 137–167.

Davis, B. & Sumara, D. (1997). Cognition, complexity, and teacher education. *Harvard Educational Review, 67*, 105–125.

Davis, B. & Sumara, D. (2002). Constructivist discourses and the field of education: Problems and possibilities. *Educational Theory, 52,* 409–428.

Davis, B. & Sumara, D. (2005). Complexity science and educational action research. *Educational Action Research, 13,* 453–464.

Davis, B. & Sumara, D. (2006). *Complexity and Education: Inquiries into Learning, Teaching, and Research.* Mahwah, NJ: Lawrence Erlbaum Associates.

Davis, B. (2008). Complexity and education: Vital simultaneities. *Educational Philosophy and Theory, 40,* 50–65.

Doll, Jr, W. E. (1993). *A Post Modern Perspective on Curriculum.* New York: Teachers College Press.

Edwards, R. (2010). Complex global problems, simple lifelong learning solutions. In D. Osberg and G. Biesta (Eds.), *Complexity Theory and the Politics of Education.* Rotterdam, The Netherlands: Sense Publishers.

Eenwyk, van J. (1997). *Archetypes and Strange Attractors.* Toronto: Inner City Books.

Ely, M., Vinz, R., Downing, M. & Anzul, M. (1997). *On Writing Qualitative Research.* London: Falmer.

Engles, F. (1987). *The Condition of the Working Class in England.* New York: Penguin.

Ennis, C. D. (1993). Reconceptualizing learning as a dynamical system. *Journal of Curriculum and Supervision, 7,* 115–130.

Eve, R., Horsfall, S. & Lee, M. (Eds.). (1997). *Chaos, Complexity and Sociology.* London: Sage.

Fogel, A., Lyra, M. & Valsiner, J. (1997). *Dynamics and Indeterminism in Development and Social Processes.* Hillsdale, NJ: Lawrence Erlbaum Associates.

Friensen, N. (2009). *Re-Thinking E-Learning Research: Foundations, Methods, and Practices.* New York: Peter Lang Publishing.

Gleick, J. (1987). *Chaos: Making a New Science.* New York: Penguin.

Goldstein, J. (2000). Emergence: A construct amid a thicket of conceptual snares. *Emergence, 2,* 5–22.

Gordan, D. (1999). *Ants at Work: How an Insect Society is Organized.* New York: Free Press.

Haggis, T. (2008). Knowledge must be contextual: Some possible implications of complexity and dynamic systems theories for educational research. *Educational Philosophy and Theory, 40,* 158–176.

Hawken, P. (1994). *The Ecology of Commerce.* London: Phoenix.

Holland, J. H. (1998). *Emergence: From Chaos to Order.* Reading, MA: Helix.

Horn, J. (2008). Human research and complexity theory. *Educational Philosophy and Theory, 40,* 130–143.

Horn, J. & Wilburn, D. (2005). The embodiment of learning. *Educational Philosophy and Theory, 37,* 745–760.

Jacobs, J. (1961). *The Death and Life of Great American Cities.* New York: Vintage.

Johnson, S. (2001). *Emergence.* London: Penguin.

Johnson, N. (2007). *Simply Complexity: A Clear Guide to Complexity Theory.* Oxford, UK: Oneworld Publications.

Kauffman, S. (1993). *The Origins of Order.* London: Oxford University Press.

Kauffman, S. (1995). *At Home in the Universe: The Search for the Laws of Self-Organization and Complexity.* New York: Oxford University Press.

Kuhn, L. (2008). Complexity and educational research: A critical reflection. *Educational Philosophy and Theory, 40,* 177–189.

Kuhn, T. S. (1957). *The Copernican Revolution: Planetary Astronomy in the Development of Western Thought.* Cambridge, MA: Harvard University Press.

Kuhn, T. S. (1962). *The Structure of Scientific Revolutions.* Chicago, IL: Chicago University Press.

Landow, G. P. (1999). Hypertext as collage-writing. In P. Lunenfeld (Ed.), *The Digital Dialectic: New Essays on New Media.* London, UK: The MIT Press.

Lemke, J. L. & Sabelli, N. H. (2008). Complex systems and educational change: Towards a new research. *Educational Philosophy and Theory, 40,* 118–129.

Lewin, R. (1992). *Complexity: Life at the Edge of Chaos.* New York: Macmillan.

Lewin, R. (1995). *Complexity.* London: Phoenix.

Lewin, R. & Regine, B. (2000). *Weaving Complexity and Business: Engaging the Soul at Work.* New York: Texere.

Lorenz, E. N. (1963). Deterministic nonperiodic flow. *Journal of the Atmospheric Sciences, 20,* 130–141.

Marcus, P. (1985). Numerical simulation of Jupiter's great red spot. *Nature, 331,* 693–696.

Mason, M. (2008). Complexity theory and the philosophy of education. *Educational Philosophy and Theory, 40,* 4–18.

Maturana, H. (1980). Autopoiesis: Reproduction, heredity and evolution. In M. Zeleny (Ed.), *Autopoiesis, Dissipative Strutures, and Spontaneous Social Orders.* Boulder, CO: Westview.

Maturana, H. R. & Varela, F. J. (1980). *Autopoiesis and Cognition: The Realization of the Living.* Boston, MA: D. Reidel Publishing Co.

Middleton, J. A., Sawada, D., Judson, E., Bloom, I. & Turley, J. (2002). Relationships build reform: Treating classroom as emergent systems. In L. D. English (Ed.), *Handbook of International Research in Mathematics Education.* Mahwah, NJ: Lawrence Erlbaum Associates.

Mitchell, M. (2009). *Complexity: A Guided Tour.* New York: Oxford University Press.

Morin, E. (2001). The concept of system and the paradigm of complexity. In M. Maruyama (Ed.), *Context and Complexity: Cultivating Contextual Understanding.* New York: Springer-Verlag.

Morin, E. (2008). *On Complexity* (translated by Robin Postel). Cresskill, NJ: Hampton Press.

Morrison, K. (2008). Educational philosophy and the challenge of complexity theory. *Educational Philosophy and Theory, 40,* 19–34.

Nicolis, G. & Prigogine, I. (1989). *Exploring Complexity.* New York: Freeman & Co.

Osberg, D. (2005). Curriculum, complexity and representation: Rethinking the epistemology of schooling through complexity theory. Unpublished doctoral thesis. Open University, Milton Keynes.

Osberg, D. & Biesta, G. (2010). *Complexity Theory and the Politics of Education.* The Netherlands: Sense Publishers.

Prigogine, I. & Stengers, I. (1984). *Order Out of Chaos: Man's New Dialogue with Nature.* New York: Bantam Books.

Prigogine, I. & Stengers, I. (1997). *The End of Certainty: Time, Chaos and the New Laws of Nature.* New York: Free Press.

Radford, M. (2008). Complexity and truth in educational research. *Educational Philosophy and Theory, 40,* 144–157.

Richardson, K. A. & Cilliers, P. (2001). What is complexity science?: A view from different directions. *Emergence, 3,* 5–22.

Rucker, R. (1987). *Mind Tools: The Mathematics of Information.* New York: Penguin.

Richardson, K. A. (Ed.). (2005). *Managing the Complex: Philosophy, Theory, and Application* (Vol. 1). Greenwich, CT: Information Age Publishers.

Sakai, K. (2001). *Nonlinear Dynamics and Chaos in Agriculture Systems.* Amsterdam: Elsevier.

Sawada, D. & Caley, M.T. (1985). Dissipative structures: New metaphors for becoming education. *Educational Researcher, 14,* 13–19.

St. Julien, J. (2005). Complexity: Developing a more useful analytic for education. In W. Doll, Jr, M. J. Fleener, D. Trueit, & J. St. Julien (Eds.), *Chaos, Complexity, Curriculum, and Culture.* New York: Peter Lang Publishing.

Stanley, W. (2005). Pragmatic complexity: Emerging ideas and historical views of the complexity sciences. In W. E. Doll, M. J. Fleener, D. Trueit, & J. St. Julien (Eds.), *Chaos, Complexity, Curriculum, and Culture: A Conversation.* New York: Peter Lang Publishing.

Thrift, N. (1999). The place of complexity. *Theory, Culture and Society, 16,* 31–69.

Valsiner, J. (1998). *The Guided Mind.* Cambridge, MA: Harvard University Press.

Waldrop, M. M. (1992). *Complexity: The Emerging Science on the Edge of Order and Chaos.* New York: Simon and Schuster.

Watts, D. (2003). *Six Degrees: The Science of the Connected Age.* New York: W. W. Norton.

8

Re-imagining the Conditions of Possibility of a PhD Thesis

Jude Fransman

BECOMING A PHD THESIS: SELECTION, CLASSIFICATION, RECONTEXTUALISATION

How does a PhD thesis emerge from the matter of doctoral research? And what is the influence of the social *idea* of the thesis-as-text and the conditions of possibility[1] set by the material *actualisation* of the thesis on the doctoral research process? Philosophers such as Gilles Deleuze have referred to any instance through which social-material matter (such as that of doctoral research) is fixed (into forms such as a PhD thesis) as virtual–actual becoming. In some of his earlier work,[2] Deleuze argues (against Plato's transcendent assumption) that life does not rest on an ideal or original model, but rather that all social and physical matter exists on a plane of *difference* and the boundary-setting through which social or material *identities* are defined occurs through discursive practices which act as copying devices (Deleuze, 1994, p. 38). In this way, the real is always *actual–virtual* (Deleuze, 1994, pp. 207–212). An actual thing is produced only from virtual possibilities. There must already be some general image of a PhD thesis in order to build, recognise and perceive an actual PhD thesis. What something *is* (actually) is also its power to *become* (virtually). A PhD thesis can become a reference in a library search engine, a citation in another publication, a chapter in a Sage Handbook, a justification for postdoctoral funding or any number of other possibilities. Virtual potentialities are only recognised once they have been actualised and an actual thing has also a virtual dimension: a plant is not just its matter but is also a need or expectation of light and water and a PhD thesis is also an expectation of (amongst other things) a defence. So while academic standards might result in some measure of what constitutes a PhD thesis, there is always evolution and deviation whether this occurs on an individual, institutional or societal level. Colebrook (2002, p. 99) refers to this philosophy as an 'ethics of potentialities'. However, it is important to note that a focus on *becoming* does not preclude attention to *being*. Or to put it another way, what is needed is both attention to the processes through which human, material and conceptual identities develop and to the ways in which they are fixed or defined to serve particular purposes. It is here that a distinction made by Deleuze and Guattari (1987) between 'rhizomatic' maps and 'aborescent' tracings is helpful. A tracing replicates existing structures and is linear: 'All tree logic is a logic of tracing and reproduction' (1987, p. 12). By contrast, maps are creative open systems producing an organisation of reality rather than reproducing some prior representation. 'The map is ... detachable, reversible, susceptible to constant modification. It can be torn, reversed, adapted to any kind of mounting, reworked by an individual, group or social formation' (ibid.). Later on in this chapter, I go on to suggest how a digital thesis might facilitate new mappings of the PhD identity against the institutionalised tracings of the traditional thesis. I start, however, by proposing a conceptual framework to show how doctoral matter is fixed into a PhD thesis through the inter-related processes of selection, classification and recontextualisation.

Like any research text, the PhD thesis materialises, to paraphrase Karen Barad (2003) through an ongoing process of *mattering*. As Law points out (2004, p. 2), Barad's play on words gets to the heart of the relationship between matter as *material, stuff, mess* and matter as *significance, value, concern*. This relationship has been formulated in a range of ways by social theorists. Latour, for example, has distinguished between matters of fact and matters of concern (Latour, 2004); Kress has explored the motivated translation of 'stuff' into the analytical category of 'data' (Kress, 2010) and Law (2004) has unpacked the relationship between 'mess' and 'method assemblage'. Importantly, Barad's pun emphasises the inter-relationship between the material and meaningful dimensions of 'matter' (both in terms of the putative realities which form the 'raw' data of research and the research apparatus or the methods and texts which configure and represents these realities). Her formulation of matter as a verb or process (rather than a noun or thing) also suggests a performative dimension: that *mattering* is something which is *done* rather than something which exists independently of social interaction.

For doctoral students, matters of concern might be grounded in personal and professional interests and may well also be influenced by the interests of other actors such as supervisors or the research council that might be funding the PhD. As students confront the other type of (material) matter that emerges through their processes of data collection and engagement with the 'literature' (human bodies, spoken words, artefacts, statistics, graphs, diagrams, references) these matters of concern manifest as assumptions that guide the students' *selection* and *classification* of what they are absorbing: assumptions about the distinction between theory and methodology, assumptions about the aptness of particular theories and conceptual models and assumptions about the interest of different thematic foci. Such choices about what of the matter *matters* to the students (*selection*) and how those matters relate to each other (*classification*) are also highly political in nature. But decisions about what matters also relate initially to the *virtual idea* of what a PhD thesis looks like and later to the *actual materiality* of the realised thesis which plays an inevitable role in *recontextualising* the stuff of the research. These inter-related processes are complex and deserve some elaboration.

SELECTION (OR HOW THINGS ARE INCLUDED OR EXCLUDED)

In his influential handbook, *After Method: Mess in Social Science Research*, John Law (2004) proposes an expansion of Deleuze and Guattari's (1987) notion of the 'assemblage'[3] into the concept of the 'method assemblage' in order to show how research performs and, in doing so, makes selections which include or exclude. A method assemblage might be defined as 'the process of crafting and enacting the necessary boundaries between presence, manifest absence and Otherness' (Law, 2004, p. 161). So, for instance, a method assemblage based on a survey approach will generate presences (e.g. data about a sample of a particular population at a specific moment in time); manifest absences (e.g. data from those of the sample who did not respond to the survey but are acknowledged as 'non-respondents' in the survey methodology) and produce Others (e.g. data which cannot be contained as individual reports of attitudes and behaviour, or data which is not captured by the conditions of possibility set by the survey instrument). In questioning why certain things are Othered or de-selected, Law suggests that Otherness tends to take three key forms. First, what is 'routine' might be Othered. For example, in the survey approach, assumptions about how individual statements can be aggregated to account for societal trends is taken for granted. Second, what is 'insignificant' may also be Othered. For example, a survey may collect 'background data' based on factors such as age, gender and ethnicity but is less likely to collect data about whether a respondent is an oldest, youngest or only child. Third, Othering can also serve to 'repress' certain things which might risk compromising present things. For example, a survey which is interested in explaining the influence of class on a particular phenomenon may Other the influence of gender, age, ethnicity or language in order to strengthen the explanatory power of socio-economic background.

While Law focuses exclusively on the performativity of method in research, I would argue that another aspect of the research apparatus: the research text also plays an important role in distributing presences, absences and Others. For example, the representation of research as a PowerPoint presentation tends to condense lengthy analysis into a list of bullet points or visual diagrams (Othering the more complex elements of the process, authorial style, lengthy quotations, etc.). So *selection* is about decisions relating to what is included or excluded in a text. These decisions are not based on comparative evaluations of discrete things alone but also on the nature of these things in relation to each other and the form of the text(s) into which they will be assembled – an issue which is really a matter of *recontextualisation*.

RECONTEXTUALISATION (OR HOW MATTER IS TRANSPORTED FROM ONE TEXT OR MEDIA TO ANOTHER AND HOW THINGS CHANGE AS A RESULT)

To the three forms of Othering catalogued by Law above I would like to propose a fourth. Things are excluded simply because they don't *fit* with the (social or material) form of the text into which they are packaged. Or conversely, things are included – in part – because of the ease with which they can be moved from one media to another. So, for example, if a conference PowerPoint presentation is represented in the notebook of a student in the audience it is less likely that the student would attempt to replicate a photograph from one of the slides than a series of bullet points from the same slide – even if the purpose of both bullet points and photograph was to illustrate the same argument. Similarly, a policy report emerging from a quantitative research project is likely to represent the data as a series of graphs and charts rather than in its 'rawer' form of pages of statistical annexes.

The movement of meaning across contexts is an issue which has preoccupied social scientists from a variety of disciplines who have developed innovative concepts and methods through which to trace flows and reconfigurations of people, concepts and things as they travel across multiple sites[4]. Scollon and Scollon (2004), for example, employ the notion of 'nexus analysis' to trace pathways and trajectories of texts, actions, practices and objects, of people and communications across time and space and multiple modes. Iedema (2003) uses the term 'resemiotisation to explain the movement and transformation of meaning across events, spaces, times, modes and media. Others, such as Callon (1986), Bernstein (1996), Silverstein and Urban (1996), Wenger (1998), Lemke (2002), Thibault (2004) and Barton and Tusting (2005) have used a variety of terms (such as 'translation', 'traversal', 'recontextualisation', 'reification', 'entextualisation' and 'reinvoicement') to capture different aspects of this process (see Scollon, in Bhatia et al., 2008, p. 241).

From a social semiotics perspective, Kress (2010) has provided a helpful distinction between two types of movement of meaning across time and space. In the first, called *transduction*, meaning moves across modes (e.g. from speech to thought to writing) or genres (e.g. from a PhD thesis to a conference presentation) or cultures (e.g. from Spanish to English) and in doing so, changes its entities and its logic too. In the second, called *transformation*, the movement of meaning involves no change in mode and so the process operates on and with the same set of entities though these entities are reordered. So, for example, the translation of my written PhD thesis into this written chapter is an example of transformation. The mode remains that of writing and (broadly speaking) the same elements manifest in each. However, the *ordering* of the elements has changed and this ordering is reflected not only in *selection* (what is included and excluded in the transformed text) but also in *classification* (how the different elements of the text are positioned in relation to each other).

CLASSIFICATION (OR HOW MATTER IS SORTED AND HOW THINGS ARE POSITIONED IN RELATION TO EACH OTHER)

As scholars have pointed out (Kress, 2010; Bowker & Star, 1999), classification is an intensely political activity and very much related to *selection* and *recontextualisation*. Once classification systems are established, anything that does not fit into one or another category is likely either to fall through the cracks of recognition and become Othered or to be mutilated or *torqued* (Bowker & Star, 1999, p. 223) until it resembles something that meets the conventions of a particular category. As such, Bowker and Star suggest that classifications are intrinsically linked to standards and that each standard and each category valorises certain points of view and silences others. Choices regarding classification are consequently highly ethical (1999, p. 5). They are also attached to institutional discourses and broader social orderings. Kress (2010, pp. 122–123) suggests that classification stabilises the social world in particular ways, reflecting the social organisation which has produced them and which is constantly reaffirmed, remade and naturalised through them. The seemingly innocuous character of classification also helps to make its political effects more effective. In their book *Sorting Things Out: Classification and its Consequences*, Bowker and Star explore the ways in which classification systems (ranging from medical classifications of tuberculosis to classifications of race in apartheid South Africa) manifest as innocuous by becoming 'naturalised':

> The more naturalised a type of classification becomes, the more unquestioning the relationship of the community to it; the more invisible the contingent and historical circumstances of its birth, the more it sinks into the community's routinely forgotten memory. (Bowker & Star, 1999, p. 299)

Examples of this type of naturalisation in academia include the highly political yet taken for granted boundaries of many 'core' disciplines. On a somewhat smaller scale the classification of elements of a thesis (literature review, methodology, findings, etc.) provides a further example of this process at play.

So *classification* is fundamentally related to *selection* and *recontextualisation* as a means of explaining how matter is reduced, ordered and packaged. All of these inter-related processes involve political negotiations around what of the *matter* is significant and why it *matters*. In the following section, I introduce the concepts 'interest' and 'affordance' from social semiotics to show how these processes are influenced by the social and material form of the texts into which they are packaged.

INTERESTS AND AFFORDANCES

According to a social semiotic perspective (Halliday & Hasan, 1985; Hodge & Kress, 1988; Kress & Van Leeuwen, 1996; Van Leeuwen, 2005; Kress, 2010), a PhD thesis-as-text might be understood as *a momentary fixing and framing of* (doctoral) *semiosis* guided by the *interest* of the text-maker – most probably the doctoral researcher. The idea of interest here is important[5]. In social semiotics, the notion of the *arbitrary* sign developed by Ferdinand de Saussure is replaced with the *motivated* sign in the design of 'semiotic resources both to produce communicative artefacts and events and to interpret them – which is also a form of semiotic production – in the context of specific social situations and practices' (Van Leeuwen, 2005, p. xi). To understand the social and material conditions of possibility of meaning making, social semiotics offers the reformulated concept of *affordance*[6]. All instances of communication involve the use of *semiotic resources* or *modes* (such as speech, writing, gaze, gesture). According to Van Leeuwen (2005), these modes have a *theoretical* semiotic potential (constituted by all their past uses) and an *actual* semiotic potential (constituted by those past uses that are known to and considered relevant by the users of the mode and by potential uses that might be uncovered by the users according to their specific needs and interests). Since all instances of communication take place in a social context, different contexts may have different rules or best practices that regulate the ways in which specific semiotic resources can be used, or alternatively, leave the users relatively free in their use of the resource (Van Leeuwen, 2005, p. 4). So, affordance in this context is shaped by the different ways in which a mode has been used, what it has been repeatedly used to mean and do, and the social conventions and material possibilities that inform its use in context. In this way, the affordance of a mode is related both to materiality and meaning (or *matter* in both senses of the word). It is also related to the specific logic of each mode (Jewitt, 2008, pp. 25–26). The sounds of speech for instance unfold sequentially in time, and this sequence in time shapes what can be done with (speech) sounds. This sequence constitutes an affordance: it produces the possibilities for ordering things in relation to each other. Conversely, (still) images tend to be governed by the logic of space where the mechanics of ordering play out very differently (Jewitt, 2009, p. 25).

Distinguishing between the notion of 'affordance' and Halliday's similar notion of 'meaning potential', Van Leeuwen argues that while the latter notion focuses on meanings that have already been introduced into society, 'affordance' also includes meanings that have not yet been recognised:

> ... no one can claim to know all the affordances of a given [mode or semiotic resource] yet as semioticians we do not need to restrict ourselves to what is, we can also set out to investigate what could be ... (Van Leeuwen, 2005, p. 5)

This distinction is not dissimilar to the distinction between Deleuze and Guattari's map and tracing discussed in the introduction to this chapter and also embraces Deleuze's notion of *virtual–actual becoming*. However, Van Leeuwen reminds us that the fact that resources have no objectively fixed meanings does not mean that meaning is a free-for-all:

> In social life people constantly try to fix and control the use of semiotic resources and to justify the rules they make up although more so in some domains than others. (Van Leeuwen, 2005, p. 5)

The question is, how are these conditions of possibility set in the domain of doctoral research and what is the mapping-affordance (as opposed to the tracing-affordance) for those students engaged in designing and producing research texts which matter? As a response, social semiotics provides a set of tools for unpacking textual affordance in two key ways: first, by showing how the affordances of a text interact with the process through which texts are assembled; and second, by showing how the affordances of a text interact with its content and form.

With regards the first set of tools, social semioticians have suggested that texts are assembled through the somewhat sequential stages of rhetorical process, design and production (see Kress, 2010). *Rhetorical processes* occur before (though are also concurrent with and can conceivably follow) the moment of design (when a text is fixed and framed). In these processes the sign maker:

> makes an assessment of all aspects of the communicational situation: of her or his interest; of the characteristics of the audience; the semiotic requirements of the issue at stake and the resources at stake and the resources available for making an apt representation; together with establishing the best means for its dissemination. (Kress, 2010, p. 126)

In other words, this stage involves an assessment of the virtual and actual affordances of the text to be designed. So before developing a PowerPoint presentation for a conference, presenters will asses the theoretical, methodological, empirical and ideological messages they want to send (negotiating between their own personal interests and what they imagine will be the interests of the conference organisers and attendees); the integrity of their data and how best to represent it and the texts and media into which their messages will be packaged (or the conditions of possibility afforded by the presentation software). The rhetor's task is therefore a political one, namely 'to provoke and produce the rearrangement of social relations by semiotic means' (ibid. p. 121). By contrast, the *design stage* involves the transformation of 'political intent into semiotic form' (ibid. p. 121). So in this stage, the presenters start to navigate the virtual affordances of the media of the PowerPoint presentation (in terms of issues like how to condense pages of dense academic writing into a single practitioner-friendly slide and how to order the text as a linear presentation); and the virtual affordances of the conference itself (in terms of issues like how to respond to the timing of the conference, the nature of the audience and the topical focus). And finally, the *production stage* constitutes the stage in which the virtual is actualised (e.g. a PowerPoint presentation is created in space and a conference unfolds in time). So:

> Design meets the interests of the rhetor ... in full awareness of the communicational potentials of the resources which are available in the environment and needed for the implementation of the rhetor's interests. Design gives shape to the interests of both rhetor and the designer ... Production is the implementation of design with the resources available in the world in which the communication takes place. In production meaning is made material. (Kress, 2010, pp. 26–27)

If the rhetorical, design and production stages explain the process of text-making, how then might one identify the various configurations within the text (classification) and the implications for what is included or excluded (selection)? To answer this question, Kress proposes the concept of 'fixing' (which involves choices about *mode* and of *genre*[7]) and argues that these choices are always inter-related. According to social semiotic theory, texts are the products of communicative interaction and are multimodal (Kress, 2001). This means that there is always a choice of *modes* (or semiotic resources) through which to fix meaning:

> Depending on the media involved there are different possibilities: do you wish to realise meaning as image or as gesture, as moving image or as speech or as ensembles of these? (Kress, in Jewitt, 2009, p. 64).

Kress shows that the choice of mode or multimodal ensemble in which the text is realised (which might include speech, writing, image, gesture, gaze, movement, music or components of these such as colour, volume, pace, font, layout) and the *generic* form that the text takes (e.g. a PowerPoint presentation, PhD thesis or a chapter in a handbook) matters:

> Once particular means of mixing meaning have become habituated it is likely that the world as represented through the affordances of mode and genre will come to seem like this 'naturally' (Kress, 2009, p. 66).

So *genre* addresses the semiotic mergence of social organisation, practices and interactions. It names and 'realises' knowledge of the world as social action and interaction and occurs through participation in events (like academic conferences or doctoral defences) formed of such actions experienced as recognisable practices (like presenting a PowerPoint or defending a PhD).

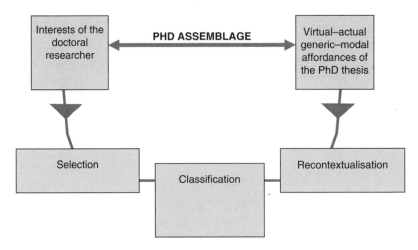

Figure 8.1   The conditions of possibility of a PhD thesis

Together the inter-related concepts of *genre* and *mode* can help show how meaning is fixed. *Genre* answers the question: 'Who is involved as participants in this world; in what ways; what are the relations between participants in this world?' and so fixes meaning socially (as a conference where participants are ascribed roles such as 'organiser', 'chair', 'presenter', 'audience member'). And *Mode* answers the question: 'How is the world best represented and how do I aptly represent the things I want to represent in this environment?' and so fixes meaning materially and ontologically (e.g. as a diagram in a PowerPoint presentation) (Kress, 2010, pp. 116–121).

So, to summarise, the notions of interest and virtual–actual, generic–modal affordance help to explain the relationship between doctoral matters of fact (the raw data or stuff of research), the doctoral researcher matters of concern (assumptions, agendas, ideologies, ethics, epistemological frameworks) and the representation of this social-material matter in the social-material PhD thesis. This relationship is visualised in Figure 8.1.

In the following section, I provide examples of some of the tensions between my own interests as a doctoral researcher and the affordances of the Institute of Education (University of London) PhD thesis before going on to show how they might have been mitigated by a representation of my PhD as a digital thesis.

NEGOTIATING INTERESTS THROUGH THE AFFORDANCES OF A PHD THESIS AT THE INSTITUTE OF EDUCATION (UNIVERSITY OF LONDON)

My PhD involved collecting, analysing and representing multimodal ethno-graphic data on the (different but overlapping) ways in which a selection of academic and community-based researchers enacted the same migrant community through their research practices. One of these case studies was a community-based oral history project which resulted in a number of research texts including a museum exhibition. In this section, I show how the processes of selection, classification and recontextualisation which informed my design, analysis and representation of this case study were influenced by a negotiation between my doctoral interests and the conditions of possibility set by the affordances of an Institute of Education (University of London) PhD thesis.

THE INFLUENCE OF MY DOCTORAL INTERESTS

As a doctoral researcher my personal and professional background and the ideological, epistemological and ethical frameworks I had inherited from previous research experience had a profound influence on my PhD interests. Three sets of interest were particularly significant.

First, my pre-doctoral professional familiarity with participatory frameworks prompted an ethical and methodological emphasis on the importance of collaborative research. This led to an interest in the different representational properties of researcher-generated, participant-generated and collaborative texts and prompted me to question how my own representations of events and practices compared with those representations of my research participants. In the oral history project case study, I attempted to capture the representational texts that the lead researcher had generated (in the form of exhibits in the museum exhibition); generated my own texts (in the form of photo-collages of the exhibition) and created a collaborative text (in the form of a guided tour of the exhibition by the lead researcher which I filmed).

Second, my research agendas were also significantly influenced by my ethnographic methodology and particularly by the six-month exploratory fieldwork I conducted at the start of my study (which elicited the emic frameworks of my research participants). While the advantages of ethnography as a method include its flexibility (enabling the emergence of an iteratively developed research question); its mobility (allowing research practices to be identified across a variety of 'physical', 'virtual' and imagined spaces) and its self-conscious reflexivity (holding to account the researcher herself as primary research instrument), the method inevitably generates an enormous corpus of data. And since at the time of collection it is not altogether clear which of the data will be useful, it is very difficult to reject anything on the basis of relevance. Consequently, the matter of selection becomes critical. However, the selection of data is also informed by the shape-shifting etic classification systems which inform collection and representation as well as analysis. In the oral history project case study, I collected data in the form of video, photographs, interviews and observation of events such as the curation and launch of the exhibition. As I go on to discuss, very little of this made it into the final draft of my PhD thesis.

Finally, my interests were also influenced by the theoretical frameworks I developed over the course of my PhD. The work of my supervisors nudged me in particular theoretical directions and the all-important doctoral aim of making an 'original contribution to knowledge' prompted me to merge their approaches with a third theoretical perspective. This final agenda relates in part to the generic affordances of the PhD as an institution and to the corresponding primary interest of any doctoral researcher: to successfully obtain a doctoral degree. In line with this agenda, the time allocated for the study (and the corresponding duration of my ESRC studentship grant) delimited the parameters of my fieldwork. Moreover, the ascribed audience for this type of text (supervisors and examiners) also played a role in my rhetorical positioning as the author of my thesis.

THE INFLUENCE OF THE AFFORDANCES OF THE PHD THESIS-AS-TEXT

In addition (and at times in tension) to these interests, the generic and modal affordances of the PhD thesis conventions set by the Institute of Education also had a profound influence on both my research process and output. So what exactly are these affordances? For a start, the PhD is constrained both spatially and temporally. According to the conventions set out in the Institute of Education doctoral handbook,[8] the thesis should not exceed the length of 80,000 words (including footnotes, endnotes, glossary, maps, tables and diagrams) though extensions of up to 100,000 words may be requested in advance. Appendices are not included in this count but 'should only include material which examiners are not required to read in order to examine the thesis, but to which they may refer if they wish' (p. 91). Interestingly, the guidelines state that 'if appropriate to the field of study' a candidate may submit a portfolio of their 'artistic or technological' work accompanied by an extended analysis or dissertation which amounts to no more than 40,000 words (p. 53). Candidates are also allowed to submit 'illustrative material' (p. 53). While guidelines are given for audio recordings (in the rather outdated form of the 'compact cassette tape C60 or C90') and photographic slides (measuring '35 mm in a 2" x 2" frame') candidates are advised to enquire well in advance about the inclusion of illustrative material in other forms (p. 53). The thesis should also be presented as a bound document typed in double-spaced English on one side only of 'good quality' plain white A4 paper with margins of not less than 20 mm (p. 52).

These conventions inevitably embed a series of assumptions: that the thesis is physically recognisable as a thesis; that the thesis is fixed and transportable in a hard form (precluding devices such as embedded video and audio); that written language is of a higher (explanatory or analytical) order than images (which serve only as illustrations) and that the thesis is ordered uni-directionally (precluding the use of devices such as hyperlinks which might result in more multidirectional navigation).

Generically, the thesis is also expected to meet a variety of social conventions. While acknowledging that 'this does not work for everyone', the doctoral handbook sets out a model structure which 'organises the content [of the thesis] in a conventional manner' (p. 23). This structure (represented in Figure 8.2) is interesting for its exclusion of an explicit theoretical framework and for its separation of the presentation of data from a theoretical discussion of findings.

Generically, the thesis is also shaped by the criteria through which it will be evaluated. These include: demonstration of the candidate's proficiency as an independent researcher; evidence of an original contribution to knowledge; demonstration of critical engagement with the relevant academic literature, a coherent argument and structure and evidence that the thesis is of an overall standard to merit publication in whole or in part or in a revised form (pp. 88–91). While the evaluation of the PhD is made primarily on the basis of the thesis-text, the defence or 'viva' (as a secondary representational text) is used to demonstrate the candidate's ownership and understanding of their work.

- Title (This needs to be clear and informative, so that readers know from the title what the thesis is about. It is a good idea to formulate a working title at an early stage; this usually helps to focus your work.)

- Abstract of 300 words

- Chapter 1:
  This should provide a clear rationale for the study and the context of the work and will normally be a statement of the problem in practical and theoretical terms.

- Chapter 2:
  A concise and critical review of and engagement with relevant literature providing a synthesis of any work which has been done in the field, and drawing out conceptual aspects:

- Chapter 3:
  A chapter in which you discuss the methodology that you have chosen to use for the empirical or theoretical work. This chapter should include sections on ethical issues, methods of data collection and analysis and mode of dissemination.

- Chapter 4:
  A chapter presenting and analysing the data.

- Chapter 5:
  A discussion of your findings; here you might relate your findings to the initial theory or theories you have discussed and to the methodology used.

- Chapter 6:
  In the final chapter, you should summarise very briefly the contribution of your work, and draw you own conclusions; these may include implications for further study and improvements you would have made if you were to repeat the study, implications for the wider context and the dissemination of your findings (how, to whom and for what purpose), and any implications of publication or dissemination.

Figure 8.2 'Conventional' thesis structure as set out in the IOE MPhil/PhD student handbook 2010/11

SELECTING, CLASSIFYING AND RECONTEXTUALISING A COMMUNITY-BASED ORAL HISTORY PROJECT

With the dual influence of my doctoral interests and the affordances of the thesis-as-text described above, what then were the implications for the way that my doctoral matter was selection, classified and recontextualised? And crucially, what was Othered in the process?

Given the material affordances of the PhD thesis described above, the process of selection is imperative but ethically charged. Like any other doctoral student, as my writing developed I became increasingly aware of the ill-matched relationship between the capacity of my chapters and the data I wanted to fit into those chapters. The 'oral history project' case study posed a particular challenge since I had just a few chapters to analytically represent a dynamic, colourful, emotive exhibition and in doing so to reconcile my hours of video footage with photographs, interviews and fieldnote observations. However, my process of selection had started even prior to my data collection of the exhibition. In fact, the oral history project was to be represented as three distinct texts: the exhibition as well as a documentary film and a book. I selected the exhibition as the focus of my study for a number of reasons: pragmatically, because the publication of the book was delayed until after the expiration of my doctoral funding; methodologically, because the curation of the exhibition was a more collaborative process (involving the project participants as well as the lead researcher/ curator) and easier to observe than the editing practices of the lead researcher/ documentary maker which occurred in isolation at her home and often late into the night and empirically because, the exhibition provided an excellent example of an 'unconventional' research text and an interesting point of comparison with the other research texts I was analysing. However, as I go on to discuss in relation to recontextualisation, squeezing an entire exhibition into a space of approximately 15,000 words was far from easy. In response, I selected matter largely on the basis of the lead-researcher/curator's guided tour which I filmed. This data served to condense the exhibition according to the researcher-curator's own representation of her project (and in line with my own ideological interests which emphasised a participatory approach to research). However, in doing so it also Othered certain elements of the exhibition (such as the dynamic audio–video exhibits which could not be accommodated by the timing of our tour) and while it represented the exhibition from the perspective of the curator it nonetheless Othered the representations of the other participants whose artefacts and interviews constituted the matter of the exhibition. Another selection practice involved my choice of visual data, which I represented as a series of photo-collages. I drew on photographs and stills from my video footage to provide a feel of the exhibition as a sensory experience and also to illustrate the visual manifestation of some of the discursive patterns[9] I had identified through the language-based data of my interviews and the written information plaques that framed the exhibition. As such, my selection mirrored the generic affordances of the PhD thesis-as-text which suggests the use of the visual to illustrate language-based analysis rather than providing a source of analysis in itself. In this way, language-based data might be regarded as the primary presence in my analysis of the exhibition while my visual data is a manifest absence (there but lacking analytical power) and other data such as audio extracts is Othered.

Selection is of course also deeply influenced by classification systems. To represent the exhibition in its entirety, I started by mapping the layout (see Figure 8.3) resulting in a spatial classification of the exhibition into ten sections. This initial classification process was primarily guided by the structuring of the exhibition through the information plaques which introduced each of the ten sections. I initially planned to represent each section through a photo-collage (see Figure 8.4). However, the material affordances of my thesis-text implied that ten discrete sections of description would impinge on my space for analysis. Consequently, I decided to condense the sections further into just five categories (Acknowledgements and Introduction; The History of the Community; Cultural

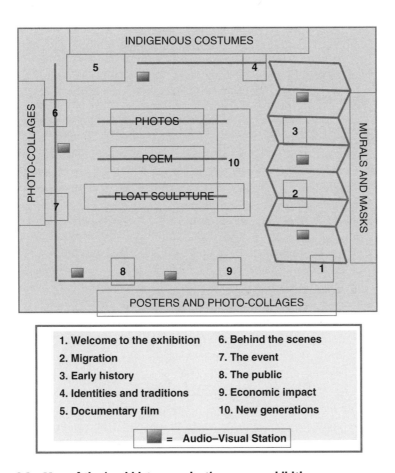

Figure 8.3   Map of the 'oral history project' museum exhibition

Identities; Economic Impact and New Generations). As a result, elements of the exhibition were manifest as absences or Othered. For example, the 'carnival event', which constituted a large focus of the exhibition, but was less relevant to my interests in the history-making practices of the community, was significantly reduced. Moreover, my classification also Othered the documentary film (another of the research texts which was shown in a small cinema within the exhibition). This was partly because the film was just too complex to summarise in the context of the exhibition and partly because the focus of the film undermined some of my analysis of the exhibition as the primary research output of the 'oral history project'. Further classification was made of the exhibition matter itself. I differentiated personal artefacts (referred to in the exhibition as 'objects of memory') from artworks, interview extracts in the form of written quotations, audio or video clips) and written analysis (in the information plaques). Once again my analysis drew primarily on the written data, using the visual artefacts for the purpose of illustration and Othering the audio artefacts (and particularly the non-verbal audio extracts such as music).

Finally, the affordances of the PhD thesis-as-text also played a strong role in the recontextualisation of data, or rather in my attempts to recontextualise data since often, when things don't fit they are simply omitted. This cumulative process of distilling the exhibition data occurred over several phases. In the first phase, I reduced the exhibition as a whole to a two-hour video of a guided tour by the researcher–curator. Since the tour was highly selective and since the mode of realisation was moving image (recorded through digital media) this resulted in a recontextualisation of 'lived experience' into a selectively framed and time-bound video artefact. However, the video footage was incompatible with the generic–modal affordances of the thesis-text and so I continued to recontextualise (and in doing so, to filter down) the data by generating a large number of stills according to a selection of classification systems (e.g. representations of the different sections, exhibits, artefacts, multimedia stations and information plaques in the museum). From this archive (and drawing on my own experiences of the museum space), I then attempted to recreate some of the emotive response that I had felt by assembling a selection of photo-collages to represent items in these different categories (see Figure 8.4). And finally, I selected just a few of these artefacts to illustrate my arguments. So my photo-collages might be considered (in the words of Bruno Latour, 1990) as 'immutable mobiles'. They are transportable devices that retain their integrity as they move (in a way that a museum exhibition in its entirety can do far less easily). At the same time, however, with each stage of filtering, things are lost and the form of the text is changed. As with the other processes of assembling the matter of the exhibition into the material PhD thesis-text, what is Othered is primarily the non-language-based elements and particularly the sensory, intangible experience of the exhibition which is hard to recreate in a video, never mind a written text.

Figure 8.4   Photo-collage of one of the sections of the exhibition

DIGITAL RE-IMAGININGS OF A PHD THESIS

This chapter has shown how the (virtual–actual) social-material affordances of a thesis-text interact with the interests of the doctoral researcher to influence the selection, classification and recontextualisation of doctoral matter into a PhD thesis. While it must be stressed that all research involves (indeed necessitates) reduction, simplification and Othering of matters of fact in line with matters of concern, there remain instances when the 'conditions of possibility' of the research apparatus risk undermining the central interests of the researcher. I offer here an example of this from my own doctoral research relating to the central interest of my research: to explore the (different but overlapping) ways in which a selection of academic and community-based researchers enacted the same migrant community through their research practices. As such, my thesis aimed to represent the 'enactments' of multiple participants but also to show how they related to each other and indeed to my own meta-enactment. As the discussion in the previous section has demonstrated, this was extremely hard to achieve. Merely *describing* the non-language-based representations was frustrated by their recontextualisation as written words and static images in my thesis. And as I have shown, my *analysis* of the representations was also influenced by the modal hierarchy implicit in the thesis-genre with the visual matter deferential to the language-based matter and the non-verbal audio matter lost completely. Moreover, my ethical interest in eliciting the response of my participants to my representations of their work was also undermined by the linear and bounded nature of the PhD thesis-text. While I might have included a section in my conclusion which consolidated the responses of my participants to my thesis as a whole, this would have at best involved a summary of quick interviews or questionnaire responses and would certainly have existed as a kind of appendage, separate from the data chapters and my own analysis.

How then might these conditions of possibility be re-imagined in a way that would accommodate a more democratic representation of non-language-based modes of representation, a more participatory engagement with the thesis my the research participants and a more flexible and non-linear reading of the text? I suggest that the limitations which derive from the affordances of my PhD thesis-as-text might have been mitigated by developing my thesis as a virtual document. Such a document might employ devices such as embedded video or hyperlinks (see Lemke, 2002; Dicks, Soyinka, & Coffey, 2006) to facilitate connections between text, image and sound as well as providing multiple options for navigation of a non-linear nature). This might have better preserved the research texts of my participants in their original forms, capturing elements that are Othered through written language. Such a text would also accommodate participatory interests by allowing participants to respond to my representation of their texts, to re-configure the (re)presentations of their texts and to respond to each other's texts through the use of discussion spaces. However, it is important to recognise the additional affordances which would be imposed by this re-imagining. The loss of authorial control over a research text may undermine the integrity of the research itself. Moreover, allowing editorial access to multiple contributors (particularly if tensions run rife among them) may result in non-participation or even incite further antagonism. Nevertheless, (re)presenting my thesis as a digital document would provide an interesting experiment in reconfiguring my data, process and outputs, contributing to a better understanding of the relationship between these aspects of research.

NOTES

1. Latour and Woolgar (1979), Mol (2002) and Law (2004) all adopt the notion of 'conditions of possibility' from Michel Foucault (see, e.g. Foucault, 1970, 1972) who argued that the apparatuses of scientific production sets limits to what is possible. In his earlier work, Foucault (1970) argued that these limits (as well as the social practices which set them) are established by historical epistemes. Later on he altered his position (see, e.g. Foucault, 1972) insisting that there is endless potential for variation and creative innovation within these limits (Rose, 1999). The notion of 'conditions of possibility' as used by Latour and Woolgar, Mol and Law differs slightly from Foucault's use in that it is drawn on a more modest scale suggesting that 'the limits to scientific knowledge and reality are set by *particular and specific sets of inscription devices*' (Law, 2004, p. 35, emphasis in original) rather than by larger epistemes. It is therefore probably closer to Foucault's later notion (1980) of the dispotif (see Savage Ruppert, & Law 2010) which includes an array of material, human and behavioural elements and so extends beyond the discursive reach of the episteme.

2. *Bergsonism*, first published 1966; *Difference and Repetition*, first published 1968.

3. Law highlights the disjuncture between the French 'agencement' (the term used by Deleuze and Guattari) and the English translation 'assemblage' with the result that the English translation 'has come to sound more like a state of affairs' than an uncertain and unfolding process (2004, p. 41).

4. Indeed, some have suggested that (at least within the School of Science and Technology Studies) academics in recent years have tended towards 'reificaphobia' or the fear that anything within the discipline should settle or solidify for too long (Hallfman, in Wyatt, 2007).

5. As Kress uses the term, 'interest' in an instance of sign-making arises out of the sign-maker's position in the world and shapes attention which in turn frames a part of the world and 'acts as a principle for the selection of apt signifiers' (Kress, 2010, p. 70).

6. Jewitt explains that the use of the term by social semioticians evolved from work on cognitive perception by Gibson (1977) and design by Norman (1988, 1990). See Jewitt (2009, p. 24) though she argues that neither Gibson nor Norman's notion of affordance adequately acknowledges how tools (conceptual and material objects) are shaped by people's use of them in specific social situations (Jewitt, 2008).

7. Kress also considers the role of 'discourse' which is less to do with the form of the text and more about the content.

8. See the Institute of Education MPhil/PhD student handbook 2010–2011 available at: http://www.ioe.ac.uk/MPhilPhD_handbook1011.pdf

9. Examples include the contrast of colour and light to illustrate dichotomies such as 'now and then'; 'visible and invisible', etc.

REFERENCES

Barad, K. (2003). Posthumanist performativity: Toward an understanding of how matter comes to matter. *Signs, 28*, 801–831.

Barton, D. & Tusting, K. (Eds.). (2005). *Beyond Communities of Practice: Language, Power and Social Context.* Cambridge, UK: Cambridge University Press.

Bernstein, B. (1996). *Pedagogy, Symbolic Control and Identity: Theory, Research, Critique.* London: Taylor and Francis.

Bhatia, V. K., Flowerdew, J. & Jones R. H. (Eds.). (2007). *Advances in Discourse Studies.* London: Routledge.

Bowker, G. & Star, S. L. (1999). *Sorting Things Out: Classification and its Consequences.* Cambridge, MA: The MIT Press.

Callon, M. (1986). Some elements of a sociology of translation: Domestication of the scallops and the fishermen of St Brieuc Bay. In J. Law (Ed.), *Power, Action and Belief: A New Sociology of Knowledge.* London: Routledge.

Colebrook, C. (2002). *Gilles Deleuze.* London: Routledge.

Deleuze, G. (1988). *Bergsonism* (translated by H. Tomlinson & B. Habberjam from *Le Bergsonisme*, 1966, Paris: PUF). New York: Zone Books.

Deleuze, G. (1994). *Difference and Repetition* (translated by P. Patton from *Différence et répétition*, 1968, Paris: PUF). New York: Columbia University Press.

Deleuze, G. (1990). *The Logic of Sense* (translated by M. Lester, with C. Stivale, from *Logique du sens*, 1969, Paris: Minuit). New York: Columbia University Press.

Deleuze, G. & Guattari, F. (1987). *A Thousand Plateaus.* Minneapolis, MN: University of Minnesota Press.

Dicks, B., Soyinka, B., & Coffey, A. (2006). Multimodal ethnography. *Qualitative Research, 6*, 77–96.

Foucault, M. (1970). *The Order of Things.* New York: Pantheon.

Foucault, M. (1972). *The Archaeology of Knowledge.* New York: Pantheon.

Foucault, M. (1980). *Power/Knowledge.* New York: Pantheon.

Gibson, J. J. (1977). The theory of affordances. In R. Shaw & J. Bransford (Eds.), *Perceiving, Acting and Knowing.* Hillsdale, NJ: Lawrence Erlbaum Associates.

Halliday, M. A. K. & and Hasan, R. (1985). *Language, Context and Text: Aspects of Language in a Social–Semiotic Perspective.* Oxford: Oxford University Press.

Hodge, R. & Kress, G. (1988). *Social Semiotics*. London: Polity Press.

Iedema, R. (2003). *Discourses of Post-Bureaucratic Organization*. Philadelphia, PA: John Benjamins Pub.

Jewitt, C. (2008). Technology, Literacy and Learning: A multimodal approach. In J. Kleine, K. Littleton, C. Wood, & C. Staarman (Eds.), *Handbook of Educational Psychology*. London: Elsevier.

Jewitt, C. (2009). *The Routledge Handbook of Multimodal Analysis*. London: Routledge.

Kress, G. (2010). *Multimodality: A Social Semiotic Approach to Contemporary Communication*. London: Routledge.

Kress, G. & Van Leeuwen, T. (1996). *Reading Images: The Grammar of Visual Design*. London: Routledge.

Kress, G. & Van Leeuwen, T. (2001). *Multimodal Discourse: The Modes and Media of Contemporary Communication*. London: Arnold Publishers.

Latour, B. (1990). Visualisation and Cognition: Drawing things together. In M. Lynch & S. Woolgar (Eds.), *Representation in Scientific Practice*. Cambridge, MA: The MIT Press.

Latour, B. (2005). *Reassembling the Social: An Introduction to Actor-Network-Theory*. New York: Oxford University Press.

Latour, B. & Woolgar, S. (1979). *Laboratory Life: The Social Construction of Scientific Facts*. Beverly Hills, CA: Sage.

Law, J. (2004). *After Method: Mess in Social Science Research*. London: Routledge.

Lemke, J. L. (2002). Travels in Hypermodality. *Visual Communication, 1*, 299–325.

Mol, A. (2002). *The Body Multiple: Artherosclerosis in Practice*. Durham, NC: Duke University Press.

Norman, D. (1988). *The Psychology of Everyday Things*. New York: Basic Books.

Rose, N. (1999). *Powers of Freedom: Reframing Political Thought*. Cambridge, UK: Cambridge University Press.

Savage, M., Ruppert, E. & Law, J. (2010). *Digital Devices: Nine Theses*. CRESC Working Paper Series, No. 86.

Scollon, R. & Scollon, S. W. (2004). *Discourses in Place: Language in the Material World*. London: Routledge.

Silverstein, M. & Urban, G. (Eds.). (1996). *Natural Histories of Discourse*. Chicago, IL: University of Chicago Press.

Thibault, P. J. (2004). *Agency and Consciousness in Discourse: Self-other Dynamics as a Complex System*. London: Continuum.

Van Leeuwen, T. (2005). *Introducing Social Semiotics*. London: Routledge.

Wenger, E. (1998). *Communities of Practice: Learning, Meaning and Identity*. Cambridge, UK: Cambridge University Press.

9

Traditional Theses and
Multimodal Communication

Dylan Yamada-Rice

INTRODUCTION

> ... four momentous changes are taking place simultaneously: social, economic, comm-
> unicational and technological change. The combined effects of these are so profound
> that it is justifiable to speak of a revolution in the landscape of communication. (Kress,
> 2003, p. 9)

The changes described by Kress above are now commonly regarded as having
brought about a communication 'revolution' in 'Western' societies away from
the predominantly written into multimodal practices (Kress, 2005). This is the
combined use of a range of resources such as image, writing, music, gesture and
speech known as modes. Although multimodality has always existed, contemporary multimodality utilizes a vast array of digital technologies, which seem to
emphasize the lacking of a monomodal written thesis challenging it to evolve.
This gap between contemporary use of multiple modes in communication
and the traditional postgraduate thesis that centers on one written mode is very
apparent in my own doctoral studies on the visual mode of multimodality. This
interest has developed through my previous postgraduate research on young children's use and access to primarily visually based media in communication practices in Japan (Yamada-Rice, 2010) and differences in the variance and quantity
of visual types and their relationship to the written mode in texts found in the
urban landscapes of Tokyo and London, using *Google Street View* to make comparisons (Yamada-Rice, 2011a,b). It is the latter that I will draw on for discussion
in this chapter because it was during that project that I became increasingly

frustrated with the difficulties in presenting data and discussion on contemporary multimodal communication practices in a traditional format.

As a result, this chapter is split first to describe the changing face of 'Western' communication, so it can be better understood how the primarily written thesis has become outdated in its means of presenting data. Second, this view is supported with a case study of difficulties and questions that arose from the writing up of my own research on the visual mode of multimodality. It is hoped that this chapter will allow reflection on how the changing landscape of 'Western' communication provides opportunities for research methodologies to be extended and presented in new and exciting ways that are better connected to research aims and evolving communication practices in general.

THE CHANGING FACE OF 'WESTERN' COMMUNICATION

This section provides insight into the history and issues surrounding contemporary multimodality. It emphasizes changes in communication practices and the resulting necessity for means of data collection and presentation to be extended in academia. It first describes changes in the areas or media 'the means for the distribution of messages' (Bezemer & Kress, 2008, p. 69) before showing how media advances have altered modal use. Lastly, the Japanese context of my research is offered as a point of comparison for evolving understanding of the relationship between modes currently being focused on in the 'West'. Throughout, the visual mode is foregrounded in discussion as it relates to the case study illustrating my own research experiences in the second part of this chapter. It is also the dominant mode in multimodality, which raises questions for traditional academic presentation that centers on the written mode.

ADVANCES IN MEDIA AND THE IMPACT OF SOCIAL CHANGE

Communicative history provides an understanding of how present practices have come into being. In chronological order of emergence this history can be seen as: word of mouth, drawn and painted images, books, photographs, movies, television and digitally based media. As a result of this chronological sequence, recently emerged digital media are often termed new media, but as others point out this can be confusing (Woolsey, 2005; Kress & van Leeuwen, 2001; Moje, 2009). Many digitally based media are more a radical 'repackaging' of traditional media than anything specifically new (Kress & van Leeuwen, 2001, p. 90). On the one hand, I agree that the term 'new' causes confusion in that it tends to isolate the connection of new technology from its historical development through past media and related practices. This view tends to ignore the fact that all media, even traditional, are technologies; instead adapting the meaning of technology itself to mean 'new' (Lankshear & Knobel, 1997). In reality, many new practices use traditional communication skills within new media (for research in this area see Chandler-Olcott & Mahar, 2003; Moje, 2009). On the other hand, the 'new' in new media is insightful when considered as a reference to the status of digitally based media as the forerunner in the way in which communication is interacted with and distributed and the ability of these media to 'simultaneously deliver' multiple modes (Woolsey, 2005, p. 5). Whether we agree with the term 'new' media or not, few would disagree that one of the biggest changes has been the rate of development of digitally based media in recent history. Geo Panch (2007) illustrates this increased developmental pace of modern communication well in *A Brief History of Modern Communication* (Figure 9.1). This illustrates how recent media development has changed the constructs of communication from analog into digital means. In this sense, 'new' can be used to distinguish analog from digital processes. It is this history that also allows an understanding of how a split in agreement around the term 'new' has arisen. 'One mindset affirms the world as the same as before, only more technologized; the other affirms the world as radically different, precisely because of the operation of new technologies' (Lankshear & Knobel, 2003, p. 81). Such discussions are particularly important to the study of contemporary multimodality as the newness of interest in the topic is often tied with new media but these new interests should not be isolated from communication history.

Figure 9.1 further illustrates how the recent surge in digital-based technology spans the last generation and shows how children growing up in the present communicational environment are immersed in this technology (wealth and access providing). It shows that the development of writing/print is marginal compared with computing. The most recent evolution of technology have been formed through the development of wide spread broadband access. The accumulation of Figure 9.1 is smart-phone technology which combines camera, telephone and broadband access, blending computing, print and broadcasting into one digital multimodal medium; providing a full range of interactive communication options. In other words, contemporary society provides multiple media through which to make meaning and communicate compared to even two decades ago. As a result, the younger generation are highly used to textual developments and change (Mackey, 2002). Thus, higher education needs to respond to the digital changes outlined above to allow students, many of whom know less of traditional than new media, to continue to make meaning in multiple ways.

In traditional literacy studies, 'there was no consideration that becoming literate might be a social process' (Hall, 1987, p. 3). In present times this notion is widely contested. Instead, it is commonly believed that 'representation and communication are motivated by the social; its effects are outcomes of the economic and the political' (Kress, 2005, p. 6). Thus, within contemporary multimodality studies an extended version of Halliday's (1978) social semiotic theory is commonly subscribed to. Such beliefs mean that media advances and social changes cannot be separated from one another. There is not the space in this chapter to outline social changes in depth but Kalantzis and Cope (2000)

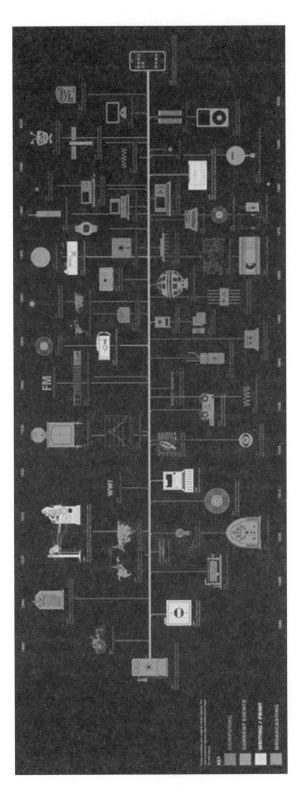

Figure 9.1   A brief history of modern communication (Geo Panch, 2007)

describe these changes in the 'West' from the 1940s Fordism model of work based on nationalism and mass culture to the present day emphasis on 'production diversity' and individualism. Kress (2010) outlines these social changes as a 'move from a relative stability of the social world over maybe the last two centuries ... to an often radical instability over the last three decades or so' (Kress, 2010, p. 6). This can be summarized as a move from the stability of 'communicating on a primarily local level [such as was the case in the 1940s to the instability of] global level' (Kress & van Leeuwen, 2001, p. 47). In other words, evolving communication practices tie with globalization and a move toward greater emphasis on individualism as opposed to collective audience and are realized through new digital technologies that allow modes to be combined to both better present individual identity and convey increasingly complex meaning to wider global audiences whose foregrounding of modes and logics of representation differ (this will be emphasized further later in this chapter when the Japanese semiotic is outlined). The 'instability' to which Kress (2010) is referring to above is also a product of the relationship between communication practices and changes in social authority. That is, from a period of stability through criticality and then to present instability, which is reflected in the changing power relationship between authors of texts and their audiences; traditionally authors of texts were in a position of power talking to a collective known audience; however, this led to authority being questioned and eroded so that presently being an author of a text widely disseminated is accessible to all and the audience can be both known or unknown (Kress, 2005), these points combined with the high pace of technological advancement prevents communication and meaning-making practices becoming fixed. These differences bring about a complexity in both social and communication patterns that are unlikely to have been felt before. It is worth noting that the contemporary situation may be even more complicated than I have had the space to illustrate as 'the range of different technological devices [provided by new media] that operate in a chain of materialization processes are largely invisible to the lay person' (Bezemer & Kress, 2008, p. 172). For example, the fact that digital image manipulation takes place within advertising processes is well known but still the exact changes that appear in the final product will remain largely invisible to people without specialized knowledge. In this sense, how digital media allow manipulation and crossovers between modes is exceedingly complex. Changes in mode and modal preferences will be discussed next.

CHANGES IN MODE: FROM PRIMARILY FIXED MONOMODAL TO UNSTABLE MULTIMODAL

Mode is a socially shaped and culturally given semiotic resource for making meaning. Image, writing, layout, music, gesture, speech, moving image, soundtrack and 3D objects are examples of modes used in representation and communication. (Kress, 2010, p. 79)

Overall, 'Western' modal preferences have evolved alongside media and social changes. The most noticeable change is that the previous centuries-long dominance of written texts in books and documents (Kress & van Leeuwen, 2001, p. 1) has been undermined (and arguably replaced) by communication through digital media. Digital media foreground the screen as the new site for communication and meaning-making (Kress, 2003; Bezemer & Kress, 2008). This has created a shift from a primarily fixed period of monomodal focus on the written to a new unstable era which preferences multimodal representations (Cope & Kalantzis, 2000). A lot of early multimodality research in education focused on science (see Kress & van Leeuwen, 2001; Jewitt, Kress, Ogborn, & Tsatsarelis, 2001; Jaipal, 2009; Marquez, Izquierdo, & Espinet, 2006; Prain & Waldrip, 2006). Generally, this work challenges the previous assumption that education revolves around the written and spoken modes and illustrates instead how contemporary multimodality in the science classroom evolves as a 'complex interplay of a range of modes' (Jewitt, 2002, p. 172). Away from education it is likely that there is an ever more complex relationship between modes where access to varied media will be wider and the process of configuring modal resources using media outside of the classroom will likely be less restricted.

While communication practices have ultimately moved into a new multimodal era, changes are arguably greatest in the visual mode which is foregrounded by new screen-based media that rely on the 'logic' of visual rules (Kress, 2003). This new foregrounding of the visual mode has a twofold impact on communication. First, it means that communication practices center more strongly on the affordances of the visual mode which utilize the properties of 'space, size, colour, shape [and] icons of various kinds – lines, circles', etc. (Bezemer & Kress, 2008, p. 171). Second, the visual mode conveys information and meaning in different ways than writing. In 1936, Benjamin wrote that the success of photography was that it accelerated the process of visual reproduction to allow the visual mode to keep pace with speech (p. 1). Since 1936, the desire to communicate instantaneously has been heightened by digital technologies, which extend such possibilities beyond traditional communication media (The New Media Consortium, 2005). Van Dijck (2008) allows us to see how these advances have changed the use of photography in present times away from a means of recording memories to 'become more like spoken language as photographs are turning into the new currency for social interaction' (p. 62). He states that they have become 'a tool for an individual's identity formation and communication' (p. 57). The addition of cameras and internet access on phones allows different constructions of identity. Smart-phone technology provides a good example of how images provide a 'new currency for social interaction' and with a 'heightened sense of immediacy'. In present times, photographs, particularly those taken with smart phones, are increasingly used to share and record information (Okabe & Ito, 2006; Van Dijck, 2008; Davies, 2006).

> ... the environment may be being lived so as to represent it; and the life-world may be turned into an artefact to be (re)used. That can be done on the spot, by uploading the artifact on

the Web or sending it to friends, for example. As a consequence, life lived offline is directly connected to life lived online, for instance to one's YouTube or MySpace profiles which now are 'literally' lived and enacted by means of representations. Life lived offline may become subordinated to life lived online or lived for life online. (Kress, 2010, p. 189)

Smart phones make it particularly easy to record and exchange images. Indeed as Kress (2010) points out the phone hardware is itself built to give preference to the logic of the visual screen above the alpha/numerical keypad, which is usually hidden behind or less dominant than the phone's screen. Smart phone technology makes 'representing reality by selecting and 'capturing' a 'naturalized' activity. In this way, present reality is conceived in terms of possible future needs of representations of past event, in terms of usability as representation and artifact, rather than of living experience' (Kress, 2010, p. 189). By which I believe Kress is referring to the social practice of recording 'present reality' in images taken with cameras and mobile devices with the intention that they will be disseminated in the future through social networking sites or blogs, etc. In this way, 'present reality' is captured with the future aim of dissemination in mind. Importantly, both the recording of events through photographs and the act of sharing through screen-based technologies foreground the visual mode and its logics causing archiving the present to be more reliant on images than on words which was the tradition. Further, such practices have implications for research when it is viewed as a means of studying the present and data presentation is acquainted with archival practices.

Lastly, there are additional reasons why the visual mode is foregrounded in present times. Contemporary communication cannot be separated from globalization. It is likely that the use of screen-based media, for speed and their prioritization of the visual mode, better fit the global climate where they are more able to overcome language and geographical barriers. Further, Kress and van Leeuwen (1996) suggest that it is possible that 'information is now so vast, so complex that, perhaps, it has to be handled visually, because the verbal is no longer adequate' (p. 32). Therefore, in numerous ways it seems likely that modern societies have advanced to the point where oral and written languages and related media are no longer adequate. Likewise, technological advances have affected social changes. One of the significant factors in increased access to digital media is rapid cost decline. Only in recent times have digital media been available for use by the average person. The previous low cost of book production in comparison with screen-based technologies is likely one of the reasons that only recently has the reign of the book begun to be replaced by the screen as the 'central medium of communication' (Kress, 2003, p. 9).

EVOLVING UNDERSTANDING OF THE RELATIONSHIP BETWEEN MODES

So far, I have focused my discussion on the historical division between the written and visual modes and their separate affordances into two distinct areas.

I have also suggested that through the use of digital media, this division is beginning to blur. There are large implications of this blurring if we agree with Kress (2010) that 'mode provides its specific lens on the world and with that lens the world seeks organized as specific arrangements in space, in time, or both' (Kress, 2010, p. 155). In other words, not only is there a need to understand the specific lenses of each mode, but also there will become an increasing need to understand how these differ and support one another – to develop an understanding of a 'multimodal lens'. This is perhaps hard to imagine when cultures that use English have historically largely separated modes into distinct areas of specialism. That is why I will draw on the Japanese context of my research and offer a glimpse at an alternative historical perspective between language and the visual mode; specifically a habitual blurring of the two that is especially relevant to this discussion on digital theses, which will incorporate screen technologies that preference the visual mode. It is also helpful to see an alternative view in order to escape our historical perspective and think in new ways.

The specific lens of the written mode in the 'West' and Japan differ from one another. English is organized around the specific arrangements in time and sequence compared with Japanese, which is organized in relation to space as well as time. Japanese language primarily uses three different script systems, kanji, hiragana and katakana, alongside a fourth lesser used and more recent romaji, which uses the Roman alphabet. Kanji are pictorial-based characters while hiragana and katakana are both phonetic scripts of fifty-two sounds each. Kanji is of primary importance to understanding the ingrained logics of Japanese language as it influenced the other two dominant Japanese scripts. Kanji are split into either pictographs which relate to physical objects, ideographs which combine pictographs to create a related idea or phono-ideographs which combine a phonological aspect and an ideogram (Rowley, 1992). For example, the pictographic origins for the kanji, meaning 'tree', can be traced to the original physical object – a tree. When this kanji for tree is repeated twice within one kanji it forms an ideogram meaning 'wood', repeated three times it means 'forest'. Contrastingly, in English 'speech and writing are, above all, modes founded on words in order ... a sound sequence' (Kress, 2005, p. 15) which can be further broken down into twenty-six phonetic letters. English words need to be placed in a sequence for the message to be conveyed. This sequence is linear. Although kanji are also written in linear paths, there is a difference in that each character contains a pictorial meaning that can be understood when isolated from the rest of the sentence or even when isolated from other parts of the same kanji. This can be seen in phono-ideographs which 'combine an element that gives a clue to pronunciation with an element that hints at the subject matter ... The theme element called a radical, may itself be a stand-alone kanji or some graphic variant of one. Tree, for example, is a character by itself. Used as a radical ... it usually indicates something made of wood or relating to trees' (Rowley, 1992, p. 7). In this way, construction of kanji is based on visual logics such as vision and space which are the same as those used for constructing other messages in the visual mode. This is evident in distinct stroke order and patterning of each kanji character, the multi-directionality and the use of space being orientated from a central point (Kenner, 2003). This would seem to mirror the logic of screen-based media, which offer multiple entry points and undermine linear movement. Therefore, 'the phonological representation is neither the only, nor primary, function. It is only a part of the language and the other aspect, visual representation, is also a key component' (Shelton & Okayama, 2006, p. 158). As a result, visual logics play an important role in both the Japanese written and visual modes; there is a historical 'semiotic overlap' between the two (McGovern, 2004). This makes the use of the visual mode more habitual in Japan as it has always linked with, rather than been separated from, the written mode.

All this makes the affordances of the Japanese written mode (the Japanese 'language lens') very different to that of English. If we consider that the conventions and principles of the dominant written mode have influenced wider communication practice, it is possible to see how Japanese communication practices beyond the written might have been influenced by the strong visual connection to the written mode. In other words, the historical connection to the visual mode in Japan, even in the written mode, makes it plausible that the habitual understanding of the visual mode will be different from the 'West'. Understanding such ideas is, I believe, relevant to the discussion here because in 'Western' contemporary multimodality, image is becoming a fully representational mode which is infringing on and influencing the previously dominant written mode. 'Engagement with text, even if much of it is still alphabetic, is now a more complicated affair. In contemporary texts, words may be printed or sounded or both. Pictures, still or moving, may argument, contradict, or replace words' (Mackey, 2002, p. 3). Such contemporary practices will certainly be carried over into a digital thesis. Thus, it is important to understand that there are other cultures that can help support our understanding of the use of multimodality in presentation. Where 'Western' academia may previously have assumed that processes could only be described in writing, other cultures can help us see that there is a history of representing information in other ways. Such ways will become increasingly relevant to the way in which 'Western' academia will need to display information to keep up with digital media that convey messages in multiple modes. Finally, it is worth bearing in mind that with globalization, the internet and digital technologies, Japanese semiotics and the use of the visual mode that I have just discussed (as well as those of other cultures) will travel and be shared globally. Thus, whereas all 'makers of signs, no matter their age, live in a world shaped by the histories of the work of their societies; the results of that work are available to them as the resources of their culture' (Kress, 2010, p. 74), we should consider that the societies in which we draw on are no longer only locally specific. Instead, there will also be an increasingly global influence on the way in which information is conveyed – a digital thesis would be well centered to take account of these practices.

It is hoped that this section has shown how the ingrained affordances of the written mode that have dominated communication and meaning-making practices until recent times are likely to be tied to wider cultural understandings. In other words, 'the social configuration of a group and its concerns, the social meanings and values of that group, have their effects on the habitual use of the resource and, in this way, in the longer-term shaping of the resource in that domain' (Kress, 2003, p. 65). However, contemporary communication and meaning-making practices have evolved to use multiple modes. Although as I have shown multimodality is not new, digital technologies allow a greater flexibility in the way that modes are adapted for meaning-making and also allow the visual mode to be foregrounded through screen technologies. Finally, this section outlined how we need to be aware that screen-based technologies also break down the ingrained logics of a culture's communication system (the dominant means of communication until present times) as globalization allows ways of making-meaning to be shared. Overall, such discussion shows clearly how a traditional thesis that primarily centers on one mode will be lacking in the way in which meaning is constructed and understood. I hope to illustrate this point further in my next section, which provides an overview of questions and difficulties that arose in the presentation of my own work on the visual mode in a traditional thesis.

RESEARCHING THE VISUAL MODE IN THE DIGITAL AGE: A CASE STUDY

My MA in Education Research thesis: *New media, new literacy, new visual learning environment: a comparative study of images in the urban landscapes of Tokyo and London* (2009) considered differences in the variance, quantity and location of visual types and their relationship to the written mode which are combined in the dissemination of texts in the urban landscapes of Tokyo and London. By 'text' I refer to Halliday's (1978) definition of a cohesive unit of meaning used for purposes of communication rather than a paraphrase for written language. The aim was to understand better differences in young children's exposure to the visual mode through the urban environment of two countries with very different historical connections between language and the visual mode. This section will discuss the methodology, ethics and analysis of the data that focused on the visual mode and how this process fits with presenting the findings in a traditional written thesis.

METHODOLOGY

The research manifested as a whole-context, comparative study of the diversity and placement of visual components in two areas of the urban landscapes of

Shibuya, Tokyo, and Camden, London. As my research interests connect to visual aspects of new multimodal technologies and communication practices, I wanted to utilize a method that would both answer the research questions: 'In what ways do images in the urban landscapes of Tokyo and London vary?' and 'What is the relationship between text and images in both countries?' and use new visual technologies. I believe educational researchers working in the area of digitally influenced communication practices can use new media in the methodology to undertaken research in ways better connected to the aims and purpose of such studies. These wishes, the comparative nature of my research questions and the heavy time constraint of this project (preventing me from flying to Japan) led me to collect data using *Google Street View* images of the two landscapes. *Street View* is one part of the *Google* search engine's online maps. The maps provide 360° horizontal and 290° vertical photographic images taken from city streets. *Street View* maps can be viewed by dragging a 'pegman' and navigating with horizontal and vertical arrows displayed in the top right-hand corner of each photograph and on the road, which is highlighted by a horizontal line. There is also a zoom function providing close-up images. *Google* launched the service in May 2005 and maps are presently available of some major cities in the 'West' and Japan. The ostensible purpose of *Street View* from the point of view of the creators, *Google*, is about new ways of mapping and navigation which is apparent from the site's emphasis on offering directions each time you search for a location.

In order to compare Tokyo and London's landscapes, I copied *Street View* images without cropping and pasted them together using *Photoshop* to form a static, two-dimensional montage of two similar sized inner-city areas. I developed the idea through my interest in exploring the visual mode in the city from the perspective of early childhood education. I began to imagine the visual components a young child would see walking through the streets. I was further drawn to the idea by Grimshaw's (2001) definition of montages as using 'radical juxtaposition and violent collision of different elements in order to suggest new connection and meanings' (p. 11). The importance of considering the entire context was fundamental to my methodological decisions. Foremost, 'photographs get meaning … from their context' (Becker, 1998, p. 88). Second, like Prosser and Schwartz (1998) I believe, 'full contextual detail (if this is ever possible) enables the trustworthiness and limitations of photographs to be assessed' (p. 125). One of the arguments I have against photographs in research that discuss individual texts separate from the landscape in which they were taken is that they do not allow an understanding of what surrounds them. It is my belief that these areas also provide a message and it is therefore imperative to present the entire context. For example, looking at Siber's (2005) individual photographs of advertisements in the environment, I wonder what lies outside his framing. Therefore, the images I copied into montages were taken at consistent intervals in height and length along the street using the arrow function keys provided by Google, but unfortunately, this technique led to periodic gaps and overlapping in the images. This was the first methodological problem I encountered in trying to alter a 360° resource to fit the two-dimensional page. With more time, I began to think that I could have created a three-dimensional environment using *Google Sketch Up*, which allows three-dimensional computer generated models to be added to *Google Maps*. Here I would like to raise my first concern as a student, not only do universities need to be susceptible to the digitalization of the thesis though the incorporation of new media but they also need to be aware that presenting data in such ways might require substantially more time than a written thesis if the true benefits are to be felt. The use of three-dimensional modelling would have addressed my concerns about contextual detail further still – that is not to say that any photographic collection 'can be claimed as the "natural", unobtrusive way' (Adelman, 1998, p. 149). Of course, any image selection, montage or three-dimensional modelling technique will make selections from the whole but they can offer a broader understanding than individual photographs/ images, one that is closer to the experienced environment, and avoid the overlapping and missed material caused by turning a three-dimensional space into two dimensions to fit a thesis. A selection that also fits better with the use of new media to communicate as discussed in the first part of this chapter. To highlight this further in my final thesis, I also needed to display something as simple as the data collection areas as a highlighted route on two screen shots from *Google Maps*. A digital thesis would have allowed web links to the *Street View* maps to have been added providing the reader with the means to better immerse themselves in the data collection areas. More will be said on presentation of data later.

It is worth mentioning that there were unforeseen challenges resulting from the use of *Street View*, such as differences in the times footage was taken and the incomplete mapping of many areas, making the selection of sample areas challenging. This suggests that students working with new technologies need to be prepared for methodological errors different from traditional means of data collection. However, I feel a level of methodological error is inevitable if researchers are to avoid 'fixed, preconceived expectations of what it will be possible to achieve by using visual research methods in a given situation' (Pink, 2001, p. 32). Freedom to experiment is what will allow visual research methods to evolve away from 'most photographs in journals and newspapers which confirm our beliefs and are taken by the photographer with that rather than the discovery in mind' (Adelman, 1998, p. 148). As long as adequate consideration is given to ethics, visual analysis, planning, data collection, editing, exhibition and descriptive image communication components (Chalfen, 1998), this margin of error seems to justify potential findings from spontaneity in image-based data collection and analysis using new media. On the discussion of image-based data collection, it is worth pointing out that it is likely that the development of such methods will become increasingly important to the majority of educational researchers, as communication and meaning-making in general are increasingly foregrounding the visual mode (as discussed in the first part of this chapter).

Therefore, methodologies will also need to foreground the visual mode to collect data in better connected ways.

ETHICS

I would like to mention briefly how the use of new media in data collection and presentation also requires researchers to think differently about ethics. My own use of *Google Street View* as a research tool highlights some of these concerns.

Street View is publicly accessible and my research did not involve engagement with human participants and so I was not required to seek University ethics approval. However, the newness of the service, especially in the UK at the time my research was conducted (which only became available in April 2009) meant ethical discussions surrounding the interactive maps were rarely out of the news. These discussions still continue today. Clearly, big ethical considerations are involved. Most discussions center on whether *Street View* is an invasion of privacy. It is interesting to note that this ethical question raises different responses in different countries. In the US, the home of *Google*, a legal claim that the maps violated the privacy of a couple was thrown out of court. It was held that the couple had not made use of *Google's* online tools to request the offending images be removed (Shiels, 2009). In this case, it is easy to take the position, as the judge did, that *Google* had done everything possible. Certainly, the couple could have used the *Google* online tools; however, I struggle with whether this is enough when online sites such as *Funny Street View Google Maps*, collate and dissemi-nate embarrassing images. This is a clear example that: 'once visual … represen-tations … have been produced and disseminated publicly neither author nor subjects of the work can control the ways in which these representations are interpreted and given meanings by their readers, viewers or audiences' (Pink, 2001, p. 43). The power of new technologies to produce and disseminate images exceedingly fast is one of the positives of evolving communication practices but it is also an ethical concern. Harper's (1998) words on images are interesting to this discussion on ethics: '… art reflects the social organization- specifically, the class structure which produces it' (p. 33). To some degree this is also true of *Street View*, as only a proportion of people have access to broadband. Therefore, although *Google* has created systems for the removal of images by request, these are only accessible through a high speed internet connection, even though the people affected by the images will not be limited to those with broadband. In the UK, the Information Commissioner declared that the risk of privacy invasion is minimal and *Street View* could continue. This decision was based on the belief that 'there is no law against anyone taking pictures of people in the street' (Anon, 2009c). The US and UK consensus is that the images are acceptable because the focus of the cameras are not on any individual (Anon, 2009b). But *Google's* easy access and well know label make it very different from individuals on the street with cameras. This is a point that would likely be agreed by residents in a village near Milton Keynes who opposed *Street View* to the extent that they prevented *Google* image-making cars from entering the village (Anon, 2009c). *Google* clearly needs to give greater thought to the words of Berger (1972) that 'soon after we can see, we are aware that we can also be seen. The eye of the other combines with our own eye to make it fully credible that we are part of the visible world' (p. 9). While the maps are undoubtedly popular, they also evidently highlight people's sensitivity that they can be seen. In comparison, the stance taken by Greece has been stricter. The Athens's Data Protection Agency has prohibited *Google* from collecting images, as it does not provide enough information regarding how long it keeps images or alert residents well enough that they are to be photographed and their rights in these circumstances (Smith, 2009), evidence that 'permission has to be understood in a socially or culturally appropriate context' (Banks, 2001, p. 131). In its defence, *Google* believes the public are just not yet used to the new mapping technology (Shankland, 2008) so are working hard to ensure residents in areas being photographed are familiar with the service and local governments are informed of the privacy measures they have put in place (Anon, 2009a). These include the online removal request form and automatic face blurring procedures. Unfortunately, the accuracy of *Google's* face-blurring technology is imperfect, leaving many individuals visible (Anon, 2009c). The technology was so patchy in my own Street View samples that I decided to blur missed faces in data collection images, so identity would be protected in the data presentation. I felt ethically uncomfortable leaving visible faces within my own work even though *Google* is posting them on the World Wide Web. There are further concerns 'that *Google* is keeping the original, unblurred images' (Anon, 2009a). As an overall defence *Google* also claims they are not recording anything that is not already publically visible (Wray, 2009) a position that I have already shown is ethically flawed. *Google* also claim that the 'photos will be updated periodically, but the company has not specified a timetable' (MacDonald, 2009). Overall, *Google* needs to address ethical concerns better. Like others, I believe *Google* should provide information and seek opinions from wider sources in the pre-photographing stages, not after they have been uploaded to the internet (Anon, 2009c). Prosser and Schwartz (1998) suggest good photographic research takes a 'softly softly' approach when initially settling into a community. Perhaps *Google* could take a more 'softly softly' approach by listing the dates and routes that it will be recording on its hugely utilized website. Presently, *Google* fails to realize that the 'production of photographic images is a social event, involving communication and mutual understanding on the part of both image-maker and image-subject' (Banks, 2001, p. 117). I do not think, as some do, that the service should be pulled. I see it as an inevitable technological change in ways of mapping. It is also a valuable tool for research and education but *Google* could do much more.

The ethical questions raised by *Street View* can easily be applied to the wider consideration of ethical issues that will need to be considered in a digital thesis (see chapter by Fitzgerald in this volume). Namely, ethics stemming from the wider dissemination of a digital compared to a traditional thesis, the ways in which data on the internet are appropriated for new means (not always good) and the ways in which we seek permission from participants for inclusion will need to be considered deeply. If these concerns are addressed, there are certainly many positives to the inclusion of new media in data collection and dissemination. Keeping with the example of Street View, I believe there is potential for it to be used in other research, especially to add context to comparative research. Perhaps all research in the future will provide co-ordinates to Street View maps, so that readers will be better able to understand details of the research context. In this way, I see future research products as multimodal packages, reflecting wider communication trends. On a basic level, as discussed previously, the use of multiple modes furthers our understanding of the everyday world.

VISUAL ANALYSIS

The analysis was informed by a belief that 'the purpose of [visual] analysis is not to translate 'visual evidence' into verbal knowledge, but to explore the relation-ship between visual and other knowledge' (Pink, 2001, p. 96). In this section, I shall discuss the analysis that identified the relationship between written text and the visual mode in the urban environment of both countries.

This was addressed by color coding the montages, using separate colors to represent the written mode, the visual mode and texts where the two were inseparable, for example, when a written price list overlaid a photograph. In order to color code the maps, the complete space given over to each mode was filled by the corresponding color. The overall affect was a series of landscape montages with blocks of color that depicted the location, size and context of mode. Overall, this method addressed the fact that 'particular modes of commu-nication should be seen in their environment, in the environment of all the other modes of communication which surround them' (Kress & van Leeuwen, 1996, p. 33). As described earlier visual context is important. Ideas presented in Scollon and Scollon (2003), suggesting that language patterns manifest in the environ-ment in layers and complex interactions, are a vital part of this project's wider hypothesis that connections could exist between young children's learning of visual communication skills and the diversity, density and location of visual components in the urban landscape. Full visual context also addresses the 'criteria [that] requires each image be filled with as much contextual detail for the researcher to engage in a systematic and iterative analysis of the image record' (Adelman, 1998, p. 158). This last quotation also shows how the overlay of this color coding technique onto a three-dimensional environment built in *Sketch up* and shown on *Google Maps* as discussed earlier, could address these concerns much fuller.

VISUAL PRESENTATION

During the presentation of my data within a traditional thesis with appendices I struggled with how to address the importance of visual context. Ideas presented in Scollon and Scollon (2003), that language patterns manifest in the environment in layers and complex interactions, were a vital part of my belief that connections exist between visual communication skills and the situation and location of the visual mode in the urban landscape during the initial stages of formulating the research. On one level the montages provided context to address the 'criteria [that] requires each image be filled with as much contextual detail for the researcher to engage in a systematic and iterative analysis of the image record' (Adelman, 1998, p. 158). However, deciding how to present montages and mapping websites in a traditional thesis was problematic. Primarily due to time constraints I finally choose to present the montages in the appendixes. This was far from ideal, as I believe that the analysis of images in research extends to their placement within the written text. Like Barthes' (1970) study of signs in *Empire of Signs*, I think 'images contextualise the analysis, place it in history and give it a framework' (Trifonas, 2001, p. 27). By placing the montages as an appendix separate from the thesis I was detracting from the importance of these images by giving preference to the written section, which was embodied in the structure of the written thesis.

I was acutely aware that the use of images in educational research, like all areas, has its own history. Therefore, I felt that the positioning of data was also a positioning of myself within this historical framework – one that I felt was outdated for the presentation of my work on contemporary communication practices where the visual mode is prioritized. While visual means of data collection, once confined to natural science and anthropology, have been given a new lease of life in educational research by the advent of new visual technologies (Larsen, 1991), in the field of presenting educational research images are incorporated into research as surplus decoration more often than not, not because they bring unique qualities to the discussion. In other words, they are still supporting written text in a way Banks (1998) suggested was necessary by being referenced in the body of a written piece. I agree that photographs must bring unique qualities to research but no longer believe that they must always be referenced. In the same way that images are now incorporated in multimodal texts, for example websites, to convey meaning without a written description, so too can the affordances of different modes be realized within academic presentation. This will be easily realized in the move to presenting a thesis digitally. Pink (2001) argues that to incorporate images well in research, researchers must develop new objectives and methodologies 'rather than attaching the visual to existing methodological principles and analytical frames' (p. 4). I agree. It seems likely that digital technologies that center on the visual mode will become increasingly incorporated into research and as such new ways need to be found to explore how the data using these technologies might support alternative especially digital means of not only undertaking but also presenting research data. The same should also be considered in the inclusion of other modes in a digital thesis. As communication patterns continue to evolve along the lines laid out at the beginning of this chapter, it seems likely that we will (if we haven't already) be able to make meaning between modes in ways that need different explanations than those suggested by Banks (1998).

CONCLUSION

This chapter has discussed how new digital technologies allow communication to be constructed multimodally to an extent previously unknown. Meaning-making across a range of modes allows messages to be fine-tuned to define and convey knowledge in new ways. While such processes have always existed, the use of modes other than the written has until recently primarily been confined to specialist producers. Nowadays, the design process has become an important part of contemporary multimodality as the need to switch modes and create messages that will stand out from the mass of communication is vital in present times. Messages in research are no different. These new-found means of allowing non-specialists to produce and receive messages through the process of design by media selection, modal choice and arrangement, changes the constraints on how we define knowledge. This has huge implication for the future of the academic thesis. Limiting the discussion of literature and presentation of data primarily to the written mode not only constrains how we define knowledge but it is out of sync with how meaning-making and communication is occurring outside academia as described earlier. In many cases, it is also at odds with the multiple modes through which data are being collected. Further, at the very least the ideas engaged with in the initial stages of formulating research are no longer sourced solely though the written mode either. I have already felt such limitations first-hand with my research on the visual mode and the difficulties of presenting this in a different, written mode such as outlined in the case study in this chapter. It can no longer or should no longer be the case that:

> There is a general assumption that language is a communicational and representational medium which is fully adequate to the expression of anything that we might want to express: that anything that we think, feel, sense can be said (or written) in language. The obverse of this assumption is that if something cannot be expressed in language...then that thing is in any case outside rational thought, outside articulate feeling, and therefore need not be said or should not be said. (Kress, 2000, p. 193)

Instead we need to take account of the fact that, as Kress (2010) writes more recently, there is now a 'move towards multimodal communication with a strong interest in the visual mode' and as a result we need to take better account of the 'affordances they offer – what they facilitate, what they hinder and inhibit – influences how we make meaning' (p. 185). Thus, there is now a fundamental need to understand how the shift to foregrounding the visual mode in communications (and in the future in digital thesis) will change how knowledge is constructed and stored.

This chapter has attempted to show how a digital thesis could close the gap between contemporary multimodal communication practice and academic traditions that still primarily focus on the written mode and it suggests that there are direct implications for how knowledge can be defined and presented, as my own experiences illustrate. Evolving digital technologies and practices further the potential for creating new methodologies (such as my use of *Google Street View*) and ways of presenting data. The implication of undertaking research in a digital and multimodal age are huge and more space needs to be given in academia to discuss this and its implications for research presentation, the research process and ethics.

REFERENCES

Adelman, C. (1998). Photo context. In J. Prosser (Ed.), *Image-based Research. A Sourcebook for Qualitative Researchers* (pp. 148–161). London: Falmer Press.

Anon. (2009a). Google alerts Canadians about Street View filming. *CBC News,* March 26. Retrieved April 15, 2009, from http://www.cbc.ca/canada/british-columbia/story/2009/03/26/tech-090326-google-street-view.html

Anon. (2009b). Call to 'shut down' Street View. *BBC News,* April 23. Retrieved 23 April 23, 2009, from http://news.bbc.co.uk/1/hi/technology/7959362.stm

Anon. (2009c). All Clear for Google Street View. *BBC News,* April 23. Retrieved April 23, 2009. from http://news.bbc.co.uk/1/hi/technology/8014178.stm

Banks, M. (1998). Visual Anthropology: Image, Object and Interpretation. In J. Prosser (Ed.), *Image-based Research. A Sourcebook for Qualitative Researchers* (pp. 9–23). London: Falmer Press.

Banks, M. (2001). *Visual Methods in Social Research.* London: Sage.

Barthes, R. (1970). *Empire of Signs* (translated from French by R. Howard; 1982). Canada: Douglas & McIntyre Ltd.

Becker, H. S. (1998). *Visual Sociology, Documentary, Photography, and Photojournalism: It's (Almost) All a Matter of Context.* In J. Prosser (Ed.), *Image-based Research. A Sourcebook for Qualitative Researchers* (pp. 84–96). London: Falmer Press.

Benjamin, W. (1936). *The Work of Art in the Age of Mechanical Reproduction.* Retrieved May 23, 2009, from http://www.marxists.org/reference/subject/philosophy/works/ge/benjamin.htm

Berger, J. (1972). *Ways of Seeing.* London: Penguin Books Ltd.

Bezemer, J. & Kress, G. (2008). Writing in multimodal texts: A social semiotic account of designs for learning. *Written Communication, 25,* pp. 166–195.

Chalfen, R. (1998). Interpreting Family Photography as Pictorial Communication. In J. Prosser, (Ed.), *Image-based Research. A Sourcebook for Qualitative Researchers* (pp. 214–234). London: Falmer Press.

Chandler-Olcott, K. & Mahar, D. (2003). Tech-savviness meets Multiliteracies: Exploring adolescent girls' technology-mediated literacy practices. *Reading Research Quarterly, 38,* 356–385.

Cope, B. & Kalantzis, M. (2000). Introduction: Multiliteracies: The beginnings of an idea. In B. Cope & M. Kalantzis (Eds.), *Multiliteracies: Literacy Learning and the Design of Social Futures* (pp. 1–3). London: Routledge.

Davies, J. (2006). Affinities and Beyond! Developing ways of seeing in online spaces. *E-Learning, 3,* 217–234.

Geo Panch, G. (2007). *A Brief History of Modern Communication.* Retrieved September 6, 2010, from http://www.geopanch.com

Grimshaw, A. (2001). The *Ethnographer's Eye: Ways of Seeing in Modern Anthropology.* Cambridge: Cambridge University Press.

Hall, N. (1987). *The Emergence of Literacy.* London: Hodder & Stoughton.

Halliday, M. (1978). *Language as a Social Semiotic.* London: Edward Arnold.

Harper, D. (1998). An Argument for Visual Sociology. *Image-based Research. A Sourcebook for Qualitative Researchers* (pp. 24–41). London: Falmer Press.

Jaipal, K. (2009). Meaning making through multiple modalities in a biology classroom: A multimodal semiotics discourse analysis. *Science Education, 94,* 48–72.

Jewitt, C. (2002). The move from page to screen: The multimodal reshaping of school English. *Visual Communication, 1,* 171–195.

Jewitt, C., Kress, G., Ogborn, J., & Tsatsarelis, C. (2001). Exploring learning through visual, actional and linguistic communication: The multimodal environment of a science classroom. *Educational Review, 53,* 5–18.

Kalantzis, M. & Cope, B. (2000). Changing the Role of Schools. In B. Cope & M. Kalantzis (Eds.), *Multiliteracies: Literacy Learning and the Design of Social Futures* (pp. 121–148). London: Routledge.

Kenner, C. (2003). Embodied knowledges: Young children's engagement with the act of writing. In C. Jewitt & G. Kress (Eds.), *Multimodal Literacy* (pp. 88–106). New York: Peter Lang.

Kress, G. (2000). Multimodality. In B. Cope & M. Kalantzis (Eds.), *Multiliteracies: Literacy Learning and the Design of Social Futures* (pp. 182–202). London: Routledge.

Kress, G. (2003). *Literacy in the New Media Age.* Oxon, UK: Routledge.

Kress, G. (2005). Gains and losses: New forms of texts, knowledge, and learning. *Computers and Composition. 22,* 5–22.

Kress, G. (2010). *Multimodality: A Social Semiotic Approach to Contemporary Communication.* London: Routledge.

Kress, G. & van Leeuwen, T. (1996). *Reading Images. The Grammar of Visual Design* (2nd Edn.). New York: Routledge.

Kress, G. & van Leeuwen, T. (2001). *Multimodal Discourse: The Modes and Media of Contemporary Communication.* New York: Oxford University Press.

Lankshear, C. & Knobel, M. (1997). Literacies, texts and difference in the electronic age. In C. Lankshear, J. P. Gee, M. Knobel, & C. Searle, (Eds.), *Changing Literacies* (pp. 134–163). Buckingham: Open University Press.

Lankshear, C. & Knobel, M. (2003). *New Literacies: Changing Knowledge and Classroom Learning.* Buckingham: Open University Press.

Larsen, P. (1991). Media contents: Textual analysis of fictional media content. In: K. B. Jensen, & N. W. Jankowski (Eds.), *A Handbook of Qualitative Methodologies for Mass Communication Research* (pp. 121–134). London: Routledge.

MacDonald, C. (2007). Google's Street View site raises alarm over privacy. *The Herald,* June 4. Retrieved April 23, 2009, from http://www.theherald.co.uk/news/other/display.var.1444323.0.0.php

Mackey, M. (2002). *Literacies Across Media.* London: Routledge.

Marquez, C., Izquierdo, M., & Espinet, M. (2006). Multimodal Science Teachers' Discourse in Modeling the Water Cycle. *Science Education, 90,* 202–226.

McGovern, S. (2004). The Ryoan-ji Zen garden: Textual meanings in topographical form. *Visual Communication, 3,* 344–359.

Moje, E. B. (2009). Standpoints: A call for new research on new and multi-literacies. *Research in the Teaching of English, 43,* 348–362.

Okabe, D. & Ito, M. (2006). *Everyday Contexts of Camera Phone Use: Steps Toward Technosocial Ethnographic Frameworks.* Retrieved June 11, 2009, from http://www.itofisher.com/mito/publications/everyday_context.html

Pink, S. (2001). *Doing Visual Ethnography: Images, Media and Representation in Research.* London: Sage.

Prain, V. & Waldrip, B. (2006). An exploratory study of teachers' and students' use of multi-modal representations of concepts in primary science. *International Journal of Science Education, 28*, 1843–1866.

Prosser, J. & Schwartz, D. (1998). Photographs within the Sociological Research Process. In J. Prosser, (Ed.), *Image-based Research. A Sourcebook for Qualitative Researchers* (pp. 115–130). London: Falmer Press.

Rowley, M. (1992). Kanji Pict-O-Graphix: Over 1,000 Japanese Kanji and Kana Mnemonics. Stone Bridge Press.

Scollon, R. & Scollon, S. W. (2003). *Discourses in Place: Language in the Material World*. London: Routledge.

Shankland, S. (2008). Google begins blurring faces in Street View. *CNET News Blog*. May 13. Retrieved April 24, 2009, from http://news.cnet.com/8301-10784_3-9943140-7.html

Shelton, B. & Okayama, E. (2006). Between script and pictures in Japan. *Visible Language, 40*, 157–176.

Shiels, M. (2009). Judge dismisses Google lawsuit, *BBC News*, February 19. Retrieved May 24, 2009, from http://news.bbc.co.uk/1/hi/technology/7898407.stm

Siber, M. (2005). Visual literacy in the public space. *Visual Communication, 4*, 5–20.

Smith, H. (2009). Google Street View banned from Greece. *Guardian*, May 12. Retrieved May 21, 2009, from http://www.guardian.co.uk/technology/2009/may/12/google-street-view-banned-greece

The New Media Consortium. (2005). *A Global Imperative: The Report of the 21st Century Literacy Summit* (Adobe). Retrieved May 5, 2009, from http://nmc.org/pdf/Global_Imperative.pdf

Trifonas, P. P. (2001). *Barthes and the Empire of Signs*. Cambridge: Icon Books Ltd.

Van Dijck, J. (2008). Digital photography: Communication, identity, memory. *Visual Communication, 7*, 57–76.

Woolsey, K. (2005). *New Media Literacies: A Language Revolution*, New Media Literacies Project. Retrieved May 30, 2009, from http://www.nmc.net/summit/Language_Revolution.pdf

Wray, R. (2009). Google Launches Street View in the UK. *Guardian*, March 19. Retrieved April, 2009, from http://www.guardian.co.uk/business/2009/mar/19/google-street-view-uk

Yamada-Rice, D. (2010). Beyond words: An enquiry into children's home visual literacy practices. *Journal of Early Childhood Literacy, 10*, 341–363.

Yamada-Rice, D. (2011a). New media, evolving multimodal literacy practices and the potential impact of increased used of the visual mode in the urban environment on young children's learning. *Literacy, 45*(1), 32–43.

Yamada-Rice, D. (2011b). A comparative study of visuals in the urban landscapes of Tokyo and London. *Visual Communication, 10*, 175–186.

Ethical and Intercultural Issues

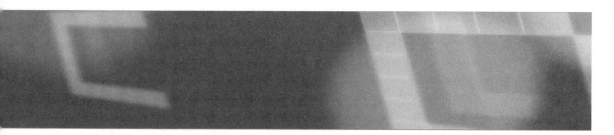

If digital media have created new possibilities for research and the dissemination of new knowledge, they have also created new issues in the representation of research and research participants. The contributors to this section of the book discuss the ethical and legal implications of this changed landscape, as well as how research into virtual worlds can entail traditional intercultural conflict and prejudice. However, the final chapter of the section concludes with a strong argument that, in ethnographic research that crosses the boundary of digital and place-based observation, it is not ethical solely to represent participants' practices with the flatness of the written page.

Williams and Brydon-Miller discuss the new ethical issues that arise from digital research and dissemination. Digital research and dissemination have created new opportunities as well as the need for research that investigates society's use of digital technologies. As a result of these technologies, research can represent participants more directly, through images and sound, than was ever possible through transcripts and written description, and research outcomes can be distributed digitally beyond traditional routes. However, these new opportunities simultaneously create new responsibilities for researchers. Williams and Brydon-Miller argue that, in addition to the traditional principles of ethical research of justice, beneficence and autonomy, transparency and demo-cratic practice must be considered. Images, which in traditional theses were frequently relegated to appendices but now can be easily included in the text body, may, because of their immediacy, overwhelm thoughtful evaluation. Further, because information, once digitized, can be easily reconfigured and redistributed, the traditional relationship between researcher and participant has inexorably changed. As a consequence, they argue that ethical research in digital environments requires new, non-hierarchical relationships between participants and researchers. They provide a helpful heuristic to guide institutions, supervisors and researchers in the new landscape of digital research.

Besides creating new ethical dimensions for research and dissemination, dissertations and theses that include digital material raise new and complicated intellectual property management issues. Copyright law developed in the eighteenth century to protect the rights of publishers and authors (Woodmansee, 1984), and the nineteenth century saw the emergence of the research-based doctorate and, with it, the dissertation or thesis that reported the outcomes of the research project. These text-based dissertations had relatively few conflicts with intellectual property law; if they reported new knowledge they were unlikely to infringe copyright. Since the dissertation was largely textual and universities established regulations on the use of secondary sources, plagiarism was a more likely risk than copyright infringement. Digital dissertations, however, disturb this settled understanding. When copyright material is directly included in dissertations, the candidate who creates a digital dissertation may move beyond the traditional areas of plagiarism and fair dealing. Fitzgerald and O'Brien discuss the implications of these changes. They lay out the scope of copyright law, and the balance that the law seeks to create between the rights of the creator and the public's (and research community's) interest in dissemination. The electronic dissertation or thesis can be disseminated more easily, allowing scholarship that would have remained seldom read in traditional paper form to be circulated by institutions including university repositories and larger projects such as the British Library's EThOS (Electronic Theses Online Service) project, which is intended to create a single online point of access for all British theses. However, copyright infringement can implicate these schemes to disseminate scholarship, if the dissertation creator does not obtain full rights to all the material included in the digital dissertation. Fitzgerald and O'Brien outline a series of steps that the doctoral candidate should undertake to assure that all third party material has been assessed for copyright status, and, if necessary, to assure that permission of copyright owners has been obtained to protect the candidate and institutional repositories.

The old *New Yorker* cartoon that 'on the Internet, nobody knows you're a dog' is not entirely true. While some researchers hoped that online environments would allow the creation of a space in which social interaction would be voluntary and equal, rather than compelled and laden with status markers, researchers investigating interactions in virtual worlds may find that cultural barriers exist which reflect offline divisions. Cheong's chapter describes how researchers engaged in multimodal research may find that, far from leaving behind real-world identities when researching online, gender, race and class, among other markers of difference, may pursue the researcher. Offline hierarchies may be replicated and even reinforced in virtual worlds. While engaging in virtual worlds can bring new opportunities for research into intercultural and social interaction, researchers must be sensitive in how they identify themselves and how others portray them.

In the last chapter in this section, Domingo reminds us that literacy is something that people do, not a skill that they have. She describes the literacy practices of the participants in her study, a group of Filipino British youths and connects their multimodal literacy practices with her own research. She developed 'migratory research practices' to encompass her participants' 'migratory literacies', that is, literacy practices that moved from one physical location to another and, more importantly, practices that moved from offline to online. Her participants' literacy practices were digitally layered across many modes, including text, speech, image, music and gesture. They used digital tools to create texts while travelling on public transport; these digital texts could then be disseminated globally. In a similar way, she accessed the digitized journals and books from her institution, New York University, as she traveled to the site of her study in London, and then created a web presence to archive the digital data that she generated. Through the research process, she realized that her own practices would have to change, and with them, the representation of her research in her dissertation. Given the need to fairly and fully represent her participants, the report of their practices could not be adequately presented in a written text. She could not ethically 'fossilize' their literacies on a page, but instead needed to create a digital dissertation.

REFERENCE

Woodmansee, M. (1984). The genius and the copyright: Economic and legal conditions of the emergence of the author. *Eighteenth Century Studies, 17*, 425–447.

10

Ethics and Representation

Bronwyn T. Williams and
Mary Brydon-Miller

INTRODUCTION

The dissertation has left the page and this shift toward new forms of scholarship demands a fundamental reconsideration of the ethical implications of research using digital media. There are an increasing number of examples of such scholarship. One dissertation on creating connections between deaf and hearing cultures includes video clips of rehearsals, performances and discussions with the participants involved in the project (Davis Haggerty, 2006). Another, this one on the leadership qualities of community activists, incorporates videos of interviews with the participants (Gutierrez, 2008). A Masters thesis on the relocation of residents from an urban public housing project contains a full-length film documentary of the research including interviews and other footage (Schippling, 2007). These examples, as well as the work contained in other chapters of this volume, demonstrate instances in which the research in a dissertation or thesis is being presented not only through print, but also through combinations of video, image and sound.

When it comes to research ethics, there have long been concerns among scholars about what happens when research participants are represented in writing (Kirsch, 1999; Newkirk, 1996; Powell & Takayoshi, 2003). Besides questions of whether participants consent to be written about and how they are treated during the gathering of data, there has been a sustained and productive conversation focused on issues of identity and representation. Among the questions that scholars have considered are: how do we deal with negative portrayals of participants? Should participants have the opportunity to respond to the research before it is published? How will research benefit the participants involved? In the past, such questions assumed that representations of research participants would take place through printed words on paper. Technology and tradition dictated that scholarly publication took place in print, as most still does today, where these questions continue to be important.

As this volume illustrates, however, the advent of digital media is substantially changing how research is both conducted as well as reported. Digital media have made it easy to compose images, video, sound as well as print. What is more, the combination of new media and online technologies have made possible, even easy, the publication and distribution of multimedia scholarship. Scholars now have the opportunity to choose which medium – or multiple media – through which to compose their research. In rhetorical terms, as Welch (1999) points out, delivery, or how we choose to communicate, has again become a concern for scholars.

In this chapter, we explore the ethical concerns involved when researchers have the opportunity to collect, analyze, compose and publish their work in multiple media. The move to digital research and writing raises questions about how research participants will be represented through multiple media as well as how readers of digital research will interpret such representations. Digital media are changing ethical considerations in ways that reach far beyond issues of informed consent. In particular, we will explore how digital research writing complicates questions of identity and representation.

We begin by providing a brief overview of the existing literature on ethics in digital research settings, identifying the need for further consideration of issues of identity and representation as key locations of potential contention in digital research. Following this, we outline a model for ethical reflection that involves the generation of a set of critical questions designed to guide researchers in identifying the ethical principles which inform their practice and examining the ways in which these values are enacted throughout the research process. We then discuss how this general model might be applied to questions of ethics and representation in digital research and consider which ethical principles are of greatest salience in this research arena, moving beyond the more conventional principles of justice, beneficence and autonomy to focus specifically on the principles of transparency and democratic practice. In doing this, we draw upon the current conversations about ethics in conducting digital literacy research and how new technologies have complicated previous questions of research ethics, and in particular, the ways in which new media texts change questions of representation for readers. Finally, we consider the implications of this process of ethical reflection for informing the further development of digital research.

CURRENT DISCUSSIONS OF THE ETHICS OF DIGITAL RESEARCH

With the growing sophistication and use of digital media there has been an accompanying discussion of the ethics of conducting research online. This robust and thoughtful discussion has come from a variety of disciplines, including literacy studies and rhetoric and composition. Most of the attention in these discussions has been about issues of data gathering and working with research participants. One result is that a number of professional organizations have adopted policy statements, or included references in existing ethical guidelines, concerning research practices online, from the American Psychological Association and the British Sociological Association to the Association of Internet Researchers. In addition, a number of books have focused on the subject including *Online Social Research* (Johns, Chen, & Hall, 2004), *Readings in Virtual Research Ethics* (Buchanan, 2004) and *The Ethics of Internet Research* (McKee & Porter, 2009), plus there is now a journal, the *International Journal of Internet Research Ethics.*

Broadly speaking, the concerns of much of the scholarship on digital research ethics have centered on three sets of issues that involve online interactions. First, there has been an ongoing set of concerns about how informed consent is obtained in online settings. Some articles outline the difficulty in gaining consent from individuals who are not physically present, particularly in ways that will satisfy local Institutional Review Boards that may be less flexible or even resistant to dealing with online research (Jones, 2004). The other concern in obtaining informed consent has involved verifying the authenticity of a person whom the researcher cannot see and who may be thousands of miles away. Echoing the famous *New Yorker* cartoon's question of whether, online, anyone can know whether you're a dog, scholars (Hine, 2000; Keller & Lee, 2003; Lee, 2000; Robinson, 2010) have raised questions and proposed possible solutions for determining the identity of participants in online research, and in particular in determining whether or not participants are adults.

A second area of concern in online research ethics has focused on the questions of what material is available online, and how long digital material might be available. For example, just as research with subjects in face-to-face settings raises questions of when or how the researcher should act if the actions or words of participants raise concerns about safety or legality, scholars have explored how researchers might respond to similar concerns when coming across material on websites or blogs (Kaplan & Howes, 2004; Stern, 2003). Other scholars have pointed to issues involving the storage and access to data online. Heverly (2008) points out that the Internet, far from being a world in which information is ephemeral, is actually one where information posted online, even in the course of conducting research, might remain available long after the researcher and participant believe it has been removed. Barnes (2004) meanwhile notes that automatic data gathering is common online, often for commercial purposes, but that data from online research may be archived or logged in places and databases that are not clear to the participants, or even the researchers.

Perhaps the most widespread discussion of online research ethics, however, has revolved around questions about the assumptions of privacy people have, or feel they can expect, when they are online. As McKee and Porter point out:

> for print-based and face-to-face research contexts, there are some agreed-upon guidelines and well-established research customs for determining what constitutes 'public' or private' communications. But for researchers studying venues such as blogs or interactive media, the guidelines are less clear. (2009, p. 7)

At the core of these discussions seem to be two sets of questions. First, there is the question of whether information posted online should be regarded as 'published' text in the same way that a book is published (Bruckman, 2004), or individual communication that is much more akin to private speech (Berry, 2004). If a researcher regards the words posted on an online forum as published text because they are words that are made available to others through media, then there is no more reason to worry about quoting those words, obtaining consent from the authors, or publishing articles about them than there would be in doing the same with a book from the library and the same conventions regarding citation would hold. On the other hand, if the words in an online forum are closer to speech happening between mutual members of a community, then the ethical obligations of the researcher are obviously much different and might include gaining informed consent and insuring confidentiality of sources. As Berry (2004) points out, online communities often behave as if there are mutually understood expectations of respect and privacy. Such community expectations result in online participants of forums or social networking sites often behaving as if they are addressing friends in more private, protected settings, including revealing personal or emotional information. The intimacy of sitting at a computer in a private room, responding to what seem to be individual members of a community only increase this sense of privacy (Barnes, 2004). There are numerous case studies of researchers who have become aware that they have somehow violated the privacy expectations of online communities and found the response of participants in the research to be one of anger and betrayal (Hall, Frederick, & Johns, 2004; McKee & Porter, 2009; Sidler, 2007).

The unstable, hybrid and rapidly evolving nature of online environments makes it all the more difficult to determine what should be considered private and what considered public. Such concerns are not only those of researchers, as ongoing public debates over the privacy policies of Facebook should remind us. Instead, what seems to be increasingly necessary is an awareness that online spaces require not only different conceptions of private and public than face-to-face communities, but also that there is a need for different metaphors in online research to describe the role of both research and the researcher (Sidler, 2007).

Through most of these discussions of digital research online, however, there is an implicit, or sometimes explicit, assumption that, once the research has been completed, it will be written about in print.

As digital media have changed issues of data gathering, however, they are now changing how scholars can approach issues of composition, publication and distribution. Now that digital media allow individuals to easily incorporate video, images or sound into composing texts about research, the questions and implications of how researchers represent participants in multiple media have become more complex.

A MODEL FOR STRUCTURED ETHICAL REFLECTION

Before examining the specific ethical issues involved in this shift toward digital forms of research production, presentation and dissemination, however, we would like to offer a new model for guiding a critical reflection of the ethical implications of research more generally. This model was developed as an attempt to operationalize the more theoretical reframing of research ethics away from the existing contractual model toward a model that takes into account the relationships of commitment and caring found in more engaged forms of research like action research and many feminist research methods (Brydon-Miller, 2008, 2009). But we believe this model has broader implications for informing the examination of ethical issues in a variety of research settings, including digital research.

This model begins by identifying the basic ethical principles which inform the researcher's practice. The principles outlined in the Helsinki Declaration and the Belmont Report serve as a starting point, but, as shown in Table 10.1, there is also room to identify additional principles which might be relevant to a particular methodology, participant population or research question. In the case of digital research, two additional principles seem to us to be especially salient: transparency (i.e. the extent to which the entire research process is clearly articulated to participants and those using the research) and democratic practice (i.e. the extent to which participants are able to contribute to the research process from the creation of research questions through decisions regarding dissemination of results).

Once the basic principles have been articulated, and this process itself should whenever possible involve collaboration with research participants, researchers

Table 10.1 Model for structured ethical reflection

Basic ethical principles	Developing partnerships/ identifying participants	Creating research questions	Collecting data	Analyzing data	Publishing and disseminating data
Autonomy					
Beneficience					
Justice					
Transparency					
Democratic practice					

are challenged to ask how their actions and decisions at each stage of the research process reflect the basic principles they have identified. So, for example, in the early stages of the research process the researcher might ask, 'Is the process by which I am identifying potential participants for this study clear (i.e. does it reflect the principle of transparency)? Does it provide equal opportunities for all potential participants to take part (i.e. does it reflect the principle of justice)? And are potential participants aware of what is being studied, of what they are being asked to do or to contribute, how the information will be collected, stored, and used, and aware that they are free to choose whether or not they wish to take part (i.e. does it reflect the principle of autonomy)?'

This same process of developing critical questions is then revisited at each stage of the research process. For the purposes of this discussion, however, we will focus specifically on the two final stages, analyzing the data and publishing and disseminating the results of the research, since they offer particular challenges to those conducting digital research which have not been adequately addressed in the literature to date.

THE ETHICS OF IMAGES AND EMOTIONS

Let us first consider why we believe these two principles of transparency and democratic practice are particularly critical in the development of new understandings of the ethical challenges involved in digital research. The revolutionary power of digital technology, as Manovich (2001) has argued, is that, once information is converted into a series of 1s and 0s, it can potentially be converted into any form of representation, from print to moving image. What is more, it can be compressed, transmitted and reconstructed across great distances almost instantly. Finally, compared with the media that preceded it, such as photographs or books, it is also easy to store and copy.

These qualities of digital technology have allowed individuals to engage in the production of multiple media in ways that were unimaginable little more than a quarter century ago. The model for producing and distributing images or recordings or moving pictures that marked mass popular culture in the twentieth century is one that required large amounts of capital in order to produce and distribute content. Labor, with specifically defined jobs such as sound engineers or camera operators, produced the work rather than individual artists. Large corporate organizations were necessary to reproduce and distribute the content, by producing films or recordings, building theaters or television broadcasting stations and the role of the audience was to consume the content, but not have the material means to alter it. During the last century, this model of mass popular culture was compatible with a model of corporate economic relations where large organizations mass produced goods that were then sent to be consumed by those who did not have the same production capabilities, but could consume the goods. The capital required to produce the content in film or music was substantial, while the capital required to consume it, such as film projectors, television sets or record players, was much smaller. This same corporate model has also typified the research endeavor where academic credentialing, access to large research grants and closely guarded systems of publication and presentation maintained control of knowledge generation within the domain of a small academic élite. Digital technologies, however, allow for a single individual to create, manipulate and distribute multiple media, including print, as easily – perhaps more easily, than a person typing on a page – signaling a move away from a hierarchical model of media production to a more accessible process that allows more democratic participation in the production process[1]. This same shift toward more open access to the means of production translates into research processes in which knowledge generation as well might be more egalitarian and participative.

What we also want to emphasize, however, is what happens on the reception end of digital media texts. For if digital technologies have changed the practices of composing, we should also be aware of how they may have changed the practices of interpreting texts that include multiple media, particularly in ways that influence how readers might respond to representations of research participants. In particular, we want to focus on three ways in which multiple media change the interpretation of texts: the different challenges presented by reading visual texts, the genre influences of new media texts and the ability of readers to sample, alter and redistribute digital new media texts.

One of the great advantages of digital media is the capability to reproduce, edit, and distribute images as easily as print. Although most people understand in a general sense that images and print transmit information in different ways, the reasons we might interpret and respond to information in images differently than print requires some specific attention. For example, the linear and symbolic nature of print requires time to interpret, and can only be interpreted over time by reading one word after another. Images, on the other hand, allow for much faster interpretation as we respond to multiple layers of information as quickly as evolution allows us to process visual information. The speed with which we can interpret visual information is the reason, for example, that airline consoles provide visual representations of vital data, rather than providing written descriptions of speed, direction or altitude (Kress, 2003). Such visual representations allow pilots to interpret information at a glance and make decisions almost instantaneously, if necessary. By contrast, reading words, one after another, slows down interpretation and allows for a more reflective, systematic interpretation of information.

The speed at which we can interpret images has several implications when it comes to composing with multiple media. Images often provide layers of information very quickly. For example, if I encounter an image of a student reading in a classroom, I not only immediately register the action of the student, but I also register information about clothing, age, sex, race, the setting of the classroom from materials on walls to the kind of furniture and lighting, the kind of material the student is reading and so on, far faster than I can type this sentence. I also make inter-textual connections, and judgments, about the layers of information I am seeing, whether it is the intention of the researcher providing the image to have me make those judgments or not. The potential of images to provide such layers of information can be positive, in that lengthy descriptions of classrooms or participants are no longer necessary in the same way. On the other hand, the layers of information may also distract me from the writer's point in using the image or lead me to judgments that may or may not be accurate. As one example, a colleague related to me an incident from a literacy workshop where middle-school students were asked to do a photo-voice type project in which they documented literacy practices in their homes through the use of photographs. These images were to be included in a course website and also potentially used in the scholarship of the researchers. One student presented images from his home that included magazines, postcards and other literacy artifacts, as the assignment had required, but in the images it was also clear that his family was poor and the household was in disarray – at least that was the interpretation of the researchers. What troubled the researchers was both that the clutter in the photographs overwhelmed the focus on literacy artifacts, but also that publishing the images might embarrass the student or reinforce negative stereotypes about poor families.

The latter concern points to another implication created by the speed and layers images provide, that images tend to work more powerfully on emotions. Images are not necessarily more emotionally potent than a print text – both forms depend on content and context. That said, the speed with which we interpret images, and the connections we make to reach those interpretations have implications for issues of emotion. First, interpreting any text requires making inter-textual connections to previous texts and experiences. Images often offer connections to visual memories of lived experiences that include embodied, emotional responses. In the example of the image of the student reading, for example, we might be immediately reminded of childhood experiences of a similar classroom and connected to the accompanying emotional memories. Even if we do not make direct, personal emotional connections, our ability to comprehend images quickly and holistically, rather than at the slower systematic speed of reading print, may give the image greater immediate emotional power. As Hill (2004) notes, in a situation where images and words are both offering information, vivid images may overpower the written descriptions or arguments. Hill notes:

> In short, because our minds prefer to take the fastest and easiest route to making a decision, and because image or imagistic texts offer shortcuts toward the endpoint of making a decision, then images (or, to a lesser extent, imagistic concrete language) will prompt the viewer to make a relatively quick decision, largely ignoring the more analytical, abstract information available in verbal form. (2004, p. 33)

The researchers in the middle-school project, with their response to the images of the poor student's house, illustrate this concept. Their concern was that people encountering the images would reach a quick decision, perhaps based on previous emotions, about the content of the photograph that would overwhelm any print text provided for context. In a similar example, at one presentation about a classroom ethnography, a scholar chose to read a transcript of a student's comments, rather than show the video the researcher had recorded, because she was concerned that the student's emotional and tearful delivery of the comments might overwhelm the content. Images, both moving and still, already authorize a kind of staring, sometimes almost a sense of voyeurism, when an image is particularly connected to strong emotional connotations (Boxall & Ralph, 2009). In the context of representing research participants, if the emotional response to a specific image is pity or sympathy or distaste arising from different positions of privilege, the use of images or video may intensify issues of power imbalances between research participants and the scholars writing and reading about them.

The last implication of our ability to read images, with their various layers, quickly and holistically, has to do with the arrangement of visual images. Where print, again, is linear and sequential and plays to the strengths of narrative and analysis, images are spatial and immediate. The nature of images, however, does not mean they are without qualities of arrangement that shape interpretation. As Kress argues, the placement of visual elements in space also often carries cultural meaning. 'Placing something centrally means that other things will be marginal, at least relatively speaking. Placing something at the top of the space means something else will be below' (2003, p. 2). We ascribe cultural meaning to these spatial arrangements – though, of course, they may vary by culture – very often expecting the central element of an image to be the most important. The cultural frames we use to interpret the arrangement of elements in images have their own influences of genre and history that we must take into account, as we will discuss below. The point here is that there is no neutral way to arrange visual elements. In research terms, then, there is no neutral, objective place to locate a video camera or frame an image when composing a digital text. To paraphrase Kress (2003), placement has meaning. When composing with images, then, it is important to consider how these other ways of interpreting images may shape an audience's response to research participants.

Here is where the principles of transparency and democratic practice begin to emerge as important ethical considerations in guiding the research process. Both research participants and those who will later serve as the audience for the research need to understand these processes of representation and interpretation. Research participants, such as the students engaged in the photo-voice study described earlier, should be guided through a process of viewing and interpreting photographs themselves so that they come to understand the impact that images can have on the viewer and should be provided with training in composing images that capture their experiences in the ways in which they choose to represent themselves, their families and their communities (Miller, 2010).

There should also be consideration given to others who might be affected by the images created through such processes. If relatives or community members are included in photographs or video used in digital research, they too should have the opportunity to participate in deciding how these images are used and how they are later distributed. If information is collected from websites or online forums, contributors should be aware of the presence and intentions of the researcher before any data are collected.

The dilemma here is that these democratic processes can also result in community members engaging in uncritical depictions of the lives and interactions being studied. The responsibility of the researcher, then, must include the recognition that there may be multiple truths, as well as opportunities for community members to engage in critical education and dialog with the researcher about the interpretations. We are not suggesting that researchers shirk their responsibility to tell the truth as they see it, but rather that they recognize the possibility of multiple truths and provide opportunities for those being represented to offer their own interpretations alongside those of the researcher.

In a similar fashion, it is important that readers of digital media develop strategies that enable them to both respond to the emotional content of the work, while simultaneously engaging in a more critical process of interpretation that allows them to evaluate their emotional responses.

POPULAR CULTURE, GENRE AND INTERPRETING DIGITAL TEXTS

The second area in which digital media change the way texts are composed and interpreted has to do with the genre expectations that shape both the writing and reading of texts. In part, genre questions about new media revolve around the ways in which technological capabilities allow for conventions regarding the creation and interpretation of texts to be developed and repeated so that readers can approach a text with certain expectations in mind. For example, web pages have evolved, at this point, so that the title of the page is at the top, drawing on our cultural familiarity with important information being at the top of print pages (Kress, 2003), while also conforming to the technological limits of a web page that only allow us to see one screen at a time, and that then load those screens from the top down.

Yet it is also the case that digital media genres and expectations have not developed without antecedents. New technologies and genres develop first through experiences with existing genres and forms (Stephens, 1998). So, for example, early movies looked like filmed plays and movies have often been analyzed critically using the same theories and approaches as plays and novels. The genres of film making and film criticism that were distinctive to cinema took time and experimentation to develop. There has been a similar development of online and digital forms, from the early 'bulletin boards' to current video games that use movie-like scenes and camera angles. Websites often look like magazine covers and billboard ads on websites have that label for a good reason. Although new forms are evolving online and often influence existing forms of popular culture, the influences for crafting and interpreting digital texts are still often grounded in existing genres from newspapers, magazines, television and film. As a number of scholars have pointed out (Cope & Kalantzis, 2010; Manovich, 2001; Williams, 2009), these forms draw from earlier genres, very often mass popular culture such as television, film, music and video games. While this phenomenon may be changing, it is still the case that the broadest and deepest rhetorical experiences we have with visual information on screens come from popular film and television. When we encounter new images on computers screens, then it is likely that we will include popular culture texts in the inter-textual and interpretive frameworks from which we draw.

We may not be explicitly aware that we are making these connections to our experiences with film and television, but our emotions and values may be influenced by them nonetheless. For example, in one research project, a video clip of two students holding hands seemed to suggest that they had reconciled their differences. Researchers who only saw the video clip assumed the gesture of holding hands indicated friendship, while researchers who had been present in the classroom, and aware of the larger context of the moment, realized that the two students were still arguing and that one was actually forcefully holding down the hand of the other (Schuck & Kearney, 2006). Not only did the researchers watching the video not grasp the larger context of the exchange, but 'the use of such clips in commercial film-making has created "movie clichés" which encouraged the researchers to jump to a conclusion that they had seen previously enacted in television or movie stories' (Schuck & Kearney, 2006, p. 459). Another example might result from the suggestion that is sometimes made to digitally obscure the faces of research participants being shown in video clips so as to protect their anonymity (Pauwels, 2006; Schuck & Kearney, 2006). Yet the obscured face on video is most often seen in popular culture on reality programs about crime or news reports depicting either criminals or victims. Video images of research participants might be read with connotations of shame or guilt, even if not explicitly, in such clips. In a similar way, poor production values in film, which in popular culture contexts often signal a degree of unprofessional or even illicit content, can shape the reading of digital texts. The point is that if we are not explicitly aware of, or reflect on, how we have learned to interpret images or video on screens, we may well be influenced in our response to digital texts – and our response to the participants represented in the texts – by our previous experience with images and videos and issues such as whether we perceive the production values to be of high or low quality.

Clearly, the stakes are different when we represent a participant in an image, rather than through words. Even as digital technologies have allowed for the easy manipulation and editing of still and moving images, there is a still a cultural expectation that images are somehow more trustworthy and allow readers an opportunity to 'see things for themselves'. Yet, any image or video that is used in composing digital texts about research is selected information and no more inherently trustworthy than a printed paragraph. Anonymity, for example, is more difficult to create for an image or video clip than it is to simply change a name in print. Cameras can be positioned so as not to show participant faces, or a still clip representative of the larger video could be extracted or faces obscured by editing. Yet, in doing, so we are making decisions about the nature of the representation of the participants that we must reflect on and communicate to both readers and participants if we are to honor the principles of transparency and democratic practice. Not only does trying to obscure a face perhaps also obscure the voice of the participant and deny the participant credit for being part of the research, and thus add to the power imbalances between researcher and participant, but it demonstrably changes the nature of what was observed. Such editing, which always happens, may hide as much as it reveals.

One implication of the effects of writing with digital media then, is that there needs to a more explicit focus on the nature of visual rhetoric. Because we do not have to learn to read visuals in the same way we have to learn print, as a culture we have the tendency to regard images as easy and obvious to interpret. Yet images and video are employed, and interpreted, rhetorically and are involved with the same issues of context, inter-textuality, audience, and authorship that shape writing in print. If we plan to create digital texts with multiple media, then we must learn more about visual rhetoric, and teach more about it to students, and to readers of our texts.

SAMPLING AND REMIXING DIGITAL TEXTS

A final concern about the ways that abilities to compose with digital media may affect issues of ethics and representation has to do with the potential for unintended consequences if digital multimedia texts are made available to a wider audience online. For example, referring to a website might result in unwanted attention and traffic in the same way publishing a phone number might (Pauwels, 2006) or discussion of an online forum might lead to trolls or stalkers who use the information from an article to harass members of online communities (Barnes, 2004).

To consider one example of the potential for unintended consequences in depth, it is important to focus on the ease with which digital texts can be searched for, sampled, and remixed. The same technologies that so easily allow individuals to compose and transmit multimedia texts also allow individuals to copy and remix those same texts. What is more, digital media technologies have changed the relationship of audience members to text by allowing them to respond to producers and other audience members, and so made the concepts of sampling and remixing more common and accepted. In print culture, reading was an activity that made meaning from a text but did nothing to the text itself, recognizing the autonomy and authority of the writer to create the text. Readers could interpret and analyze the meaning and structure of texts, but regarded the texts as coherent wholes that should remain that way. Most scholars, in reading and writing about texts continue to regard them in this way. Digital media technologies, however, create reading activities that are better described by ideas of textual poaching and bricolage.

de Certeau (1984) argues that it is not enough to study representations of culture separately from individual behavior. Instead, he maintains that we must be aware that 'everyday life invents itself by *poaching* in countless ways on the property of others' (p. xii). In other words, we not only interpret texts, but we appropriate pieces of the texts and make new things from them that serve our own interests and experiences. This is a common and accepted practice in academic writing when writers quote or paraphrase from one text in the service of a new or connected argument. Yet, the ability of individuals to appropriate and reuse pieces of a text has been limited, until the advent of digital media, by our limited means of production and cultural power. We might copy a quotation from an article in our own writing, but would not actually copy and paste the page from the book into our text and publish it ourselves. Now, however, digital media technologies have enabled all audience members to be able to read with an eye toward textual poaching, and to have the capabilities to actually sample sections of a work, manipulate the content and distribute the remixed text.

More to the point, however, the practices of sampling and reusing material to create new texts have become an integral part of online culture. Around any corner on the Internet, you can find individuals sampling from existing texts to combine media and genres on video websites, blogs, and social networking pages. Digital technologies allow for material used in one text to be appropriated over and over again by audience members who are composing their own texts. In a study of online memes – the viral bits of information that get shared online – Knobel and Lankshear (2007) point out that one of the characteristics of the memes they studied was that they were not passed along intact like multimodal chain letters. Instead, the video or image or text was both appropriated and remixed. For example, an image of Kanye West disrupting the Grammy Awards was soon juxtaposed with new words and new contexts, from a presidential press conference to the moon landing. Indeed, the allure of memes is, in part, the ability to participate in spreading the meme both in copying and manipulating it.

> In many ways these 'mutations' often seemed to help the meme's fecundity in terms of hooking people into contributing their own version of the meme. A concept like 'replicability' therefore needs to include remixing as an important practice associated with many successful online memes, where remixing includes modifying, bricolaging, splicing, reordering, superimposing, etc. (Knobel & Lankshear, 2007, p. 209)

The point of this discussion of the culture and practices of sampling and remixing online, is to point out that, as digital media allow for the publication of video and images, if that material is available online it will always run the potential risk of being appropriated and reused. Video and images, in particular, are much more inviting for this kind of sampling and reuse than print texts. It is not at all beyond the realm of possibility for an individual to come across a video clip from a piece of digital research, sample it, re-dub it or re-edit it, and post a new video that quickly goes viral. If this seems far-fetched, consider the case of the 'Star Wars Kid' where an obscure home video of a Canadian teenager pretending to wield a light-saber has been sampled and remixed hundreds of times and those videos have been watched by tens of millions of people.

Digital technologies that now provide the opportunity for broader, more democratic access to the production and distribution of knowledge, also allow for the use of digital texts in ways their producers could scarcely imagine. At a recent presentation a scholar studying the home literacy practices of middle-school children said her institutional review board approval would not allow her to show video of her participants, but she instead showed a video she had found posted on YouTube of young people involved in similar activities. Because the YouTube video had been posted to the public, her assumption was that it was available to show in this context. Certainly, however, the boys who made the video could not have imagined that it would end up being displayed in this context for an academic audience. If researchers can find and reuse digital texts for their purposes, it should not be surprising if digital scholarly work is similarly available for sampling and remixing.

CONCLUSIONS

Just as strategies for creating and interpreting new forms of media grow from our experiences with existing forms, so our expectations regarding digital research methods and the research ethics that will apply to them are based on our prior notions of research practice. Sometimes this prior knowledge can help us to navigate the unknown territory of research in these new contexts, but just as often our assumptions turn out to be misleading and our imposition of pre-existing principles and practices inappropriate.

The existing systems for determining whether research is ethical and the principles that have guided this evaluation reinforce an antiquated notion of the research process in which distinguishing researcher from research subject was clear cut and expectations regarding control of the research process, ownership of data and authorship were well articulated and agreed upon. In this context, the principles of justice, beneficence and autonomy served us well as reminders of our responsibilities to our subjects and to the broader community of scholars. At the same time, however, they served to reinforce systems of power and privilege by putting researchers and our institutions in the position of determining what research would be conducted, and by whom.

The democratization of the process of creating digital media blurs the lines between researcher and researched by putting the means of knowledge production in the hands of anyone with internet access and imagination. The possibility of having the results of digital research accessed, altered and redistributed challenges claims of ownership of data. And when research participants become the directors and stars of our digital dissertations, it raises the question of who can claim credit and who is granted the credentials associated with the final product.

The principles of transparency and democratic practice provide strategies for examining the ethical implications of our work more consistent with the ways in which digital media and the approaches to understanding and distributing knowledge regarding these practices actually function. The principle of transparency requires us to be honest and direct in communicating our intentions as researchers. Explaining who we are, what we want to learn, and how we plan to collect information to help understand our research question allows others to decide whether they wish to participate in our research.

Toward this end, we also must not assume we know more than others involved in the research process. This is new territory for all of us and whatever theories we have read, whatever courses we have taken or taught, have not fully prepared us for what we have to learn. Our knowledge can contribute to a deepening understanding of the impact and implications of new forms of communication, but the experience and insights of other participants are just as important. This demands that we develop more democratic spaces for knowledge to be created, challenged and shared.

In addition, our institutions will have to catch up. Those of us who are conducting digital research are often still tethered to the constraints of institutional review boards that demand that we maintain confidentiality, where none exists or insist that we remain outside of the communities that we study, rather than recognizing the value in working collaboratively. At the same time, reappointment and tenure processes will need to come to terms with the notion that digital research takes many forms and that distributing the knowledge created through such practices may take place in a blog or website or YouTube video with greater impact and relevance than any peer-reviewed journal article.

Finally, recognizing the ways in which digital media shape our understanding of the world, and of one another, requires us to develop new strategies for teaching our students and one another how to use these new sources of information and entertainment wisely. We must challenge ourselves to critically examine our own interpretations and assumptions while at the same time allowing ourselves to explore, invent and play.

NOTE

1. This process of personal production and participation in the creation of new information and artistic expressions through digital media seems familiar to us because it harkens back to days before the development of mass popular culture when people connected directly to one another through music, performance, storytelling and other more intimate forms of communication. What we have not yet fully grasped, however, is how the scope and scale of current media outlets fundamentally alter what was personal interaction into what is now a form of global networking.

REFERENCES

Barnes, S. B. (2004). Issues of attribution and identification in online social research. In M. D. Johns, S.-L. S. Chen, & G. J. Hall (Eds.), *Online Social Research: Methods, Issues, and Ethics* (pp. 203–222). New York: Peter Lang.

Berry, D. M. (2004). Internet research: Privacy, ethics, and alienation, an open source approach. *Internet Research, 14*, 323–332.

Boxall, K. & Ralph, S. (2009). Research ethics and the use of visual images in research with people with intellectual disability. *Journal of Intellectual & Developmental Disability, 34*, 45–54.

Bruckman, A. S. (2004). Introduction: Opportunities and challenges in methodology and ethics. In M. D. Johns, S.-L. S. Chen, & G. J. Hall (Eds.), *Online Social Networks: Methods, Issues, and Ethics* (pp. 101–104). New York: Peter Lang.

Brydon-Miller, M. (2008). Ethics and action research: Deepening our comitment to principles of social justice and redefining systems of democratic practice. In P. Reason & H. Bradbury (Eds.), *The SAGE Handbook of Action Research: Participative Inquiry and Practice* (pp. 199–210), 2nd edn. Los Angeles: Sage.

Brydon-Miller, M. (2009). Covenantal ehics and action research: Exploring a common foundation for social research. In D. M. Mertens & P. E. Ginsberg (Eds.), *The Handbook of Social Research Ethics* (pp. 243–258). Los Angeles: Sage.

Buchanan, E. (2004). *Readings in Virtual Research Ethics: Issues and Controversies.* Hershey, PA: Information Science Publishing.

Cope, B. & Kalantzis, M. (2010). New media, new learning. In D. R. Cole & D. L. Pullen (Eds.), *Multiliteracies in Motion: Current Theory and Practice* (pp. 87–104). London: Routledge.

Davis Haggerty, L. R. (2006). Adjusting the margins: Building bridges between deaf and hearing cultures through performance arts. Ph.D. Dissertation. Antioch University.

de Certeau, M. (1984). *The Practice of Everyday Life* (Translated by S. Rendall). Berkeley, CA: University of California Press.

Gutierrez, R. D. (2008). Life-affirming leadership: An inquiry into the culture of social justice. Ph.D. Dissertation. Antioch University.

Hall, G., Frederick, D., & Johns, M.D. (2004). "NEED HELP ASAP!!!" A feminist communitarian approach to online research ethics. In M. D. Johns, S.-L. S. Chen & G. J. Hall (Eds.), *Online Social Research: Methods, Issues, and Ethics* (pp. 239–254). New York: Peter Lang.

Heverly, R. A. (2008). Growing up digital: Control and the pieces of a digital life. In T. McPherson (Ed.), *Digital Youth, Innovation, and the Unexpected* (pp. 199–218). Cambridge, MA: The MIT Press.

Hill, C. A. (2004). The psychology of rhetorical images. In C. A. Hill & M. Helmers (Eds.), *Defining Visual Rhetorics Mahwah* (pp. 25–40). Mahwah, NJ: Lawrence Erlbaum Associates.

Hine, C. (2000). *Virtual Ethnography.* London: Sage.

Johns, M. D., Chen, S.-L. S., & Hall, G. J. (Eds.). (2004). *Online Social Research: Methods, Issues, & Ethics.* New York: Peter Lang.

Jones, S. (2004). Introduction: Ethics and internet studies. In M. D. Johns, S.-L. S. Chen, & G. J. Hall (Eds.), *Online Social Research: Methods, Issues, and Ethics* (pp. 179–186). New York: Peter Lang.

Kaplan, I. & Howes, A. (2004). "Seeing through different eyes": Exploring the value of participative research using images in schools. *Cambridge Journal of Education, 34*, 143–155.

Keller, H. & Lee, S. (2003.) Ethical issues surrounding human participants research using the internet. *Ethics & Behaviour, 13*, 211–219.

Kirsch, G. E. (1999). *Ethical Dilemmas in Feminist Research: The Politics of Location, Interpretation, and Publication.* Albany, NY: SUNY Press.

Knobel, M. & Lankshear, C. (2007). Online memes, affinities, and cultural production. In M. Knobel & C. Lankshear (Eds.), *A New Literacies Sampler* (pp. 199–228). London: Peter Lang.

Kress, G. (2003). *Literacy in the New Media Age.* London: Routledge.

Lee, R. M. (2000). *Unobtrusive Methods in Social Research.* Buckingham, UK: Open University Press.

Manovich, L. (2001). *The Language of New Media*. Cambridge, MA: The MIT Press.

McKee, H. A. & Porter, J. E. (2009). *The Ethics of Internet Research: A Rhetorical, Case-Based Process*. London: Peter Lang.

Miller, B. (2010). Photovoice as a needs assessment to explore stress in teens. Unpublished doctoral dissertation. University of Cincinnati, Ohio.

Newkirk, T. (1996). Seduction and betrayal in qualitative research. In P. Mortensen & G. E. Kirsch (Eds.), *Ethics and Representation in Qualitative Studies of Literacy* (pp. 3–16). Urbana, IL: NCTE.

Pauwels, L. (2006). Ethical issues of online (visual) research. *Visual Anthropology, 19*, 365–369.

Powell, K. M. & Takayoshi, P. (2003). Accepting roles created for us: The ethics of reciprocity. *College Composition and Communication, 54*, 394–422.

Robinson, L. C. (2010). Informed consent among analog people in a digital world. *Language and Communication, 30*, 181–191.

Schippling, R. M. (2007). Public housing redevelopment: Residents' experiences with relocation from Phase 1 of Toronto's Regent Park revitalization. Masters Thesis. University of Waterloo.

Schuck, S. & Kearney, M. (2006). Using digital video as a research tool: Ethical issues for researchers. *Journal of Educational Multimedia and Hypermedia, 15*, 447–463.

Sidler, M. (2007). Playing scavenger and gazer with scientific discourse: Opportunities and ethics for online research. In H. A. McKee & D. N. DeVoss (Eds.), *Digital Writing Research: Technologies, Methodologies, and Ethical Issues* (pp. 71–88). Cresskill, NJ: Hampton Press.

Stephens, M. (1998). *The Rise of the Image The Fall of the Word*. Oxford: Oxford University Press.

Stern, S. R. (2003). Encountering distressing information in online research: A consideration of legal and ethical responsibilities. *New Media & Society, 5*, 249–266.

Welch, K. (1999). *Electric Rhetoric: Classical Rhetoric, Oralism, and a New Literacy*. Cambridge, MA: The MIT Press.

Williams, B. T. (2009). *Shimmering Literacies: Popular Culture and Reading and Writing Online*. London: Peter Lang.

11

Copyright Management Approaches

Brian Fitzgerald and Damien O'Brien

INTRODUCTION

This chapter examines the relationship between copyright law and the creation and dissemination of electronic theses and dissertations.

COPYRIGHT LAW PRINCIPLES

Copyright is an area of the law known as intellectual property law. It enables the copyright owner to control certain acts (such as the reproduction and the communication to the public of their copyright material) and to prevent others from using copyright material without the copyright owners' permission, through the granting of a group of exclusive rights to the copyright owner, subject to certain conditions and exceptions[1]. As a result of the increasing move towards standardised intellectual property laws through international organisations, such as the World Intellectual Property Organization (WIPO) and World Trade Organization (WTO), most countries now have developed laws which specifically address copyright, for example in Australia, copyright law is governed by the Copyright Act 1968 (Cth)[2].

From a theoretical perspective, copyright serves (at least) an economic function by granting creators or authors monopoly rights in their creations for a limited time and thereby enabling them to receive remuneration for the use of those creations[3]. This, in turn, provides an incentive for further creativity and innovation. However, most copyright laws have been structured to provide a balance between providing incentives in the area of innovation and creativity and ensuring access to information for users of copyright material, while also being careful not to restrict competition in the marketplace.

Copyright law also provides protection for moral rights which are personal rights belonging to the author or creator of the copyright work, which exist independently of economic rights[4]. Australian copyright law recognises three types of moral rights:

- The right of attribution of authorship
- The right not to have authorship falsely attributed
- The right of integrity of authorship

The first of these moral rights, the right of attribution of authorship involves the right to be identified as the author of the work if any 'attributable acts' are done in respect of the work. The second moral right provides the author of the work the right not to have authorship of the work falsely attributed. The third moral right of integrity involves the right not to have the work subjected to derogatory treatment which would demean the creator's reputation[5].

At the international level, copyright law has long been considered to be a balance of competing policy objectives. The Preamble to the WIPO Copyright Treaty (WCT) recognises the need to maintain a balance between the following interests: 'the rights of authors and the larger public interest, particularly education, research and access to information, as reflected in the Berne Convention'[6]. To give effect to this balance, copyright legislation in most jurisdictions also provides for a range of 'fair use' or 'fair dealing' exceptions to copyright infringement, which allow copyright material to be used free of charge without the permission of, or a licence from the copyright owner[7]. Such provisions are an important mechanism that is designed to ensure the right to access information is preserved and to achieve the public interest goal of encouraging education, research, the free flow of information and freedom of expression[8].

One of the fundamental principles of copyright law is that copyright does not protect ideas, information or facts. Instead copyright protects the form or manner in which those ideas, information or facts are expressed[9]. Generally, this requirement will be satisfied where the expression is in a tangible form in the sense that it has been written down, recorded or stored. In response to new technologies, this principle has been interpreted broadly, and includes material that has been recorded in any digital form, such as on a computer or portable storage medium (e.g. a CD, DVD or thumb drive).

There are a number of different categories of material which copyright law protects in most jurisdictions. For example, under the Australian Copyright Act 1968 (Cth) the types of material which are afforded protection by copyright are divided into two broad groups or categories: works and subject matter other than works[10]. The category known as 'works' includes literary, dramatic, musical and artistic works, while 'subject matter other than works' extends copyright protection to sound recordings, cinematograph films, published editions and sound and television broadcasts[11].

As noted above, in order to ensure that an appropriate balance is struck between the rights of copyright owners and the public interest in the dissemination of material, copyright laws in most jurisdictions include a range of free use exceptions which allow material protected by copyright to be used without the permission of the copyright owner, known as fair use or fair dealing.

This doctrine of fair use, which operates in the US allows for limited use of copyright material without the permission of the rights holder or copyright owner for individual activities such as criticism, comment, news reporting, teaching, scholarship and research[12]. It should be noted that this doctrine allows for more open-ended use of copyright material to be made and is not restricted to use by way of specific purposes, such as the defence of fair dealing which operates in some jurisdictions. In determining whether the use made of the particular copyright work will be deemed to be a 'fair use', there are a number of factors which require consideration in each particular case; these include:

- The purpose and character of the use, including whether such use is of a commercial nature or is for non-profit educational purposes.
- The nature of the copyrighted work.
- The amount and substantiality of the portion used in relation to the copyrighted work as a whole.
- The effect of the use upon the potential market for or value of the copyrighted work[13].

The doctrine of fair use which operates in the US can be contrasted with the concept of 'fair dealing' which operates in a number of other jurisdictions, including Australia, the UK, Canada and Singapore. These fair dealing provisions permit the use of copyright material for certain purposes, providing the dealing with the work is deemed to be fair[14]. In these particular circumstances, copyright in the material will not be infringed, without the permission of the copyright owner, providing the dealing falls within one of the purposes outlined in the relevant fair dealing provisions in each jurisdiction; for example, it is for the purposes of research or study, criticism or review, parody or satire, reporting news or judicial proceedings or professional advice, and the dealing with the material is deemed to be fair. Most copyright laws do not provide a precise definition of what will amount to 'fair'. However, 'fair' is generally determined with reference to all of the circumstances relating to the dealing, for example, the nature and purpose of the dealing, the amount taken from and impact on the potential market for the material being copied[15].

THE LEGAL STATUS OF ELECTRONIC THESES AND DISSERTATIONS

Copyright protection

In almost all jurisdictions, theses and dissertations will be deemed to be a subject matter protected by copyright law and will in most cases fall within the category of copyright protection known as 'works', in particular literary works. While most copyright laws, for example the Australian Copyright Act 1968 (Cth), do not provide an exhaustive definition of a literary work, it is generally accepted that the term 'literary work' will include any work which is expressed in either print or written form[16]. Importantly, the term 'literary' does not prescribe that the work must reach any particular standard of literary style or merit, that is, there is no quality requisite, simply that the work must be original[17]. Therefore, as a general rule, most theses and dissertations will automatically be protected by copyright[18].

Copyright ownership

When considering issues of copyright ownership in theses and dissertations as a starting point and subject to any express agreement to the contrary (such as an agreement in writing assigning copyright to an educational institution or a third party), it is the PhD candidate (the author who has created it) who will own copyright in the original expressions in their thesis or dissertation[19]. However, in some cases it is possible that a third party, such as a funding body, educational institution or even supervisor may obtain copyright in the PhD student's thesis or dissertation. This is an issue which requires careful management from both the host educational institution and PhD student. If any funding or other financial contributions have been made available for the completion of the dissertation, it is important to ascertain the terms of these agreements and whether the funding body or institution providing the funding will seek an assignment (transfer of ownership) of the copyright in the PhD student's thesis or dissertation.

Similarly, in some disciplines which are heavily dependent upon input and guidance from a PhD student's supervisor, the student and supervisor will need to clarify copyright ownership issues, in particular whether the supervisor has made a significant enough contribution to the thesis or dissertation in order to constitute some form of copyright ownership. As a practical measure it should be noted that any agreement to assign copyright to an educational institution or a third party should be made in writing, in order to be enforceable at law and should generally be made at the time of the PhD candidate's enrolment or before the candidate commences work on their thesis or dissertation[20].

The Oak Law Project Report No 1 identified four distinct stakeholders in the process of creating and disseminating electronic theses and dissertations:

- *The student.* As the contributor of original material, the submitting student will have intellectual property (IP) rights in most, if not all of the content. ...

- *The supervisor.* Depending on the discipline, there may be some content of the thesis or dissertation that is directly or co-contributed by the student's supervisor. This may give IP rights to the supervisor and/or the supervisor's employer, the relevant academic institution.
- *University, granting agency and industrial partner.* Universities, granting agencies and industrial partners typically have IP rights agreements and policies that may govern some of the content of electronic theses and dissertations (ETD).
- *ETD disseminating institution (repository).* Institutions that have a repository of electronic theses and dissertations (ETD) need clarification of IP rights ownership. What is the status of the repository? (Is it a publisher?) What are the permissions required for cited materials and are there any exemptions available (such as fair dealing for research or study, or criticism or review)? There may also be tortuous issues arising in rare circumstances (such as defamation or passing off)[21].

MANAGING THIRD PARTY COPYRIGHT IN ELECTRONIC THESES AND DISSERTATIONS

One of the most common copyright issues which arise in the thesis or dissertation process involves third party materials which are protected by copyright and for which no permission or licence has been sought/granted for the re-use of such material in the PhD student's thesis or dissertation. The ease at which content, particularly in a digital format can be reproduced, sometimes unintentionally, means that there is always a likelihood that some ETDs may contain third party materials, in the form of text, drawings, photographs, reproductions of paintings, video and sound recordings, which are protected by copyright law.

This is a significant copyright issue, which has the potential to subject the PhD student, educational institution and other third parties involved in this process, such as repositories, to litigation for copyright infringement. Therefore, it is essential for educational institutions or repositories hosting ETDs to develop and implement strategies to avoid incurring liability (whether through an action for copyright infringement or through a request for payment of equitable remuneration to a copyright collecting society) due to the unauthorised use of any third party copyright materials included in ETDs.

As noted above, 'third party copyright' will typically consist of copyright material which is owned by someone other than the ETD author. Problems for students/institutions/repositories will arise where third party copyright is reproduced in the thesis or dissertation without the copyright owner's permission. Educational institutions and repositories should not simply assume that the theses or dissertations consist only of original material, as in practice theses and dissertations regularly include third party content, whether it be text, diagrams, pictures or other works. Furthermore, if the copyright owner of the third party content has given permission for the work to be used, educational institutions and repositories must ensure that the terms of such permission are not only confined to use in the original thesis or dissertation but extend to reproducing or communicating the content for the purposes of digitisation and public access via the repository[22].

There are a number of options available to educational institutions and repositories in order to mitigate the risk of copyright infringement in relation to third party copyright for born digital theses and dissertations. These include:

- Ensuring that ETD candidates are provided with sufficiently extensive information and, if necessary, practical training on the basic principles of copyright law, so they understand when they can use third party content in their thesis or dissertation without permission (i.e. an insubstantial part or a substantial part which can be used because of the operation of the fair dealing or other exception to infringement) and when they will need to obtain permission ('clearance') from the copyright owner to use third party content and how to obtain permission[23].
- Requiring the ETD candidate to be responsible for identifying all third party content included in the thesis or dissertation, determining which third party content they require permission to use and obtaining all necessary licences (typically a non-exclusive, perpetual licence) from the owners of such third party content, which must be broad enough to permit the thesis or dissertation containing the third party material to be reproduced and communicated via the Internet (whether by the student, the university or the disciplinary repository).
- Requiring the ETD candidate to 'self manage' any third party content which is not authorised for digital distribution[24].

PRACTICAL COPYRIGHT MANAGEMENT APPROACHES FOR ELECTRONIC THESES AND DISSERTATIONS

The best approach to minimise any potential exposure to issues of copyright infringement for all parties in the ETD process is to develop and implement copyright management practices in relation to ETDs. The key objective of copyright management in this context is to ensure that the student and repository/ educational institution hosting the ETDs have appropriate authorisation to be able to legally carry out all the acts involved in putting the ETDs online.

In this regard, there are two important steps which must be strictly followed in any copyright management strategy in this field. First, in the event that any third party copyright material has been included in the ETD, it will be necessary to ensure that all appropriate permissions have been obtained to use that material in the ETD, unless permission is not required under law, for example, the doctrine of fair use or fair dealing applies. This is a vital step, which will require the PhD student, with the assistance of their educational institution to ensure that all the permissions have been obtained and on terms which cover the intended use/ dissemination of the thesis or dissertation 'downstream'. For example, if it is contemplated that the ETD will be communicated and disseminated on the Internet, then this must be included in the permission.

Second, the hosting repository/educational institution must be granted a licence (preferably in written form) by the copyright owner authorising the relevant repository/educational institution hosting the ETD to reproduce and communicate or otherwise disseminate the thesis or dissertation via the Internet. In this regard, the repository/educational institution will need to be proactive in ensuring that the PhD student has correctly obtained permissions where any third party copyright material is present in the ETD and that these permissions have been obtained on terms which allow the repository/educational institution to use the ETD in such manner that they wish, for example, communicating and disseminating the ETD online.

A five-step practical copyright management approach

The most practical way to manage copyright issues in the ETD process is to have the ETD candidate self manage the process from the very first day of their candidature. To achieve this, the ETD candidate could be required to keep a 'Copyright Compliance Table' (which could be incorporated in an e-diary or e-portfolio commonly used in many universities or potentially embedded in the metadata of an ETD though machine readable 'tags') of the third party copyright material utilised in the ETD. Based on materials or training provided to the student through their candidature, support from their supervisor and in difficult cases the university, the student would be asked to record all third party copyright materials included in the thesis or dissertation, to make an assessment of the copyright status of these materials and to note this in their Table on a continuous basis. Where permission is required, they would be expected to seek and obtain that permission and record it in their Table. This management process in itself would be an excellent tool for assisting students to develop continuous learning skills in the increasingly important skill of copyright management.

In managing these situations the following steps are suggested:

- *Step 1. Identify all third party copyright materials* included in the ETD.
- *Step 2. Determine whether a copyright is exercised in relation to 'substantial part'.* Examine each item of third party copyright content included in the ETD to assess if its inclusion involves the exercise of acts (e.g. reproduction, adaptation) in relation to a substantial part of the third party copyright content; where only an insubstantial part of any item of third party content is used, there is no need to take further steps as use of an insubstantial part is not an infringement and does not need to be authorised by the copyright owner. Establishing guidelines for what is a substantial part is integral to the risk management process. It is not possible to provide absolute and firm guidelines for all situations, but it must be understood that any figures stated in the guidelines will essentially become the *de facto* rule.
- *Step 3. Determine whether there has been an act of fair dealing/fair use.* If a substantial part of an item of third party copyright content is included in the ETD, consider whether use of that part is justified under the notion of fair dealing or fair use. Consider also whether the communication to the public (dissemination) of third party copyright in the thesis or dissertation by the student or repository/educational institution will be covered by any of these defences.
- *Step 4. Determine whether there are any other exceptions to copyright infringement which may apply.* For example, in some jurisdictions it is not an infringement of copyright law to take a photograph of a sculpture or work of artistic craftsmanship that is on permanent public display, so if a student reproduces and/or publishes an image of a work of artistic craftsmanship in a public place there is no need to obtain permission from the owner of copyright in the publicly displayed work[25].
- *Step 5. Assess whether permission should be requested.* If, after going through these steps there is still uncertainty about whether the use of the third party content in the thesis or

dissertation or its dissemination is authorised, a request should be sent to the copyright owner specifying the third party materials which are to be included in the thesis or dissertation and the use to be made of that material and seeking express permission for such use; any licence obtained for the use of third party content must be broad enough to permit the thesis or dissertation to be reproduced in digital form and communicated online (whether by the student, the university or a disciplinary repository). Since there will be doubt about whether the reproduction and communication to the public of some materials included in theses and dissertations is permissible, in some cases there will be no option but to seek express permission.

CONCLUSIONS

There are many copyright issues in the theses and dissertations process, which all concerned parties, the PhD student, educational institution and repository, need to be aware of and carefully manage. In this regard, it is essential that a clear copyright management policy is developed which provides protocols for the handling of these issues by the particular parties involved in each stage of the theses and dissertations process. To this end, this chapter has attempted to provide some best practice guidelines in managing these copyright issues. While these guidelines and steps may not comprehensively address all of these issues in each particular context, they will, however, be a useful starting point in helping PhD students, educational institutions and repositories understand copyright issues and minimise any potential liability in theses and dissertations.

Some have suggested that the current legal regime which governs these issues, copyright law, is outdated and that there is a need for reform in this area of the law and the possible introduction of a specific defence or exception which permits certain dealings with theses and dissertations without the need to obtain relevant copyright permissions. However, such proposals for reform, in the authors' view, are unlikely to become accepted as a part of copyright law in the near future. Therefore, in the absence of any specific exception or defence in the theses and dissertations context, it is imperative that repositories and educational intuitions have an effective copyright management protocol/guideline, which works for PhD students and all interested parties, to ensure that correct copyright permissions are obtained where third party material is involved, and ETDs can ultimately be made available to the public in accordance with the law.

ACKNOWLEDGEMENTS

The authors owe special thanks to Professor Mark Perry and Professor Anne Fitzgerald for their assistance. The authors also acknowledge that this work is derived from research undertaken as part of the Open Access to Knowledge (OAK) Law Project: Creating a legal framework for copyright management of open access within the Australian academic and research sector (http://www. oaklaw.qut.edu.au).

NOTES

1. For an overview of the origins and evolution of copyright law, see Fitzgerald, A. & Fitzgerald, B. (2004). *Intellectual Property in Principle* (pp. 82–85); Atkinson, B. & Fitzgerald, B. (2011). *Copyright Law*, Vol. 1.

2. For other examples of copyright legislation, see the Copyright Act of 1976 in the US, the Copyright, Designs and Patents Act 1988 in the UK and the Copyright Law 2001 of the People's Republic of China.

3. It should also be noted that in commercial reality authors commonly assign copyright in their works to commercial entities such as publishers. In this regard, copyright also serves as an economic function to reward and encourage investment in the publishing sector.

4. See Article 6, Berne Convention for the Protection of Literary and Artistic Works (1886). For an overview of the moral rights regime under Australian law, see Fitzgerald, A. & Fitzgerald, B. (2004). *Intellectual Property in Principle* (pp. 118–124); Fitzgerald, B., et al. (2006). *OAK Law Project Report No 1: Creating a Legal Framework for Copyright Management of Open Access within the Australian Academic and Research Sector* (pp. 51–52).

5. For example, see *Snow* v. *The Eaton Centre Ltd* (1982) 70 C.P.R. (2d) 105 (Ont. H.C.); *Huston* v. *La Cinq* Cass. civ. 1re (28 May 1991). See also the notion of performers' rights which are a mix of both personal and economic rights and now exist in many jurisdictions.

6. WIPO Copyright Treaty, Geneva 1996.

7. Fitzgerald, A. & Fitzgerald, B. (2004). *Intellectual Property in Principle* (pp. 166–167); Fitzgerald, B., et al. (2006). *OAK Law Project Report No 1: Creating a Legal Framework for Copyright Management of Open Access within the Australian Academic and Research Sector* (pp. 37–43).

8. *Harper & Row* v. *Nation Enterprises*, 471 U.S. 539 (1985); *Statute of Anne 1709* (UK).

9. For an overview of the idea/expression dichotomy, Fitzgerald, A. & Fitzgerald, B. (2004). *Intellectual Property in Principle* (pp. 84–86).

10. See Fitzgerald, A. & Fitzgerald, B. (2004). *Intellectual Property in Principle* (pp. 95–104).

11. See Part III and IV of the Copyright Act 1968 (Cth).

12. 17 USC § 107.

13. 17 USC § 107.

14. For example , in the context of research or study see ss 40(1) and 103C(1) of the Copyright Act 1978 (Cth).

15. *CCH Canadian Ltd* v. *Law Society of Upper Canada* 2004 SCC 13.

16. See *University of London Press Ltd* v *University Tutorial Press Ltd* [1916] 2 Ch 601, 608.

17. See Fitzgerald, A. & Fitzgerald, B. (2004). *Intellectual Property in Principle* (pp. 97–98).

18. This will include protection under the moral rights and performers' rights (where applicable) provisions of the copyright law, although some countries have limited or no express moral rights protection, for example, the US. It should also be noted that electronic theses and dissertations will increasingly be made up of integrated or standalone copyright protected audio and/or visual material.

19. Fitzgerald, B., et al. (2006). *OAK Law Project Report No 1: Creating a Legal Framework for Copyright Management of Open Access within the Australian Academic and Research Sector* (pp. 170–171).

20. For a further discussion on this issue see, Monotti A and Ricketson S (2003) *Universities and Intellectual Property: Ownership and Exploitation*, Chapter 7.

21. See Fitzgerald, B., et al. (2006). *OAK Law Project Report No 1: Creating a Legal Framework for Copyright Management of Open Access within the Australian Academic and Research Sector* (p. 177).

22. Fitzgerald, B., et al. (2006). *OAK Law Project Report No 1: Creating a Legal Framework for Copyright Management of Open Access within the Australian Academic and Research Sector* (pp. 181–182).

23. See O'Brien, D., et al. (2007). *Copyright Guide for Research Students*.

24. See Fitzgerald, B., et al. (2006). *OAK Law Project Report No 1: Creating a Legal Framework for Copyright Management of Open Access within the Australian Academic and Research Sector* (p. 182).

25. For example, in Australia see ss 65 and 68 Copyright Act 1968 (Cth).

REFERENCES

Atkinson, B. & Fitzgerald, B. (2011). *Copyright Law* (Vol. 1). London: Ashgate.

Fitzgerald, A. & Fitzgerald, B. (2004). *Intellectual Property in Principle*. Sydney: Lawbook C Company, pp. 82–86, 95–104, 118–124, 166–167.

Fitzgerald, B., Fitzgerald, A., Perry, M., Kiel-Chisholm, S., Driscoll, E., Thampapillai, D., & Coates, J. (2006). *OAK Law Project Report No 1: Creating a Legal Framework for Copyright Management of Open Access within the Australian Academic and Research Sector.* Canberra: Elect Printing, pp. 37–43, 51–52, 170–171, 177.

Monotti, A. & Ricketson, S. (2003). *Universities and Intellectual Property: Ownership and Exploitation,* Chapter 7. New York: Oxford University Press.

12

Understanding Identity Representations in Multimodal Research

Pauline Hope Cheong

INTRODUCTION

Accompanying the alacritous developments in the Internet and web-based technologies are increased opportunities to engage in multimodal research experiences that are mediated online. Moreover, in light of 'media's intrusive ubiquity' (Silverstone, 2005, p. 191), the fecundity of transmediation whereby messages are appropriated, reconfigured and retransmitted across different media platforms (Jenkins, 2006), and the alleged emergence of the 'mediation of everything' (Livingstone, 2009), research into offline phenomena is now inextricably linked to its online manifestations and expressions, which must be understood in order to augment ecological validity in published studies. Correspondingly, we are witnessing new formats of research presentations including electronic theses and dissertations that strive to incorporate and present online and hybrid data.

Significant attention on digital theses has been placed on the improvement of library instructions, technical tools and open access mechanisms to enhance the preparation of student work into electronic formats for long-term archival and dissemination (Fox, McMillan, & Srinivasan, 2009). However, in the relatively recent and rapid push toward digital engagement in tertiary education, what are often obscured or overlooked are the challenges related to the creation of multimedia data and researcher participation in virtual worlds, which increasingly occupy a central place in multimodal research and global scholarship. Rice (2009) recommends that in light of the 'social and technological interdependencies of new media' which 'forces us to collaborate with people and systems not rewarded or designed to do so with us', research attention should be focused on understanding the developing, embedded and pervasive 'tensions among interdependence, collaboration and dysfunctional sociotechnical interactions' (p. 718). These tensions also apply to academic researcher experiences as scholars adopt and use new media, communication technology applications and platforms. New formats of mediated communication implicate new forms of social stratification, which constitutes secondary digital divides (Cheong, 2008) and multi-layered cultural challenges for e-learning and scholarship in higher education (Cheong & Martin, 2009). Beyond primary Internet access, wireless infrastructures and networked repositories that are increasingly available in tertiary institutions, virtual communication and participation represent new areas that affect access and agency for graduate students and researchers.

In this chapter, I discuss the intercultural dialectics that underlie digital participation, particularly the stratification processes in which researchers who engage multimodal research about, in, and through virtual communities may experience as an integral component of their scholarship and research. In the following section, I propose a critical cultural framework to understand the experience of multimodal research in order to unpack intercultural questioning, discovery, tensions and rewards implicated in online ethnography and data collection encounters. To illustrate these intercultural dialectics, I draw upon the small but growing corpus of new media and intercultural communication research, as well as interdisciplinary Internet and informatics studies. Next, I explicate how intercultural dialectics regarding the tensions between the personal–contextual, static–dynamic, differences–similarities and the privileged–disadvantaged affect the perception and communication of researchers' identities, with recent examples related to interaction in virtual worlds. Finally, I conclude the chapter with pedagogical implications as professors, lecturers and instructors encounter supervisory and mentoring prospects in the digital dissertation process.

INTERCULTURAL DIALECTICS AND SECONDARY DIGITAL DIVIDES

Attention to intercultural dialectics experienced by researchers helps highlight differences experienced within groups and individuals, since the notion of 'Internet use' may be broadened to include the management of conflicting tensions, uneven gains, multiple opportunities, ambivalences and challenges in online and offline experiences (Cheong, Martin, & Macfadyen, 2012). While there is a great deal of scholarly focus on the digital divides in terms of access and connections, there is a relative lack of critical research that examines secondary digital divides. More attention needs to be paid to the cultural complexity and transitivity in mediated interactions (Orgad, 2006), as well as the 'fluid relationality' between technical processes and social inequalities (Halford & Savage, 2010). This lacuna is significant for the digital dissertation process given how researchers may experience tensions in their self-representations and online interactions within digital platforms. Academic fieldwork in hierarchical virtual worlds can be understood as cross-cultural adaptations, fraught with potential and actual cultural tensions, including how researcher identities are formed and practiced in cyber-ethnography research in virtual spaces. According to Ward (2010), virtual worlds constitute real cultures as they manifest 'distinctive organizations of shared knowledge into schematic cognitive models' that construct significant meaning for interactants (p. 11). As such, newcomers and interactants, including researchers in the virtual cultures act as 'sojourners' who 'employ communication to acculturate themselves', 'accommodate the cultural others they encounter, and negotiate viable identities' (p. 1).

From a critical perspective, analysis of intercultural dynamics shaping online participation in multimodal experiences is crucial to understanding the data collection, composition and interpretation process undertaken by graduate students and researchers. The practice of cross-cultural adaptation by researchers who want to undertake mediated fieldwork is often underscored by stress and growth as they encounter diversity in other interactants' demographics, backgrounds, identities, affiliations, interests and competence. Access to online communities does not automatically equate to empowering research outcomes. Post-Internet adoption divides exist and usually intensify as they are enfolded in historical social stratification patterns (van Dijk, 2004). In an attempt to describe and interpret the contradictions in research endeavors in virtual environments, a dialectical intercultural perspective is advanced here to draw attention to the dynamic character of online cultures (Lunenfeld, 2000), as well as our knowledge about cultures and communication and cultural 'others' (Collier, 2005; Halualani, Mendoza, & Drzewiecka, 2009).

A dialectical intercultural perspective is a meta-theoretical framework. This framework focuses on the simultaneous presence of two relational forces of interaction in recognition of their seeming opposite, interdependent and complementary aspects, akin to eastern philosophies on the completion of relative polarities. Communication scholars have historically applied the dialectical perspective in face-to-face interpersonal relationships (Baxter, 1990; Baxter and Montgomery, 1996), organizational settings (Putnam, 2004) and critical rhetorical analysis (Whittle, Mueller, & Mangan 2008). Borrowing from Mikhail Bakhtin's (1981) work on language and culture, Martin and Nakayama (1999) offered the dialectic perspective as a way to advance research of cultural communication phenomena beyond rigid traditional paradigmatic scholarship. Dialectics in intercultural communication research refer to the processual, relational and contradictory logics of intercultural knowledge and practices, including the cultural–individual, personal–contextual, differences–similarities, static–dynamic, history/past–present/future and privilege–disadvantage dimensions (Martin & Nakayuma, 2009).

Here, the notion of mediated intercultural dialectics in multimodal research is employed given that the Internet affords liberating and dominating, empowering and fragmenting, universalizing but non-totalizing research experiences, which are produced by and in turn produce culture. Interactive norms in cyberspace may be invented and resisted but at the same time reproduced in ways that are retrograde. Such invention implies that as researchers enter and interact in virtual worlds, advisors and advisees alike need to embrace the notion of both – and, not an either – or orientation to cultural tensions and dis/empowerment.

In spite of the celebratory rhetoric of increased informational retrieval online, not all online experiences are equal and beneficial. Assumptions that all scholars who use the Internet will garner returns, in the form of greater access to data and knowledge they value and to enhanced publication chances, are problematic. Cultural factors, including intercultural dialectics implicating researchers' identities and the intersectionality of race, class, age and gender, may serve as secondary digital divide factors to influence researchers' agency and their ability to choose and enact online interactions. In particular, the 'Matthew Effect' suggests that the digital divide is a newer manifestation of the greatest benefits accruing to resource rich individuals who employ new technologies sooner and more productively, thereby increasing the extent they reap benefits from going online (Robinson, DiMaggio, & Hargittai, 2003). In parallel, a 'research Matthew effect' may function to widen the disparities in the digital dissertation process. For researchers engaged and immersed in new media research, the multimodal and multilayered nature of virtual worlds and their complex technological affordances for self-representations compel attention to the tensions that accompany the performativity of their identities (Latour, 2005). Tensions in self-representations exist because online identities are still often constituted through gender, race, class and other markers of differences (Gajjala, Rybas, & Altman, 2007). In the next section, I discuss two key views on mediated identities and subsequently, the role in which various intercultural dialectics play in virtual worlds, with implications for researcher engagement.

CULTURAL IDENTIFICATIONS AND TENSIONS ONLINE

Participation in new digital environments is conventionally understood to be effortless and expedient, particularly for younger students and scholars who have been labeled 'digital natives' (Palfrey & Gasser, 2008). In this sense, younger researcher cohorts are perceived to be more proficient and amenable to online research processes than older faculty members. In parallel, the dominant view on researcher engagement online focuses on its concealment and adept management, related to the erasure of identity derived from anonymity afforded by new technologies and the liberatory manipulation of selves created and shaped through computer mediated communication. The online environment is posited as Oldenburg's 'great good place', which hosts equitable, voluntary, informal and convivial 'third places' of sociability between people of different cultures (Soukup, 2006; Steinkuehler & Williams, 2006). Virtual worlds are commonly described (and critiqued) as the post-racial 'new world'. This 'new frontier' is conceived as a space where individuals are able to re-figure and form identities in self-expression without corporeal constrains (Gunkel & Gunkel, 2009). In a related manner, it is a common belief that online experiences are conducive for minority researchers, who are protected from offline disparities. For cultural 'others' and those occupying marginal standpoints, cyberspace has been described as a safe place for the expression of their ethnic identity (Mitra, 2006).

Yet an alternative perspective regards researcher engagement online as contested since identity is contextually embedded, negotiated, co-created and challenged through online interaction. Multiple identifications are constructed and emergent in social and relational contexts (Collier, 2005). Identity negotiation is a 'transactional process whereby individuals in an intercultural situation attempt to assert, define, modify, challenge, and/or support their own and others' desired self images' (Ting-Toomey, 1999, p. 40). Kennedy (2006) for instance argues that anonymity online exists but to a certain degree. This is because conceptualizations of the free floating, unidentified self are limited by developments in digital media that are becoming more integrated. These convergent spaces increasingly tie online and offline personas which are then subject to corporeal and corporate influences in online environments. Similarly, Brookey (2009) in an expressively titled essay, *Paradise Crashed*, emphasizes that disjunctures between promotional hype related to Internet use and digital praxis exist. He underscores how virtual communities are riddled with reproductions of corporeal limitations and the import of real world disparities in terms of social roles, performances and compensations.

In this way, mediated intercultural dialectics related to researchers' identities encompass the complexities of both empowering and disempowering developments. Because cultural identifications are expressed and emerge online, virtual worlds are not just utopic, dystopic or ontologically neutral spaces that are conducive for research, as some researcher interactants are attributed less privileged identities and traits to varying extents. Correspondingly, mediated intercultural dialectics involve the enactment and presentation of identities through processes of avowal and ascription online. Avowal refers to the self an individual portrays whereas ascription is the process by which others attribute identities to an individual, commonly via the expression of stereotypes which are widely held beliefs of some groups, and prejudice and racism through symbols, norms and labels (Collier, 2005). Online intercultural conflicts occur when there are felt and expressed incongruities between avowed and ascribed identities. These conflicts can manifest in uncivil discourse and disruptive behaviors like flaming and griefing which can affect researcher experiences. Flaming refers to negative antisocial behaviors, including the expression of hostility, the use of profanity and the venting of strong emotions (Thompsen, 1996) while griefing refers to the intentional harassment of online interactants (Warner & Raiter, 2005; Foo & Koivisto, 2004).

Given that intercultural dialectics are by definition plural and that diverse forms of intercultural dialectics interrelate (Martin & Nakayuma, 2010), in the next section, the treatment of researcher dis/empowerment in the context of mediated identities will be discussed via the personal–contextual, static–dynamic, differences–similarities and privilege–disadvantage dialectics. Specifically, I explicate these intercultural dialectics and illustrate their dynamics and asymmetries using contemporary examples related to mediated identities in virtual worlds. The dialectics refer to and expand upon examples discussed in a commentary on identity performances in virtual worlds (Cheong & Gray, 2011), since they are a fertile and emergent platform for digital media research.

In brief, virtual worlds refer to environments utilizing three-dimensional and Internet technologies to bring people together in real-time. In light of contemporary multimedia convergence, this significant and increasingly popular site of study encompasses stand-alone games, local and wide network games, multiplayer and massively multiplayer games, massively multiplayer online role-games, online console gaming and virtual social worlds (de Freitas and Griffiths, 2008). Popular examples with thousands and even millions of subscribers include *World of Warcraft*, *EverQuest*, *Final Fantasy*, *Xbox Live*, *Second Life* and the like. While earlier online communication was mostly text-based, many newer virtual world platforms have textual and audio capabilities and are three-dimensionally graphical, 'modeled after real-world cities and have large public spaces as well as buildings with clearly identifiable functions ... As such, they represent a fascinating laboratory to observe sociability online ...' (Ducheneaut, Moore, & Nickell, 2007, p. 3). As virtual worlds expand and develop, their potential for facilitating synchronous interaction between multiple users increases (Castronova, 2005; Seay, Jerome, Lee, & Kraut, 2004). Beyond instrumental tasks, interactants in virtual worlds are increasingly required to engage in relational activities with strangers and friends that encourage them to develop collaborations (Nardi & Harris, 2006) and maintain overlapping community bonds with their offline identities and relationships (Lehdonvirta, 2010). These social affordances of virtual worlds allow researchers and scholars to create identities, histories, interpersonal relationships and observe rich discourse via multiple and immersive communication modes.

MEDIATED INTERCULTURAL DIALECTICS AND THE CONSTRUCTION OF IDENTITY

The mediated personal–contextual dialectic involves the role of personal characteristics as well as contextual features of intercultural relationships, as identity and social roles are enacted in virtual environments to give meaning to online messages. The identification/s created by interactants has/ve certain personal qualities, but emergent tensions can also be experienced with role enactments within virtual environments. For instance, various online activities and tasks involve individual personality and motivations as well as compliance to group activity, rules and requirements. In an example in virtual worlds, massive multi-player online role playing games have complex group activities and specific and hierarchical role structures (Ducheneaut, Yee, Nickell, & Moore, 2007). These online group activities include: (a) mobs, which are usually formed by players who need to complete a quest, to experience points of avatar promotion, (b) raids five man groups that are needed to finish the most challenging in game tasks, and (c) guilds which require a minimum of ten players to form. Community sanctions regulate guild rankings, membership and recruitment, status and prestige (Kaluza & Golik, 2008). Therefore, the performances of specific social roles in virtual worlds also implicate intergroup competence, which entail the expression of social identities in practices that are perceived to be appropriate for intergroup interactions (Baldwin & Hunt, 2002). In this way, researchers and interactants online may experience and observe the need to negotiate their social roles with in/outgroup tensions, when communicating with others in virtual environments.

Contextual features affecting individual and group game participation also interrelate with the static–dynamic dialectic, whereby intercultural communication tends to be at once static and dynamic. Some cultural and communication patterns are relatively stable while other aspects of cultural identification shift over time. For example, task performance is a cultural constant in many virtual worlds, although conditions of interactivity may change. Online environment settings and interactive user interfaces allow for opportunities to construct multiple and context-dependent personas. Talamo and Ligorno (2001) found that users in virtual worlds strategically exploit cues and technological resources available to perform tasks and interact with others while dialogically creating and repositioning their identities. The dynamic evolution of virtual groups is also affected by its size, history and status, which are key factors that shape the chronemics of their formation, growth and demise (Chien-Hsun, Chuen-Tsai & Hsiesh, 2008). Thus, although online interactions may reflect differences in individual personality and motivations, there are contextual constraints on participation tied to normative group structures and sanctions, as well as cyclical developments in the creation, development and dissolution of virtual communities online.

It is also instructive to attend to the differences-similarities dialectic in digital participation since online intercultural communication is characterized by both differences between groups of people but also various similarities in human experiences and ways of interaction. Emphasizing the similarities can negate cultural variations while looking at the differences can lead to identity ascriptions that reaffirm cultural stereotypes online. Of particular interest is research on groups using computer mediated communication which suggests a status leveling or equalization effect in terms of participation. These scholars argue that the absence of non-verbal cues in some forms of textual computer-mediated-communication suggest no 'line of sight data' (e.g. information on racial, ethnic, age, gender, class social cultural identities) (Postmes, Spears, & Lea, 1998) that can minimize prejudicial reactions. Amichai-Hamburger and McKenna (2006) suggest that virtual communication facilitates more fruitful intergroup contact than face to face communication as interactants experience reduced levels of anxiety and the lowering of costs to enable positive intercultural contact between geographically distant partners. Yet more recent scholarship also highlights how stereotypes may be recontextualized in virtual worlds and lead to intercultural conflicts and prejudices developed out of perceived threats and negative experiences with cultural others. Avatar culture can reinforce sexual and heternormative gender norms that are rooted, practised and commoditized in corporeal contexts (Brookey & Cannon, 2009). At the same time, online worlds allow users to function through avatars, which often appear similar to their sense of an ideal self that embodies socially desirable and personally favorably attributes (Bessière, Seay, & Kiesler, 2007). Online intercultural communication also includes non-verbal codes which are reflective of offline cultural norms. Non-verbal codes like eye gaze transfer and cultural proxemics of avatars involve intercultural communication via spatial positioning of interpersonal distance (Yee, Bailenson, Urbanek, Chang, & Merget, 2007).

Furthermore, researchers who are online interactants need to negotiate the differences–similarities dialectic, in particular when ascriptions about cultural others takes the form of essentializing views from visual and linguistic profiling alongside contrastive comparisons between us and them online. On multimodal virtual worlds, visual profiling is typically related to the personification of online interactants' characters via three-dimensional representational or two-dimensional iconic avatars. Visual profiling is manifest in biased portrayals of avatar content in virtual worlds. Although avatar culture simultaneously provides a reflexive recess with pre-existing facets of social identity, some scholars stress that it recurrently affirms group differences and stereotypes or cybertypes, particularly as they relate to gender and sexuality (Webb, 2001; Nakamura, 2002). For example, Downs and Smith (2010) found that female characters were more likely to be represented by avatars showing partial nudity, have unrealistic body images and wear sexually revealing clothing. In virtual world environments, gender stereotypes of male characters as aggressive and female characters as sexualized are perpetuated by online interactants' perceptions that these stereotypes are acceptable (Brenick, Henning, Killen, O'Connor, & Collins, 2007) and commonly held (Dill & Thill, 2007). In addition, racial identifications matter in virtual interactions because the construction and deployment of racial stereotypes tends to affirm the status quo, and augment racial inequality. Sisler (2006) for example highlights how digital stereotypical representations of Arab and Muslims as hostile, cruel or exotic leads to the erasure of diverse ethnic and religious identities, disadvantaging interactants who are non-White.

Accordingly, within the unequal power structures of virtual world cultures, attention needs to be paid to intercultural dialectics that influence online research processes. For instance in relation to gender, Kendall (2009) writes that in the online research process, 'sexual attention both regulates and delineates status positions. Unwanted sexual attention that women receive positions them as sexual objects, limiting their role and status. However, sexual attention also illuminates finer distinctions, positioning some women to benefit more from the existing hierarchy than others' (pp. 110–111). As such, vigilant negotiation of identities is warranted as female researchers must manage their own status with regard to their gendered identity within hierarchical constraints, particularly on online environments that value hegemonic masculinity over emphasized femininity.

In this way, cultural ascriptions also implicate the privilege–disadvantage dialectics as power is negotiated in online communication where some identities may be simultaneously privileged and disadvantaged, or be privileged in some contexts and disadvantaged in others. This dialectic enjoins us to be aware of social differentiation and power relations that shape interactions of researchers from different cultural groups, while acknowledging the structural role of sociohistorical contexts in knowledge development in virtual spaces. Virtual game environments have historically reinforced Eurocentric, masculine, hegemonic notions of power, privilege and inequality (Chan, 2005). The power structure of the game industry is a predominantly white and secondarily Asian, male dominated elite (Fron, Fullerton, Morle, & Pearce, 2007). This economic and cultural characteristic tilts the online playing field in favor of majority participants and subjugates various aspects of minority identities. Everett (2009) points out that key stakeholders invested in the gaming industry including the popular media, often depict the typical gamer as the adolescent white male. Analysis of avatar representations show a systematic over-representation of males, white and adults and under-representation of females, Hispanics, Native Americans, children and the elderly (Williams, Martins, Consalvo, & Ivory, 2009). This disjuncture is significant to note because demographic data as well as recent analysis indicate the popularity of virtual games among older interactants in their thirties and more intensive online participation by females (Williams, Yee, & Caplan, 2008).

Given the globalization of e-learning and scholarship (Garcel-avila, 2005), it is significant to also note how intercultural dialectics implicate mediated identities in terms of linguistic backgrounds that are tied to power and political histories. Asymmetries in intercultural dialectics function when in-group members who attempt to maintain a positive group identity through language alienate linguistic minorities. Chua (2009) contends that while open communication is fundamental to the creation of cohesive collective identity in virtual communities, emergent regulations and censorship practices on speech is enacted to silence cultural others who are perceived to be intimidating and adversarial to other groups. Although online settings are increasingly cosmopolitan and potentially open to participants of different linguistic backgrounds, the *de facto* dominance of the use of English language as a currency of exchange has historically existed in virtual world interactions among members of diverse linguistic backgrounds (Allwood & Schroeder, 2000). Thus, non-native English interactants may require language socialization for their identity development and management in online settings (Thorne, Black, & Sykes, 2009).

Beyond textual interactions in online environments, the recent addition of voice communication brings an added set of countervailing influences on identity and online participation. Linguistic profiling is related to the perception of language competency in textual expressions as well as increasingly to vocal intonations as more interactants use voice over Internet protocol in computer networks to carry digitalized voice signals. Experimental research findings suggests that guild players interact with others from diverse backgrounds when using voice (Williams et al., 2006), and it was found that while a combination of voice and text facilitated stronger trust and liking among interactants, the formation of in-group insularity over time curtailed bridging engagements with others who have different textual and linguistic practices (Williams, Caplan, & Xiong, 2007). Moreover, auto-ethnographic accounts from the standpoint of a female, African–American graduate student researcher also explain how linguistic profiling leads to hate speech in virtual worlds (Gray, 2010). Gamers who engage in racism typically seek to confirm the linguistic profile and racial position of players from language cues by explicitly questioning and calling out their identity, provoking them via bringing up racial stereotypes and labels in online discourse, and then instigating parties to conflicts.

Finally, it is pertinent to note how intercultural collaborations in virtual communities may be affected by stereotypes linked to nationality and ethnic identifications associated with perceived skills and motivation to engage with others. For instance, Kaluza and Golik (2008) documented conflicts between European and Asian players as the former group displayed racism and hateful expressions toward: (a) Chinese who were labeled 'farmers' as they were perceived to play primarily for profit to sell their in-game currency, rather than for leisure, and (b) Indians who were labeled as 'e-bays' as they were perceived to have compensated for their lack of technical skills and motivation by purchasing their highly skilled avatar online. Nakamura (2009) also found profiling activity and racial wars online since the purchase and possession of others' avatars, subsequently leads to the suppression or denial of avatarial self-possession by some communities like Chinese players. In this way, virtual world participation extends offline structural and cultural inequalities.

In sum, as illustrated above, intercultural privilege–disadvantage dialectics intimately intertwine with digitally mediated identities, with impact on digital participation. Correspondingly, tensions in self-presentations lead some online interactants to practise constant monitoring, self-policing and censorship in their discourse for fear of being discriminated and excluded in select virtual spaces

(Chua, 2009; Nakamura, 2002). In practical terms, the fieldworker needs to be aware that he or she will be sensitive to certain intercultural dialectics, affected by some asymmetries, while being oblivious to others. For researchers' inhibiting virtual worlds, the extent to which they suppress or disclose their majority and/or minority identities may risk their credibility and therefore affect their socialization, learning and engagement.

CONCLUSION

New modes of virtual engagement bring new opportunities and possibilities for multimodal research and diversity in global scholarship. Intercultural dialectics of digitally mediated identities have heuristic value for the electronic dissertation process because they outline critical points of departure from attention and discourse centered on digitalization, technical infrastructure, institutional practices and organizational logistics, which tend to separate social inequalities from technical processes. Before the digital point-of-publication there are necessary research practices that increasingly implicate scholarly engagement in virtual spaces. This chapter discussed how intercultural dialectics may function as secondary digital divides to influence the extent and multiplicity of online participation at the interface level and beyond. Consideration of the ways that intercultural dialectics implicate digitally mediated identities asks us to reflect carefully on cultural dynamics and asymmetries. As several examples in this article demonstrates, in the latest digital environments like virtual worlds, accessibility and engagement are nonetheless shaped by cultural ascriptions, underscoring the complex interrelationships with dynamic cultural positioning and dialogical interactions with digital affordances.

Accordingly, members of the academy need to recognize that intercultural dialectics are real and inherent in multimodal research and cannot be simply eliminated or resolved. Academic advisorship could be sensitized to respecting the mediated fieldwork opportunities that extend students' communication and research experiences but also to differences in digital participation that are dependent on varied factors and literacies, including researchers' standpoints and their negotiation of mediated intercultural dialectics. The exploration of 'rich points' in 'teaching the conflicts' beyond 'teaching the norms' (Belz, 2005) in patterns of online engagement is helpful for opening up active interpretation to a multiplicity of emerging multimodal research experiences. As such, encouragement of graduate students toward research reflexivity and articulation of their experiences may provoke increased understanding of the cultural dynamics and tensions that confront them. As Markham and Baym (2008) argue, compounding the challenges of Internet inquiry and constructing research studies in a mediated age is the slim discussion dedicated to reflexive responses to methodological challenges in research reports and peer-reviewed journals. This absence of discussion or debate about research participation tied to challenges and tensions they have to negotiate, in effect suppresses how the researchers' online experiences and emotions inform their work. Hence, it is important to provide budding scholars an avenue in electronic theses to discuss and document the processes that underlie their production from fieldwork to composition, particularly challenges which may seem opaque to administrators and supervisors unfamiliar with virtual worlds that are increasingly engaged for research in a digital and multimodal age. Ongoing naming and mindfulness of intercultural dialectics underscores the dual nature of scholarly research which is rewarding and challenging, confining and liberating (Allen, Orbe, & Olivas, 1999) and asks us to carefully reconsider the liberatory and friction-free promise of digital scholarship.

REFERENCES

Allen, B. J., Orbe, M. P., & Olivas, M. R. (1999). The complexity of our tears: dis/enchantment and (in) difference in the academy. *Communication Theory, 9*, 402–429.

Allwood, J. & Schroeder, R. (2000). Intercultural communication in a virtual environment. *Intercultural Communication, 4*. http://www.immi.se/jicc/index.php/jicc/article/view/142/109

Amichai-Hamburger, Y. & McKenna, K. Y. A. (2006). The contact hypothesis reconsidered: Interacting via the Internet. *Journal of Computer-Mediated Communication*, 11, article 7. http://jcmc.indiana.edu/vol11/issue3/amichai-hamburger.html

Bakhtin, M. M. (1981). *The Dialogic Imagination: Four Essays by M. M. Bakhtin* (trans. by C. Emerson & M. Holquist) (M. Holquist, Ed.) Austin, TX: University of Texas Press.

Baldwin, J. R. & Hunt, S. K. (2002). Information seeking behavior in intercultural and intergroup communication. *Human Communication Research, 28*, 272–286.

Baxter, L. A. (1990). Dialectical contradictions in relationship development. *Journal of Social and Personal Relationships, 7*, 69–88.

Baxter, L. A. & Montgomery, B. (1996). *Relating: Dialogues and Dialectics.* New York: Guilford.

Belz, J. A. (2005). Intercultural questioning, discovery, and tension in internet-mediated language learning partnerships. *Language and Intercultural Communication, 5*, 3–39.

Bessière, K., Seay, F., & Kiesler, S. (2007). The ideal elf: Identity exploration in world of warcraft. *Cyberpsychology and Behavior, 10*, 530–535.

Brenick, A., Henning, A., Killen, M., O'Connor, A., & Collins, M. (2007). Social evaluations of stereotypic images in video games: Unfair, legitimate, or just entertainment. *Youth Society, 38*, 395–419.

Brookey, R. A. (2009). Paradise crashed: Rethinking MMORPG's and other virtual worlds. An introduction. *Critical Studies in Media Communication, 2*, 101–103.

Brookey, R. A. & Cannon, K. (2009). Sex lives in second life. *Critical Studies in Media Communication, 26*, 145–164.

Castronova, E. (2005). *Synthetic Worlds: The Business and Culture of Online Games.* Chicago, IL: The University of Chicago Press.

Chan, D. (2005). Playing with race: The ethics of racialized representations in E-Games. The Ethics of E-Games. *International Review of Information Ethics*, 4, 24–30.

Cheong, P. H. (2008). The young and techless? Internet use and problem solving behaviors among young adults in Singapore. *New Media and Society, 10*, 771–791.

Cheong, P. H. & Martin, J. N. (2009). Cultural implications of E-learning access (and divides): Teaching an intercultural communication course online. In B. A. Olaniran (Ed.), *Cases on Successful E-Learning Practices in the Developed and Developing World: Methods for Global Information Economy* (pp. 78–91). Hershey, PA: IGI Global.

Cheong, P.H. & Gray, K. (2011). Mediated Intercultural dialectics: Identity Perceptions and Performances in Virtual Worlds. *Journal of International and Intercultural Communication*, 4(4), 265–271.

Cheong, P.H., Martin, J.N., & Macfadyen, L. (2012). Mediated intercultural communication matters: Understanding new media, dialectics and social change. In P.H. Cheong, J.N. Martin, & L. Macfadyen, (Eds.), *New Media and Intercultural Communication: Identity, Community and Politics*. pp. 1–20. New York: Peter Lang.

Chien-Hsun, C., Chuen-Tsai, S., & Hsieh, J. (2008). Player guild dynamics and evolution in massively multiplayer online games. *Cyberpsychology and Behavior, 11*, 293–301.

Chua, C. E. H. (2009). Why do virtual communities regulate speech. *Communication Monographs, 76*, 234–261.

Collier, M. J. (2005). Theorizing cultural identifications: Critical updates and continuing evolution. In W. B. Gudykunst (Ed.), *Theorizing About Intercultural Communication* (pp. 235–256). Thousand Oaks, CA: Sage.

de Freitas, S. & Griffiths, M. (2008). The convergence of gaming practices with other media forms: What potential for learning? A review of literature. *Learning, Media and Technology, 33*, 11–20.

Dill, K. & Thill, K. (2007). Video game characters and the socialization of gender roles: Young people's perception mirror sexist media depictions. *Sex Roles, 57*, 851–864.

Downs, E. & Smith, S. L. (2010). Keeping abreast of hypersexuality: A video game character content analysis, *Sex Roles, 62*, 721–733.

Ducheneaut, N., Moore, R., & Nickell, E. (2007). Virtual 'third places': A case study of sociability in massively multiplayer games. *Computer Supported Cooperative Work, 16*, 129–166.

Ducheneaut, N., Yee, N., Nickell, E., & Moore, R. (2007). The life and death of online gaming communities: A look at guilds in World of Warcraft. Paper presented at CHI 2007 Proceedings, San Jose, CA.

Everett, A. (2009). *Digital Diaspora: A Race For Cyberspace*. State University of New York Press: New York.

Foo, C. Y. & Koivisto, E. M. (2004). Defining grief play in MMORPG's: Player and developer perceptions. *The Australasian Computing Education Conference, 74*, 245–250.

Fox, E. A., McMillan, G., & Srinivasan, V. (2009). Electronic theses and dissertations: Progress, issues and prospects. In T. Luke & J. Hunsinger (Eds.), *Putting Knowledge To Work And Letting Information Play*. Blacksburg, VA: The Center for Digital Discourse and Culture.

Fron, J., Fullerton, T., Morie, J. F., & Pearce, C. (2007). The hegemony of play. *Situated Play, Proceedings of DiGRA 2007 Conference*. Authors and Digital Games Research Association, pp. 1–10.

Gajjala, R., Rybas, N., & Altman M. (2007). Epistemologies of doing: E-merging selves online. *Feminist Media Studies, 7*, 209–213.

Garcel-avila, J. (2005). The internationalization of higher education. A paradigm for global citizenry. *Journal of Studies International Education, 9*, 121–136.

Gray, K. (2010). Racializing gender in Xbox live: The need for a black cyber feminist theory. Paper presented at the 4th International Multi-Conference on Society, Cybernetics, and Informatics, Florida.

Gunkel, D. J. & Gunkel, A. H. (2009). Terra Nova 2.0 – The new worlds of MMORPGs. *Critical Studies in Media Communication, 26*, 104–127.

Halford, S. & Savage, M. (2010). Reconsidering digital social inequality. *Information, Communication and Society, 13*, 937–955.

Halualani, R. T., Mendoza, S. L., & Drzewiecka, J. A. (2009). 'Critical' junctures in intercultural communication studies: A review. *The Review of Communication, 9*, 17–35.

Jenkins, H. (2006). *Convergence Culture: When Old and New Media Collide*. New York: New York University Press.

Kaluza, M. & Golik, E. (2008). Intercultural communication and the Internet. The role of intercultural communication in internet societies. *Informacijos Mokslai, 45*, 22–34.

Kendall, L. (2009). How do issues of gender and sexuality influence the structures and processes of qualitative internet research? In A. Markham & N. Baym (Eds.), *Internet Inquiry: Conversations About Method* (pp. 99–118) Thousand Oaks, CA: Sage.

Kennedy, H. (2006). Beyond anonymity, or future directions for internet identity research. *New Media and Society, 8*, 859–876.

Latour, B. (2005). *Reassembling the Social: An Introduction to Actor-Network Theory.* New York: Oxford University Press.

Lehdonvirta, V. (2010). Virtual worlds don't exist: Questioning the dichotomous approach in MMO Studies. *Game Studies: The International Journal of Computer Game Research, 10,* http://gamestudies. org/1001/articles/lehdonvirta

Livingstone, S. (2009). On the mediation of everything: ICA presidential address 2008. *Journal of Communication, 59,* 1–18.

Lunenfeld, P. (Ed.). (2000). *The Digital Dialectic: New Essays on New Media.* Cambridge, MA: The MIT Press.

Markham, A. N. & Baym, N.K. (Eds.). (2008). *Internet Inquiry: Conversations About Method.* Thousand Oaks, CA: Sage.

Martin, J. N. & Nakayama, T. K. (1999). Thinking dialectically about culture and communication. *Communication Theory, 9,* 1–25.

Martin, J. N. & Nakayama, T. K. (2009). *Intercultural Communication in Contexts.* New York: McGraw-Hill.

Martin, J. N. & Nakayama, T. K. (2010). Intercultural dialectics revisited. In T. K. Nakayama & R. T. Halualani (Eds.), *The Handbook of Intercultural Communication,* (pp. 59–83). Oxford, UK: Wiley–Blackwell.

Mitra, A. (2006). Towards finding a cybernetic safe place: Illustrations from people of Indian origin. *New Media and Society, 8,* 251–268.

Nakamura, L. (2002). *Cybertypes: Race, Ethnicity, and Identity on the Internet.* New York: Routledge.

Nakamura, L. (2009). Don't hate the player, hate the game. The racialization of labor in world of warcraft. *Critical Studies in Media Communications, 2,* 128–144.

Nardi, B. & Harris, J. (2006). Strangers and friends: Collaborative play in World of Warcraft. In *Proc. CSCW 2006* (pp. 149–158). New York, NY: ACM Press.

Orgad, S. (2006). The cultural dimensions of online communication: A study of breast cancer patients' Internet spaces. *New Media & Society, 8,* 877–899.

Palfrey, J. & Gasser, U. (2008). *Born Digital: Understanding the First Generation of Digital Natives.* New York: Basic Books.

Postmes, T., Spears, R., & Lea, M. (1998), Breaching or building social boundaries? SIDE-effects of computer-mediated communication. *Communication Research, 25,* 689–715.

Putnam, L. L. (2004). Dialectical tensions and rhetorical tropes in negotiations. *Organization Studies, 25,* 35–54.

Rice, R. (2009). Sociological and technological interdependencies of new media. *Journal of Computer-Mediated Communication, 14,* 714–719.

Robinson, J., DiMaggio, P., & Hargittai, E. (2003). New social survey perspectives on the digital divide, *IT & Society, 1(Summer),* 1–22.

Seay, A. F., Jerome, W. J., Lee, K. S., & Kraut, R. E. (2004). Project massive: A study of online gaming communities. In: *Proceedings of CHI 2004* (pp. 1421–1424). New York, NY: ACM Press.

Silverstone, R. (2005). The sociology of mediation and communication. In C. J. Calhoun, C. Rojek, & B. S. Turner (Eds.), *The SAGE Handbook of Sociology* (pp. 188–207). London: Sage.

Sisler, V. (2006). Representation and self-representation: Arabs and muslims in digital games. In M. Santorineos, N. Dimitriadi, & Fournos (Eds.), *Gaming Realities: A Challenge for Digital Culture,* (pp. 85–92). Athens.

Soukup, C. (2006). Computer-mediated communication as a virtual third place: Building Oldenburg's great good places on the world wide web. *New Media and Society, 8,* 421–440.

Steinkuehler, C. & Williams, D. (2006). Where everybody knows your (screen) name: Online games as 'third places'. *Journal of Computer-Mediated Communication, 11,* http://jcmc.indiana.edu/vol11/ issue4/steinkuehler.html

Talamo, A. & Ligorio, B. (2001). Strategic identities in cyberspace. *CyberPsychology and Behavior, 4*, 109–122.

Thompsen, P. A. (1996). What's fueling the flames in cyberspace: A social influence model. In L. Strate, R. Jacobson, & S. B. Gibson (Eds.), *Communication and Cyberspace: Social Interaction in an Electronic Environment* (pp. 297–315). Creskill, NJ: Hampton Press.

Ting-Toomey, S. (1999). *Communicating Across Cultures.* New York: The Guilford Press.

Thorne, S. L., Black, R. W., & Sykes, J. (2009). Second language use, socialization, and learning in Internet interest communities and online gaming. *Modern Language Journal*, 93, 802–821.

van Dijk, J. (2004). Divides in succession: Possession, skills, and use of new media for societal participation. In E. P. Bucy & J. E. Newhagen (Eds.), *Media Access: Social and Psychological Dimensions of New Technology Use* (pp. 233–254). Mahwah, NJ: Lawrence Erlbaum Associates.

Ward, M. (2010). Avatars and sojourners: Explaining the acculturation of newcomers to multiplayer online games as cross-cultural adaptations. *Journal of Intercultural Communication*, 23, http://www. immi.se/jicc/index.php/jicc/article/view/205

Warner, D. & Raiter, M. (2005). Social context in massively-multiplayer online Games (MMOGs): Ethical questions in shared space. *International Review of Information Ethics*, 46–52.

Webb, S. (2001). Avatarculture: Narrative, power and identity in virtual world environments. *Information, Communication and Society, 4*, 560–594.

Whittle, A., Mueller, F., & Mangan, A. (2008). In search of subtlety: Discursive devices and rhetorical Competence. *Management Communication Quarterly, 22*, 99–122.

Williams, D., Caplan, S., & Xiong, L. (2007). Can you hear me now? The impact of voice in an online gaming community. *Human Communication Research, 33*, 427–449.

Williams, D., Ducheneaut, N., Xiong, L., Zhang, Y., Yee, N., & Nickell, E. (2006). From tree house to barracks: The social life of guilds in World of Warcraft. *Games & Culture, 1*, 338–361.

Williams, D., Martins, N., Consalvo, M., & Ivory, J. (2009). The virtual census: Representations of gender, race, and age in video games. *New Media and Society, 11*, 815–834.

Williams, D., Yee, N., & Caplan, S. E. (2008). Who plays, how much, and why? debunking the stereotypical gamer profile. *Journal of Computer-Mediated Communication, 13*, 993–1018.

Yee, N., Bailenson, J. N., Urbanek, M., Chang, F., & Merget, D. (2007). The unbearable likeness of being digital: The persistence of nonverbal social norms in online virtual environments. *The Journal of CyberPsychology and Behavior, 10*, 115–121.

13

The Social Life of Digital Texts in Multimodal Research

Myrrh Domingo

INTRODUCTION

All about our digitally connected world interactive texts abound that display new ways for making meaning across social contexts (Appadurai, 1996). This assertion takes into account that what counts as text includes both permanent (e.g. published books, written reports) and performative (e.g. oral storytelling, informal conversations) formats (Wade & Moje, 2001). With the rising use of digital technologies[1] and the Internet, performative texts are now more commonly practiced in most urban settings. It is not uncommon to see people communicating via text messaging or even video chatting using FaceTime on their smart phones. Daily routines now often involve reading current events via digital newsprint, retrieving mail using the Internet, and interacting with friends through social networking sites like Facebook or Twitter and sometimes even meeting virtually on Skype. As these examples demonstrate, digital texts communicate in new ways that no longer privilege static print as the primary conveyor of meaning (Hull & Nelson, 2005). This is to say that multimodality combined with new media technologies extends grammars to also include interactive features (Mills, 2009; Pahl, 2007). For example, websites and blogs (e.g. YouTube, WordPress) permit layering of sound, image, music, among other modes for articulating ideas beyond inscribed language (Hull & Nelson, 2005; Kress, 2010).

Whereas print-based approaches to reading and writing often restrict the movement of meaning to fit onto the linear page, digital spaces more readily embody noisy and moving[2] textual elements (Kress, 2010). This evolved notion of literacy includes more participatory engagement with digital texts that draw on multiple senses for articulating and receiving meaning (Howes, 2009). As such, written words can now be 'touched' or 'clicked' on screen to reveal hyperlinks, play audio and video files that allow readers to migrate across digital spaces (Domingo, 2011b). In what ways does this shift in textual production also transform the process for meaning making? How might dissertations and theses be re-envisioned given this shift in textual production?

To attend to these questions, this chapter explores the ways in which digital texts take on a social life given their interactive qualities. I will discuss issues surrounding dissertation and thesis design that articulate meanings not only using written language but also multimodal meaning making (Ivarsson, Linderoth, & Säljö, 2009; Kress, 2010). This is to say that digital textual production transcends place-based settings to also include migratory spaces. To this end, I argue that when interactive texts are fossilized to adhere to linear research formats, there are social and cultural insights that may be lost in the representational shift.

The chapter is divided into three main sections. It begins by providing background for an empirical study conducted about interactive textual design among a group of Filipino British youth. It also explains unconventional ethnographic issues associated with researching their textual production using digital technologies. Throughout this chapter, examples will be drawn from this context to illustrate key points. Next, a review of literature is presented that explores the movement of textual production from page to screen not as contradictory practices but as extending multimodal design possibilities. Lastly, this chapter also offers practical approaches for empirically working with digital data that communicate social and cultural insights using interactive design. Thus, the overall aim of the chapter focuses on exploring how interactive design representations have implications for the dissemination of cultural knowledge.

MULTIMODAL RESEARCH CONTEXT: THE PINOYS AND THEIR MIGRATING LITERACIES

This section provides the ethnographic research context about a group of Filipino British youth who call themselves Pinoys. Throughout this chapter, selected findings about their textual production will be referenced as examples. I find it useful to begin by providing background about their distinctive ways of reading and writing using digital technologies. Examining the Pinoys' interactive texts makes discernable unconventional research problems that arise from study-ing multimodal textual production in digital settings.

RESEARCH CONTEXT AND PARTICIPANTS

The Pinoys and I first met three years ago while I was studying abroad in London. I was drawn to their multimodal approach toward languages and literacies as their distinctive ways with words involved new forms of meaning making in digital contexts (Cope & Kalantzis, 2000; Jewitt, 2008; Kress & van Leeuwen, 2001; New London Group, 1996). For the Pinoys, digital textual production was a pliable artform for designing meaning beyond written words (Bakhtin, 1981). As Kyd, one of the main participants posited, 'We like to, like to hide some stuff, do puzzles, and for those who thinks it's just music, it's just music'. In his video 'Flow Ko' (*My Flow*), Kyd's artistic design moved beyond written and spoken text to also include image, color, gesture and sound; and as the title suggests, Kyd's distinctive 'flow' – his rhythmic orchestration of modes as a pliable artform – functioned beyond the aesthetics of music to also enable expression of his diverse social and linguistic identities[3] (Domingo, 2011a). Kyd digitally crafted beats, rhyme and lyrics not only as a medium for making music but also for multimodally asserting social and cultural meanings in his digital textual pro-duction. For example, he aligned spoken words to the rhythm of the music in rap patterns that blend British grime with classic American hip hop beats, and he integrated the Filipino and British flags as the primary colors for the music video. Similarly, Aziatik and Lucky QBall – among the main participants – articulated their remix of a beloved traditional Filipino folk song called 'Tinikling' into a hip hop rendition titled 'Pinoy Ako' (*I am Filipino*) as creating a 'culture song'. As Aziatik stated, 'Kids nowadays they don't know this kinda stuff, obviously they don't learn it in school … so we want something for them to yung maalala nila yung culture nila' (*remember their culture*). As these examples show, the social and cultural significance embedded in the Pinoys' digital texts were also educa-tive in nature. Yet, while it is possible to articulate the intent of their meaning making using written language, it is an entirely different encounter through multimodal participation. Experiencing the performance of their songs, whether on the digital screen or at a live venue, more visibly displays how the Pinoys merged their social and cultural affiliation as situated across hip hop, Filipino and British cultures.

While I theorized about their engagement of hip hop music in the larger research project, this chapter focuses on this participatory practice as concerned with digital design. This choice was determined primarily by the purpose of this chapter on empirically and ethically handling digital data in multimodal research. To this end, I explore the social life of their hip hop texts as offering insight into how their multimodal meanings migrate.

Migrating literacies

The study encompassed a three-year period for generating data about the ways in which the Pinoys languages and literacies traveled across diverse discourse communities (Bakhtin, 1981; Rampton, 1995). As such, I use the term migrating literacies to describe how the Pinoys multimodally engaged reading, writing and speaking across social contexts that are both physically and digitally navigable. My purpose in examining the Pinoys' migrating literacies[4] was to understand how they layered their linguistic diversity and cultural knowledge to navigate the discourses of their social worlds.

Recruitment of the Pinoys involved reaching out to various community centers in England to gain access into working with youth whose reading and writing practices encompassed digital, multimodal and transnational contexts. A member of a Philippine Community Center responded to my visitation request and introduced me to several youth groups. The Pinoys were among these groups, and the six participants featured in my ethnography voluntarily opted to partake in the project after they were informed of the research purpose.

The six Pinoys are affiliated through their hip hop production group that includes members around the world. Their sense of community and belonging is held together by their joint interests in their Filipino heritage and hip hop as a platform for expressing their cultural knowledge and social identities (Canagarajah, 2006; Lave & Wenger, 1991). As a community, they participate in producing shared textual projects (e.g. writing lyrics, making hip hop beats, performing at live venues, designing clothing) that articulate their language loyalty and cultural affiliation to the larger world. Arriving at this understanding of the Pinoys' distinctive digital textual production necessitated the development of migratory research practices.

ETHNOGRAPHIC ISSUES IN MULTIMODAL RESEARCH

The specific problems I discuss in this section were not traditional concerns addressed in ethnographic or multimodal literature during the time in which this research was conceptualized and carried out. This is partly due to the nature of this research in documenting digital literacy practices that were at the forefront of online innovations. Of prime example would be how the Pinoys were already utilizing YouTube and Facebook by the time I started researching them in 2007. Given that the former was made public in 2005 and the later in 2004, the Pinoys were rather advanced in engaging these online platforms as rhetorical resources for communicating their ideas and asserting their identities.

In our increasingly global world, the prolific use of digital technologies and the Internet have become linked with practices of multimodal textual production in most daily urban settings (Appadurai, 1996). Yet, linear texts that pervade most Western schools and universities often still privilege written language for communicating meaning. As a doctoral student studying the Pinoys and their migrating literacies, I was faced with the challenge of trying to communicate my participants' interactive meaning making using primarily written language throughout the research process – from data collection, analysis and finally presenting the work as a formal dissertation. I found that fossilizing the interactive texts of my participants resulted in more than shifting the representational format but also altering the migratory meanings embedded in their multimodal designs. For example, the Pinoys did not participate in digital textual production merely for entertainment purposes. Rather, they used new media technologies to facilitate transcultural exchanges with youth around the world (Hull & Nelson, 2009; Lam & Rosario-Ramos, 2009; Yi, 2009). Aziatik created radio podcasts that were circulated among the Pinoys and their peers worldwide. These songs in these podcasts were artistically crafted to blend Tagalog[5] and English. Thus, both the performers and listeners engaged in multilingual exchanges.

In the case of this particular research, participatory notions of language and literacy invariably intersected with the challenge of creating a traditional dissertation that lacked spatial dimensions for containing the social qualities of interactive texts (Domingo, 2011b). This is to say that even a traditional paper-based appendix could not fully contain the Pinoys' animated designs, which layered written language with other modes like sound, image and music.

While my research was focused on documenting the Pinoys migrating literacies, ethical considerations necessitated new approaches for attending to the social and cultural meanings embedded in their digital textual designs. Thus, I had to consider new ways for empirically attending to multimodal data. To document the Pinoys' textual production and participation across these digital spaces, the scope of my research also necessitated my participation in migratory research practices. In the following section, I describe this shift in my research approach.

Migratory practices in research

Murthy (2008) points to a balanced combination of physical and digital ethnography for providing researchers with a broader array of methods. This approach was applied in the large-scale Digital Youth Project by the MacArthur Foundation, which examined the ways in which digital media are shifting the learning of young people as they socialize and participate in civic life across varied social contexts (Ito et al., 2008). I also carried out a similar approach of balancing physical and digital data collection; however, I differentiate my research approach beyond the notion of 'balancing' to that of 'migrating' to better understand how transcultural reading and writing transpires across physical and digital contexts. This migratory approach emerged as I became aware of the problematic nature regarding the study the Pinoys' everyday interactions with texts as rooted only in the placed-based structures that they frequented. Thus, enacting a migratory practice stems from understanding the Pinoys' social spaces as an extension of their everyday communities, whereby research traversals serve not only as additive ways for collecting data but an inextricable process for comprehending youth literacies in digital and transnational contexts.

By enacting a migratory research practice, I also was able to examine the digital textual production of the Pinoys not as isolated events but as an intricate process of meaning making that unfolded over time, across social spaces and as embedded in the lived realities of my participants (Lemke, 2007). For example, access to each of the participants' social networking sites (e.g. YouTube, MySpace, Facebook) enabled ethnographic observations to also include online spaces. These digital spaces made it possible to stay updated about the Pinoys' social activities through their posted photographs and news feeds. This collective constellation of empirical data opened new ways for layering 'thick descriptions' that more attentively documents multimodal meaning making (Geertz, 1973). Therefore, this ethnography focused not only on the finished digital literacy artifacts but the entire process of the Pinoys' generative practices of textual design. Participant observations and interviews spanned both the world navigable by the body and the world mediated online. I physically traveled with them across social contexts and participated in their online communities.

Further, visibly documenting the Pinoys' digital textual production necessitated that I expand beyond traditional ethnographies of language and literacy research. Though my research builds upon this tradition, I also drew from ethnographies of media[6] to enhance my understanding of culture from rooted-space orientations to more fluid arrangements (Condry, 2006; Dornfeld, 1998).

While ethnographic methods can provide insight into everyday practices of languages and literacies as situated in social interaction, these lived realities in transcultural contexts were only liminally published during the time in which this study was conducted (Hull & Nelson, 2009; Lam & Rosario-Ramos, 2009; Yi, 2009). Thus, there was limited research literature that documented how researchers might attend to interactive data that did not easily fit standard research conventions (e.g. online literacy artifacts like music videos and web design that could not be archived like traditional paper documents). In addition, collecting such data as literacy artifacts meant having to develop new ways for analyzing their noisy and moving features.

The developed migratory research practice enabled understanding of meaning making to transpire beyond place-based settings to also include additional everyday learning spaces in the lives of the Pinoys (e.g. composing music on a mobile phone while riding public transportation or listening, creating a radio podcast for global circulation). Studying these migratory learning spaces made it possible to display how the Pinoys, their ideas, and their interactive texts were migrating across discourses of schools, homes, communities and workplaces.

In the following section, I offer a review of literature that takes into account how some of the migratory practices of the Pinoys are becoming more mainstream experiences. In examining multimodal literature, I also continue to demonstrate how cultural knowledge is embedded in interactive textual designs.

MULTIMODAL MEANING MAKING: INTERACTIVE DESIGN FROM THE PAGE TO THE SCREEN

This section explores the movement of textual production from page to screen not as contradictory practices but as extending multimodal design possibilities (Mills, 2009; Pahl, 2007; Williams, 2009). I posit that this dialogic approach towards textual design has implications for the research process. Given that interactive texts carry cultural meanings, subscribing to a linear dissertation and thesis invariably restricts the social life of texts to circulate. To this end, the latter part of this section examines how multimodal design promotes the sharing of cultural knowledge (Alvermann, 2008; Ivarsson, Linderoth, & Säljö, 2009; Kress, 2010).

Multimodal design and digital textual production

Everyday encounters with texts have increasingly become saturated with images and sounds for circulating ideas and thoughts beyond traditional print media. Modes once considered supplementary to written words now comprise design capabilities that layer the inextricable relationships among language, oral and written; images, still and moving and sound, voice and music (Cope & Kalantzis, 2000; Jewitt, 2008; Kress & van Leeuwen, 2001; New London Group, 1996). Among the ways in which a multi-sensory approach to meaning making transforms the act of reading and writing is through the notion of design.

There is shared recognition that while paper-based texts are necessary, they are no longer adequate for communicating across the various new media technologies and online platforms in our global world (Andrews & Haythornwaite, 2011; Kress, 2010). As Jewitt (2009) argues, 'Multimodality is gaining pace as a research approach, as speech and writing no longer appear adequate in understanding representation and communication in a variety of fields, and the need to understand the complex ways in which speech and writing interact with 'non-verbal' modes can no longer be avoided' (p. 3). Such perspectives on languages and literacies research recognize the role of print and other symbol systems as integral to textual production (Kress, 2003; Scribner & Cole, 1981; Street, 1993). In this regard, reading and writing practices are not restricted to written language but also acknowledge other forms of human communication as a means for designing multimodal meaning making (e.g. body language, speech acts, visual representations).

This shift has implications not only for the study of literacies that engage such multimodal textual practices but also for students' production of texts for research purposes. Consider how the dissertation and thesis as a final product tends to be represented in a linear format. While students often produce these formal paper-based documents as required by their programs of study, the steps leading to its production have often shifted to include more interactive textual design. For example, students frequently create outlines and map their paper topic using interactive online programs (e.g. Mindomo). It is also becoming more common for students to create blogs and websites that document their thinking about their thesis. To this end, I argue that converting multimodal representation to fit page-bound documentation not only alters the textual arrangement but also the analytic path of students. This is to say that certain modes cannot be fully converted to fit flat or silent formats, which invariably impacts the ways in which intended meanings are conveyed. For example, understanding some of the Pinoys' video texts required developing a multimodal analytic approach that could more fully attend to both the temporal and spatial dimensions of their meaning making (see Figure 13.1). This analytic path differs from transcription approaches that are more temporally fixed. Further, transcribing multimodal data to account for

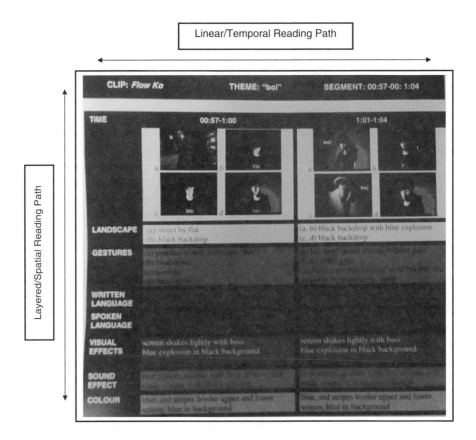

Figure 13.1   Multimodal analysis and transcription

written language, image, music as disparate parts would not have made the Pinoys' migrating literacies visible.

Multimodal analysis and transcription made it possible to 'read' the Pinoys' interactive texts using both a linear/temporal path and a layered/spatial path (Domingo, 2011a). The analytic approach also accounted for the cultural, linguistic and social migrations embedded in the textual design. Lastly, applying the layered/spatial reading path provided insight into the new ways that meanings circulate in digital contexts.

In the following section, I share specific examples of everyday interactivity with texts to demonstrate how reading and writing practices are breaking from still-representations to more dynamic configurations.

Mobility and digital texts

Interactivity in digital textual production is perhaps most evident in the digitizing of everyday texts. The introduction of e-readers, Dropbox, GoogleDocs, among other online platforms for archiving digital texts provides reading and writing experiences that are both mobile and interactive. In terms of mobility, books, manuscripts, movies, document files, photo reels and music albums are no longer restricted to placed-based archives. Thus, access to a collection of literacy texts are possible whether on the train, at work, in school or even at home. To this end, the structure of learning has extended beyond liminal spaces of classrooms to allow readers opportune moments for interacting with texts even 'on the go'. While learning in out-of-school contexts has long been an interest in literacy studies, research suggests that engagement with digital texts and popular media is central to developing critical readers and writers in our increasingly global and digital world (Buckingham, 2003; Doering, Beach, & O'Brien, 2007; Stone, 2007; West, 2008).

Digitizing of everyday texts is also an advantage for students studying abroad or traveling from their home universities. Having access to one's portable library affords mobility without the constraints of physically moving textbooks and other educational materials from place to place. For example, I conducted my ethnography of Filipino British youth in London while I remained a doctoral student at New York University, New York. While I physically migrated between the two cities, the digitizing of texts made traveling easier to maintain, as I did not have to ship books and other educational resources to sustain my research studies across these two places. Given the storage and retrieval facility of digital texts, access to a personalized collection of literature made it possible for data collection and analysis to inform each other. Topics and patterns that emerged through this approach were further explored by reviewing relevant literature (Dyson & Genishi, 2005). In having a digital archive of the seminal literature for my research, as well having online access to New York University's library collection, it was possible to bridge the learning that transpired in the field to larger bodies of relevant work. As such, my participants' distinctive literacy practices across digital contexts were made more visibly apparent. Heath and Street (2008) posit that this ongoing exchange between inductive and reflexive analysis assist to 'refine questions' during the course of data collection, leading away from 'loose generalizations' and into credible empirical evidence rooted in qualitative records and comparative cases (p. 100). Having an archive of digital files enabled research pursuits abroad without having to relinquish access to seminal works that informed and guided my ethnography.

In the aforementioned examples, the use of digital texts was addressed to focus on solving an issue of mobility. What follows is a discussion centered on the transformative meaning making processes that transpires given the interactive quality of digital texts. I identify design interactivity as a feature of multimodal meaning making in students' participation in digital textual production.

Interactivity and digital texts

Yet another shift toward interactivity in digital textual production is evident in increasingly design-oriented reading and writing experiences (Kress, 2010). Rather than reading for meaning, meaning is achieved through the process of interactive design. Further, students are able to interact with digital texts in ways that embody the notion of language as a living artifact. For example, when reading a journal article or even a book chapter digitally, meanings are not merely accessed via reading line by line. The act of reading is a process that transpires through an embodied engagement with text. With the touch of a finger, the linear page suddenly comes to life to reveal an alternate landscape. Words can literally become virtual portals for understanding the context of meaning beyond inference. Such is possible when readers have the option to literally read 'beneath the surface' by looking up the meaning of individual words via the Internet. A similar transitory experience happens when online articles include embedded links to other related texts. Thus, readers and writers are not passive interpreters of text but actively engaged in making meaning. This active engagement with text is also evident when using digital platforms such as iAnnotate and GoodReader. Both permit individuals to 'talk back to the text' given their advanced options for note taking. In many ways, this process resonates a dialogic process for meaning making (Bakhtin, 1981). As Barton and Hamilton (1998) argue:

> Literacy is primarily something people do; it is an activity, located in the space between thought and text. Literacy does not just reside in people's heads as a set of skills to be learned, and it does not just reside on paper, captured as texts to be analyzed. Like all human activity, literacy is essentially social, and it is located in the interaction between people. (p. 3)

Applying Barton and Hamilton's perspective of literacy as social, the interactivity of digital texts enables students to enact literacies that are in conversation with the larger world (Freire & Macedo, 1987). The shift from page to screen as a process has extended reading and writing processes to include both physical and metaphorical interactivity. For students, interactivity as a design expands the ways in which they can represent knowledge.

As these examples demonstrated, digital texts afford students research mobility to expand their learning spaces beyond the classroom. In the continuing discussion, attention is given to the new ways in which digitizing texts affords students a new sense of research interactivity when working with dialogic data. Specifically, I focus on the ways in which digital and multimodal design promotes the sharing of cultural knowledge.

CULTURAL KNOWLEDGE AND THE SOCIAL LIFE OF DIGITAL TEXTS

In this section, I explore how a multimodal approach toward textual design has implications for the research process. Given that interactive texts carry cultural meanings, subscribing to a linear dissertation and thesis invariably restricts the social life of texts to circulate (Ivarsson, Linderoth, & Säljö, 2009; Kress, 2010).

By contrast, viewing digital texts with a dialogical frame opens possibilities for layering of modes not only as a communicative resource but also as a medium for expressing one's diverse social identities and linguistic repertoire in digital communities. As Lemke (2007) states, 'In some very basic sense the use or function of every media work is not just to link a producer and a user, but to link across the timescales of production, circulation, and use' (p. 143). This view suggests that speech, language and utterance are not encapsulated in a vacuum but alive in living interaction with the social world (Bakhtin, 1981; Landay, 2004). For example, it was problematic to analyze the Pinoys recorded speech, image, music and gestures, among other modes, in isolation from one another because they articulated cultural knowledge using multimodal meaning making. Thus, transcribing their interactive texts linearly and not accounting for the other modes beyond written language would have yielded limited understanding of their digital textual production (see Figure 13.1).

Cultural knowledge and digital texts

Whereas print materials restrict meaning to fit page-bound dimensions, interactive texts enable fluid migrations of meaning across digital contexts. This shift in textual production offers insight into reading and writing practices that do not yield a finite production of cultural artifacts but become part of an 'interanimating relationship' with new contexts (Bakhtin, 1981). This is to say that multimodal designs can more attentively carry dynamic and fluid notions of culture as lived practices of sharing ideas, thoughts and texts across diverse communities. This perspective deviates from past language and literacy traditions that championed the development of explicitly written text to autonomously represent meaning (Goody & Watt, 1968; Levi-Strauss, 1962; Olson, 1977; Ong, 1982). By contrast, viewing multimodal texts as encompassing a social life takes into account that people's relation with language is a pliable artform (Bakhtin, 1981). Andrews and Haythornthwaite (2007) have previously articulated this process as *dialectical*, whereby the relation between technology and literacy are co-evolutionary. Their viewpoint emphasizes that the learner both shapes and is shaped by specific digital engagements, whereby learning happens as a reciprocal rather than causal practice. In this regard, daily reading and writing practices encourage literacy experiences beyond the visual sense to also include tactile and auditory participation, among other sensory perceptions (Domingo, 2011a; Howes, 2009).

In my research, I saw this pattern displayed when the Pinoys remixed music to embody social and cultural meanings. This process was previously described in Aziatik's creation of a 'culture song' titled 'Pinoy Ako' (see section on Ethnographic Issues in Multimodal Research). This example illustrates what Williams (2009) posits as participatory reading and composing opportunities in digital contexts. He described how such practices provide youth with rhetorical devices for expressing diverse identities and building community through the reproduction and reconstruction of texts that resemble 'bricolage' and 'collage' rather than traditional linear formats (p. 8). Studies have also examined how digital textural production not only cultivates identity and community building but also fosters cultural knowledge (Alvermann, 2008; West, 2008). Kress (2010) posits this human engagement of social semiotics as culturally variable, whereby modes convey different meanings depending on the sociocultural source. To this end, I detail how today's digital texts possess social qualities.

Social life and digital texts

As multimodal meanings can more readily be constructed and circulated using digital texts, consider how some of the everyday texts that circulate are increasingly displaying social qualities. Note how digital newsprints like *The Wall Street Journal*, *The New York Times* and *BBC* websites enable subscribers to interact with textual features that include playing videos and photo slides. In this regard, reporting of current events moves beyond written language to also include interactive design. As such, digital textual production integrates a dialogic experience that beckons both the mind and the body to interact in multimodal meaning making. Further, this movement not only transforms the 'reading path' but also extends possibilities for meanings to circulate (Kress & van Leeuwen, 2001). For example, the layering of modes in digital news promotes a social dimension to reading current events given that sharing a link to an article is increasingly accompanied by at least three design elements: image, text and color. This is often the case when articles are shared via Facebook posts, which prompts users to write about the link by providing a text box that include statements such as 'What's on your mind?' or 'Say something about this ...' I refer to this interactive feature among people, thoughts and texts on Facebook as one vivid example of the social life of digital texts. Not only are people able to share what they read via updates to their wall but also by sending direct links to the primary source via feeds to their connected friends and networks. When such posts are shared via a communal newsfeed, the article is not the sole conveyor of meaning. Readers may continually comment on the news itself or in response to what others wrote about the article. Thus, the text takes on a social life, transforming through the ongoing act of reader and writer response. In this regard, it is not uncommon to see discussions that ensue among wide networks about the news articles or other similar current events that are posted on social networking sites like Facebook.

The integrative view of speech and writing as situated within a larger world poses concern for examining research data as isolated from its social context (Kress, 2010). This section demonstrated how sociocultural perspectives provide conceptual tools for thinking about the social nature of texts and the cultural knowledge embedded in their design. This section also offered insights into empirical and ethical approaches for attending to the problem of collecting the noisy and moving features inherent in multimodal data.

CONCLUSIONS

This chapter aimed to complicate discussions surrounding the design of dissertations and theses beyond issues of representation to also include concerns about the social and cultural insights embedded in textual arrangements. To attend to this focus, this chapter demonstrated how multimodality and new media technologies permit new ways of sensing multimodal meanings that exhibit social qualities. Whereas linear and paper-bound text often privileges the visual sense, digital data saturates multiple senses and necessitates their collaborative activity (Howes, 2009). As such, linear arrangements of texts are increasingly inadequate for articulating cultural knowledge expressed using modes beyond written language.

Two questions were posed to guide this chapter: In what ways does this shift in textual production also transform the process for multimodal meaning making? How might dissertations and theses be re-envisioned given this shift in textual production? While the former was discussed in detail using both conceptual tools and research references, the latter was addressed by offering empirical and ethical approaches to handing multimodal research data. In what follows, I refer back to my own ethnography to detail implications for future research about digitizing dissertations and theses.

At the start of my ethnography, there was no formal intent to produce or participate in digital textual production or to consider digital components for my dissertation; however, it became apparent that understanding the Pinoys' interactive ways with words would require alternative research approaches for handling multimodal data. The Pinoys engaged language as alive in social inter-action rather than adhering to fixed definitions of literacy (Bakhtin, 1981; Barton & Hamilton, 1998; Brutt-Griffler, 2002; Freire & Macedo, 1987). Among the ways that I was able to attend to the Pinoys' interactive texts was by using online platforms and new media technologies that permitted manipulating noisy and moving data. For example, I created my own website to archive their work. It allowed for quick retrieval and visual display. Rather than using the site to lin-early arrange dialogic data, I spent considerable time designing a more layered configuration of the data collected, research analysis and relevant literature.

Another means by which my dissertation moved beyond linear display was by altering my learning path to include migratory research practices. Applying a multimodal analytic approach revealed much about my participants' distinctive ways with layering modes as a form of textual production. Rather than serving as additive features of design, their layering of these modes opened new ways for interacting and making meaning with texts (Hull & Nelson, 2005). This dialogic feature of digital design allowed them to play with words, ideas and texts to design interactive meaning rather than fossilizing their languages and literacies to lie flat on the page.

I purposely refer to these two examples as they demonstrate how digitizing texts has implications not only for representational purposes but also for extend-ing the analytic path of students. Given the design features made available by multimodal meaning making, it was possible to handle digital data interactively. While I submitted both a traditional and digital dissertation, it was actually during the data collection and analysis process that I found the digitizing of texts more productive for sensing data in new ways.

The shift in textual production from page-bound inscriptions to interactive designs, made it possible for meanings to migrate beyond place-based settings. To this end, it is critical to consider the representational choice for sharing cultural knowledge in educational contexts. As this chapter demonstrated, fossil-izing dialogic texts has ethical implications for conducting empirical research that lends social and cultural insights.

NOTES

1. The terms 'digital technologies' and 'new media technologies' are used synonymously in this chapter to refer to textual production in online contexts. In both cases, interactive participation distinguishes these communicative resources from page-bound tools (e.g. paper and pen, written language).

2. I would like to differentiate my literal use of the term 'noisy and moving' to describe digital texts from studies in dyslexia that also reference words as having animated qualities despite being page bound. Throughout this chapter, I apply the term to conceptually allude to the nature of language and literacy practices as socially and culturally mediated (Scribner & Cole, 1981; Street, 1983; Vygotsky, 1978).

3. The participants in this study blend English and Tagalog, native language of the Philippines, to communicate with one another and their peers. In some cases, Spanish was also integrated in their reading and writing practices.

4. A working definition of migrating literacies identifies design and circulation of multimodal texts as rhetorical resources for managing linguistic variety and cultural affiliation across discourse communities. Migrating literacies takes into consideration youth agency and dialogic participation as predominant features of multimodal textual

production, whereby youth remix and reconstruct multisensory texts that deftly configure modes to embody social and cultural significance (Domingo, 2011b).

5. Tagalog is the native language of the Philippines.

6. Just as my work moves away from a causal relationship between orality and writing, ethnography of media moves away from causal effects of technology on the lives of people. Instead, there is an emphasis on the social practice of media, which attends to understanding how people manipulate technologies to attend to their own culture and ideology.

REFERENCES

Alvermann, D. E. (2008). Why bother theorizing adolescents' online literacies for classroom practice and research? *Journal of Adult and Adolescent Literacy, 52,* 8–19.

Andrews, R. & Haythornthwaite, C. (Eds.). (2007). *The SAGE Handbook of E-Learning Research.* London: Sage.

Andrews, R. & Haythornwaite, C. (2011). *E-Learning: Theory and Practice.* London and New York: Sage.

Appadurai, A. (1996). *Modernity at Large. Cultural Dimensions of Globalization.* Minneapolis, MN: University of Minnesota Press.

Bakhtin, M. M. (1981). *The Dialogic Imagination: Four Essays. Bakhtinian Perspectives on Language, Literacy and Learning.* Cambridge: Cambridge University Press.

Barton, D. & Hamilton, M. (1998). *Local Literacy: Reading and Writing in One Community,* London: Routledge.

Buckingham, D. (2003). *Media Education: Literacy, Learning, and Contemporary Culture.* Cambridge: Polity Press.

Brutt-Griffler, J. (2002). *World English: A Study of its Development.* Clevedon: Multilingual Matters.

Canagarajah, A. S. (2006). Constructing a diaspora identity in English: The case of Sri Lankan Tamils. In J. Brutt-Griffler & C. Evans Davies (Eds.), *English and Ethnicity* (pp. 191–213). New York: Palgrave Macmillan.

Condry, I. (2006). *Hip-Hop Japan: Rap and the Paths of Cultural Globalization.* Stanford, CA: Duke University Press.

Cope, B. & Kalantzis, M. (Eds.). (2000). *Multiliteracies.* London: Routledge.

Doering, A., Beach, R., & O'Brien, D. (2007). Infusing multimodal tools and digital literacies into an English education program. *English Education, 40,* 41–60.

Domingo, M. (2011a). Analysing layering in textual design: A multimodal approach for examining cultural, linguistic and social migration in digital video. *International Journal of Social Research Methodology, 14,* 219–230.

Domingo, M. (2011b). Migrating literacies in global and digital worlds: Exploring linguistic diversity, cultural knowledge and social identities of urban youth. Unpublished Dissertation, New York University, New York.

Dornfeld, B. (1998). *Producing Public Television, Producing Public Culture.* Princeton, NJ: Princeton University Press.

Dyson, A. & Genishi, C. (2005). *On the Case: Approaches to Language and Literacy Research.* New York: Teachers College Press.

Freire, P. & Macedo, D. (1987). *Literacy: Reading the Word and the World.* South Hadley: Bergin & Garvey.

Geertz, C. (1973). *The Interpretation of Cultures.* New York: Basic Books.

Goody, J. & Watt, I. (1968). The consequences of literacy. In J. Goody (Ed.), *Literacy in Traditional Societies* (pp. 27–68). Cambridge: Cambridge University Press.

Heath, S. B. & Street, B. (2008). *Ethnography. Approaches to Language and Literacy Research.* New York: Teachers College Press.

Howes, D. (2009). Anthropology and multimodality: The conjugation of the senses. In C. Jewitt (Ed.), *The Routledge Handbook of Multimodal Analysis* (pp. 225–236). Abingdon, Oxon: Routledge.

Hull, G. A. & Nelson, M. A. (2009). Literacy, media, and morality: Making the case for an aesthetic turn. In M. Prinsloo & M. Baynham (Eds.), *The Future of Literacy Studies* (pp. 199–227). New York: Palgrave MacMillan.

Hull, G. & Nelson, M. E. (2005). Locating the semiotic power of multimodality. *Written Communication*, *22*, 224–262.

Ivarsson, J., Linderoth, J., & Säljö, R. (2009). Representations in practices. A sociocultural approach to multimodality in reasoning. In C. Jewitt (Ed.), *The Routledge Handbook of Multimodal Analysis*. Abingdon, Oxon: Routledge.

Ito, M., Horst, H. A., Bittanti, M., Boyd, D., Herr-Stevenson, B., & Lange, P. (2008). *White paper – Living and learning with new media: Summary of findings from the Digital Youth Project*. Chicago, IL: The John P. and Catherine T. MacArthur Foundation.

Jewitt, C. (2008). Multimodality and literacy in school classrooms. *Review of Research in Education*, *32*, 241–267.

Jewitt, C. (2009) (Ed.). *The Routledge Handbook of Multimodal Analysis*. Abingdon, Oxon: Routledge.

Kress, G. (2003). *Literacy in the New Media Age*. London: Routledge.

Kress, G. (2010). *Multimodality. A Social Semiotic Approach to Contemporary Communication*. London: Routledge.

Kress, G. & van Leeuwen, T. (2001) *Multimodal Discourse: The Modes and Media of Contemporary Communication*. London: Hodder Arnold.

Lam, W. S. E. & Rosario-Ramos, E. (2009). Multilingual literacies in transnational digitally mediated contexts: An exploratory study of immigrant teens in the United States. *Language and Education*, *23*, 171–190.

Landay, E. (2004). Performance as the foundation for a secondary school literacy program: A Bakhtinian perspective. In A. Ball & S. W. Freedman (Eds.), *Bakhtinian Perspectives on Language, Literacy, and Learning*. Cambridge: Cambridge University Press.

Lave, J. & Wenger, E. (1991). *Situated learning: Legitimate Peripheral Participation*. Cambridge: Cambridge University Press.

Lemke, J. (2007). Video epistemology in- and outside the box: Traversing attentional spaces. In R. Goldman, R. Pea, B. Barron & S. J. Derry (Eds.), *Video Research in the Learning Sciences* (pp. 39–51). Mahwah, NJ: Lawrence Erlbaum Associates.

Levi-Strauss, C. (1962). *The Savage Mind*. Chicago, IL: University of Chicago Press.

Mills, K. A. (2009). Multiliteracies: Interrogating competing discourses. *Language and Education*, *23*, 103–116.

Murthy, D. (2008). Digital ethnography: An examination of the use of new technologies for social research. *Sociology*, *42*, 837–855.

New London Group. (1996). A pedagogy of multiliteracies: Designing social futures. *Harvard Educational Review*, *66*, 60–92.

Olson, D. R. (1977). From utterance to text: The bias of language in speech and writing. *Harvard Educational Review*, *47*, 257–281.

Ong, W. J. (1982). *Orality and Literacy: The Technologizing of the Word*. New York: Routledge.

Pahl, K. (2007). Creativity in events and practices: A lens for understanding children's multimodal texts, *Literacy*, *41*, 86–92.

Rampton, B. (1995). *Crossing: Language and Ethnicity Among Adolescents*. London: Longman.

Scribner, S. & Cole, M. (1981). *The Psychology of Literacy*. Cambridge, MA: Harvard University Press.

Stone, J. (2007). Popular websites in adolescents' out-of-school lives: Critical lessons on literacy. In M. Knobel & C. Lankshear, (Eds.), *A New Literacies Sampler* (pp. 49–66). New York: Peter Lang.

Street, B. (1993). *Cross-Cultural Approaches to Literacy*. Cambridge, UK: Cambridge University Press.

Wade, S. E. & Moje, E. B. (2001). The role of text in classroom learning: Beginning an online dialogue. *Reading Online*, 5. Retrieved April 6, 2009, from http://www.readingonline.org/articles/art_index.asp?HREF=handbook/wade/index.html

West, K. C. (2008). Weblogs and literacy response: Socially situated identities and hybrid social languages in English class blogs. *Journal of Adolescent and Adult Literacy, 51,* 588–598.

Williams, B. (2009). *Shimmering Literacies. Popular Culture & Reading and Writing Online.* New York: Peter Lang.

Yi, Y. (2009). Adolescent literacy and identity construction among 1.5 generation students from a transnational perspective. *Journal of Asia Pacific Communication, 19,* 100–129.

Multimodality, Including the Representation and Presentation of Theses and Dissertations

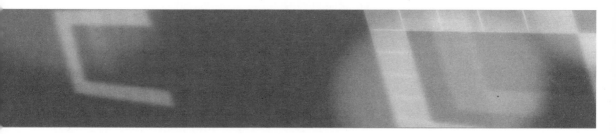

As we pointed out in the Introduction to this handbook, multimodality is not synonymous with digitization. Multimodality preceded the digital by several centuries, but its revival and re-formulation has been brought about partly by the affordances of the digital. A conventional thesis or dissertation can be multimodal by virtue of its texture (e.g. a dissertation about hand-made paper typed on to hand-made paper); its inclusion of images (e.g. Japanese manga in a study of the emergence of study manga); its inclusion of figures and tables and its inclusion of other modes of representation in an accompanying CD Rom. One could even argue that a 'purely' written verbal text is multimodal in that its layout is visual (e.g. its use of space, its typography, its generic structure). The digital, however, offers another dimension to multimodality: the potential inclusion of sound and moving image, as well as still images, in the main body of the text. In the present section, we include chapters on the social and economic context for thinking about the thesis or dissertation in an age of provisionality; and chapters on music, performing arts and visual research.

Gunther Kress' work on multimodality is seminal, and continues to inspire new thinking about modes of representation, not only in academia but beyond. In the chapter he has written for this collection, he considers the nature of research and postgraduate students' work – specifically the PhD – in highly provisional social, economic and political contexts. He sees the move taking place as one 'from theory to methodology and from the PhD as a contribution to knowledge to the PhD as a high-level certification of competence in research methods'. The shift from substantial 'contribution to knowledge' to knowledge about the processes of undertaking high-level research is one manifestation of the changing nature of the thesis and dissertation in its social context. What emerges from this chapter is the sense of the increasing tension between what students might wish to do to remain true to the shifting targets of their own research, and the real and complex multimodalities of communication in the twenty-first century on the one hand; and the often rigid and certainly conventional requirements for success at doctoral level on the other. While it may be the case that universities, supervisors and examiners are attentive to the shift toward method, it may not always be the case that they are open to the experimentation that can take place as students try to navigate their way through a problem, or try out new formats in order to better represent their understanding of a field.

In a chapter on practice-as-research in music performance, Mine Dack discusses a different but related shift from score-based studies in music to performance-based studies. The emphasis is seemingly different from that of Kress, in that the focus is not so much on method in the contemporary thesis or dissertation, but on how to represent music-in-action. However, the seeming difference is counter-balanced by a similarity, which is the problem all research students face: how to capture what is live, tangible, present experience in advanced research; and how to represent it in academic form. There is another shift going on, as described in Dack's chapter: the movement away from secondary written languages ('scores' in this case) which are used as a means to conveying the nature of a work (again, musical in this case), to a more digitized and direct communication of the modalities of the experience in question. This shift is a profound one, because it begs the question as to why we need second-order symbolic systems – like written language – to explore and understand first-order experience. The classical humanists would argue that written language provides a means of abstraction or conceptualization that enables one to stand back from a phenomenon in order to understand it better.

In exploring the tensions and movements occurring in the field of advanced study, this present section sits closely alongside the pre-occupations of students, writing in the earlier section on their own perspectives of the changing landscape of postgraduate research. In the rest of the present section, Anna-Marjatta Milsom, Susan Melrose and Juliet MacDonald discuss, from different perspectives, their experience as students or lecturers/professors in navigating the interface between the arts, digitization and the thesis/dissertation. Milsom's own thesis, submitted at London Metropolitan University, consisted of a DVD consisting of images, documents, translations, photographs and other items, beautifully presented on its opening page as if in a workshop or desk of a student or artist with drawers to be opened (which contained the various texts). This 'artifact' was accompanied by the conventional written thesis. It is a case of the artifact being appended to the body of text, and yet the artifact being the central creative core of the claim to new knowledge. In due course, we are seeing a shift from the artifact as the edge of the written work to the reverse: the written work as supplementary to the artifact.

Susan Melrose's chapter draws attention to the need of performance-based research to have the skills of a digital producer to enable representation of the work in a suitable format for examination. In this sense, she highlights the fact that universities like to see, through their regulations and requirements for high-level academic awards, work submitted that can be examined in its entirety and that can be lodged in the library, once approved. This accords with the notion of a 'portfolio' of work, again sometimes accompanied by written critical commentary, that is examinable and store-able. Juliet MacDonald, in the final chapter in this section – which has focussed on the difficulties facing students as they try to find the right balance between what they want to do and the needs of the university – looks at drawing practices and their modes of reproduction. In doing so, she asks us to consider the changes that take place when work in one mode (e.g. a pencil drawing on paper) is transformed to another, through digitization. Again, we are invited to consider issues of transcription, second-order representation and 'authenticity' as we try to make sense of what counts as new knowledge, what is mandated by universities, and what are the various affordances of different modes and media. In moving her work from paper to digital form, questions are raised about the currency and/or longevity of each of the media and what this means for future generations of artists and researchers.

14

Researching in Conditions of Provisionality: Reflecting on the PhD in the Digital and Multimodal Era

Gunther Kress

INTRODUCTION

Technologies come in all shapes. When they appear in the form of gadgets – 'appliances' – for the production and dissemination of messages, they attract attention, much more than the less 'noticeable' technologies of representation, such as speech, writing, image, gesture. This chapter deals with technologies of both kinds; and sets a consideration of both in their relation to research and 'the PhD' in the context of 'the wider social'.

A question about the 'standing' and the characteristics of the PhD is at the same time a question about the function of research in relation to producing (academic/disciplinary) knowledge: the PhD has been – and still remains, ostensibly at least – a certification of competence in the production of such knowledge. It is impossible to talk about the one without invoking both. A discussion might therefore appropriately start with Lyotard's *Report on knowledge* (Lyotard, 1984 [1979]), which foreshadows with astonishing prescience the developments around 'knowledge' now in full flood. In this chapter, the concern here is with PhDs in the broad are of the Social Sciences, Arts and the Humanities; criteria of different kinds apply in other disciplinary areas.

SOCIETY, 'KNOWLEDGE', REPRESENTATION

In the context of this Handbook, my interest is in the PhD as a social, academic and intellectual phenomenon which is everywhere connected with meaning and with identity. Over some thirty years as a supervisor of PhD researchers, I have also had a somewhat different, more specifically professionally oriented interest: overtly concerned with matters such as regulations, finding examiners, opportunities for publication, jobs and so forth, all organized by the wish to assist the PhD researcher in successful completion. The two perspectives are everywhere connected; yet as a 'responsible' supervisor the ontological and the social status of the PhD were less in the foreground of everyday 'supervision' than the immediate need 'to get the job done'.

The other focus, on meaning, knowledge, identity, power, has given me more than a bystander's interest in the changes which have characterized the award over that thirty-year period. In the 1980s, it was taken for granted in the 'English-influenced' anglophone world – in the UK, in Australia, in South Africa, for instance – that the PhD was defined by its constituting 'a contribution to knowledge'. Now, while that phrase may still exist (or not, increasingly), in many of the same places the PhD is effectively seen much more as a high level certification of competence for research. 'The' PhD does have very different forms throughout the world, even throughout the anglophone world, and its forms are subject to continuous change. Here the discussion is set in the narrower frame of the PhD now, in the Social Science/Humanities/Arts in the 'English-influenced' world.

Assume that the PhD is about a contribution to 'knowledge'. Semiotically speaking, 'knowledge' is an issue of meaning. 'Meaning' is a social matter; it is generated in social action and interaction: action in the social world, whether by myself or with others, using socially made cultural tools. The two kinds of tools at issue here in relation to the PhD are 'modes' and the digital media: 'modes' are tools for making meaning in representation, now frequently discussed under the heading of multimodality; the digital media are tools for the production and dissemination of 'messages'. The two form an integral, mutually interacting partnership – as media and representation have always done.

Consequently, in relation to the PhD in the digital and multimodal era there are three factors to consider. One, the overarching larger frame of 'the social' and what it enables and constrains. Both the digital media and the technologies of representation – the modes of 'multimodality' – are the effects of 'social work'. The necessary first question is whether either the facilities of the digital media or the affordances of modes could and would be used as they now are, if the social conditions of the sites of use were other than they are? If, for instance, distributions of power and possibilities for exercising agency were as they had been say even thirty years ago. Or, turning that round, one can ask whether some of the effects attributed to the digital media or to 'multimodality' could have been – and were – achieved with earlier technologies of mediation – and which could not?

Take, as an example, the topical issue of 'cutting and pasting'. I have a stack of primary school children's exercise books from the 1970s and 1980s. They contain many examples of 'cutting and pasting' – not then used as a metaphor as it is now, but as a description of something done with actual scissors applied to real paper-based media and actually glued – pasted – into a very material exercise book.

The social conditions then demanded such practices in primary schools as part of a beginning interest in 'project work', itself a response to economic conditions (i.e. an assumed need to make 'the school' relevant to everyday work-place demands). The technologies of the time were perfectly adequate for both the material and the intellectual/conceptual work of 'cutting and pasting'. The practice did not then produce the moral panic which the contemporary version has produced, and it is worth asking why not. There were, then, debates about 'standards' in writing, which were quite like debates now, with, then as now, 'the economy' looming as the unyielding master of all the school should be. Yet the big difference was that the debate was not, then, overshadowed by digital technologies, which are now seem as so threatening to writing, at every turn. In those different conditions, 'real' cutting and pasting produced no panics because it was not seen as a threat to writing. Now, using the facilities of digital technologies, 'cutting and pasting' is seen as a fundamental threat to that touchstone of civilizing technologies, to 'writing'.

The changes in both kinds of technologies – those of representation and those of production and dissemination – have been astonishingly – nearly frighteningly – rapid. To give an example: in a research project (funded by the UK's Economic and Social Science Research Council, the ESRC) conducted in 2000 – 'The social production of School English' – we found that the subject 'English' at that time existed as a paper-based, writing and speech focussed, practice. As one instance, in a class discussion of a seventeeth-century poem, the spoken and written exploration of the poem was supported by the technologies of overhead projector and the Oxford English Dictionary. By 2005, in a research project on the effects on classroom practices of Interactive Whiteboards, IWBs (Kress, et al., 2005; Moss and Jewitt, 2006), this newly introduced technology had led to a teaching of poetry which now was image (and speech) based – (coincidentally, in this later project, one school and one of the teachers of the earlier project participated). By 2005, 'ideas' that were central to the poems to be discussed, were introduced by images; and the students' *spoken* contributions were typed on keyboards and projected on the IWB. The ontological/epistemological foundation of the school-subject had been pretty radically remade in the intervening five or so years.

Clearly, the technology of the IWB facilitated this practice. Yet it would have been possible to have an image-based discussion using an overhead projector, even if with somewhat greater expenditure of pedagogic and semiotic effort. What is not clear is whether in 2000 social conditions and policy – a closely framed and heavily supervised, nationally mandated curriculum – would have permitted the later practice of foregrounding the mode of *image* as a route to the understanding of a seventeeth-century poem. The policies of the school, of its subject departments and the 'understandings' of the teachers, or indeed the expectations and demands of anxious parents might all have worked to prevent that. By 2006 however, the political and social conditions as well as the surrounding policies, had changed sufficiently for the new practice to become possible: for the school subject English to be mediated via the mode of *image* and for that to have become – astonishingly – unremarkable, naturalized.

That is the perspective which shapes my discussion: the social as prior and as the essential frame in which to discuss the shape and characteristics of the PhD in the environment of the uses and effects of digital and multimodal technologies. In the 'world', all three are always inextricably intertwined. The facilities of the digital media – the 'media of the screen' – have social consequences and effects; the resources of multimodality for their part have affordances with ontological, epistemological and therefore also social effects. All affect the conception of what the PhD is, should and can be. All affect identity.

THE SOCIAL AND ECONOMIC FRAME

The issues under this heading are now commonplace, and so I will simply assert several which bear directly on the topic, without elaboration or justification. Social conditions in most 'Western' (as indeed in many 'non-Western') societies, are affected by 'globalization': of economies, in finance and manufacturing; of cultural production and commodities; by competing value systems; whether for people at upper educational levels or those at the lowest. Speed and potentials of 'movement' and transport – whether of commodities, finance, values, people – has led to conditions where the global is an effective force everywhere, even if very differently, always in interaction with the forces of the local.

One wide-spread effect of these processes is the fraying of what had previously been – or had been taken to be – strong boundaries: whether those between or within nation states, in societies, between communities and other social groupings, around class, gender, generation, profession and not least in relation to 'disciplines' and hence with effects on the PhD. All such boundaries are fraying or disappearing where they have not already done so. Stability has been and still is giving way to instability. At every level stability and certainty are replaced by provisionality, which I take to mean a condition in which we know that what had seemed 'givens' yesterday are likely not be there in that or possibly in any form tomorrow. In a social world marked by provisionality every action I am about to take has to be newly considered in relation to an assessment of the social conditions which might obtain at the point of taking that action.

Two areas to feel the impact of these social conditions immediately are *conventions* and the *status of knowledge*. (I take *convention* to name the solidified routines which are the result of the regulation of social relations in fields of power over time.) *Semiotic* conventions are shaped by, reflect and in turn maintain *social* conventions; and inevitably they, too, have frayed. The social–semiotic category most immediately and evidently affected is that of 'genre', that is, the semiotic–textual instantiation of social relations among those interacting in a specific social setting. Social and therefore semiotic conventions are established, enforced and maintained with the application of lesser or greater degrees of power, so that changes in power–relations quickly manifest themselves in changes in social and semiotic practices.

As a slight yet telling example, not all male PhD examiners in the UK now wear a tie for a PhD viva. On the one hand, the award of the PhD is becoming too common place to warrant the continuing support of ritually specific attire; on the other, the social relations demonstrated by dress are now used, frequently, to signify a down-playing of hierarchy. The genre of the PhD itself had been, and still is, held in place by significant exertion of power: differently in different cultural places and differently in different disciplines. Hence the strength of convention and its maintenance, the *generic form* of the PhD acts as one touchstone and indicator of social change – an academic canary in the social cage.

The other consequence has been the effect on 'knowledge' itself. Grammatically speaking, some forty years ago, the word 'knowledge' was not (used as) a 'count-noun'; to use the plural form 'knowledges' was frowned on as 'ungrammatical', and 'faddish'. However, with the fraying of former distributions of *power-as-authority*, the status of 'knowledge', based on the authority of those who had been designated to produce it, has come into severe crisis. Of course, academics themselves had worked assiduously to dig a deep ditch of scepticism to divert the waters of social and cultural support away from the fields which had previously been kept fertile by their labor and that 'source'. With postmodern theories cutting off what had formerly been the criterial support of the PhD thesis, that is, its contribution to 'knowledge', that prop has been knocked away. It leaves the award in a precariously unstable state.

The undermining of the security of the category 'knowledge' has had very similar effects in representation: that is, modal effects, in terms of the former 'canonicity' of modes which had been and now are becoming admissible for use in PhDs. I will turn to that later.

THE PHD AND THE DIGITAL MEDIA OF PRODUCTION AND DISSEMINATION

Apart from the traditionally central requirement of 'constituting a contribution to knowledge', a PhD thesis had to meet other, often seemingly banal, requirements. One of these, in part related to *medium* and in part related to *epistemological* and *ontological* considerations, is that of 'length'. Most PhD theses in the Social Sciences and Humanities in the English-influenced anglophone area, are about 80,000 words in length. This does vary from social–cultural site to social–cultural site and from discipline to discipline, and has done so over history. (During a one-year stint as a Lector at the University of Kiel, in 1966, I recall seeing doctoral theses in the library of the English department, from the pre-WWII era. They were around twenty pages or so in length. Of course, it would be important to know what other forms of 'examination' had been part of the larger social/academic frame in which the twenty-page theses had been produced and were 'acceptable'.) 'Length' is a reliable signifier of (academic) significance.

Nevertheless, the bound thesis, as 'medium' – or the printed version, published as a 'book', as is demanded still in many places in Europe – does impose a limitation in length. Eighty thousand words corresponds roughly to the size of a 'monograph' – itself a genre fast fading in relevance. It 'stands for' an amount of work, of time spent on the task, an indicator of the kind of work expected and of the seriousness of the enterprise of 'making a contribution to knowledge'. The characteristics of the chapters and their sequence were and still are themselves subject to regulation. For instance, in many places there is still a requirement for a 'Literature Review', both as a review of 'the field' and a statement of the place of one's own work in that field. Conceptions of how disciplinary work is conducted – how knowledge is 'advanced' – are implicit in such generic aspects of the PhD text: ranging from what a PhD chapter 'is'; to what kinds of chapters are to be included, an insistence for instance, on demonstrating in a 'theory chapter', the relevance of the theoretical framing in relation to other possibilities that might have been chosen; to the sequencing of chapters; in many disciplinary areas the presence of empirically oriented chapters as the demonstration of a capacity to handle significant amounts of material and the capacity to turn that material into data; of competence in description and analysis.

In their characteristics and their ordering, chapters constituted – and still often do – an organization which exemplified the notion of 'a coherent 'body' of knowledge' and of 'coherent components' within that body of knowledge. A chapter was and often still is underpinned by a conception of 'completeness' of the 'treatment' of a topic and of 'knowledge'.

By contrast, writers of theses now, thoroughly embedded in the digital era as they are, might refuse notions of 'coherence', of 'a body of knowledge' as in '… setting forth "a coherent body of knowledge" …': an effect of postmodern theory. They might also refuse notions of 'completeness' inherent in phrases such as 'a "satisfactorily thorough and complete treatment" of the topic …' What becomes clear now is that the seemingly simple notion of 'length' provided a necessary – and at the time conceptually invisible – frame within which 'coherence' could and would be established and 'completeness' taken for granted. One might venture to sloganize: 'without "length" no "frame"'; 'without "frame", no "coherence"'; 'without "coherence" no "completeness"'. 'Frame' certainly guaranteed (attempts at) 'coherence' and was essential to ensure 'completeness'.

'Completeness' always has been an epistemological/ontological issue, though relatively invisible; now it is visible, yet entirely unresolved and insecure.

The facilities of the digital media can of course be used to construct 'completeness'; though their characteristics tend away from 'frame', 'limit', 'completeness'. They offer 'connection', and ubiquity of access. These facilities coincide with the skepsis of postmodern theory. The metaphors of the 'rhizome' for instance (Deleuze, 1978), of 'the' or of 'a' 'web', of 'network', are all metaphors which explicitly or implicitly oppose 'framing' (Bateson, 2000; Goffman, 1974). They are apt signifiers for signs which describe the foregrounded facilities of the digital media. Both the facilities and the metaphors differ radically from older metaphors of order: of hierarchy, of notions of an author's ordering; of the seemingly necessary and 'naturally' sequential order of chapters in the thesis text. Contemporary facilities and metaphors also work against the (in any case always fictive) chronological ordering of the research process and work: where it is assumed that the orderliness of theory produced method; method (or methodology/-ies) in turn underpins 'data-collection'; 'data description and analysis' together lead to 'findings'.

Everything about the explicit and implicit assumptions of the process of research and knowledge production, as that stately process in a world whose order is revealed by the results of that work: everything of that is inimical to the explicit and implicit assumptions of what research might be in a social world of provisionality, of the theoretical positions of postmodernity; and of the facilities of contemporary digital media. It would have been perfectly possible to use the digital media, even in their present form – in some mind experiment – in the more stable social world of thirty or forty years ago though those uses would have been profoundly different; or they could be used now, in a society that enforced specific social constraints with strong external prohibitions: designed to lead to a deliberate refusal of the use of all or of specific aspects of the potential of their inherent facilities.

The crucial issue is that there is now a congruence of social givens, of the arrangements of social environments, of theoretical conceptions following on from postmodern theories, and of the ubiquitously available potentials of current digital technologies. That conjunction and congruence has profound effects on the PhD now; it exerts enormous pressures now and will continue to do so more intensively into the near future.

Problems which had long been debated in the philosophy of knowledge are now starkly evident in the contradictions of the traditional thesis (its social/generic/medial/modal/semiotic/epistemological/ontological assumptions) and of these assumptions, though now articulated through the potentials and facilities of the digital media in contemporary social arrangements. The development of the digital media is bound to continue, with a trajectory which is relatively clear, barring the super- or inter-vention of social moves away from present trends. There is every reason to imagine the thesis of the quite near future as an *open text* (an idea which, for me at least, is, at present, still, a contradiction in terms); no longer bounded by the figure of the author, as in Foucault's conception in the 1950s (Foucault, 'Orders of Discourse', 1971); not limited by the producer now or for a future time; infinitely interpretable as all interpretations always are – though always limited by the bounds of what the thesis provides as the *prompt* for the basis of interpretation (Kress, 2010). Paradoxically, that thesis will in some ways be using contemporary digital means to produce an equivalent of the potentially open and infinite network of the footnote apparatus of the traditional scholarly text, a tradition rooted in medieval traditions of scholarship: a time when authorship was also *not* an issue.

Two further points on the implications of present social conditions and the facilities of the digital medium on the PhD. The turning away from stability and coherence which is evident in 'the social', whether in the domain of social practices, of public policy and practice or in theory, is matched – in the Humanities, the Arts, the Social Sciences – by an emphasis in academic work on *process* and *practices*. If stability is rejected in conceptions about 'the social', then that same rejection is mirrored and entrenched, at present, in academic work. In that respect, the digital media offer better means for dealing – for purposes of research – with the materials, the 'stuff' of social life, which current theory and research overwhelmingly present as processes – both in terms of (relatively) straightforward recording as well as of transcription/'transposition'. They offer tools for turning these materials into 'data' that remain relatively close to the material in its original social sites. I will return to that point in considering the PhD and multimodality.

The second point concerns 'coherence'. If the social is marked by the absence of coherence, then it follows that a large range of contemporary texts will also be characterized by that absence: it should be no surprise if it is absent in the PhD. If PhD researchers take seriously the requirement of providing apt accounts of *process* and *practices*, using one or another version of ethnography as means of description, then it is difficult to see in what ways such PhDs can be either 'coherent' or 'complete' – always assuming that to be an aim of the researcher. Whatever else 'ethnography' – of whatever form does or does not offer – it insists necessarily on the always provisional position of the ethnographer. This is reflected in an at times extreme anxiety by researchers – and in particular PhD researchers, who fear the sceptical eye of the examiners – in insisting on chains of 'reflexivity', as the refusal of the possibility of secure points of view.

PhDs will, in all these respects, be characterized by the signs of provisionality.

The (facilities of) media technologies always have their impact on research. Examples of this are readily to hand. I shall mention two. At the beginning of the twentieth century, first the wax-cylinder and then the phonograph as means of recording of sound, led to a burgeoning development of phonetics and phonology. In the 1950s to 1960s, the development of the reel-to-reel tape recorder led to the possibility – and then the explosion – of Conversation Analysis, of Discourse Analyses of various kinds, as of methodological developments in forms of ethnographic analysis. Digital media offer the potential of opening up vast areas for research in the Social Sciences, the Arts and the Humanities, with major impact on the scope and 'reach' of research; on the re-visiting of questions previously investigated with older technologies; as well as on methodology. Given contemporary social environments, the joint effect of linking *technologies of recording* – such as (digital) video; or the recording/tracking/documenting of activities in digital production – with the as yet still quite unexplored *facilities of digital media* in description and analysis of practices and processes, of turning such materials into 'data', research in these areas will experience a quantum leap: in 'reach', in research methods and in theorizing.

This will constitute an ever more insistent imperative for PhD researchers, to fully explore and use both the range of recorded materials and to explore and expand the range of means of transposition of such materials into data. In that context too, the digital media are bound to have a large effect in the acceleration of the move from 'theory' to 'method'. That is now clearly on the cards: the facilities of the digital media will emphasize method over theory – whatever that may (come to) mean.

The effects on the PhD are tangibly evident now; and they will intensify. Most (are beginning) now to focus on methods rather than on theory. Or to put this more clearly, for many PhD researchers, this is no longer a visible, existent choice, that is, of theory and its method versus the use of increasingly multiple methods. Where before methods were shaped by theory, frequently now no theoretical frame is evident, though there is a strong presence of (often multiple) methods. PhD work will, in my view, be shaped by the much enhanced facilities for recording and managing (video-recorded materials as) data and by an accompanying shift in emphasis from theory to methods.

One consequence will be an increasing concern with 'transcription'/ 'transposition', an essential part of the change from 'stuff' in the world, of 'material' to 'data'.

THE PHD AND MULTIMODALITY

The increasing focus on 'multimodality' has four causes at least. There is, first and foremost what we might call the 'world itself' – the constitution and shape of the social world which I sketched above; and the social semiotic effects of that changed social world. That links, second, to the softening of social boundaries, also mentioned earlier. Maintaining the fiction that 'language' is sufficient to all meaning needed great expenditure of social and semiotic effort; that effort or the power to exert it, now no longer exists. Third, in and out of that social change, there is the recognition that neither speech nor writing, nor both together ('language') can account for more than a part only of the domain of meaning; each separately and even both together are always partial means of making and accessing meaning. There is then, fourth, the intensification of the social/semiotic trends through the technological potentials of the digital media. The ready availability of the means of recording and production now available exert enormous pressure in the direction of recognizing what the world of meaning is actually like.

Once the multimodal character of meaning is acknowledged, the problem of 'transcription'/'transposition', a problem of a theoretical and practical kind, emerges. The term 'transcription' indicates in its name the route from *sound* to *script*, from *speech* to *writing*; and it points to the many problem in the transposition of material from speech to a written form. For one, the alphabet is an enormously limited resource for 'capturing' the vast potentials of sound, socially shaped, in the many affordances of speech. Only a small fraction of these can be 'transcribed'/'transposed' into script by means of letters. That which appears in transcriptions is never that which was there in the interaction: it is an always massively reduced account, a set of features reduced both by the interests of the researcher evident in the principles of the research question and the always inadequate resource for the transposition of meaning through 'letters' – as well as the other affordances of writing. The alphabet, differently in various speech and writing cultures, severely limits what can be transposed. What cannot be transposed tends to disappear from view, either entirely – it does not appear in the theory or even in 'common-sense' – or else it is relegated to the margin, acknowledged only to be dismissed as marginal: as in 'yes of course we are aware that these things (loudness, pace, rhythm, "tone of voice", indications of sex, gender, age and so on) matter, but let's now get on with the real issue'. Those things which are not 'the real issue' are the names as the extra-linguistic, the para-linguistic; they are not rule-governed but individual and idiosyncratic and as such not possible to account for, beyond the reach of theory.

A multimodal approach to meaning insists on encompassing all the potentials of making meaning. For the PhD researcher this poses two problems: one is a question of 'recognition': how can I 'recognize' what bits of the world need to be within the frame of my Research Question; and what are the means of 'transposing' these things into 'data' in the thesis text? It is at this point where I think the term 'transcription' becomes problematic because on the one hand the metaphor of 'script' introduces the severe limitations of that resource while offering, seemingly, a solution; and on the other hand the existence of the label becomes an obstacle to seeing the problem and thereby limits work in solving it (Bezemer and Mavers, 2011). But it also urges the PhD researcher to take account of the wide variety of modal resources which are essential in providing a full range of data for the Research Question posed.

The second problem is of an ontological and epistemological kind: modes (themselves transcriptional resources of 'the world') offer differing affordances: distinct and different takes on the world, and, in that they raise the question around 'knowledge' yet again, though differently to the (postmodern theory inspired) manner mentioned before. Now that recording of the world of meaning around us in all its manifestations is possible, a question which had remained a distant concern now becomes central: all modes have their specific affordances, so that choosing this mode rather than that brings with it the affordances – epistemological and ontological of each mode. Multimodality introduces the issue of ontology and epistemology into all research, and therefore into PhD research.

The digital media now make it possible to *show* what happened in time *in time*; and to demonstrate that taking such material 'out of time' is to produce serious misrepresentations of what that material is. Yet even the 'transposition', the 'transduction' of ontological material – 'knowledge' – from one spatially instantiated mode, writing, to another, image, shows the problem.

A simple example I use – mildly adapted from research in science classrooms can make the point (Kress, Tsatsarelis, Jewitt, & Ogborn, 2001). After four lessons on 'cells' the teacher asks, in class: 'Can someone tell me something about cells?' A young woman says: 'A cell has a nucleus, Miss'. Ontologically, the statement projects the world as one in which an entity, the 'cell', 'has' something, a 'nucleus'. Now the teacher says, 'Very good! Can you come to the front and draw what you have said?' This demand poses a quite different (implicit and unavoidable) question: the student now has to make a decision about how to draw the 'shape' of the cell, where in that shape to place the cell – in the centre, more or less, or nearer the cell wall; she has to decide whether the nucleus is a small dot or large, a small circle or a large one and so on. What the science teacher may be regarding relatively straightforwardly as 'knowledge about cells' is profoundly dependent on the potentials of modal representation and realization. In one case, the written account, there is a 'statement' about two entities and an indication/ naming of their relation (one of 'ownership'); in the other case there is a depiction of spatial relations, of size, of positioning. In each case there are relations, though they are not straightforward by any means; and there are real differences: the spoken utterance does not provide (sufficient) information to allow the drawing to be made; nor could the drawing be used to predict the relation of ownership.

Choice of mode construes the world distinctly and differently so. Each representation in each mode forces the maker of the representation into an epistemological/ontological commitment: 'this is how the world is'. With digital media, making modal choices is relatively easy. Yet the researcher is forced, willy-nilly, into making decisions about the kind of epistemological commitment she or he wishes to make; how she or he wishes to represent 'the knowledge' at issue. That choice construes the world for the person who will engage with that representation, so that epistemological commitment is at the same time an ideological positioning.

Difference in modal choice and representation exposes the age-old issue of what has been named implicit and explicit knowledge. This becomes a huge problem in sites where practices – knowledge which precise and embodied but not spoken or written – are the issue. 'Transcription' by means of the alphabet, now that other possibilities exist through digital media, would constitute an ongoing, now *wilful*, and massive misrepresentation.

This is not the place to discuss the theoretical issues around 'transcription'. Rather it is to point out that at a time when (a) the significance of *all* modes in communication has come into the foreground; (b) when the technology exists to provide 'apt' means of presenting what counts or what should count as data and when (c) the social conditions are such that institutional blindness to matters other than the linguistic is coming under severe challenge, the effect on research, whether in a PhD or elsewhere, have to be seriously looked at. Different distributions of power and agency, now compared with several decades ago, as well as, connected with that, an insistence on the *recognition* and apt *valuation* of semiotic work performed in all the means a culture makes available, makes it no longer feasible to overlook such meanings.

In a multimodal view, the *materiality* of modes is one of the central concerns. In relation to *writing* it now becomes apparent that 'writing' has existed as an abstraction. Materially, 'writing' exists in different forms; it is produced as handwriting, as print, as inscriptions of various kinds – each with the potential for making meaning. Materiality connects with the sensuousness of modes, the body and its senses. These are issues which have been theoretically debated since the 1980s, especially in feminist theory (Gross, 1989; Butler, 1988), though now with the facilities of the digital media and the understanding of the affordances of different modes these matters will become a more insistent presence in very many more PhDs. If, as is clear, many PhDs had not dealt with the 'materialness' of meaning, or, putting it differently, with the materiality of modes, it was at least in part because 'materiality' was not amenable to being 'accountable' in ways that other stuff in the world could be turned into 'data'. After all, what was left out was not visible, audible or evident to any theory that would have underpinned a transcription. Embodiment was a large area of theorizing, though without the recording, documenting and transcribing now possible with digital media and the theoretical frame of social semiotics and multimodality.

These effects, in some ways similar to what I have already pointed to, link with the larger social frame. Where there had been not just canonical genres but also canonical modes for representation – writing dominantly; though also images in Art, or in Science; or numerical modes; etc. – now the link of 'canonicity' and mode is challenged everywhere: whether in discourse, in genre or in mode. This poses the problem of 'recognition', for the PhD no less than for the teacher in a class.

The recognition of multimodality is posing an agenda which is entirely traditional in some ways and entirely new in others. A big issue for the PhD now is to assist in a whole set of questions which are the result of social matters as much as of the technologies of dissemination, representation and production. PhD researchers are called on to provide tools for recognition of that which has hitherto not been recognized, left aside. They will increasingly be asked to do the unusual, the entirely innovative, in a genre beset by still relatively tightly controlled convention. That is, PhD researchers for a while to come will face the problem of a mismatch between their university's regulation and what the world around the discipline and the university both enables and demands. Just as the social conditions have loosened the grip of power on certain generic and modal aspects of the PhD, so do the social conditions now permit and increasingly *demand* apt means of representing the world to be accounted for in the 'frame' of the PhD in means that are apt to the materials and what is being asked of them.

CONCLUSIONS

There are times when the social is in a period of *relative* stability, and with that conventions around knowledge and representation are relative stable. Depending on dispositions of power, the agency of the PhD researcher is stronger or less so, foregrounded or subsumed under requirements of conformity to power and convention.

It is clear that conventions are not stable and under continuing, ongoing challenge, on every front. Every aspect of what the PhD was securely 'about', even some twenty years ago, is now a matter of careful positioning: socially, medially and modally. All this, while the very status of the award itself is subject to constant challenge.

Here I have pointed to the different and yet convergent effects of three factors: the overarching – and for me 'semiotically generative' – social frame; the technologies of production and dissemination – the digital media and the technologies of representation, technologies for making meaning material. These are everywhere connected, all with social origins and social effects; yet all also independently effective, socially, ontologically and epistemologically. It is the coming together of certain social (as well as economic, political) conditions with the facilities of the technologies of digital media and the technologies for making meaning material – the modes of contemporary multimodal communication – which are posing profound problems for research done under the category of the PhD. And all this at a time when there is a profound theoretical scepsis about the very category of knowledge itself.

REFERENCES

Bateson, G. (2000). *Steps to an Ecology of Mind.* Chicago, IL: University of Chicago Press.

Bezemer, J. & Mavers, D. (2011). Multimodal transcription as academic practice: A social semiotic perspective. *International Journal of Social Research Methodology, 14*(3), 191–206.

Deleuze, G. & Guattari, F. (1987). *Thousand Plateaus: Capitalism and Schizophrenia.* Minneapolis, MN: University of Minnesota Press.

ESRC (UK Economic and Social Science Research Council). (2000). The social production of school English. A 3-year research project funded by the ESRC of England.

Foucault, M. (1971). Orders of discourse. *Social Science Information, 10,* 7–30.

Goffman, E. (1974). *Frame Analysis: An Essay on the Organization of Experience.* Cambridge, MA: Harvard University Press.

Gross, L. (1989). *Sexual Subversions.* Sydney: Allen and Unwin.

Hodge, B. (1995). Monstrous knowledge: Doing PhDs in the new humanities. *The Australian Universities Review, 38*(2), 35–40.

Jewitt, C., Moss, G., & Cardini, A. (2007). Pace, interactivity and multimodality in teacher design of texts for IWBs. *Learning, Media and Technology, 32*(3), 302–318.

Jewitt, C., Bezemer, J., Jones, K., & Kress, G. (2009). Changing English? The impact of technology and policy on a school subject in the 21st century. *English Teaching: Practice and Critique, 8*(3), 21–40.

Kress, G. R. (2010). *Multimodality. A Social Semiotic Approach to Contemporary Communication.* London: Routledge.

Kress, G. R., Tsatsarelis, C., Jewitt, C., & Ogborn, J. (2001). *Multimodal Learning and Teaching. The Rhetorics of the Science Classroom*. London: Continuum.

Kress, G. R., Bourne, J., Franks, A., Hardcastle, J., Jewitt, C., Jones, K., & Reid, E. (2005). *English in Urban Classrooms*. London: Routledge.

Lyotard, J. F. (1984). *The Postmodern Condition: A Report on Knowledge*. Minneapolis, MN: University of Minnesota Press.

15

Practice-as-Research in Music Performance

Mine Doğantan-Dack

INTRODUCTION: ISSUES IN CONTEMPORARY PERFORMANCE STUDIES

Even though sound recordings have been available for over 120 years[1], evolving from the wax phonograph cylinder through the shellac disc to the digital MP3 to become ubiquitous artefacts in our contemporary culture, their acceptance as valid documents for musicological research did not happen early on and naturally during the twentieth century. Since its nineteenth-century beginnings as an academic discipline rooted in German philology and hermeneutics, musicology has been dominated by a textual approach to knowledge production and presentation such that its primary source material, namely the musical score, has been conceptualised as a 'final, fixed, immortal text' (Bowen, 1999: 429), the meanings of which can be revealed through the reading and deciphering of abstract musical relationships embedded in the notated symbols. Furthermore, the communication of any understanding and knowledge thus gained about a piece of music would typically be achieved through the creation and dissemination of written texts[2]. Placing its foundations on the tangible score, musicological research throughout the larger part of the twentieth century displayed a dismissive attitude towards not only recordings but to what recordings document, namely musical performances[3]. This attitude is epitomised in Arnold Schönberg's famous words that:

> Music need not be performed any more than books need to be read aloud, for its logic is perfectly represented on the printed page; and the performer, for all his intolerable

arrogance, is totally unnecessary except as his interpretations make the music understandable to an audience unfortunate enough not to be able to read it in print. (in Newlin,
1980: 164)

In this chapter, I first discuss the cultural and historical background for the
recent paradigm shift within musicology from a score-based to a performance-
based understanding of music, evaluating the role of digital technologies in
the establishment of performance studies as a musicological discipline. The
first section also offers a critique of the status quo in performance studies by
reference to examples from the dominant disciplinary discourse, which continues to sustain the assumptions of a score-based ideology of music and thereby
marginalises the role of performance skill and expertise in knowledge production
and dissemination within the discipline. In the second section of the chapter,
I explore the conceptual problems surrounding the notion of 'practice-as-research
in music performance', and comment on the possibilities offered by digital technologies to processes of research and to the shaping of research outcomes, and
on the continuing role of knowledge production in written, textual formats within
practice-based musical performance research. In the final section, I present
my practice-based research project titled *Alchemy in the Spotlight*, discussing the
challenges the project poses to the dominant discourse and methodologies in
contemporary performance studies, and arguing for the necessity of multimodal
approaches to knowledge presentation and dissemination when researching live
musical performances.

The impressive rise of performance studies as a musicological discipline over
the last couple of decades, which according to Cook and Clarke moved musicology away from a text-based ideology[4] and an overriding pre-occupation with the
score 'towards an understanding of music as performance' (Cook and Clarke,
2004: 10), is the result of a felicitous meeting of various complex cultural trends
at a specific historical juncture: first, following recent scientific advances that
revealed the intimate relationship between the bodily and mental experiences,
the decline of the Cartesian model of a disembodied mind in philosophy put an
end to the primacy of the mental – and thereby of the abstract – in the construction, representation and reception of knowledge (Damasio, 1994). Contrary to
what Descartes believed, 'our bodily experience is the primal basis for everything we can mean, think, know, and communicate' (Lakoff and Johnson, 1999:
xi), and our physical interactions with the material world are fundamental to any
cognitive and affective experience and thereby to knowledge; music is no exception since musical experiences do not originate in the disembodied mind of a
listener contemplating abstract musical structures, but rather in the intentional
movements of the hand, of the vocal cords, of the musician's whole body in producing musical sounds. Second, the post-modernist emphasis on the role of the
body in the construction of subjectivity and knowledge inevitably motivated a
change from an understanding of music as abstract structure embodied in the
score to one that regards performance as the true site of musical embodiment
such that in its absence the notated 'text' remains mute and lifeless; this new

conception turned attention to the creation of embodied knowledge, that is knowledge attained in and through practice of performance in a particular cultural context.

Another catalyst in the move towards the emergence of performance studies within musicology has been the recent shift away from monomodality to multi-modality in Western culture (Kress and van Leeuwen, 2001). The waning of the dominance of textual practices and the increasing deployment of a mixed set of modes or semiotic resources, including images and sounds, in the making and communication of meanings brought into focus the important role played in contemporary practices by qualities such as colour, layout, font type and size, etc., which for the longest time were regarded as inessential as far as the content of the communicated knowledge is concerned. The implication for performance studies of such a multimodal turn has been to emphasise the importance of expressive qualities such as tone colour, touch, articulation, phrasing, tempo and dynamic variations in processes of musical communication. Because such expressive qualities, which preoccupy performers in their efforts to create musical meaning, cannot be notated accurately and cannot, therefore, be textualised, musicology traditionally regarded them as secondary qualities of musical sounds and structures in comparison with the primary qualities of pitch and rhythm, the two most precisely notatable aspects of music. The influence of multimodality moved the centre of scholarly research from an almost exclusive focus on musical sound as written to musical sound as heard, listened to and made by human beings – with all its vibrating, every-changing, rising and falling tonal shades.

The influence of these complex cultural developments would, nevertheless, have been insufficient to firmly establish performance studies as a thriving research area without the powerful impetus of *the* prime mover behind the scene, namely digital technologies. In the absence of digital technologies, the paradigm shift in musicological thought from a perspective on music as a text in written form to music as enacted and embodied in human performance could not have been realised. First, the appearance of commercially available keyboard instruments, such as the Musical Instrument Digital Interface (MIDI), which can be directly monitored by a computer to record and store all instrumental events of a performance, meant that performance data could be captured with considerable precision from expert performers playing music. Second, it is only after the advent of sophisticated software programs that it became possible for researchers to scrutinise in detail the century-old legacy of recorded performances and thereby validate them as primary musicological source documents. Although research on expressive qualities of musical performances go back to the last decade of the nineteenth century[5], the great majority of data in these early studies derived from measurements of keyboard performances given specifically for research purposes in a 'laboratory' setting; without digital technologies the expressive properties of truly inspired – and inspiring – performances by some of the greatest musicians captured in commercial recordings could not be studied in any systematic and rigorous manner. Digital technologies for the first time allowed musicologists to 'navigate and browse [sound] recordings' (Cook, 2007: 186) and obtain rich data, providing 'the same kind of empirical grasp on performance that we take for granted when writing about scores' (Cook, 1999: 42). As Clarke has observed 'the perennial problem with the study of performance is its temporality and hence ephemerality, and if nothing else, concrete performance data [obtained by digital means from recorded performances] at least gives analysts and other parties the assurance that they are dealing with the same thing' (Clarke, 1995: 52). In this sense, the most significant factor behind the establishment of performance studies has been the reification afforded musical performance by digital technologies, which at the same time paved the way for the frequent inclusion, in mainstream disciplinary discourse, of spectrograms, tempo-graphs and corresponding sound files alongside the written text, further supporting the move to a multimodal approach to knowledge production and dissemination.

Ironically, while providing empirical rigour, and thereby scientific status to the study of musical performances, recent digital technologies at the same time have been instrumental in sustaining the values of a score-based, textual ideology that musicologists of a 'performative turn' (Cook, 2001, 2003) ardently wished to leave behind. The increasing multimodality in knowledge presentation and dissemination within performance studies is not, in this sense, a reflection of a move to a *multimodal conception* of musical performance, which is still largely regarded to function similarly to a *musical score-cum-literary text*. The great majority of the data gathered digitally from recordings – for example, information about the tempo and dynamics of a performance – is represented visually by means of static, spatial graphs, which are rather 'disturbingly like a score' (Clarke, 2004: 99). Since it is now possible to go back and forth a recorded performance represented by means of visual graphs, and to dwell on a chosen segment by magnifying it temporally and 'freezing' the fleeting event, the temporal essence of a musical performance is transformed into and comprehended in spatial terms, similar to a text on the printed page or the screen. While a performance in real life is unidirectional, cannot be compressed or expanded temporally, and moves from the first note to the last inexorably without any breaks, its spatial representation invites a 'reading' of the performance as if it is a written text, by going back and forth at one's leisure, pondering on selected passages and even stopping half-way to return to it the next day.

The greatest peril for research in musical performance of such tangible, spatial representations that objectify performance data is the illusion they perpetuate that they capture and reflect the dynamics, the artistic experience and expert knowledge involved in the making of a musical performance. In other words, they can – and often do – easily lead to the assumption that empirical research on performance gives researchers access to the artistic principles behind performance making. This misapprehension has been exacerbated by the fact that historically performers and musicologists never interacted sufficiently to develop the tradition of a shared conceptual platform and discourse: consequently, the dominant disciplinary ideology and protocols in performance studies have by convention failed to assign performers themselves any authority over the mechanisms of knowledge production, representation and dissemination. The most serious charge to emerge from such a situation is that performance studies has been explaining musical performance without performers, and without any representation of the insider's expert view. The words of theatre practitioner and performance theorist Schechner fittingly sum up this predicament: 'The great big gap between what a performance is to people inside and what it is to people outside conditions all the thinking about performance' (Schechner, 2003: 300).

Consequently, the dominant disciplinary discourse in contemporary performance studies within musicology is shaped not only by a textual approach to music and music making, but also through attempts to assimilate musical performance into a domain of knowledge within which the researcher, studying performances from the outside as it were, can exercise his or her theoretical expertise. For example, Cook argues that 'the study of music as performance is part and parcel of the shift within musicology as a whole towards reception history; performance is self-evidently a form of interpretation, *in just the same way as* are critical or historical writing about music, iconographic representations, or TV and film adaptations' [my italics] (Cook, 2007: 184). Any expert performer would object to such a formulation on the grounds that the embodied-aesthetic quest that drives a musical performances does not overlap in any significant sense with the features defining the kinds of interpretation mentioned by Cook: indeed, there is an all-important ontological disparity between musical performance and critical writings, film adaptations, etc. in that the former is an action, constituted by the *intentional* movements and gestures of the performer driven by artistic principles and aims, while the latter are not. Within the multiplicity of interpretative practices in relation to music, performance stands out as being inexorably connected to the actions of a human agent in a given space at a given time: whether heard live or on a recording, the sounds of a performance are causally related to the aesthetically driven activity of producing the sounds[6]. Research that aims to understand the sounds of a performance – and the physical movements generating the sounds – without consideration of the artistic processes of aesthetic judgement and choice informing them is bound to remain inconclusive in accounting for what happens in a musical performance. Hence, while the strategy of representing musical performance in terms of what is familiar for the musicologist might seem innocent, this practice has been marginalizing performance expertise and its vital role in the generation of knowledge about performances.

The pervasiveness of a textual ideology in studying and conceptualising musical performance is also evident in the introduction of the term 'acoustic text' (Cook, 2007) to refer to recorded performances, which are regarded as the basic 'repository of evidence' (Leech-Wilkinson, 2001: 1) in performance studies. First, the term conceals the aesthetic primacy of live performance as the golden standard in the art of music making within the tradition of Western classical music, by insinuating that a performance is always crafted in the same way as a written text, and that the two activities have similar histories of becoming. Although the frequently articulated folk-psychological opposition between live and recorded musical performances has been critically disavowed by various scholars (Auslander, 1999; Fabian, 2008; Johnson, 2010), there is ample evidence indicating that for performing musicians there are significant phenomenological, aesthetic and indeed existential differences between the experiences of performing live and in the recording studio. It is, of course, correct to argue that the technological possibilities offered by the recording studio allow a performer to construct a performance from multiple-takes *after* reflecting upon and evaluating his or her artistic 'product' in the manner of a writer who reflects upon his or her drafts before finalising the text. Nevertheless, in a live context on stage, which is where all recording musicians start out and develop as performers by cultural necessity, the kind of control a performer has over the performance that unfolds publicly in real time is fundamentally different from the control an author exercises over the final textual artefact that is publicly available. Second, and more importantly, the term 'acoustic text' obscures the fact that there is always the potential for failure in the actual making of a live performance unlike in the making of a text, which succeeds or fails according to public verdict following its completion and dissemination as a product. A textual conception of musical performance thus minimises the value of the skill and expert knowledge involved in performance making, which at the professional level is one of the most complex and demanding tasks human beings accomplish, combining remarkable physical and mental achievement (Altenmüller and Gruhn, 2002; Clarke, 2002).

PRACTICE OF MUSICAL PERFORMANCE AS RESEARCH: CONCEPTUAL CONSIDERATIONS

It is, therefore, a fortunate – and much desired – historical coincidence that various recent cultural and economic factors led to transformations in the structuring and operations of the Higher Education sector and in the funding strategies of Research Councils, creating favourable conditions for the introduction of expert performers into academia and the potential integration of their expert professional knowledge and artistic experience into traditional research cultures[7]. Currently, more and more universities and conservatories offer opportunities for performers to undertake research projects that are specifically structured around their artistic practice, and creative outputs in multimodal formats resulting from such undertakings (e.g. audio and/or audio–visual documentations and representations of the artistic processes and products) are increasingly regarded as valid research outcomes. In this connection, digital technologies offer unprecedented opportunities to the performer–researcher for incorporating his or her practice into the processes of documenting and disseminating his or her research work.

The web-based, open-access, peer-reviewed online multimedia repository PRIMO (Practice as Research in Music Online), for example, makes it possible for performers to disseminate their research outputs in audio, video, graphics and/or multi-media formats to the wider research communities[8].

Because the development of a cultural environment in Higher Education Institutions where the performer can undertake artistic practice of musical performance with an imperative to contribute knowledge and insight to performance studies is a very recent phenomenon, there are, as yet, no firmly established models and methodologies, and no discursive cohesion among the presentations of knowledge that is generated by this kind of research. Furthermore, as 'the latest (the last) scion in the family of knowledge in Western society, a descendant that is currently in a frank phase of growth through trial and error' (Coessens, Crispin, & Douglas, 2009: 44), such research-driven artistic practice poses fundamental challenges to the basic paradigms of traditional research. Consequently, there are ongoing debates concerning the conditions under which performance can be regarded as research, the ways it establishes and advances knowledge in the discipline of musicology, and the nature of the research outcomes.

Among the various terms that are used to describe research undertaken by practitioners and which involves practice as an integral part of its methodology and output, one in particular requires conceptual deconstructing since it complicates the relationship between practice and research by entailing their identity: this is 'practice as research'. In other words, when applying the term to musical performance, one would conceptually identify performance, and therefore the performing activity that produces the performance as product, as a research activity. Clearly, not all musical performance is *ipso facto* research: there is a distinction – an important distinction – between professional practice of musical performance, and the practice of musical performance as part of a research enquiry[9]. Is there any basis then on which a given musical performance can be identified as constituting a research activity? What could it mean to say of a musical performance as it unfolds – while performers make it and listeners listen to it – that it *is* a research activity, as distinct from a 'research-informed performance', for example, which is conceptually quite clear?

My position in this regard is that performing music in the Western classical tradition is *never, as it unfolds in real time, identical to a research activity*[10]. I do not make this assertion based on folk-psychological prejudices against traditional research that regard it as an objective, distanced, unemotional undertaking. On the contrary, I believe that both artistic practice and traditional research can be creative, passionate, and involve complex cognitive and affective processes as well as theorising. Nevertheless, performing music does not – indeed cannot – involve any reflective component by the performer, at least not in the way we understand it to be a crucial aspect of any research activity: as a defining feature of research, reflection always offers the researcher the possibility to change, improve, transform, expand, and re-work his or her ideas and their manner of presentation *before* the research outcome is made publicly available.

This possibility is simply not present for the performer during the making of a live performance.

Even when the performance takes place as part of an ongoing research activity, *while it happens* it is bracketed as an artistic undertaking that is continually striving towards singularity and is concerned not with the creation, representation, dissemination of new insight, understanding or knowledge, but rather with the making of an affectively charged, hopefully magical and transformational experience. While performing music, the performer's devotion is to the music and not to any research question. It is important to note that other processes that are part of the totality of musical performance practice, such as the preparatory processes that take place in practice sessions and rehearsals, can indeed be identified as research activities in the sense that the temporal structuring of these processes allows the performer to interrupt the unidirectional flow of the music, to stop and reflect on what he or she has just played, and to experiment with the music. Nevertheless, the fact that performers think about what they do rigorously, that they experiment on a daily basis with the music they play, that they are involved in complex cognitive and affective operations and implicit theorising, is not sufficient to render the resulting live performance a research activity; that there is expert knowledge and skill embodied in the activity of performance-making does not automatically qualify the performance as research. To hold such a view would all but collapse the distinction between research and virtually any other kind of activity that involves expertise and skill, and as such would not offer any substantial arguments to clarify the issues surrounding artistic activities integrated within research enquiries. For conceptual clarity, then, when musical performances and certain research imperatives meet in a broader set of activities by practitioner–researchers, the totality of the undertakings can be referred to as 'practice-as-research (or practice-based research) in musical performance' rather than as 'musical performance-as-research'. Musical performance in the Western classical tradition as a real-time, embodied, unidirectional phenomenon can be integrated into a research activity only as artistic practice, and it is the particular dynamics between this practice and the reflective exploration and theorising that shapes this particular kind of research.

Such a stance has significant implications regarding the appropriate forms and formats in which the findings of practice-based research can be (re)presented in that if a performance itself is not a research activity, then an audio or audio–visual recording of it does not constitute a research output. As part of a research enquiry any musical performance needs to be contextualised by means of pre- and/or post-performance reflection, meaning that the practitioner–researcher reflects on the relationship between the research questions being explored and the particular performance in question, and subsequently presents this reflection in a medium that is separate from the audio-(visually) documented performance, so that the knowledge, creativity and experience generated during and through the performance does not remain simply locked into it. Ongoing discussions about the nature this medium should assume is one of the divisive issues in practice-as-research in music: on the one hand, some claim that a musical performance is its own argument in its specifically musical language and that no other medium should be required to establish the knowledge-bearing status of a musical performance. On the other hand, some argue that what is required is not a demonstration of the knowledge-bearing status of performance but of the processes of knowledge production in a form that allows other researchers to retrace its history of becoming. I have argued elsewhere (Doğantan-Dack, 2008) that because the foundations of knowledge production and research in the Western tradition prioritise reason and propositional knowledge over and above affect and know-how, all too often even the obvious fact that musical performance embodies expert knowledge has to be argued for and demonstrated with ample evidence[11]. When the performance is part of a research enquiry, it becomes even more urgent to demonstrate the processes of creativity and knowledge that form part of pre- and post-performance reflection in a medium that is different from the documented performance, such as a text, further audio-visual or multimodal material so as to contribute to the research context. PRIMO, for example, requires a textual supplement that describes and gives a summary of the submitted item's content 'and an insight into its contribution to current research'[12].

The reflective component of practice-based-research in musical performance further problematises the discourse of performance studies by seeking to represent situated knowledge derived from the performer's perspective. The dominant disciplinary discourse is still very much the product of an attitude relentlessly pursued in the name of objective, scientific research since the beginnings of musicology as an academic discipline, and as such it continues to largely shun away from expressions of the subjective, of the affective and the ephemeral. As Cumming has observed:

> ... the 'quest for certainty' can have interpreters [theorists] avoiding comment on any aspect of musical content for which they cannot find an empirical foundation. Comment on such things as sound quality and its signification, or the affective connotation of a phrase, do, for example, present a greater risk to an interpreter [theorist] who wishes to project the image of secure knowledge, because the factors informing aural judgments of this kind are not always readily accessible ... and they cannot be specified by reference to a score. (2000: 46)

Consequently, aesthetic value judgements in relation to musical performance – regarded too vague and subjective – remain outside the purview of performance studies. Studies that analyse and compare recorded performances invariably refrain from making assertions about the aesthetic quality of the performances being explored, and as such do not reveal knowledge about the very fundamentals of the performer's artistic activity, which is continuously driven by value judgements of one kind or another. For the performers, aesthetic evaluations motivate the acceptance or rejection of various musical possibilities that are entertained as an interpretation of a piece develops. The insider's view on what happens in a musical performance – and why – can only be articulated through a discourse that takes account of and thrives on the situatedness, the very subjectivity of the aesthetic judgements made by the performer in relation to his or her performance. In the words of Cox, 'artistic research must be rigorous, but it cannot be simultaneously objective and artistically engaged. Yet another turn is required, a fundamental re-appraisal of the role and legitimacy of the interposed sensibilities of the researcher – one which perceives them as validating the research, rather than compromising it' (in Coessens, Crispin, & Douglas, 2009: 10). One of the most significant contributions of practice-based research projects to contemporary performance studies is the increasing awareness they bring regarding the fundamental artistic principles, methods, practices and values that drive and sustain musical performance; indeed, an awareness that 'the relationship between studying performance and doing performance is integral' (Schechner, 2002: 1). Within the totality of all activities that define 'performance practice' in the Western classical tradition, it is in the processes of live public performance that the artistry of 'doing performance' is fully represented; and it is, therefore, in these processes that the fundamental principles of artistic performance should be explored.

THE ALCHEMY PROJECT

Questions relating to the nature and experience of performing live have rarely been asked in performance studies, which built its epistemological as well ontological foundations on recorded performances. 'Musicology's perpetually absent objects' (Abbate, 2004: 514), live performances nevertheless continue to be the touchstone in the artistic practice of performance making in the Western classical tradition. The artistry of a performer that is revealed during a live performance is culturally highly valued since on stage he or she has to achieve a successful performance in an environment that is doubly constrained by the inherent indeterminacy of the event and the necessity of uninterrupted flow, mobilising a remarkable range of skills and experiences. In cultural terms, it is particularly important to articulate the significance of live musical performance as the ultimate norm in classical music practice when performances recorded and edited in the studio provide the context for an overwhelming majority of musical experiences. The practice-based research project titled *Alchemy in the Spotlight: Qualitative Transformations in Chamber Music Performance,* funded by the AHRC[13], and directed by this author is the first research undertaking to explore live performance from the perspective of professional performers[14].

The Alchemy project concerns investigating the individual and collective cognitive and affective processes involved in performing live in public in the context of a professional piano trio, which has been specifically established for this project (Marmara Piano Trio)[15]. The practices of the piano trio in rehearsals, workshops and live performances are central in addressing the research questions posed. One of the aims of the project is to identify and explore the magic that performers sometimes experience during a live performance. In formal terms, performance magic is related to certain qualitative transformations, referring to certain processes that are peculiar to live performance contexts as distinct from the processes involved in rehearsals and practice sessions. During a live performance, the cognitive-affective world of the performers and consequently the interpretation of the music they perform often undergo certain qualitative transformations. These transformations are related to such phenomena as increasing expressive freedom, increasing affective involvement, unplanned creative interpretative choices and certain alterations in time-consciousness, which turn the ordinary into something special on stage: a process of alchemy. The Alchemy project explores the conditions of emergence of such transformations in the context of a professional piano trio preparing and performing selected works from the classical, romantic and contemporary repertoire; it compares and contrasts the processes that take place in rehearsals/practice sessions with those that unfold during a live performance. Existing research on chamber music practice focuses on the preparatory processes rather than the live event itself[16]. However, because live performance is characterised by an inherent indeterminacy such that the individual and collaborative cognitive–affective processes involved in the preparatory phase do not lead to those that shape the live event through the logic of linear causality, it is not possible to understand all that happens in a live performance by reference to the preparatory processes alone. There is, in this sense, a qualitative difference between preparatory processes and the performance itself. Neuroscientist Damasio articulates this difference as a passage over a threshold:

> I have always been intrigued by the specific moment when, as we sit waiting in the audience, the door to the stage opens and a performer steps into the light; or, to take the other perspective, the moment when a performer who awaits in semidarkness sees the same door open, revealing the lights, the stage, the audience. I realized some years ago that the moving quality of this moment, whichever point of view one takes, comes from its embodiment of an instance of birth, of passage through a threshold that separates a protected but limiting shelter from the possibility and risk of a world beyond and ahead. (1999: 3)

One of the most significant hypotheses of the Alchemy project is that the intentional processes that performers undertake to achieve positive qualitative transformations during a live performance do not invariably lead to such transformations, which may or may not take place during the actual event; consequently, investigating them is contingent on making them happen in the first place. Rather than planning and predicting them, performers can only take risks and wish for them to happen. In this sense, the professional practice of live performance is the only valid instrument of research for exploring the qualitative transformations in question.

The Alchemy project challenges some of the received and established notions about music performance within contemporary performance studies. One of these concerns the way live performance has been conceptualised. Accordingly, the purpose of all preparatory processes is to get the musicians ready for the final stage of public performance, where an interpretation that is more or less fixed in its details during the practice sessions and rehearsals is unfolded for an audience. Indeed, it is in part this conception that has led researchers who aim to understand how performers work to focus exclusively on the processes involved in practice sessions and rehearsals, and to neglect issues relating to performing live in public. Performers, however, do continue to learn on stage, which can be regarded as their workplace, and it is the new knowledge thus acquired that becomes the basis for future superior performances. In other words, there is a kind of expert musical knowledge that simply cannot be acquired in the practice room. Pianist Sviatoslav Richter, for instance, is known to have said that it was only at his fourth public performance of Mozart's Piano Sonata in A minor that he achieved what he considered a satisfactory interpretation (in Neuhaus, 1993: 206). The Alchemy project aims to articulate this knowledge and to change the dominant conception of live performance by arguing that from the performer's perspective, it represents only an intermediary arrival point in the unfolding 'life' of a piece of music in 'the hands' of performers, so to speak, rather than a final, fixed state.

In this connection, the project provides further support for the hypothesis that a musical performance is not identical to a research activity. One of the research findings of the Alchemy project is that the way performers attain new knowledge about performance making on stage, that is the way they continue to learn through live performance, does not fit the model that represents learning or coming to know in traditional research.

The origins of this model go back to Plato's *Allegory of the Cave*: the prisoner who can break away from his or her chains of ignorance in the darkness of the cave and undertakes the difficult journey to the outer world and towards the light, ultimately *beholds* the Platonic Forms, that is the essence of each and every phenomena. It is at this moment of visual beholding that he or she comes to know reality[17]. This is a conceptual manner of knowing in that the internal structuring and outer form of the Idea or Platonic Form is clearly 'grasped'. Nightingale argues (2004) that this kind of culminating vision represents the basis of what we understand by theorising in the West; in fact, originally, the word *theoria* was used in ancient Greece to refer either to the activity of an audience watching a spectacle or the spectacle gazed at. There are indeed many examples from the history of music theory, that confirm the model. Schenker, for instance, has famously declared that he did not invent the *Urlinie* but was given a vision of it[18]. Similarly, nineteenth-century music theorist Fétis recounted, at the beginning of his *Traité* (1849), how the nature of the tonal system was revealed to him in a flash of intellectual synthesis while sitting under a tree in the woods.

The Platonic model for acquiring knowledge does not fit what happens when performance magic takes place during a live event: learning through live musical performance is rather similar to what Tekippe has called 'primordial knowing' (1996), which can be modelled on mystical experiences of becoming-one-with or, perhaps, rites of passage. The metaphor of 'alchemy' aptly describes this kind of experience without necessarily invoking any mystical dimensions. As in alchemy, during a live performance, the performer at his or her best turns the ordinary into something highly valued, and in the process gets transformed himself/herself. The experience has the peculiar quality of triggering in the performers and audiences alike a powerful affective way of knowing: while in conceptual knowing, the subject beholds the object of knowledge in a clear and distinct manner (*à la* Descartes), in primordial knowing, the passing of the threshold from not-knowing to knowing takes place as the subject merges with the object so as to grasp it from within, as it were. And in this sense, primordial knowing moves beyond traditional concepts of knowledge and understanding associated with research, into *wisdom*, which involves acting with just the right aesthetic decisions at the right moment during the live event so as to produce performance magic.

The Alchemy project also provides data corroborated with ample anecdotal evidence that the conditions of emergence of qualitative transformations are bound up with the social dimension of the live performance. For many performers, going on stage is a highly charged positive – and at times euphoric – affective experience; the famous tenor Enrico Caruso, for example, is known to have said that 'he could achieve the correct mental state in order to sing his top Cs convincingly when he was in the presence of an audience' (Davidson, 1997: 215). There is, in this sense, a distinct social ontology to live performance. Although the performer's artistic skills and capabilities are the most important determining factors for the emergence of high-quality performances, the magic does not emerge only out of the performer's own resources but also requires audience presence as in a live context. This is why many performers feel that the recording studio, while offering a safer environment for performance making, also takes away the magic of the live event that thrives on the inspiration the artist draws from his or her listening audience on stage[19]. Another aspect of the live event that is seldom mentioned is the impact of the performance space on the performance making both acoustically and socially: according to the findings of the Alchemy project, mechanisms of knowledge production – in the sense of practising alchemy and magic on stage – start functioning if and when performers, with the intention of interacting with the performance space so as to 'draw' the audience into their music making, succeed in making subtle expressive adjustments that simply could not have been rehearsed.

CONCLUSION

Because a live musical performance resists translation into a conceptual object of understanding in the absence of a tangible phenomenon that could represent it, a necessary starting point for any research on live music performance, whether traditional or practice-based, is a recorded documentation of it, which nevertheless is not sufficient to provide a full picture of the vanished event. Given that the artistic features of live performance making are so closely related to social factors, it becomes imperative to represent and disseminate the findings of this kind of practice-based research project on live music making by multimodal means in that it is not possible to document the complex social and cultural web that surrounds the event monomodally, through, say, only an audio–visual recording of the performance, or only a written reflective account of it. In this endeavour, the performer–researcher would take the value of the live event for him or her as a starting point and thereby move beyond the interests of merely gaining new knowledge and understanding into an area where artistic engagement with and commitment to the 'object' of research, namely the live performance, necessitates an interested and subjectively valorised positioning of him- or herself as a researcher. One of the greatest challenges for contemporary performance studies is to recognise and theorise the situated expert knowledge live musical performance generates and to honour it as the epistemological foundation of the discipline. As Rink has commented, performance studies as a discipline within musicology will continue to thrive 'only to the extent that performers – as artists and artist-researchers – come to assume greater priority within the discipline' (2004: 41) and are recognised as authorities in the generation of knowledge about musical performances. Towards this aim, the ever-expanding potentials for multimodal discourses offer unprecedented opportunities to expert performers, who wish to undertake practice-based research projects with the aim of producing dissertations and theses in academic contexts. I believe it is through such projects that it will be possible to put to rest the remnants of the textual ideology in musical performance research, by putting forward the insider's view through multimodal means, where the performer's artistry and scholarship meet in aural-discursive, multimodal discourses that would be listened to and read both as artistic practice and research.

NOTES

1. The first commercially available cylinder recording was produced in the USA in 1890 (Day, 2000: 2).

2. Schenker's (1868–1935) musical analyses are an exception in that while also containing textual commentaries, they are essentially presented in the form of graphs that employ traditional music notational signs.

3. Various scholars probed the nature of recordings as musicological documents. Trezise, for example, questions the validity of assuming familiarity with the performances of musicians only through their recordings (Trezise, 2008), while Fabian convincingly argues that recordings in the classical genre can indeed be regarded as documents of the interpretative styles of performers (Fabian, 2008). Rumsey draws attention to the fact that in the context of recorded music 'fidelity to an original' is a problematic concept (Rumsey, 2008).

4. The term 'text-based ideology' refers to the received set of musicological values that regards the essence of musical meaning to reside in the notated musical score, which is conceived as functioning similarly to a literary text. According to such an ideology, understanding music is a textual, that is, score-based endeavour. However, while it implies a monomodal conception of music, a textual ideology does not necessarily result in a monomodal presentation and dissemination of musicological knowledge in the form of written texts: it is perfectly possible for a text-based ideology in the sense defined above to employ multimodal means to present and disseminate knowledge. In reality, music notation, which has been part of written music theoretical discourse for centuries, is a system of graphic signs

and in this sense always introduces an element of multimodality to the written text. The term 'textual ideology', therefore, refers to a conceptual approach.

5. For a review of the history of empirical studies of musical performance, see Gabrielsson (1999).

6. Levinson writes that there is a:

well-entrenched process/product ambiguity in regard to the concept of a performance. On the one hand, there is the activity of producing sounds for an audience, on the other hand, there are the sounds that are produced. (1987: 378)

As I have argued elsewhere, although:

sound-recording technology is often regarded as having broken the singular, causal ties between the performer and her performance in the listener's experience by abstracting the acoustical features of a performance from its original place, time and social context of occurrence, as the direct and immediate consequence of the performer's actions, a performance – whether live or recorded – is always indissolubly linked to its maker. Research in sound perception and cognition provides substantial evidence that images of sound and sound production are closely linked such that actions of the performers that produce the musical sounds are represented as part of the musical sounds themselves in the listener's experience. (Doğantan-Dack, 2008: 298)

7. For a brief history of the 'institutional validation of practice as research' see PARIP website at URL: http://www.bris.ac.uk/parip/t_ap.htm. PARIP (Practice as Research in Performance) was a five-year project directed by Kershaw and the Department of Drama: Theatre, Film, Television at the University of Bristol and funded by the AHRC (Arts and Humanities Research Council of the UK).

8. PRIMO is developed and managed by the Institute of Musical Research, University of London, with technical support from the University of London Computer Centre and from JISC (Joint Information Systems Committee). For more information on PRIMO visit URL: http://primo.sas.ac.uk

9. In a comprehensive review of a conference organised by NAMHE (National Association for Music in Higher Education) in 2004 and titled 'Practice as Research: Towards Consensus', Bayley points out that:

there are different roles in which performance can function but evidence from the inappropriate submissions in RAE [Research Assessment Exercise] 2001, commented upon in the overview report, suggested that not everyone knew where to draw the line between performance as research and performance as professional practice. (NAMHE, 2004: 8)

10. I make this assertion in reference to Western classical music performance practice since in the performance tradition of other musical genres such as jazz, the improvisatory element introduces components that are similar to composing music and thereby changes the creative relationship of the performer to the unfolding music and his or her reflective stance.

11. 'To challenge the disciplinary status quo, which is deeply rooted in this tradition giving priority to discursive knowledge, and to reclaim for performance studies the long-neglected epistemological primacy of the act of music making require using the tools of that very tradition, namely arguing and convincing. It will indeed take much discoursing to establish the fact that the possibility of any musicological knowledge about music is contingent upon the existence of a musical way of knowing that originates in music making' (Doğantan-Dack, 2008: 302).

12. See 'About PRIMO' in http://primo.sas.ac.uk. Approaching this issue from a pragmatic perspective, Ritterman argues that evidently:

if one chooses to present one's practice-based research without supporting documentation – leaving the work to 'speak for itself' – this puts a high premium on the 'musical ears' and range of experience of assessors. Few musicians can rely on having their work publicly reviewed in ways that provide informed and perceptive comment on its distinctive or original aspects. So it seems only reasonable that artists submitting examples of their practice in any competitive funding exercise would wish to take the precaution of making the case for themselves. (2006)

13. The AHRC (Arts and Humanities Research Council) funds postgraduate training and research in the arts and humanities, from archaeology and English literature to design and dance. The quality and range of research supported not only provides social and cultural benefits but also contributes to the economic success of the UK. For further information on the AHRC, visit URL: http://www.ahrc.ac.uk

14. The project website, designed by Boyd Davis (Research Leader in the School of Design, Royal College of Art) and maintained by Middlesex University can be visited at URL: http://wwwmdx.ac.uk/alchemy

15. For more information on the Marmara Piano Trio, visit URL: http://www.marmaratrio.com

16. For example: (i) Gruson, L. (1988). Rehearsal skill and musical competence: Does practice make perfect? In J. Sloboda (Ed.), *Generative Processes in Music: The Psychology of Performance, Improvisation and Composition* (pp. 91–112). Oxford: Clarendon Press; (ii) Hallam, S. (1995). Professional musicians' approaches to the learning and interpretation of music. *Psychology of Music*, 23, 111–128; (iii) Weeks, P. (1996). A rehearsal of a Beethoven passage: An analysis of correction talk. *Research on Language and Social Interaction*, 29(3), 247–290; (iv) Davidson, J. & King, E. C. (2004). Strategies for ensemble practice. In A. Williamon (Ed.), *Musical Excellence: Strategies and Techniques to Enhance Performance* (pp. 105–122). Oxford: Oxford University Press; (v) Ginsborg, J., Chaffin, R., & Nicholson, G. (2006). Shared performance cues in singing and conducting: A content analysis of talk during practice. Psychology of Music, 34(2), 167–192.

17. Some of the ideas in this and the following paragraph were first presented in a conference paper titled 'Practice and Theory: Ways of Knowing Music', 8th Conference on Systems Research in the Arts, Baden-Baden, Germany, August 2007.

18. In Schenkerian music analysis, Urlinie, or the fundamental line, refers to the particular melodic pattern that takes place at the hierarchical background of every tonal piece of music, holding the surface elaborations of it together.

19. Canadian pianist Glenn Gould (1932–1982) was an exception in this connection as he preferred practising his art in the recording studio exclusively after retiring from the stage permanently at the age of 32.

REFERENCES

Abbate, C. (2004). Music – drastic or gnostic? *Critical Inquiry, 30*, 505–536.

Altenmüller, E. & Gruhn, W. (2002). Brain mechanisms. In R. Parncutt & G. E. McPherson (Eds.), *The Science and Psychology of Music Performance* (pp. 63–82). New York: Oxford University Press.

Auslander, P. (1999). *Liveness.* London: Routledge.

Bowen, J. (1999). Finding the music in Musicology: Studying music as performance. In N. Cook & M. Everist (Eds.), *Rethinking Music* (pp. 424–451). Oxford: Oxford University Press.

Clarke, E. (1995). Expression in performance: Generativity, perception and semiosis. In J. Rink (Ed.), *The Practice of Performance* (pp. 21–54). Cambridge: Cambridge University Press.

Clarke, E. (2002). Understanding the psychology of performance. In J. Rink (Ed.), *Musical Performance: A Guide to Understanding* (pp. 59–74). Cambridge: Cambridge University Press.

Clarke, E. (2004). Empirical methods in the study of performance. In E. Clarke & N. Cook (Eds.), *Empirical Musicology. Aims, Methods, Prospects* (pp. 77–102). Oxford: Oxford University Press.

Coessens, K., Crispin, D., & Douglas, A. (2009). *The Artistic Turn: A Manifesto.* Ghent: New Goff.

Cook, N. (1999). Words about music, or analysis versus performance. In N. Cook, P. Johnson, & H. Zender (Eds.), *Theory into Practice: Composition, Performance, and the Listening Experience* (pp. 9–52). Belgium: Leuven University Press.

Cook, N. (2001). Between process and product: Music and/as performance. *Music Theory Online* 7/2. URL: http://www.societymusictheory.org/mto/

Cook, N. (2003). Music as performance. In M. Clayton, T. Herbert, & R. Middleton (Eds.), *The Cultural Study of Music: A Critical Introduction* (pp. 204–214). New York: Routledge.

Cook, N. (2007). Performance analysis and Chopin's mazurkas. *Musicae Scientiae, XI*(2), 183–207.

Cook, N. & Clarke, E. (2004). Introduction: What is empirical musicology? In E. Clarke & N. Cook (Eds.), *Empirical Musicology: Aims, Methods, Prospects* (pp. 3–14). Oxford: Oxford University Press.

Cumming, N. (2000). *The Sonic Self.* PLACE: Indiana University Press.

Damasio, A. (1994). *Descartes' Error: Emotion, Reason and the Human Brain.* New York: Putnam.

Damasio, A. (1999). *The Feeling of What Happens: Body and Emotion in the Making of Consciousness.* New York: Harcourt Brace.

Davidson, J. W. (1997). The social in musical performance. In D. J. Hargreaves & A. C. North (Eds.), *The Social Psychology of Music* (pp. 209–228). Oxford: Oxford University Press.

Davidson, J. and King, E. C. (2004). Strategies for ensemble practice. In: A. Williamon (ed.) *Musical Excellence: Strategies and Techniques to Enhance Performance*. Oxford: Oxford University Press, pp. 105–122.

Day, T. (2000). *A Century of Recorded Music: Listening to Musical History*. New Haven, CT: Yale University Press.

Doğantan-Dack, M. (2008). Recording the performer's voice. In M. Doğantan-Dack (Ed.), *Recorded Music: Philosophical and Critical Reflections* (pp. 293–313). London: Middlesex University Press.

Fabian, D. (2008). Classical sound recordings and live performances: Artistic and analytical perspectives. In M. Doğantan-Dack (Ed.), *Recorded Music: Philosophical and Critical Reflections* (pp. 232–260). London: Middlesex University Press.

Fétis, F.-J. (1849). *Traité complet de la théorie et de la pratique de l'harmonie*. Paris: Brandus.

Gabrielsson, A. (1999). The performance of music. In D. Deutsch (Ed.), *The Psychology of Music*, 2nd edn (pp. 501–602). San Diego, CA: Academic Press.

Ginsborg, J., Chaffin, R. and Nicholson, G. (2006). Shared performance cues in singing and conducting: a content analysis of talk during practice. *Psychology of Music, 34*(2) 167–192.

Gruson, L. (1988). Rehearsal skill and musical competence: does practice make perfect? In: J Sloboda (ed.) *Generative Processes in Music: The Psychology of Performance, Improvisation and Composition*. Oxford: Clarendon Press, pp. 91–112.

Hallam, S. (1995). Professional musicians' approaches to the learning and interpretation of music. *Psychology of Music, 23*: 111–128.

Johnson, P. (2010). Illusion and aura in the classical audio recording. In: A. Bayley (Ed.), *Recorded Music: Performance, Culture and Technology* (pp. 37–51). Cambridge: Cambridge University Press.

Kress, G. & van Leeuwen, T. (2001). *Multimodal Discourse: The Modes and Media of Contemporary Communication*. London: Hodder Arnold.

Lakoff, G. & Johnson, M. (1999). *Philosophy in the Flesh: The Embodied Mind and its Challenge to Western Thought*. New York: Basic Books.

Leech-Wilkinson, D. (2001). Using recordings to study musical performances. In A. Linehan (Ed.), *Aural History: Essays on Recorded Sound* (pp. 1–12). London: The British Library.

Levinson, J. (1987). Evaluating musical performance. Reprinted in J. Levinson (1990), *Music, Art and Metaphysics: Essays in Philosophical Aesthetics* (pp. 376–392). Ithaca: Cornell University Press.

NAMHE (Autumn 2004). Newsletter. R. McGregor (Ed.).

Neuhaus, H. (1993). *The Art of Piano Playing* (trans. K.A. Leibovitch). London: Kahn and Averill.

Newlin, D. (1980). *Schoenberg Remembered: Diaries and Recollections* (1938–76). New York: Pendragon Press.

Nightingale, A. W. (2004). *Spectacles of Truth in Classical Greek Philosophy*. Cambridge: Cambridge University Press.

Rink, J. (2004). The state of play in performance studies. In J. W. Davidson (Ed.), *The Music Practitioner: Research for the Music Performer, Teacher and Listener* (pp. 37–51). Aldershot: Ashgate.

Ritterman, J. (2006). Knowing more than we can tell. Paper presented at *Symposium on Artistic Research* held by the Music Department, Middlesex University.

Rumsey, F. (2008). Faithful to his Master's Voice? Questions of Fidelity and infidelity in music recording. In: M. Doğantan-Dack (Ed.), *Recorded Music: Philosophical and Critical Reflections* (pp. 213–231). London: Middlesex University Press.

Schechner, R. (2002). *Performance Studies*. New York: Routledge.

Schechner, R. (2003). *Performance Theory*. New York: Routledge.

Tekippe, T. (1996). *Scientific and Primordial Knowing*. Lantham, MD: University Press of America.

Trezise, S. (2008). Distortions and masks: Transmutations of the 'performing breath' in the studio take. In: M. Doğantan-Dack (Ed.), *Recorded Music: Philosophical and Critical Reflections* (pp. 261–292). London: Middlesex University Press.

Weeks, P. (1996). A rehearsal of a Beethoven passage: an analysis of correction talk. *Research on Language and Social Interaction*, 29(3) 247–290.

16

Translating Lydia Cabrera:
A Case Study in Digital
(re)presentation

Anna-Marjatta Milsom

INTRODUCTION

While the traditional route towards completing a doctoral thesis is to research, write and eventually submit a word-processed document, alternative modes of examination are increasingly being regarded as valid. Alternative techniques may be particularly suited to Humanities subjects, where objects and artefacts, practice and performance, rather than words alone, can contribute positively towards the 'original contribution to knowledge in the field' that is the key requirement for a PhD. What follows is an examination of the content, theoretical underpinnings and rationale behind the multimodal, digital element of a PhD thesis in translation studies (Milsom, 2008). The departure from the norm was supported from the outset by open-minded and infinitely patient supervisors and was, ultimately, well-received by the examiners. The university already offered PhD examination 'by artefact' for doctorates in performance-related subjects, so that, while a thesis in translation studies had never before been presented in such a way, a useful precedent existed. The final submission consisted of a DVD-Rom that held source documents, translations, photographs, drafts, drawings and annotations, accompanied by a correspondingly shorter written text of 40,000 words. The written text was also contained on the DVD-Rom, so that, technically, the submission might have consisted of the DVD alone. However, the traditional bound volume was still submitted, with the DVD-Rom in a pocket inside the back cover. That this is already something of an anachronism is an example of just one of the many issues in the ongoing debate on the future of the doctoral thesis.

Examination by artefact was not, in fact, envisaged at the start of the project. Rather, the path emerged organically and somewhat ponderously, out of the research process itself. It was first prompted by an unexpectedly emotional reaction to the published work and archived source material of its subject, the Cuban ethnographer and author, Lydia Cabrera (1899–1991)[1]. What began as a fairly straightforward interest in translating her folktales from Spanish into English, ended in a radical rethinking of the final presentation. At times, the process became almost impossibly circular, with Cabrera's own explorations in ethnography and art foreshadowing directions taken in the search for an appropriate way to relay her texts into the 'after-life' afforded by linguistic translation (Benjamin, 1923/2004). The very fact that Cabrera's tales often encompass both the scientific (ethnographic) and the artistic (literary), made the process of translating them particularly rich and complex, and it was partly in response to this complexity that a digital format was finally adopted.

BACKGROUND OF THE STUDY

Lydia Cabrera was, by any standards, an unconventional woman, whose life and work spanned most of the twentieth century. She was an ethnographer, writer, historian and artist. She restored buildings, produced translations and was a compulsive doodler. She published twenty-two books in all, which provide a unique insight into Afro-Cuban religions, customs and folktales. She also explored the vestiges of African languages still just extant in early twentieth century Cuba and produced three *vocabularios*[2]. Two further volumes of her work were published posthumously[3]. Cabrera wrote scores of lyrical short stories inspired by Afro-Cuban mythology and the four resulting collections were among the first to document the enormous contribution that African lore and religions make to Cuban culture[4]. These four literary volumes were the focus of the research, but all Cabrera's work nimbly traverses the boundaries between ethnography, poetry, testimony, art, fact and fiction. Despite its significance, her oeuvre remains relatively unknown outside Spanish-speaking academic and ethnographic circles. Given that she left Cuba in 1960 and eventually settled in Miami, it is perhaps surprising that comparatively little has so far been translated into English. The PhD aimed, in part, to address this, by presenting translations of twelve of her Afro-Cuban tales – which at that point had not appeared anywhere in the English language[5] – alongside hitherto unpublished archival material.

Early on in the research, polyvocality was identified as a key feature of Cabrera's work and the multiple ways in which 'voice' operates in her tales were analysed. It soon became important that all the participants in the chain of story-telling should be given the opportunity to speak in any new representation. This meant paying due attention to Cabrera as author of the published stories, but also to the informants who were her oral sources and to the mediating presence of the translator. In formulating a creative response to this multiple voicing, insights were drawn from visual art, poetry and ethnography.

A study trip to the Lydia Cabrera archive was a pivotal factor in the decision to seek alternative ways of presenting the research findings. When Cabrera left Cuba, many of her ethnographic notes travelled with her. Along with photographs, letters, unpublished stories, essays and other artefacts, these are now housed in the Cuban Heritage Collection of the Otto G. Richter Library at the University of Miami. Dating back as far as the early 1930s, they constitute a fragile treasure which can be freely handled and examined (much of the paper gives off a fine, sneeze-inducing dust). Notes are written on the backs of envelopes, on both sides of file cards or on torn up sheets of paper carefully stapled together. Most are hand-written in a looping, hard-to-decipher script, but some have been meticulously typed up by her assistants. Others have been traced over in biro where they threatened to fade altogether. Cabrera's own annotations indicate whether a reference has been used, and often in which volume it appears, by the Spanish 'ya' ('already' or 'done') being written beside or across the text.

The experience of having physical contact with Cabrera's field notebooks, photograph albums, drawings, letters and hundreds of index cards, immediately turned her from an object of academic and literary interest into an emotionally engaging presence (see Figures 16.1 and 16.2). Crucially, from the point of view of the research, the archive contained evidence of the sources behind some of her published work. Slowly, the whispered presence of Cabrera's Afro-Cuban informants became audible and the idea of presenting multiple layers of text emerged. The combining of a written thesis with an interactive artefact, therefore, sought to represent both the scholarly activity of research writing and the overwhelmingly vocal nature of the archival encounter. The digital artefact aimed to allow user-readers to mirror these explorations by encouraging them to make their own way through the weight of written, aural and visual material that screen-based (re)presentation permitted.

TRANSLATION AS ETHNOGRAPHY

In any work of translation, the translator is engaged in a kind of literary ethnography, bridging time, distance and cultures in and through the texts produced. Within translation studies theory, a great deal has been written, especially since the 1980s, about how ideology, inequalities of power and the tendency for the target system to dominate and control the source affect the way cultures and their literary products are regarded and understood (Bassnett and Lefevere, 1990; Álvarez and Vidal 1996; Venuti, 1995/2008). Some similar concerns over the

Figure 16.1   Lydia Cabrera (left) with Josefa Tarafa (far right), with whom she made extensive recordings of Afro-Cuban sacred music in the 1950s. Unknown woman in car
Courtesy of the Cuban Heritage Collection, University of Miami Libraries, Coral Gables, Florida

Figure 16.2   Lydia Cabrera (right) with Josefa Tarafa (left)
Courtesy of the Cuban Heritage Collection, University of Miami Libraries, Coral Gables, Florida

vexed notion of representation have been voiced in anthropological circles more or less contemporaneously, much of the debate being crystallised in and flowing from the essays collected in Clifford and Marcus's *Writing Culture* (1986/2010). Since then, ongoing reappraisals of both translation and ethnographic practices have shared a concentration on the wider cultural context and the real social and political effects of the representations of culture that we, as translators and ethnographers, make. Bassnett and Lefevere go so far as asserting that, 'Rewriters and translators are the people who really construct cultures on the basic level in our day and age. It is as simple, and as monumental as that. And because it is so simple and yet so monumental, it is also transparent: it tends to be overlooked' (1998: 10). In recognition of this, a number of translators and academics have experimented with broader ways of actively contextualising translations (Cheung, 2006). Those who have done so are often working in the light of interdisciplinary influence stemming from postcolonial studies, where ideological concerns inevitably mean a head-on engagement with issues of power, authority and representation. To give an example, *Imaginary Maps*, a volume of stories by the Bengali writer Mahasweta Devi (1995) and translated by Gayatri Chakravorty Spivak, has been cited approvingly for Spivak's way of framing the narratives (Simon, 1996: 147–149). Spivak's interaction with both author and context is made manifest through her translations and through the unusually weighty paratext with which she surrounds them. In the 'Translator's Note', she explains that 'All words in English in the original have been italicised. This makes the English page difficult to read. The difficulty is a reminder of the intimacy of the colonial encounter' (in Devi, 1995: xxxi). Unsettling the text on the page and potentially discomfiting the reader speak very directly to Appiah's notion of 'thick translation' (1993/2004), a concept which was to become central to the research project.

'THICK TRANSLATION'

Appiah's coining of the term 'thick translation' derives from Geertz's call for 'thick description' to be employed in ethnography (1973/1993). Geertz talks of the need to recognise the interpretive – as opposed to objective – nature of ethnography, not least because, 'Doing ethnography is like trying to read (in the sense of "construct a reading of") a manuscript – foreign, faded, full of ellipses, incoherences, suspicious emendations, and tendentious commentaries, but written not in conventionalized graphs of sound but in transient examples of shaped behavior' (1973/1993: 10). How well this relates to translating Lydia Cabrera's work, where real 'foreign, faded' manuscripts figured so prominently in the background research. While one survey of anthropologists' attitudes to their own field notes showed that they often regarded them as, 'worthless … in some ways because they were indecipherable, incomplete, disordered, and so on' (Jackson, 1995: 42), the inclusion of such comparatively unmediated material is exactly the kind of self-reflective practice Geertz recommends. His comments on the scarcity of experimentation in anthropology might have been applied just as appositely to translation, 'Self-consciousness about modes of representation (not to speak of experiments with them) has been very lacking …' (1973/1993: 19). Even where such self-consciousness is in evidence, theorists have often drawn a distinction between the ways in which literary translation and ethnography are, or should be, presented. Herzfeld, for example, insists that, '… where the transla-tor of fiction may insert unobtrusive aids to understanding, the ethnographer's aids *must* obtrude, *must* serve as constant reminders that the job is never done even as they seek to achieve that impossible closure' (2003: 130).

It is, however, just this type of deliberate intrusion that is exemplified in Spivak's 'difficult to read' italics and lies at the heart of Appiah's definition of thick translation. Rooting his discussion in the context of translating proverbs from a dialect of the Twi language spoken in Ghana, Appiah makes a compelling case for the existence of a gap between 'getting meaning right' and facilitating understanding (1993/2004: 390). In acknowledging the 'Geertzean vocabulary' of his title, he equates 'thicker' with 'richer' contextualisation (1993/2004: 394). Locating his area of concern within the context of higher education and with a broadly ethical aim, he explains:

> … it seems to me that such 'academic' translation, translation that seeks with its annotations and its accompanying glosses to locate the text in a rich cultural and linguistic context, is eminently worth doing. I have called this 'thick translation' … A thick description of the context of literary production, a translation that draws on and creates that sort of understanding, meets the need to challenge ourselves and our students to go further, to undertake the harder project of a genuinely informed respect for others. (1993/2004: 399)

Hermans (2003) sees thick translation partly as a critique of the reductive tendency in contemporary translation studies which generalises, rather than acknowledges, the complexity of difference. For Hermans, thick translation means making the translator's subjectivity evident and disrupts the easy accep-tance of some of the prevailing norms which bolster translation theory and studies in the West. In terms of how to actually imagine thickness, he says one example (albeit 'probably the most unlikely') is:

> Erasmus' *New Testament,* as much a comment on translation as a translation, engulfed as it is by footnotes, annotations, explications and digressions, their very excess signalling the original's inexhaustible fecundity and hence the inadequacy or at least the provisionality of any and all translation. (2003: 387)

Appiah and Hermans provide convincing theoretical justification for adopting thickness in approaching the task of translation. Following Appiah's lead, I looked first to contemporary ethnographic practice for further ways of achieving it. With Hermans exhortations to 'disturb the prevailing vocabularies of transla-tion studies by importing other conceptualizations and metaphorizations of trans-lation' (2003: 387) very much in mind, I also had recourse to two additional disciplines. These were visual art and poetry, sources of inspiration validated in terms of the project by the rising ascendancy of the 'seen' over the 'read' within modern modes of communication in the West (Kress and Van Leeuwen, 2006).

Applying thickness: ethnographic insights

The nature of written texts that purport to represent a prior oral event has attracted the scrutiny of ethnographers who see an essential paradox in a textual product representing an oral performance. The crux of the matter lies in whether by fixing a spoken text in writing, the source performance may be misrepresented or irreparably damaged in some way:

> The whole enterprise of inscribing the oral presupposes a questionable conception of orality and literacy that pits the two practices against one another. ... Can one revive the Other's oral memories without doing violence to the very traditions one seeks to vindicate? (Millay, 2005: 13)

Millay examines the spoken-textual dichotomy at work in the writing of several Latin American anthropologist-writers, Lydia Cabrera chief among them. She comments on the inherent complexity which resides in Cabrera's work because it can only ever achieve an illusion of orality. This illusion is at its densest where Cabrera herself seems to 'become' the Other in her tales. However, Cabrera also speaks to us in and through other voices. These include those of the observer-in-the-culture and ethnographer, and the translator and mediator, thus giving very clear signals about the nature of the illusion that is being conjured up. That orality should be emphasised, even reinvigorated, through new (re)presentations of the story texts, was central to the PhD project. The digital format allowed emphasis to be placed very literally on the spoken word by including readings of Cabrera's tales in Cuban Spanish and in their new English versions.

Cabrera's position within (although not of) the Afro-Cuban culture she wrote about, is rather unusual. Compared with the traditional fieldworker who visits from 'outside', observes, records and then goes away to write, Cabrera was Cuban, brought up listening to Afro-Cuban tales, and maintained relationships with many of her informants that spanned decades. Doane (1991) talks of the role of scribes who, while engaged in the task of writing down oral stories, form part of the oral culture themselves. We should consider Cabrera as falling into this category:

> ... they do not merely mechanically hand [the tales] down; they rehear them, 'mouth' them, 'reperform' them in the act of writing in such a way that the text may change but remain authentic, just as a completely oral poet's text changes from performance to performance without losing authenticity. A textualist perspective will show scribally reperformed texts to have a different textual form from their 'originals', but these texts reperformed in their writing will be *new originals* ... (1991: 80–81; my italics)

Re-performance eloquently describes one aspect of Cabrera's storytelling, and thinking of her as a re-performer may be set against any lingering unease that she somehow compromises oral texts by making them 'literary'. Much of her more literary work is, in large part, creative re-performance rather than straight report, and its description as 'antropoesía' [anthropoetry] is a fitting one (Cabrera Infante, 1992: 89). The tales she relates are both her own and reverberate with the presence of other, previous speakers. Theirs are the voices that reach furthest back in time and space and which I wished to ensure were also audible in the new translations.

The increasingly sharp focus on the interpretive nature of ethnography links it to contemporary developments in translation theory and practice. The search for new ethnographic forms to reflect this change of emphasis, such as the use of film and web-based interactive media, informed the trend towards digital interactivity and the visual. In translation and in ethnography (but far more commonly in the latter), form may be considered in terms of its potential to empower and reposition the reader or user (in addition, obviously, to its potential to empower and reposition the subject). In his discussion of the innovative possibilities for ethnographic film, it is worth quoting Nichols at some length:

> An interpretive method that centres on the form and texture of the text, and our experience of it, also holds the potential to bridge the divide between the practice of interpretation as the scientific derivation of data, facts or 'ethnographicness' ... and interpretation as a hermeneutic act that locates the interpreter, viewer, and text in the midst of both a formal and an ideological, aesthetic and social, web of significance, stylistically inflected, rhetorically charged, affect-laden. In short, bridging the gulf between interpretation as content analysis and interpretation as discourse analysis, between seeing *through* a film to the data beyond and *seeing film* as cultural representation, may reorient visual anthropology toward questions of form and their inextricable relation to experience, affect, content, purpose, and result. (1994: 83)

The word 'film' here might constructively be replaced by the word 'translation', opening up space for a discussion about the double experience of 'seeing through' a translation to the data behind (such as source texts), and seeing translation as 'cultural representation', defined by factors which include the expectations of the target audience, attitudes towards translator (in)visibility and so on. In the PhD project, both types of seeing were taken into account in designing a digital container to hold the 'web of significance' which radiated from the re-voicing of Cabrera's work in English.

Applying thickness: visual insights

The creative possibilities inherent in written text have long been a source of inspiration for visual artists. Some have brought writing directly into the gallery space – think, for instance, of Weiner's highly conceptual work post-1970s (see his retrospective, 2007–2008), Sinclair's 'Real Life' paintings (see, e.g. 2006), or the narrative thread (literally) running through Emin's embroidery and appliqué pieces (such as 1995). For others, urban streets provide the space for daringly scrawled tags in injury-defying locations. Whatever the setting, many practitioners blur the distinction between visual art as writing and writing as visual art.

Their words, whether spelt out in glass tubing, painstakingly stitched together or tattooed onto their own skin, require the viewer to act as a very careful reader indeed, yet may also trigger a purely aesthetic response. Because human engagement so often stems from a reaction to the visually pleasing, it was always intended that the Cabrera artefact should operate positively on an aesthetic level as well as on a functional, information-holding one. Visual or concrete poetry is perhaps the ultimate example of such cross-fertilisation between creative writing and visual art. From Apollinaire's 1914 poem 'Lettre-Ocean' via the work of the Italian Futurists and Cubist text collages, the same sensibility was later to find itself expressed in the word-pictures of poets such as Cummings and Pound in the 1950s and 1960s[6]. The history of these boundary-pushing types of poetry shows them to be far from static in terms of geographic location and influence. While some text-based artists continue to work on paper alone, it is increasingly common for new forms of visual and concrete poetry to be produced for and disseminated via the wide open spaces of the internet.

Applying something of the sensibility of new visual poetic forms to the Cabrera project made sense both aesthetically and conceptually. On the one hand, the more visually intriguing and stimulating the artefact, the more readily it would, it was hoped, foster user-reader engagement. On the other, the presence of pre-texts and drafts would make visible the processes of change and revision that every piece of writing undergoes (including this chapter, see Figure 16.3).

My position within the project as subjective initiator, compiler and translator was made explicit through the inclusion of handwritten and hand-corrected draft translations. The deletions and rewritings on even the most 'finished' versions of each of the twelve stories serve as graphic reminders that they remain in the process of being (re)written. User-readers are aware, even if only subconsciously, that they are dealing with texts in which choices have been made and, it is implied, still others might be made in the future.

Applying thickness: back to Cabrera

A concern with multiple versions has parallels with Cabrera's own methodology, perhaps seen most emphatically at work in *El monte* (1954/1992), a book often considered to be her most significant ethnographic achievement. This judgement resides only superficially in the weighty physicality of its 600 or so pages. Constructed in such a way that it interleaves the verbatim testimony of a chorus of informants with Cabrera's distinctive authorial voice(s), it makes for extremely dense and demanding reading. This is a text that defies easy classification, just as it defies easy absorption. Almost every page is stippled with the inverted commas of direct speech, as differently told versions of Afro-Cuban creation stories, religious ceremonies and the activities of the gods are ranged alongside one another in a veritable clutter of (often contradictory) alternatives. Although *El monte* is divided into subject-related chapters, many of the narrative loops

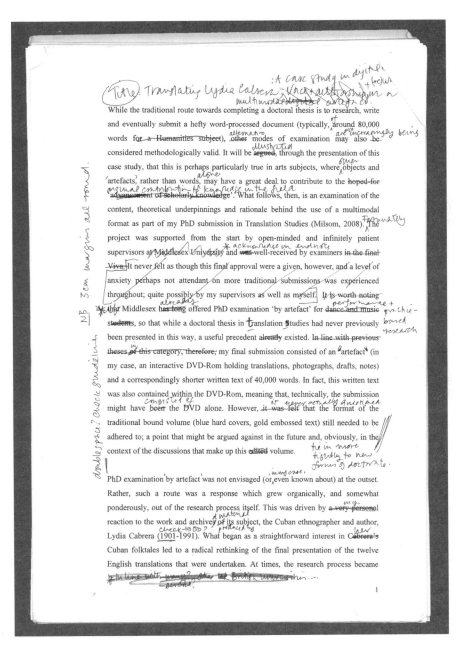

Figure 16.3   An early draft of this chapter

fracture and repeat themselves in an unsettlingly non-linear fashion. Far from detracting from the authority of Cabrera's work, this almost overwhelming accretion of material confers a multiple authority that departed radically from the norms of ethnographic publishing in the 1950s (and would still be unusual today). The following extract is taken from a review of a new edition of *El monte*, published in Cuba in 1989:

> Every time I've read *El Monte,* with no little fatigue but an equal amount of delight, I've wondered whether an editor could have put this jungle in order and concluded that no, it's better as it is, that the reader should seek in this conglomeration of popular poetry and philosophy the kernel of a thinking different to 'logic', and that it possesses a special logic of its own. (González, 1990: 88; my translation)

The textual 'jungle' alluded to here may be seen as a manifestation of something approaching the kind of thickness Appiah and Hermans envisage for translation. Placing my English renderings of Cabrera's stories into a format which allowed for text and context to co-exist could, therefore, be seen as following her lead. Three years after Cabrera's death, Castellanos compiled and edited *Páginas sueltas* (Cabrera, 1994) (literally, *Loose Pages*), which edged towards doing something similar within standard book format. Writings from different periods of Cabrera's life were presented chronologically, couched within the paratextual framework of Castellanos' detailed footnoting, over fifty pages of introduction, a definitive bibliography and reproductions of photographs and illustrations. Here we return to the visual aesthetics of the artefact; a reproduction of Cabrera's handwriting engages the reader in a different and infinitely more intimate way than its word-processed substitute could ever do, bridging print and picture by falling somewhere between the two. All written text, of course, is visual in the sense of its 'physicality and materiality as *graphic substance*' (Kress, 1998: 67), but the handwritten document inevitably encourages greater reader engagement than does one in which variables such as font selection and paragraphing conform to strict norms. In the Cabrera artefact, the inclusion of handwritten pages from the author's notebooks reflected more than the desire to pursue documentary authenticity (although this too was important). Where it seemed likely that an oral telling occasioned a notebook entry, these pages come as close as it is possible for us to now get to that event. The informants' presence is often explicit in their non-standard Cuban Spanish (*Bozal*), which is sometimes smoothed out of Cabrera's published stories, and the immediacy of the telling seems to be reflected in her apparently hurried and abbreviated script. Reproducing such documents, then, was another way of applying thickness to a re-presentation of Cabrera's Afro-Cuban tales.

BEYOND THE BOOK

Ever since Vannevar Bush first exhorted scientists to put their technological expertise into the compilation and compression of the sum of man's knowledge – 'The *Encyclopaedia Britannica* could be reduced to the volume of a matchbox' – the idea of written texts on screens, linked to one another through a network of associations, has been a fast-approaching reality (1945/1996: 39). Two decades later, Nelson coined a new term to refer to the links, now so familiar to users of the internet, that operate between documents stored in electronic format, 'Let me introduce the word "hypertext" to mean a body of written or pictorial material interconnected in such a complex way that it could not conveniently be presented or represented on paper' (1965: 96). Explorations in the use of hypertext, exploiting the range of possibilities afforded by a newly multimodal approach to the making of texts, are now common in areas as diverse as archive-based resources, digital arts, fiction and visual ethnography. And, of course, changes in ways of writing texts inevitably mean changes in the experience of reading them. The effects which any such moves may have on the reader are by no means universally agreed. In preparing the Cabrera DVD, however, two much-discussed and related aspects were of particular relevance: (a) the destabilisation of the author as authority and the increased potential for user-readers to construct their own readings; and (b) the way that 'gaps' in the text facilitate the above and hold the potential to become positive prompts for creativity and interpretation.

The first of these relates directly to the ethnographic nature of Lydia Cabrera's project and the multimodal nature of mine. The second can be linked to the literary dimension and the act of translation itself.

Technically speaking, the PhD project is an experiment in hypermedia rather than in hypertext. Nielson defines the computer-based writing known as hypertext as 'non-sequential' writing in which there is 'no single order that determines the sequence in which the text is to be read', while 'hypermedia' or 'multimedia hypertext' are terms coined later to indicate the possibility of incorporating image and sound into the plain text (1995: 1–5). All hypertexts and hypermedia, however, share one essential characteristic: that of linking (Lavagnino, 1995: 109). Feustle talks poetically of the '… *texture* of threads that reach out by means of the computer program and connect original works, critical studies, bibliographies, and historical backgrounds' (1991: 299). However described, this means that narratives become open to gentle (and not so gentle) disruption. As they are explored, the texts become the fabric from which multiple readings may be spun. It is the inherent 'radical instability' of hypermedia (Bolter, 1997: 269), which makes it so appropriate a platform for a translated literature that seeks to show its own mutability at every turn.

It is, of course, legitimate to question whether engaging with hypermedia is so very different from the reading that might be made from a traditional printed book. There is a broadly post-structuralist tendency in printed literature that has been particularly richly exploited in Latin American fiction, which plays with and undermines conventional ways of reading[7]. And in any case, it has always been possible to:

> … depart from the main axis of the book by looking up words in a dictionary, researching
> allusions contained in the text, checking footnotes, seeking out critical commentary,

researching aspects of historical and biographical context ... and so forth. For an active, writerly reader reading a text is not really a linear experience. (Gaggi 1997: 101)

Nonetheless, a multimodal artefact such as the Cabrera object makes this type of reading experience far more marked, as links to annotations, visual images and audio files offer the user-reader a thicker interaction without having to physically leave the main text(s).

The book form most closely associated with this type of rich reading is perhaps the critical edition; a product of literary scholarship in which minutely edited textual material lies between the (usually hardback) covers. Footnotes and other forms of scholarly apparatus may imply authority and fulfil an explanatory role in such texts, but annotations and glosses hold the potential not only to explain and clarify, but also to subvert and undermine (Cosgrove, 1991). They are also, we remember, central to ideas about applying thick translation and can be used to facilitate other readings and insert other voices. Jackson's highly personal dissection of the footnote emphasises the role that potentially subversive marginal notes can play (a discussion which, it goes without saying, is heavily footnoted), 'Footnotes ... might turn out to be not foundation stones but landmines, exploding upwards into the soft black-and-white underbelly of the main text on contact with the reader's gaze' (1999: 140). It was this sort of unsettling of the linear reading experience that was aimed for in annotating the translations on the Cabrera artefact. The form this annotation took will be discussed in the next section. Having looked at the theoretical basis of the project, the rationale and sources of inspiration behind its production, what follows brings practical considerations such as navigation, user interaction and the content of the artefact to the fore.

THE DIGITAL ARTEFACT

As already discussed, the decision to combine a shorter written thesis with some type of creative artefact emerged over the course of the research. Before settling on the DVD-Rom format, other possibilities were considered, including an art installation (in which texts might have been projected and story recordings made accessible through speakers or headphones), a live story-telling performance and a printed paper object (e.g. a folding map where texts in different languages combined to build up a fictitious two-dimensional landscape). In the end, the sheer volume of material involved in the project made the digital artefact a pragmatic choice.

Given that research played such a central role in translating Cabrera's short stories, it was decided that this should be overtly alluded to in the opening screen of the DVD-Rom (see Figure 16.4).

User engagement begins with a black and white photograph of an actual (rather than computer) desktop on which are ranged manila folders containing the twelve stories, a sketchbook, a telephone, a computer and CDs of photographs.

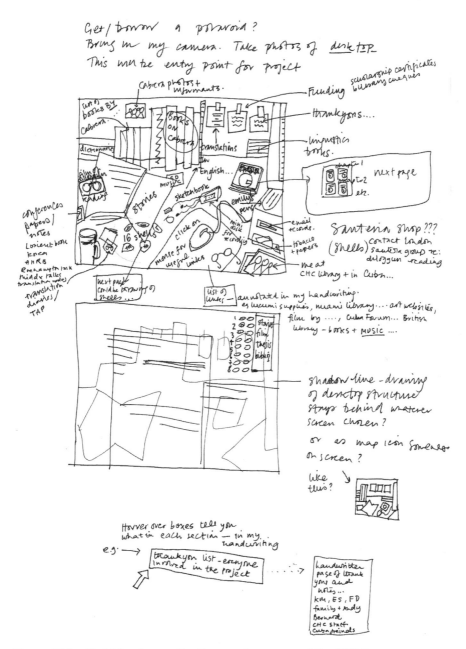

Figure 16.4   Sketchbook page for the opening screen of the DVD Rom

A shelf stacked with relevant literature occupies the space above the desk. In all, there are six pictorial links, these being:

- Twelve folders leading to the individual collections of texts, field notes, source documents and draft translations, each folder pertaining to a single story
- CD Roms leading to an 'album' of photographs – my own and a selection from the Lydia Cabrera archive in Miami
- A sketchbook leading to a small selection of the pages within it which document different aspects of the project as it developed
- An A4 envelope leading to instructions for using the navigation
- A 'post-it' note leading to a list of acknowledgements and thanks
- A computer monitor leading to the complete text of the written thesis

From the desktop, the user-reader is able to roll over the various links that operate like hyperlinks directing them to further pages. Links are indicated by objects on the desk changing from black and white to muted colour on roll-over, and the user chooses where to 'go' simply by single mouse-clicks. The tale texts (Cabrera's notes and published Spanish stories) and their translations are by far the densest source of data linked to the desktop. They are accessed by clicking on the pile of twelve manila folders, which leads to a screen that allows the selection of an individual story (as shown in Figure 16.5). Subsequently, a further screen offers choices about voice-overs (see Figure 16.6). Every effort was made to keep the navigation simple and the aesthetic 'hand-drawn'. Basic on/off buttons are scribbled onto 'post-it' notes for the audio selection, instructions are jotted on a piece of lined paper (as shown in Figure 16.7) and the 'back' and 'quit' options on each screen are operated by single mouse clicks. The artefact looks very evidently authored (voiced), rather than slick, technical and anonymous.

As far as initial design decisions were concerned, a fundamental consideration in the production of any interactive product is whether, in Joyce's terms, the finished hypertext is destined to be 'exploratory' (in which case users can only investigate the body of material made available to them by the author), or 'constructive' (in which case users are able to interact more fully with the text object, adding additional material to it) (1995: 41–43). The Cabrera artefact is exploratory and the data contained on the artefact cannot exceed pre-set parameters. The user-reader is unable, for example, to choose the events which make up the unfolding narrative of each tale, as is commonly the case in classic hypertext fiction. Nevertheless, it was thought important that the artefact should allow a sufficiently broad range of options to permit an individualised reading. It was also important that all the voices in the texts be given space, without any one being overly dominant. To this end, the sequencing of field notes, source texts and draft translations in each of the twelve story files is deliberately arranged to be circular and, although the documents appear in chronological sequence, there is, strictly speaking, neither a beginning nor an end. True, access to the texts begins at the most 'finished' draft translation, but once user-readers have entered at this level, they are able to travel in either direction without ever reaching a

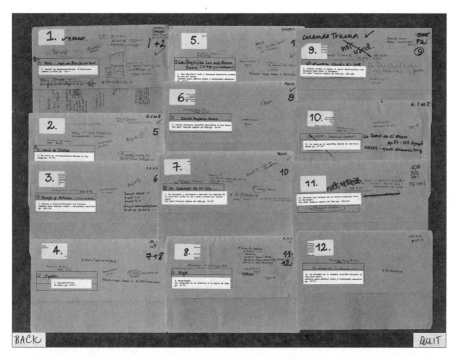

Figure 16.5 Selecting a folder allows readers to explore one of twelve tales on the DVD Rom

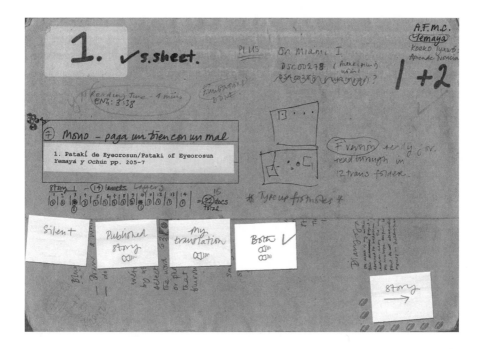

Figure 16.6 Once a folder on the DVD Rom is selected, the user-reader can choose whether or not to hear audio recordings (Spanish, English or both) as they scroll through the written texts

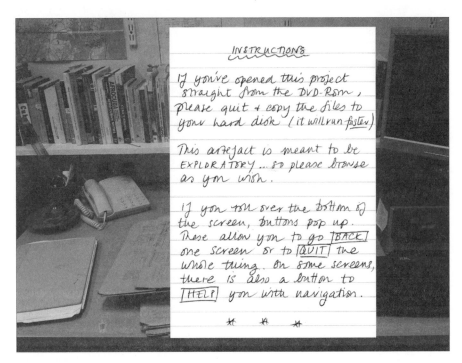

Figure 16.7   On-screen instructions for navigating the DVD Rom, with the 'desktop' visible behind

stopping point. Further development would involve incorporating randomness, so that the point of entry changed each time the texts were accessed. The written documents making up each story fade and blend visually into each other, with the earliest source notes and the latest draft translation standing next to one another within the loop (see Figure 16.8).

Depending on the quantity of drafts, transcripts and source documentation (such as field notebooks) collated for each tale, the layers of text range from six to eleven. The tales themselves run from around three hundred words to over six thousand. Once inside a story folder, the user-reader can stay with a single document (scrolling up or down using the mouse in a conventional way) or go back and forth (using the arrow keypad) to obtain an overview of all the documents held in the folder. Sound (voice-over) and image (photographs and scans) may contribute to the reading.

The final layer of text consists of the footnotes linked to the most 'finished' translation of each tale. Whereas in a printed edition the reader has no option other than to be aware of accompanying notes – whether they read them or not – hypermedia makes it possible for each user to decide whether, how often and to what extent to digress from the main thread of their reading. So, in the Cabrera artefact, any word or phrase in the translation which is linked to an annotation is, quite literally, blurred. This simple visual metaphor is intended to mimic the

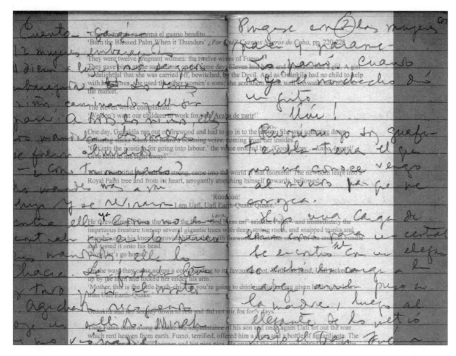

Figure 16.8   Translation and field notes blend into one another as they are scrolled through within the DVD Rom.
Cabrera's field notebook reproduced courtesy of the Cuban Heritage Collection, University of Miami Libraries, Coral Gables, Florida

potential fuzziness of comprehension which may, at that moment, be affecting the reader. A single mouse click on the smudge that is semi-obscuring the word(s) makes a 'post-it' note annotation appear, blocking out part of the text and interrupting the user's reading until a further mouse-click makes it disappear (see Figure 16.9).

The notes themselves contain personal reflections on translating a particular word or phrase, references to scholarly resources, comments on pre-texts and photographs, and constitute a physical manifestation of thickness.

CONCLUSION

The Lydia Cabrera case study is an example of a form of doctoral thesis in which creative artefacts are accorded the same scholarly weight as the written words that make up the more traditional thesis. It has been shown how a thick aesthetic was applied to this particular project and how the most significant decision made in arriving at the final form was to use a screen-based, digital format. The platform lent itself to the placing of annotations within the translated texts and

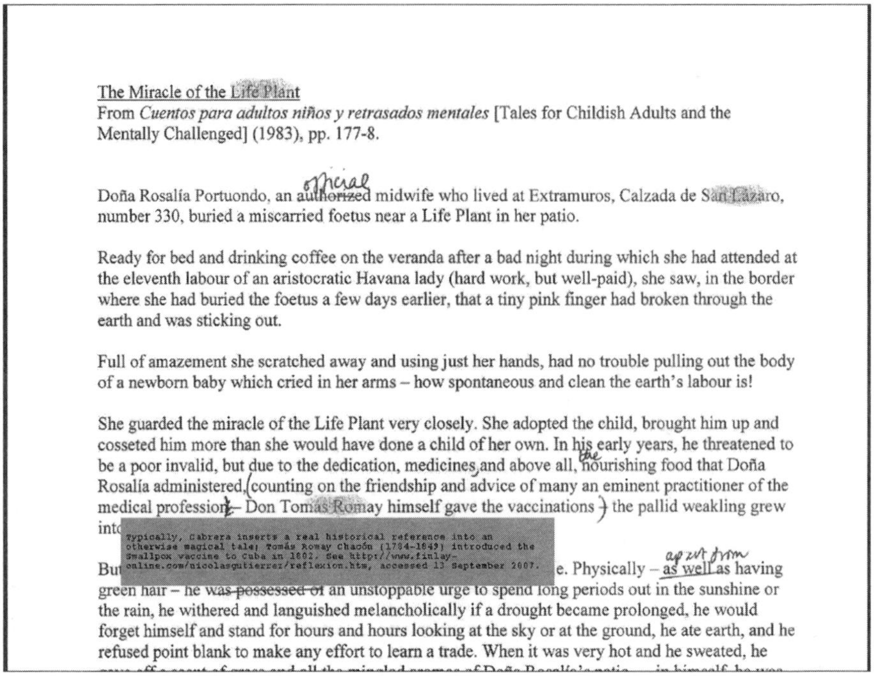

The Miracle of the Life Plant
From *Cuentos para adultos niños y retrasados mentales* [Tales for Childish Adults and the Mentally Challenged] (1983), pp. 177-8.

Doña Rosalía Portuondo, an ~~authorized~~ *official* midwife who lived at Extramuros, Calzada de San Lázaro, number 330, buried a miscarried foetus near a Life Plant in her patio.

Ready for bed and drinking coffee on the veranda after a bad night during which she had attended at the eleventh labour of an aristocratic Havana lady (hard work, but well-paid), she saw, in the border where she had buried the foetus a few days earlier, that a tiny pink finger had broken through the earth and was sticking out.

Full of amazement she scratched away and using just her hands, had no trouble pulling out the body of a newborn baby which cried in her arms – how spontaneous and clean the earth's labour is!

She guarded the miracle of the Life Plant very closely. She adopted the child, brought him up and cosseted him more than she would have done a child of her own. In his early years, he threatened to be a poor invalid, but due to the dedication, medicines and above all, *the* nourishing food that Doña Rosalía administered (counting on the friendship and advice of many an eminent practitioner of the medical profession – Don Tomás Romay himself gave the vaccinations) the pallid weakling grew into

But [typically, Cabrera inserts a real historical reference into an otherwise magical tale: Tomás Romay Chacón (1764-1849) introduced the smallpox vaccine to Cuba in 1802. See http://www.finlay-online.com/nicolasgutierrez/reflexion.htm, accessed 13 September 2007.] e. Physically – *apart from* ~~as well~~ as having green hair – he ~~was possessed of~~ an unstoppable urge to spend long periods out in the sunshine or the rain, he withered and languished melancholically if a drought became prolonged, he would forget himself and stand for hours and hours looking at the sky or at the ground, he ate earth, and he refused point blank to make any effort to learn a trade. When it was very hot and he sweated, he

Figure 16.9   A 'finished' translation as it appears on the DVD Rom, with a footnote selected

these, along with the inclusion of drafts scored with crossings-out, question marks and rewritings, made the translator's presence, subjectivity and fallibility supremely evident. The monolithic authority of the text was undermined by allowing the fluid, creative nature of the translation process to become visible, while the status of each text as one version amongst many was emphasised. The capacity of the DVD-Rom to store large quantities of information meant that it was possible to show texts existing in a chain of prior textual events, capable of infinite revision and rebirth. The multimodal character of the DVD-Rom, in which writing, image and sound are stacked up against each other in a consciously cluttered way, was designed to encourage a particularly intense form of reader engagement. Such an exploration simply would not have been possible within the standard written format of a traditional thesis.

The Cabrera project illustrates ways of translating that celebrate the shifting nature of the activity and look beyond conventional publications in which the translator's foreword often marks the full extent of transparent, creative practice. Enabled by the adoption of digital technology, the research ultimately suggested that one future direction for interlingual translation might involve taking a consciously 'visual turn', privileging thickness and recognising that the translated text holds the potential to do a great deal more than offer one string of words as the linguistic equivalent of another.

ACKNOWLEDGEMENTS

Pursuing thickness became, in this case at least, a distinctly collaborative act. I thank my supervisors at Middlesex University, UK – Kirsten Malmkjær, Gordon Davies and Francisco Dominguez – for their insight and encouragement. Computer skills did not, in themselves, form part of the PhD submission, and I am immensely grateful to Gordon Davies for writing the code that supports the artefact and to Kate Milsom, Mimi Son and Alex Chase for manipulating the majority of the images that appear on the DVD-Rom. I am also indebted to Robin Scobey for patiently directing the sound recordings made at London Metropolitan University, UK, and to Elizabeth Silva for reading Cabrera's Cuban texts so beautifully.

NOTES

1. There is some uncertainty over whether Cabrera was born in 1899 (as reflected in official documents) or in 1900, as she herself affirmed. See Castellanos's introduction to *Páginas sueltas* (Cabrera, 1994:14).

2. Cabrera's dictionaries are *Anagó, vocabulario Lucumí: El Yoruba que se habla en Cuba* (1957/1986), *Vocabulario Congo: El Bantú que se habla en Cuba* (1984) and *La lengua sagrada de los Ñáñigos* (1988).

3. Edited and introduced by Isabel Castellanos, *Consejos, pensamientos y notas de Lydia E. Pinbán* (1993) and *Páginas sueltas* (1994) were published within three years of Cabrera's death.

4. Cabrera's four volumes of tales are *Cuentos negros de Cuba* (1940/1993), *¿Por qué? cuentos negros de Cuba* (1948/1972), *Ayapá: cuentos de Jicotea* (1971), and *Cuentos para adultos niños y retrasados mentales* (1983).

5. To date, two book-length translations into English of Cabrera's fiction have subsequently been published. *Afro-Cuban Tales* (2004), translated by Hernàndez-Chiroldes and Yoder, is Cabrera's complete first volume of tales (originally published in French in 1936 as *Contes nègres de Cuba* and four years later in Spanish as *Cuentos negros de Cuba*). *Afro-Cuban Short Stories by Lydia Cabrera (1900–1991)* (2008), translated by Gutiérrez and Richards, comprises forty tales selected across all four volumes of short stories. Two of the tales translated for the Cabrera DVD-Rom, *The Branch on the Wall* and *The Miracle of the Life Plant*, are translated in the latter.

6. For a selection of the manifestoes and statements which have underpinned the development of visual poetry (an art form that has often functioned as an overtly political act of expression), see Cobbing and Mayer (1978: 14–19).

7. A classic example of the undermining of conventional ways of reading is Cortázar's 1963 novel, *Rayuela* [Hopscotch] which begins:

> In its own way this book is many books, but above all it is two books. The reader is invited *to choose* one of the following two possibilities: The first book can be read in the normal way and finishes at Chapter 56 ... The second book can be read starting at Chapter 73 and then following the order shown at the end of each chapter. (1963/1977: 'Guide'; my translation)

REFERENCES

Álvarez, R. & Vidal, M C-Aì (Eds.). (1996). *Translation, Power, Subversion*. Clevedon: Multilingual Matters.

Appiah, K. A. (1993/2004). Thick translation. *Callaloo, 16*, 808–819; reprinted in L. Venuti (Ed.), *The Translation Studies Reader*, 2nd edn (pp. 389–401). London: Routledge.

Bassnett, S. & Lefevere, A. (Eds.). (1990). *Translation, History and Culture*. London: Pinter.

Bassnett, S. & Lefevere, A. (Eds.). (1998). *Constructing Cultures: Essays on Literary Translation*. Clevedon: Multilingual Matters.

Benjamin, W. (1923/2004). The task of the translator: An introduction to the translation of Baudelaire's *Tableaux Parisiens* (trans. H. Zohn). In L. Venuti (Ed.), *The Translation Studies Reader*, 2nd edn (pp. 75–85). London: Routledge.

Bolter, J. D. (1997). The rhetoric of interactive fiction. In P. Cohen (Ed.), *Texts and Textuality: Textual Instability, Theory, and Interpretation* (pp. 269–290). New York: Garland Publishing.

Bush, V. (1945/1996). As we may think. *Atlantic Monthly, 176*(1), 101–108, reprinted in *Interactions, 3*(2), 35–46 *ACM Digital Library* [Online]. Available at http://portal.acm.org/ (accessed December 1, 2010).

Cabrera, L. (1936). *Contes nègres de Cuba* [Black Tales from Cuba] (trans. Francis de Miomandre). Paris: Gallimard.

Cabrera, L. (1940/1993). *Cuentos negros de Cuba* [Black Tales from Cuba]. Havana: Imprenta La Verónica. Reprint, Miami: Ediciones Universal.

Cabrera, L. (1948/1972). *¿Por qué? cuentos negros de Cuba* [Why? Black Tales from Cuba]. Havana: Coleccíon del Chicherekú; Ediciones C.R. Reprint, Madrid: Ramos.

Cabrera, L. (1954/1992). *El Monte (Igbo-Finda; Ewe Orisha. Vititi Nfinda)*. Havana: Ediciones C.R. Reprint, Miami: Ediciones Universal.

Cabrera, L. (1957/1986). *Anagó, vocabulario Lucumí; el Yoruba que se habla en Cuba* [Anagó, Lucumí Vocabulary: The Yoruba Spoken in Cuba]. Havana: Coleccíon del Chicherekú; Ediciones C.R. Reprint, Miami: Ediciones Universal.

Cabrera, L. (1971). *Ayapá: cuentos de Jicotea* [Ayapá: Tales of the Turtle]. Miami: Ediciones Universal.

Cabrera, L. (1983). *Cuentos para adultos niños y retrasados mentales* [Tales for Childish Adults and the Mentally Challenged]. Miami: Ediciones Universal.

Cabrera, L. (1984). *Vocabulario Congo: el Bantú que se habla en Cuba* [Congo Vocabulary: The Bantu Spoken in Cuba]. Miami: Ediciones C.R.

Cabrera, L. (1988). *La lengua sagrada de los Ñáñigos* [The Sacred Language of the Ñáñigos]. Miami: Ediciones C.R.

Cabrera, L. (1993). *Consejos, pensamientos y notas de Lydia E. Pinbán: Edición de Isabel Castellanos* [Advice, Thoughts and Notes by Lydia E. Pinbán: Edited by Isabel Castellanos]. Miami: Ediciones Universal.

Cabrera, L. (1994). *Páginas sueltas: Edición, introducción y notas de Isabel Castellanos* [Loose Leaves: Edition, introduction and notes by Isabel Castellanos]. Miami: Ediciones Universal.

Cabrera, L. (2004). *Afro-Cuban Tales*. (trans. Alberto Hernández-Chiroldes and Lauren Yoder). Lincoln, NE: University of Nebraska Press.

Cabrera, L. (2008). *Afro-Cuban Short Stories by Lydia Cabrera (1900–1991)*. (trans. M. A. Gutiérrez and M. D. Richards). Lewiston, NY: Edwin Mellen Press.

Cabrera Infante, G. (1992). *Mea Cuba* [My Cuba]. Madrid: Grupo Santillana de Ediciones S.A.

Cheung, M. P. Y. (Ed.). (2006). *An Anthology of Chinese Discourse on Translation, Volume 1: From Earliest Times to the Buddhist Project*. Manchester: St. Jerome.

Clifford, J. & Marcus, G. E. (Eds.). (1986/2010). *Writing Culture: The Poetics and Politics of Ethnography*. Berkeley, CA: University of California Press.

Cobbing, B. & Mayer, P. (1978). *Concerning Concrete Poetry*. London: Writers Forum.

Cortázar, J. (1963/1977). *Rayuela* [Hopscotch]. Buenos Aires: Editorial Sudamerica, S. A. Reprint, Barcelona: EDHASA.

Cosgrove, P. W. (1991). Undermining the text: Edward Gibbon, Alexander Pope, and the antiauthenticating footnote. In S. A. Barney (Ed.), *Annotation and its Texts* (pp. 130–151). New York: Oxford University Press.

Devi, M. (1995). *Imaginary Maps* (trans. G. Chakravorty Spivak). London: Routledge.

Doane, A. N. (1991). Oral texts, intertexts, and intratexts: Editing Old English. In J. Clayton & E. Rothstein (Eds.), *Influence and Intertextuality in Literary History* (pp. 75–113). Madison, WI: University of Wisconsin Press.

Emin, T. (1995). *Everyone I Have Ever Slept With 1963–95* [Installation]. London: South London Gallery.

Feustle, J. A. Jr (1991). Hypertext for the PC: The Rubén Darío project. In P. Delany & G. P. Landow (Eds.), *Hypermedia and Literary Studies* (pp. 299–313). Cambridge, MA: The MIT Press.

Gaggi, S. (1997). *From Text to Hypertext*. Philadelphia, PA: University of Pennsylvania Press.

Geertz, C. (1973/1993). *The Interpretation of Cultures: Selected Essays*. New York: Basic Books. Reprint, London: Fontana Press.

González, R. (1990). El monte nuestro de cada día [Our Everyday Wilderness], *Unión, 10*, 87–90.

Hermans, T. (2003). Cross-cultural translation studies as thick translation. *Bulletin of SOAS, 66*(3), 380–389.

Herzfeld, M. (2003). The unspeakable in pursuit of the ineffable: Representations of untranslatability in ethnographic discourse. In P. G. Rubel & A. Rosman (Eds.), *Translating Cultures: Perspectives on Translation and Anthropology* (pp. 109–134). New York: Berg Publishers.

Jackson, J. E. (1995). Déjà entendu: The liminal qualities of anthropological fieldnotes. In J. Van Maanen (Ed.), *Representation in Ethnography* (pp. 36–78). Thousand Oaks, CA: Sage.

Jackson, K. (1999). *Invisible Forms: A Guide to Literary Curiosities*. London: Picador.

Joyce, M. (1995). *Of Two Minds: Hypertext Pedagogy and Poetics*. Ann Arbor, MI: University of Michigan Press.

Kress, G. (1998). Visual and verbal modes of representation in electronically mediated communication: The potential for new forms of text. In I. Snyder (Ed.), *Page to Screen: Taking Literacy into the Electronic Era* (pp. 53–79). London: Routledge.

Kress, G. & Van Leeuwen, T. (2006). *Reading Images: The Grammar of Visual Design*. London: Routledge (1st edn, 1996).

Lavagnino, J. (1995). Reading, scholarship, and hypertext editions. *TEXT: Transactions of the Society for Textual Scholarship, 8*, 109–124.

Millay, A. N. (2005). *Voices from the Fuente Viva: The Effect of Orality in Twentieth-Century Spanish American Narrative*. Lewisburg: Bucknell University Press.

Milsom, A.-M. (2008). Picturing voices, writing thickness: A multimodal approach to translating the Afro-Cuban tales of Lydia Cabrera. PhD dissertation, Middlesex University, London.

Nelson, T. (1965). Complex information processing: A file structure for the complex, the changing and the indeterminate, Proceedings of the 1965 20th National Conference of the Association for Computing Machinery, Cleveland, OH (pp. 84–100). *ACM Digital Library* [Online]. Available at http://portal.acm.org/ (accessed December 1, 2010).

Nichols, B. (1994). *Blurred Boundaries: Questions of Meaning in Contemporary Culture*. Bloomington, IN: Indiana University Press.

Nielson, J. (1995). *Multimedia and Hypertext: The Internet and Beyond*. Boston, MA: AP Professional.

Simon, S. (1996). *Gender in Translation: Cultural Identity and the Politics of Transmission*. London: Routledge.

Sinclair, R. (2006). *Real Life Painting Show* [Exhibition]. Glasgow: Centre for Contemporary Arts (CCA).

Venuti, L. (1995/2008). *The Translator's Invisibility*. London: Routledge.

Weiner, L. (2007–2008). *As Far as the Eye Can See* [Exhibition]. New York: Whitney Museum of Contemporary Art.

17

Disciplinary 'Specificity' and the Digital Submission

Susan Melrose

INTRODUCTION

My main concern in this chapter, given the relatively recent entry of expert performance-practitioners into the postgraduate and higher degree programme of the British university and more widely, is with some of the implications for the higher degree/postgraduate submission and its examination, when the research enquiry is itself pursued, in significant part, through a creative practice that continues, in the digital age, to involve a performance-making whose outcome is real-time and event-based, combining live performance and spectating – hence that continues to cohere with certain notions of disciplinary specificity and identity.

In other words, these are creative practices that might still be called 'dance' or 'movement-based performance', or 'dance theatre', or 'collaborative performance', in the postgraduate/higher degree arena, even if it is also the case that each is more likely than not to bring together a number of instances of disciplinary mastery – lighting and sound design, dance but also choreography, electronic arts and music performance – upon whose contribution the researcher-practitioner's research activity and submission will in part depend, even if it does not seem to be the case that those of us who oversee and supervise such projects have necessarily legislated as to the status, with regard to a candidate's examinable submission, of another practitioner's input to it that is both itself creative *and* cannot therefore be 'owned' as such by the researcher-practitioner.

I want at this point to add what may or may not be a further and not unrelated complication in the case of higher degree/postgraduate submissions by expert performance-practitioner-researchers: where the indicative disciplinary markers sketched out above apply, and where either a live performance event or documentation of the same, or both (as is more generally required), are submitted for examination, then it seems to be almost always the case that the documentation submitted for examination will be digital, generally DVD-based; and, where it is at least 'adequate', both in terms of digital and 'dissertational' production values, and in terms of the 'knowledge-project' undertaken by the candidate, it is still likely to be the case that the performance-practitioner-candidate will have needed the expert input of a digital practitioner, in the production of the documentation. It will have needed, furthermore, *control* over that input that is appropriate to the performance register/s engaged with, in the overall research project, as a mode of advanced enquiry; and a degree of expertise with regard to managing the interface between the performance(-making) and the digital, that allows the candidate to ensure that the seductive play and potential of the digital does not seem to 'magic away' the 'resistant materialities' (Hayles, 1999: 245) (and their own seductive play and affective capacity) of the live.

PRACTITIONER-CENTRED MODES OF KNOWLEDGE, EXPERTISE AND THE SET-UP

The notion that disciplinary specificity might engage modes of knowing, 'knowledge objects' (Knorr Cetina, 2001: 175–188) and models of intelligibility (ways of seeing, knowing and doing) that differ from those that have been normalised within – for example – the mainstream traditions of schooling that applied to my own generation is one whose complexities lie beyond the reach of this chapter. (I mention my generation – and that of many senior university colleagues involved in higher degree supervision – specifically because I would categorise its own infancy, at least, as 'pre-digital', possibly lacking, on this basis, that so-called 'cognitive mapping' (Jameson, 1991) that is now apparently shared by a younger generation now entering higher degree programmes.) For the purposes of the present enquiry, the focus of which is disciplinary specificity, practitioner-centred knowledge modes and their implications for the formal submission in the digital era, I want to cite the work of Knorr Cetina on what she has called 'epistemic cultures' and subcultures (Knorr Cetina, 2001: 1–25), and to add to this perspective the notion of 'set-up' introduced by Rabinow (2003: 44–56).

My argument here is simple: it is that the expertise of professional performance practitioners whose interest is such as to direct them to the postgraduate/ higher degree programme of the university, is likely already to entail complex modes of enquiry that take place not so much *through* creative practice – this might suppose an enquiry that pre-exists, drives and conditions the enquiry that follows – but *as* creative practice, where that creative practice is, as I have suggested above, complex, often multi-participant, relationally complex and internally differentiated. There are two different set-ups within which the expert-practitioner-researcher operates: the wider arts community/ies within which her or his expertise has been externally acknowledged as such, and the higher degree context. The set-up, according to Rabinow, is a network of heterogeneous and loosely linked institutional arrangements, pre-suppositions, expectations, attitudes, laws, ways of seeing and doing, concern with provenance and evidence, evaluative and interpretative models and understandings and so on. Each of these elements plays its part in disciplinary practice, and in the research context and culture; only some of them are consistently articulated discursively, but all of them participate in judgements of taste and value. In the case that concerns me here, where higher degree research is overlaid upon the economy of performance production, we might well expect to find certain elements of these two set-ups that 'fit', and some that do not; some might even be in sharp contradiction with each other.

Knorr Cetina is a sociologist with a particular interest in what she calls 'knowledge practices' (2000: 175–188) and how these operate within cultural contexts. Her reference to 'epistemic' or 'knowledge cultures' and subcultures seems to me to be particularly useful to my concern with expertise (in the performing arts and in the higher degree context): epistemic practices are 'knowledge-centred practices' – I would identify choreography as one such; while 'epistemic objects' are those that 'bind[...] experts to knowledge things in creative and constructive practice[s]' (1999: 182). These knowledge 'objects', she clarifies, are 'processes and projections rather than definitive things'. They are 'in the process of being materially defined' by the very research practices that identify them as being of research interest in the first place. To give you a sense of what I think Knorr Cetina means here, I want to identify 'integrity (in performance)', 'affective potential', the 'expert-intuitive processes in creative decision-making' and the 'logics of production specific to the discipline/s' as four such apparently nebulous, but vital 'epistemic objects' which an expert performance practitioner-researcher might identify to be of particular interest to explore in the higher degree research set-up, precisely because they have proved to be of interest in expert or professional performance-making presented to and validated in terms of the wider arts communities. Each of these four, it seems to me, unwritten/unspeakable in terms of some decades of published enquiry in the field, presents a particular challenge to researcher-practitioners, not least in those set-ups, like that of higher degree research, where research practices (knowledge practices) need to be documented precisely because the research activities and their 'objects' are action and process oriented, 'rather than definitive things' – although some may mistakenly assume that the available 'definitive things' of performance (e.g. 'the performer' or 'the body' or ' the show', that seem to lend themselves more readily to certain attempts at 'capture'), are indeed what performance and performance research are made of.

What Knorr Cetina understands by a 'knowledge-thing' is revealed in her account of 'epistemic cultures', which recalls Rabinow on set-ups. Epistemic cultures are once again more apparently nebulous than definitive; they are:

> ... amalgams of arrangements and mechanisms – bonded through affinity, necessity and historical coincidence – which, in a given field, make up *how we know what we know.* (1999: 1)

'Epistemic cultures' or subcultures, she adds, 'create and warrant knowledge', and the analysis she proposes is one that explores 'the meaning of the empirical, the enactments of object relations, [and] the construction and fashioning of social arrangements' within a disciplinary field (Knorr Cetina, 1999: 1).

I have described discipline-specific creative practices, above, as complex and internally differentiated. The qualifiers are important to what follows for a number of reasons: first, the noun 'practice' has become a major discursive player in certain fields and areas of research over the past decade; yet its ubiquity and apparent usefulness in these fields – it allows some of us, for example, to challenge the classic philosophical divide between something conventionally primary called 'theory' and something secondary called 'practice' – means that some of its users seem to me to run the risk of overlooking the fact that anything identified as 'a practice' is likely to entail a *set* of different and indeed uneven processes, performed within a particular set-up, to particular ends, where that set-up momentarily lends to those processes their particular identity. Rehearsal practices in the performing arts, for example, may function to elicit work from a performer or performers that will constitute new performance material, but they may also involve processes of repetition, aiming at detailed development and mastery of predetermined performance material. In both cases, the work of director or choreographer is delicate, painstaking and developmental, and likely to be characterised by highly individualised and often idiosyncratic processes, but these tend to differ remarkably when the projected outcome is identified as 'devised' or 'text-based', 'work in progress' or 'research led'. What characterises all of the rehearsal or workshop processes, however, is their radical difference from the performance outcome, where that outcome is presented to an audience, real-time event-based and involving the active presence of live spectators.

The 'knowledge objects' specific to the making, the ongoing enquiry that they enact, their developmental status at any moment-hence their incompleteness at any time-are constitutively *un*-likely to be crystallised in the performance outcome *as such*; *un*-available *as such* to spectating, what tends to be made available in the performance event is their transformation into the performance *effects* of the making. In terms of the higher degree/postgraduate research enquiry itself, carried out *as* creative process, the performance event, despite its capacity to refocus attention on spectating and thereby on 'the enactments of object relations, [and] the construction and fashioning of social arrangements' within the expert or professional performance subculture (Knorr Cetina, 1999: 1–25), is rarely itself the research-specific 'knowledge object', even if it is indeed the case that it can stand as one momentary instantiation of the project, which allows that refocus on the spectatorial social and inter-relational. In research terms, 'we' – by which I mean the postgraduate/higher degree performance economy – *want to know something other* than what we see in the performance event (where, in some senses, what we actually see is our own relationship in and with 'the work').

Not only, then, does spectating, in the public event, involve practices and processes which are incommensurable with those specific to the making as an advanced enquiry; not only do the models of intelligibility that inform spectating – present but distanced, omni-attentive, often objectifying ('the performer'); visually focused and meaning-productive – differ radically from those engaged in performance invention; but, more importantly for the present enquiry, those 'knowledge objects' identified by Knorr Cetina, the 'processes and projections rather than definitive things' specific to the making, *are unavailable as such to spectating*. The outcome made available (in the present example, to spectating) is, in terms of the research enquiry, a momentary instantiation of a research undertaking that is non-identical with the research undertaking itself (2001: 181–183).

As non-identical – effectively – with itself, a momentary and incomplete instantiation of the enquiry itself, and unavailable as such to spectating – upon which the very status of expert performance-making does however depend – these aspects of performance-making are equally unavailable to those who might lend their digital expertise to the postgraduate/higher degree candidate seeking to document her or his work. The 'real work' was the developmental creative process, yet it is likely to be the case that what that creative decision-making constitutively entails is invisible to the documenting eye. I have written elsewhere at length on the difficult history, as 'knowledge object', of what I have called the 'expert-intuitive processing' that I see as central to the practices of expertise in the creative and performing arts[1]. For historically specific reasons, something hypostasised as 'intuition' – a noun, rather than a process word – has been largely marginalised, indeed erased from, much of the published writing of Critical Theory, Cultural and Performance Studies – as largely have, by the way, enquiries into the expert and the professional in the creative arts. My argument in this chapter concerned with the postgraduate/higher degree enquiry turns on the need to recuperate expert-intuitive processes as key to expertise in the creative arts. Expert-intuitive processes are both constitutive to creative decision-making, *and* their output systematically undergoes, in the hands of the expert/professional practitioner and in the developmental processes of the making, a degree of transformation when that output come into contact with the production logics specific to the discipline.

What are the implications for that documentation that is indispensable to the research submission, where documentation alone can guarantee to live performance in the higher degree context its capacity to be disseminated to the wider research community? Put simply, as expert spectator and performance document-maker, *I can neither see nor hear* expert-intuitive processing at work, precisely at that moment when I know it is working – and nor, then, can the camera or sound recorder; and if I can, in many instances of working with expert practitioners, see or hear its outcome or effect in the making processes, I cannot see either the cause of that effect, nor what happens in performance-making developmental terms, when the outcome of intuitive processing meets the production processes equally vital to expert performance-making in one or another discipline. Along the same lines, the higher degree candidate/expert-practitioner-researcher cannot begin to see the processes constitutive to her own creative practices unless and until we allow her to acknowledge their vital role, as 'knowledge objects' in enquiry into the set-up specific to the making; she cannot begin to see what Knorr Cetina calls the 'amalgams of arrangements and mechanisms – bonded through affinity, necessity and historical coincidence – which, in a given field' (1999: 1), make up *how she knows what she knows as an expert practitioner.*

How then might the higher degree candidate identify, document and archive disciplinary specificity, in performance-*making* practices, as distinct from the practices of expert spectating, upon which much performance-documentation tends to be modelled? What is at stake in this question is the issue of the university's failure, over recent decades, to engage theoretically with disciplinary specificity, in contrast with the widely preferred and marketable 'interdisciplinarity.'

CAN WE RE-*MEMBER* THE UNSEEN, THE MARGINALISED, THE UNSPOKEN AND THE ERASED *DIGITALLY*?

I have made a number of points, above, with regard to knowledge made widely available through published writing in the university, contrasting that knowledge with expert performance-making set-ups, 'knowledge things' and models of intelligibility that are both constitutive to disciplinary practices in the arts professions and largely erased from, unspeakable within or invisible to that published writing which attempts however to concern itself with decision-making in the creative and performing arts. I have drawn on the insight of Knorr Cetina (2001: 181), to suggest that in some of these cases, key 'knowledge things' specific to the making are 'processes and projections rather than definitive things', which quality tends to lend itself to their overlooking. I have suggested, equally, that the input of digital technology to the research degree documentation project might, with the very best of intentions, overlook or magic away precisely what needs to figure in documentation if we are to attempt to do justice to creative decision-making as a significant part of the postgraduate/higher degree enquiry.

I have intimated, indeed, drawing on the notion that different generations involved in the same higher degree programmes might be differently 'cognitively mapped' when it comes to 'knowledge things' and processes in the digital age; and I have argued that some of us, expert though we may be, *do not necessarily know what we need to know*, or say, or show, if we are to begin to account for the specificity of disciplinary practices in the field. I want at this point to clarify my *sense* (I use the term advisedly, lacking an adequate evidential basis) that where certain knowledges in expert practice have been widely erased or marginalised – in part because the established and scriptually based research degree programme prioritises older knowledge objects – expert performance-maker-researchers may well *not know what they have forgotten* in the making processes. It follows that the not-known or forgotten is unlikely to be documented as such, however well-meaning the team that attempts to document the process.

It is on these sorts of bases that I propose to identify certain categories of knowledge-object (or objectual practices) that are widely omitted from post-graduate programmes in the university, despite the sense (once again) of their pertinence that most expert practitioners retain; these are 'knowledge objects' that the expert practitioner and those who evaluate her work hold onto, but that, in my experience at least, relatively rarely constitute a major research focus in postgraduate work and that research documentation, as a consequence, rarely remembers. The first is *expert-intuitive processing* in creative decision-making that is expert in kind; the second is *signature practices* which – for knowledge-historical reasons – many in Cultural Studies continue to overlook in their preference for knowledge systems in place of the name of the artist, even though it is through her or his ability to identify and engage with these that the named expert practitioner's work is known. Signature, it is worth noting here, is *practised*, tends to be im-*pressed*, rather than to have its own 'thingness'.

The third, rehearsed to some extent in the Deleuzian tradition (Deleuze, 2001: 26) and taken up more recently by Brian Massumi (Massumi, 2002), is *singularity* (or the aspiration to the same in the named arts practitioner's work); the fourth is the *sensibility* of the expert practitioner. A fifth objectual practice, bound up in the previous three, has been identified in Massumi's work (2002) with regard to the artist as a working practitioner, as *qualitative transformation* (162) – the need, in the artist, as futurologist, to focus on the next piece of work (which might 'be better' able to articulate the artist's own ongoing quest and enquiry), rather than earlier work or the previous work, which tends to be the piece with which the academic researcher, whose work is necessarily backward-looking, wants to concern herself.

If these are both articulated in and indeed constitutive to the making processes and outcome of the researcher-practitioner's work, yet their name is rarely spoken as such when it comes to the usual reading in the higher degree programme in the university, how might any of us proceed to re-member them, when it comes to the effective documentation of 'own creative practices' in the higher degree set-up? I have indicated that I sense that these objectual practices are constitutive; I would argue, in addition, that 'we' *know them when we see them*, in the university, rather better than we know how to instruct others to identify them.

On the basis of these sorts of observations, my question continues to be *who should and can* document and archive expert performance-making practices, in a practice-led-research context? I have argued elsewhere (Melrose, 2007) that it is solely on the basis of the higher degree programme's recognition of the disciplinary expertise of the practising artist, and on our ability to discursively articulate – on her and our own behalf – what is specific to her expert practices, that we can begin to identify what is needed of the IT-practitioner who would effectively document another's postgraduate or doctoral research. We do need to acknowledge that, *like* the expert arts practitioner and the expert performance researcher, the digital practitioner is similarly expert. But what this shared expertise means in terms of practice, given my argument above, is that all three of us, as experts in our disciplines, tend to make decisions via the operations of a discipline-specific expert intuition.

I proceed to argue in this chapter that it is time for some of us in the higher degree programme to identify expert-intuitive processing, signature practices and the aspiration to singularity in expert decision-making *as such,* if we are to begin to master some of the implications of these knowledge things, not least for documentation or archiving of an other's expert-practices in the higher degree set-up. As long as some of us fail to do so, we run the risk of replicating, in the higher degree documentation produced, precisely that erasure of data specific to disciplinary specificity, disciplinary expertise and performance-making processes – rather than spectatorial practices and their secondary processing – that seems to me to characterise much current research degree work presented for examination. 'We' – in generational terms – run the risk, in the higher degree programme, of drawing on that ('pre-digital') writing whose importance figured in our own higher degree studies, despite the clearly demonstrated fact that such writing, almost by definition, is expert but spectatorially positioned, with regard to what it has taken to be its analytical object. Is it provocative to observe here that the writing of Judith Butler, Michel Foucault, Roland Barthes, Gilles Deleuze and Felix Guattari, Jacques Derrida, is both expert, and in general spectatorially positioned with regard to its target object? As an expert practice of writing, it is embedded within and operates *within* expert writing, even if some of it attempts systematically to target practice modes that lie outside writing. When we come back to Knorr Cetina's notion of the 'amalgams of arrangements and mechanisms – bonded through affinity, necessity and historical coincidence – which, in a given field, make up *how we know what we know*', we might need to acknowledge that the amalgams of arrangements and mechanisms, the knowledge objects and the models of intelligibility that make up how the critical theorist knows what she knows, tend to be scriptural (de Certeau, 1984), writerly, to operate within and in terms of a writing mastery of whose registers often lie outside the established expertise of the arts practitioner.

WHERE/HOW TO BEGIN?

Memory, remembering and forgetting – if not in their specific relationship with arts practitioner expertise – do figure in and in some instances are explicitly thematised in the work of a number of twentieth century writer-philosophers, as are certain questions relating to the nature and performative power of art itself. The writing of Jean-Francois Lyotard, concerned notoriously with the postmodern and with master narratives (Lyotard, 1971/1984), has also observed more recently, of the artwork, that the signature artwork tends to disarm the viewer; it tends to disarm 'thinking machines' or 'representing machines' (Lyotard, 1991: 17) – hence, those engaged by the critical writer. If Lyotard's judgement of the 1980s was valid, it might seem that something 'in' that art tended to locate itself, on or outside the margins of written and possibly digital inscription. In the face of art's powers to disarm, however, the response of the academic and critic is to seek at great haste to write 'twenty or one hundred pages', in an attempt 'to pick up the [mind's] pieces, and [to put] the plot together again'. That expert writerly picking up of the mind's pieces, by the academic and critic, immediately renders that experience historical, and the critical commentary both reactive, spectatorially centred, and other to that art with which it nonetheless purports to engage. Attention has shifted hence from cause to effect, from artwork to art effect; with the consequence that enquiry has shifted to the spectator, and away from any sense of either the artwork or the signature and sensibility of the artist as inventor and futurologist. This is a curious but widespread peculiarity of what might be called 'art-writing'. Art-writing, in turn, 'stages' and reproduces the dominant models of intelligibility that informed critical perspectives from the 1970s onwards and that are widely taught in postgraduate seminars; it replicates a schism between the communication sciences, on the one hand, and aesthesis, or the operations of aesthetic judgement, on the other hand[2]. What I have called *'signature practices'* in the making, and the singularity and qualitative transformation the artist aspires to, have as a consequence of this sort of schism, been systematically under-theorised in the set-ups that have dominated in the older university, not least under the headings of critical theory and the critique of representation.

On this basis, 'the show' is not 'the [research] thing', and nor does 'the show' constitute, in itself, whatever I am recognising as signature: the signature of the artist is likely, instead, to emerge with time, on the basis of performance regularities identifiable *across the researcher's body of work*. In performance-making terms, *choreographic* regularities tend to be identified through engagement with a complex, historically differentiated practice-memory, which informs and conditions expert-intuitive process and decision-making, where these are equally conditioned by the aspiration to the new, to qualitative transformation (Massumi, 2002), and, in Knorr Cetina's terms (2001: 185), these are 'under-girded' affectively.

Can we require of the digital document-maker that he or she be concerned with the enquiry into signature practice, into the indices of affective investment and where and how these might be identified, and into the practitioner's own drive to qualitative transformation? Such a concern would mean that the documentation processes need to enquire into their own capacity for presentation and representation. We might need, if that were to be the case, to call for a reflective digital practice and practitioner, a capacity for praxiological enquiry (an enquiry through expert practices into expert practices) in the digital document-maker, which I would argue is likely to lie within her or his competence – yet this might suggest that the digital document-maker needs herself to be a researcher. Any such praxiological enquiry needs to be attentive to the different *registers* and peculiarities of practice, as these are deployed in different discipline-specific set-ups. The encoding scheme or schemes adopted, and the meta-data that apply, need to take onboard, and to categorise, not only knowledge complexity, but the ongoing speculative nature we might expect of the practice-led enquiry in the higher degree set-up.

Lyotard's *The Inhuman* (1991) is subtitled with deliberate informality, in the French, *Causeries sur le temps*, or 'chatting about time', and these chats include the subject of the times of art-making. In Lyotard's terms, the artist's signature practices might equally be resistant to *digital* inscription – at least if the latter is pursued unreflexively. His 1980s use of the term 'digital inscription' is unlikely to have come out of much hands-on experience of digital inscription; he was, after all, a professional philosopher-researcher and writer. It is rather more likely to have come from others' *written* observations on the digital, including Adorno's observations on music, which Lyotard cites. As far as the twenty-first century digital is concerned, then, Lyotard's 'conversations' of the 1980s are 'history'. His expertise as philosopher, meanwhile, was writing-based, and it took writing as its means of production as well as its outcome. His interest in aesthetics in the 1980s, then, 'comes out of' the registers of writing specific to the discipline of philosophy, and out of the perspective of expert spectator – whence my caution. As philosopher, Lyotard tried nonetheless to focus on what, according to his own disciplinary orientation at the time, might seem to resist writerly inscription.

The art-*effect* (we need to recognise the implications of the final term) *dis*-arms, for Lyotard, in the way it brings uniquely together an abiding enigma and the work's technicity; the greater its technicity, he argues, citing Adorno (Lyotard, 1991: 'Matter and Time'), the greater the likelihood that it will make itself available to digital inscription; but as a direct consequence, the less its abiding enigma is available to be grasped as such. There are a number of points I want to make here: first, Lyotard's clear concern is with the impact of the work on a perceiver, and not with the work of making the work. Second, while Lyotard's highly conventional attempt to dissolve the art into two qualities – the technical and the enigmatic – has a certain appeal, my own approach has been to argue that creative decision-making proceeds through the catalytic interrelationship of – for example – (the outcome of) expert-intuitive processing and the production logics specific to the discipline. My identification of expert-intuitive process in creative decision-making as a model of intelligibility vital to the making sets out quite particularly to recuperate that expert-intuitive processing from the realm of the other-than-rational, where so many have sought to locate it, to the detriment of performance theoretical writers' understanding of creative process. Expert-intuitive outcomes, in other words, partake of both the enigmatic and of the technical, are constantly tested in terms of the technologies (in the widest sense) of performance-making and its events.

My third point returns to issues already raised above: the 'picking up of the mind's pieces', by the academic and critic immediately renders the initial, spectatorial engagement historical: the 'is it happening?', of Lyotard's sublime (1994) is thereby rendered – and recuperated – as 'it happened'. The academic and critic, on this basis, are history. Yet Lyotard hardly seems to be unaware of some of these difficulties: one remedy to be found in his essay on time, which might seem to allow us to document while abstaining from these instances of secondary appropriation in the case of the expert practitioner's work, would be to undertake a process of documentation that might 'mediate [...] what happens before reacting' to it (1991: 58–77). The timing of documentation, on behalf of the expert arts practitioner-researcher, is thus critical. By my use of the words 'on behalf of ...', I mean a documentation carried out in terms that relate as tightly as possible to the practitioner's creative practice pursued as an advanced research enquiry. I would argue that it needs to begin to be undertaken before it seems to be necessary or useful, and visited systematically throughout the schedule for the development of the research project.

The research undertaking and its documentation needs to begin to engage with the making processes, well in advance of the performance event (which is not necessarily its primary focus), in a set-up activated on the basis of an evaluation of the practitioner's already-evidenced expertise. One should, thereafter, be able, with expert process in mind, to begin to engage with and document the time of the work's evolution, leading up to something like 'the work that finishes the work' – as Lyotard has so neatly put it, albeit in reference to Freudian psycho-analysis (1991: 56). Without that engagement with the making processes, in the research context, the academic researcher's attempt to seem to put the work back together again, *after experiencing it*, is likely to be *other* to the signature effect that I am targeting, and would thus 'owe[...] nothing', in Lyotard's words, 'to the place [the work] can take (and which in a sense it never takes) in the intrication of sensory positions and intelligible meanings' (56–57) specific to the practitioner's understanding and undertaking.

EXPERTISE, DISCIPLINARY SPECIFICITY AND ITS DOCUMENTATIONS

We might expect that the practitioner herself, bringing her expert recall of what she was looking at and staging, in the developing work, and how she then realised it in terms of professional production logics and production values, is best placed to provide valuable input to the effective documentation of what we widely accept to be 'her work' in the higher degree set-up. Her insight, in the terms I have set out, should lie in her ownership of and ability to recall the initial impetus and the making processes themselves, as distinct from their outcome. Yet a number of factors come into play here, particularly when the candidate is constrained to seek to find some kind of empirical fit between the higher degree set-up and its own knowledge project and those specific to creative practice.

I have argued that certain models of intelligibility and 'knowledge-objects' are highly particular to her disciplinary mastery and expertise, and added that these tend to be non-identical with the models of intelligibility and 'knowledge-objects' to be found in the higher degree seminar that widely continues to be preoccupied with the production of writing in complex registers, pursued from particular positions with regard to its analytical object. Lyotard's identification of the abiding enigma of the artwork, regardless of the fact that his concern is with the art-effect, may well apply to the artist's own grasp of her 'process', not least in the sense that a creative 'unknowing' is often cited by the arts-practitioner as a way of seeing and knowing that is vitally important to making new work. Lyotard's concern with what he called 'digital inscription', in the mid-1980s, and apparent failures of that inscription when it comes to art's abiding enigma, promotes me to ask, at this point, whether we can now anticipate a better 'fit' between the operating systems available to the digital documentation of creative process more generally, and their effects, when our concern is with the digital documentation of discipline-specific creative process.

Massumi's qualitative transformation and the futurology he attributes to the practising artist (Massumi, 2002: 4) together seem to suggest a willingness in many artists to shake themselves free of certain sorts of knowledge acquired at particular points in the making. What I have sometimes seen as a wilfully retained 'expert unknowing' in expert practitioners' process is plainly likely to manifest itself with regard to the expert-intuitive operations themselves, to the impact of contingency and happy accident on production processes, and to the notion of what the emerging work might or might not seem to thematise. Yet at the same time, in expert practice, mastery of modes of production, taken in the fullest sense, grows in the doing of it, as a set of practices few of which are developed discursively in the same practitioner. In his 'Derridean dispersion and Heideggerian articulation', practice theorist Charles Spinosa (in Schatzki et al., 2001: 199–212) accounts for this sort of practice mastery in terms of its acquisition through what he calls a 'tendency of [practice] elaboration' (200) that both contributes to expertise and is likely not to require either full awareness of that process, or any discursive articulation of it.

Similarly, that the artwork lends itself notoriously to endless unfoldings suggests a complexity of signifying potential that the professional arts practitioner (Francis Bacon's painting in Deleuze's account [2005] comes to mind) might well *sense,* without aspiring to participate in those processes of meaning-production.

Sensing is taken by that practitioner not merely to be a wholly adequate mode of knowing but one that is preferred to discursive articulations – a fact that we might need to explore from the perspective of the range of models of intelligibility that apply, rather than disparage. That sense and sensing, here, are bound-up with an exercise of judgement, in the expert arts practitioner, that parts at least of the wider arts community/ies have validated is, once again, a matter whose complexity lies beyond the reach of this chapter.

I have rehearsed some of the knowledge 'difficulties' of expert creative process and its anticipated digital documentation in the field of the higher degree submission, in order to raise the question of how we might test these knowledge specificities against the epistemic specificity, the 'amalgams of arrangements and mechanisms – bonded through affinity, necessity and historical coincidence – which, in a given field, make up *how we know what we know'* in the field of digital practice. In order to begin that task, I want to cite Rudi Laerman and Pascal Gielen's 2007 web-published, 'The Archive of the Digital An-Archive', as an example of writing in the field that comes out of what I persist in identifying as the disciplinary set-up specific to the sociology of the arts.

The writers announce an explicit Foucauldian interest in 'the law of what can be said', as their starting-point. In terms of the notion of a disciplinary set-up that I have begun to identify, their published article itself suggests to me that the authors write, if I might put it this way, *out of writing* itself, and out of what I would identify as a critical 'belief in' writing as the dominant knowledge-medium. Despite a stated concern with 'contemporary cyber-reality', their disciplinary set-up seems – again on this limited evidence – not merely to privilege writing, but their text is repeatedly concerned with what they identify as the 'ongoing *discourse* "on" the digital archive' (my emphases). The archive users they reference, in turn, typically '*read* data' (my emphasis), rather than viewing it, thereby prioritising the orders of writing and reading; and the writers themselves openly observe that even in the case of 'the treatment of images and sounds (both need words in order to become meaningful) [in archival terms]'.

Meanwhile, Laermans and Gielen (2007) set out observations on the differences between a database, which is user-need oriented and hence open to constant update, and an archive, which is a necessarily closed and hence stabilised database. They note the fairly widespread argument that 'the digital' and 'the archive' 'are clashing notions because they refer to the basic, and opposite, characteristics of old and new media', and, as a consequence, that the digital archive is differently evaluated by traditional archivists and 'new media' archive specialists. Where their work seems to me to become more compelling, is in their identification of what they call the 'hidden performativity of computer programs, which make information production simultaneously possible and impossible'.

'The archive of the [digital] archive' itself, note the writers, is 'not neutral'. They cite Wolfgang Ernst's observation (2002) that 'Behind every collection [of information] that is dressed up in a narrative or iconic way stands a bare technological structure, an archival skeleton that is with strategic consciousness withdrawn from discursive access on the level of the interface (…)'. 'Apparently without irreversible hierarchies', they note, still citing Ernst, 'the system of technical transfer and storage protocols is, beyond the visible surfaces, much more rigid than a traditional archive ever was'. In media-theoretical terms, the writers add, 'most users do not actually observe the […] mediating and performative role of the different sorts of programs on which they rely when storing, retrieving or processing information'. What is at work, the writers point out, at this unobserved and generally speaking unobservable level, is a 'sub-media space within which hierarchies of carriers of signs lead into dark opaque depths'.

From the point of view of the known and knowable in expert performance-making practice that I have set out in this chapter, the writers' uses of qualifiers like 'dark', 'opaque' and 'unobserved' are momentarily appealing: there is an order of the unknowable here; yet it is an order identified by the writers as operating performatively in a 'sub-media space' of 'dark opaque depths', from where it exercises a control that might seem to *perform the performers*, removing from them a capacity for choice that they might otherwise take to be their own. If we were to review this sketch for a model of knowledge against the disciplinary specificity of performance-making practices, we might be obliged to acknowledge that what I have identified throughout in terms of the specificity of the discipline pre-exists and provides the constitutive ground to the practices of expert performance-making engaged in the higher degree set-up by the candidate concerned. We do not need to dramatise these in terms of 'dark opaque depths'; indeed I should prefer to draw on the Deleuzian model of a 'plane of immanence' (Deleuze and Guattari, 1994: 49), whose reach and power are such that all instances of new practice are always already given. 'Dance', in other words, predetermines, regulates and controls certain constitutive aspects of inventive practice even in the hands of the edgy, challenging practitioner, and it informs the expectations and modes of engagement of performance's spectators; yet it is almost certainly the case that this order of control is extra-discursive. It is 'held', and it is progressively elaborated, for one or another expert practitioner, in the practice of it.

When Laermans and Gielen note an order of control operating in the digital realm that is relatively inaccessible to and unownable by the user, my own *sense* is that the expert user, in the higher degree set-up, will have insight into these complexities. After all, the determining player operating in the writers' 'dark sub-medial space', in mediological terms, surely emerges on the basis of industry standards, regulated by Relational Database Management Systems (RDBMS). These industry standards, as I understand it, are agreed not only between multiple authors but between authors and vendors of these systems, in order to maximise 'inter-operability' between systems.

Unlike the plane of immanence in dance, however, all operate in the digital arena within a linguistic frame and use 'pseudo-code' (programming statements) which resemble language, and programming algorithms which are normally stated in standard language before being translated into programming 'languages' (e.g. SQL, C++, PERL, Java). These are rules-based systems, and all users rearticulate them, regardless of their own aspiration to digital difference.

The performance document-maker, in other words, in seeking to inscribe digitally what is particular to the expert practice concerned, has a wide but strictly limited range of options available, but cannot otherwise intervene in the display options that these control. Hence in adhering to standards, she attempts to obtain a best approximation of how the end user will receive the material; and in the higher degree set-up, that end-user can be expected to be expert at least in terms of the disciplinary field within which the candidate's work is located. That user may well not (yet) be expert in the fields of digital inscription, and will need as a consequence to be guided by the candidate's own account, included in the mixed-mode postgraduate or higher degree submission, of some of the meta-praxiological issues at stake.

My argument, thus, is that by taking the adequate digital inscription itself of the 'knowledge objects' specific to expert performance-making process *as external measure of* the latter, the expert-practitioner postgraduate/higher degree candidate will begin to obtain an insight into the knowledge specificity of her practice that is currently unusual in the higher degree set-up. In such an undertaking, where knowledge systems are overlaid, the one upon the other, it is likely that the performance practitioner will begin to be able to dissolve complex notions that an unreflective language use has the capacity to render monolithic.

In this context, Lyotard's observations on time, memory effects and digital technologies (Lyotard, 1991: 50–87) seem to me to be of interest, despite rapid technological development and cultural dissemination over the past two decades: for Lyotard, remembering is not monolithic but internally differentiated, and I would argue that it is in part this internal differentiation that lends itself to the sort of praxiological enquiry into documentation that I am calling for here. Plainly the terms he used re-engage with the philosophical tradition that provides his own disciplinary expertise, and his enquiry into what he terms 'temporal syntheses' revisits Kant, on apprehension and reproduction, Bergson on recognition, and Freud, on memory; yet his suggestions seem to me to resonate with certain sorts of distinctions we might make between certain sorts of material used in documentation.

From the perspective of 'preservation' of a past that needs, in fact, to be reconstructed (since the cyber-realm otherwise has no memory), Lyotard focuses on what might be the bases for the practitioner-documenter's selection of already digitised data, already delocalised and detemporalised, and on how simulacra – one of which is 'the past' itself, and another of which is 'signature' – are produced, and might be grasped auto-reflexively as well as expert-intuitively (1991: 50). It is these simulacra, once constructed, he argues, that re-anchor data in a number of conceptual frames which are likely in turn to trigger their own memory effects on behalf of an expert user-researcher, provided we make awareness of those sorts of frames available discursively.

The three memory effects noted by Lyotard, in the mid-1980s, he argues, 'coincide more or less with three very different sorts of temporal synthesis linked to [digital] inscription' (50): the first mode of temporal synthesis, 'breaching' renders the past in terms of habit, including habits of thought and feeling; it coincides with the identification of elements drawn together on the basis of affinity, habit or habit-memory. The second, 'scanning', effects its own temporal synthesis and seems to evoke the experience that attaches to that synthesis: it 'implies not only the retention of the past in the present as present, but the synthesis of the past as such and its reactualization as past, in the present (of consciousness)'. Remembering, 'implies the identification of what is remembered through its classification in a calendar and a cartography' (51), and it is self-referential: 'it remembers its own presuppositions and implications' (53). The third mode of temporal synthesis, 'passing', coincides with that involuntary but often puzzling memory, which can seem, as though uninvited, to 'come to the practitioner': it is associated with 'working through', in the Freudian psychoanalytic sense of the term. Passing, Lyotard adds, uses up more energy than other techniques, because 'it is a technique with no rule, or a negative rule, deregulation'. It involves an ongoing 'working through', where elements retained trigger again, in the practitioner, an ongoing enquiry that seems, even as one's work reaches its momentary, public instantiation – always a compromise with resistant materialities – to be unanswerable.

CONCLUSION

If 'we' are to work together, as differently skilled expert practitioners, on the digital documentation of signature creative *process*, with a mixed-mode dissertation in mind, I would argue that a meta-theoretical engagement, on the part of the expert digital practitioner, working with the artist on the expert-practitioner document, is important. First, the latter needs to be in a position to advise the former, as to what is constitutive to the making processes, and what has most commonly been overlooked; and the former needs, on that sort of basis, to be able to trial and test digital solutions for disciplinary problems. 'We' may need to re-invent historically precise set-ups, and to provide alternative perspectives with regard to missing data, if we are to overcome long-established and naturalised prejudice.

The inventiveness and the professional virtuosity of the digital practitioner are central here, as soon as we recognise that in order to document the shift in perspective to practitioner expertise and experience, creative digital solutions need to be found. Second, the expert digital practitioner needs to learn to make explicit and therefore transparent to the artist, the existence and operation of rules in setting the parameters of the digital document. Third, and finally, all partners need to recognise the limits which the existence of a rules-bound digital system imposes on any attempt to record material, requiring that the higher degree candidate constitute a rich meta-narrative, derived through collaborative invention, if its complexities are to be understood by an eventual user.

NOTES

1. http://www.sfmelrose.org.uk
2. Osborne, P. (2000). *Philosophy in Cultural Theory*. London: Routledge.

REFERENCES

de Certeau, M. (1984). *The Practice of Everyday Life* (trans: S. Randall). Berkley, CA: University of California Press.

Deleuze, G. (2001). *Difference and Repetition* (trans: P. Patton). London: Continuum Publishing.

Deleuze, G. (2005). *Francis Bacon; The Logic of Sensation* (trans: D. W. Smith). London: Continuum Publishing.

Deleuze, G. & Guattari, F. (1994). *What is Philosophy?* (trans. G. Burchell & H. Tomlinson). London: Verso Books.

Hayles, K. N. (1999). *How we Became Posthuman. Virtual Bodies in Cybernetics, Literature and Informatics.* Chicago, IL: University of Chicago Press.

Jameson, F. (1991). *Postmodernism, or, The Cultural Logic of Late Capitalism*. London: Verso Books.

Knorr Cetina, K. (1999). *Epistemic Cultures: How the Sciences Make Knowledge*. Cambridge, MA: Harvard University Press.

Knorr Cetina, K. (2001). Objectual practices. In: T. Schatzki, K. Knorr Cetina, & E. Von Savigny (Eds.), *The Practice Turn in Contemporary Theory*. London: Routledge.

Laermans, R. & Gielen, P. (2007). The archive of the digital an-archive. *Image and Narrative*, Issue 17 *The Digital Archive*, April 2007; http://www.imageandnarrative.be/inarchive/digital_archive/digital_archive.htm

Lyotard, J.-F. (1984). *The Postmodern Condition: A Report on Knowledge* (trans. G. Bonnington and B. Massumi). University of Minnesota Press; first published in France as *La Condition postmoderne: rapport sur le savoir* (1979), Paris: Les Editions de Minuit.

Lyotard, J.-F. (1991). *The Inhuman: Reflections on Time* (trans. G. Bonnington and R. Bowlby). Stanford, CA: Stanford University Press.

Lyotard, J.-F. (1994). *Lessons on the Analytic of the Sublime: Kant's Critique of Judgment* (trans. E. Rottenberg). Stanford, CA: Stanford University Press.

Massumi, B. (2002). *Parables for the Virtual: Movement, Affect, Sensation*. Durham, NC: Duke University Press.

Melrose, S. (2007). *Still Harping on (About Expert Practitioner-centred Modes of Knowledge and Models of Intelligibility)*. Available at: www.sfmelrose.org.uk

Osborne, P. (2000). *Philosophy in Cultural Theory*. London: Routledge.

Rabinow, P. (2003). *Anthropos Today: Reflections on Modern Equipment*. Princeton, NJ: Princeton University Press.

18

Digits and Figures: A Manual Drawing Practice and its Modes of Reproduction

Juliet MacDonald

INTRODUCTION

In 2006, I conducted a literature search of PhD theses on the subject of drawing. I found a few, by researchers in the UK, that I was able to order from the British Library. They arrived on microfilm. I remember sitting at the large viewing apparatus, having struggled to thread the film, scrolling through pages in linear fashion. In some cases, the thesis was reproduced onto the film in negative, and unless there was an optical mechanism to reverse it, words would appear glowing from a darkened ground on the large screen above me, often accompanied by a constellation of other bright spots and scratches – noise from the photographic process of reproduction or dust on the film itself. The theses I viewed (Bailey, 1982; Leake, 1993; Pigrum, 2001; Saorsa, 2004; Wallis, 2003) included drawings and other visual material, but these were also in negative, without half-tones, reduced to a binary pattern of dark or light. The full-colour paintings and tonal drawings of Karen Wallis, for example, appeared to me as clusters of more-or-less illegible marks. Copyrighted material was excluded, or else reproduced with a cross through it. Any material the author had supplied on disc was missing altogether. Although these researchers wrote ably and extensively about their investigations, it was clear that valuable evidence of their processes, methods and findings that had been submitted as part of the thesis, was not reproduced.

In this chapter, I describe my own PhD project, as a case study of an art practitioner's research into drawing. I consider the implications of producing the thesis in a format aimed at facilitating online access. This case study is set within the context of a growing international community of researchers investigating aspects of drawing using practical methodologies, and the need for platforms that facilitate the dissemination of visual, procedural and inter-textual aspects of our research.

My thesis (MacDonald, 2010) addresses drawing as a process of enquiry, figuration and knowledge-making, the primary method and object of research being my own practice of observational drawing[1]. I define this more specifically as a manual and visual practice of direct mark-making in response to perceptual experience. The drawings conducted as part of the project are descriptions of bodies and embodied experience, and the fluency of bodily action and sensory experience in the act of drawing is central to the investigation of corporeality and knowledge at its heart.

The drawing practice could be described as low-tech, utilising economical, readily available equipment of pencil, ball-point pen and paper but drawings were scanned, digitally manipulated, layered and animated in a creative re-working of the figurative content. The final thesis comprises: Part I, a written overview containing a narrative of the research process; Part II, a digital archive of drawings and animations, cross-referenced numerically to the narrative and Part III, a set of 12 texts forming an interconnected diagram/website. Part I was submitted in print and in Portable Document Format (PDF), Parts II and III were on disc and online, viewable using a web browser[2].

Here, I consider the aspects of my drawings that are replicable digitally, and those that remain as properties of the singular artefact. This requires a consideration of drawing as a process, as the artefact of a process and as a configuration or figure. I go on to describe in some detail how the configuration of marks is materially copied in the analogue/digital process of scanning, before being manifested in, and framed by, the screen.

During the production of my thesis, my writing processes were informed by the spatial and diagrammatic thinking constituted by drawing. HTML (Hypertext Mark-up Language) provided the means to connect texts in a non-linear structure. In the final part of this chapter, I note the desire to integrate fully text and image and factors that constrain this. Finally, I consider the longevity of my own digital thesis. As universities struggle to establish consistent and lasting modes of storage, Internet technologies evolve and software monopolies are contested, how can we ensure that the knowledge constituted by the thesis remains accessible?

AN EXPANDING FIELD OF RESEARCH

Until the late twentieth century, drawing was often seen as occupying a support-
ive or preparatory role in relation to painting or sculpture. However, the Museum
of Modern Art's exhibition, *Drawing Now: 1955–1975* (Rose, 1976), set the
scene for a recognition of drawing within contemporary art, as an autonomous
discipline. The Drawing Center established the following year, also in New York,
was to develop into a major focal point for the study of drawing.

In the 1960s, a few authors set out to provide an overview of the practice
across cultures and historical periods. Hill's book, *The Language of Drawing*,
describes a reflexive process: 'Drawing turns the creative mind to expose its
workings' (1966: 1). Rawson's 1969 publication, *Drawing*, includes a systematic explanation of the way in which drawn lines, marks and blobs operate.
Rather than simply describing representational functions, he suggests a fabric
of analogies and references that are relayed through drawing. Publications
by Rawson and Hill can be criticised for presenting too universal a picture
of drawing, but they identify a topic for further investigation. Adopting a more
scientific approach, Beittel studied college students seeking to categorise their
cognitive processes in drawing. Speculating on the conjunction of being both
artist and researcher, Beittel writes of an 'immersive understanding' that is
unable to predict or control but can only describe and interpret (1972: 246).
Bailey's phenomenological study of 1982, stands out as one of the few PhD
theses from the period before 1990 to address the process of drawing as a form
of reflection: 'Knowledge that arises from the drawing process is a *coming to
know*, not a knowledge achieved prior to the on-going dialectic of the process
itself' (1982: 41).

Neither Beittel nor Bailey makes a first-person study of their own artwork,
rather they record and analyse the drawings of others from a position evidently
informed by practice. The phenomenon of art practitioners researching into, and
by means of their own drawing practices is a relatively recent one. A number of
exhibitions and their associated publications provide a further context to this
(Petherbridge, 1991; Rose, 1992; Craig-Martin, 1995; de Zegher and Newman,
2003). The involvement of practising artists in the selection and curation of some
of these shows is significant, as it parallels the growing importance of practitioner research in an academic context.

Since 1990, there have been a growing number of conferences, MA programmes and research initiatives devoted to various aspects of the topic, that
have brought together not only artists but also designers, architects, psychologists and those of other disciplines that use drawing[3]. International partnerships
have been instigated and individual institutions have also established their own
centres, such as the NAS Study Centre for Drawing in Sydney. In addition to
institutional initiatives, independent projects for the study of drawing have started
to emerge. Since its inception in 2008, Drawing Spaces in Lisbon has gained

importance internationally as a focal point for the theoretical and practical investigation of drawing. This developing academic context includes journal articles (Schneckloth, 2008), publications (Duff and Sawdon, 2008) and a growing number of PhD completions and Masters dissertations[4].

THE INTERNET AS A CONTEXT FOR DRAWING RESEARCH

Until recently, the primary means to make the outcomes of drawing processes public was either through exhibitions or printed books. For example, Phaidon's *Vitamin D* (Dexter, 2005) is a weighty, full-colour volume, offering an international survey of contemporary drawing. The reader or viewer has the luxury of leafing through pages of high definition images printed on good quality paper with deckled edges – a tactile reference to hand-crafted art materials.

By contrast, the exhibition catalogue of the annual Jerwood Drawing Prize, established in 1994 to promote and gauge contemporary drawing practice, is now available for download as a PDF document (see Jerwood Visual Arts website). Similarly, the Manifest Gallery in Ohio displays every successful entry in its *International Drawing Annual* online (see Manifest website). However, in both cases the digital resource, of small, heavily compressed images, is supplemental to the primary dissemination method, that of exhibition or print.

Although vital as modes of public access to the arts, neither exhibitions nor printed books are ideal formats for the worldwide reproduction of research knowledge. Digital technologies have made possible the speedy production of full colour books, printed on demand, but the cost of each copy is a serious consideration for researchers. Exhibitions have the benefit of providing access to the original products of research, but it is expensive and time-consuming to tour exhibitions internationally.

Consequently, the academic community is increasingly making use of Internet technologies to share research. The Drawing Research Network, established in the UK in 2001, now has an international membership contributing to its email network and its revamped website has facilities for sharing news, setting up a profile and linking to online dissertations and theses. Since 2002, the online journal for contemporary drawing research, *TRACEY*, has provided the opportunity for peer-reviewed publication of research outputs. Making use of its web platform to encourage contributions in any format, it forms an important archive of recent investigation into drawing.

However, despite the willingness to submit articles to *TRACEY*, until very recently, few PhD theses have been made available online. Cain's thesis has recently been published by Intellect (2010). If it had already been widely disseminated online it is possible that this would have disqualified it in the eyes of the publisher. Meanwhile, a number of researchers maintain their own websites as artists, often with a small section for their written outputs (Schneckloth, 2010; Talbot, 2010). In the wider context of art practice, the drawing blog is now a means by which a flow of drawings enters the public domain, from photographs of finished works in galleries to scans of quick sketches and doodles.

The British Library no longer supplies theses on microfilm. The programme of digitisation has begun, at least in the UK, and it is now possible to download Wallis's thesis with full-colour images, as a PDF document. However, the videos that formed part of her submission on disc, although already digitised, have not been made available in this way[5]. The standard PDF works best to support text and still image content. It corresponds well to the printed book or the bound thesis, support for moving image content being still at an early stage. In the submission of my own thesis, the inclusion of moving image content was an important factor in choosing an HTML format, and this is one area of future development for the digital thesis.

In his influential essay of the 1930s, *The Work of Art in the Age of Mechanical Reproduction*, Benjamin marks out key developments in the technologies of image reproduction: stamping of coins in ancient Greece; woodcut printing, etching and engraving in the Middle Ages; lithography at the beginning of the nineteenth century; photography a few decades later and finally film. He argues photography exceeded all previous techniques: 'For the first time in the process of pictorial reproduction, photography freed the hand of the most important artistic functions which henceforth devolved only upon the eye looking into a lens' (1999: 213). The continued use of manual drawing processes by artists, designers, architects and many other disciplines, demonstrates that the lens did not displace completely all other means of figurative production. However, the multiplicity of reproductive methods made possible by digital technologies, marks a further step change in Benjamin's narrative of the democratisation of image and sound. As broadcasting becomes a possibility for almost anyone with a computer connected to the Internet, and as access to knowledge is devolved from libraries to laptops, the visual, auditory, filmic and textual products of artistic research are now replicable to an extent that even Benjamin might not have imagined. This multiplying effect brings with it concerns about the ease of plagiarism, but it can be assumed that as the technologies of duplication improve so too will those of comparison and detection. The British Library example shows that institutions responsible for safeguarding and distributing knowledge products are adjusting to this changing context, but there is still some way to go.

DRAWING AROUND THE BODY: A DIGITAL THESIS

My own research project was based on the hypothesis that drawing can operate as a form of reflection or enquiry. I had experienced shifts in my thinking that I attributed to the activity of drawing. During slow, careful study of organic things, such as pieces of fruit or leaves, resemblances (vein structures or skin-like surfaces) became meaningful as a suggestion of the commonality of living processes. This complicated the subject/object relationship I had assumed. Seeping into my visual experience was the colouring of other senses, for example, the roughness or softness of a surface, the smell of the fruit ripening. This sensory encroachment asserted the presence of something living, dying or harbouring life and also acting upon me. The combined effect of resemblance and proximity made its mark. In the ecological repositioning that this brought about, drawing had been a catalyst.

Within this revised context, I was particularly concerned with the question of corporeality: the body as a contained or containing unit; as individual entity or part of collective being; as structure or process; as the locus of subjectivity or the surface of cultural inscription; as a taxonomic specimen or as the basic fact of animal commonality. I set out to test drawing as a means to investigate these ontological concerns. My primary research method was to draw from immediate perceptual experience and to direct my attention towards others (human and other animals). I viewed this as a process in which I marked affective significance, faces being of most importance.

The inter-subjectivity of this process was informed by the work of Merleau-Ponty, who disputes notions of the embodied subject as a self-sufficient entity, able to make detached observations of the world without being affected by it:

> Visible and mobile, my body is a thing among things; it is caught in the fabric of the world, and its cohesion is that of a thing. But because it moves itself and sees, it holds things in a circle around itself. Things are an annex or prolongation of itself; they are incrusted into its flesh, they are part of its full definition; the world is made of the same stuff as the body. (1974: 284)

Hass highlights Merleau-Ponty's description of the body's intentionality as having a figure-ground structure or schema: 'the behaving body is a projective being: its most basic function is to project out of and against itself toward things' (1999: 94). Hass argues the sense of other possible perspectives is implicit in the perceptual process, as described by Merleau-Ponty, and this enables us to recognise the projective behaviour in others, 'behavior … is not only something that I prepropositionally live, it is also something I can *perceptually figure* and in doing so sense that this is another perceiving being, another corporeal schema' (1999: 97). These descriptions, retrospectively, provide me with an explanation of the figurative outcomes of my drawing process.

Initially responding to Merleau-Ponty's proposal of 're-learning to look at the world' in *Phenomenology of Perception* (1962, p. xx), I set out to draw without pre-conception, reacting with immediacy to phenomena rather than operating within a set of received modes, aspirations, styles and aesthetic values. However, the difficulty of setting aside the practice I had been taught, to start with a 'clean sheet', became increasingly apparent. First, I abandoned the conventional practice of studying the *still* body, posed at a convenient distance. Instead, I positioned myself in public places, in crowds or fields, where others around me were following disparate trajectories (as shown in Figure 18.1).

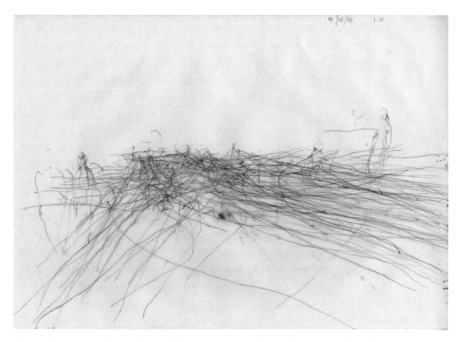

Figure 18.1   Drawing of people's movements through a busy shopping area

Second, I set out to destabilise received skills by drawing with various restrictions to my usual manual and visual operations (Figures 18.2 and 18.3 are examples of this).

Around the central practice of observational drawing, or 'drawing from life', were other graphic modes: note-making and diagrams moved towards written formulations and I extended this mode of working to arranging texts and drawings around a room and connecting them with threads; I used doodling as an alternative mode of unplanned figuration, and repetitive tracing of a double loop as a means to consider bodily movement and the action of re-inscribing.

This creative methodology involved the re-working of drawings rather than their interpretation or analysis. For example, I drew over existing drawings. As one set of traces became the ground for another, the meaning of marks was partially effaced by each fresh deposit of material, and by sections accidentally rubbing off or being deliberately erased. Rather than being fixed and framed, the artefact of the drawing process was subject to a history of re-drawing (see Figure 18.4).

I also scanned drawings in order to re-work them. I will go on to describe the mechanical, optical and digital procedures that this entails, later in the chapter. For now, I will summarise this move by saying that the *configuration* of marks constituted by the drawing process was digitally reproduced by means of scanning. This enabled me to recombine groups of figures spatially and sequentially,

Figure 18.2   Left-handed drawing

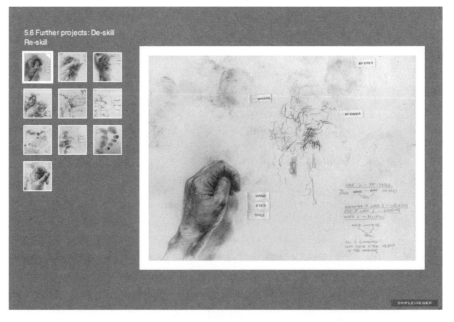

Figure 18.3   Screenshot of a page constructed using the SimpleViewer web gallery software. The drawings are outcomes of the author's *De-skill Re-skill* residency at Drawing Spaces, Lisbon, in 2008

Figure 18.4　The re-working of drawings such that one drawing becomes the ground for another

layering, blending and morphing from one to another. I produced moving image sequences that function for me as re-animations.

Part II of my thesis is a digital archive of around 250 drawings and animations that constitute a large part of the research process I have just outlined (not all the drawings I made are included but this is a representative selection). They are cross-referenced numerically to a written narrative of the research process, in Part I. The decision to use freely available web gallery software[6] to display these rather than designing my own web pages was partly governed by time constraints. A format based on HTML was chosen rather than PDF because it provided better support for interactivity and the embedding of video. Given the large amount of data, downloading this body of work as a single PDF would have been extremely slow. The page design I have used is based on the notion of an interactive portfolio rather than on the model of a printable document (see Figure 18.3). The quantity of drawings, displayed in this way, makes clear that the drawings I have reproduced are the substance of the research, not merely the illustration of a theoretical study.

As I developed an understanding of drawing as being more than simply a space for reflection, and considered its figurative processes as constituting knowledge, it became increasingly imperative to question the paradigm of artistic discourses that had shaped my own practice. I found a paradoxical aspect to my practice; at times, as I started to draw I seemed to constitute myself as an observer with some sense of detachment, whereas at other times I found myself drawn towards, and lost in, the complexity or affectivity of the subject matter. I noted oscillations between different modes of looking.

The third part of my thesis responds to the contradictions of my practice. I considered histories and discourses of drawing in relation to discussions of knowledge in order to examine critically how these histories inhabit my own practice and have shaped its figurative outcomes. Critiques of Cartesian dualism, particularly by feminist writers, are of particular importance to this. For this part of the thesis, I viewed 'drawing' as a constellation of diverse practices, intersecting with both art and science.

I was particularly concerned with the values accorded to the hand and the eye, as parts of the body considered instrumental in drawing and celebrated in its rhetoric, finding an important intersection in the significance accorded to manual and visual operations in discussions of both drawing and knowledge. In English, to 'grasp' and to 'see' are both used synonymously with the verb to understand. In humanist discourse the hand and the eye are tropes for capability and knowledge; manual dexterity and visual acuity are presented as defining traits, indicative of uniquely human ingenuity and insight. In the academic theorisation of observational drawing during the Renaissance, the trained hand and the judging eye appear as instruments of the knowing mind. Drawing is considered productive of knowledge but only within this triangulation, the rest of the body being omitted from the description. I found that so long as I was holding the drawing tool in the usual way and focussing my eyes in such a way as to flatten and fix the objects of perception, I was to some extent continuing a tradition.

Influenced by Foucault, Barad uses the term 'apparatus' to include not only the equipment and devices employed in knowledge projects but also the set of discourses, material arrangements, institutions and subjectivities that contribute to their production and use (2007: 63 and 199–201). Considered in this way, the apparatus of drawing is a dynamic process, a coming together of material configurations, discursive practices, bodies and tools. If the body of the practitioner is considered as a unitary entity, then manual and visual practices are integral to the whole mode of being of the embodied subject. However, if this body is operating as part of a wider apparatus of drawing, the hand and eyes take on additional values as the nexus of a pre-established mode of doing. In the first case, they are integral parts of the body's sensory, motor and cognitive systems; in the second case, they are also the instruments of a habitual grip and focus that are tied to the history of artistic and academic systems of practice.

My research process could be described as a type of excavation. Having dug into my own practice and found the paradoxes, contradictions and tensions outlined above, I considered these as traces of a history beyond my own. I began a writing process informed by the practice of drawing diagrams and connecting texts in the three-dimensional space of a room. The texts that emerged from this process contained overlap and cross-references to each other. Some were ambiguous and apparently contradictory in their arguments. Some were later abandoned. In many respects, this process was analogous to drawing, in that the cross-references between and within texts were as important as the linear development of their arguments. Overall, this historical investigation could be described as a process of knotting together, rather than unravelling.

Part III of the thesis, *Hand Eye Practice* is the digital outcome of this writing process. It consists of twelve texts as HTML pages. Cross-references are made using hyperlinks so that texts and some drawings are brought together in one inter-connected structure. A simple diagram on the opening page is the index to the inter-textual body or drawing behind it (Figure 18.5).

The structure is not closed; there are links to external websites, even though these may not remain live. Not restricted to paper, or even the bounded space of a room, this divergent structure is fully activated in the expansive context of the Internet.

Not every aspect of my drawing processes and products were reproduced in the digital submission that I made. To evaluate the extent to which drawings, (particularly drawings made on paper using conventional materials) can be understood using digital technologies, it is worth considering three aspects of drawing: its process, the artefact that is produced by the process and the arrangement of marks or figure that is constituted.

Figure 18.5 The opening page of *Hand Eye Practice*, Part III of the thesis. The titles link to 12 texts that are connected to each other by hyperlinks

DRAWING AS PROCESS

Serra famously commented in 1977: 'Anything you can project as expressive in terms of drawing – ideas, metaphors, emotions, language structures – results from the act of doing' (1994: 53). Others have noted the graphic fusion of spatial and temporal experience as the line is drawn. 'Drawing is an inscription of space, and the line, through all its passage, is the animation of this spatiality. The line is, par excellence, the spatial image of all process' (Bailey, 1982: 261).

In the submission of my thesis, I relied on scans of drawings as the primary record of figurative process, each drawing containing the traces of many actions and tacit decisions. Written commentary provided another means to share my findings about processes. However, anyone seeking to research the dynamic event of the line becoming visible might argue that the drawn artefact is no more than a fossil record of this, in which case it is necessary to witness, or failing that to record, the event itself.

Film and video have been an important means of documenting art practice for many years (Jackson Pollock's action paintings of the 1950s are one example). Researchers investigating the performative, kinesthetic, transitive, iterative or other durational aspects of drawing are likely to choose video for its documentation. The moving image produced on screen is clearly not the same as the event witnessed by the artist or audience, if this was ever in fact, a unified experience. The viewer of the screen image sees *something* from a distance, but this may yet be recognisable and usable for research purposes. Likewise, researchers may chose to record the making of drawings stage by stage using time-lapse techniques. Digital formats that readily support the moving image would be required for any of these approaches.

DRAWING AS ARTEFACT

Benjamin's re-examination of art discourse in the context of new modes of reproduction questions the values attributed to the unique presence of the artwork, which he calls the 'aura' (1999: 215). Implicit in the value system he critiques are notions of originality and authorship. The artwork is considered a new configuration of materials, relations of forms, colours, textures, marks, that have not been made before. This material configuration must then persist over time, substantially unchanged apart from a few allowable additions (dust, grime) and subtractions (worn edges, faded pigment) to retain the status of being the *original* object, connected to its author by an unbroken historical connection. Driven by concerns about the commodification of the art object, a century of artists have critiqued values of originality and authorship by means of many appropriations. However, within a research context these values retain an important status. The knowledge produced in the thesis must be new knowledge; it must be primarily the researcher's own work, and traceable as such. For the purposes of examining a thesis or dissertation, the assessment of authenticity is centred on the individual researcher as the origin of the work produced.

However, this is not the only reason that the physical artefact of drawing may be necessary in the examination or sharing of research. In my own *viva*, I decided not to present sketch books, files and stacks of drawings, feeling that the figurative output of my drawing processes would be sufficiently manifested in the digital archive I had created, as I will go on to explain in the next section. However, this absence of the drawn objects themselves was commented on by the examiners, and I take their concerns seriously. If I scan one of my drawings and upload the resulting image to a webpage, the thing you see on screen is not the *same* as the drawing I made. That is not to say that it is less real, or that it belongs to an immaterial realm of cyberspace. On the contrary, difference lies in the specifics of material constitution. The statement that they are not the same may seem self-evident – if my research was located in large painted canvases it would hardly be worth making, but a small monochromatic drawing might seem completely transferable. To demonstrate the difference, I will describe some of the characteristics that may be occluded, for research purposes, when the event of copying takes place.

Take, for example, a drawing made using conventional media of pencil and paper: in many places, deposits of graphite dust are caught up or ground into the tooth of the paper; other particles have a more tenuous hold, lightly resting on the surface and are subject to displacement if touched. The tactile qualities of a drawing and its instabilities are apparent when it is closely inspected (assuming that it is not behind glass). Graphite has a smoothness and a reflective sheen in its densest areas that becomes apparent if the drawing is encountered from an oblique angle. By contrast, charcoal has a warm, powdery depth of black. Ink drawings are characterised by the way in which the fluid has run across and settled in pools on the surface, or, in a less resistant paper, seeped and bled into it. Many of my drawings were made using a ballpoint pen. They include lines that are heavily laid into the paper, leaving a groove and others that are so light and fine they barely rest on the surface.

The paper, sometimes described as the 'support' for the drawing, is actually fully part of it, and not detachable. The thinness of the paper constitutes the drawing's overlooked, third dimension, and determines how much it can be flexed and warped in various ways. Handling it in such a fashion opens the possibility of folding, scrunching, tearing, cutting, burning or shredding. As interactive objects, paper drawings are vulnerable.

Any of these properties of the artefact might be the subject of research, from an aesthetic, phenomenological or forensic point of view. The drawing presents a history of the bodily actions that produced it, and examiners or other researchers may wish to inspect or touch this material record, in order to understand the scale, texture or weight of a drawing, to read its minute details or to see the faintest records of erasure. Although it is possible that in the future a combination of haptic technologies and three-dimensional imaging at high resolution, might generate a useable copy that not only presents these qualities before the viewer, but also visualises details, properties and data that are currently unseen, it is currently necessary to be in close proximity to see and feel these things.

As I have discussed in relation to my own research, the drawn artefact is not an entirely novel object, but rather the product of many histories of practice and technologies of making. Multiple contexts inform both its production and reception such that no two people will have the same experience of it. However, it constitutes a material record of its production and will therefore continue to be valued for many aspects of research.

DRAWING AS CONFIGURATION

When Merleau-Ponty embarks on his account of the perceptual process he uses a very simple example: 'a white patch on a homogeneous background' (1962: 3). He goes on to explain how the patch is perceived as a shape rather than a collection of white points. Areas of white near the edges of the patch are perceived as belonging to it even though they border on the background. 'Each part arouses the expectation of more than it contains, and this elementary perception is therefore already charged with a *meaning*' (1962: 4).

Here he is making use of Gestalt theory, which describes perception as operating according to a figure-ground structure. Gestalt psychologists made studies of child development and conjectured the very earliest perceptual experiences of the infant:

> ... we ought not to say that the child sees a luminous point; but rather that the child sees a *luminous point upon a relatively indifferent background;* or, in the case of touch, that pressure is felt upon the hand, which before had been lacking in phenomenal distinction. Generally stated, *from an unlimited and ill-defined background there has arisen a limited and somewhat definite phenomenon, a quality.* (Koffka, 1928: 145)

There are two aspects of this theory, particularly as it is developed by Merleau-Ponty, that are relevant to the consideration of perception, drawing and also to the mechanical or digital reproduction of drawings. One aspect is the theory's emphasis on the context of sensations rather than sensations in isolation. As Merleau-Ponty puts it, 'an isolated, objective line and the same line taken in a figure, cease to be, for perception, "the same"' (1962: 11). The other is that the figure-ground structure constitutes a differentiation. Merleau-Ponty, elsewhere, describes the line as 'a certain disequilibrium kept up within the indifference of the white paper' (1974: 305). At its simplest level, drawing makes a distinction. Even a single point on an otherwise uniform surface creates some kind of differential. A line intensifies this imbalance and opens into other possibilities: enclosing areas, connecting points, crossing and transgressing boundaries, following trajectories.

Merleau-Ponty employs Gestalt theory as a starting point, but goes far beyond it in his challenge to scientific positions that would posit the world as an objective reality independent of the observer, and would reduce perception to a matter of data-processing. Instead, he argues that the world is already meaningful for the embodied being enmeshed in it, and it has a physiognomic character. Perception is therefore charged with bodily intentionality; it is an active process of seeking out meaningful configurations.

Hass argues that the figure-ground structuring of perception, as Merleau-Ponty describes it, becomes more of 'a meaning-laden complex' (1999: 94). There is a sense of the visible extending beyond the areas that I can see at this moment – behind the objects I can already determine, beyond the periphery of my immediate field of vision. In a two-dimensional example, the background seems to continue behind the figure, as though the difference between them constitutes a gap.

In my own research, I was concerned to work with aspects of figuration. I tested figure ground distinctions by working back over previous drawings (see Figure 18.4), in order to understand more about drawing as a meaning-making or knowledge-making process. Merleau-Ponty also puts a stress on ambiguity: 'We must recognize the indeterminate as a positive phenomenon. It is in this atmosphere that quality arises. Its meaning is an equivocal meaning; we are concerned with an expressive value rather than with logical signification' (1962: 6). My drawings show not only distinctions and relationships but also the grey areas in between. Reproductions in print or on screen are never an exact replica of the drawing, but a sufficient resemblance to the *figure* can be generated by photographic or electronic means as I shall go on to explain.

THE ANALOGOUS PROCESS OF SCANNING

As Hayles noted in 1999, 'a defining characteristic of the present cultural moment is the belief that information can circulate unchanged among different material substrates' (1999: 1). Like Hayles, I would dispute this commonly held view and rather than describe information as *something* that 'circulates' at all, I would prefer to say that sets of *relationships* reappear in the configuration of different materials. These copies result from chains of events. The contiguity of materials in the making of a copy is important. Each reproduction is materially and contextually different to any other, but each retains a reference, by analogy or by resemblance, to the thing it touched.

To demonstrate this I will describe one part of the process of reproduction. When I place one of my drawings face down on the glass of my ordinary desktop scanner and issue an instruction from the computer to start scanning, a combination of mechanical, optical and electronic events is set in motion. The following is my understanding of the process (Matteson, 1995; Gann, 1999).

A thin strip of light illuminates one narrow section of the drawing. Light bounces off the paper, the darkest portions of the drawing reflecting least and a lens then directs the light onto a line of sensors, known as a charge-coupled device (CCD). Each minute sensing element produces a photoelectrical charge relative to the intensity of the light it receives. These charge packets are then passed down the line by means of a shift register. A few electrons may be lost at each shift, in which case those charge packets with the greatest distance to travel are subject to the greatest degradation. This succession of charges is then converted to an output voltage.

The process just described is completed in milliseconds, after which the scanner carriage moves mechanically a tiny distance along the bed, where it pauses and captures another slice of the exposed drawing. The process is repeated, the carriage moving incrementally each time, until the entire two-dimensional surface of the drawing has been scanned – or rather *sampled*. Matteson points out that 'The x-direction scan is therefore done electronically, while the y-direction scan is done mechanically' (1995: 32).

The output of this sampling process is a linear sequence of voltages. The order in which the voltages are received corresponds to the spatial co-ordinates of the drawing. Differentials of tone or colour are recorded as differences in the strength of the voltage. Thus, *spatial* relationships have been reproduced *serially*, and relationships of light or dark have been reproduced as relative amplitudes in an electrical signal.

The output signal is then passed through an analogue-to-digital converter. This electronic device operates a second sampling process, such that differentials of amplitude are reproduced as electronic on/off patterns, readable using micro-processors as sequences of numerical values – in other words, binary data.

In the context of communication systems, an analogue signal is a continuous one, such as might be constituted as a waveform, a pulse or perhaps as hand-writing. By contrast, a digital signal is made up of discrete units of information. The word *digit* can be applied to separate figures, such as 1 2 3 4 5, or to the fingers of a hand, understood as five individual parts (rather than as the cognitive extremities of a whole body), that constitute an elementary counting system. In binary systems, the digits are represented simply as zeros or ones. In the process of analogue-to-digital sampling, no matter how frequently a sample is taken, certain values in between are missed.

It should be stressed at this point, that once the digital signal is created and sent to the computer's memory, it does not become immaterial. The configuration of digits exists in physical locations and is even given an address. Whether it is maintained as on/off charges in the semiconducting substances of minutely printed circuits, or stored as directions of attraction on the surface of magnetic film, it has a place in the physical world. But like the 'points' that make up Merleau-Ponty's patch of white (1962: 3), these charges and magnetisms have meaning only given their position in relation those around them.

There are various additions and subtractions in this copying process; not only are nuances missed in sampling, and electrons lost in the shift register, but even the reflection of light is not completely clean and tidy. As Barad points out, descriptions of optics that treat light as a simple ray reflecting off a surface in predictable, geometric fashion, are useful as an 'approximation tool' but leave out the complexity of wave and particle behaviours that lead to multiple diffractions around the edges (2007: 84–85). Further down the line, software algorithms are applied to the digital information in order to compress the quantity of data. The JPEG compression standard for images (developed by the Joint Photographic Experts Group) works by predicting the value of a pixel based on neighbouring pixels. High compression rates, described as 'lossy', leave their own marks and traces within the image, called 'artefacts', as details around edges are subject to the distortions of this process of levelling.

In summary, the chain of events described above produces a pattern of digits, and this pattern refers to the configuration of marks in my drawing. The pattern, or set of relations, can be reconstituted as differentials of coloured pixels on a screen or monitor, the serial information having been re-aligned to a matrix of spatial co-ordinates. Copies can be made to appear on desks, on knees or in hands as part of the material constitution of various devices of display. However, given that they are constituted by the scanning apparatus itself, and the collision of physical processes that goes on in it, the pattern is not simply a human-made thing, it is in part the product of optical, mechanical and electronic operations and circumstances. Each time a group of screen pixels changes colour somewhere in the world, and the configuration of a drawing coalesces into view, it does so as a unique physical event, and with the added signature of the device that renders it.

Before its current usage in the context of communication systems, the word *analogue* had a different sense. In 1989, *The Oxford English Dictionary* defined it as a noun: 'An analogous word or thing; a representative in different circumstances or situations; something performing a corresponding part'. This relates closely to the meaning of *analogy* as 'Equivalency or likeness of relations' (OED, 1989). The procedures described above enact a number of analogies, from light reflected to electrical current relayed, from spatial to temporal position, from relations of amplitude to those of discrete numerical value. These all operate on the principle of sampling differentials and producing a rough resemblance of relations.

But the other sense of analogue is also useful in thinking through the scanning process because it stresses continuity. In each part of the process a direct reference is made: the light touches the paper and then hits the sensors, which sets in motion a series of electrical and electronic movements and conversions. The contiguity of elements in the process means that a continuous line of reference is maintained back to the object I placed on the scanner.

'How can resemblance result from this rarely described series of exotic and miniscule transformations obsessively nested into one another so as to keep something constant?' (Latour, 1999: 61). Latour's words are quoted by Kirby as part of her critique of the perceived dichotomy between nature and culture. For Kirby, Latour's emphasis on the 'bridges of translation' enacted as forms of knowledge are transformed and circulated, does not go far enough in explaining the linkages between technologies, languages, bodies and the coded interchanges that go on between them (2008: 227). She describes organic processes as themselves articulate and differentiating, 'the meat of the body *is* thinking material' (2008: 221). According to this line of reasoning, any reproductive strategies – organic, mechanical or digital – could be interpreted as the 'figuring out' processes of living matter. In her 1997 publication *Telling Flesh: The Substance of the Corporeal*, Kirby argues that bodily matter is graphically and meaningfully productive. 'Our attempt to rethink corporeality in a way that wrests it from the role of dumb and passive container will need to grant that the body is already a field of information, a tissue of scriptural and representational complexity' (1997: 148).

Rawson writes of the 'analogising faculty' at work in drawing (1969: 26). When things drawn refer to things seen, viewing a drawing becomes a matter of recognising similarities, imputing oblique references and recalling prior experiences and the feelings associated with them. Writing more recently, Newman turns drawing towards something less centred on the human. He suggests that drawing could aspire to a similar status as photography, as 'a resemblance produced by contact' (2003: 105). It could be argued that this phrase aptly describes not only the singular artefact of drawing, but also its singular reproductions.

CURRENCY VERSUS LONGEVITY

In 2004, I published an article in the online journal *TRACEY*, called *Out of Hand* (MacDonald, 2004), which made use of Adobe's Flash® software to integrate text and drawings with interactivity and animation. At the time I assumed that this would become the norm for submissions to the journal, that Flash® would become easier to use and more ubiquitous, and that the final submission for my thesis would be similarly integrated. All these assumptions turned out to be wrong. To author websites with interactivity using Flash now requires programming or at least scripting knowledge, and disputes between Adobe Systems Inc. and its competitor Apple Inc. have meant that some platforms do not currently support the Flash® plug-in. In the final submission of my thesis, Part II is mainly drawings and Part III is mainly text[7].

A concern, when considering the integration of text, image and moving image, is accessibility. In the drive for a fully semantic web it is preferable to keep text and image separate rather than having words bound up in the pixellations of image content. Supplying appropriate metadata for images is a challenge in itself, without also having to extract alternative versions of text from embedded formats. Although as the software for reading text and image gets smarter this too may change.

The continued difficulty of authoring complex websites from scratch is a limiting factor when considering the production of an online thesis, unless web design is the topic of research. Added to this, is the awareness that software becomes obsolete, which has implications for the longevity of the thesis.

Perhaps the digital thesis, and particularly the online thesis, represents a shift in expectations. Traditionally, theses have been protected by hard binding and stored within the walls of the library. Not many copies have been produced, and the loan of these has been carefully controlled. The emphasis has been on preservation, that future generations of researchers should be able to access this knowledge object has been a paramount concern.

By contrast, the digitisation of the thesis facilitates the lateral spread of research knowledge, at high speed. In this open access context, longevity can be sacrificed for currency, and the possibility of widespread reproduction. By this reckoning, a thesis may still achieve long-term impact if it is extensively copied and becomes a point of intersection for multiple chains of reference.

NOTES

1. I treat the term 'observational drawing' with some reservation in the thesis and note that it carries connotations of a detached stance in relation to the objects of vision.

2. Although Parts II and III were submitted for examination on disc, it is my hope that they will be hosted online as part of the institutional repository at Leeds Metropolitan University.

3. For example, in the UK, Loughborough University hosted the *Drawing Across Boundaries* Conference in 1998, and *Drawing – The Process* followed at Kingston University in 2003.

4. In addition to those listed in my introduction, there are now many other theses that develop the notion of thinking through drawing (Riley, 2001; Wilson, 2005; Stackhouse, 2005; Cain, 2008).

5. Portable Document Format (PDF), developed by Adobe Systems Incorporated was initially designed to support the production of printed material and the dissemination of printable documents. Although the PDF format now supports the inclusion of video and audio, some PDF viewing software will not play this. The production of standard PDFs from printed originals can presumably be automated by the British Library, whereas the copying and insertion of digital video would be more time-consuming and expensive. It would also create a problem of large file sizes and consequently slow downloads.

6. The software is called SimpleViewer and can be downloaded from www.simpleviewer.net/products/

7. The examiners commented that I should have included more cross-referencing between the three parts of the thesis.

REFERENCES

Bailey, G. H. (1982). Drawing and the drawing activity: A phenomenological investigation. PhD thesis, University of London.

Barad, K. (2007). *Meeting the Universe Halfway: Quantum Physics and the Entanglement of Matter and Meaning.* Durham: Duke University Press.

Beittel, K. R. (1972). *Mind and Context in the Art of Drawing: An Empirical and Speculative Account of the Drawing Process and the Drawing Series and of the Contexts in Which They Occur.* New York: Holt, Rinehart and Winston.

Benjamin, W. (1999). The work of art in the age of mechanical reproduction. In: *Illuminations* (edited and with an Introduction by H. Arendt; translated by H. Zorn) (pp. 211–244). London: Pimlico.

Cain, P. (2008). Drawing as coming to know: How is it that I know I make sense of what I do? PhD thesis, The Glasgow School of Art, University of Glasgow.

Cain, P. (2010). *Drawing: The Enactive Evolution of the Practitioner.* Bristol: Intellect.

Craig-Martin, M. (1995). *Drawing the Line: Reappraising Drawing Past and Present.* London: The South Bank Centre.

de Zegher, C. & Newman, A. (Eds.). (2003). *The Stage of Drawing: Gesture and Act. Selected from the Tate Collection.* London: Tate Publishing.

Dexter, E. (2005). *Vitamin D: New Perspectives in Drawing.* London: Phaidon.

Drawing Research Network [http://www.drawing-research-network.org.uk]

Drawing Spaces [http://drawingspacesen.weebly.com]

Duff, L. & Sawdon, P. (eds) (2008). *Drawing – The Purpose.* Bristol: Intellect.

Gann, R. G. (1999). *Desktop Scanners: Image Quality Evaluation.* Upper Saddle River, NJ: Prentice Hall.

Hass, L. (1999). Sense and Alterity: Rereading Merleau-Ponty's Reversibility Thesis. In D. Olkowski & J. Morley (Eds.), *Merleau-Ponty, Interiority and Exteriority, Psychic Life and The World* (pp. 91–105). Albany, NY: State University of New York Press.

Hayles, N. K. (1999). *How we Became Posthuman: Virtual Bodies in Cybernetics, Literature, and Informatics.* Chicago, IL: The University of Chicago Press.

Hill, E. (1966). *The Language of Drawing.* Upper Saddle River, NJ: Prentice Hall.

Jerwood Visual Arts [http://www.jerwoodvisualarts.org/page/3158/Jerwood+Drawing+Prize]

Kirby, V. (1997). *Telling Flesh: The Substance of the Corporeal.* New York: Routledge.

Kirby, V. (2008). Natural Convers(at)ions: or, what if culture was really nature all along? In S. Alaimo & S. Hekman (Eds.), *Material Feminisms* (pp. 214–236). Bloomington, IN: Indiana University Press.

Koffka, K. (1928). *The Growth of the Mind: An Introduction to Child-Psychology* (translated from the German by R. M. Ogden), 2nd edn. London: Kegan Paul (1st edn, 1924).

Latour, B. (1999). *Pandora's Hope: Essays on the Reality of Science Studies.* Cambridge, MA: Harvard University Press.

Leake, I. (1993). Apprehending movement of the human figure through the medium of drawing, with comments on its possible relationship to computer mediated interaction. PhD thesis, University of Brighton.

MacDonald, J. (2004). Out of hand. *TRACEY online journal of Contemporary Drawing Research.* http://www.lboro.ac.uk/departments/sota/tracey/journal/narr/index.html

MacDonald, J. (2010). Drawing around the body: The manual and visual practice of drawing and the embodiment of knowledge. PhD thesis, Leeds Metropolitan University.

Manifest [http://www.manifestgallery.org/nda/index.html]

Matteson, R. G. (1995). *Introduction to Document Image Processing Techniques.* Boston, MA: Artech House.

Merleau-Ponty, M. (1962). *Phenomenology of Perception* (translated from the French by C. Smith). London: Routledge.

Merleau-Ponty, M. (1974). Eye and mind (translated from the French by C. Dallery). In J. O'Neill (Ed.), *Phenomenology, Language and Sociology: Selected Essays of Maurice Merleau-Ponty* (pp. 280–311). London: Heinemann Educational Books.

Newman, M. (2003). The marks, traces, and gestures of drawing. In de Zegher, C. & Newman, A. (Eds.), *The Stage of Drawing: Gesture and Act. Selected from the Tate Collection* (pp. 93–108). London: Tate Publishing.

Petherbridge, D. (1991). *The Primacy of Drawing: An Artists View: A National Touring Exhibition From the South Bank Centre.* London: South Bank Centre.

Pigrum, D. (2001). Transitional drawing as a tool for generating, developing and modifying ideas: Towards a programme for education. PhD thesis, University of Bath.

Rawson, P. (1969). *Drawing.* London: Oxford University Press.

Riley, H. (2001). The intelligence of seeing. An inquiry into the relationships between perception theory, communication theory, and the practice and teaching of drawing. PhD thesis, Swansea University.

Rose, B. (1976). *Drawing Now.* New York: Museum of Modern Art.

Rose, B. (1992). *Allegories of Modernism: Contemporary Drawing.* New York: Museum of Modern Art.

Saorsa, J. (2004). Drawing as a method of exploring and interpreting ordinary verbal interaction: An investigation through contemporary practice. PhD thesis, Loughborough University.

Schneckloth, S. (2008). Marking Time, figuring space: Gesture and the embodied moment. *Journal of Visual Culture*, *7*(3), 277–292.

Schneckloth, S. (2010). http://www.saraschneckloth.com/sara_schneckloth/h_o_m_e.html

Serra, R. (1994). *Writings, Interviews*. Chicago, IL: University of Chicago Press.

Stackhouse, A. M. (2005). Trahere: The sense of unease in making a mark; the practice of drawing and the practice of thinking. PhD thesis, Duncan of Jordanstone College of Art and Design, University of Dundee.

Talbot, R. (2010). http://www.richardtalbot.org

The Oxford English Dictionary (1989). Vol. I, 2nd edn. Oxford: Clarendon Press.

TRACEY online journal of Contemporary Drawing Research. [http://www.lboro.ac.uk/departments/ac/tracey/index.html]

Wallis, K. (2003). Painting and drawing the nude: A search for a realism for the body through phenomenology and fine art practice. PhD thesis, Faculty of Art, Media and Design, University of the West of England.

Wilson, K. (2005). Mimesis and the somatic of drawing – in the context of 20th century Western fine art practice. PhD thesis, Loughborough University.

Archiving, Storage and Accessibility in the Digital Age

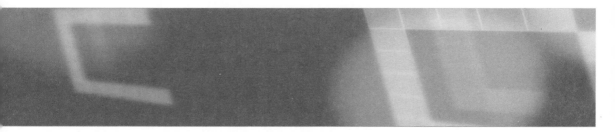

In this section, we turn to archiving and preservation of digital and multimodal dissertations and theses. Here, technological advances open up access to content, encourage peer review and facilitate user involvement in ways that could not have been envisaged ten years ago. Michael Schwab argues that artistic research and its understanding of the impact of presentation has much to offer contemporary research in all disciplines. He notes that while a practice component is clearly essential within artistic research projects, the required written component may be the only archived, and remembered, part, depending on the ability of institutions to store material, visual or acoustic content. Schwab describes the development of The Research Catalogue (RC), software specifically designed for the publication and preservation of artistic research. The aim of RC is to extend the options researchers have when preparing material for publication, combining four applications: academic repositories, museum catalogues, on-line publishing and e-research; placing 'format' at the centre of the production process and, facilitating further critical analysis of the data.

Joanna Newman points to the growth of the virtual networked library, and discusses research carried out by the British Library which identifies a number of challenges. First, how to ensure researchers remain aware of the wealth of non-digital resources and the context within which material was originally produced. Second, that the apparent technological ease of the generation born since 1993 disguises a significant lack of information-seeking and information literacy skills. Third, use of emergent technology is less prevalent than might be expected, with the encouragement (or not) of supervisors playing a critical role in take-up. She suggests that research libraries, librarians and information specialists have a key role to play in addressing these issues, as well as in the medium- and long-term preservation of, and access to, digital material. The chapter concludes by outlining a number of collaborative initiatives addressing the latter.

Martin Reiser's chapter describes the development, use and potential of locative media projects in literary and historical interpretation, as research tools and as a way of bringing archives alive. His work builds on the use of situated learning, which posits that learning is enhanced if it takes place within an authentic context. Reiser's examples include a research pilot which logged journeys through the fictional landscape outlined in Iain Banks' novel *The Crow Road* and explored the relationship between literature, group scholarship, located technologies and their supporting databases. Similar technology explored the relationship between writer and place further, using the landscape of D.H. Lawrence's childhood. Original texts were annotated by layered audio-visual information and analysis, and used via mobile technologies to explore the context of the work. A third project, 'Riverains', was piloted in 2010, also drawn from archival sources; this time user-generated content was added, so participants became simultaneously user and author.

Lisa Stansbie considers the digital thesis produced as a website, whereby the website is the submission itself, containing practice and context. This format allows the inter-disciplinary nature of much creative research to be an integral part of the thesis, showing process and development as well as the final 'gallery exhibition'. Stansbie draws attention, though, to the challenge that more experimental sites pose the reader, and examiner, and stresses that conventional elements such as abstract, overview and critical content, as well as clear signposts and routes to the practice, should remain. She discusses the implications for PhD submissions as to whether a website thesis is ever complete and of hyperlinks which allow the reader freedom of movement. So, while the move to e-theses opens work to a wider audience than print; the website PhD expands the readership far further and facilitates much easier access. 'Sharing the results of research to such a large audience potentially allows for peer review on an international scale ... '. Stansbie acknowledges that, while such open access might be daunting, website submissions offer great potential to reflect the multi-layered hybrid nature of creative thought in art and design.

19

The Research Catalogue: A Model for Dissertations and Theses

Michael Schwab

INTRODUCTION

Arguably, the traditional paper-based academic publication format has proved disadvantageous for practice-led fields of research and study, such as art and design. A move into digital formats promises to remedy such disadvantages, while it must remain clear that any format will at the same time enable *and* limit the preparation and publication of all academic or artistic propositions. However, it can also be argued that contemporary artists are specialised in the negotiation of formats, since a definition of modern art without consideration of notions such as 'medium' or 'technology' seems to be impossible. This line of thought provides just one reason why the voice of artists and artistic researchers matters when it comes to the definition of new formats for dissertations and theses. Even more provocatively, it is possible to argue that artistic research might offer a point of reference for any form of contemporary research, because an understanding of the impact of the presentation format not only enhances the communicative powers of a research project, but also shapes the research process and is reflected in its findings. This is not to say that art and science are identical or that something like a 'third culture' (Snow, 1998) exists; the point is rather that artistic research despite its comparatively short life and confusing definition may offer an important and potentially essential reference point when methods of research and modes of publication are being discussed.

On a more pragmatic level, even if such a radical position is not shared, artistic research remains a fact. The UK has been at the forefront of the developments in this field since the 1992 *Further and Higher Education Act* paved the way for research in art and design allowing MPhil and PhD degrees to be awarded by art schools that since have become universities[1]. Other countries and regions, such as Australia or Scandinavia, have been similarly active while often naming their degrees differently[2]. In the European context, it is specifically the 1999 *Bologna Declaration* that has given artistic research a much greater relevance in several countries, introducing the possibility for awarding doctorates in art and design, together with bachelor's and Masters degrees. It appears that our culture has accepted and is actively promoting practice-led research in art and design, which warrants the question of how artistic research compares with research in other fields, such as science or the humanities, in particular when it comes to assessment, publication, dissemination and accessibility.

At present, although a practice component is essential for the successful delivery of an artistic research project, no guidelines exist addressing how this component is to be presented in the context of a thesis[3]. The written component on the other hand, since it is formally similar to research outputs in other fields, is required to adhere to standards of academic writing, and it is this component that is archived in the libraries and accessible, for example, via the British Library's *EThOS*[4] programme. It appears that whatever is accepted as 'academic writing' and technically supported by institutions such as universities or the British Library will define how much 'practice', that is, material, visual or acoustic research will be stored and remembered, and thus allowed to impact on the future meaning of the findings. From an artistic researcher's point of view, the current situation artificially cuts through most of his or her artistic research projects, requiring an adaptation of potentially foreign formats through which results may be compromised. Assuming that reflective distance is still required, it would be much more favourable if the form of instantiation was determined by the research project itself. In the case of artistic research, the materials, methods and communicative requirements make an institutionally and technically flexible approach to the 'writing' of a thesis desirable. Moving to digital and potentially multimedial dissertation and thesis formats is thus relevant not only because it allows more media to be attached and submitted, but also because it promises a more creative and formally precise negotiation of academic, reflective and critical work. This would have the advantage of being technically compatible with traditional forms of academic writing while opening up the intellectual potential of such negotiation even to non-artistic research fields.

The development of the *Research Catalogue* (RC)[5] may be seen as a first step in this direction. The RC emerged from discussions around the *Journal for Artistic Research* (JAR)[6] at Y, the Institute for Transdisciplinarity, at the University of the Arts in Berne, Switzerland, where, together with experts from the field of conservation, forms of documentation and referencing of artistic research have been discussed. The development of the RC is funded by the Dutch government as part of the *Artistic Research Catalogue* (ARC) project, organised through the University of the Arts, The Hague, and led by Henk Borgdorff and myself. The project brings together eighteen academic and non-academic partner institutions, which contribute individual research projects that are analysed for the development of the RC, a prototypical software specifically designed for the publication of artistic research. The RC is used for JAR and can function as institutional repository as well as serve as a model for dissertations and theses in art and design in general. Both the RC and JAR illustrate current developments in the field, which hope to bring together institutional and intellectual requirements by engaging with digital publication formats. Before I go on to explain the RC in more detail and indicate its relevance for the discussion concerning digital dissertations and theses, a further explanation of artistic research is required in order to contextualise the particular challenge artistic research poses and the solution the RC offers.

WHAT IS ARTISTIC RESEARCH?

'Artistic research' is a troubled concept, but the term has gained popularity, in recent years, specifically in the context of the continental European engagement with the question of research in art and design. In the UK, notions such as 'studio-based' or 'practice-based' have been popular to describe such research activities while the Arts and Humanities Research Council (AHRC) currently prefers the term 'practice-led research'. This term, like any of the others, reflects the AHRC's position according to which it 'expect[s] … practice to be accompanied by some form of documentation of the research process, as well as some form of textual analysis or explanation to support its position and to demonstrate critical reflection,' while it states that without such support artists 'would be ineligible for funding from the Council' (AHRC, 2009: 59). With these sentences the AHRC provides a pragmatic definition for research that in an essential manner involves artistic practice. However, the definition given by the AHRC is also an elaborate construction, which while solving some problems creates others.

As far as research methodology is concerned, the most important problem created by such definitions is the lack of an identifiable site for research in the arts. In fact, it appears that the definition is set in place precisely to avoid such a site, since neither should practice on its own be seen as research nor should research be found in the written part, which is there only to 'support' and to 'demonstrate'. Research thus requires a studio-practice supplemented by writing. The site for research is as a consequence always double, with one aspect referring to the other. On the one hand, such a deferral can be perceived as a problem, because no clear instruction can be given to a researcher of how he or she is supposed to orchestrate the relationship between art practice and writing.

On the other, deferring the site for research also offers an opportunity to a researcher, who is encouraged to do valuable groundwork in order to explain a project's particular methodological position. A notion such as 'artistic research' rather than 'practice-based' or 'practice-led' research has the benefit of not making a categorical decision concerning orders within diverse methodologies of research and the origin of a particular finding. It is also of importance that the notion of 'artistic research' connects better with non-academic modes of research within the wider artistic community, indicating that a cultural agreement may be reached in relation to what generally counts as 'artistic' but less towards the more specific driving factors of research[7]. All of this happens, of course, against the backdrop of a post-deconstructive cultural climate where metaphysical notions such as 'origin' or 'presence' have virtually disappeared (cf. Derrida, 1997) and where a re-defined understanding of art promise a way forward (cf. Badiou, 2005; Rancière, 2004; Nancy, 1996).

In recent years, a shift has occurred in the discussions around artistic research, which has had the effect of emphasising the primary rather than secondary status of writing[8]. Questions such as if or how artefacts in general may embody knowledge (cf. Biggs, 2004) have become less relevant when compared with engagements with concrete research projects and, importantly, the way they (re)present themselves, that is, the different ways in which they engage with writing. In their introduction to *Thinking Through Art: Reflections on Art as Research* (2006), Katy MacLeod and Lin Holdridge reference Stephen Melville, who in his catalogue essay *Counting/As/Painting* starts with the assumption that 'theory is not something that needs to be brought to objects. It is something at work within them, a constitutive part of what or how they are' (Melville, 2001: 8). Based on such understanding he can claim that '"[t]heory" here would be less something a critic or historian brings to the work … than something to be traced in it, and writing would belong to such work as part of its unfolding, a continuation of the conditions of its appearing' (Melville, 2001: 19), which in the context of artistic research makes MacLeod and Holdridge demand that '[w]e need to bring our writing nearer to our making' (MacLeod and Holdridge, 2006:12). Notions similar to that of 'unfolding' can be found in Florian Dombois' approach via 'modes of depiction (*Darstellungsformen*)' (Dombois, 2006) in Mika Elo's discussion of Walter Benjamin's use of 'translation' (Elo, 2007), my own remarks on 'reflection' (Schwab, 2008) or 'deconstruction' (Schwab, 2009) or Jonathan Miles' work on Jacques Derrida's concept of 'invention' (Miles, 2012) which he pits against an instrumental notion of 'method'. The usefulness of the latter term in the context of artistic research is also questioned by Henk Slager (Slager, 2009).

Using these and other concepts, the discussions leading to the *Journal for Artistic Research* identified what may be called modes of writing that can be found in the *practice* of artistic research. This preliminary list is being further extended in the *Artistic Research Catalogue* (ARC) project to include notions such as:

- *Exposure.* In the RC, research aspects of works are exposed shifting an emphasis or highlighting particular aspects.

- *Staging.* In the RC, artistic work is staged as research; staging implies that the form of the work is transformed into a 'stage form' that performs its research contribution.
- *Performance.* Like 'staging', 'performance' indicates the utilisation of a register of presentation and the creation of an experience.
- *Translation.* An artwork is translated into the language of the Research Catalogue; form and elements of the work shift, whilst meaning is conveyed.
- *Reflection.* What is invested in the work is reflected upon through additional ideas and concepts potentially 'dormant' in the work that increase its relevance and/or understanding, which is reflectively transformed.
- *Unfolding.* A research aspect is unfolded as other folds are created when the work is entered into the Research Catalogue.
- *Exhibiting.* As exhibition, a Research Catalogue entry does not represent an artwork but its context dependant publication.
- *Curating.* Content is arranged in such as a way as to open up meaning between pieces of visual, acoustic or textual information.

Such exemplary descriptions of modes of artistic publication are beyond the traditional practice/theory divide. They require a re-consideration of 'academic writing' as taking place in-between not only theory and practice, but also academic and non-academic modes of working that point not to a 'definitive difference' but only to '*différance*' (Öberg, 2010: 41f).

RELATIONS TO SCIENTIFIC RESEARCH

To date, there has been no comprehensive attempt to empirically link methodological or epistemological developments within the theory or history of science to artistic research; studies such as Florian Dombois' work, for example, that links scientific with artistic modes of research remain the exception (cf. Dombois, 1998; Kunsthalle, 2010). However, in particular the work of Bruno Latour and Hans-Jörg Rheinberger lends itself to such a perspective and has started to enter the discourse. Noteworthy in this respect is the work of the artistic researcher Hannes Rickli, who worked with Rheinberger for his 2009 exhibition *Videograms* at the Helmhaus in Zürich. The exhibition is part of a long-term research project, in which Rickli collects and artistically analyses the original video documentation used for scientific experiments in order to display:

> everything that is aesthetic about the research process, and thus everything that is perceptible by the human eye and ear. The trace reveals precisely that which is obliterated as scientific activity evolves: concrete objects, spatial constructions, temporal sequences, lighting conditions, gestures, and manual actions. Precisely this twofold character of the trace, which cannot be wholly controlled by the producers, interests me as an artist. (Rickli, 2012: 108)

Here, an artistic interest meets an epistemological interest, because for Rheinberger too, what may be seen as the 'messy' practice of laboratory research (an expression that already implies aesthetics) is not sub-ideal but rather essential to the development of a field. What Rheinberger terms an 'experimental system' is a complex, ambiguous and only partially directed setup for the creation of 'epistemic things', which 'present themselves in a characteristic, irreducible vagueness. This vagueness is inevitable because, paradoxically, epistemic things embody what one does not yet know' (Rheinberger, 1997: 28). Epistemic things may be material objects, but they can also be concepts, structures or functions that play a role in knowledge generation processes. For the pragmatic reasons of mastering vagueness, the development of collaborations between scientists and artists appear productive for science, and have been funded by the Wellcome Trust, for example, as part of its *sciart* scheme (cf. Bergit and Thackara, 2003). For the present argument, however, it is not the possible instrumentalisation of art for scientific research that matters; rather, it is the proposed re-conceptualisation of science as *practice* that makes epistemic things comparable with works of art when it comes to research. Being practically defined, 'thing' or 'work' are essential parts of making processes (the making of knowledge in this case), an aspect that is important when research is described as situated (cf. Holert, 2009; Haraway, 1988) or performative (cf. Haseman, 2006; Bolt, 2008). In an attempt to describe artistic research, Henk Borgdorff suggests the notion of 'boundary work' (Borgdorff, 2010; 2012; Schwab, 2012), which he explicitly links to Rheinberger's concept of epistemic things, stressing that artistic research takes place not only on the border between art and academia but also on the border where the border between art and academia meets life (Borgdorff, 2012). It is in this sense, that Rickli's work exemplifies the capture of epistemic things while the boundaries are still fuzzy, adding to their scientific relevance a co-present artistic relevance, both of which are aspects of the 'work to be done' (Borgdorff, 2012: 120) when thinking meets life.

Epistemic things/boundary works have a public dimension. They are not 'objective' in a distanced and 'true' sense, but rather involved in the hands-on creation of objectivity, that is, the reality-in-flux of our shared understanding of the world (cf. Daston and Galison, 2007). Without such public dimension epistemic things or boundary works could not do their work, which is the reason why if one wants to know how knowledge comes into being and communicate knowledge in action, one needs to be sensitive with regard to the moment at which an external register, such as the writing of a thesis, over-determines and thus fixes identity in knowledge[9]. To be sure, such fixture is an academic achievement which I am far from dismissing; I only want to indicate that fixture requires depth for which universities also need to cater should the knowledge they produce remain culturally credible and relevant. In reference to the ideas of both Michael Gibbons and Helga Nowotny (Gibbons et al., 1994; Nowotny, Scott, & Gibbons, 2001), Borgdorff proposes to explain artistic research in relation to Mode 2 knowledge production emphasising, however, that artistic research may also be used to question the very distinction between Mode 1 and Mode 2 research (Borgdorff, 2008: 18). Nevertheless, he makes a case for much artistic research to fit the criteria for Mode 2 research (context of application, transdisciplinarity, heterogeneity and diversity, accountability and reflexivity and extended peer review) indicating that negotiations between artistic and scientific research when understood as Mode 2 knowledge production have become possible, if not timely. Discussions around the importance of practice for research or the particularities of Mode 2 knowledge production shed a light on the fact that limited and idealised registers of research and the associated constituents of knowledge are being transformed even outside the debates around artistic research, which adds to these debates an extreme reference point and a challenge.

ACADEMIC WRITING

Seen against such a backdrop, academic writing is not something one simply learns and applies; rather, it is the labour of creating and transforming epistemic things or boundary works into their public and discursive form that can be understood and evaluated by a group of appropriate peers in order to judge their relevance for research and society. The traditional model for academic writing is propositional text, while for the debates around artistic research the use of other media such as image or sound is of importance for a piece of writing. To employ multimedia in the context of academic writing is not unheard of, but it is their relationship to the text that is of concern if it is thought of as representational. If an image, for instance, appears to illustrate a text, we do have the sense that what is to be said resides in the text, while the image has a mere communicative function; conversely, if a text explains an image, we think that the image holds the meaning while the text merely elaborates on that meaning. Both cases use different voices, but it is the importance of representation (that text is represented through an image or vice versa) that makes it so difficult for artists, because contemporary art is defined aesthetically rather than representationally, at least if we are to follow Jacques Rancière's assessment of the situation, when he claims that the representational regime of the arts has been replaced by the aesthetic regime (Rancière, 2004). Even if one does not follow Rancière in calling what is occurring in contemporary art 'aesthetics', there is widespread consensus that however one may refer to the present situation, it has to be defined outside of representational registers[10]. However, if this is the case, how do we build a bridge to academic writing?

We teach academic writing to students in order to improve their use of language, with the aim of helping them to make a more precise and generally better argument. The most important features of academic writing may be identified as: complexity, formality, precision, objectivity, explicitness, accuracy, hedging and responsibility (Gillett, 2010). Admittedly, not all notions on this list lend themselves to an easy transposition into the field of artistic research, although once one operates in material, visual or acoustic cultures most of these terms will make sense outside of a limited propositional, textual use. For an artist, for example, complexity means that a work also speaks of its reflective implications and its position within a context of practice, making 'easy' solutions often impossible. Such explicitness need not, however, be literal, for a work's proposition may very often lie in what it does not explicitly say. Accuracy in the context of artistic research may refer to the use of tools, devices or materials, not, however, as a demonstration of skill, but rather as the creation of an accurate relationship between any of these elements and the work's meaning. Accuracy may be understood like a tuning or calibration process, in which a single experience is shaped from accurately interrelating diverse elements. Precision[11] may be required, because even if a work does not look precise, this very character of not-looking-precise may be a precise way of entering the material, adding, for instance, justification to a transformative appropriation (which would be a 'misquote' if it did not work). Hedging, on the other hand, is not often openly discussed in the arts, but most people are very aware of the limits that a work accepts in order to remain comprehensible, that is, art. If everything was to be mobilised in an extreme artistic effort, the work may have a claim, but this claim may be hermetically sealed off. While these features may be found in academic and non-academic contexts alike, formality, objectivity and responsibility appear to be more specific to artistic research than to art in general[12].

In respect to responsibility, a fake account of a research project, or the use of fake references within one, might be essential to an art work but counterproductive to its relevance as artistic research. This would be particularly the case if the account does not produce new understandings on the basis of such inaccurate referencing, which, however, as understanding would have to be accepted as genuine (the means are fake, but the result is not). Formality thus means that artistic research as a form different to art is accepted and embraced, including a shared concern with regard to artistic contributions to knowledge and understanding. Objectivity, however, as discussed above cannot mean the assumption of a detached world and its equally detached understanding, but is a transpersonal strife, which as artists but not as researchers we have the luxury to ignore.

The lack of objectivity, however, also means that assessments are grounded in subjective negotiations between peers also when it comes to the status of an artistic research publication as academic writing. On this side, too, the field is constantly shifting. The *Journal for Artistic Research*, for example, has discussed what rules, if any, might apply to its reviewing process and, perhaps more importantly, from what vantage point a review can speak *about* a publication. *JAR* has resolved at present to a learning-by-doing approach in an attempt to avoid simply replicating reviewing processes from different fields that might not be appropriate to artistic research. Nevertheless, the goal is an expanded notion of academic writing that includes a multiplicity of voices, diverse forms of presentation and an artistic re-negotiation of what it means to add to knowledge and understanding.

THE RESEARCH CATALOGUE

The Research Catalogue is best described by explaining its key concepts: exposition, page, aspect, tool and work. An exposition is comparable with what articles are in traditional journals. It has a title, one or more authors, an abstract, a media file that can be used to represent the exposition and a set of closed-vocabulary metadata. As the name suggests, the purpose of an exposition is to 'expose' practice as research rather than simply document or refer to it. Given that there is no ready-made template for an exposition, each exposition represents a choice as to how a material is exposed within the constraints of the RC. To mention two extremes, the RC supports traditional text-based propositional formats, while it also supports a collage of sound, image or video files that might not be textually linked or commented upon. The choice as to how an exposition is constructed adds to its meaning and plays an important role during the reviewing process.

An exposition consists of one or more pages, where a pages is the two-dimensional surface on which content is organised. A page is a fabric made up from different elements brought together at particular positions so as to facilitate a constellation that results in a meaningful exposition. Other than a computer screen, a page is not limited to a pre-determined size. Rather, a user of the RC will see at any given time only a particular aspect of the page, that is, he or she will see only a limited part of a page through a window or frame. The user can scroll horizontally or vertically to move around the page or can use hyperlinks to reposition the aspect on a page or to navigate to an aspect on a different page. Additional navigational tools attached to the frame offer navigation from page to page, that is, from the default aspect of one page to the default aspect of another page. The ordering of the pages in relation to each other forms an important part of the way in which an exposition may be unfolded through user interaction. (Pages may be compared with rooms in an exhibition: we move from one room to the next, but also have choices how we move. Using hyperlinks, we can tele-transport to exact locations in a room, but also to a page-cum-archive or a page-cum-studio in order to drill down into particular details.)

All the content on a page is displayed through rectangular tools. Tools are specific and can be configured by the author(s). For example, the text tool might be used to display a block of text, while it can also be edited to allow emphasising words or captions, etc.; the image tool displays an image, while the amount of metadata that is displayed can be chosen in the settings; the slide show tool displays a sequence of images and so on. The RC has started with a limited set of tools, and we expect the toolbox to grow in time as researchers from diverse fields may require particular visualisation or sonification tools[13]. Tools offer structured ways in which to display information on a page the same information displayed through different tools may look different. The tool position and the tool size are configured by the author(s) as part of the exposition writing process.

Some but not all content may be grouped together in works. A work is an identifiable entity with title, author(s), description, metadata, etc. that brings together one or more files that form a presentation of the work. For example, a painting may be depicted in its entirety, but additional photographs of details may be important. Sketches may also belong to a work and so will photographs or recordings of the work in different contexts or during different performances. Textual elements concerning how the work has been made or how it may be read may equally belong to a work on the RC. Semantic tags will eventually allow the navigation of a work through its supporting media files. Works or, in fact, any piece of content are displayed via tools at particular positions on the pages of an exposition.

Files that do not belong to a work must be part of an exposition[14]. Such files are most often text elements that explain relationships between works or introduce critical discourse that is of relevance for the exposition. It is, however, also possible that an exposition does not utilise the work structure at all even for content that might otherwise be considered a work. The reason for this is that a 'work' is not a neutral entity as it delimits and objectifies what might require a less determined place in the overall architecture of an exposition. Despite this, it is important that the RC supports what may be considered traditional modes of art writing, artistic research publications and museum-type repository structures, because the RC is not intended to replace any of these, but rather to extend the options a researcher has when preparing his or her material for publication. This is to say that the form an exposition adopts and the way its material is structured become, in fact, part of its content. On a technical level, this means that all design choices by the author(s) are actually part of the content of an exposition (and have to be stored appropriately in the database). Depending on the context in which the RC is used (as part of *JAR*, as an institutional repository, etc.), a consistent default style has to be agreed upon and stored with an author's material so that they can edit this to sustainably reflect expositional choices. It also means that the RC cannot be too experimental, because it will have to reproduce exactly what was submitted and agreed upon on publication.

TECHNICAL CONTEXT AND BACKGROUND[15]

The Research Catalogue may be novel, but it is nevertheless part of a more fundamental transformation of the use of information technology in art and design. The RC combines four usually separate fields of applications: academic repositories, museum catalogues, online publishing and e-research. In theory at least, in the field of art and design, digital dissertations and theses will require an engagement with all four areas in order to reap the potential benefits from advanced uses of information technology.

Academic repositories usually hold institutional research output, if not in downloadable form as reference or as a link to the publisher's website. Given that artistic research extends the format research output can take, academic repositories need to adapt. *Kultur*[16], for example, is a JISC-funded project with the purpose to enhance the existing *EPrints* institutional repository software for the use in art and design. As part of the project, the *EPrints* metadata schema was extended when the original generic term 'artefact' was developed into 'art/design item' to support categories such as 'Animation', 'Architecture', 'Audio Work', etc. a number of which can apply to a single work (Sheppard, 2009). Additional uploads of media files serve to illustrate the item, without, however, being embedded in a structured model of their interrelationships and their different roles in representing the research output. Nevertheless, *EPrints* is a good example for the extension of an academic repository into areas usually covered by museum catalogue software. At the same time, such an extension adds an additional overhead to deposit processes. As far as digital dissertations and theses in art and design are concerned, such enhanced institutional repositories already allow for digital versions of traditional, paper-based texts that can also be supported by online multi-media content, while the dissertation or thesis itself will not be prepared online. Repositories spring into action after the fact.

Online publishing software is usually independent from repository software. Items from a repository may be used for the preparation of a publication, but they are normally used as a reference, a copy or they may sometimes be embedded. However, in these cases the publication does not integrate with the repository and making copies is often preferred over making links. Copies can be controlled while links might break or linked content might change making publication platforms that use such features questionable, in particular when it comes to dissertations and theses, but also in the case of peer-reviewed articles where what is reviewed has to stay the same and has to function as reference even in the future. Artistic research, for which design and modes of presentation are essential, adds an even greater difficulty to this, because not only has the content of a contribution to remain identical, but also the way it appears on screen. This poses an enormous challenge, because changes in technology, such as new browser generations or server software updates, impact on the way in which a publication appears on screen. Despite such difficulties, the arrangement of content and the overall design of an online, institutionally supported publication has become important in e-portfolio applications such as *Mahara*[17]. *Mahara* allows users to drag-and-drop content from their *Mahara* file repository onto a single portfolio page, which can even be submitted for marking to a tutor. As mentioned, it can be difficult to be certain which elements on a portfolio page are fixed when this page is submitted, because RSS feeds, blogs or embedded media cannot be locked. Equally, changes to the uploaded files on repository level are reflected in the submission, as well as site-wide style changes, which can alter the design substantially. If content could be locked, html use limited and the page style made independent of the site style, *Mahara* e-portfolios could (almost) be useable as dissertation platform in art and design.

A combination of repository and online publication software, as proposed for enhanced publications, could go a step further. An enhanced publication is, for example in the context of the EU funded *DRIVER II*[18] project, defined as 'enhanced with research data, extra materials, post publication data, database records ... and that has an object-based structure with explicit links between the objects' (Woutersen-Windhouwer et al., 2009: 31). Enhanced publications in the field of art and design are rare if not non-existent, while they have become essential tools in other areas. Henry Rzepa, Professor of Computational Chemistry at Imperial College London, for example, states that 'to truly understand a chemical phenomenon, you benefit from having the data that constitutes the model being presented' (Rzepa, 2009). The claim to be made for art and design and artistic research in particular would be of a similar nature: an artistic phenomenon will be better understood if the model of thinking that is proposed for its comprehension and communication can enable an active engagement with the material assembled during the research process, keeping in mind that any representation of artistic material in a repository or a publication will have transformed this material from a reality into an intellectual model.

TRANSDISCIPLINARITY

The RC may not so much offer a new format for dissertations, theses and artistic research publications in general than a meta-format or a framework that allows format choices to be made, represented and evaluated. Like any (academic) publication format, the RC is limited to what can be done and sustained technically, but it need not prescribe how a particular argument is presented or a case is made. As much as one may focus on the technical development of the RC, it is not so much the variety of required and supported media formats, for example, that give the RC and with it artistic research a particular position in the field; rather, it is the acceptance of the format as content-relevant and thus necessarily internal to the unfolding of a research project that makes the RC unique and may indicate artistic requirements when new digital formats for dissertations and theses are discussed.

If digital technologies enhance what may have been limited format choices in the past, one has to admit that thinking about formats puts into disposition their historical, institutional, ideological and disciplinary role as regulators for academic research and study. Art's role in this context is more fundamental than the question whether an artwork may or may not contribute to the development of knowledge and understanding; the moment the question of form is touched upon and considered relevant, we are on artistic territory. This does not mean that the form is dependent on the content, which it truthfully reveals in a modernist kind of way, but rather that its transformational interdependence with truth throws up new types of questions that disallow, at least when it comes to research, the separation of art as 'assertion of form' from philosophy (or science) as 'assertion of truth' (cf. Steinweg, 2004; 2009). Transdisciplinarity may be defined as a confusion of form and truth processes, which is beneficial for the understanding of a phenomenon and the creation of epistemic things or works of art. Seen from a transdisciplinary point of view, as Latour suggests, reality stops being different for scientific or artistic researchers, since artists now 'can work on the same realities as scientists' (Latour, 2009). To this, one should, however, also add the reverse: that what counts as reality to an artist must also be accepted as part of scientific reality. Accepting each other's reality does not mean that art and science are identical. Esa Kirkkopelto is right to point out that other than with approaches external to art, 'artistic research does not question the existence of art or an artistic experience, but takes it as a given fact' (Kirkkopelto, 2008). It is this particular perspective that allows artistic research to add a wealth of new methods and approaches to the canon of research for which an intimate understanding of how art works is fundamental.

Returning to the question of digital dissertations and theses, with the RC a transdisciplinary definition for a research publication is attempted that accepts all formats, artistic or scientific, by making the format choice part of the writing process. The writing process is a data preparation process, which adds the creation of new data and new data relations to the engagement with existing data. The reader can, in a potentially self-directed fashion, enter into and even enhance the data or use the data actively, that is, not just as reference, in a different context. Needless to say that, for more than purely technological reasons, both *JAR* and the RC have to be an experiment and a research project in their own right, since although both can project what many voices in the field of artistic research require, making it work remains a tremendous challenge.

NOTES

1. Due to their special status, a limited number of art schools in the UK could award practice-based research degrees before that date (cf. Mottram, 2009).

2. In many countries, a Doctor of Arts (DA) rather than a Doctor of Philosophy (PhD) is awarded. The former appears to emphasise the specifically artistic element while the latter seems to place emphasis on the comparability of the research to other fields and methodological approaches all of which converge in this unifying 'research doctorate'.

3. I am focusing on the MPhil/PhD thesis, because for MA dissertations the question of practice is less of a problem. In effect, an MA dissertation has the luxury of not relating in any direct manner to a student's practice, while for a practice-based PhD thesis its relationship to practice is essential making the thesis a more radical case in point.

4. http://ethos.bl.uk

5. http://www.researchcatalogue.net

6. Both the RC and JAR are initiatives of the Society for Artistic Research (SAR). For more information and a list of the, at present, thirty-eight international supporting institutions see: http://www.jar-online.net

7. According to Stephen A.R. Scrivener, historically the art world has failed to develop a 'professional research class' if compared with other fields of research (Scrivener, 2006). A strictly intra-academic discussion of artistic research might, thus, miss out on essential aspects of artistic research, which the academy has not represented or, indeed, cannot represent.

8. This is true even outside the question of research, as the popularity of artists' writing and publication projects and the number of new writing degrees at art and design schools in the UK indicate.

9. Bruno Latour's notion of 'circulating reference' is also relevant in this context. Reversible 'chains of transformation' maintain reference while reducing and amplifying phenomena as they are turned into compatible, standardised text that can enter circulation due to its relative universality (Latour, 1999: 69 ff.). The 'gap' between world and language is not radical but rather gradual creating space not for a single leap of understanding, but for multiple, transformative processes towards 'objectivity'.

10. Rancière is aware of the problems associated with the notion of 'aesthetics', but chooses to maintain that word (Rancière, 2009). Alain Badiou, for example, dismisses representation and also aesthetics both of which are regulatory principles outside of which art operates (Badiou, 2005).

11. Notions such as 'simplicity' or 'consistency' may be added to 'precision' in order to describe the characteristics of research. A series of symposia (2005–2007) at Y, Institute for Transdisciplinary, University of the Arts, Berne, discussed these notions in the context of artistic research (Dombois, Yeboaa, & Schmidt, 2009).

12. I am aware that this distinction is difficult to maintain. Voices such as Dieter Lesage's, for example, conflate art and artistic research (cf. Lesage, 2009), while I insist that such a position predetermines what art can be (art need not care about knowledge) rightly adding to the fear that artistic research, in particular on an institutional level, might actually be part of an attempt to control art (cf. Sheikh, 2006).

13. The development of new tools may be an important part of a research project and budgeted for in a funding application. The development of new tools allows responding to the particular needs of specialised research communities.

14 The museum, theatre, music hall or gallery context offers little if no registers for art outside the notion of the work. That the RC offers such a place may be significant, in particular when positions such as Michel Foucault's link the questioning of the notion of 'work' to the practice of writing (Foucault, 1984). Concerning authorship, the RC is less radical, although seen in totality, the interlinkage through tagging and search algorithm as well as the re-usability of material dissolves authorship to some degree.

15. A word to my personal background, which will explain the choices of examples in this section: outside of my role as ARC project leader, I work at the Royal College of Art in London as tutor in Critical and Historical Studies and have been employed as e-learning coordinator for a number of years. The RCA uses *Mahara* for its e-portfolios and is currently introducing *Kultur* as its repository software; I am sure that different examples from other institutions can be found to illustrate the point I make.

16. http://kultur.eprints.org/
17. http://mahara.org/
18. http://www.driver-community.eu/

REFERENCES

AHRC. (2009). Research Funding Guide. http://www.ahrc.ac.uk/FundingOpportunities/Documents/Research%20Funding%20Guide.pdf

Badiou, A. (2005). *Handbook of Inaesthetics.* Stanford, CA: Stanford University Press.

Bergit, A. & Thackara, D. (Eds.). (2003). *Experiment: Conversations in Science and Art.* London: Wellcome Trust.

Biggs, M. A. R. (2004). Introduction: The role of the artefact in art and design research. http://www.herts.ac.uk/artdes1/research/papers/wpades/vol3/mbintro.html.

Bolt, B. (2008). A performative paradigm for the creative arts? *Working Papers in Art & Design* 5. http://sitem.herts.ac.uk/artdes_research/papers/wpades/vol5/bbfull.html.

Borgdorff, H. (2008). Artistic Research within the Fields of Science. http://www.ahk.nl/ahk/lectoraten/theorie/download/artistic-research-within-the-fields-of-science.pdf.

Borgdorff, H. (2010). Artistic research as boundary work. In C. Caduff, F. Siegenthaler, & T. Wälchli (Eds.), *Art and Artistic Research: Music, Visual Art, Design, Literature, Dance*, Zurich Yearbook of the Arts, Vol. 6 (pp. 72–79). Zürich: Zürcher Hochschule der Künste/Scheidegger & Spiess.

Borgdorff, H. (2012). Boundary work: Henk Borgdorff interviewed by Michael Schwab. In F. Dombois, U. M. Bauer, & M. Schwab (Eds.), *Intellectual Birdhouse: Artistic Practice as Research.* London: Koenig Books: Rodopi, 117–123.

Daston, L. & Galison, P. (2007). *Objectivity.* New York: Zone Books.

Derrida, J. (1997). *Of Grammatology.* Baltimore, MD: The John Hopkins University Press.

Dombois, F. (1998). Über Erdbeben. Ein Versuch zur Erweiterung seismologischer Darstellungsweisen. Text. PhD Thesis. Berlin: Humboldt-Universität zu Berlin. http://deposit.ddb.de/cgi-bin/dokserv?idn=957588704.

Dombois, F. (2006). Reflektierte Phantasie. Vom Erfinden und Erkennen, insbesondere in der Seismologie. *Paragrana Beiheft, 2,* 101–111.

Dombois, F., Yeboaa, O., & Schmidt, S. (Eds.). (2009). G*enau – leicht – konsequent.* Basel: Schwabe.

Elo, M. (Ed.). (2007). *Here Then: The Photograph as Work of Art and as Research*. Helsinki: Finnish Academy of Arts.

Foucault, M. (1984). What is an Author? In P. Rabinow (Ed.), *The Foucault Reader* (pp. 10–120). New York: Pantheon Books.

Gibbons, M., Limoges, C., Nowotny, H., Schwartzman, S., Scott, P., & Trow, M. (1994). *The New Production of Knowledge: The Dynamics of Science and Research in Contemporary Societies*. London: Sage.

Gillett, A. (2010). *Features of Academic Writing*. http://www.uefap.com/writing/feature/featfram.htm.

Haraway, D. (1988). Situated knowledges: The science question in feminism and the privilege of partial perspective. *Feminist Studies, 14*(3), 575–599.

Haseman, B. C. (2006). *A Manifesto for Performative Research*. http://eprints.qut.edu.au/3999/

Holert, T. (2009). Art in the knowledge-based Polis. *e-flux journal*, no. 3 (February). http://www.e-flux.com/journal/view/40.

Kirkkopelto, E. (2008). New start: Artistic research at the Finnish Theatre Academy. *Nordic Theatre Studies, 20*, 17–27.

Kunsthalle, B. (Ed.). (2010). *Florian Dombois. What Are the Places of Danger. Works 1999–2009*. Berlin: Argobooks.

Latour, B. (1999). *Pandora's Hope: An Essay on the Reality of Science Studies*. Cambridge, MA: Harvard University Press.

Latour, B. (2009). The theatre of proof: A series of demonstrations. In H. U. Obrist & O. Eliasson (Eds.), *Experiment Marathon* (194–199). Reykjavik: Reykjavik Art Museum.

Lesage, D. (2009). The academy is back: On education, the Bologna process, and the doctorate in the arts. *e-flux journal*, no. 4(3). http://www.e-flux.com/journal/view/45.

MacLeod, K. & Holdridge, L. (Eds.). (2006). *Thinking Through Art: Reflections on Art as Research*. London: Routledge.

Melville, S. (2001). Counting/as/painting. In P. Armstrong, L. Lisbon, & S. Melville (Eds.), *As Painting: Division and Displacement* (pp. 1–26). Columbus: Wexner Center for the Arts, The MIT Press.

Miles, J. (2012). Fine art and research. In F. Dombois, U.M. Bauer, C. Mareis, & M. Schwab (Eds.), *Intellectual Birdhouse: Artistic Practice as Research*. London: Koenig Books, 217–227.

Mottram, J. (2009). Researching research in art and design. In J. Elkins (Ed.), *Artists with PhD: On the New Doctoral Degree in Studio Art* (pp. 3–30). Washington, DC: New Academia Publishing.

Nancy, J.-L. (1996). *The Muses*. Stanford, CA: Stanford University Press.

Nowotny, H., Scott, P. & Gibbons, M. (2001). *Rethinking Science: Knowledge and the Public*. Cambridge: Polity Press.

Öberg, J. (2010). Difference or différance? In C. Caduff, F. Siegenthaler, & Wälchli, T. (Eds.), *Art and Artistic Research: Music, Visual Art, Design, Literature, Dance*, Zurich Yearbook of the Arts, Vol. 6 (pp. 40–45). Zürich: Zürcher Hochschule der Künste/Scheidegger & Spiess.

Rancière, J. (2004a). *The Politics of Aesthetics*. London: Continuum.

Rancière, J. (2009). *Aesthetics and Its Discontents*. Cambridge: Polity Press.

Rheinberger, H.-J. (1997). *Toward a History of Epistemic Things: Synthesizing Proteins in the Test Tube*. Standford, CA: Stanford University Press.

Rickli, H. (2012). Precarious evidence: Notes on art and biology in the age of digital experimentation. In F. Dombois, U.M. Bauer, C. Mareis & M. Schwab (Eds.), *Intellectual Birdhouse: Artistic Practice as Research*. London: Koenig Books, 101–115.

Rzepa, H. (2009). Interview: Making logical connections. *Highlights in Chemical Science*. http://www.rsc.org/Publishing/ChemScience/Volume/2009/05/Henry_Rzepa_interview.asp.

Schwab, M. (2008). First, the second: Walter Benjamin's theory of reflection and the question of artistic research. *Journal of Visual Art Practice, 7*(3), 213–223.

Schwab, M. (2009). The power of deconstruction in artistic research. *Working Papers in Art & Design, 5*.

Schwab M. (2012). Between a rock and a hard place. In: F. Dombois, U.M. Bauer, C. Mareis and M. Schwab (eds) *Intellectual Birdhouse: Artistic Practice as Research*. London: Koenig Books, 229–247.

Scrivener, S. A. R. (2006). Visual art practice reconsidered: Transformational practice and the academy. In M. Mäkelä & S. Sara Routarinne (Eds.), *The Art of Research: Research Practices in Art and Design* (pp. 156–179). Helsinki: University of Art and Design Helsinki.

Sheikh, S. (2006). Spaces for thinking: Perspectives on the art academy. In *Artistic Research*. http://www.textezurkunst.de/62/spaces-for-thinking/

Sheppard, V. (2009). *Kultur. Metadata Report Final.* Southampton: University of Southampton. http://kultur.eprints.org/Metadata%20report%20Final.pdf.

Slager, H. (2009). Art and method. In J. Elkins (Ed.), *Artists with PhD: On the new Doctoral Degree in Studio Art* (pp. 49–56). Washington, DC: New Academia Publishing.

Snow, C. P. (1998), *The Two Cultures.* Cambridge: Cambridge University Press.

Steinweg, M. (2004). *Kunst, Philosophie und Politik.* http://artnews.org/texts.php?g_a=index&g_i=4099.

Steinweg, M. (2009). Nine theses on art. *Art & Research, 3*(1, October). http://www.artandresearch.org.uk/v3n1/steinweg.html.

Woutersen-Windhouwer, S., Brandsma, R., Hogenaar, A., Hoogerwerf, M., Doorenbosch, P., Dürr, E., Ludwig, J., Schmidt, B., & Sierman, B. (2009), *Enhanced Publications: Linking Publications and Research Data in Digital Repositories.* Amsterdam: Amsterdam University Press. http://dare.uva.nl/document/150723

20

The Changing Role of Library and Information Services

Joanna Newman

INTRODUCTION: THE LIBRARY AND INFORMATION LANDSCAPE

Research, and the library and information services support research have been transformed by information communications technology, with the pace of change accelerating rather than slowing down. At the same time there is considerable uncertainty in the wider higher education environment stimulated by financial, demographic, global and economic factors. Following the recent review of the UK higher education chaired by Lord Browne of Madingley[1], wide-ranging changes may now lead to a concentration of research funding, divergence of the sector and potential mergers. Taken together, these trends will impact to a greater or lesser extent on all library and information service provision.

The role of research library and information services within the UK higher education have been transformed over the last few years through technology and changes in the way that researchers operate in a substantially digital environment that transcends institutional and discipline boundaries. The virtual networked library is growing at the expense of the physical library where space is re-purposed for scholarly interaction, the sharing of information and research and collaborative work. In a networked world, the future lies in collaborations and partnerships – between individual higher education library and information services and between the national library and the higher education sector.

In this chapter, I look at the overall implications of these changes for research libraries in the UK and for the British Library, whose core role is to underpin research nationally and to support research internationally. While the focus is on the UK, the case studies and examples have wider applicability.

THE LIBRARY AND INFORMATION LANDSCAPE OF THE FUTURE

In response to the fast pace of external change in its operating environment, the British Library has undertaken wide-ranging research and consultation to develop a picture of its likely operating environment in 2020. This has helped define a long-term vision statement and a roadmap for the next phase of organisational transformation (British Library, 2010a). As part of the project, the Library sought contributions from leading thinkers in universities, the research councils, research funding bodies and university libraries, and in the other UK national libraries. This consultation sought to address questions such as: What do changing technological and user expectations mean for the research library? What will it look like in ten years' time? Will it exist in its current physical form? What role will library and information professionals play in supporting learning and research in the digital age? What will be the impact of repositories and open access on the delivery of library resources; of the need to digitise and make more widely accessible key scholarly resources and of the calls for libraries to play a central role in the promotion of 'information literacy'?

Predicting the future has always been a notoriously difficult science and whatever we forecast for 2020, the reality will almost certainly be very different. We could not have predicted the technological changes that have taken place since 1999; in a period of increasing technological change the future is even less certain, while the current economic downturn and consequent insecurity has made trend-gazing across the higher education landscape more difficult. Nevertheless, most people consulted in the higher education sector thought the current climate offered opportunities as well as challenges. Those opportunities include prospects for the higher education sector to form new collaborations and partnerships with other UK and overseas institutions. Many people also identified the potential for harnessing digital technology to provide economies of scale and enhance communication and resource sharing across the sector. There will be an increased emphasis on collaborations helped by a technological infrastructure that enables shared resource discovery, library management systems and virtual research environments linking researchers by projects not institutions. Despite increasing reliance on virtual provision, physical space will continue to matter in enhancing collaborations and understanding, and new buildings or re-purposing space will continue to play an important role in enhancing research. This is evidenced by a number of inspirational new learning spaces that have been built in the UK over the last few years, for example, Glasgow Caledonian's Saltire Centre, Sheffield Universities' the Information Commons and the new University Library at Leicester (British Library, 2010b).

HOW LIBRARIES ARE USED BY RESEARCHERS

Advances in technology have transformed the research experience and user expectations. Users expect to search for and access content and information instantly and however, wherever, and whenever they need it.

In some scientific disciplines, digital resources have already entirely replaced the need to consult physical library holdings. Instead, researchers rely on the laboratory and use of e-resources, often working in a virtual research environment, shifting between physical locations in offices, libraries, laboratories, coffee bars and homes. These research environments include the increasing use of resources kept in their own institutional repositories. By comparison, although some new subjects and research areas are beginning to emerge in the humanities, not all humanities researchers may yet be making full use of digital material and technology – while social science researchers fall somewhere in between.

There are however dangers and pitfalls in relying solely on digital resources. The process of historical discovery, for example, is compressed and simplified if sources are accessed only through the digital copy and can skew results because researchers can easily forget the context in which material was originally produced. Digital resources also give an illusion of completeness and accuracy although choices are made about what and how much to digitise and copyright also has an influence here. However soundly based on evidence and market testing, these choices can lead to false assumptions in research. What if students assume the digitised content is all there is? How do we ensure an awareness that not everything is available digitally and how do we help build the skills needed to make the most of the born-digital?

The Google Generation

It has been clear for some time that new generations of researchers have very different expectations from those who grew up before Google. The 'Google Generation' study (CIBER, 2008) focused on young people born after 1993. Its aim was to determine how this generation is likely to use digital resources in five to ten years' time and the implications for library and information services. The study, commissioned jointly by the British Library and JISC in 2007 and undertaken by the CIBER research team at University College London, overturned the common assumption that the Google Generation are actually the most web-literate. Their apparent ease with technology belies a significant lack of information-seeking and information literacy skills. While they are naturally at ease and familiar with computers, they rely heavily on search engines. They 'view' rather than 'read'. They are 'promiscuous' in their information seeking, and do not possess the critical skills to assess the information they find on the web.

The study also revealed that behaviour traits that are common in this age group – impatience in search and navigation, and zero tolerance for any delay in satisfying their information needs – are now becoming the norm for all age-groups, from younger pupils and undergraduates through to professors. The report concludes by calling for libraries to respond urgently to the changing needs of researchers and other users. It points out that going virtual is critical and learning what researchers want and need is crucial if libraries are not to become obsolete. Libraries need to keep up with the demands of students and researchers for services that are integrated and consistent with their wider internet experience. The report also highlights the need for educational research into the information behaviour of young people and training programmes on information literacy skills in schools to ensure that the UK remains as a leading knowledge economy with a strongly skilled next generation of researchers.

Researchers of Tomorrow

The Library and JISC are currently building on the Google Generation research with another major three-year study focusing on 'Generation Y', that is those born between 1982 and 1994. The crucial difference from the Google Generation, still in school, is that these students are not 'digital natives'. It is therefore assumed that they will at least have acquired information-seeking and enquiry skills before Google was available. The 'Researchers of Tomorrow' study (British Library, 2009b, 2010c; http://explorationforchange.net/index.php/rot-home.html) is tracking the research behaviour of seventy Generation Y doctoral students, analysing their activity and habits in online and physical research environments and assessing their usage of library and information resources, both on and offline. Again the results are counter-intuitive and interim findings show, surprisingly, that they are failing to make any greater use of emergent technology such as Web 2.0 tools to support their research. Only a small proportion of students are using these tools, although they generally find them valuable. Researchers with supervisors without Web 2.0 skills, in particular, were unlikely to use these tools in their research. Their main sources are Google and Google Scholar. They are no more likely than other age groups to use technology such as virtual research environments, social bookmarking, data and text mining, wikis, blogs and RSS-feed alerts.

An emerging theme from the study is the importance of the supervisor's role in encouraging the use of Web 2.0 research tools. The study has found that if supervisors are not using technology, their students are also likely not to. The study is also evidencing a reluctance to share data with other researchers during doctoral study. Despite supporting, and in many cases being funded on the condition that the resulting research is made available, students perceive the traditional doctorate as an impediment to sharing data before it is produced for the Viva, as the doctorate is judged and awarded in many cases for the originality of the data and research produced. Students in interviews expressed reluctance to share material which they would be judged on.

There is also substantial overlap between information-seeking habits of Generation Y and older students – challenging initial assumptions that they are more digitally dependent, technology savvy and willing to share their research. Like students of other ages, Generation Y researchers express a desire for an all-embracing, seamless and accessible research information network in which restrictions to access do not restrain them. However, most do not have a clear understanding of what open access means and this negatively impacts their use of open access resources.

Both Generation Y and older students express exasperation about restricted access to research resources due to the limitations of institutional licenses. This is born from a sophisticated knowledge of the networked information environment. Students regularly speak favourably about sector-wide shared services and resource sharing though they are reluctant to share the results of their own research until it has been published.

There are some interesting and important divergences between Generation Y and older doctoral students. Generation Y scholars are more likely to turn to their supervisors for research resource recommendations than older doctoral students. Also, 33 per cent of Generation Y students say they have never used library staff for their support in finding difficult to source material. Only 11 per cent of Generation Y, compared with an average of 17 per cent for other age groups, regularly use library staff support to find research resources and only 4 per cent, compared with 9 per cent average, take advice from subject specialist librarians.

More Generation Y respondents (46 per cent) than any other age group turn to their fellow students and/or supervisors for support in using emergent technologies. Around half of this group have not been trained to find journal articles and even fewer have been trained in use of e-research and other advanced tools. Library collections are used heavily by students in their own institutions, but only 36 per cent of Generation Y students have used inter-library loan services compared with 25 per cent of older students, with 42 per cent of arts and humanities students using these services regularly compared with 13 per cent among science students. This highlights the fact that library and information services need to raise awareness of ways in which libraries are able to support researchers and, in particular, the ways in which library and information professionals can help improve and develop information seeking and enquiry skills.

There is already a huge amount of detailed information from this large group of doctoral students as well as over 10,000 responses from more than seventy higher education institutions taking part in an annual quantitative survey – the largest survey of its kind in Europe. The aim is to feed information back to libraries, so they can adapt what they are doing in support of researchers. The study will provide a benchmark for assessing the needs of coming generations. It will provide crucial guidance to the community of library and information specialists.

Clearly one of the priorities must be to adapt the way that libraries present information to make it far more accessible to people who are used to a Google interface. It is vital to focus on the end user to ensure that resources provided by all research libraries remain both relevant and used. In a fast-changing environment, the research library world needs to continue to investigate the impact of technology on learning and research behaviours to inform the development of relevant new products and services.

THE CHANGING NATURE OF RESEARCH

Developments in technology are transforming the nature of research, facilitating work across discipline and geographical boundaries and across different data sources thus enabling both virtual and actual collaboration. This move to collaborative research – between departments in the same institution, between institutions nationally and internationally – will continue, despite some apparent reluctance to work collaboratively both across and within disciplines because of the difficulty researchers have in understanding briefs outside their own areas of expertise. Collaboration will be driven both by technology and by the growing complexity of the research environment and interconnectivity of research issues. It will also be influenced by directive research programmes, such as those from the European Union and the UK Research Councils, on major issues such as climate change, spread of infectious diseases, global security, etc. which require a cross-disciplinary approach (British Library, 2010b).

Internal research carried out for the British Library in 2009 (British Library, 2009a) demonstrates an increase in the numbers of collaborative research papers between 1992 and 2007 in a sample of eight UK universities and across all disciplines:

- In the arts and humanities multi-authorship increased at a faster rate than the overall publication rate of research papers (26 per cent), from 16 per cent to 21 per cent, an increase of 31 per cent.
- In the social sciences the total number of papers published annually increased by 209 per cent, while the overall incidence of multi-authorship increased from 50 per cent to 81 per cent, a growth of 62 per cent.
- In Science, Technology, Engineering and Mathematics (STEM), the total number of papers published annually increased by 88 per cent, while the overall incidence of multi-authorship increased from 88 per cent to 96 per cent, a growth of 9 per cent.
- Bringing all three disciplines together, there was a steady increase in the proportion of papers with multiple authors, from 82 per cent in 1992 to 92 per cent in 2007.

The research also examined the websites of nineteen higher education institutions for information about collaborative and multi-disciplinary projects. As might be expected the numbers were greatest in STEM and lowest in arts and humanities disciplines:

- 14 per cent of projects were found in arts and humanities, 37 per cent in social science and 49 per cent in STEM disciplines.
- 76, 35 and 11 multi-disciplinary projects were listed for STEM, social science and arts and humanities, respectively, and 224, 137 and 62 collaborative projects for STEM, social science and arts and humanities, respectively.

- Considering the *proportion* of projects in each discipline that were either multi-disciplinary or collaborative, far more projects were found to be collaborative rather than multi-disciplinary, with between 38 per cent and 48 per cent of projects in all three disciplines being collaborative. Collaborating with experts based at other academic or non-academic institutions in your own field appears to be par for the course, especially in STEM research areas.
- Working *across* the disciplines is much more unusual, with just 13 per cent of projects being multi-disciplinary.

To be most effective, collaborative research needs to be underpinned by a joined-up library and information service infrastructure and support within and across disciplines, institutions and countries. The ability to search for and access research material easily across the entire library and information network will be critical, together with the provision of virtual and real research environments that facilitate collaborative working.

Research in environments other than higher education is also expected to increase over the next few years and new research players could emerge in the UK, such as from the voluntary sector; for example, the National Trust, and other bodies concerned with conservation of the environment like the Natural History Museum which already employs over 300 research scientists. In addition, more individual research may take place in other contexts such as national libraries, archives, museums and galleries as well as in commercial research consultancies. In the global digital landscape researchers will expect content from all libraries, museums, archives to be seamlessly accessible to all and the national Resource Discovery Taskforce (http://rdtf.jiscinvolve.org/wp/scope-and-terms-of-reference/) is focusing on requirements for a shared UK infrastructure to address this issue. This trend will also provide an opportunity for research libraries to diversify their core audiences and meet the needs of professional and commercial research consultancies who can be encouraged to research in new and more productive ways.

Because of the current emphasis on the benefits and impact of research, it is likely that arts and humanities research funding will be dependent on applications that align themselves to global research challenges during the economic downturn[2]; while social science research is, in general, likely to remain flat as it more readily demonstrates impact; STEM research is unlikely to show much change but will continue to remain important because of its central role in global challenges and the economy. The abolition of government funding for the teaching of arts and humanities and social science subjects will also impact on the size of the future research community in these disciplines. However, the distinction between disciplines is becoming less clearly defined and teams addressing global challenges include researchers across all disciplines, with STEM researchers supported by arts and humanities and social science researchers looking at the creative and social consequences. Innovation too draws on the entirety of the research base.

Research library collections across all disciplines will therefore continue to be of key relevance to an inclusive research sector with thematic programmes.

However, if the focus of research funding shifts markedly from arts and humanities to social science and STEM disciplines, arts and humanities collections may seem to be less relevant and may therefore be at risk. For research libraries with large heritage collections another major issue is whether future generations of researchers will know their collections exist. The challenge for these libraries will be to provide remote access to their content and, given the current funding climate, working across the sector to develop a national digitisation strategy would make good sense.

DIGITAL RESOURCES

The volume of digital content and data is expanding exponentially though for the research library the future will be a hybrid model in which born-digital and digitised materials sit alongside analogue heritage collections and a dwindling, but continuing, output of print-only publications and works published in parallel print and digital versions.

More and more research outputs are published electronically either in e-books and e-journals. 'We estimate that by 2020, 75 per cent of all titles worldwide will be published in digital form only, or in both digital and print [form]' (British Library, 2010a). 'It is now estimated that 96.1 per cent of journal titles in science, technology and medicine, and 86.5 per cent of titles in the arts, humanities and social sciences are now available online' (Cox and Cox, 2008). Researchers with UK higher education affiliation have free access on site and online to a wide range of electronic books, journals and other resources via their university library through subscriptions and licensing arrangements though, in many cases, because these resources can easily be accessed outside the physical library building, researchers may not realise that the resources they are accessing are provided from their university library. In constrained financial circumstances, however, libraries may not be able to afford to maintain e-journal subscriptions at the same level. In this scenario they, and their users, are likely to put increasing pressure on the national library to fill the gap.

There is also a growing trend towards free, open-access scholarly works to enable access, remove barriers to participation and serve the public good. Support for open access publishing models is being driven by a number of institutional mandates. For example, the US National Institute of Health, which distributes US$29 billion of grants resulting in 80,000 articles annually, now insists on articles being available to all within a year of publication. A range of models including author-pays, hybrid open access (where authors pay to have their articles made freely available immediately) and time-delayed open access exist. Public and third sector funded research will drive research increasingly towards open access models.

Bi-directional forms of discussion through blogs and wikis are breaking down the role of creator, editor and peer reviewer, and leading to scientific articles released in a state of constant beta testing. Already, textbooks are being developed collaboratively: the first chapter/volume will be 'published' before others are complete; some beta versions will also make it online, and will be updated in response to feedback from students. These open models are enabled by open licensing schemes such as Creative Commons and the open source software movement. Open research and learning is also being driven by transparency and open government initiatives.

Research outputs are now likely to include databases, data sets, web sites and other forms of digital scholarship. This is due in part to the impact of user generated content, self-publishing trends as well as the significant level of replicated content and data. Increased computing power allows for the generation of significant data outputs for scientific research. Data itself will become a published commodity as demonstrated by the journal *Nature* providing access to data in parallel with print publications.

More and more print resources are being made available digitally to researchers through publicly funded or sponsored digitisation projects or commercial partnerships. Digitisation releases content and information for research across the world. Researchers no longer have to travel to access content in special libraries and repositories in other countries or in other institutions in their own country. For many researchers, the virtual library has become more important than the physical library. Digitisation has also transformed access to content, enabling researchers to search and make new connections in ways not previously possible or imaginable. The availability of digital versions of a whole corpus of work, such as the Proceedings of the Old Bailey (http://www.oldbaileyonline.org/), containing records of criminal trials held at London's central criminal court from 1674 to 1913, has enabled new forms of research such as data mining and key word searching. It has also inspired new forms of engagement with the public in the form of the award-winning *Garrow's Law*, a BBC legal drama inspired by the life of an eighteenth century barrister whose defence style fundamentally altered the nature of the English criminal trial. The programme makers relied heavily on the online archive when researching and writing the script.

JISC collections

In the UK, the JISC has been instrumental in creating resources and services for the further and higher education communities. JISC Collections (http://www.jisc-collections.ac.uk/) is a shared service established by the UK Higher and Further Education funding councils, to support the procurement of digital content for education and research in the UK. It makes available a wide range of digitised resources from research libraries and other repositories that are free to the UK further and higher education communities or for which it has negotiated a special price (http://www.jisc-collections.ac.uk/Catalogue/).

The maintenance of digitised collections once project funding has come to an end has been problematical and there is a danger that links may become dysfunctional and digital material may no longer be accessible. JISC's future strategy will therefore focus on ensuring sustainability and connectivity of resources and facilitating resource discovery.

Nineteenth century newspapers and archival sound recordings

Two examples of JISC-funded digitisation projects are the British Library's nineteenth century newspaper and archival sound recording collections (http://www.bl.uk/reshelp/findhelprestype/news/newspdigproj/database/; http://sounds.bl.uk/). The online resource of nineteenth century newspapers now contains two million pages and is available free at over 300 UK higher and further education institutions and for a subscription fee to non-affiliated researchers. The Archival Sound Recordings collection is also free to the UK higher and further education institutions and contains 45,200 selected recordings of music, spoken word and of human and natural environments. In addition, both services are freely available to researchers in the British Library's reading rooms.

Digitised resources like these have the potential to change research behaviours and lead to new subjects for study. One student in Cambridge, for example, used the digitised newspaper collection to trace the reception of Darwin's *Origin of Species* when it was published. In the past, this type of research would have involved going to see the physical newspaper collection at Colindale, and, unless a researcher was doing a PhD or a very specialised research project, it is unlikely they would have done that. So instead of just a few people making use of these resources, hundreds of thousands across the world can now potentially make use of the resource to enhance their research and/or explore new research avenues.

Researchers are also discovering how they can treat material in different ways, through text and data mining, for example. Here the sciences are leading the way but the same kinds of opportunities exist for the humanities. Newspapers in hard copy, for example, are explored in linear fashion. They are rarely indexed and are difficult to search for specific items or themes. Digitised or born-digital newspapers, however, allow the user to search for a specific item within an individual newspaper title or to search across different newspaper titles to draw together materials relating to a wide range of research topics.

Because of copyright or licensing restrictions some of the British Library's digitised collections can only be accessed in its reading rooms. The Library's aim, however, is to digitise more and more of its heritage material and make it available to researchers worldwide. Both JISC and European Union digitisation strategies encourage collaboration across Europe.

Europeana

The British Library is a partner in the Europeana initiative which (http://www.europeana.eu/portal/) offers over 14.6 million items of digitised cultural and scientific resources – images, text, sound and video – from some 1500 of Europe's archives, museums, libraries and audiovisual collections, making them available through a single portal and promoting discovery and networking opportunities in a multilingual space. As more content is added the portal will transform the way global researchers interact with Europe's rich heritage in the digital age.

The IMPACT project

Another important European initiative in which the Library is engaged is the IMPACT project ('Improving Access to Text'; http://www.impact-project.eu/) for optical character recognition. Mass digitisation across Europe is proceeding slowly. By speeding up and enhancing the quality of mass text digitisation, the technology, which is being developed collaboratively, will help build a critical mass of material and improve digital access to historical printed text.

Copyright issues

The adaptation of copyright is essential to ensure that it is no longer a barrier but appropriate for the digital age. A major UK initiative in this area is the Strategic Content Alliance (http://www.jisc.ac.uk/contentalliance), funded by JISC and involving the British Library, the BBC, the British Educational Communications and Technology Agency, the Museums, Libraries and Archives Council and the National Health Service's National Library for Health. The Alliance has two key aims. One is to ensure that copyright is fit for purpose. The other is to develop a common approach to key issues like metadata standards, web archiving, cataloguing and copyright.

The British Library has long argued for the resolution of issues on copyright and improved access to research material that is necessary to boost the knowledge economy. Current copyright legislation developed in and for the print world, hinders research in the digital age in a number of ways. Access to a considerable body of digitised material – data, text, newspapers, sound, images, film, etc. – that would be of great benefit to researchers, can only be provided onsite in library and information services and not opened up to the wider research community online because they are protected by copyright. Publicly funded or sponsored digitisation programmes are obliged to focus on older, out-of-copyright material. Orphan works, that is, works that are believed or known to be in copyright but whose copyright owner is unknown or untraceable, cannot be exploited creatively or commercially because of the uncertainty of copyright ownership. Without a solution, a large proportion of historical collections cannot be made freely available for research worldwide.

Library and information services need to be able to make 'fair dealing copies' available for research – that is, copies from in-copyright works without permission from the rights-holder for non-commercial research and private study purposes – of anything in their collections, including sound and film recordings that are not currently covered. It is also vital that libraries are able to preserve copies of material they acquire, including web harvesting, in order to maintain long-term access for research.

Resolving issues of public policy such as these while balancing the needs of publishers is perhaps as important to the future of digital information as understanding the latest technological developments and the changing behaviour of research students.

THE ROLE OF THE INFORMATION SPECIALIST

In a world where more and more material is available in digital form and much can be delivered to the user however, whenever and wherever she wants it, where users increasingly assume everything is on the web but lack search and appraisal skills, where users are not aware of the support for research that libraries and information services can provide and where collaborative research across disciplines, institutions and countries is increasing, what is the role of the information specialist?

In a student-centred world post-Browne Review, the physical university library sits at the heart of the Institution. The library and information specialist in the digital world becomes a guide to, and interpreter of, the increasing amount of information available. He understands and anticipates the needs of researchers and assists them in discovering and accessing the resources, data and statistics that will be both relevant to, and trusted by them. The role of the data manager becomes more prominent.

The library and information specialist has to become more adept at promoting the services they can offer in support of research, using the media that researchers and their supervisors use. Web 2.0 and associated social networking services, for example, offer libraries significant opportunities to engage much more easily with those who use their services, and tap into their expertise and involvement – as well as reaching out to those who otherwise might not think that the library is for them.

With fewer print resources being published and more content available online, individual libraries and information services are already re-configuring space for collaborative and interactive research and the sharing of knowledge. Examples of inspiring new learning and research spaces include Warwick University's Wolfson Research Exchange (http://www2.warwick.ac.uk/services/library/research exchange/), Glasgow Caledonian University's Saltire Centre (http://www.gcu.ac.uk/thesaltirecentre/), the University of Sheffield's Information Commons and Graduate Research Centre (http://www.sheffield.ac.uk/infocommons/index.html) and the Rolex Learning Centre at the École Polytechnique Fédérale in Lausanne, Switzerland (http://rolexlearningcenter.epfl.ch/). In the future, collaborative research space may be provided jointly by a number of library and information services and individual information specialists may work virtually or actually with research teams and content outside the library and information service. At the British Library there are a number of initiatives that are beginning to address some of these issues.

National postgraduate training days

The British Library's on site Postgraduate Research Training Days were developed to introduce new doctoral researchers to the Library's rich resources. They offer specially tailored workshops and networking opportunities, focusing on specific disciplines – currently history, modern foreign languages, English literature, social sciences, creative research and entrepreneurship. Each day includes a general introduction to the range of research materials available in the Library together with special curator sessions and workshops in a range of topics, and guidance on how to access the catalogues and carry out bibliographic research. Researchers are introduced to specialist Library curators and have the opportunity to network with postgraduate students from other universities across the UK. The Training Days contribute to national subject-specific and generic research skills training. They are however limited to those who are able to travel to the physical library in London. The next step will be to extend the reach of the Training Days with online versions and to include the STEM disciplines.

The Business and IP Centre

The Business & IP Centre at the British Library, which has been used by over 200,000 entrepreneurs and SMEs (Small and Medium Enterprises) since its launch in March 2006, is increasingly developing as a virtual space (http://www.bl.uk/bipc/index.html) as well as a physical one. Users can access free online courses on intellectual property. They can network with fellow users on the Centre's Facebook and other networking sites and view video of events on YouTube. One of the Centre's aims is to continue with development of an online portal that could extend virtual access for users everywhere.

Growing knowledge

The research environment is changing so quickly that researchers need to get to grips with the issues raised and experience the kind of technology that is being developed now.

In order to inform its long-strategy, the British Library held a major digital research exhibition, Growing Knowledge, from October 2010 to July 2011 (http://www.growingknowledge.bl.uk/Default.aspx), to give a vision of how research content might be accessed, used, manipulated and shared in the future.

The exhibition demonstrated a range of cutting-edge research tools and services and visitors could try out the latest multimedia applications and collaborative technologies designed to enhance research. Visitors to the exhibition were able to search large audio files and uncover clips that were relevant to their research, explore maps using advance geospatial technologies, manipulate content across multiple media and save work to return to later, and find out about new online resources and collections specific to their research. Many of these tools are also accessible online and the exhibition web site also included blogs written by the Growing Knowledge Researcher in Residence and the Library's lead curator. The aim was not just to showcase the latest developments but also to consult and engage with existing users and new researchers, and, crucially important, to get their feedback. All the findings will be formally evaluated and used by the Library and its partners to inform future developments.

PRESERVATION AND ACCESS

The role of the research library is not just about access to material for researchers today, it is also concerned with medium- and long-term preservation of, and access to, digital material. The diversity of digital resources and the continuing development of computer technology together present major challenges to library and information services for both long-term preservation and ongoing access to digital content. The library and information services community is addressing these challenges through various collaborative initiatives:

Digital Preservation Coalition

The Digital Preservation Coalition (http://www.dpconline.org/) was established in 2001 as a membership organisation in order to address the preservation of digital resources in the UK and to work internationally to secure the global digital memory and knowledge base. The Coalition supports its members in ensuring long-term access to and management of their digital assets and collaborates with national and international partners to take forward the digital management and preservation agenda. It also acts as a broker and an agent of knowledge transfer.

The Planets Consortium

The EU-funded Planets Consortium (Preservation and Long-term Access through NETworked Services; http://www.planets-project.eu/) brings together expertise from across Europe from national libraries and archives, leading research universities and technology companies in order to ensure long-term access to European cultural and scientific assets. Although the formal project is now completed, the practical services and tools that were developed are available on the Planets web site and the outputs are being maintained and developed by a follow-on organisation, the Open Planets Foundation, a not-for-profit company, registered in the UK (www.openplanetsfoundation.org).

There are a number of not-for-profit solutions to storage[3]. As of now national libraries do not provide this service.

The role of the national library

Collecting, preserving and making available the memory of the nation has always been a fundamental role of the British Library. The Library has the statutory function of legal deposit which, for printed books and papers, has existed in English law since 1662. That responsibility was extended to digital materials in 2003 but legislation giving the Library the right to collect online and digital material is, at the end of 2010, still not in place. Speedy enactment of the necessary legislation is critical for the support of research in the digital age.

Ensuring that current and future generations of researchers are aware of the resources held in libraries and archives presents a number of challenges. It is not enough just to get content out there: it needs to be sufficiently innovative that researchers want to use it. The Library has recently provided free access to its 14 million catalogue records, comprising a wealth of bibliographic data. This initiative exposes the vast dataset to users worldwide and allows researchers and other libraries to access and retrieve bibliographic records for publications dating back centuries in every conceivable subject area. For libraries this can reduce the effort involved in cataloguing their holdings; for the wider research community this is a valuable source of research data.

The UK Web Archive

Deciding how much digital material can be preserved is another vital issue. It is clear that one institution, no matter how big, cannot possibly collect and preserve everything. Nor could they provide access to the wealth of digital and digitised resources.

There are, for example, millions of UK websites. They are constantly changing and even disappearing. Often they contain information that is only available online. Researchers of the future need to be able to access information given at a specific moment in time for example government advice about swine flu, or sites relating to a specific event such as the London Olympics. Ensuring complete coverage of all versions of all web sites would be a huge undertaking.

New business models and partnerships are increasingly essential to preserve the nation's memory in the digital age, and avoid the danger of what's been called a 'digital black hole' in the knowledge base.

In February 2010, the British Library officially launched the UK Web Archive (http://www.webarchive.org.uk/ukwa/) in partnership with the National Library of Wales, JISC and the Wellcome Library, as well as technology partners such as IBM. The purpose of the archive is to offer generations of researchers access in perpetuity to UK websites that have research value or are representative of British social history and cultural heritage. This includes blogs, wikis, tweets, web-based community databases, Facebook groups, YouTube and micro-blogging which are arguably as much a part of the nation's memory as formal publications.

The Library is working with a number of other key UK institutions to collect these resources but is hampered by the existing legal position – permission has to be sought to harvest each web site – which will make it feasible to collect only 1 per cent of free UK websites by 2011. Finding legitimate ways of providing access to harvested social networking sites within the law is equally important.

SHARED SERVICES

Collaboration between libraries, universities, museums and other institutions is essential if they are to provide the broadest possible access to resources, including books, audio, films and other visual material – and ensure researchers have a seamless experience in accessing them.

Developments in technology enable the development of shared infrastructure and other services across library and information services in higher education. In the current economic climate, there is even more incentive to develop shared services primarily to maximise resources, manage risk and develop academic activities on a broader basis, but also to share back-office functions, improve delivery and free up resources to support research and to share skills and knowledge. The sector must become smarter at working together and creating more integrated services; services that harness the expertise of different organisations in a way that is joined up and easier for people to find and access digital content and which stimulates collaborative research.

Shared services in higher education can be delivered on various levels: within individual institutions, locally or regionally, for example, joint procurement and administration, shared repositories, shared library management systems; and nationally, for example, research infrastructure such as JISC shared services. They could also include non-higher education partners such as other national research libraries, museums or galleries. Service providers could be another higher education institution or a third party for example for procurement, help-desk services, management of primary research data or provision of large-scale computing facilities.

The British Library is involved in a number of shared and collaborative services and initiatives.

The UK Research Reserve

The UK Research Reserve (UKRR) is an example of collaborative working that is more about print than digital resources and which illustrates how shared services can make a huge difference in preserving material and making it available to researchers cost effectively (http://www.ukrr.ac.uk/). UKRR is a collaborative distributed national research collection managed by a partnership between the higher education sector and the British Library. It frees up campus space for other purposes such as collaborative learning and research space, while guaranteeing long-term preservation of the journals at the British Library and enhanced digital delivery of requested items to individual researchers. Twenty-nine universities have taken up membership, which offers higher education libraries a secure solution to storing and preserving lower-use print research journals. Funded by the UK Higher and Further Education funding councils as a national shared service, it is estimated that it will save the higher education sector £37 million over five years.

The Electronic Theses Online Service

The Electronic Theses Online Service (EThOS; http://ethos.bl.uk/Home.do) provides secure internet access for researchers to the UK higher education theses. Users benefit from quick and easy access, in one place, to a previously scattered and hard-to-access body of unique and unpublished research material, thus extending the reach of the original research, providing an overview of research in a particular field, giving new students a flavour of a finished thesis and providing a stimulus for new research. Students are also encouraged to deposit their own completed theses to extend the body of knowledge and raise the profile of their research. Library and information services benefit because the digitised theses are permanently available to students, staff time is saved in retrieving hard copy for consultation or loan and shelf space is saved. In addition, the research profile of an institution is raised.

Collaboration with participating universities has therefore created a global window to the UK research, enriching the knowledge pool for everyone. The total population of the UK theses is estimated at approximately 500,000 and the database at the British Library already offers free search access to more than 250,000 electronically stored theses. This central hub provides a single point of access, automatically harvesting electronic theses and digitising paper ones.

Other niche projects have been developed on the back of EThOS such as Digital Islam through which almost 1000 PhD theses in the field of Islamic studies have been digitised and added to the database.

UKPubMed Central

The life sciences website UKPubMed Central is a gateway for the UK's biomedical, health and social care researchers (http://www.bl.uk/reshelp/experthelp/science/ukpmc/ukpmc.html). It has made some 1.9 million full text articles and 19 million abstracts available on the web. The consortium led by the British Library includes partners from the University of Manchester and the European Bioinformatics Institute. It is supported by the principal funders of biomedical and health research in the UK – a group of government organisations and leading medical research charities including Cancer Research UK, Medical Research Council and the Wellcome Trust. Research publications arising from grants awarded by these organisations are submitted to UK PubMed Central, lending further visibility to this research and enabling others to benefit from it.

CONCLUSIONS

What can we learn from this snapshot of research library and information services? The higher education sector as a whole is currently undergoing a period of transformational change caused by uncertainties in the global financial, economic, demographic, social and technological environment. The make-up of the landscape in three, five or ten years' time remains uncertain, not least because of increasing pace of technological change.

Research library and information services are playing a strategic role at the forefront of change. They have re-shaped services to provide virtual access to networked resources and re-configured space to encourage scholarly interaction and collaborative working. There has not been scope in this chapter to consider developments in Europe and elsewhere in the world, but the issues and examples given from a UK perspective offer pointers to the way forward which have wider applicability.

The findings from the Google Generation and Researchers of the Future projects highlight the need for library and information services to respond to the changing requirements and experience of users in order to remain relevant and used. At the same time, library and information specialists need to be much more visible in the research environment, sharing their information seeking and enquiry skills and helping to make sense of the vast amount of data and information in the digital world.

The ever-growing corpus of digital resources is widening access and transforming both search and research – but how do we ensure that all relevant resources are accessible and continue to be available for research in the future? Research is becoming more collaborative driven both by technological developments and funding bodies – but, if the balance of research funding shifts away from arts and humanities disciplines, what will happen to legacy arts and humanities collections?

In this world, the need for joined-up research infrastructure and support across the sector is imperative because of the scale and financial implications of the issues involved: to safeguard the nation's heritage collections, to develop and roll-out a national digitisation strategy, to ensure the preservation of and access to digital resources in the medium and long-term futures, to enable seamless searching across global digital resources, to share skills, good practice and lessons learned. The future lies in the development of partnerships, collaborations and shared services within the higher education sector and between research libraries and national libraries.

ACKNOWLEDGEMENT

My thanks to Stephanie Kenna for her contribution to this chapter.

NOTES

1. *Securing a Sustainable Future for Higher Education: An Independent Review of Higher Education Funding & Student Finance*, 12 October 2010. Available at http://hereview.independent.gov.uk/hereview/report/

2. Full details of the allocation of the UK science and research funding for 2011/12 to 2014/15 can be found at http://tinyurl.com/2evrkjm

3. These include:
   - The US-based JSTOR (http://www.jstor.org/) which helps scholars, researchers and students discover, use and build upon a wide range of e-journal and other scholarly content in a trusted digital archive. It contains most twentieth century journal articles in arts and humanities and social science disciplines. It enables libraries to reduce storage costs and free up shelf space.
   - LOCKSS (Lots of Copies Keep Stuff Safe; http://www.lockss.org/lockss/Home), based at Stanford University Libraries, an international initiative that provides libraries with digital preservation tools and support in order to facilitate the collection and preservation of collections of authorised e-content.
   - CLOCKSS (*Controlled* LOCKSS; http://www.clockss.org/clockss/Home), a collaboration between scholarly publishers and research libraries with the aim of building a sustainable, geographically distributed dark archive in order to ensure the long-term survival of web-based scholarly publications.

REFERENCES

British Library (2009a). *Project Gateway, Market Research B: Statistics to Inform Project Gateway Planning: Research Trends*. Internal working paper.

British Library (2009b). *Mapping the Needs of a Generation*. Press Release. London: British Library. Available at http://pressandpolicy.bl.uk/Press-Releases/Mapping-the-needs-of-a-generation-2fb.aspx

British Library (2010a). *2020 Vision*. London: British Library. Available at http://www.bl.uk/aboutus/stratpolprog/2020vision/index.html

British Library (2010b). *2020 Vision Project: Trends in Universities, Research and Higher Education*. Internal discussion document. Available at http://www.bl.uk/aboutus/stratpolprog/2020vision/further%20information/index.html

British Library (2010c). *Emerging findings from 'Researchers of Tomorrow' Study*. Press Release. Available at http://pressandpolicy.bl.uk/Press-Releases/Emerging-findings-from-Researchers-of-Tomorrow-Study-294.aspx

CIBER (2008). *Information Behaviour of the Researcher of the Future*. London: UCL. Available at http://www.jisc.ac.uk/media/documents/programmes/reppres/gg_final_keynote_11012008.pdf

Cox, J. & Cox, L. (2008). *Scholarly Publishing Practice (Third Survey)*. Association of Learned and Professional Society Publishers. Quoted in Research information Network, *E-journals: their use, value and impact*, April 2009, page 14.

21

Animating the Archive

Martin Rieser

INTRODUCTION

Karlis Kalnins coined the phrase 'locative media' as the title for a workshop hosted by RIXC, an electronic art and media centre in Latvia during 2002. Whilst Locative media is closely related to *augmented reality* (reality overlaid with virtual reality) and to *pervasive computing*; locative media usually concentrates on social interaction with a *specific* place through mobile technology. Hence, many locative media projects have a background in social, critical or personal memory[1]. In this chapter, I will describe attempts to use location-specific media in literary and historical interpretation contexts, both as a researcher's tool and a way to bring archives alive, both for the focused student and the interested public.

Now that physical space can be technologically overlaid with augmented information, our modified understandings of information in the landscape are only just beginning to be documented and analysed. This new learning methodology, using Locative Media, has been identified by Nesta's FutureLab[2] as a form of *Situated Learning*[3]. FutureLab has experimented extensively with locative and situated learning, in conjunction with both Mobile Bristol (a research collaboration between Hewlett Packard and Bristol Universities), and with Nottingham University's Mixed Reality Lab. Early projects included *Savannah*, a mobile educational game, which mapped an African savannah environment over familiar open spaces in Bristol. FutureLab concluded that *Savannah* provided an interesting test-bed for exploring ideas in the three areas of: mobility, collaborative learning and games. *Savannah* highlighted the real strengths and weaknesses of games-based learning, in particular, it emphasised the real engagement and enthusiasm that children demonstrate in these environments, but also the relative limitations of rules-based worlds for teaching complex issues where children act as participants within, rather than as manipulators of the games world (i.e. where they cannot control or reflect upon the rules of the world).

Futurelab also developed *MobiMissions*[4]. The idea of the *MobiMissions* project was that the players set each other 'missions', leaving them in a particular mobile cell. Players wandering into that particular cell are able to see any missions left there and decide whether to accept them. A five-week trial was carried out with seventeen students (aged between 16 and 18) from a post-16 centre. Each student was equipped with a Nokia phone for the duration of the project. All the missions, and the responses to them, were loaded onto a central web server, where they could be viewed later. In that study, sharing the phone and its content implied a level of trust and reciprocity, strengthening social ties between co-located friends. Students found this co-located play more inspiring than playing alone, commenting: 'You get better ideas'. The group co-created meaning for their *Missions and Responses*, using each other as a source of inspiration. Although both projects took place in real-world locations, the content and location were arbitrarily related. True *situated learning* pre-supposes a cultural relation between content and location, as in the following definition (and as in my described projects):

> *Situated* – activities that promote learning within an authentic context and culture. Situated learning posits that learning can be enhanced, by ensuring that it takes place in an authentic context. Mobile devices are especially well suited to context-aware applications simply because they are available in different contexts, and so can draw on those contexts to enhance the learning activity. The museum and gallery sector has been on the forefront of context-aware mobile computing by providing additional information about exhibits and displays based on the visitor's location within them[5].

THE USE OF LOCATIVE MEDIA FOR LITERARY DECONSTRUCTION

This situated aspect of mobile learning inspired the first of my examples. In 2006, inspired by D.H. Lawrence's writings on the role of landscape in Hardy's novels in the essay *Study of Thomas Hardy*[6], it became clear to me that tracking the transformation of space via such literary imaginaries was susceptible to illustration and field analysis through these new technologies of location awareness, mobile delivery and interaction.

In July 2006, we developed a research pilot into *Locative Technology and Literary landscapes,* which involved the logging of locative journeys through a well-known fictional landscape related to the novel *The Crow Road*, written by Iain Banks in 1992. Conceived by myself and Professor Tim Middleton, the project was a participation between the Department of English at Bath Spa University and two Centres in Excellence in Teaching and Learning (CETLs): BroadcastLab and DesignLab, both part of the overarching organisation known as ArtsWork at the Artswork CETL at Bath Spa University. While the Crow Road is a district near Glasgow, it is also a Scottish euphemism for death. This was very much the subject of the novel, also made into a BBC serial in 1996. Part of the novel is set around Crinan on the West Scottish Coast in Argyllshire. Over four days in July 2006 staff and Student Fellows from the Labs photographed, filmed and inscribed the locations in this beautiful part of Scotland. *The Crow Road* was the first inter-disciplinary project to get under way in Artswork. A Blog also records that journey[7]. The production of the pilot involved programmers, designers, photographers and filmmakers working in close collaboration with literary experts. The tracing of the points where real landscapes overlap the fictional world was undertaken using GPS-enabled PDAs and mobiles and turned into a locative tour of sites mentioned or fictionalised in the book.

In March 2007, Iain Banks was in Bath for the Bath Literature Festival, to answer questions and read from his new novel *The Steep Approach to Garbadale* (published in the UK by Little and Brown in March 2007). Prior to the reading, Banks endorsed the research approach as a fruitful one and confessed that the process by which the landscape had transmuted into the final literary imaginary as being highly serendipitous. In a sense, the first case study of *The Crow Road* was a proof of concept, but much of this paper deals with new research projects predicated on that pilot (Figure 21.1).

Whilst tourist guides using GPS were no longer novel even in 2006 (Node, Stuttgart2Go, GUIDE), The Crow Road Pilot addressed a different problematic, exploring the relationship between literature, group scholarship, located technologies and their supporting databases. At the time, papers had addressed some of the issues on location (e.g. Benford, Tummala) and semantic blogging (e.g. Cayser, Potter), but not from a field-study perspective. Some examples of early Mobile systems that situated learning in authentic contexts include the Ambient Wood (Rogers et al., 2002), MOBIlearn (Lonsdale et al., 2003, 2004)[8] and the multimedia tours offered at the Tate Modern (Proctor & Burton, 2003).

FutureLab further identified the social participation aspect of situated learning as follows:

> The situated learning paradigm, as developed by Lave et al. (1991), holds that learning is not merely the acquisition of knowledge by individuals, but instead a process of social participation ... Situated learning requires knowledge to be presented in authentic contexts (settings and applications that would normally involve that knowledge) and learners to participate within a community of practice. By developing appropriate context-based teaching strategies with mobile technologies, we can fulfill both of these requirements[9].

As to the collaborative aspects of the project FutureLab adds this definition:

> *Collaborative* – activities that promote learning through social interaction.

Collaborative learning has sprung out from research on computer-supported collaborative work and learning (CSCW/L) and is based on the role of social interactions in the process of learning. Many new approaches to thinking about learning developed in the 1990s, most of which are rooted in Vygotsky's socio-cultural psychology (Vygotsky, 1978), including activity theory (Engeström, 1987).

The Crow Road by Iain Banks
Pilot Demonstrator

A GPS-based interactive tool based on the real geography which in-spired Iain Banks' novel The Crow Road. Developed by Professor Martin Rieser and Dr Tim Middleton at Bath Spa University. Programmed by Amy Bonham, using Flash Lite mobile programme complete with video, audio, text and still image related to each location mentioned in the novel and cross-referenced to the exact position of the user.

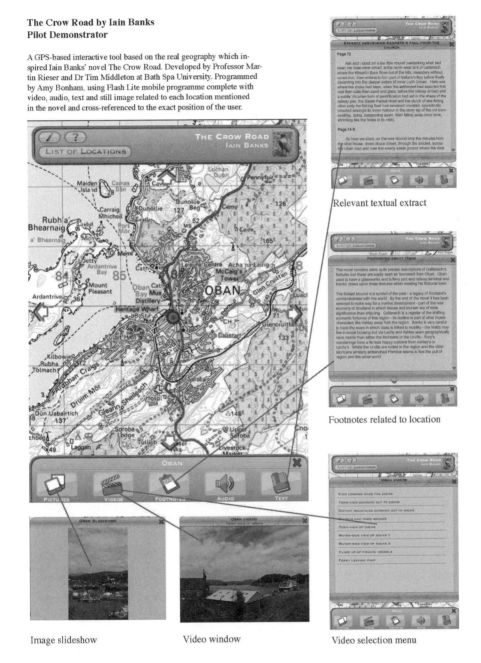

Relevant textual extract

Footnotes related to location

Image slideshow   Video window   Video selection menu

Figure 21.1   The Crow Road

Though not traditionally linked with collaborative learning, another theory that is particularly relevant to our consideration of collaboration using mobile devices is conversation theory (Pask, 1976), which describes learning in terms of conversations between different systems of knowledge. Mobile devices can support *mobile computer supported collaborative learning* (MCSCL) by providing another means of coordination without attempting to replace any human–human interactions, as compared with say, online discussion boards which substitute for face-to-face discussions (Zurita et al., 2003; Cortez et al., 2004; Zurita & Nussbaum, 2004)[10].

The learning experience in the field was in itself instructively collaborative, using two groups of students from English and Art and Design to both document the landscape and the process of documentation itself. We utilised sound recording, location logging, video and digital photography at every identified location, which matched a fictional scene in the novel. The two teams from very different cultures worked very well together in both complementary tasks and in sharing the filming and editing each evening. Assembly of the pilot involved a team of multimedia design students, although the final realisation was by Amy Bonham, an MA student in Multimedia. The accidents of engagement included the acquisition of a local professional Scottish storyteller who agreed to contribute all of the readings. Even with limited field testing, it soon became clear to us that any successful future use as a learning tool required that the data needed to be opened up to augmentation by further field users and that any subsequent model should be based on a more wiki-like approach to the data gathering process, so as to provide a fully enriched learning environment.

The next instance of location-aware technologies using both modes of mobile situated learning was in relation to another fictionalised landscape: that of D.H. Lawrence's childhood in Eastwood in Nottinghamshire, in order to tease out the complex relationship between writer and place through this new methodology. Funded by Renaissance[11], via MUBU, the project team worked closely with the D.H. Lawrence Centre at Durban House in Eastwood and with Nottingham University's D.H. Lawrence Research Archive through 2010. In addition, there were Museum/Heritage group partnerships with D.H. Lawrence Festival, Broxtowe Borough Council and The D.H. Lawrence the Birthplace Museum. The research team included De Montfort University, where I was now based, and representatives of Cuttlefish Multimedia, Loughborough (who were developing the mobile platform *Empedia* for iphones and Android platforms in conjunction with the IOCT at De Montfort University via a short Knowledge Transfer Partnership).

Original texts were 'annotated' by layered audio-visual information and analysis, and situated use via mobile technologies, exploring the cultural and physical contexts within which the work resonated: making literature accessible by 'animating the archive'. The project explores how we might better understand and evaluate the ways in which mixing the performances, sounds, images and objects from both the past and present could be captured and disseminated at the point of their inspiration for academic study. In trying to understand how technologies might newly recover or change research practice we utilised moving image, still image, texts and audio. The project also addressed the issues of transmission and memory: how we might capture the sensory experiences of the past and what this might mean in terms of cultural memory and identity. The use of vocalised and relevant Lawrence poetry, annotations by school workshops and local history groups all contributed to this attempt to bring the past alive and to make it relevant to contemporary users.

This ongoing study investigated appropriate forms of content and delivery for locative textual, aural and visual field guides to literary landscapes through the development of a shared 'animated' archive, and should ultimately help us to evaluate the scholarly and public uses of the system and the reactions of users. In doing so, it will also attempt to establish the best forms of open-source website and wiki to support scholarship, and updating and distributing locative guides through the *Empedia* platform[12]. It was intended as a demonstrator of the potential for locative and web technologies, combined with collaboration in the field, in creating knowledge networks mapped to topography. As in *The Crow Road*, contextually relevant texts were annotated through appropriate forms of aural and visual inscription for interpretation in the field using locative triggers. A key objective at the project's end will be to evaluate user behaviours and reactions to both interface and content – this is still work in progress, but we anticipate huge interest from the museums sector to this pilot. As in *The Crow Road*, the final version will only use information relevant to its location to avoid on-screen clutter. In other words, the menus will only reveal the specific assets available at that location.

Further demonstrators may be constructed in Bath looking at Jane Austen's relationship with the city in the three novels: *Persuasion, Northhanger Abbey* and *Mansfield Park*. This research would also examine Bluetooth and RFID way marking and the use of large public screens in conjunction with the University of Bath[13].

The key research questions in the D.H. Lawrence study emphasised how a locative re-imagining of a literary text enhanced cultural heritage in ways that are both scholarly *and* accessible to a wider public. As the project rolls out we will be examining relationships between scholarly practice and wider enjoyment of texts and open online databases and mobile devices. Mobile locative technologies offer an opportunity to change the nature of literary interpretation, through new understandings of the imaginative transformation of landscape by authorial imaginaries. Whether the participatory accumulation of local/specialist knowledge via web and mobile technologies can be successfully engineered is yet to be proven. But we hope and anticipate that a combination of field research and user responses will generate new knowledge, particularly through representation of local histories via collective knowledge. The first part of this trajectory was a school's workshop offering local texts for visual and written interpretation, which annotated parts of the Council's *Blue Line* trail. Part of the project involved readings by professional actors and by the school children from the workshop, so we are also asking whether a revival of oral and performative modes of interaction can be predicated on these technologies and how useful in such experiential forms of delivery are oral readings and dramatisations? It remains to be tested as to which forms of text and oral delivery are most effective and appropriate for locative and mobile media.

As described, the project simultaneously addresses two audiences, the *scholarly* and the *interested reader*. The process of production was complex: essential preparatory project activities included field research mapping, visually documenting locations related to texts, an exegesis of relevant texts and the transfer of texts to screen, implementing and testing downloadable journeys in Eastwood, collecting local histories, and directing dramatised professional readings of selected texts. User evaluations with literary specialists and reading groups in Eastwood will follow as the project is developed.

The relationship between *group scholarship* and *located technologies* will be tested in three ways:

1. The use of co-located scholarship and co-communication in the field
2. The construction of an expandable *geowiki* for global use and augmentation both by specialist scholars and local knowledge holders
3. The evaluation of appropriate interface models and information content for such tools

Further new knowledge is expected to result from field interviews with local residents.

The use of professional actor readings, overlaid through mobile technologies on the actual spaces mentioned in the literature, will create unique experiences of location. Permission to use sections of film for relevant interpretations is also being sought as I write. Although targeted at undergraduates upwards and the intelligent reader or literary enthusiast, it must be remembered that in such a pervasive learning environment, context is determined not only by location (identified by GPS, triangulation or RFID) but also by the user's experience, the light levels, the weather, efficiency with technology, etc. The project website will disseminate ideas to a broad audience; the wiki will be used as outreach beyond the research community into a wider public interest, providing downloadable software and content to enhance accessibility and focus further scholarship (Figure 21.2).

RIVERAINS: HISTORY AS EXPLORATION

Riverains creates a story trail along Old Street and Shoreditch High Street, accessible through the user's mobile phone. It maps both the imaginary underground world of the *Riverains* and London's history onto the urban landscape. Through text messaging, Augmented Reality, GPS location sensing and QR barcode code reading, participants can use their mobile phone to discover this hidden underground world, which will correspond to real locations in Shoreditch. Participants can hear the *Riverains* voices at sixteen sites and fully experience these video narratives. (From *Riverains* Illumini handout)

Demonstrators for Locative Journey interactions in Bath around a Literary Imaginary

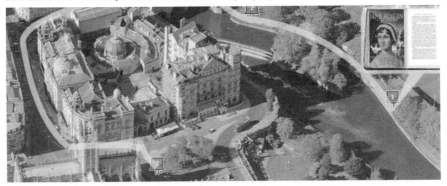

GPS triggered locations in BATH as part of a locative journey demonstration for hypothetical Jane Austen demonstration

Waymarking demonstrator using Bluetooth becons to interact with mobile on-screen displays

Public Interaction with large screen data

Schematic of interactive data mapped on building facade

Figure 21.2   University of Bath CityWare experiments ©Department of Computer Science University of Bath.

Riverains was first commissioned as an experimental locative work by the B'tween Festival in Manchester, in 2008. It has since been piloted in London at the *Illumini* Festival in Shoreditch in September 2010. *Riverains* approached local history by creating a multi-user story space accessible through mobile phones, which collaboratively mapped an imaginary world and a city's history onto an urban landscape. *Riverains* were imagined as historical souls tied to watery energies, running under our cities in rivers, cables, sewers, tunnels and caves. They travel unseen by these invisible routes and cluster around sites of past experience. Through GPS and QR code reading, participants were encouraged to use their mobile phone like a douser, to discover this hidden world, which corresponded to real underground locations aligned with the sites of past events. In future versions, they would then use the *Riverains'* overheard tales to map those sites and find clues and give directions to others. The added game elements would enable one to play as a team and to eventually add one's own stories enhancing the collaborative learning aspects of the project.

The intended sites of Manchester, London and Nottingham have rich underground worlds of hidden or 'lost' rivers, nuclear fallout facilities and Command Centres and Second World War bunkers, in addition to Victorian sewers and underground railway systems. They also have an archaeology going back through medieval to Roman times. The *Riverains* were drawn from this rich history and from the cities' annals of poverty, industrial revolution, immigration, political protest, commerce and innovation, gang warfare, crime and uncanny happenings (Figure 21.3).

The anticipated public benefits include: learning about heritage, reaching out to diverse UK communities, teaching about the past, engaging various ethnic groups in the experience, including as many as possible by going beyond the limitations of incompatible and/or different mobile platforms through use of browser-based software. The project plans to map video and photo-stories across central areas of all the respective cities. The project also allows the public, using a combination of website and GPS-enabled mobiles or mobiles with image and QR code recognition, to discover the *Riverains* presences, which will follow participants around, suddenly appearing at seemingly random times and places to participating individuals. The presences will either emerge on screen and speak when automatically triggered by pre-tagged locations, or send text messages to identify locations (Figure 21.4).

In the final version, users will also be able to use the *Riverains'* tales to discover new sites and find clues and directions to the mysterious *Gatekeeper*. Once they find the *Gatekeeper* they will be able to further create and animate their own video contributions, which can be added through a collective web interface. In the final version, a dark map of the city would be progressively lit by a virtual torch or lantern as the teams or individuals discover the stories and the stories can be stored and replayed by participants. While a basic terrain and story map has been placed online in advance, the database is intended to form a growing urban map of user-generated stories. To guard against unwanted spamming an editorial level has been built into the project.

Figure 21.3   Riverains on Empedia platform showing media locations

Riverains was run in pilot form at the Illumini Festival in September 2010, tracing a portion of Old Street and Shoreditch High Street. *Secret Subterranean London* was the third Illumini event, curated by Jane Webb, and located in the basement of Shoreditch town Hall. Over fifty artists/artist groups exhibited and performed during the week-long festival, which also included guided underground tours, artist talks and workshops. Over 3300 people attended the opening evening, Thursday 9th September 2010, and 9247 people in total visited Illumini during the whole week's event[14].

Riverains at Illumini was designed to comprise four elements, offering interaction to users with varying levels of technical requirement (users are expected to provide their own mobile phone). The work built on *Riverains* development for Manchester's B'tween festival, extending it through collaboration with artists Ximena Alarcon (Sounding Underground)[15], Kasia Molga[16] (Mirror of Infinity) and technical development by Sean Clarke and Phil Sparks (Empedia by Cuttlefish Multimedia) and Gareth Howell (using Layar).

In addition to a talk and workshop, on Sunday 11th September (2010), two 'guided walks' followed in which participants were supported in using the QR code[17] reader version, and Layar[18] (for those with suitable phones), as they followed the trail along Old Street and Shoreditch High Street. Those without appropriate phones were able to share the experience using spare iPhones during the walks. *Riverains* was aimed at the broad spectrum Illumini audience.

Figure 21.4   Riverains workshop interaction in Shoreditch. Photo: Jackie Calderwood

The guided walks targeted people with iphones and were promoted in the online 'artist talks' programme (first walk) and by word of mouth at The Illumini exhibition itself (second walk). More people joined the walk whilst gathering at the street level outside the venue.

The video pieces by Alarcon and myself were triggered by photographing QR codes distributed on stickers along the route; carrying visual clues as to locations associated with the video content. Whilst encouraging audiences to download in advance in areas of free wifi, the 3G downloads took no more than a minute, and in fact began streaming almost instantly. The *Layar* version was equally successful and it is hoped that the next incarnation will fully develop all the intended game elements and the user software to upload further stories.

As it was, the rich history of Shoreditch was explored with pieces on early Shakespeare using imagined voices of characters or actors from the plays *Henry IV* and *Romeo and Juliet*; verbatim readings from the coroner's report of the 'Ripper' murder of Mary Kelly held in the Town Hall site of the exhibition, with interjections by the Ripper's imagined persona; immigrant voices from Jewish, Huguenot and contemporary narratives were available, as were reflections on the Great Plague in London, creating dramatised monologues based on Daniel Defoe's *Journal of the Plague Year.* Suffragette histories became audio–visual sound–image montages echoing their treatment in Holloway Prison. Finally, there were reflections on the early history of underground rivers that criss-cross the area and notionally hold the historical presences, which are the *Riverains*.

PERVASIVE MEDIA AND INTELLIGENT TAGGING

The widespread development of device independent 'cloud computing' is the next emergent technology, which when combined with semantic web[19] and Wimax[20] technologies will ensure that the infrastructure for continuous locative learning within urban centres will be installed effectively over the next ten years. The research pilot Electronic Media Metadata Acquisition (EMMA) was predicated on this assumption and the need to automate aspects of meta-tagging, so that rich media information is useful regardless of context, particularly in mobile delivered information. The 'EMMA' product was prototyped under an East Midlands Innovation Fellowship Grant at De Montfort University as a multidisciplinary research collaboration between the Institute of Creative Technology and the Faculty of Technology in 2008–2009. It proposed a commercial software package bundled with specialised hardware (patent pending) to enable required connectivity direct to any professional video camera. The primary aim of the software tool (usually based on a PDA platform) was developed for re-purposing of data related to the planning and implementation of media production in the field, so creating XML tagged assets fit for a variety of linear and non-linear forms. Meta-tagging all generated media at the moment of production was seen as a means of simplifying the future archiving and retrieval of video and audio assets for re-purposing and re-use. We scoped integrated in-house tagging and archiving software for rapid recognition and retrieval of any asset and attempted to automate the meta-tagging process and eliminate manual input wherever possible. The in-house tagging system was specified with a proper taxonomy developed to go forward as an IEEE standard in this area. To rationalise the taxonomic hierarchy of tags to ensure that all sections of media are marked and create an effective Digital Rights Management and asset tracking system, the system developed as a result of comparing existing tagging taxonomies in use and their suitability for the task. A seven-level taxonomy was developed to allow fine-grain and generic descriptors to co-exist.

The pilot project's innovation was threefold: it re-purposed all the existing data from production notes and planning sources; it created a rational layered taxonomy, which was context independent; and through its physical interface allowed for the permanent embedding or stamping of digital video for asset-tracking and Intellectual Property management, as well as future reuses in unforeseen contexts within online (semantic) databases. While at the time a number of research projects were addressing elements of this project, none are approaching the problem in such an integrated manner, and none were developing hardware solutions for on-camera use. It was assumed that when the product came to market it would still be unique and under patent protection. The development of similar systems by Adobe Premiere's *Story* and *Script to Screen* additions and Avid *iNews*, meant that the crucial commercial advantages for professional production were lost. A credible bid for £500,000 with six commercial partners was prepared for the TSB and made it as far as the last sixteen in the second round.

While the exploitable output was to be a custom hardware–software product – a custom plug-in for most professional cameras using USB input with wireless connectivity to electronic clapperboards, laptop computers, smart phones and PDAs an Extensible Markup Language-based (XML) system with maximum compatibility to archives, using a new taxonomic layered methodology, was coupled to a bid for an new IEEE standard for meta-tagging.

The metadata was to be encoded and referenced in such a way that any asset fragment would be traceable to its original source greatly assisting in the enforceability of Intellectual Property rights. All preproduction notes and shot list data can be repurposed for the tagging process, additions can be made at any stage prior to shooting, thereby rationalising production. Archiving of all digital production materials is a complex, difficult and costly operation for most SMEs and as a consequence large amounts of materials are stacked or remain unindexed in any useful way, certainly for further exploitation. The system offered a painless and economically advantageous route to archiving which is always up to date. The system also allowed for the rational and systematic archiving of all materials, regardless of current use or context, to allow for further exploitation in unexpected future contexts.

A trackable asset code could also be easily linked to a pay-per-view or download payments system. We envisaged a spin-off company to marketise the product and drive through production. The loss of the TSB bid has put this temporarily on hold. However, EMMA remains an innovative attempt to integrate digital production technologies at the point of production and is unique in its proposed development of the XML schema which encompasses the requirements of the media industry for meta-tagging media files, since it raises an awareness of the need to make decisions at the start of production rather than trying to create the metadata at some later stage (which is always more complex and less satisfactory).

The concept of building the collection of the metadata into the media as soon as production starts and making it an integral part of the production process, and later rights management, is still key to the success of low cost effective metadata collection in the media industry. However this approach is still not reported in such direct terms in the literature and therefore is still an important and largely unexploited approach which has significant benefits. There are still major opportunities in adapting the technology for mass domestic use through further research bids, particularly in relation to the emerging semantic web and cloud storage of personal and social media and adaptation for mobile platforms; it will form an essential requirement in future pervasive information databases and archives, as the pilots in this paper have implied.

CONCLUSION

Integrated pervasive learning and research is best achieved through situated and contextualised media explored through collaboration and action-based learning, aligning with dialogue methods of research. All the projects described aimed to include participants both as active consumers of information in context using mobile platforms, but also to become authors, augmenting and tagging data with their own additions and digging into local and personal information to expand the archive in innovative ways. Our experience has shown us that interfaces need to be as simple, and as automated, as is feasible; and that browser-based content combined with efficient semi-automated semantic tagging and open source software allows for the maximum engagement, simplicity of production and two-way participation.

NOTES

1. See: http://socialnets.wikispaces.com/Definitions (accessed October 2010).
2. See: http://www.futurelab.org.uk/ (accessed October 2010).
3. See: http://www.learning-theories.com/situated-learning-theory-lave.html (accessed October 2010).
4. Thomas, Kim A Mobile with a Mission FutureLab, March 2007.

5. Hundebøl, Jesper, Pervasive e-learning in Situ Learning in Changing Contexts, Niels Henrik Helms, Knowledge Lab, http://www.dream.dk/uploads/files/Hundeboel%20Jesper%20Niels%20Henrik%20Helms.pdf (accessed 16 March 2008).

6. D. H. Lawrence, In: B. Steele (Ed.), *Study of Thomas Hardy and Other Essays*. The Cambridge Edition of the Works of D.H. Lawrence.

7. *The Crow Road* http://thecrowroad.blogspot.com (accessed October 2010).

8. See: http://www.mobilearn.org/standards/standards.htm (accessed October 2010).

9. See http://elearning.typepad.com/thelearnedman/mobile_learning/reports/futurelab_review_11.pdf (accessed October 2010).

10. ibid.

11. See: http://www.mla.gov.uk/what/programmes/renaissance/regions/east_midlands (accessed October 2010).

12. See: http://empedia.info/ (accessed October 2010).

13. See: http://www.cityware.org.uk/ (accessed October 2010).

14. See: www.illuminievent.co.uk (accessed October 2010).

15. See: http://www.mti.dmu.ac.uk/~xalarcon/soundingunderground/info/ (accessed October 2010).

16. See: www.mirror-of-infinity.net/ (accessed October 2010).

17. See: http://www.mobile-barcodes.com/about-qr-codes/ (accessed October 2010).

18. See: http://www.layar.com/ (accessed October 2010).

19. See: http://semanticweb.org/wiki/Main_Page (accessed October 2010).

20. See: http://www.wimax.com/general/what-is-wimax (accessed October 2010).

REFERENCES

Engeström, Y. (1987). *Learning by expanding: An activity–theoretical approach to developmental research*. Orienta-Konsultit Oy.

Lave, J. & Wenger, E. (1991). *Situated learning: Legitimate peripheral participation*. Cambridge, UK: Cambridge University Press.

Proctor, N. & Burton, J. (2003). Tate Modern multimedia tour pilots 2002–2003. In J. Attewell, G. Da Bormida, M. Sharples, & C. Savill-Smith (Eds.), *M Learn 2003: Learning with mobile devices* (pp. 54–55). London: Learning and Skills Development Agency.

Rogers, Y., Price, S., Harris, E., Phelps, T., Underwood, M., Wilde, D., Smith, H., Muller, H., Randell, C., Stanton, D., Neale, H., Thompson, M., Weal, M., & Michaelides, D. (2002). *Learning through digitally-augmented physical experiences: Reflections on the ambient wood project*. Equator Technical Report. Available online at: <http://machen.mrl.nott.ac.uk/ PublicationStore/2002-rogers-2.pdf>

Vygotsky, L. S. (1978). *Mind in society: The development of higher psychological processes*. Cambridge, MA: The MIT Press.

BIBLIOGRAPHY

Benford, S. D. & Rowland, D. (2005). Life on the edge: Supporting collaboration in location-based experiences. In *Proceedings of ACM CHI 2005 Conference on Human Factors in Computing Systems: Public life, Portland, OR* (pp. 721–730). New York: ACM Press.

Cayser, S. (2004). Semantic blogging and decentralized knowledge management. *Communications of the ACM – The Blogosphere 47* (12).

Pask, A. G. S. (1976). *Conversation theory: Applications in education and epistemology*. Amsterdam: Elsevier.

Page, K. R., Michaelides, D. T., Buckingham S., Simon J., Chen-Buger, Y.-H., Dalton, J., Eisenstadt, M., Potter, S., Shadbolt, N. R., Tate, A., Bachler, M., & Komzak, J. (2005). Collaboration in the Semantic grid: A basis for e-learning. *Applied Artificial Intelligence, 19* (9–10), 881–904.

Proctor, N. & Burton, J. (2004). Tate Modern multimedia tour pilots 2002–2003. In J. Attewell and C. Savill-Smith (Eds.), *Learning with Mobile Devices* (pp. 127–130). London: LSDA.

Tummala, H. & Jones, J. (2005). Developing spatially-aware content management systems for dynamic, location-specific information in mobile environments. Proceedings of the 3rd ACM international workshop on Wireless mobile applications and services on WLAN hotspots, pp. 14–22.

22

Establishing the Cybertextual in Practice-Based PhDs

Lisa Stansbie

INTRODUCTION

This chapter discusses how a digital online thesis can be a suitable model for practice-based PhDs within the discipline of *art and design*. It draws from precedents within the field, including my own PhD submission *Zeppelinbend: multiplicity, encyclopaedic strategies and non-linear methodologies for a visual practice* (2010) Leeds Metropolitan University. It investigates how a digital submission offers a differentiated approach for a reader, who then becomes an active *user*, drawing parallels with Aarseth's (1997) perspectives on digital literature and interactivity. Part of this discussion will necessitate a brief consideration of how such theses might generate greater dissemination of the work while the immaterial form may pose questions of authorship and copyright.

It is important to note that in contrast to other academic disciplines the *creative* PhD allows for the submission of *practice* that might include works of art, design, compositional scores and audio–visual material amongst other artefacts. The term *practice-based* (or practice-led) has evolved from this specific approach. This practice is usually submitted with supporting written documentation varying in length[1] that acts as a contextual framework[2].

This discussion will specifically consider the website format of a digital thesis, whereby the website is the submission itself (usually its design is an integral element of the submission) with no other supporting documentation in material form. It is 'digital born' (Hayles, 2008) and designed specifically for the web, taking advantage of the multimodal possibilities this platform offers. The need to state this as the form is because currently there exists a myriad of practices under the umbrella of a digital PhD submission which include, but are not limited to: the digitally distributed thesis that exists as a digital copy via an online version (uploaded to portals and collections such as the Australian Digital Thesis Program[3]) and the CD Rom submission and the material thesis supported by visual/creative work in a digital form. In *The Challenge of the Paperless Thesis* (2006), Bostock states that the CD Rom is the most effective format for a digital PhD submission due to 'storage demands'. However, the development of software for image and audio–visual processing has developed rapidly to enable web friendly use particularly over the last five years; servers have also evolved in line with these developments so that they are able to handle with speed the growing necessity for sites that rely on a heavy audio–visual content.

In his essay *Innovative Hypermedia ETDs and Employment in the Humanities*, Katz (2004) refers to the website thesis as an '*innovative hypermedia*' work and states that in comparison with the other forms of electronic theses and submission formats, outlined above, they are '... the most different from conventional print theses and dissertations. These innovative documents receive different degrees of acceptance in different professions and academic disciplines' (Katz, 2004). The examples of website submissions discussed later fall within the area of *art and design* and it has become apparent that as practice-based PhD study is increasing within the UK university art and design departments, the boundaries have shifted relating to what format a submission can take. The art and design PhD submission is becoming potentially more experimental. The notion of the website as the thesis that contains both the practice and related contextual framework in its entirety, opens up this format question further, particularly in relation to the longevity of a website submission and its potentially unstable dissemination within the geography of the internet.

PRACTICE-BASED DOCTORAL STUDY IN ART AND DESIGN

Non-standard formats for PhD submission have developed over time as art and design research has evolved. Within the UK the PhD in art and design is relatively new in terms of the broader field of doctoral research in other disciplines. Early (late 1950s to 1970s) art and design PhD degrees were sited within the theoretical framework of a traditional art history thesis or theses related to architectural subjects[4].

The expansion of practice-based PhD study in the UK within art and design has grown in line with the *new universities*. Polytechnics with their long-standing tradition of studio-based programmes largely led the way in approaching the idea of research through and by practice. The art and design practice-based PhD uses 'making' to investigate research questions, the making is the methodology and vehicle for generating new knowledge. In order to contextualise how this practice embodies knowledge, it is usually framed by critical contexts/commentaries that make analytical connections with precedents in the field and states how the study demonstrates new knowledge.

During the 1980s and 1990s doctoral study within art and design[5] in the UK had started to develop '… experimental methods [that] provided the dominant research strategy for investigation' (Mottram, 2009). As practice-related submissions increased particularly from 2000 onwards we begin to see a shift in submission formats, largely the presence of the practice itself in the form of objects and artefacts alongside consideration given to their presentation in the form of documentation and exhibition(s).

The first entirely non-standard submission at Leeds Metropolitan University, in which the text and work are interwoven as one was *A Place of constraint, a promise of happiness: scrutinising structures of surveillance and control in suburbia* (2007) by Liz Stirling. The PhD was submitted as a series of five digitally printed AO sized maps, also available as large PDF documents. The thesis combined fictitious and factual material, image and text, documentation and new imagery, challenging the notion of truth in material. Its originality was the methodology of the practice and the presentation of this as a whole piece; a methodology drawing on methods from different *disciplines* from history to sociology, photography to print, performance to creative writing in order for the subject to be scrutinised and critiqued from an interventionist viewpoint rather than a passive observational position. Although Stirling's PhD format is a material form, it has many similarities with a website submission, particularly in its use of a bricolage of image and text and the presentation of cross-relationships via linking. With regard to actual whole website submissions currently it seems that there are still very few, although this is itself difficult to ascertain[6].

The multimodal website submission reflects the recent currency of digital dissemination practices already present in many university courses where e-learning and online practices are actively encouraged. In practice-based creative doctoral study, the website format allows for the inter-disciplinary nature of creative research to become an integral part of the thesis. In his essay *The Three Configurations of Studio-Art PhDs*, Elkins (2009) poses models of what shape practice-based PhDs within art might take. In his 'third model', which is stated, as 'The Dissertation *Is* the Artwork, And Vice Versa' he asks the reader to imagine a scenario where '… the scholarly portion of the thesis (is) inextricably fused with the creative portion, so that the artwork is scholarly and the scholarship is creative' (Elkins, 2009). He cites examples of multimedia submissions which consist of CD Roms and practical work but states that he is yet to see an example of a creative PhD where the '… scholarship melts into the creative work, or asks to be read as creative work'. The website format offers such a possibility and allows for a fusion of practice and 'scholarship'. Through this mode of presentation the blurring of artwork and scholarship enables the website to be an integral part of the research, its structure can reflect the nature of the research and potentially give further insights into the methodology of the practice. Theses in this sense might act to reflect a more personal approach of the practitioner, drawing on the aesthetic/design possibilities offered by website construction processes and software. They can also demonstrate a gathering of perspectives from a wide variety of sources and reference particular practices first hand: moving image and sound, for example. When presented as a website the relationship between the 'practice' and the surrounding theory can be illuminated for a reader who might have to transverse back and forth between these elements, with the act of doing so revealing their inextricable connection.

However, the website submission for a practice-based doctoral study may only successfully contain the research in its entirety where the digital medium is an intrinsic element of the research and/or its methodology (www.zeppelinbend.com)[7] is framed from the outset by methodologies that state an interrogation of the material and immaterial processes of art production and dissemination and so the digital nature of the submission could be seen to extend particular research questions.

The submission is structured as a website so that holistically the presentation of the research mirrors the methodology of the practice itself, connecting the separate parts as a net. Its online presence reflects the fact that the digital plays a central role in the research and the practice it generates from its conception to its presentation. This enables the practice to be cross referenced with theoretical concerns discussed in the form of four pieces of writing titled under 'critical context', including extended footnotes and internal and external links that provide an overview of the research. This also makes it possible for the visual work to be accessed online at different points throughout the commentary when it is referred to (Stansbie, 2010).

Within www.zeppelinbend.com even previously constructed material-based installation and object works are presented through digital images, which act as documentation and set up a screen relationship with the viewer/reader rather than a tactile one. An additional layer of commentary is used in the documentation of the physical making and subsequent audience experiences of object-based work, which is revealed through separate connected blogs. The blogs act as satellite digital sites where the works can be experienced developmentally and the writing contained within each blog can be more analytical, reflective and ultimately experimental. In the Spitfire Beach Blog (2010), the narrative of the blog is structured around the making of the art works that form the project Spitfire Beach[8]. However, the writing in this form becomes more than documentation, as interwoven narratives unfold and a process of remembering is engaged. The blog combines a wandering through memories and recollections as the work is produced. Connections are generated through daydreaming that takes place during the making and writing process. This creates parallel stories; one descriptive account of the actual project and the other of nostalgic personal remembering retold through paths that journey back into the past. Through the blog there is one voice but two interwoven narratives. These narratives are reflective and descriptive when talking about the work and anecdotal story telling through the accounts of seemingly arbitrary personal experiences and thoughts, set off by the wandering of my mind. The practice evokes a whole new set of paths of potentiality as detailed in the blog. Calvino (1988) describes the process of writing used by the novelist Carlo Emilio Gadda in his *Risotto alla Millanese* as episodes in which '... the least thing is seen as the centre of a network of relationships that the writer cannot restrain himself from following' (Calvino, 1988). In the writing of the blog I am allowing a tangling of associations but it is ultimately confined, structured and ceased by the blog format.

Within digital art where the works are created, edited and stored using technology, such as *The Archive* (2005–2010)[9] on www.zeppelinbend.com, fluidity exists between the means of production and presentation as a website. A different method of utilising a website occurs when the 'practice' is materially object-based. The website can provide a means of documentation and presentation where the maker feels that a material interaction with the art object itself is not a prerequisite for understanding the research; in this instance the website is a tool to present work. This is similar to Christiane Paul's (2007) analogy between different types of digital art 'Within the category of digital art, one needs to distinguish art that uses digital technologies as a tool as opposed to a medium' (Paul, 2007). This distinction between website as medium or tool is blurring as more variations on the format develop; www.zeppelinbend.com capitalises on the potential to use the website as both documentation and medium. With the possibility to creatively experiment with the format of the website thesis an in-depth consideration of the design/interface may be required. An experimental site with an unconventional interface may ultimately challenge the accessibility for a reader/examiner, who might need direction when unpicking the website as a PhD submission. The www.zeppelinbend.com interface is still recognisable as a PhD study. It contains the pre-requisite elements of an abstract, overview, critical contexts and area containing the practice. As an interface the menu enables an ease of use and the separate categories of the research each contain introductory pages that outline what is contained on preceding pages. The practice itself is presented as documentary pages, many of which contain the actual film works and a contextual framing for each work. It maintains this fixed pattern so that although the research discusses non-linearity and multiplicity the structure retains clarity of orientation.

As a practitioner producing art works over a period of the PhD study, it can be difficult for a supervisor to experience the material art objects and their associated processes at each stage of the research. The means of digital documentation and the ease with which images can be collated and organised offers potential to archive the research and allows for its sequential presentation. This digital approach might be seen to challenge the traditional documenting processes of art studio practice, such as the '*sketchbook*' and also question the long held tradition of a *final* material gallery exhibition that provides a showcase at a specified submission date of selected products. Such an exhibition is also time-limited, available to view between given dates, whereby an online presentation can be revisited and re-experienced at the pace of the viewer.

In particular relation to the PhD thesis, the notion of a final submission at a given date does not sit comfortably with a website format. Lev Manovich (2002) describes the format of websites as a database that '… never have to be complete; and they rarely are. The sites always grow. New links are being added to what is already there. It is as easy to add new elements to the end of the list as it is to insert them anywhere in it'. This is where CD Rom discs are usually requested as a record of the website at a given date[10]. With the development of www. zeppelinbend.com and its stated methodology of multiplicity and ever-expansion, the organic form of the website has allowed these methods to be used in the production of the research and the way in which the website is experienced. However, the notion of multiplicity is somewhat at odds with the confines of a doctoral study final submission, meaning the site had to stop 'growing' on a given submission date.

INTERACTIVITY AND HYPERLINKING[11]

Hyperlinking is essentially a constructed path, designed for the user to follow through a site. Hyperlinking allows for navigation and access. 'In contrast to conventional texts (and perhaps especially conventional PhD theses), there is no linear sequence in which a hypermedia documents pages are meant to be read and understood' (Bostock, 2006). The use of a link also offers the potential to make relationships and ideas manifest and exposes the potential of the Internet a '… potential that we're actively creating and expanding' (Weinberger, 2008).

The website www.zeppelinbend.com requires that a reader exercises modes of selection/point-and-click, reading, listening and watching, often switching between these functions via selected hyperlinks. There are deliberately numerous hyperlinks (both internal and external) that change the reader's direction, so that the structure and the way in which a reader interacts with them creates rhizomatic tangents intentionally disrupting a linear path. With an interactive PhD thesis the participation required from a user starts from the initial entrance to the site. As Lev Manovich (2002) states in his description of websites as databases '… from the point of view of user's experience a large proportion of them are databases in a more basic sense. They appear as collections of items on which the user can perform various operations: view, navigate, search. The user experience of such computerised collections is therefore quite distinct from reading a narrative or watching a film'.

Textual portions of the writing in a digital online thesis are most likely (as with zeppelinbend.com) to be a hyperlinked thesis, allowing a reader to navigate away from the writing and view/read other online associated works and references, bringing the external internet into thesis as a form of citation.

The ease of '… cutting, copying and otherwise manipulating text permits different forms of scholarly composition, ones in which the researcher's notes and original data exist in experientially closer proximity to the scholarly text than ever before' (Landow, 2006).

Due to the internal and external linking and layering of the online submission it can reference a wide variety of current sources and embed different methods of writing typically incorporating '… varieties of webbed structure, in which support for an initial thesis may be conceived of as radiating out from a common centre … rather than a tree structure that is intended to be traversed by a single path, the structure of an innovative hypermedia document will incorporate repetition, circles, return loops, tangents, dead-ends, and even entire documents authored by others' (Katz, 2004).

The work contained as part of the zeppelinbend.com PhD submission titled *The Archive* (2005–2010) poses different possibilities via hyperlinking for a user compared with zeppelinbend. Part of The Archive's function is to demonstrate explorations into connecting the unconnected, using combinations of mundane and unusual objects, text, images and film. The Archive also attempts to explore the notion of multi-choice for a user through the use of forking paths and multi-choice hyperlinking. The use of forking paths, looping and dead ends on the scale applied within The Archive is perhaps not appropriate in the larger submission site itself, which might become unusable should it use the same structure. Aarseth (1997) describes how the creation of such 'forking' reminds a user of the '… inaccessible and the missed choices … creating an absence of possibility' this often encourages a desire on the part of a user for re-visiting. In *Semiotics and The Philosophy of Language* (1986), Umberto Eco states there are different types of labyrinths, the linear, the maze and the net. The Archive's structure sits between a maze and a net. It is not entirely net like in structure, as every point is not connected with every other point, which would allow a user entirely free movement throughout; some pages cross-link but due to the process used for linking archive pages it is not possible to hyperlink every one to each other. This is largely due to the use of associative words that make the hyperlink to the next archive page. If the archive entries were all inter-connected the threads that connected them would become increasingly tenuous and nonsensical, whereas currently an associative pattern can be understood by a user, enabling an understanding of navigational possibilities. Pages within the archive have multiple paths stemming from them whereby the user can choose a predetermined direction from around one to four possible options: an example of forking to various degrees. Bolter (1991) suggests that hypertext links work in much the same way that a user reads a dictionary: '… in a printed dictionary, we must move from page to page looking up definitions, if we are to set in motion the play of signs'. The act of clicking the link activates the work, and subsequently activates a chain of signs, setting up a procedure for interpretation and interaction.

Aarseth (1997) also discusses interactivity with text through his term 'cybertext' where he states that electronic text or 'cybertext' focuses importance on an exchange with the reader centring attention on '... the consumer, or user, of the text, as a more integrated figure'. In relation to Leishman's PhD website submission *Creating screen-based multiple state environments: investigating systems of confutation* (2004) completed at Glasgow School of Art, the notion of Aarseth's *ergodic* is pertinent to the submission whereby a reader/user must use '... non-trivial effort ... to transverse the text' (Aarseth, 1997). In Leishman's online submission the creative interactive works form part of the site[12] so that a reader has to use the interactive narrative animation works, alongside reading the written component. This interactivity asks a reader to contemplate the thesis on a different level transforming the reader into active participant and the 'success' of the thesis relies on the reader's ability to interrupt and assimilate the varied layers contained within it. This creates a co-dependency between author and reader/user. Leishman's thesis states that a primary intention is '... to investigate the interplay between Internet-based digital narrative, image and interaction, and ultimately develop new practice, which is primarily within the experiencing of the artwork and articulates a new contribution to the field of study' (Leishman, 2004). With the central aspect of the research positioned around interactivity and residing within digital practices it is pertinent to the thesis that it is submitted as an interactive online document that allows for a dynamic multisensory interaction with the thesis and crucial that the user can experience the interactive animation works which become *eventised*, as points of experiential reference:

> The structuring of this thesis is done in a manner that reflects the epistemological grounding for the research. This grounding was contextually multiplicious and interwoven. Thus the body of commentary texts where appropriate contain links to the practice, live external websites, and extended commentaries. The extended commentaries are of a richer than normal footnote style and are intended to offer to you, the reader, a further discursive vein. Please note if you choose not to explore the various links or the extended areas of reference you will experience another type and more surface reading of this thesis. (Leishman, 2004)[13]

A particular signature of the website is the screen space through which the thesis is mediated. The confines of the screen space differ in a multiplicity of ways to the printed text space, perhaps most obviously in the lack of pages. In the examples of PhD submission cited in this chapter, the written components contain scrollable text portions. For a reader this can pose difficulties, largely in navigating the text, particularly when footnotes are present. Footnotes can act as the (printed) material theses' version of a hyperlink – opening out particular areas of the writing and adding a further layer of insight. Digitally footnotes have to be re-considered as their traditional printed position in the 'footer' is impractical with the scrollable text space of the screen. In www.zeppelinbend.com, in particular, the writing has been separated into chapters, each of which is accessible via the *critical context* page, which acts as an index to the writing (the design also allows for a display of the key-terms defined within each written piece). The footnotes are contained in a separate section to the side and are hyperlinked from the writing with a link from the footnotes themselves (a bidirectional link) that re-orientates the reader back to the place from which they were reading.

This process is intended to alleviate the need for scrolling back and forth and seems to be the practised method used by the small number of online PhD submissions available (including Leishman's). This practice also avoids linking whereby a new browser window opens or changes, and keeps the reader in the same space as the body of text, allowing for cross-referencing and an almost uninterrupted reading experience if the reader requires.

AUTHORSHIP/DISSEMINATION

A new form of production has been enabled by the Internet: that of sharing and re-using through new technology and networks. More than ever before a generation of web users are becoming the web makers; it is an era of appropriation and the hack. It is appropriation in the form of Nicholas Bourriaud's (2002) 'post-production' linked to the contemporary deejay, a remix culture that borrows, represents, simulates and innovates. 'In our daily lives, the gap that separates production and consumption narrows each day. We can produce a musical work without being able to play a single note of music by making use of existing records' (Bourriaud, 2002).

Currently, technology is implicit in a great deal of creative work and its dissemination through the Internet. This is not how it used to be and the technology has made it easier and quicker to 'hack'. Wark (2004) describes the notion of the hack through discussion of the 'hacker class' and how hacking involves the 'production of production':

> We produce new concepts, new perceptions, new sensations, hacked out of raw data. Whatever code we hack, be it programming language, poetic language, math or music, curves or colourings, we are abstracters of new worlds. Whether we come to represent ourselves as researchers or authors, artists or biologists, chemists or musicians, philosophers or programmers, each of these subjectivities is but a fragment of a class still becoming, bit by bit, aware of itself as such. (Wark, 2004)

The Internet provides potential for a new form of production outside the existing market system; however, the open-access of the web poses a multitude of questions relating to authorship, copyright and privacy. The place of the digital thesis in this landscape could be seen as somewhat problematic. As an 'academic' piece of original work its presence (particularly solely) online, while having the potential to be easily accessed, also means it can be easily copied, edited, hacked and re-used. In zeppelinbend.com, this position is acknowledged and also forms an active part of the contextual framework of the research itself. Forms of appropriation from the Internet are utilised in both the making of the work and the critical context titled *Appropriation and the Hack*. As the creator of a website submission the author should consider that the work they upload has the possibility to be re-used itself as with any other website in the contemporary landscape of the Internet. The authenticity associated with original 'art work' in particular is challenged via www.zeppelinbend.com as the film works presented as part of the submission are deliberately unprotected and remain downloadable at source. In the same way that Benjamin (1983) described photography as a reproductive method that has the potential to destroy the aura of the traditional art object, the use of the internet to create and disseminate art can be seen as even more comprehensive in its ability to challenge the traditional notions of authenticity and value attached to material art objects. Importantly its seemingly effortless 'means of production' for replication, editing, copying and multiplying can devalue the 'original'.

'The place of writing is again in turmoil' (Hayles, 2008). This quotation from Hayles introduces her book *Electronic Literature* (2008) and is taken from the first chapter where she suggests that the idea of printed books and writing is currently under threat from electronic sources. The proliferation of Internet 'writing' from an increasing number of authors has resulted in an explosion of Internet text(s). In this jungle of words it can be difficult to decipher the worth of pieces of writing in their myriad of formats that the web enables, and as such online writing is deemed by many as inferior in its authority and authenticity.

A number of authors have embraced the potential of Internet publishing and have uploaded 'soft books' for readers to freely download. This also enables ease of 're-printing' and often the books can be in a continual state of flux. Manovich's (as yet unpublished at the time of writing) electronic book *Software Takes Command* (2008) states on the first page 'One of the advantages of online distribution which I can control is that I don't have to permanently fix the book's contents. Like contemporary software and web services, the book can change as often as I like, with new "features" and "big fixes" added periodically. I plan to take advantage of these possibilities. From time to time, I will be adding new material and making changes and corrections to the text' (Manovich, 2008). In the traditional PhD a log book or journal often records the journey of the PhD and also encourages a '... dialogue between researcher and supervisor and (is) a point of reference in reviewing progress and reflecting on further development of it' (Jones, 2009). Outside of the discipline of art and design this logging of the journey and maintaining lines of communication with supervisors that enable reflection is undertaken by a number of students currently utilising online technology to continually update their writing as it progresses. In this sense, their research journal is almost entirely digital. Belshaw[15] a researcher into new literacies and twenty-first-century education practices is studying for an EdD at Durham University titled *What is Digital Literacy: a pragmatic investigation*, due to complete in 2011[16]. Belshaw uses Google docs[17] to upload portions of his 60,000 word thesis periodically (each section is dated), which can then be commented on (with permission) and worked with fluidly as the thesis develops organically and in the public domain. Belshaw has also inserted links within the writing and that enable a reader to interrelate his concepts so that readers can return to earlier ideas or other sections of the writing where hyperlinked. This approach reflects the nature of the research question itself, the methods, processes and form of dissemination have an active relationship with digital literacy. This system also shares some similarities with a blog format[18], which moves away from a reading only experience, in that it asks for reader comments so that a reader can effectively become a writer via the commentary. Developing work that utilises blog formats might be considered as collaborative authorship with the potential to change not only the reading experience but to move away from sole authorial and intellectual property. These formats allow for a reading of the development of ideas by external parties and as such provide a vehicle to reconsider the 'summative' assessment of the digital submission, encouraging the possibility for an ongoing formative analysis. The desire to share research and to disseminate the unfinished work so that anyone can see the writing develop in this way is unusual within academia where the knowledge can be held as specialised.

The material thesis is read by select examiners and external interested parties with access to the material document available by request. Traditionally, material papers/essays in journals and PhD studies are measured by their distribution and impact within the field, so how might the dissemination of a digital thesis or submission be measured? The website PhD thesis expands the readership enabling vast potential through the audience of the web and facilitating an ease of access on a worldwide level via search engines[19]: '… web-based electronic publications are more available and more easily searched for useful information than *any* print text, even if that print text is right on the shelf in one's home or office' (Katz, 2004). The server with which the site is located will automatically log information ('hits') and this currently has the potential to measure unique visitors, time and duration of visit (even time spent on particular pages), geographical location and linkage to other sites, which could be a form of measuring the use and citation of the work. The opening up of access to scholarly works via websites allows for a freer dissemination of knowledge and can challenge the notion of specialised controlled documents with limited access. The potential to disseminate research on this scale can be both liberating and intimidating. Sharing the results of research to such a large audience potentially allows for peer review on an international scale and as an author one might be apprehensive in situating their work in this arena.

Most examples of digital theses discussed (including my own) have clearly stated viewing recommendations for the site, including browser versions and associated software requirements. This issue of access can be essential in maintaining the accessibility of the site and is also an aspect that cannot remain a 'fixed' element of the submission, as over time browsers evolve and so the digital thesis requires a technical support mechanism or ongoing 'maintenance', something a bound copy of a material submission will not require. This has led to a view that the online thesis is unstable as a long-term work. A particular concern is that hyperlinked websites contain links that may become broken over time (link rot) and particular aspects of multimodal approaches may need to be re-configured to be correctly displayed as generations of web browsers are updated and versions of software evolve. This is where periodic 'migration' (or upgrade) might be used, to update the site so that it functions on newer versions of software. This does necessitate a continued responsibility on the part of the author of the work (or assigned 'keepers'). This need for continual maintenance of websites has led some writers to describe the format as 'fragile' (Bostock, 2006).

There are a variety of strategies of preserving the longevity of websites and associated digital artworks that may form part of them and this issue has been the topic of ongoing extensive research within 'digital art'. One strategy specific to net art (online art/interactive art work) is the use of emulators:

> ... computer programs that 'recreate' the conditions of hardware, software, or operating systems, so that the original code can still run on a contemporary computer. The latter may work well for some projects and turn out to be problematic for others, which might still look 'dated' in their recreation: if the latest technology had been available to the artists at the time of the work's creation, they might have done a different project in the first place. (Paul, 2007)

With the development of net art various agencies have developed research initiatives that focus on the preservation of digital work[20] and it may be that as PhD submissions evolve into non-standard website submissions, similar initiatives are used to maintain, upgrade, preserve and document sites that exist outside the already defined digital theses repositories.

As an author of a digital online theses the interface becomes a crucial tool – readers may be approaching the submission from a less familiar standpoint and examiners who are used to the traditional thesis might look for parallels in the digital counterpart. In this sense, a consideration must be given to how it might be accessed by others, with differing experience, so that its future can be preserved for researchers. Access to a website submission is most likely to be via search engine generated results and the author of such a submission may have to program search engine optimisation tools such as meta-tag elements, which will provide information about the site and enable search engines to categorise the site efficiently. While the digital thesis that is uploaded to a portal may only be accessible via a particular site such as an online library or database, search engines rarely excavate as deep as this so called 'deep web'[21] meaning that the website submission is generally easier to locate and access.

CONCLUSION

There is much to be taken from the development of electronic literature and its interactive presentation methods in relation to the future of the online thesis. Experimental multimodal process utilised in online literature projects such as *The Jew's Daughter* by Morrissey, '... an interactive, non-linear, multi-valent narrative, a storyspace that is unstable but nonetheless remains organically intact, progressively weaving itself together by way of subtle transformations on a single virtual page' (Morrissey, 2000) pose different experimental and increasingly interactive possibilities for the online submission and specifically written components.

There are multiple possibilities in utilising the code that constructs web pages itself as a form of thesis[22]. Within electronic literature many precedents exist where embedded hidden information within the code works to activate the screen page but contains another layer of context and meaning for the work. This creative use of code might act as a further layer of potentiality functioning as discrete footnotes. The website format creates a space where, as discussed (in relation to literature) by Hayles (2008), a hybrid exists, the space becomes a '… trading zone … in which different vocabularies, expertises and expectations come together'. There is a multiplicity of experimental precedents within digital art and literature involving websites that activate the reader/user and involve text, however the 'trading zone' in which a PhD submission might be situated will need to involve the vocabulary of doctoral research and the expectation that it can be understood as such. Using a digital format is appropriate where it acts as an imperative tool in the progress, processes, methodology and presentation of the research itself. The website submission offers greater potential to reflect the hybrid nature of creative thought in art and design and can promote a greater depth of contextualisation and its form can reveal personal artistic vision.

As Katz (2004) states the future of the website PhD submission will no doubt evolve and potentially expand outside the confines of the arts and humanities and authors of such 'innovative' publications might be better placed in networked digital fuelled institutions of the future because they are '… comfortable producing, revising and using highly flexible electronic publications in their teaching and research'.

NOTES

1. The length of the written component of a practice-based PhD within art and design is dependent on individual institution protocols and these can vary widely within the UK.

2. Largely students undertaking doctoral research in art and design frame and relate the project to their own individual interests, differing from other disciplines which might attach doctoral study to a particular institutions stated area(s) of research or funded projects.

3. The aim of the ADT programme is to establish a distributed database of digital versions of theses produced by the postgraduate research students at Australian universities: http://adt.caul.edu.au

4. Judith Mottram (2009) states that the first art and design PhD on record in the UK is B.A. Chew (1957) 'Some recent British sculptors: a critical review' (University of Manchester).

5. For a more expansive historical overview of the development of art and design PhDs, see Mottram, J. (2009). Researching research in art and design. In J. Elkins (Ed.), *Artists with PhDs: On the New Doctoral Degree in Studio Art* (pp. 3–30). Washington, DC: New Academia Publishing.

6. It has been extremely difficult to obtain current information relating to the number of existing website submissions, as they slip between libraries and digital portals. The examples used have been suggested by other academics with knowledge of the students.

7. The website name/address itself is the title of the PhD, reflecting the fact that the website is the PhD.

8. 'Spitfire Beach' was a week-long project that took place during February 2010 in the T1 Project Space at The University of Huddersfield and involved an exploration of sculpture and film through the use of Airfix model aeroplane kits. This project culminated in a film work titled *Spitfire Beach* (2010).

9. The archive is an interactive ever-expanding digital archive that explores the notion of connecting the unconnected, using combinations of mundane and unusual objects, text, images and film. Information contained within its

web pages is both fictional and factual, using Internet search engines and my own writing to weave a network of associations.

10. Potentially useful in gathering proof of the fixed submission is the Internet Archive's 'Wayback Machine', a continually growing archive of the internet at given dates, meaning that previous versions of sites can be viewed. The Internet Archive Wayback Machine contains almost 2 petabytes of data and is currently growing at a rate of 20 terabytes per month. This eclipses the amount of text contained in the world's largest libraries, including the Library of Congress, http://www.archive.org

11. The development of the term 'hypertext' is associated with Vannevar Bush who wrote an article in *Atlantic Monthly* in 1945 where he called for '… mechanically linked information-retrieval machines to help scholars and decision makers faced with what was already becoming an explosion of information' (Landow, 2006, p. 9).

12. It is important to note the geographic siting of Donna Leishman's website submission. Leishman's PhD website 'Creating screen-based multiple state environments: investigating systems of confutation' (2004) is a clearly placed separate entity within a larger website that documents her previous and subsequent practice, but it not part of the actual submission itself.

13. Leishman's site also contains 'snapshots' of the website as it evolved over the period of the doctoral research, allowing a reader to see the development of the interface and its relationship to the work.

14. A similar view on the value attached to digital/electronic art works opposed to object material-based practices exists.

15. Doug Belshaw's research was found via a search on Twitter.

16. Available at: http://www.dougbelshaw.com/thesis/

17. Google documents allow you to upload documents (with a Google account) to a website, where you can access them at any time to edit and it also allows for real-time collaboration.

18. Belshaw also provides links via the Google doc thesis to a less formal blog where the narrative and thoughts relating to the development of the project are described in a reflective personal manner.

19. Search engine manufacturers have developed tools designed for scholarship with engines such as Google Scholar:

> Google Scholar provides a simple way to broadly search for scholarly literature. From one place, you can search across many disciplines and sources: articles, theses, books, abstracts and court opinions, from academic publishers, professional societies, online repositories, universities and other web sites. Google Scholar helps you find relevant work across the world of scholarly research http://scholar.google.co.uk/intl/en/scholar/about.html

20. Variable Media Network: http://www.variablemedia.net/ http://www.bampfa.berkeley.edu/ciao/avant_garde.html is an example of one.

21. 'With an estimated 500 billion webpages hidden from search engines, companies like Google and Yahoo have entered into agreements with major libraries to index their collections' (Landow, 2006, p. 39).

22. Currently, an online thesis itself can only be viewed on a screen when the code is at work.

REFERENCES

Aarseth, E. J. (1997). *Cybertext: Perspectives on Ergodic Literature.* Baltimore, MD: The John Hopkins University Press.

Benjamin, W. (1983). *The Author as Producer in Understanding Brecht.* London: Verso.

Bolter, D. (1991). *Writing Space: The Computer, Hypertext and the History of Writing.* Mahwah, NJ: Lawrence Erlbaum Associates.

Bourriaud, N. (2002). *Postproduction Culture as Screenplay: How Art Reprograms the World.* New York: Lukas & Sternberg.

Bostock, W. (2006). The challenge of the paperless thesis: Issues in the implementation of a regime of electronic theses and dissertation. In T. Nguyen & D. S. Preston (Eds.), *Virtuality and Education: A Reader.* New York: Rodopi Press.

Calvino, I. (1988). *Six Memos for the Next Millennium.* New York: Vintage.

Eco, U. (1986). *Semiotics and the Philosophy of Language.* Bloomington, IN: Indiana University Press.

Elkins, J. (2009). *Artists with PhD's: On the New Doctoral Degree in Studio Art.* Washington, DC: New Academia Publishing.

Fleishman, D. (2004). *Creating Screen-based Multiple State Environments: Investigating Systems of Confutation.* Scotland, UK: University of Glasgow, http://www.6amhoover.com/viva/

Hayles, N. K. (2008). *Electronic Literature: New Horizons for the Literary.* Notre Dame, IN: University of Notre Dame Press.

Jones, T. E. (2009). Research degrees in art and design. In J. Elkins (Ed.), *Artists with PhD's: On the New Doctoral Degree in Studio Art.* Washington, DC: New Academia Publishing.

Katz, S. (2004). Innovative hypermedia ETDs and employment in the humanities. In *Electronic Theses and Dissertations: A Sourcebook for Educators, Students and Librarians.* New York: Marcel Dekker Inc.

Landow, G. P. (2006). *Hypertext 3.0: Critical Theory and New Media in an Era of Globalization.* Baltimore, MD: The John Hopkins University Press.

Manovich, L. (2002). *The Language of New Media.* Cambridge, MA: The MIT Press.

Morrissey, J. (2000). *The Jew's Daughter.* http://judisdaid.com/thejewsdaughter/

Mottram, J. (2009). Researching research in art and design. In J. Elkins (Ed.), *Artists with PhD's: On the New Doctoral Degree in Studio Art* (pp. 3–30). Washington, DC: New Academia Publishing.

Paul, C. (2007). *Challenges for a Ubiquitous Museum: Presenting and Preserving New Media.* http://www.neme.org/main/571/preserving-new-media

Stansbie, L. (2010). *Zeppelinbend: Multiplicity, Encyclopaedic Strategies and Nonlinear Methodologies for a Visual Practice.* Leeds Metropolitan University, http://www.zeppelinbend.com

Wark, M. (2004). *A Hacker Manifesto.* Cambridge, MA: The MIT Press.

Weinberger, D. (2008). The morality of links. In J. Throw & L. Tsui (Eds.), *The Hyperlinked Society: Questioning Connections in the Digital Age.* Ann Arbor, MI: University of Michigan Press.

Research Methods

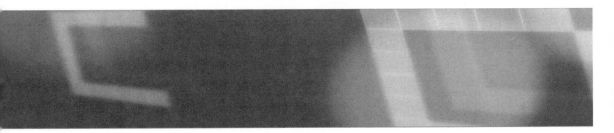

The final section of the Handbook opens with Snyder and Beale's broad view of the cultural, institutional and national perspectives that shape a research environment, moves through Wilson's analysis of the changes in meaning-making produced by technologies and modes of representation, and focuses on the issues encountered by Vasudevan and DeJaynes in their own research, especially the multiple literacies required to deal with disparate digital media. Follwing Yee's analysis of changes generated by practice-centred research, a discussion vividly illustrated by individual recent doctoral dissertations, Nuhn concludes by probing the issues raised by his doctoral research.

It would be easy to imagine that the shift to digital technologies for inquiry, representation and dissemination might be the most important influence on the modern PhD. Snyder and Beale paint a corrective picture, showing the complex influences on national and individual institutional practice of tradition, local and wider competition for prestige, for income and for completions and the interaction between state policies for the economy and for education. They show how the debate about the nature of the PhD has been concerned with whether it principally develops a product (an original contribution to knowledge) or a person (the newly skilled researcher).

They set their own Australian experience in its international context. National characteristics include the strong influence of government which has historically provided much of the financial support for research degrees and which desires a system which will benefit the economy. Years of rapid growth in enrolments for higher degrees are now under threat from financial and political pressures. Digital technologies have wrought several changes. They have made dissertations rapidly available internationally; Monash University (Snyder and Beale's own institution) has led the ARROW project, making theses and other research outputs searchable and available over the Web. The speed of digital collaboration has facilitated the university's involvement in international education, where study across multiple sites is now a reality. The shift to digital has a clear role in influencing the character of doctoral programmes, but it is the complex ecology of people, institutional frameworks and governments that determines how the technologies are used.

Amy Alexandra Wilson's discussion of the changes in meaning-making induced by the shift to the digital is focused on three questions. How do digital media afford and constrain the expression of content? What happens to the author's message when data are resemiotised? How might this resemiotisation influence the learning of the author of the dissertation or thesis? Wilson approaches this through consideration of four kinds of modal change. She presents two opposing aspects of the digital. On the one hand, optimism that digital texts may have greater semiotic potential for conveying certain types of messages when compared with printed texts, offering multiple changing combinations that the student can select to most fully support an argument or establish expertise within the field. On the other hand, there is concern at the many constraints. These can be local concerns such as an individual's lack of familiarity with available technologies, lack of access or lack of training in how to use them to create a variety of representations. But the constraints of digital media may also be due to the nature of screens themselves: electronic formats can limit the types of knowledge that a graduate can demonstrate because they suppress materiality, smell, taste and other qualities, and because of their tendency to abstract the object of interest from its spatial and other contexts.

What counts as knowledge, including the methods by which one can legitimately obtain it and demonstrate it, are crucial to the selection of modes of representation. Depending on the student's field and the communication objectives, some combinations of modes will enable the clear and compelling expression necessary to the thesis more fully than others. It may also mediate the development of the student as he or she is able to think about a subject in a more complex and generative way. The effects on the student are fundamental to the perspective of Lalitha Vasudevan and Tiffany DeJaynes. They have both researched the multiple media literacies in the lives of adolescents, increasingly characterised by virtual explorations, multimedia self-representations and digital mediation. They argue that in ethnographic research focused on these multimodal practices of meaning-making and knowing, their subjects are themselves engaged in the research as documentarians and co-investigators. Digital technologies, far from introducing any kind of homogeneity, have led to communication formats which are not only varied but are enmeshed one with another. Meaning-making takes place across modes, spaces and times. To the stationary and handheld video game consoles, televisions, cameras and computers of a few years ago have been added blogging, instant messaging, media-making and social networking. How can one engage in research within this hybridised information economy? The authors' research involved multimodal research protocols that they designed and shaped iteratively as their work progressed. When media technologies are in the highly active hands of the subjects of the research, the authors argue, any pre-definition of the limits of the site would be untruthful to the nature of what turns out to be going on.

As new forms of literacy become evident in the subjects, so new literacies are also required of the researcher. Within these media-saturated research spaces, new forms of data collection emerge. New formalisms are called for to represent and analyse interconnections, relationships, texts, identities and communicative patterns. The authors found themselves compelled to amend (and sometimes altogether redesign) their initial research protocols in response to their encounters with the collective and interwoven nature of the literacy practices they had set out to examine, especially in relation to their digital practices.

Joyce Yee's analysis of the changes in research models within design is of interest both within and beyond that discipline. Though Yee argues the emergence of distinctive designerly ways of thinking (and potentially therefore of researching), many other scholarly communities will also be interested by the efforts of the design community to develop its research culture and to identify appropriate forms of inquiry and representation. Using recently completed design dissertations as exemplars, Yee describes four possible characteristics of designerly enquiry: 'bricolage', reflective practices, visual approaches and thesis-structural innovation. In research inspired by bricolage, multiple methods adopted from different disciplines enable the researcher to compare and contrast multiple points of view. This allows researchers to deploy available and established strategies and methods, but also grants them the license to create new tools and techniques. At the heart of the chapter, Yee looks at the role of practice. Is practice in itself a research method? Perhaps practice alone cannot constitute research, reflection on the work being essential in order for design knowledge to be validated? But by contrast, examples are offered where designing is itself a critique of current design and consumption practices, with little need for textual exegesis. These invite consideration of how design practices can succeed in being both productive and reflexive.

Visual approaches of course are not unique to design, but Yee argues that the visual has a distinctive place in design research, supporting reflection and exploration, analysis and knowledge-generation, communication and discussion. Visuals are used by the designer–researcher for private exploration and knowledge construction as much as for communicating to others. Looking at the structure of the dissertation, Yee juxtaposes exemplars for and against linearity, for and against the dominance of words and of novel physical forms. The implications are discussed for two of the key characteristics associated with academic research: rigour and validity. How do traditional notions of rigour sit with the nature of design and practice? Thinking pragmatically about validity, if the design dissertation is to be *useful*, perhaps it needs to communicate to other designers using forms to which they are receptive. Whether something 'works' in this sense acquires a higher value than traditional notions of truth. Yee concludes with a plea that, though perhaps aimed at the design community, might apply to any area of research. In the spirit of bricolage we need to be constantly on the lookout for methods which can be adopted, adapted and made appropriate to our own fields. The shift to the digital is one among many influences which should cause us to rethink what we believe we know.

Finally, Ralf Nuhn's chapter expresses the views of a researcher and artist on the interface between the dissertation or thesis, and the artwork itself. It looks at the tensions and possibilities between, on the one hand, the production of a verbal, textual thesis; and on the other, the creation of six interactive installations. Further tensions are explored between the 'real' and the 'virtual', and the chapter goes on to reflect on mixed mode research. With its strong visual presence, captured in the final image of the present handbook, the chapter serves as a fitting conclusion to the section and the handbook as a whole.

23

A Modern PhD: Doctoral Education in Australian Universities in Digital Times

Ilana Snyder and Denise Beale

INTRODUCTION

'Global rethink on PhD as it loses its relevance' was the headline in the higher education supplement of the *Australian Financial Review* (Mather, 2010). Although the broadsheet is aimed at a particular audience, the provocative words encapsulate several key aspects of recent academic debates, in Australia and elsewhere, that have focused on the future of the PhD. They suggest that the recognised international qualification is threatened with marginalisation unless it changes to suit new times in which digital technologies are ubiquitous, at least in the developed world and knowledge generation is at a premium. In the article, Mather represents the PhD as a superseded, highly specialised prerequisite for an academic career. Recent graduates, she argues, are seeking careers outside academia, only to find that employers are disappointed with their level of skills, particularly their ability to communicate and collaborate with others in the workplace, a 'problem apparent globally'. As the institutions responsible for doctoral education, universities are faced with a demand for change.

However, the Financial Review's depiction of the PhD as outmoded needs interrogating. The suggestion of 'a simplistic dichotomy between "before" and "now" is a linguistic construct which is "suspiciously similar to a pre-modern/ modern" framing that assumes a linear progression to development' (Pearson,

Evans, & Macauley, 2008, p. 369). The impulse to explain the history of the PhD as a neat series of chronologically and causally linked events is problematic. History presented in this way may be comforting in its familiarity and apparently illuminating but it is a construct. Such concerns over doctoral programmes are not new: scrutiny of the PhD and its purposes has been undertaken by the OECD since 1987, in the USA for longer and in Australia, at least since 1989 (NBEET, 1992).

Changes to the nature of the PhD have been constant over the last twenty years in universities around the world, even though those changes have often been gradual, incremental or piecemeal due to the complex nature of universities, the institutional frameworks within which they are embedded and their multiple stakeholders. On the one hand, universities respond to changing circumstances, including shifts in demand, the introduction of new technologies, government policy and the movements of institutional actors, but, on the other, they also anticipate and plan for change to enhance their prestige and influence (Marginson, 2007).

While offering new possibilities, the use of digital technologies in doctoral education challenges existing structures and relationships. But in the main digital technologies have been employed to provide resources and services which underpin student and staff learning and to distribute the results of research more widely through electronic publication of doctoral theses. Although the use of digital technologies in these ways has been accompanied by debate over the nature of the doctoral thesis, its ownership, the creation of new knowledge and what constitutes publication (Lang, 2002), the use of digital technologies to create new thesis formats is a reality in only a small number of disciplines.

In the renewed debate over the PhD there is considerable commonality in the 'forces and forms' (Nerad & Heggelund, 2008) creating pressures on institutions to initiate change within programmes. These pressures vary from country to country and within countries which is at least partly explained by the geopolitical reality: while universities compete internationally, they also contend with each other nationally and at a more local level (Marginson, 2007). Digital technologies are employed by universities in this competition but governments, which in Australia includes both federal and states and territories, also play a powerful role in shaping information and communications infrastructures and the purposes for which they are used.

As a settler society, Australian policy makers and institutional leaders have traditionally adopted ideas from overseas, initially from the UK and more recently from the US and other sources. The ideas are then modified to suit local circumstances and further reworked as they are applied in particular contexts (Walter, 2010). For Australia, digital technologies offer considerable opportunities to surmount the barriers of time and distance, yet that same distance means that the application of these technologies in institutional contexts can often take place after their development and implementation overseas. In this chapter, we illustrate how these patterns can play out in a case study of doctoral reform in a major

Australian university, Monash University. Monash plans to introduce a new 'modern PhD' programme at the beginning of 2012 to be rolled out over a period of two years. The analysis identifies the complex interplay of local, national and international influences and ideas that shaped the reform and their adaptation to meet the strategic goals of the institution at a particular point in its history. However, before the focus shifts to the reform agenda at Monash, some background details about global and national trends are discussed.

DOCTORAL EDUCATION'S GLOBAL TRAJECTORY

Recognised as stemming from the Humboldtian university of nineteenth century Germany, the PhD has become over time a university's pre-eminent research qualification (Pearson, 2005). Although adopted at different historical points in different countries and modified to suit particular circumstances, it is almost universally accepted: the PhD 'lies at the core of a university's research capacity'(Nerad, Trzyna, & Heggelund, 2008, p. 3). PhD candidates contribute to a university's research output but their enrolment is also tied up with its status and prestige, with the number of doctoral students being one measure of a university's research intensity. Universities are nested within a complex and interlocking system of stakeholders, regulatory bodies including governments, with histories, established relationships, practices and varying levels of resources.

It is within the very density and complexity of these frameworks that the challenge of digital technologies is negotiated and new practices emerge which build on the old (McKitterick, 2003). Universities develop strategies to build their reputations locally, nationally and internationally (Marginson, 2007), which also enhances their ability to attract talented new doctoral candidates. At a time of intensifying global competition between universities for capable staff and research students, with the expansion of existing universities and the entry of new ones from many different countries, reputation is an important guide to quality (Marginson & Considine, 2000). As the doctorate lies at the heart of a university's purpose, to change it is to run the risk of affecting the quality of the PhD on offer and thus the reputation of the awarding university.

Despite the risks involved, debate continues over the meaning of the PhD and its purpose, which is evident in the terms used to designate it, a point Park makes about the UK context: '[I]n recent years the UK doctorate has been reconceptualised as a training period for future researchers, rather than a piece of work that changes the course of human knowledge' (2007, p. 30). In part this reflects the dual nature of the PhD, but also the different perspectives and interests at play. Doctoral candidates gain their knowledge through research, a process of training in the methods of research in the academy which enables them to enter the workforce, possibly as researchers in universities. 'Research training', as it is widely known, can also include research Masters degrees and postdoctoral studies.

The term 'research training' is not without its critics, who deplore its vocational and instrumental connotations (Boud & Tennant, 2006). The critics point out that the term privileges government and institutional agendas rather than those of candidates, supervisors and departments. It also highlights the increasingly central nature of the university in modern societies and the primacy accorded to knowledge generation and certification, particularly at the PhD level. Universities control doctoral selection, curricula, examinations and the award of the degree. They determine the degree of change within their doctoral programmes, responding to multiple stakeholders: staff, students, professional associations, external research organisations, industry and governments (Prewett, 2006).

Growing international competitiveness and the struggle for national advantage have seen research and knowledge generation, particularly in the sciences, prioritised and linked with national innovation strategies. As a result, university research and the education of new doctoral graduates have become the targets of greater government attention and regulation, 'as the primary source of research productivity and innovation in the global knowledge economy' (Nerad et al., 2008, p. 3).

The impetus for change in doctoral programmes has received much attention from scholars. Broadly, the forces come from government policy, globalisation and internationalisation, new knowledge growth and organisation and new technologies. It is this final category that is of particular interest in a chapter focused on doctoral reform in digital times. As a driver of change, new technologies include transport technologies, and computer and communications technologies, which enable the mobility of staff, students and new ideas, as well as a new means of generating and disseminating knowledge.

While doctoral forms have undergone considerable changes, Nerad makes the point that 'many innovations are still largely local, and changes in practices are not broadly understood' (2008, p. 294). In the next section, we briefly explore recent thinking about doctoral programmes in the US, the UK and Europe. We then turn to Australia to look at Monash University's doctoral reform agenda.

CONTEMPORARY THINKING ABOUT DOCTORAL PROGRAMMES IN THE NORTH

The US model of the doctorate is widely regarded as the standard to which other countries aspire, attracting students from around the world (Altbach, 2007; Marginson & van der Wende, 2007). The US PhD is diverse, but typically includes a compulsory coursework component, which is examined, as well as a dissertation (Altbach, 2007). Over the past twenty years, newer forms of doctorates, such as professional doctorates, have been introduced, responding to concerns over PhD programmes and the preparation of graduates (Nerad, 2008). Considerable debate within the US continues over the PhD and different initiatives have been introduced from within the academic profession to examine ways of instituting change, such as the 'Carnegie Initiative on the Doctorate', 'Re-envisioning the PhD' and 'The Responsive PhD' (Nerad, 2008). However, the position of the US as the global leader in the field of doctoral education has made change less of an imperative than in other countries (Marginson & van der Wende, 2007). Notably, the role of government policy in the US is accorded less importance in the discussion of the purpose and shape of PhD programmes than in many other countries.

By contrast, in the UK, at a time of increasing demand for postgraduate qualifications from both domestic and international students (Green, 2008), the government plays a greater role in regulating the standards and quality of PhD programmes (Park, 2007). New forms of the doctorate in the UK have become more common, including doctorates by publication, professional doctorates and doctorates with taught elements (Green, 2008). For government, the sciences have been a particular focus, with Doctoral Training Centres, an initiative of the EPSRC (Engineering and Physical Sciences Research Council), established to increase the numbers of PhD students from 2009 working in the engineering and physical science fields on particular projects with an interdisciplinary emphasis. A four-year PhD programme includes coursework as part of the students' assessment. The centres aim to increase the numbers of doctoral graduates and to develop graduates with skills that are valued in industry and research (EPSRC, 2010).

New elements such as courses which offer candidates skills training have been incorporated to reflect concerns from government and industry that the skills of doctoral graduates are too narrowly focused for the workplace (Green, 2008). One aim has been to develop graduates in ways that 'further their personal and professional development' (Denicolo, 2007, p. 246). Debate over assessment of the PhD has accompanied such change, posing the question as to whether assessment should focus solely 'on the product (thesis) or the process (developing the researcher)' or a 'balance … between the two' (Park, 2007, p. 32). Green notes that UK institutions have been particularly reticent in their adoption of electronic means for thesis submission and dissemination, even though 'wider and quicker access to research findings … will bring benefits both in terms of spreading the knowledge base and in increasing the transparency of standards of doctoral work across international borders' (2008, p. 67). However, as with the US, the reputation of the UK doctorate is well-established and the pressures for change limited (Green, 2008).

In continental Europe, the diversity of institutions and forms of doctoral education is even greater, rooted in historical, national and regional traditions. Moves to work towards comparability of European degrees began in 1998, driven by a small group of countries and formalised in the Bologna Declaration of 1999 (Marginson & van der Wende, 2007). The involvement of the European Union, which viewed higher education as the key to regaining economic competitiveness at a time of increasing global competition, saw commitment to the Lisbon Strategy of 2000 (Marginson & van der Wende, 2007). Now known as the

Bologna Process, measures to 'harmonise' degree structures and standards of assessment involve a larger number of countries, forty-five as compared with the twenty-five members of the EU (Bartelse & Huisman, 2008). Initially focused on undergraduate education, then master's level, since 2003 attention has shifted to doctoral education as part of the third cycle (Bitusikova, 2009). As Kehm remarks, 'the generation of new knowledge has become an important strategic resource' (2007, p. 308).

European governments consider it essential to increase the numbers of doctoral students (Bitusikova, 2009). The length of doctoral candidature and the consequent later entry of graduates to the workforce are key concerns in the EU. Graduates' preparedness for their future careers is also at issue (Kehm, 2007; Marginson & van der Wende, 2007). The Bologna Process has been influential in bringing about new strategies to reform the doctorate, with the proposal for a 'modern PhD' by LERU, the League of European Research Universities, one such example. LERU sets out the ways in which PhD programmes should change to equip future graduates with the knowledge and skills required in diverse and complex environments. However, at the core of the modern PhD remains the importance of 'a significant original contribution to knowledge' through research (Bogle, 2010, p. 3).

While PhD programmes continue to be re-examined in the US, the UK and Europe, the role of digital technologies has come under less scrutiny. Although the rapid incorporation of digital technologies into society offers considerable opportunities for change within higher education institutions, they have been adopted primarily as enabling technologies. In doctoral programmes, digital technologies are used in the main to support research and learning and to distribute and disseminate the results of such learning.

The digital dissemination of doctoral dissertations was regarded as a way to expand access to the new knowledge produced by doctoral graduates (Lang, 2002). Since the 1990s, a number of programmes have been developed in different countries to create electronic repositories of dissertations and to make these available to scholars and other students via the Internet through portals which bring together university libraries, for instance, the NDLTD (Networked Digital Library of Theses and Dissertations) in the US (Edminster & Moxley, 2002), the DART–Europe (Digital Access to Research Theses – Europe) (Moyle, 2008) and the ADT (Australian Digital Theses) Programme in Australia (Wells & Cargnelutti, 2004).

The development and use of such repositories have raised important questions for doctoral students, supervisors, librarians, editors and publishers, as well as for the institutions that house them, related to intellectual property, copyright, archiving, authorship and status as publication (Lang, 2002). Another question is about the nature of such knowledge, whether it is private or public (Edminster & Moxley, 2002). Despite the new possibilities afforded by digital media, the form and format of theses have not been significantly altered. The focus has been on the challenges the digital form presents: the examination of electronic theses compared with those in print, their permanence in a rapidly evolving digital environment (Bellamy, 2005), authorship, particularly in collaborative research projects and limited experimentation with the possibilities of the new medium (Auld, 2005). The high-stakes nature of the PhD examination process means that candidates, supervisors and institutions are sensitive to questions relating to standards and authority (Libner & Morgan, 2004).

In Australia, global models have had considerable influence (Marginson, 2002) and, while individual institutions are often innovative, in high-stakes competition when Australia has much to lose, established conventions offer a safer path forward. The models for reconceptualisation of the PhD with most influence are those which have already been elaborated in the US, the UK and Europe, amongst them the Bologna Process (Birtwistle, 2009; DEST, 2007) and LERU's 'modern PhD'. Aspects of the 'modern PhD' and the UK's doctoral training centres are evident in the model proposed by Monash University. Also evident is the way in which digital technologies are primarily approached: as a means to support doctoral research and learning and distribute dissertations.

DOCTORAL EDUCATION IN THE AUSTRALIAN CONTEXT

The Australian higher education system now comprises thirty-nine universities and a number of other higher education institutions, the majority comprehensive public universities (Australian Government, 2008). Established mostly by state charter, they have been funded and regulated by the federal government since 1974. The growth of university education in Australia is a relatively recent phenomenon which is easy to overlook. The risk is to impose a sense of 'tradition' on the PhD in Australia which does not exist (Pearson, 2005, p. 121). The first universities were founded in the nineteenth century, with newer universities established from the late 1950s (Evans, Evans, & Marsh, 2008). However, it was not until the late 1940s that the first Australian PhD programme was introduced at the University of Melbourne at a time when Australians went abroad for doctoral education (Marginson, 2002; Pearson, 2005). In the context of limited access to upper levels of secondary education, and with only an élite attaining an undergraduate tertiary education, the numbers of doctoral students were few indeed. In 1950, only eight PhDs were conferred in Australia (Evans et al., 2008).

As in many other western countries, the growth of education in Australia in the post-war years was profound. Government policy in the 1950s and 1960s was directed to the expansion of secondary education and higher education to meet labour force demands in the professions, as well as to accommodate rising demand for education in the population (Marginson, 2000). However, even with the establishment of new universities in the 1950s and 1960s, until the late 1960s, the majority of students gaining higher education remained an élite. Doctoral education was not a government priority, although the number of doctoral students grew as a direct result of the increase in undergraduates in the 1960s and 1970s. By 1980, the number of PhD completions had risen to 836 (Evans et al., 2008).

In the 1980s, higher education increasingly became the target of government policy to reduce its costs to government in the context of expanded provision, but also to link it to national priorities in an effort to increase economic competitiveness through the development of a skilled workforce (HEC, 1989). The expansion of postgraduate research and research training was seen as providing 'research trained graduates' for future careers in higher education institutions, but also in other sectors such as government and industry (NBEET, 1992, p. 5). Nevertheless, there were limits to the desired expansion which could be funded by government. Declining real levels of government funding meant that universities had to find other sources to offset the loss, including student fees from levies on domestic undergraduates, but particularly from full fees charged to international students and domestic students undertaking professionally related courses.

The growth of universities' research capacities was only partially funded by government. Across Australia, privately funded professional postgraduate programmes for both domestic and international students subsidised research and teaching. Doctoral completions by domestic students between 1997 and 2008 grew by 66 per cent. For international students, who are privately funded, doctoral completions in 2008 rose by 102 per cent from 1997, comprising 22 per cent of total doctoral completions in 2008 (DEEWR, 2009). In 2008, doctoral completions, expressed as a ratio of bachelor degree completions for all students, was just over 4 per cent, a figure comparable with that in the US (Nerad, 2008), which represents an enormous expansion in a little over fifty years.

In Australia, government policy plays a powerful role in the higher education sector, particularly in matters relating to research training, through resourcing and accountability requirements (DEST, 2007), and with federal government funding comprising 86 per cent of university research expenditure in 2002–2003 (DEST, 2007), its leverage is substantial. Between 1999 and 2004, new federal funding policy measures limited growth in domestic doctoral enrolments, with the result that institutions developed strategies to manage doctoral candidature to assist completions (Evans et al., 2008), at the same time as targeting increased enrolments of international doctoral students (for example, Monash University, 2000).

In 2009, under a new government, a renewed focus on innovation and its connection to research in the higher education sector has resulted in pressure to lift the number of doctoral enrolments for two primary purposes: to ensure that new research-qualified graduates will be available to replace the aging academic workforce (Australian Government, 2009b) and to provide research training for those doctoral graduates who enter other research facilities, industry or government (Australian Government, 2009a). Overall, the majority of doctorate holders are employed in the public sector (Edwards, Radloff & Coates, 2009). The available data suggest that the higher education sector employs the single largest share of doctorate holders, 25.9 per cent (Edwards et al., 2009). The number holding doctorates employed in the sciences outside the higher education sector represents the next largest group with 18 per cent holding doctorates. Other sectors employ small percentages, from 6 per cent to approximately 1 per cent (Edwards et al., 2009).

A much larger proportion of Australians now achieve a tertiary education, with 32 per cent of those aged 25 to 34 holding a bachelor degree (Australian Government, 2009a) and 5786 doctoral completions in 2008 (DEEWR, 2009). Following a review of the tertiary education sector by the incoming federal government, in 2009 and 2010 reforms to funding and accountability measures were announced and a target set to increase student participation, particularly from disadvantaged groups, with the goal that '40 per cent of all 25 to 34 year olds will hold a qualification at bachelor level or above' (Australian Government, 2009a, p. 12). At the same time, the government noted 'a critical need to attract greater numbers of Higher Degree by Research (HDR) students to address the shortage of research-qualified staff entering the academic labour market' (2009a, p. 25).

The preparation of new doctoral graduates has become a priority for the government to enable it to achieve its higher education agenda. New funding allocated for research training will support larger numbers of research students for periods of candidature of up to four years, six months longer than was previously the case (Australian Government, 2009a). Incentives are thus provided for universities to add more research training places, to improve programmes to attract research students and thereby add to their standing, as well as increasing the numbers of potential staff available for future recruitment.

THE MODERN PhD AT MONASH UNIVERSITY

The state of Victoria's first university, the University of Melbourne, was founded in 1853 for the education of the élite. Rising demand for tertiary education in the period directly after WWII led to the foundation of Monash University, Victoria's second, in 1958 at the instigation of the federal government (Marginson, 2000). The circumstances of its foundation meant that Monash was strongly influenced by and responsive to government policy (Marginson, 2000). Incorporated within the Act that established Monash was the academic standard which prevailed at the University of Melbourne (Marginson, 2000): 'the new university was competing with another university whose approach was dominant in the city' (Marginson, 2000, p. 13). From its foundation, government policy and the University of Melbourne have been the most powerful influences on Monash and the policies it has adopted, although also mediated by international developments.

Monash saw rapid growth in its student body. By 1985, it was the fifth biggest university in Australia and by the early 1990s, Monash had achieved a strong reputation for research. Mergers with other institutions in the period between

1988 and 1995 enlarged Monash considerably but it was a testing process in which attention was focused internally until the end of the 1990s. Its more diverse student and staff bodies and the decentralisation of its campuses necessitated innovative approaches to teaching, learning and research in the context of federal funding constraints on higher education and the establishment of new accountability requirements. One outcome was a decline in research performance in the context of new government funding schemes which distributed grants on a competitive basis, advantaging universities that concentrated on scientific research rather than research across a broad range of disciplines (Marginson, 2000).

Constrained government funding for higher education and policy changes encouraged the enrolment of full fee-paying international and domestic students in coursework postgraduate programmes in universities throughout Australia, a policy which remains contested (Marginson, 2007). The expansion of such coursework programmes was one way for Monash to achieve growth, with the number of students enrolled in graduate and postgraduate courses increasing by 138 per cent between 1998 and 2009 (Monash University, 2002a, 2010a). In the late 1990s, the extra funding provided by students enrolled in these courses allowed Monash to direct sustained attention to postgraduate research studies, at the faculty and discipline level as well as at the administrative level. Coursework components were approved for PhD programmes in several disciplines as well as external modes of study (Monash University, 1998).

In 1999, Monash established a graduate school, Monash Research Graduate School (MRGS), to centralise and standardise postgraduate research policy, consider the development of new programmes and provide administrative services, important in a university with multiple campuses (Monash University, 2000). Its focus was on the improvement of postgraduate learning through the provision of workspaces for students, seminars in particular skill areas (exPERT programme) which were conceived as 'employment and research training' programmes and workshops for supervisors (Monash University, 2000, p. 25). New scholarships and funding mechanisms developed within the university, subsidised by full fee-paying courses in other programmes, aimed to offer further support to the most talented postgraduate research students (Monash University, 2000). At the same time, high rates of growth did not necessarily translate into improved research performance and exposed the university to new vulnerabilities, in particular, through a greater reliance on international student fees to fund research.

From 2001, when the growth of domestic HDR students was effectively capped by federal funding policy, strategies focused on ways to assist students to complete their studies and a confirmation process was introduced at the end of the first year of candidature (Monash University, 2002b). Recognition that a lower share of research students would affect research performance saw Monash target growth in postgraduate enrolments from international students, with the aim to increase the number of international doctoral students by 100 per cent in four years (Monash University, 2000). Programmes to accredit supervisors began in 2002. The MRGS programmes of skills development continued to expand, prompted in part, as in other universities, by government requirements (Borthwick & Wissler, 2003). PhD theses by publication were recognised and new programmes were added (Monash University, 2003). In 2008, agreements with overseas institutions for joint PhD programmes were signed, with the first students commencing in 2009 (Monash University, 2008a, 2009).

With these initiatives, Monash reacted to one set of pressures over which it had little control, those external to the institution. But it also acted to enhance its capacity to meet changing circumstances, including within the institution itself, and to distinguish itself from its primary competitor, the University of Melbourne, which attracted both a larger number and a larger share of research students with nearly 9 per cent of its total student load enrolled in HDR programmes in 2009. By contrast, at Monash, the equivalent share was just under 6 per cent in 2009 (Monash University, 2002a, 2010a; University of Melbourne, 2010). The focus on the expansion of undergraduate education and on fee-paying postgraduate awards saw considerable growth in these areas, but between 2002 and 2008, domestic HDR student enrolments saw little change. The completion rate of research students in the other Group of Eight universities (an association of the leading research-intensive universities in Australia of which Monash is a member) continued to outstrip that at Monash (DEEWR, 2009), with the University of Melbourne ranking first in the country for research completions between 2000 and 2009. To improve the completion rates of existing HDR students, Monash expanded the suite of programmes offered by the Monash Research Graduate School and introduced two further milestones in addition to the confirmation process at the end of the first year (Monash University, 2003). New types of PhD programmes were offered in several disciplines, for instance, professional doctorates such as the Doctor of Business Administration (DBA) as well as cotutelle doctoral programmes (Monash University, 2002b) and new scholarships to attract doctoral candidates, particularly international students (Monash University, 2001, 2009).

Digital technologies have been employed progressively to assist in the dissemination of students' research, to provide information, resources and services to support research students and allow them to access them via the internet. Since July 2005, all doctoral students are required to publish their theses electronically after examination to disseminate the results of the research more widely (MRGS, 2010a). The doctoral theses are made available via ARROW (Australian Research Repositories Online to the World), an open access digital archive that provides central storage and public access to Monash University's research publications. Monash candidates enrolled in PhDs in Visual Arts, Creative Writing and Music Composition are required to submit an exegesis electronically, which may be accompanied by multimedia presentations. PhDs under a cotutelle arrangement are exempt from submitting an e-thesis, although they can elect to submit voluntarily. Students can also opt to restrict access to their theses and/or initiate a full embargo which applies for three years in the first instance.

In addition to students' theses, ARROW contains accepted versions of academics' published works such as books, book chapters, journal articles and conference papers. Non-published manuscripts and grey literature such as technical reports, working and discussion papers, and conference posters are also collected. Research data holdings, data sets, collections of images, audio and video files are actively sought by the Monash library system which looks after ARROW.

All works held in the ARROW Repository are copyright material. Users are free to copy, distribute and transmit the work, provided they observe the conditions under the Creative Commons licence (Creative Commons, 2010). Of course, there may be copyright restrictions on the deposit of previously published works into the ARROW Repository. This has meant that doctoral candidates required to submit their theses electronically and academics wishing to deposit materials are advised to check copyright transfer agreement for any restrictions. In Australia, it is the responsibility of authors to secure permission to use any third-party material in their work, from the rights holder. Researchers can rely on a special provision in the Australian Copyright Act known as 'Fair Dealing' for the use of third-party content during the actual process of conducting research, but this provision does not apply to publication.

When ARROW was established, the argument was made that open access enhances the public value of research, increases its exposure, provides long-term preservation and permanent links, increases the potential for sharing and leads to increased information discovery via harvesters (Google, OAIster and the ARROW Discovery Service). An evaluation of the reach and take-up of ARROW resources, including doctoral theses, is yet to be carried out. These theses are also accessible through the Australian Digital Thesis portal.

As well as access to ARROW, a range of online services is available to doctoral students which allows them to enrol and apply for scholarships online. Resources provided include library tutorials on topics such as thesis preparation and skills development in information technology applications and interactive online courses. Details of awards, fellowships, scholarships and funding opportunities are all published online. Information on support services within the university is also available on the web with links to external resources suitable for research students. Presentations on topics of interest to doctoral students are provided online as podcasts, videos or PowerPoint slides, on topics such as induction to candidature, constructing a thesis, copyright issues and examination processes and procedures (MRGS, 2010b).

To assist them in their research and with storage of data, other services are available through the e-research centre, which provides digital collaborative tools to enable research students to share documents, data and ideas with their supervisors or with other students at any time in the Virtual Research Environment. Large bodies of research data can also be stored online through the centre for access anywhere in the world. While the digital environment offers many opportunities, it also means that institutions are faced with questions as to authority, authenticity and conventions (Bamford, 2005). As a result, the process of adoption and the evolution, diffusion and embedding of new digital practices is likely to be slow.

An awareness of its positioning in relation to other member universities of the Group of Eight on all indicators of research performance, including HDR enrolments, is an ever-present feature of the university's performance reporting. The introduction of the 'Melbourne Model' by the University of Melbourne, which aimed to increase its postgraduate research intake through a structural change to bachelor and Masters degree structures, commencing in 2008, brought new competitive pressures to bear (University of Melbourne, 2007). In 2008, Monash University council noted the 'need for the educational model going forward to articulate very clearly the distinctive nature of Monash programme offerings' (Monash University, 2008b, p. 10.4) in an environment in which the University of Melbourne was already the leader and offering a model that was new in Australia. Positioning itself as an international university within a globally competitive environment, in which new universities in Asia and India are presenting challenges, has become an important element of Monash's strategy (Monash University, 2008b). The international linkages the university has developed with institutions in Asia and India, such as a 'dual award PhD' from its joint venture with the Indian Institute of Technology, Bombay, and a 'split PhD model' with certain universities in Malaysia, aim to build a presence in the region (Monash University, 2009, p. 16). These initiatives too are underpinned by digital technologies which enable rapid communication, access to online resources and applications such as video-conferencing.

The appointment of a new vice chancellor in 2009 and the government requirement for universities to redefine their mission gave Monash the opportunity to align its strategy in ways that have maximised the benefits of new funding structures. It began a process of consultation with staff and students to develop a new PhD programme, one that represents an integrated approach. The design draws explicitly on the British and LERU models (Bogle, 2010), embodied within its adoption of the title, the 'modern PhD', but also retains existing elements within the new framework. In its *Interim Agreement for Mission-based Compacts* with the federal government, Monash University noted its intention to 'increase postgraduate research education with the development of PhD programmes in the areas of global grand challenge' (Australian Government, 2010, p. 7). The new PhD model is part of a repositioning strategy which aims to attract doctoral students to a more international model in a marketplace that is fiercely competitive.

The proposed 'modern PhD' maintains and reaffirms the essential focus on research as the core of the doctorate, developed through two different types of programmes. One will be discipline-based, the other interdisciplinary, similar to the British doctoral training centres. While the thesis remains an essential element of both programmes, each will also include a requirement for skills development components to be completed to gain the qualification. The skills components will range from research-based to more general skills related to such essentials as communication. The focus, reminiscent of that in the UK (Denicolo, 2007), is on the whole person rather than simply the thesis. Skills components can take a variety of forms, from short courses to cooperative teamwork, and be offered in different locations, internationally or locally, in workplaces, at conferences or in fieldwork. The new doctoral training centres, to be located in high quality research-intensive areas, will involve coursework for the first twelve months, followed by student experiential learning within a particular project. Students who have completed a bachelor degree will be eligible and their first year of coursework study within the doctoral training centre will be considered equivalent to a Masters by research degree. Only after this is completed will a student select a field for research for the following three years. Recognising the importance of supervision to research training, the model proposes the establishment of a new centre which will provide training for supervisors as well as registration of all supervisors on a time-limited basis (Monash University, 2010b).

Monash University is the largest in Australia, with nearly 60,000 students in 2010. Of these, higher degree by research students constitute 3933 enrolments, which includes doctoral candidates and students undertaking a Masters by research degree (Monash University, 2010a). It has eight campuses encompassing city, outer suburban and regional as well as two overseas campuses in Malaysia and South Africa. Approximately 35 per cent of the students are international and nearly 10,000 students undertake their studies externally (Monash University, 2010a).

Yet strategic decisions made earlier threaten elements of the university's design for a remodelled PhD. In the wake of the global financial crisis and domestic anxiety over rapid population growth, government policy changes to visa and entry regulations for international students, combined with a soaring Australian dollar, have reduced significantly the number of international students commencing study in 2011, with falls of up to 30 per cent anticipated (ABC, 2010). Melbourne's *Age* newspaper reported that the immediate impact of this fall in international student numbers has meant that Monash University is faced with the need to reduce its budget for 2011 by $45 million dollars, requiring, amongst other measures, the redundancy of 300 staff (Collins, 2010). While the significant influences on higher education in Australia have been national and local, international forces have also been substantial: unpredictable and uncontrollable factors have imposed the need for change.

As suggested at the beginning of this chapter, Australians have always looked abroad for new ideas, particularly to the UK and the US (Walter, 2010). In the development of the mission-based compacts to be agreed with the universities, the Australian Government drew on existing models in the UK and the US (Group of Eight, 2008). Monash University's development of the 'modern PhD' has been informed by PhD models, both existing and proposed, in the UK and also in Europe, but to a lesser extent. These ideas gleaned from distant shores are also melded with other elements which suit local needs and conditions. From its foundation, Australia's dependence on immigrants and foreign capital (Meredith & Dyster, 1999) has forced it to adapt ideas in new ways when global circumstances change, restricting or expanding the resources available, and hence their implementation. Monash University's 'modern PhD' will continue to be shaped by new global conditions as they emerge, but always in a recognisably Australian form.

CONCLUSION

Clearly, the place of digital technologies within doctoral programmes will continue to evolve. Already their use has expanded considerably the support available for doctoral students as well as providing others with access to their scholarship. Yet the very affordances of digital production mean that a new instability has been introduced into the print medium in an institutional environment in which the authority and validity of the printed work still reign. The reconsideration of doctoral programmes opens a space for new forms to be considered but ultimately the complex ecology of people, institutional frameworks and governments will determine how the technologies will be used. For more than two hundred years, manuscript and print co-existed, with print only slowly gaining authority (McKitterick, 2003). While the structure of doctoral programmes will continue to change, the probability that the thesis will be radically transformed by digital production in the immediate future remains unlikely.

REFERENCES

ABC (Australian Broadcasting Commission) (2010). University hit by drop in foreign student number. *Inside Business*, 17 October. Viewed 22 October 2010 http://www.abc.net.au/insidebusiness/content/2010/s3040409.htm.

Altbach, P. G. (2007). Doctoral education: Present realities and future trends. In J. J. Forest and P. G. Altbach (Eds.), *International handbook of higher education* Vol. 1 (pp. 65–82). Dordrecht: Springer.

Auld, G. (2005). Factors to consider when planning to submit a digital thesis. Paper presented at the Australian Association for Research in Education Conference, Cairns. Viewed 8 March 2011 www.aare.edu.au/05pap/aul05175.pdf.

Australian Government (2008). *Review of Australian higher education. Final report.* Denise Bradley (chair), Canberra. Viewed 27 July 2010 http://www.deewr.gov.au/he_review_finalreport.

Australian Government (2009a). *Transforming Australia's higher education system.* Canberra. Viewed 27 July 2010 http://www.deewr.gov.au/HigherEducation/Documents/PDF/Additional%20Report%20-%20Transforming%20Aus%20Higher%20ED_webaw.pdf.

Australian Government (2009b). *Powering ideas. An innovation agenda for the 21st century.* Canberra: Department of Innovation, Industry, Science and Research. Viewed 1 September 2010 www.innovation.gov.au.

Australian Government (2010). *Interim agreement for mission-based compacts.* Canberra: Department of Education, Employment and Workplace Relations and the Department of Innovation, Industry, Science and Research. Viewed 1 September 2010 http://www.deewr.gov.au/HigherEducation/Policy/Pages/InterimAgreements.aspx.

Bamford, A. (2005). The art of research: Digital theses in the arts. Paper presented at 8th International symposium on electronic theses & dissertations, Sydney. Viewed 8 March 2011 http://www.adt.caulf.edu.au/etd2005/papers/123Bamford.pdf.

Bartelse, J. & Huisman, J. (2008). The Bologna process. In M. Nerad & M. Heggelund (Eds.), *Toward a global PhD? Forces and forms in doctoral education* (pp. 101–113). Seattle: University of Washington Press.

Bellamy, C. (2005). The innovative ETD: Innovation and obsolescence. Paper presented at 8th International symposium on electronic theses & dissertations, Sydney. Viewed 8 March 2011 http://www.adt.caulf.edu.au/etd2005/119Bellamy.pdf.

Birtwistle, T. (2009). Towards 2010 (and then beyond) – the context of the Bologna process. *Assessment in Education: Principles, Policy & Practice, 16*(1), 55–63.

Bitusikova, A. (2009). New challenges in doctoral education in Europe. In D. Boud and A. Lee (Eds.), *Changing practices of doctoral education* (pp. 200–210). London: Routledge.

Bogle, D. (2010). *Doctoral degrees beyond 2010: Training talented researchers for society.* Leuven, Belgium: LERU, League of European Research Universities. Viewed 1 July 2010 http://www.leru.org.

Borthwick, J. & Wissler, R. (2003). *Postgraduate research students and generic capabilities: Online directions.* Canberra: Department of Education, Science and Training. Viewed 1 October 2010 http://www.dest.gov.au.

Boud, D. & Tennant, M. (2006). Putting doctoral education to work: Challenges to academic practice. *Higher Education Research & Development, 25*(3), 293–306.

Collins, S. J. (2010). Foreign students in retreat, *The Age,* 14 October. Viewed 22 October 2010 http://www.theage.com.au/national/education/foreign-students-in-retreat-20101013-16k03.html.

Creative Commons (2010). Viewed 31 October 2010 http://creativecommons.org/.

DEEWR (Department of Education, Employment and Workplace Relations) (2009). *Award course completions 2008.* Canberra: Department of Education, Employment and Workplace Relations. Viewed 30 August 2010 http://www.deewr.gov.au.

Denicolo, P. (2007). The metamorphosis of doctoral education in the UK and Europe: Perspectives from a teacher as learner. In J. Butcher and L. McDonald (Eds.), *Making a difference. Challenges for teachers, teaching and teacher education* (pp. 235–250). Rotterdam: Sense Publishers.

DEST (Department of Education, Science and Training) (2007). *OECD Thematic review of tertiary education. Country background report. Australia.* Canberra. Viewed 1 September 2010 http://www.oecd.org/document/5/0,3343,en_2649_39263238_35580240_1_1_1_1,00.html.

Edminster, J. & Moxley, J. (2002). Graduate education and the evolving genre of electronic theses and dissertations. *Computers and Composition, 19,* 89–104.

Edwards, D., Radloff, A., & Coates, H. (2009). *Supply, demand and characteristics of the higher degree by research population in Australia.* Canberra: Australian Council for Educational Research. Viewed 27 July 2010 http://www.innovation.gov.au/Section/Research/Documents/SupplyDemandand CharacteristicsoftheHDRPopulationinAustralia.pdf.

EPSRC (Engineering and Physical Sciences Research Council) (2010). *Home page.* Viewed 1 October 2010 http://www.epsrc.ac.uk/funding/students/centres/Pages/default.aspx.

Evans, T., Evans, B., & Marsh, H. (2008). Australia. In M. Nerad & M. Heggelund (Eds.), *Toward a global PhD? Forces and forms in doctoral education* (pp. 171–203). Seattle: University of Washington Press.

Green, H. (2008). United Kingdom. In M. Nerad & M. Heggelund (Eds.), *Toward a global PhD? Forces and forms in doctoral education* (pp. 36–74). Seattle: University of Washington Press.

Group of Eight (2008). *Mission-based funding compacts with public universities.* Group of Eight, October. Viewed 1 October 2010 http://www.go8.edu.au.

HEC (Higher Education Council) (1989). *Australian graduate studies and higher degrees.* Canberra: Australian Government Publishing Service. Viewed 30 July 2010 http://www.dest.gov.au.

Kehm, B. M. (2007). Quo Vadis doctoral education? New European approaches in the context of global changes. *European Journal of Education, 42*(3), 307–319.

Lang, S. (2002). Electronic dissertations: Preparing students for our past or their futures? *College English, 64*(6), 680–695.

Libner, K. & Morgan, K. (2004). PhDigital? Lessons from the history of the doctorate and the dissertation. Paper presented at ETD 2004, Lexington, Kentucky. Viewed 9 March 2011 http://www.uky.edu/ETD/ETD2004/libner/Libner-Morgan-ETD2004.pdf.

Marginson, S. (2000). *Monash. Remaking the university*. St Leonards NSW: Allen and Unwin.

Marginson, S. (2002). Nation-building universities in a global environment: The case of Australia, *Higher Education, 43*, 409–428.

Marginson, S. (2007). Global position and position taking: The case of Australia. *Journal of Studies in International Education, 11*(1), 5–32.

Marginson, S. & Considine, M. (2000). *The Enterprise University*. Cambridge: Cambridge University Press.

Marginson, S. & van der Wende, M. (2007). *Globalisation and higher education*. Paris: OECD Directorate for Education. Viewed 25 July 2010 http://www.cshe.unimelb.edu.au/people/staff_pages/Marginson/OECD-Globalisation&HigherEd.pdf.

Mather, J. (2010). Global rethink on PhD as it loses its relevance. *The Australian Financial Review*, 20 Septembe, 30.

McKitterick, D. (2003). *Print, manuscript and the search for order*. Cambridge: Cambridge University Press.

Meredith, D. & Dyster, B. (1999). *Australia in the Global Economy*. Cambridge: Cambridge University Press.

Monash University (1998). *Annual report 1997*. Clayton: Monash University.

Monash University (2000). *Annual report 1999*. Clayton: Monash University.

Monash University (2001). *Annual report 2000*. Clayton: Monash University.

Monash University (2002a). *Pocket statistics 2002*. Clayton: Monash University. Viewed 30 July 2020 http://www.opq.monash.edu.au/ups/statistics/summary/pocketstats-2010.pdf.

Monash University (2002b). *Annual report 2001*. Clayton: Monash University. Viewed 30 July 2010 http://www.monash.edu.au/pubs/ar.

Monash University (2003). *Annual report 2002*. Clayton: Monash University. Viewed 30 July 2010 http://www.monash.edu.au/pubs/ar.

Monash University (2008a). *Annual report 2007*. Clayton: Monash University. Viewed 30 July 2010 http://www.monash.edu.au/pubs/ar.

Monash University (2008b). *Council minutes and agenda of meetings*. Clayton: Monash University.

Monash University (2009). *Annual report 2008*. Clayton: Monash University. Viewed 30 July 2010 http://www.monash.edu.au/pubs/ar.

Monash University (2010a). *Pocket statistics 2010*. Clayton: Monash University. Viewed 30 July 2020 http://www.opq.monash.edu.au/ups/statistics/summary/pocketstats-2010.pdf.

Monash University (2010b). *Monash futures*. Clayton: Monash University. Viewed 1 June 2010 http://www.monash.edu.au.

Moyle, M. (2008). Improving access to European E-theses: The DART-Europe programme, *Liber Quarterly, 18*(3/4), 413–423.

MRGS (Monash Research Graduate School) (2010a). *Handbook for doctoral and MPhil degrees*. Clayton. Viewed 20 October 2010 http://www.mrgs.monash.edu.au/research/doctoral/index.html.

MRGS (Monash Research Graduate School) (2010b). *Resources for HDR candidates*. Clayton. Viewed 20 October 2010 http://www.mrgs.monash.edu.au/research/doctoral/index.html.

NBEET (National Board of Employment, Education and Training) (1992). *Research and research training in a quality higher education system*. Canberra: Australian Government Publishing Service. Viewed 30 July 2010 http://www.dest.gov.au.

Nerad, M. (2008). United States of America. In M. Nerad & M. Heggelund (Eds.), *Toward a global PhD? Forces and forms in doctoral education* (pp. 278–299). Seattle: University of Washington Press.

Nerad, M. & Heggelund, M. (Eds.) (2008). *Toward a global PhD? Forces and forms in doctoral education*. Seattle: University of Washington Press.

Nerad, M., Trzyna, T., & Heggelund, M. (2008). Introduction. In M. Nerad & M. Heggelund (Eds.), *Toward a global PhD? Forces and forms in doctoral education* (pp. 3–16). Seattle: University of Washington Press.

Park, C. (2007). *Redefining the doctorate*. Heslington, York. Viewed 25 August 2010 http://eprints. lancs.ac.uk/435/1/RedefiningTheDoctorate.pdf.

Pearson, M. (2005). Framing research on doctoral education in Australia in a global context. *Higher Education Research & Development, 24*(2), 119–134.

Pearson, M., Evans, T., & Macauley, P. (2008). Growth and diversity in doctoral education: Assessing the Australian experience. *Higher Education, 55*, 357–372.

Prewett, K. (2006). Who should do what? Implications for institutional and national leaders. In Chris M. Golde & George E. Walker (Eds.), *Envisioning the future of doctoral education: preparing stewards of the discipline* (pp. 23–33). San Francisco: Jossey–Bass.

University of Melbourne (2007). *Annual report 2006*. Melbourne. Viewed 1 October 2010 http://www. unimelb.edu.au/publications/annualrep/index.html.

University of Melbourne (2010). *Annual report 2009*. Melbourne. Viewed 1 October 2010 http://www. unimelb.edu.au/publications/annualrep/index.html.

Walter, J. with Moore, T. (2010). *What were they Thinking? The Politics of Ideas in Australia*. Sydney: The University of New South Wales Press Ltd.

Wells, A. & Cargnelutti, T. (2004). Australian digital theses program: Expansion, partnership and the future. *Lecture notes in computer science, 3334*, 660.

24

How Changes in Representation can Affect Meaning

Amy Alexandra Wilson

INTRODUCTION

The terms *digital dissertations* and *digital theses* call to mind different images depending on the context in which these terms are used, including the author's field of study, the norms of the degree-granting institution and the preferences of individual thesis or dissertation committees. For some, a digital thesis is nothing more than a typed document that has been encoded electronically and uploaded to a database to enable others to locate it more easily. For students in various branches of music, however, a digital dissertation may include a portfolio of audio or visual files of performances, whereas an architectural major's final thesis project can include a computer-generated blueprint for a building. Other examples include the science graduate who uses visual models of physical phenomena in motion, the communications graduate who builds an interactive website with avatars or a mathematician whose culminating thesis relies heavily on numbers, symbols and graphs.

As these examples suggest, the types of representation used in digital theses can be as diverse as the people who make them, each of whom has learned about different phenomena in the world (e.g. building design, molecular structure, eighteenth-century British novels), and each of whom has been trained to represent these phenomena using specific sets of semiotic resources organized in accordance with the conventions of their respective disciplines. Despite these differences in representation, however, many dissertations and theses increasingly have one characteristic in common: in an era that has been dubbed the Media or Digital Age (Negroponte, 1995; Kress, 2003), many graduate students' culminating projects are now encoded and transmitted through electronic bits. The purpose of this chapter is to explore what might be gained and lost when phenomena are transformed, manipulated and (re)presented via digital media. Specifically, this chapter addresses three questions:

- How do digital media afford and constrain the expression of content?
- What happens to the author's message when data are resemiotized?
- How might this resemiotization influence the learning of the author of the dissertation or thesis?

AFFORDANCES AND CONSTRAINTS OF DIGITAL MEDIA

The increasing popularity of digital dissertations suggests that electronic media must make something possible for their users; graduate students and their committees must find something of value in digital formats if they require or request them prior to graduation. The concept of *affordances* (Gibson, 1979; van Leeuwen, 2005) can be helpful in explaining the purpose, usefulness and ultimately the growing prevalence of these types of dissertations. The concept of affordances has often been associated with *modes*, or articulated systems for making meaning, such as spoken words, written words, music, gestures, layout and so forth (e.g. Kress & van Leeuwen, 2001). The mode of image, for example, affords the simultaneous visualization of spatial relationships more easily than written words, which unfold according to a temporal logic, word by word and line by line (Kress, 2009; Saussure, 1916/1986). Though images may afford the visualization of spatial relationships, an important question remains: Does an image in a printed photograph or book hold the same semiotic potential as an image online? In other words, do the affordances of modes change when the material medium through which they are expressed change?

Jewitt (2006), when she asserted that affordances are related to the material nature of modes as they are used in social settings, began to address this question. Although an image on a printed page may essentially look the same as an image on a screen, the material nature of the paper changes what is possible in the act of communication, including how and with whom the image can be shared, how the image can be combined with other modes and how others can respond to the image. Electronic media, of course, are widely lauded for what they make possible in this regard: text-makers can design online texts that use ever-changing configurations of spoken words, music, sound, written words, still images and moving images, and they can share these texts with a global audience who in turn can modify or respond to the original text in a matter of minutes. In this sense, if affordances are explained – not in terms of the communicative potential of individual modes – but in terms of what a combination of modes can do together (Hull & Nelson, 2005; Lemke, 1998), then digital texts may have greater semiotic potential for conveying certain types of messages, as compared with many printed texts, due to the myriad of changing combinations that digital media enable.

Accompanying the concept of affordances, however, is the concept of constraints. At the same time that the material nature of electronic bits enables certain types of communication, it may also limit certain types of communication. These constraints can be local concerns that restrict individual users, such as an individual's lack of familiarity with available technologies, lack of access to these technologies or lack of training in how to use them to design a variety of representations. The constraints of digital media may also be due to the material nature of screens themselves. Regardless of whether the thesis writer's primary object of study is pollution, perfumes or textiles – many electronic media require the presentation of any phenomenon in a way that inhibits the communication of its smell, taste, materiality and – to some extent – its spatial position in relation to other three-dimensional objects. Moreover, digital media easily enable the distortion and manipulation of audio and visual data, even if this distortion is unintentional and is due to specific pieces of recording equipment being unable to capture nuances of sound or sight. For these reasons, depending on the dissertation committee's criteria for determining expertise in each field of study and the purpose of the graduate's culminating project, electronic formats can limit the types of knowledge that a graduate can demonstrate.

Although digital media wield enormous semiotic potential in communicating different types of messages, each message is still bound by the communicative purpose that the graduate student seeks to achieve. The concept of affordances would suggest that, even within the digital realm, the thesis writer should select combinations of representations that would best enable him or her to craft an argument in accordance with the conventions of the discipline and the demands of the content. For example, precise changes in a relationship between two variables may be most aptly displayed by a line graph with the line extending over time as the viewer watches, whereas a literary analysis of Thomas Hardy's novels may still be aptly represented primarily through written words. Likewise, in some fields of study, graduates may desire the option of designing culminating projects whose media enable nuances of smell, texture, taste, the placement of objects in physical space or any combinations of these modes. In each case, the forms of representation selected by the graduate student can be the ones that most fully allow her or him to support an argument or establish expertise within the field.

RESEMIOTIZING DATA

As graduate students create digital dissertations and theses, selecting forms of representation that lend themselves to the communication of a particular body of content, they often have to 'transform' the data from one mode into another, from one material to another, and from one site to another. Two examples will illustrate the possible nature of these transformations. First, a graduate student in a Master of Fine Arts program specializing in interior design is required to make a thesis studio for her final project, which will be evaluated based in part on its sustainability, utility and creative capacity to resolve advanced problems in design (e.g. New York School of Interior Design, 2010). She begins to think about the plans for her studio several semesters in advance, sketching and re-sketching an office space on paper before using a CAD (Computer Aided Design) program to design a two-dimensional black and white plan of the room, followed by a three-dimensional colored image. She writes verbal justifications to accompany these images, explaining how the room meets existing codes and regulations; why she selected the colors, materials, lights and furniture; and why she spatially arranged the room as she did. In the design school's annual thesis exhibition, the computer-generated images are displayed beside a board that includes sample materials such as upholstery fabrics, window covers and paint colors. The student's images, coupled with photographs of rooms she helped to design during her internship, are uploaded to the student's electronic portfolio and a client later pays the student to implement her office plan in a house.

Second, a doctoral student in science education videotapes an earth science teacher explaining lunar phases to her students. The teacher darkens the classroom, places a light bulb in its center to represent the sun, and asks the students to stand in a circle around the light bulb. She gives each student a Styrofoam ball to represent the moon, while the students' heads represent the earth. The earth science teacher asks the students to rotate their bodies around in a circle, holding their 'moons' in front of them. The spatial position of the earth (the students' heads), the sun (the light bulb) and the moon (Styrofoam ball) changes when the students move, simulating lunar phases as a shadow falls across the 'moon' and then is lifted again.

The earth science teacher then distributes a piece of paper to her students, which contains a diagram of lunar phases as perceived from outer space. A large circle in the center of the diagram represents the earth, while various smaller circles around the earth, connected by a dotted line, represent the different positions of the moon in its orbit. A large circle to the far right of the diagram represents the sun, which lights the right half of each moon, while the left half is darkened. The earth science teacher asks her students to hold up the piece of paper to their eye level, with the thin edge of the paper near their eyes, and pretend as though they are looking from the earth outward. The students cover the outside of the dotted line with their fingers while they look at each moon from the position of the earth. This action enables students to see what the moon looks like when viewed from the earth at various positions on the diagram. Using this video as his primary source of data, the doctoral student writes an analysis of the lesson, which includes still images taken from the video and photographs of the diagram that the teacher distributed to her students. He posts his analysis on an online journal with a link to the uploaded video.

As these examples indicate, digital theses and dissertations may often require changes in representation: from moving three-dimensional objects to a video-recording; from drawn sketches on paper to computer-generated images on a screen and so forth. Given the wide variety of changes that can happen when content is resemiotized from one form to another, it is important for committees and students to think about the nature of these transformations and their effect on data, including what could be gained and lost in the process of making these changes.

CHANGES WITHIN AND ACROSS MODES, MATERIALS AND LOCATIONS

From the beginning to the end of the process of writing a digital dissertation or thesis, content can undergo countless changes in message, form and medium. These changes can be explained in terms of at least four categories: (a) changes within the same mode (e.g. using spoken words to repeat and explain somebody else's spoken words); (b) changes from one mode to another (e.g. using written words to describe and explain gestures); (c) changes from one material medium to another (e.g. an image on paper versus an image on screen) and (d) changes from one site to another (e.g. a video on a personal camera screen becomes a video on YouTube watched by another). Designing a digital dissertation or thesis may require many or all of these changes at different points.

Changes within modes

Kress (2003) has used the term *transformation* to describe changes that involve 'the forms and structures within a mode' (p. 36), such as the Masters student who sketched and re-sketched possible plans for her thesis studio, and the doctoral student who revised the written portion of his analysis, changing the structure and content of his writing. This chapter will primarily address changes across modes, but it is worth noting that even seemingly simple transformations within a mode can also be complex and can draw from multiple modes.

In most cases, a digital dissertation or thesis is a project that represents some type of synthesis of learning, a demonstration of the expertise that the graduate student has gained through a series of texts throughout her or his program: lectures, textbooks, articles, discussions and so forth. For an interior design major, texts often also include photographs, textiles the spatial layout of objects in rooms, furniture, lights, floor plans and three-dimensional models of rooms and buildings. If learning involves inward sign-making, as Kress (1997) has asserted, then by the end of their programs, graduates will have encountered a variety of signs through which they construct understandings. An apparently easy change in line or color within a sketch, therefore, can be the outward demonstration of an internalization of multimodal texts that the student had read throughout the program. In this sense, transformation can be a complex and demanding process that still requires the learner to make connections across modes.

Changes across modes

Along with changing structures within a given mode, writers of digital dissertations and theses often re-form data across modes as well in a process that is termed *transduction* (Kress, 2003). Examples include changing the computer-generated image of an office to a physical office space, or changing three-dimensional objects and bodies in space (students turning while holding Styrofoam balls) to a moving image displayed on a flat screen. As representations morph from one mode to another, questions arise as to how their message might change, how their semiotic potential might change and what is gained or lost in the process of transduction. The answer to this question depends in part on what is changed, how it is changed and what each new mode enables dissertation writers to communicate.

To illustrate the potential gains, losses and changes in meaning that can occur when representations undergo the process of transduction, I turn to the example of the doctoral student in science education, who 'fixed' the mode of three-dimensional bodies in space by video-recording it, in effect changing the lesson to a new mode (a moving image). The video of the lunar phases demonstration enabled viewers to easily see changing spatial relationships between the objects displayed on the screen, and it enabled viewers to hear the teacher's verbal narration. The original mode of his data likewise enabled participants to visualize changing spatial relationships. In this case, perhaps an immediate tactile form of embodied participation was lost: unlike the students in the classroom, people who view the doctoral student's video cannot move their bodies to cause changes in the shadow on the moon, nor do their heads represent the earth. Moreover, depending on the vantage point of the video camera, the view of the shadow on each student's earth would be different – a significant change because the shape of the shadow on the moon is important to an understanding of lunar phases.

Nonetheless, although this embodied form of participation was lost and a precise view of the shadow on each student's 'moon' may have been altered, the ability to display moving spatial relationships remained the same. A semiotic shift to written words alone would not enable the same visualization of second-by-second changes in spatial relationships among physical bodies, but would enable the doctoral student to transcribe the teacher's spoken words, to describe the students' and teacher's actions in general terms and to analyze the lesson. Other modes – such as music or still three-dimensional models – would likely not even be considered in this case due to their relative inability to represent shifts in spatial positions over time and to represent the stream of words that narrated these shifts.

The Masters student who helped to design rooms as an intern, and then posted online photographs of these rooms as part of an electronic portfolio, offers a second example of semiotic transduction. In this case, too, the shift in mode changed what was possible for those who could no longer sit in the furniture or move their fingers across the material of the curtain. Though the tactile quality of the original text was lost, photographs taken from different locations in the room would still enable the viewer to gain a sense of its general aesthetics, including its color, lighting, use of lines and positioning of different objects in relation to each other. Unlike the previous example, in this case a moving image would not necessarily be more effective than the student's photographs because the furnishings of a room do not usually move or make sounds.

In both cases, what was lost may relate to an image's inability to represent a body in three-dimensional space that influences, relates to and touches other objects with particular tactile qualities. In both cases, the ability to view spatial relationships and shapes was maintained, which is important for a text whose purpose is to communicate room design or the causes of lunar phases. Though the semiotic potential of the original texts changed, with potential losses in what the communicator was able to express, the use of digital media also enabled new possibilities for communication. Whereas the printed image and the demonstration of lunar phases were local, available only to participating students or visitors at a given time, online texts are global, available to all interested parties, accessible at the user's convenience and easily juxtaposed with other signs such as the graduate students' written words intended to shape the viewers' interpretation of the images.

Along with providing exact recordings or the creative representation of existing phenomena, digital technologies may also help to bring new phenomena into existence. Programs such as AutoCAD, for example, enable a precision of angle and measurement that would be comparatively difficult for a graduate student to draw by hand and to modify as the need arose. Architectural graduates and interior design graduates can use this software to generate plans for buildings and rooms as part of their final project (including relying on digital technologies to make quick and accurate mathematical computations), which can later be modified and turned into actual buildings or rooms. In this case, the affordances of digital technologies may be in their generative capacity as a computer-generated image later becomes a building or a room.

Epistemological changes

When representations changes from one mode to another, perhaps more than just their affordances change in terms of what they are most aptly able to communicate and to whom. Kress (2003) has suggested that a shift in mode also necessitates a shift in an epistemological commitment, including what counts as knowledge and the methods by which we can obtain it. Iedema (2003) likewise has noted that shifts in mode can also entail 'privileging different domains of human experience' (p. 234), changing more than the simply the appearance or the structure of the content. In a Masters or doctoral program, what counts as knowledge, including the methods by which one can legitimately obtain it and demonstrate it, are especially important points to consider as committees decide whether writers of the dissertations and theses have demonstrated they are knowledgeable and proficient enough in the field to have earned a degree. Because different fields address different domains of human experience, what counts as advanced knowledge and how one can come to obtain and demonstrate that knowledge may vary according to field.

For an interior design major – whose ultimate professional goal may be to demonstrate expertise regarding how to design comfortable, useful and beautiful spaces for people to work and live in – an actual room designed during an internship is an apt form through which to represent this proficiency. People play, eat, worship, relax and work in physical settings, surrounded by physical objects that affect their ability to do these things and the quality of their experiences as they are doing them. When the room later becomes a digital photograph to be placed on the graduate's online portfolio, this transduction changes the more than just the material nature, the structure and the mode of the studio – it changes the 'domain of human experience' possible for the user of the text. The user becomes a viewer who is able to evaluate a couch but cannot rest on it.

It should be noted here that new technologies are changing the domains of human experience that are possible with digital media. For example, Microsoft – the multinational, multimillion dollar computer company – is moving toward 'gesture technologies' in which users' movements can influence objects seen in three-dimensional space (Vance, 2010). Moreover, different companies such as DigiScent have experimented with a given set of digitally produced scents, albeit with limited commercial success (Paterson, 2006). As technologies move toward easy communication through a wider variety of modes, the possibilities of expression for future Masters and doctoral students are expanded as well. Even so, we as humans remain physical beings who have gustatory, olfactory and tactile experiences with the physical world. For areas of study that address certain aspects of this world, it remains for graduate students and their committees to discuss how they can best generate, represent and demonstrate knowledge, including discussions of the effects of the epistemological changes that occur in the process of transduction.

Changes in material media

Changes in modes may or may not be accompanied with a change to a different physical medium. Communications graduates, for instance, can analyze a host of messages online – YouTube videos, avatars in computer games, websites, political ads, television shows – and can design multimodal dissertations and theses without ever consulting or using a source beyond those they can call up on their computer screen. In that case, the physical medium (the screen with speakers that make sounds) remains the same, even though the modes have changed. In some fields of study – history and literature, for example – attention is not usually given to the physical medium of the original data (e.g. if a student read the US Constitution or *Huckleberry Finn* online or from a book, he could still write the same analysis of them). In other fields of study, such as some branches of science, the material nature of the data is highly significant and can even be the focal point of the thesis or dissertation (e.g. the qualities of the local soil). For some graduate students, then, changes that occur in physical media can be important considerations, whereas other students' work may not undergo this type of semiotic shift.

The example of the doctoral student's dissertation in science education can serve as a springboard to discuss how shifts in material media can change what is possible in the communication of meaning, even when the mode remains the same. In the original science lesson, the teacher held up an image depicting lunar phases, with the earth in the middle and moons placed at different positions in a circle around the earth to represent the changes in the moon's position over time. The left half of each moon was black, while the right half was white, to illustrate how the moon was lit by the sun placed to the right of the diagram. In order to see the view of the moon from the earth, the students lifted up their papers, placing the edge of the paper at their eye level and covered the part of the moon that was outside the dotted orbit with their fingers, enabling them to see the view of the moon from the earth (e.g. crescent moon, waxing gibbous moon and so forth). The material nature of the image, which was in this case photocopied and placed on a lightweight paper, enabled the students to easily manipulate the image in a way that allowed them to reach their teacher's instructional objective, which was to compare the view of the lunar phases as seen in outer space (as shown in the original diagram) to the view of lunar phases as seen from the earth (as seen when students lifted up the diagram and covered the outer half of each moon). The affordances of paper, in this case, were that it was a relatively inexpensive, lightweight medium that could be cheaply distributed to students and manipulated to reach the teacher's objective.

When the doctoral student changed the material substance of the same image – from appearing on paper to appearing on a computer screen – the image's semiotic potential also changed. Users of a desktop computer could not lift up the diagram, placing it at their eye level so they could see only the edge of the paper, and look outward from the earth to the moon. In this example, too, however, new technologies are changing the material nature of digital theses and dissertations, including where and how they can be manifested. Rather than being tied to one material medium, such as desktop computer, digital dissertations and theses can now be read on relatively portable laptops, Smartphones and digital tablets such as iPads. In this instance, the material nature of an iPad could have essentially the same affordances as paper: the reader could lift up the image on the iPad, with the thin side of the iPad at their eye level, and look outward from the earth to the moon. As this example illustrates, changes in a mode's materiality can affect its semiotic potential, depending on the graduate student's communicative purpose. These changes in semiotic potential can be tied to semiotic shifts before the electronic dissertation is published, or they can be tied to the physical properties of the medium through which the audience is accessing the dissertation or thesis.

Changes in location or frame

Even when the modes and physical properties of a given text remain unchanged, what happens when the sign moves from one location or site to another? Hodge and Kress (1988) began to address this question when they described a religious statue placed behind the altar at the front of a church and conjectured as to what would happen to its meaning if it were moved. For example, if it were placed in an art museum near paintings, its meaning would change from being a relatively inaccessible object of veneration to being a work of art that people could walk around and perhaps touch. Similarly, a three-dimensional model of a room placed in a thesis exhibition hall would change in meaning if moved to a toy room, and a computer-generated image of an office means something different if it is sent as an email attachment to a professor or if it is posted on a website for an interior design firm.

As these examples illustrate, changes in a text's frame can lead to changes in a text's meaning (e.g. Goffman, 1986; Kress, 2009). The immediate surroundings of a text can serve as a frame, setting that text apart as a separate unit. For instance, a colored space between photographs on a webpage can set apart the images in the photographs, or the walls that surround an office can set apart the furnishings in that room as being part of a cohesive unit. These physical frames can be themselves set within larger frames: The thicker walls of the office building serve to hold together all of the walls that frame each room, collectively holding the rooms together as a structure in which a group of people work. Likewise, though the photographs are separated by the colored space between them, they may also appear side by side on the same screen after somebody types in a URL to find a single website. The layout of the website as a whole can indicate the connections between the pictures as well as their separation.

Along with being framed by properties such as spatial position, texts can also be framed according to genre. Kress (2003) has defined *genre* as a relatively stable communicative pattern that arises when a social group develops a relatively stable set of interactions. For instance, people in many contemporary societies value aesthetic beauty and comfort in their homes and workplaces. Within this society, a group of people want to earn advanced credentials for room design, and the genre of the *thesis studio* arises as a means to establish people's expertise in this area. A second genre, an electronic *portfolio* for interior design firms, also arises as others seek those with expertise to help them design their rooms. When the computer-generated image of the office is placed beside an extensive technical explanation and e-mailed to a professor, it takes on the genre of a *thesis project* as the student assumes the position of novice in relation to an expert. If the same image is placed on a website for the interior design firm that hires the student, its meaning may also changes as the student assumes the role of expert to be consulted.

Changes in location – whether from one website to another or from one physical environment to another – can thus also lead to changes in meaning because the frame has changed. For makers of digital dissertations and theses, the consequences of these relocations can be especially worthy of consideration. The nature of online texts enables relatively easy reframing and remixing as viewers can take a portion of a digital text and relocate it, using it as part of a new text in a different genre (e.g. Erstad, 2008).

IMPLICATIONS OF RESEMIOTIZATION

This chapter has addressed the question: how can data be resemiotized and what happens as a result of this resemiotization? Throughout the process of designing a digital dissertation or thesis, data can be resemiotized in at least four ways: through intramodal transformations; through transductions across modes; through changes in material media and/or through changes in location, site or frame. Halliday's (1978) description of the metafunctions of language can help to explain the changes in meaning that can occur with each form of resemiotization. Halliday (1973/1978) asserted that any instance of communication fills three functions: the *ideational* function, by which people represent objects or phenomena and the relations between them, along with expressing their experiences of the world; the *interpersonal* function, which 'embodies all use of the language to express social and personal relations' (1973, p. 41), including the social roles that people assume for themselves and assign to their audience and the *textual* function that relates parts of the text to each other, relates the text to the context in which people are communicating and does so in such a way that the text is coherent both within itself and with the situation at hand.

Resemiotization can affect meaning by changing what is realized across all three domains, although what is changed and how it is changed will vary according to the specific communicative context. A graduate student assumes the role of novice appealing to expert by submitting a project, but when published online the same project can become evidence of the graduate student's expert status, changing the *interpersonal* meanings instantiated in the text. Local, transitory physical interactions in an earth science classroom – where teacher and students know each other and influence each other's communications – become 'fixed' (Kress, 2003) global objects to be viewed by anybody when posted online, entirely shifting the *textual* nature of communication as the video must cohere with the expectations of a new audience in a different way. Dissertation writers can refer to new aspects of the world when they make changes within a mode or across modes, but even the 'same' *content* in another mode (e.g. a room with furnishings versus a photograph of a room) affords an entirely different type of semiotic potential in terms of the domains of human experience that can be realized. In sum, although each example of communication may be changed in specific ways, resemiotization in all of its forms can change – not only what is expressed, but also the context in which the message is understood, including the social roles that are realized therein.

TRANSMEDIATION AND LEARNING

To this point, the chapter has discussed how resemiotization might alter the semiotic potential of a given text, but it also is important to point out that resemiotization can also alter the understandings of the graduate student. Vygotsky (1978) and those who draw from his work (e.g. Cole, 1996; Wertsch, 1998) have theorized how signs mediate the development of people's understandings of particular concepts, asserting that the nature of a sign (e.g. an image, a numerical/ symbolic combination) can shape what is possible in people's thinking as they seek to understand and solve advanced problems in their field.

For example, Rumelhart, Smolensky, McClelland, and Hinton (1986) explained how the vertical alignment of numerals with base-ten place values enables people to perform mathematical algorithms by 'reduc[ing] a very abstract conceptual problem to a series of operations that are very concrete and at which we can become very good' (p. 46). In other words, the spatial organization and syntax of numbers in mathematical problems are 'an essential part of a cultural tool without which we cannot solve [a given] problem. In an important sense, then, the syntax is doing some of the thinking involved' (Wertsch, 1998, p. 29; cf. O'Halloran, 2005). In accordance with this theory, just as numbers are culturally shaped signs that can enable users to solve particular sets of problems that could not be solved with words alone, perhaps the computer-generated, scaled image of the office also enabled the Masters student to 'resolve advanced problems in design' (New York School of Interior Design, 2010) that could not have been accomplished through written words alone. Under this view, different modes are no longer viewed primarily as representations of phenomena, with some modes more apt at representing particular types of phenomena than others. Modes also become tools that mediate graduates' thinking as they think about how to solve problems, with some modes enabling students to solve discipline-specific sets of problems more easily than others.

Working within this tradition, Siegel (1995) addressed how translations across sign systems affect learners' understandings of content. Similar to Kress's (2003) definition of *transduction* as 'a process in which something which has been configured or shaped in one or more modes is *re*configured, *re*shaped according to the affordances of a quite different mode', Siegel defined *transmediation* as 'the act of translating meanings from one sign system to another' (p. 455; cf. Suhor, 1984).

However, whereas Kress focused more on the changes in the structure and affordances of the text, Siegel's focus was on the *act* of the translation, especially on how this act can affect the understandings of the sign-maker.

Siegel (1995) asserted that the act of transmediation is generative in nature, often requiring students to develop deeper understandings as they invent connections between two or more sign systems and the concepts they are studying. As an example, she described two students who did not understand an article about mathematics until they drew and labeled a sketch that served as a graphic organizer to show how different concepts in the article were related. This act of transmediation, she argued, provided students with 'an entry into the text' (p. 468). Regardless of the final modes through which the dissertation will be presented, therefore, graduate students can 'mess about' with representing the ideas in the dissertation in various combinations of modes as a potentially fruitful and generative practice that can enable them to develop new understandings.

CONCLUSION

Ideally, a digital dissertation or thesis will be characterized by the clear and compelling expression of thought, including forms of representation structured in accordance with the conventions of the discipline. Depending on the graduate student's field and purpose for communication, different combinations of modes may enable this clear and compelling expression more fully than others. In the process of achieving this final product, the graduate student's work may undergo many semiotic changes – from one mode to another, one context to another, and one material to another. Each resemiotization can affect the semiotic potential of the text in a process that continues after the final product is posted online and an audience reads and responds to it. Each resemiotization also does more than change the meaning of the text: it may also mediate the development of the graduate student as he or she is able to think about a subject in a more complex and generative way.

If theses and dissertations are reconceptualized to account for digital forms of representation, what are the implications for advisors and their graduate students? First, advisors' mentorship can entail a willingness to supervise a final dissertation or thesis that includes multiple modes as part of either the process or the product with the understanding that these modes may facilitate their students' thinking in powerful ways. Additionally, just as many advisors' mentorship includes feedback with the intention of improving students' writing, their feedback may also include suggestions regarding forms of representation they could use to most aptly or creatively convey particular types of meanings. Lastly, graduate students' oral defences or *viva voce* examinations can include an explanation of how and why their data were resemiotized, along with a justification for why they represented ideas as they did in their final draft. This approach would require students to demonstrate expertise regarding how to communicate ideas in their respective fields as they concurrently demonstrate their understandings of major issues and trends in their fields.

REFERENCES

Cole, M. (1996). *Cultural Psychology: A Once and Future Discipline.* Cambridge, MA: Harvard University Press.

Erstad, O. (2008). Trajectories of remixing: Digital literacies, media production, and schooling. In C. Lankshear & M. Knobel (Eds.), *Digital Literacies: Concepts, Policies, and Practices* (pp. 177–202). New York: Peter Lang.

Gibson, J. J. (1979) *The Ecological Approach to Visual Perception.* Boston, MA: Houghton Mifflin.

Goffman, E. (1986). *Frame Analysis.* Boston, MA: Northeastern University Press.

Halliday, M. A. K. (1973). *Explorations in the Functions of Language.* London: Arnold.

Halliday, M. A. K. (1978). *Language as Social Semiotic.* London: Arnold.

Hodge, R. & Kress, G. (1988). *Social Semiotics.* Ithaca, NY: Cornell University Press.

Hull, G. A. & Nelson, M. E. (2005). Locating the semiotic power of multimodality. *Written Communication, 22*(2), 224–261.

Iedema, R. A. (2003). Multimodality, resemiotization: Extending the analysis of discourse as multisemiotic practice. *Visual Communication, 2*(1), 29–57.

Jewitt, C. (2006). *Technology, Literacy, and Learning: A Multimodal Approach.* London: Routledge.

Kress, G. (1997). *Before Writing: Rethinking the Paths to Literacy.* New York: Routledge.

Kress, G. (2003). *Literacy in the New Media Age.* New York: Routledge.

Kress, G. (2009). What is mode? In C. Jewitt (Ed.), *The Routledge Handbook of Multimodal Analysis* (pp. 54–67). New York: Routledge.

Kress, G. & van Leeuwen, T. (2001). *Multimodal Discourse: The Modes and Media of Contemporary Communication.* London: Arnold.

Lemke, J. L. (1998). Multiplying meaning: Visual and verbal semiotics in scientific text. In J. R. Martin & R. Veel (Eds.), *Reading Science: Critical and Functional Perspectives on Discourses of Science* (pp. 87–113). New York: Routledge.

Negroponte, N. (1995). *Being Digital.* New York: Knopf.

New York School of Interior Design. (2010). *A National leader in design education.* Retrieved from http://www.nysid.edu/NetCommunity/Page.aspx?pid=183

O'Halloran, K. L. (2005). *Mathematical Discourse: Language, Symbolism, and Visual Images.* New York: Continuum.

Paterson, M. W. D. (2006). Digital scratch and virtual sniff: Simulating scents. In J. Drobnick (Ed.), *The Smell Culture Reader* (pp. 358–370). Oxford: Berg.

Rumelhart, D. E., Smolensky, P., McClelland, J. L., & Hinton, G. E. (1986). Schemata and sequential thought processes in PDP models. In J. L. McClelland & D. E. Rumelhart (Eds.), *Parallel Distributed Processing: Explorations in the Microstructure of Cognition*, Vol. 2 (pp. 7–57). Cambridge, MA: The MIT Press.

Saussure, F. (1916/1986). *Course in General Linguistics.* (C. Bally & A. Sechehaye, Eds. & R. Harris, Trans.). LaSalle, IL: Open Court Press (original work published 1916).

Siegel, M. (1995). More than words: The generative power of transmediation for learning. *Canadian Journal of Education, 20*(4), 455–475.

Suhor, C. (1984). Towards a semiotics-based curriculum. *Journal of Curriculum Studies, 16*(3), 247–257.

van Leeuwen, T. (2005). *Introducing Social Semiotics.* London: Routledge.

Vance, A. (2010). Microsoft's push into gesture technology. *The New York Times.* Retreived from http://www.nytimes.com/2010/10/30/technology/30chip.html?_r=1&scp=2&sq=Microsoft&st =cse

Vygotsky, L. S. (1978). Interaction between learning and development. In M. Cole, V. John-Steiner, S. Scribner, & E. Souberman (Eds.), *Mind in Society: The Development of Higher Psychological Processes* (pp. 79–91). Cambridge, MA: Harvard University Press.

Wertsch, J. V. (1998). *Mind as Action.* New York: Oxford University Press.

25

Researching Adolescents' Literacies Multimodally

Lalitha Vasudevan and Tiffany DeJaynes

INTRODUCTION

During a hot, summer afternoon, three boys huddled around a small laptop computer while sitting and standing on concrete steps near the bright yellow and red sign of a McDonald's restaurant. One of them held the laptop on his lap as his two friends took turns pointing to the screen and manipulating the touchpad mouse. Peals of laughter erupted occasionally from this trio as they sat together for twenty or so minutes and reviewed video footage they had produced the previous day. Amidst their laughter could be heard ideas for the next day's filming, character revisions, commentary about the evolving story arc, and suggestions for where to go next to purchase a snack. (August, 2002)

Four girls peered over one another's shoulders, pointed out favorite lines and images, as they passed a school laptop around the table, logging in and out of social networking profiles, sharing favorite blog posts, reading lines of new fan fiction stories and role playing games, simultaneously asking questions and responding to one another's questions about their digital practices and online habits. They gathered the summer after their final year of high school to help their former English teacher reanalyze and deepen the findings of her dissertation study, in which they participated. As they purposefully and playfully moved in and out of many digital spaces together, the audio recording software on the laptop captured their words seemingly unobtrusively save the occasional redirection of participants to problematize what the various literacy practices and winding connections meant. (July, 2009)

What does it mean to research the literate lives of adolescents, which are increasingly characterized by virtual explorations, multimedia self-representations and digital mediation? This question, which we explore throughout the chapter, poses a challenge to both seasoned and emerging researchers who are concerned with understanding how young people make meaning in the world as interpreters, contributors and disseminators of meaning in the form of texts, language and other communicative artifacts. Of course, the study of meaning making is not confined to adolescents nor to literacy studies alone, but that is where we locate our ensuing discussion of multimodality and its implications for how we pursued research that was conducted across multi-mediated contexts amidst the increased availability of mobile technologies and digital tools.

Take, for example, the scenes that open this chapter which are reflective of multilayered literate engagements. Each comes from a different dissertation study of adolescents and literacies conducted six years apart. These studies encompass the period of time between the growing emergence of portable technologies (early 2000s) and a robust engagement with mobile devices and social media platforms (late 2000s). In this chapter, we draw on these complementary studies to reflect on our respective digital dissertation processes as we consider the methodological implications of conducting research across technology-saturated and digitally mediated contexts.

Both of us conducted ethnographic research with youth that was focused on multimodal practices of meaning-making and knowing. Our goal in this chapter, therefore, is to make visible how researchers might (and how we tried to) make use of methodological and pedagogical considerations of sociocultural theories of multimodality and literacies when conducting digitally mediated research across multiple contexts in which multiple modalities for investigation, interpretation and representation are engaged. In our studies, this meant paying close attention to the moment-by-moment reflection and interactions that were the hallmark of a malleable kind of research guided by multimodal inquiry in addition to the more slowly unfolding patterns of practices. Both of the dissertation studies discussed here were characterized by pedagogical spaces that were created through the research and that were rich in multimodal text production, learning and multiple forms of knowing among the participants and researcher.

While multimodality has been engaged primarily as an interpretive lens for analyzing textual artifacts such as the design of magazine advertisements, adolescents' digital stories and various forms of children's text-making (Hull & Nelson, 2005; Kress & Van Leeuwen, 2001; Stein, 2003), we use this concept to explicate our practices of recognizing, interpreting and representing meaning making across modes, spaces and times. Multimodality, Jewitt (2008) argues, 'has emerged in response to the changing social and semiotic landscape' (p. 246). In our research practice, we sought to be responsive to the multimodal practices in which our participants engaged, which included digitally mediated practices, as well as non-digital, multimodal communicative practices. For definitional purposes, we offer a discursive framing of modes of meaning (e.g. visual, aural, gestural) and modalities of expression and communication (e.g. a pen, paint, musical instrument, the body) (Jewitt & Kress, 2003). In other words, within a larger context of pedagogical responsiveness, modes and modalities are not pre-ordained in their meaning or function. A classic example of such a move away from technological determinism is a scenario in which the screen of a mobile phone is used to light a path in the dark, for example during a power outage. While the actual device has a great many technical affordances, the phone's *in situ* utility in such a moment is found in its ability to serve as a source of light.

SITUATING OUR STUDIES

Following from our inquiry-based traditions, we write from shared and complementary perspectives. Lalitha conducted her dissertation research prior to the preponderance of social media technologies and an internet landscape that is now commonly referred to as Web 2.0. The adolescents who were at the center of her study led technologically mediated lives that included everyday engagement with both stationary and handheld (and therefore portable) video game consoles, televisions, cameras and computers; and through their participation in research that was focused on their literacy and technology practices under the auspices of an out-of-school storytelling project, they became familiar with digital voice recorders, digital video cameras and video-editing software.

Tiffany conducted her dissertation research a few years later in the midst of social media landscapes of Web 2.0 platforms. She came to know her participants first through her English Language Arts classroom and subsequently across a range of digital modes of representation, some of which were directly connected to their in-school requirements and most that were reflective of the adolescents' self-directed, out-of-school lives – blogging, photography, film, music, visual design, instant message and social networking (i.e. Facebook). The youth in her study experimented with new forms of digital media and representation, many invited her into their existing social networks and through their participation in her study reflected on their experiences with various digital modalities in school and many other spaces for learning and recreation.

Like most ethnographic research, our studies were both surprising and shifted regularly to meet the demands of our participants, particularly as each of us conducted research within a pedagogical tenor. In other words, our personal histories as educators figured prominently in how we conducted our research. Lalitha accepted this role reluctantly whereas Tiffany was situated as a teacher in the high school where her study was located. (We discuss our respective research positionalities later in this chapter.) Each of us collected data by recording our research in a variety of ways – collecting and engaging with online texts, audio recordings, films, photos and other multimodal artifacts – and by sharing this recording and documenting role with our research participants. Our findings were also inevitably shaped by this deliberate messiness in which multiple forms of documentation were complemented by interpretive approaches that were equally 'messy' such that traditional methods of ethnographic data analysis and representation became hybridized through our engagement and interactions with the adolescents in our research. As such, our studies involved multimodal research protocols that we designed and shaped iteratively as data emerged.

In what follows, we document our processes in greater detail, unearthing the circular and multiple nature of our digital data collection, analysis and representation. We offer one final introductory note: Lalitha served as Tiffany's dissertation advisor, and thus this chapter is the result of our ongoing conversations about researching in a digital age.

We organize our chapter around three key ideas central to our discussion of researching multimodally. In the following section, we engage the first of these ideas and draw on Lalitha's study to describe the methodological considerations we engaged in as we created and began to explore the spaces of our research studies. Next, we emphasize the collaborative nature of participation in these studies with examples drawn from Tiffany's study in order to articulate how an interpretive stance about youth and literacies shaped how we made sense of what we were learning in conversation with our participants. The third idea around which we organize this chapter is the analysis and representation of the spaces – including the texts, practices, relationships and identities that were created and emerged within our research spaces – for various audiences. Throughout each of these intersecting dimensions of the research, we continued to document the stories of our studies. Thus, we discuss practices of documentation throughout this chapter and conclude with a discussion of methodological considerations for conducting digitally mediated research that have emerged from our respective studies.

ENACTING RESEARCH SPACES MULTIMODALLY

Youth regularly navigate multi-dimensional communicative landscapes such as social networking and video sharing sites, cloud computing services, multimedia editing programs and blogging and microblogging platforms (e.g. Alvermann, 2010; Gustavson, 2007; Hagood, Alvermann, & Heron-Hruby, 2010). Their participation in these spaces is rich with diverse literacy practices that call on youth to demonstrate discursive as well as technical fluency. Therefore, an important challenge lies in effectively investigating and interpreting these landscapes and youths' attendant practices of multimodal negotiation and navigation across diverse sociocultural contexts. Ito and colleagues (2010), for example, conducted a multi-sited, longitudinal study of young people's practices and learned of the varying ways in which youth across settings develop a relationship to the digital spaces and technologies that are a part of their lives. The findings of their study suggested that young people cultivate different practices and exhibit varying degrees of expertise in relation to their online and digital communications and navigations. Theirs was a study that required ample time observing youth, communicating with them in multiple contexts and through various modes, at times participating or drawing on personal experience with gaming or virtual worlds, in pursuit of meaning and understanding about this burgeoning and rapidly changing landscape. In this work, the research team was able to access multiple sites to comprise the space of this research project. We mention this example here to bring to the fore the importance of how research spaces are identified, constructed and traversed multimodally in pursuit of new understandings about a particular phenomenon, which in this case was the changing terrain of adolescents online practices and the resultant understandings about their texts, identities, relationships and other related meanings. Jacobs (2008) provides an astute assessment of youths' hybrid spaces and movements in her study of adolescents' instant messaging practices. She notes that asking *where* this practice takes place is not the right question, and that instead researchers need to pay attention to the many 'wheres' across which one may be engaged. In other words, Jacobs observed that instant messaging is a practice that does not only occur within the confines of a dynamic text box on a computer screen, but that when the young woman at the center of her case study was engaged in IM-ing, she was simultaneously talking on the phone, communicating via email and composing less dynamic texts via word processing programs. Portable technologies further catalyze the ability to seemingly be in two places at once (Leander, 2005).

Often, courses on research methods tend to gloss over the highly important introductory phase of conducting research, particularly ethnographic research in which relationships are of critical importance in pursuing inquiry. Questions such as *How does one enter a space?*, *How does one make oneself known – as a researcher, as a participant, as an observer?*, and *How does one initiate interactions with participants?* should be asked and kept at the forefront of an iterative and interpretive research design. Our task was complicated by our shared desire to explore the literacies of adolescents in a manner that was not tethered to predetermined labels that commonly frame the intersection of youth and literacies such as 'struggling reader' or 'struggling writer' and 'digital divide' or 'off-task'. Each of us set out to explore the nuances of adolescents' literacies by engaging with adolescents to co-construct the contexts that would eventually become the sites for our studies. To do so, we first had to appreciate the dynamic nature of contexts as understood through the prism of spatiality. The word 'context' belies the multispatial nature of the work, thus we use context interchangeably with 'spaces' in order to more fully capture the varied ways in which research relationships and practices shaped our research contexts. Gustavson and Cytrynbaum (2003) have defined spaces as places that become animated with human activity. Similarly, Leander and Sheehy (2004) advocate for a dynamic and 'spatialized' understanding of contexts in literacy research wherein contexts are not merely backdrop, but gain meaning through social practice. These and other perspectives that illustrate the contours of a 'lived' approach to research contexts were also motivating factors in how we did not merely observe but in fact *enacted* our research spaces. We were especially interested in engaging youth as knowers, which meant enacting a research space in which our adolescent participants were not merely involved in but also central to the data collection. Likewise, this meant inviting in unexpected forms of data such as spontaneously produced and scripted media artifacts, chat transcripts and text messages to name a few; and it meant extending our conceptualization of the boundaries of the research context to include unexpected geographies – physical and virtual – and temporalities.

Our example of creating a research space in this multimodal way comes from an out-of-school storytelling project[1] during which Lalitha spent fifteen months with five African–American adolescent boys in the period of time before, during and after their sixth grade year. One of the ways in which research relationships became established was through the sharing of access to technologies. Romeo[2] was a part of Lalitha's study from the beginning and he developed a penchant for the digital video camera early in the research process. While all five of the boys who were part of this storytelling project took the opportunity to experiment with the variety of technologies that were made available on a regular basis, it was Romeo who displayed the greatest facility with this medium of expression. More comfortable behind the camera than in front of it, Romeo embraced the view-finder screen like a painter approaches a painting surface – as a space in which to compose a scene, rather than a way to engage in a form of unmediated documentation of what was happening.

Within a few weeks of the initial meeting, a plan began to emerge for the first project that the group pursued for the next three months. The idea of a 'funny, scary movie' project was initiated during a conversation that took place in a local park on a hot summer day. Romeo was positioned, with the camera secure in his grip, in front of the bench where Cyrus, TJ, Rasheed (Romeo and Jamal's cousin) and Lalitha were sitting. Jamal sat across from the rest of the group on another coated wire bench dribbling a basketball. The conversation began with Cyrus and TJ making simultaneous suggestions for casting, plotlines and necessary props. As they talked, Romeo continued to interject comments that had little to do with the oral storyboarding and instead opened up another space of inquiry made available through his maneuvering of the camera.

Through his redirection of the visual gaze away from the movie planning conversation, Romeo had constructed a new narrative of the afternoon's goings on. Romeo's video documentation began with a pan between Cyrus and Jamal who were the most animated that afternoon. TJ sits playing with his durag[3] and was Cyrus's only real competition for deciding on the process for making the movie. Cyrus squints as he looks into the camera to protect his eyes from the piercing sun. Rasheed occasionally weighs in on the conversation or pokes his head directly into the frame of the camera. While filming this scene, that unfolds over the course of the seven and half minutes, Romeo experimented with a variety of visual techniques – including panning across the park, zooming into and away from different objects and people and applying some of the available filters such as the negative film screen and the fade out function – that were also documented on the video.

More significant than the fact that the image on the screen does not directly correspond with the words being spoken was Romeo's use of the negative filter to non-verbally express what he was seeing. The video suggests a parallel narrative that he constructed in this visual mode. Figure 25.1 shows three stills taken

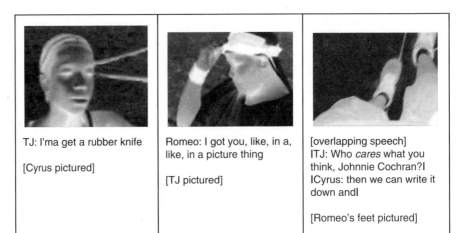

TJ: I'ma get a rubber knife [Cyrus pictured]	Romeo: I got you, like, in a, like, in a picture thing [TJ pictured]	[overlapping speech] ITJ: Who *cares* what you think, Johnnie Cochran?I ICyrus: then we can write it down andI [Romeo's feet pictured]

Figure 25.1   Stills from a video clip

from the video clip accompanied by narration underneath, which again is not necessarily aligned with the visual.

This clip signified a shift in how video came to be used in this project when it became evident that Romeo's experimentation and eventual facility with the video camera was a significant narrative activity, as was the oral construction of the scary movie. His narrative was performed across space and time, reflective of observations Blackburn (2002/2003) made of how adolescents enacted a particular narrative set of meanings using various literacy practices. She used the term 'literacy performances' to call attention to adolescents' use of both space and time to make meaning. Likewise, Rowsell and Pahl's (2007) notion of sedimented identities gains traction in Romeo's practices where his identity within the out-of-school storytelling group became sedimented across the range of video texts he would go on to create. Furthermore, the video that he created was also indicative of the space in which it was created as much as it served a representational function, much like the portraits Pink (2001) took with her camera were suggestive of the meanings given to the artifact of a photograph by local community members than of what they actually depicted.

In another moment that occurs about five minutes into the video clip, while the visual frame is fixed on Jamal's torso as he stands and bounces the basketball, Lalitha can be heard asking, 'Is he OK?' in response to a small boy who has just fallen on the playground while running to catch up with his playmates. The visual image immediately pans to the boy who quickly becomes a blur of blue as he runs forward. Romeo's camera work zooms onto the little boy as the voices of Cyrus, TJ and Jamal are filled with gentle laughter and mild concern for the boy. In doing so, the other boys momentarily acknowledge the child's fall but then resume planning the movie. As talk of fake blood and the rest of the plotline of the scary movie ensue, the camera stays focused on the boy for a bit longer, showing us that the child has some trouble putting his shoe back on. Romeo then pans across the playground for several seconds before the clip ends. When asked about his decision to film the little boy, Romeo remarked that he liked to see how other people used the park.

In these moments, Romeo the cameraman becomes Romeo the director as he re-shifts the viewer's (and the researcher's) gaze toward another simultaneous set of happenings. But he is authoring more than just this self as he zooms and pans and films in the negative. In the moment described above, Romeo authors a particular narrative space that he went on to develop throughout the duration of the study, one which is characterized by the engagement of various other visual technologies to consistently story underappreciated or overlooked aspects of social life – for example, musings on how people use the park. Thus, by disrupting the intended use of the video camera as a tool for documentation, Romeo changes not only the data available but also how he is written into the scene. It would be inadequate to note that Romeo was only documenting a group conversation or even to say that he was playing with the camera effects. It is more accurate to recognize how, through his ownership over the composing landscape of the digital video camera, Romeo authored a self of increased narrative authority and seamlessly extended the research space to include the display screen of the video camera.

In addition to a shift in ethnographic gaze, the use of the digital artifacts in this research space extends the functionality of technologies beyond assumed or deterministic purposes – for example, a video camera to create an event and not only to document events that are already occurring. Thus, the digital artifacts that were engaged, such as the expressive modalities (video camera, still camera, digital voice recorder) as well as the resultant texts (video clips, audio files, photographs), gained meaning in the ways they were situated in the storytelling space. In this sense, these artifacts served as additional sites of potential stories, identity performances and literacies (Pahl & Rowsell, 2010). Likewise, the collection, engagement and production of digital artifacts allowed the emerging inquiry to be pursued and documented in an organic way, echoing Marcus's (1995) invitation for ethnographers to follow the threads of inquiry that may transgress the boundaries of a specified research 'site'. In this case, the making of the research space was integral to the construction of the research itself. With the advent of social media and mobile devices, multiple sites can be connected by centralizing technologies such as a website, social networking site, media sharing sites and the like. As this study occurred prior to the social media and mobile technology revolution, and because there was no single site of research, all of the technologies were carried to and from and across the research geographies in Lalitha's royal blue backpack that can often be spotted in photographs and videos produced within the project space.

For Lalitha and the boys in her study, artifactual engagement with technologies was found in spontaneous acts of documentation, text production, playing with cameras, use of digital voice recorders and various software programs on a small laptop. Even in partially scripted moments, such as the production of scenes from the mock scary movie, the use and orchestration of technologies was not pre-determined and at the same was reflective of the space in which these practices occurred. Regular access to the technologies during all group meetings further cultivated an expanded palette of modes with which to orchestrate meaning making within this storytelling space (for a related and extended discussion of the orchestration of modes in digital storytelling, see Hull & Nelson, 2005).

For Tiffany, multiple sites of interaction and composing were connected through social networking sites and a connected series of blogs. The spaces of learning that Tiffany and her youth participants crafted together were filled with cameras, videocameras, ipods and laptops which were variously engaged as they took up research questions about adolescent literacies, multimodal text making and the like. Along with her youth participants, Tiffany captured important moments on the screen as participants and researcher logged into various online spaces, and traversed and collaboratively explored many different spaces, regardless of whether they were interacting online from different computers or sharing the same computer. We discuss the participatory nature of research relationships with youth in further detail in the next section.

PARTICIPATING IN DIGITALLY MEDIATED RESEARCH SPACES

Youth are emerging at the fore of discussions about globalization, cosmopolitanism and civic participation, though the nature of their participation in digitally mediated spaces is understood in a variety of ways (Hull, Stornaiuolo, & Sahni, 2010; Maira & Soep, 2005; Livingstone, 2008). Recent theorization in media studies, literacy studies and geographies reexamines and re-articulates the agency, creativity and cultural citizenship of youth in our participatory, mediated world. Affiliations beyond the nation state are increasingly common and salient for youth, and, as such, local contexts of participatory research must turn their lenses to these dynamic, often global shifts in youth cultural practices. Through their participation with digital media, youth form wide-reaching and overlapping affiliations, both deliberately and implicitly, situating their communicative practices within a broad matrix of cultural practices. As youth participate as citizens of local and global worlds, they develop cosmopolitan habits of mind and social values. Various forms of participation in our new media ecology creates new challenges and opportunities for researchers of youth, forcing us to closely consider how we study youth participation across digitally mediated spaces, how we disentangle overlapping and far-reaching flows of communication and how we involve youth in this process.

Putting participation at the heart of our research is critical, as it means seeing youth as actively engaged in their literacy practices, meaning-making, authorship and design. Additionally, it means seeing all kinds of media engagement as participation. Jenkins (2006) argues, 'Rather than talking about media producers and consumers occupying separate roles, we might now see them both as participants who interact with each other according to a new set of rules that none of us fully understands' (p. 4). New media ecologies are characterized by new kinds of social participation and authorship, rather than limited to one-sided notions of media consumption (Jenkins, 2006; Ito et al., 2008). New ways of seeing participation affect how we examine and position youth in new media landscapes, particularly in research that leans into the deeply personal and collaborative nature of youths' multimodal participation within the a global sphere. Viewing all media as social and active is particularly critical as it makes visible issues of power and agency (Ito et al., 2008).

Our multimodal research spaces were participatory in that we engaged, played, documented, socialized and experimented in digital spaces with youth rather than simply lurk in the shadows attempting to analyze what we observed. As we studied, produced media in and analyzed these multimodal spaces with participants, they became our co-investigators and collaborators. Thus, in our pedagogical spaces, we intentionally created venues to enact and explore various kinds of engagement with literacy across multiple modes and modalities.

Part of our task as researchers is to try to understand the deep-seated shifts in participation underway in our digitally mediated culture (Ito et al., 2010). As youth make their social imaginations visible in mediated ways, we must also examine our methodologies for exploring their new participatory habits of mind. Because participating in new media involves collaboration, networking and sharing, it is these social skills that become significant to explore.

Our example for how we examined participation in digitally mediated spaces comes from Tiffany's study of new media with graduating high school seniors enrolled in her English Language Arts classes. She participated with the youth in her study across a range of mediated spaces and developing new kinds of protocols for examining what was happening across the various spaces in which youth engaged, and as a result new forms of data collection emerged. Tiffany confronted what it meant to be a participant observer in digital spaces as well as her classroom (and the spaces in between, characterized by artifacts such as text messages and status updates affixed to social networking profiles). Her data collection took an interactive and naturalistic approach. This meant commenting on blogs and interacting as naturally as possible in the spaces she was invited into by the youth in her study. It also meant following the inquiry about their literate lives in surprising directions and modifying her research protocols to include various types of mediated and collaborative interactions.

Tiffany did not initially plan to use focus groups but a customized form of small group conversation as a means of participating together to understand the research emerged rather organically in her data collection. One afternoon, as she sat in her classroom interviewing one participant about her blog and other online literacy practices, the young woman's friends began entering and interjecting comments into the conversation. The group of friends gathered around the computer and began responding to the questions posed, and also began adding their own questions. As the young women clicked around from page to page and explained their interactions on social networking spaces, Tiffany understood that she needed to more deeply investigate their relationships and connections online. Hence, she modified her individual interview protocol to become a series of media-equipped focus groups with networks of friends who had built connections and interacted across a wide range of multimodal spaces. Therefore, the focus groups that she set up were in response to the digital affordances of the various communicative practices she was observing. These were not merely conversations about blogs, but in fact were moments of discursive inquiry for which the blogs provided scaffolding.

The multimodal affordances of the online spaces across which these artifacts existed and across which these practices occurred thus necessitated multimodal engagement and collaboration between and amongst participants and researcher in order to understand the practices more fully. This responsive turn resonates with Soep and Chavez's (2005) articulation of a collegial pedagogy as an approach for adults and youth to consider when they are engaged together in media production. Wissman, Vasudevan, Staples, and Nichols (in preparation) describe this pedagogically responsive stance in research using the concept of 'research pedagogies', that brings forward the attempts of researchers to meaningfully disrupt the problematic divide between research and practice. In doing so, the authors invite researchers to actively engage adolescents in the construction of spaces in which their literacies are not only researched, but in which literacy learning also takes place. In such spaces of multimodal pedagogies – where the understanding of subject-matter concepts is assessed through game play or when youth are invited to create dramatic dialogue in response to a prompt about their sense of belonging – literacies and meaning making practices are distributed across modes and artifacts. Thus, the authority of the researcher or teacher is meaningfully de-centered to create space for youths' multimodal literacies and multiple subjectivities (Janks, 2006).

Thus, the focus of the research was extended to include not only oral but visual, gestural and interactive practices across a range of texts and spaces. The participatory nature of the research work was so strong that a 'friend group case study' emerged as the best way for Tiffany to understand the various overlapping writing practices of a group of young women in her study – friends who regularly commented on one another's blogs, wrote fan fiction together, and participated in various social media websites to affiliate with others interested in visual arts, gaming and anime. To understand the traveling literacy practices of her students, the webs of connections between their online work and the way in which this connected with their social roles, Tiffany approached the friend group to meet together and reflect on their digital participation together, as a way of understanding the practices that she could only loosely see sedimented or instantiated in their digital texts (Pahl & Rowsell, 2006).

This excerpt from Tiffany's dissertation illustrates the process that evolved:

One key focal group interview, in the summer after our year together, allowed me to see their collective experiences as audience members performed. They took up roles as active listeners, co-interviewers, and collective meaning-makers during our approximately ninety-minute conversation together, sitting at a crowded café the summer after they'd graduated high school. Nicole – who had spoken with me the most about this project – acted as a leader in the group interview. She asked thoughtful questions of her friends, pushed back against some answers, and even pulled the laptop over her direction to locate blog entries she remembered in order to move the conversation certain directions she thought might be useful. As the interview continued, all of the girls began to ask one another questions, inter-mingling commentary and questioning, collectively making sense of just what it was they did with the space of the blogs in relation to one another and otherwise. Thus, the interview itself became another composing space to which they brought their writer and reader lenses and recreated audience.

Our conversation was negotiated in some interesting ways, as each girl took a turn in what we together called the 'hot seat,' giving each girl time to talk about her own blog, however, our conversation was much more organic than that depiction might suggest. What actually happened is that the laptop was passed around organically, chairs were shifted, and shoul-ders leaned over. Questions were posed by all, interjections made and a boisterous conversa-tion ensued.

In this focus group conversation, the youth and Tiffany worked from the inter-connected world they had created online: their hyperlinked web of blogs, social networks, even fan fiction and gaming sites, comparing affordances of various social networking tools and reading together the intertextual links of their many online spaces. Jane shared how she'd moved her poetry into her Facebook profile giving up some of the visual affordances of her blog in order to garner the atten-tion of a more selective audience of readers by tagging close friends and former teachers, as a way of soliciting feedback on her writing. Marie demonstrated her fan fiction writing and the group explored the explicit connections and over-lap between her blogging practices, the novel she was writing over AIM with Nicole, her anime artwork on a social media website where she had made inter-national connections, and the way that she harnessed her social network in Facebook to braid together her social and creative worlds. Irisa explained how Marie had socialized her into social media practices, by helping her start a blog, giving her feedback and pushing her to explore online outlets for sharing her hand-drawn anime artwork. Nicole acted as guide, showcasing her new online role playing game with the group, and making explicit the interconnections between the numerous local and global affiliations and social contexts of their online creative work.

As Tiffany and the youth in her study participated together in re-seeing their online writing, they remade and resituated interactions – simultaneously online and offline, past and present. Some of the fluidity, overlapping and co-constructed nature of the conversation above could be dismissed as a product of the group's closeness as a community or the young women's friendships, but the overlaps and interconnections of these relationships helped to reveal the complex terrain of their social literacy practices in mediated local and global spaces. These focus groups revealed the power of harnessing multimodal technologies in the research process, as something more nuanced and interesting than simply researching technologies. The intertextual nature of the space created by the young people in the study became clear as the youth huddled together around the laptop to deconstruct what they saw and continued interacting with one another across in-person and mediated spaces. By inviting multimodal means of engagement and communication into the research process – not just as the thing being studied but also as a means of researching and knowing – research methods were shaped and re-examined.

Participatory culture, which values affiliations and collaborations across various expressive modalities and mediums, encourages new kinds of research relationships. 'Participatory culture is reworking the rules by which school, cultural expression, civic life, and work operate' (Jenkins, 2006, p. 9). As such, we worked to understand as well as enact these new rules. Tiffany began searching for ways to understand the connections between the plethora of literacy practices she was observing, to try to understand how the various forms, artifacts, relationships and habits of mind worked together. She began asking, *What does it mean to make sense of a young person's literacies if you have so many forms and artifacts? How do you make the connections between and among participatory practices?*

Because community involvement is critical to understanding participatory culture, individual interviews were not able to reveal the depth of youths' literacy practices. Rather, the multimodal focus groups led to an understanding of how the blogs students wrote for school fit into and worked alongside (or sometimes didn't overlap with) the other participatory practices of the youth in Tiffany's study. Typically, youth made a way to fit their digitally mediated work for school somehow into the social fabric of their online lives and mediated identities. Taking an ecological approach to seeing the relationships of different communicative practices helped Tiffany understand her participants' literacies and their emerging global habits of mind. The boundaries of her research became increasingly permeable as she was invited into more spaces of knowing and began to observe how literacy practices flowed across these spaces. A multimodal focus added an observable circularity and multispatiality to both of our studies, which was both illuminating and exciting as well as overwhelming at times. Overlapping, participatory and intertextual data emerged and posed challenges for analysis and representation, as we explore in the following section.

QUESTIONS OF MULTIMODAL ANALYSIS AND REPRESENTATION

Our shared commitment to engaging in research by assuming an inquiry stance is informed, in part, by the tradition of practitioner inquiry (Campano, 2007; Cochran-Smith & Lytle, 2009) in which researcher reflexivity and the insider knowledge of participants is paramount. As we mentioned above, we also worked within a pedagogical tenor, and thus engaged multimodal pedagogies that were responsive to the identities and innovations of participants. Stein (2008) argues, 'Multimodal pedagogies acknowledge learners as agentive, resourceful and creative meaning-makers who communicate using the communicative potential and multiple resources of their bodies and their environment to interconnect' (p. 122). The technologies we employed in our studies were both part of data collection and also shaped how we worked together with our youth participants and how we interpreted the meanings about the very devices we were exploring (i.e. recording images, video and audio, being able to log in to various accounts, comment on blogs, explore websites, quickly search for something online, view fan fiction pages, or write the next segment of a script together). We attempted as researchers and youth to understand together the affordances of multimodal composing and the tensions that came along with it.

The participatory nature evident in both of our research spaces was profoundly informed by a recognition of the agency and resourcefulness evident in our youth participants' technology savvy, which guided our study of their engagement with and creation of digital artifacts. Rather than viewing this epistemic distribution as a loss of power or control over the research process, we both recognized that in order to investigate the emerging literacies of adolescents, participation had to be more than merely a dimension of the research space; our spaces were inherently participatory and participation was inherently multimodal. Likewise, this lens informed how and what we identified and documented as literacy practices by making visible our values about what counts as literacy and our understandings of young people as knowers and meaning-makers.

We continue to search for ways to examine the connections, to make visible the interconnectedness of literacy practices. We also seek ways to analyze and represent our work multimodally. When data are collected across modes, the result is files upon files of digital photos, screen shots, films, chat and text message logs, focus group interview transcripts and the residue of many additional creative projects in process. Tiffany remembers vividly looking at her data set spread out across not only many different digital spaces but also across many different mediums of representation and feeling duly overwhelmed by the 'what next?' as she looked for ways to take apart the data, dissect it, make sense of it for herself, her participants and her readers. She settled in to develop and modify strategies for multimodal analysis proposed by Kress (2003) and Jewitt (2008) among others but also found herself designing experimental approaches to analyze the interconnections, relationships, texts, identities and a host of communicative patterns, such as the focus group text analysis described above. In moving the field forward, we need to continue to make visible new ways of examining the social aspects of digital literacy practices across mediums of communication and to continue to experiment with what it means to research multimodally.

Our units of analysis, as suggested by Leander and McKim (2003), had to attend to the ways that meanings moved across spaces and modes. In Lalitha's study, this included 'group space', which was made through participants' enactments and also through their ongoing meta-discursive commentary about what it was that they were involved in creating. Exchanges between or with participants might be mined for the other texts they are suggestive of, either that were produced within or were invoked within the project space. Hagood (2004) has used rhizoanalysis as a way of visually mapping out the interrelationships between her adolescent participants' identities, communities and texts as a way of understanding the literacies and literate lives. She and others are asking of rhizomatic interactions not only 'what is this an instance of' – which is a focus that resonates with the standard practices of coding for themes and patterns – but they are also wondering to where an exchange or interaction might lead. In this vein, we might ask 'What can an artifact tell us about the space in which it was created?' and 'What are the conditions that contributed to the creation of a text or that cultivated various literacy practices evident in a piece of digital media?' Thus, the video excerpt shared above is both a multimodal marker of the origins of the group's mock scary movie and artifact that embodies the relational, communicative and pedagogical ethos of the space in which it was created.

These approaches to analyzing data are both systematic and improvised, and always responsive to the nature of the inquiry. For the two dissertation studies we have engaged in this chapter, actively engaging youth in the processes of analysis and representation was crucial. In some ways akin to the ethnographic practice of member checking, wherein emic concepts are confirmed by research participants and key informants, the adolescents involved in our studies offered interpretations on what we were seeing as well as *how* we were seeing, and thus documenting and interpreting their lives. Both of us considered and actively involved youth when composing representative vignettes, portraits, case studies and thematic arguments within our dissertations and in other writing based on our dissertation research.

Thus, a conceptualization of youth as documentarians and co-investigators was integral to both of our studies. Throughout the duration of both studies, as youth participants took up roles as photographers, videographers, visual designers and bloggers, they began to have a hand in the work of research. The ubiquity of cameras and laptops in the space of the classroom and in the hands of students meant that they quickly also became integrated into the research. In the process, youth came to understand their role as more than photographers, videographers or online writers, but also as co-researchers, sharing in the inquiry, responding to the research questions of the study as they understood them. Participants' documenting their own experiences in the spaces we traversed together led to a pool of data rich in the visual, audio, gestural and verbal artifacts and texts. The visual gaze of youth participants shaped what data was collected and how it was (re)presented.

In Tiffany's study, this meant enhancing thick ethnographic description in words with largely visual and embodied literacies landscapes of the young women and men in her study. As so much information about youth's lives is readily available across the various social media platforms in which they engage and represent themselves, conditions of anonymity become increasing challenging to navigate. For Lalitha, representation involved the creation of short videos comprising data collected with and by the boys in her study that complemented as well as extended the written ethnographic representations found within the pages of the dissertation. At the time, a CD with the movie files was supplied to her dissertation committee; today, these might be private or unlisted YouTube links.

In her current research, Lalitha has maintained a group research blog where the use of tags helps to mediate the ongoing reflective analysis as she and her team facilitate an after-school digital media arts program with court-involved youth. A private website has also been set up for program participants to revisit media artifacts that were shared or created during the weekly workshops. While the social affordances of literacies and research practices may have evolved with the advent of new technologies and media making tools, they continue to be situated within the pedagogical ethos that grounded her out-of-school storytelling dissertation study.

METHODOLOGICAL CONSIDERATIONS FOR MULTIMODAL RESEARCH IN A DIGITAL AGE

Digitally mediated research calls for researchers to consider a host of unique methodological challenges and opportunities. In our continued work with adolescents, we are reminded regularly of the collective, socially situated and multispatial nature of their literacy practices. As youth traverse the multiple spaces of their lives, they create, recreate and respond to a variety of texts. Thus, to conclude our discussion here, we return to the question we posed at the beginning: What does it mean to research the literate lives of adolescents, which are increasingly characterized by virtual explorations, multimedia self-representations and digital mediation?

We think a partial response to this question involves an awareness of how we ethically enact ourselves as researchers who are interested in understanding the digitally mediated lives of adolescents, through our use of digitally mediated methodologies. Considerations about how and why we are using and exploring digital tools, and our willingness to be surprised are a part of this ethical awareness. Likewise, in engaging in research about the literacies of adolescents, whose practices and identities have for so long been maligned by models of literacy pedagogy and research (as described in Gadsden, 2008; Hull, Zacher, & Hibbert, 2009; Luke & Carrington, 2002), we also invite researchers to consider the moral responsibility and response we bring to our participants, our inquiries and to literacy studies and related fields of study implicated in our work.

The collective and interwoven nature of the literacy practices we set out to examine and understand compel us to create and amend (and sometimes altogether redesign) our initial research protocols to respond to early findings and organic developments in documentation and data collection. Thus, we shaped and reshaped research protocols to respond to the collective nature of adolescents' literacies (especially in relation to their digital practices) in order to be responsive to these evolving literacy practices in many of the same ways that the development of social media has responded to the demands and communicative practices of its adopters. Some of the affordances of Web 2.0 resources – facilitating interaction and community, offering user-friendly tools for sharing and responding to original media content – are the same affordances that have brought together participants in our studies and what has allowed each of us to lean into the literate lives of the youth in these and subsequent research projects (Vasudevan, 2010; Vasudevan, DeJaynes, & Schmier, 2010).

Fine, Torre, Burns, and Payne (2006) have noted that often researchers who seek to involve youth in their work run the risk of asking youth to be mere parrots of existing findings and beliefs or to include their voices as mere decorations. Employing multimodal methodologies for research opens up a host of possibilities for creating conditions to not only see and hear the perspectives of participants – across modes of communication and expression – but therefore to reframe orientations and purposes of the research being conducted. Responsiveness and flexibility in this way should not be confused with a lack of rigor. Instead, willingness to critically and iteratively revisit research design proved to be a strength for both of us as we actively attended to what the participants thought worthy of capturing through the lens of the camera, watched and examined together the films and other artifacts they produced, listened for and heard the questions they asked of their peers with the voice recorder in hand and digitally exchanged ideas asynchronously in the comment sections of blogs or synchronously in AIM chats.

When we create the kinds of spaces where many perspectives are honored and many modes of exploration are employed, we begin to see youth move beyond the various tools that may be offered or available in a given context and take up and introduce new media tools for furthering the investigation, re-appropriating existing resources for research purposes and resisting technological determinism. And perhaps more importantly, we begin to see adolescents outside of the confines of often simplistic institutional labels and instead as complex, multiliterate people who are, everyday, engaged in exploring and enacting the world around them. The richness of multiple voices invites still new questions to consider, new spaces to explore, new practices to understand and new representations to render.

NOTES

1. This vignette has been adapted from an article published in *e-Learning and Digital Media* (Vasudevan, 2006).
2. All names of participants are pseudonyms.
3. A piece of fabric tied tightly around the head, sometimes worn under caps or alone.

REFERENCES

Alvermann, D. (2010). Why bother theorizing adolescents' online literacies for classroom practice and research? *Journal of Adolescent and Adult Literacy, 52*(1), 8–19.

Blackburn, M. (2002/2003). Disrupting the (hetero)normative: Exploring literacy performances and identity work with queer youth. *Journal of Adolescent and Adult Literacy, 46*(4), 312–323.

Campano, G. (2007). *Immigrant Students and Literacy: Reading, Writing, and Remembering.* New York: Teachers College Press.

Cochran-Smith, M. & Lytle, S. L. (2009). *Inquiry as Stance: Practitioner Research in the Next Generation.* New York: Teachers College Press.

Cochran-Smith, M. & Lytle, S. L. (1993). *Inside/Outside: Teacher Research and Knowledge.* New York: Teachers College Press.

Fine, M., Torre, M. E., Burns, A., & Payne, Y. A. (2006). Youth research/participatory methods for reform. In D. Thiessen & A. Cook-Sather (Eds.), *International Handbook of Student Experience in Elementary and Secondary School* (pp. 805–828). New York: Springer.

Gadsden, V. (2008). The arts and education: Knowledge generation, pedagogy, and the discourse of learning. *Review of Research in Education, 32,* 29–61.

Gustavson, L. (2007). *Youth learning on their own terms: Creative practices and classroom teaching.* New York: Routledge.

Gustavson, L. & Cytrynbaum, J. (2003). Illuminating spaces: Relational spaces, complicity, and multisited ethnography. *Field Methods, 15*(3), 252–270.

Hagood, M. (2004). A rhizomatic cartography of adolescents, popular culture, and constructions of self. In K. Leander & M. Sheehy (Eds.), *Spatializing Literacy Research and Practice* (pp. 143–160). New York: Peter Lang.

Hagood, M., Alvermann, D., & Heron-Hruby, A. (2010). *Bringing it to class: Unpacking pop culture in literacy learning.* New York: Teachers College Press.

Hull, G. & Nelson, M. E. (2005). Locating the semiotic power of multimodality. *Written Communication, 22*(2), 224–261.

Hull, G., Stornaiuolo, A., & Sahni, U. (2010). Cultural citizenship and cosmopolitan practice: Global youth communicate online. *English Education, 42*(4), 331–367.

Hull, G., Zacher, J., & Hibbert, L. (2009). Youth, risk, and equity in a global world. *Review of Research in Education, 33,* 117–159.

Ito, M., Baumer, S., Bittanti, M., Boyd, D., Cody, R., Herr-Stephenson, B., & Tripp, L. (2010). *Hanging out, Messing Around, and Geeking Out: Kids Living and Learning with New Media.* Cambridge, MA: The MIT Press.

Ito, M., Horst, H., Bittanti, M., Boyd, D., Herr-Stephenson, B., Lange, P. G., & Robinson, L. (2008). *Living and Learning with New Media: Summary of Findings from the Digital Youth Project.* Chicago, IL: The John D. and Catherine T. MacArthur Foundation. Retrieved from http://digitalyouth.ischool.berkeley.edu/files/report/digitalyouth-WhitePaper.pdf

Jacobs, G. (2008). We learn what we do: Developing a repertoire of writing practices in an instant messaging world. *Journal of Adolescent and Adult Literacy, 52*(3), 203–211.

Janks, H. (2006). Games go abroad. *English Studies in Africa, 49*(1), 115–138.

Jenkins, H. (2006). *Convergence Culture: Where Old and New Media Collide.* New York: New York University Press.

Jenkins, H., Clinton, K., Purushotma, R., Robison, A. J., & Wiegel, M. (2006). *Confronting the Challenges of Participatory Culture: Media Education in the 21st Century.* Chicago, IL: The John D. and Catherine T. MacArthur Foundation.

Jewitt, C. (2008). Multimodality and literacy in school classrooms. *Review of Research in Education, 32*(1), 241–267.

Jewitt, C. & Kress, G. (Eds.) (2003). *Multimodal Literacy.* New York: Peter Lang.

Kress, G. (2003). *Literacy in the New Media Age.* New York: Routledge.

Kress, G. & Van Leeuwen, T. (2001). *Multimodal Discourse: The Modes and Media of Contemporary Communication.* London: Arnold.

Lankshear, C., Lankshear, C., & Knobel, M. (2003). *New Literacies.* Philadelphia, PA: Open University Press.

Leander, K. (2005). *Imagining and practicing Internet space-times with/in school.* Paper presented at the National Council of Teachers of English Assembly for Research, Columbus, OH.

Leander, K. & McKim, K. (2003). Tracing the everyday 'sitings' of adolescents on the Internet: A strategic adaptation of ethnography across online and offline spaces. *Education, Communication, & Information, 3*(2), 211–240.

Leander, K. & Sheehy, M. (2004). *Spatializing Literacy Research and Practice.* New York: Peter Lang.

Livingstone, S. (2008) Taking risky opportunities in youthful content creation: Teenagers' use of social networking sites for intimacy, privacy and self-expression. *New Media & Society, 10*(3), 393–411.

Luke, A. & Carrington, V. (2002). Globalisation, literacy, curriculum practice. In M. Lewis, R. Fisher, & G. Brooks (Eds.), *Language and Literacy in Action* (pp. 231–250). London: Routledge.

Maira, S. & Soep, E. (2005). *Youthscapes: The Popular, the National, the Global.* Philadelphia, PA: University of Pennsylvania Press.

Marcus, G. (1995). Ethnography in/of the world system: The emergence of multi-sited ethnography. *Annual Review of Anthropology, 24*, 95–117.

Pahl, K. & Rowsell, J. (2006). Introduction. In K. Pahl & J. Rowsell (Eds.), *Travel Notes from the New Literacy Studies.* Clevendon, UK: Multilingual Matters.

Pahl, K. & Rowsell, J. (2010). *Artifactual Literacies: Every Object Tells a Story.* New York: Teachers College Press.

Pink, S. (2001). *Doing Visual Ethnography: Images, Media, and Representation in Research.* London: Sage.

Rowsell, J. & Pahl, K. (2007). Sedimented identities in texts: Instances of practice. *Reading Research Quarterly, 42*(3), 388–404.

Soep, E. & Chavez, V. (2005). Youth radio and the pedagogy of collegiality. *Harvard Educational Review, 75*(4), 409–434.

Stein, P. (2003). The Olifantsvlei fresh stories project: Multimodality, creativity and fixing in the semiotic chain. In C. Jewitt & G. Kress (Eds.), *Multimodal Literacy* (pp. 123–138). New York: Peter Lang,

Stein, P. (2008). *Multimodal Pedagogies in Diverse Classrooms: Representation, Rights and Resources.* New York: Routledge.

Vasudevan, L. (2006). Making known differently: Engaging visual modalities as spaces to author new selves. *E-Learning, 3*(2), 207–216.

Vasudevan, L. (2010). Education remixed: New media, literacies, and the emerging digital geographies. *Digital Culture & Education, 2*(1), 62–82.

Vasudevan, L., DeJaynes, T., & Schmier, S. (2010). Multimodal pedagogies: Playing, teaching and learning with adolescents' digital literacies. In D. Alvermann (Ed.), *Adolescents' online literacies: Connecting classrooms, media, and paradigms* (pp. 5–25). New York: Peter Lang.

Wissman, K., Vasudevan, L., Staples, J., & Nichols, R. (In preparation). *Research Pedagogies.*

26

Implications for Research Training and Examination for Design PhDs

Joyce S.R. Yee

INTRODUCTION

A designerly way of researching

It is commonly recognized by the design research community that there is a 'designerly' way of knowing articulated by Nigel Cross (1982, 2006), that is distinct from other types of knowledge. Cross positions it as a third way of knowing, distinct from a Scientific or Humanities approach. He uses this simple model to highlight the various philosophical differences between the three disciplines. Cross differentiates them (1982, p. 222) by contrasting the phenomenon of study as:

- In the *sciences*: the natural world
- In the *humanities*: human experience
- In *design*: the man-made world

When Cross and his colleagues at the Royal College of Art proposed the idea of designerly knowing in the early 1980s, design research had already been established for twenty years since the Design Methods movement (the first conference on design methods was held in 1963). However, the criticism and failure of early design research was due to its mistaken focus on 'scientizing' the discipline by adopting scientific values (objectivity, rationality and the search for 'truth'). The philosophy of design was based on the scientific model of positivistic and realist positions that set out to capture the 'truths' about design. The 'design as science' model assumes that in order to achieve intellectual maturity (Glanville, 1998), design methods and processes have to be discovered, abstracted and codified.

Cross was heavily critical of the failure of these academic leaders to develop the discipline from within, on its own terms. Despite leveraging this criticism in 1982, discourses around the philosophy and methods of a designerly way of knowing have been slow to develop, due in part to the fragmented nature of the design research community. This situation has changed somewhat in the last fifteen years as the trend to academize design has increased the number of qualified researchers.

A maturing design research paradigm

The emergence of a much larger, internationally based design research community is evident by the increased number of Design PhDs and schools offering PhD programs as the new terminal degree for design. In the UK for example, the number of Design PhDs awarded in the UK has more than doubled (Fisher, Christer, & Mottram, 2005) in the last two decades. In addition, the emergence of design-related international academic conferences and journals reflects a growing maturity within the field. In 2010 alone, there have been over 130 calls on the *Design Journal and Conference Call* website (http://designcalls. wordpress.com) for conference and journal contributions. There is a sense that design research is reaching an intellectual maturity and confidence in its own research paradigm.

It is in this changing landscape that a more established typology of design methodologies has begun to emerge, used and validated as acceptable forms of research methodology for doctoral level programs. New research paradigms have also emerged, with an increasing number of studies placing design practice as the focus of the investigation. The role of design practice and project has been hotly debated for the last few years. As yet, no conclusive research paradigm has emerged that can be distinctly described as a designerly way of enquiring.

In an attempt to address this issue, this chapter will focus on describing four characteristics of designerly enquiry using recently completed design theses as exemplars. These characteristics have been derived from an examination of a range of design theses and using a number of design research frameworks (Cross, 1999; Fallman, 2008; Frayling, 1993) to identify the epistemological and methodological models applied. Some of the PhD thesis examples have been taken from an earlier paper (see Yee, 2010) relating to methodological innovation in practice-based PhDs. New case examples have also been included, based on recommendations from the design research community. As before, the main selection criteria have been the relevance of the research subject (linked to design), the novel way in which the research methodology has been derived and the potential to reveal new insights into the ontological and epistemological context of design.

The intention is twofold: first, as a practical aid for research students to develop a clearer understanding of the design research paradigm, providing a better 'fit' of research models for design questions. In line with a 'designerly' approach, the examples should be used to inspire rather than prescribe research models to researchers. The second intention is to use the analysis to derive insights into the current state of design knowledge.

THE BRICOLAGE APPROACH: MULTI-PERSPECTIVAL AND INTERDISCIPLINARY

Origins of the term

The term 'bricolage' originated in French and is a modern equivalent to the English phrase 'making-do'. In a general sense, a bricoleur (someone who employs the bricolage method) is described as a resourceful and creative 'fiddler or tinker', and one who uses available materials to create new objects out of existing ones. This activity of re-appropriating and combining elements into new and original outcomes closely reflects the activities of a designer. This concept is also similar to the ethos of adhocism, an architectural design theory proposed by Charles Jencks and Nathan Silver in their book *Adhocism: The Case for Improvisation* (1972) in which adhocism is described as a re-appropriation of an existing system or objects in creative ways in order to solve a problem quickly and effectively.

The concept of 'bricolage' in academic studies has its roots in social research. Claude Lévi-Strauss, a French anthropologist and ethnologist, defines the term in an anthropological sense as a spontaneous creative act that uses whatever is available to reach a desired outcome. In his book, *The Savage Mind* (1966), he compares the *Engineer* (the scientific mind) with the *Bricoleur* (the savage mind) as a way of depicting two modes of acquiring knowledge (concrete and abstract).

Bricolage as a research attitude

Although Lévi-Strauss introduced the concept of bricolage as a mode of acquiring knowledge, it was Denzin and Lincoln's (2000, p. 4) articulation of it within a methodological context that offered insight into new forms of rigor and complexity in social research. Denzin and Lincoln differentiate between five types of bricoleurs – interpretive, narrative, theoretical, political and methodological. Nelson, Treichler, and Grossberg describe bricolage (in the context of cultural studies methodology) as reflecting a choice of practice that is pragmatic, strategic and self-reflexive (1992, p. 2). While Kincheloe (2001) uses the term to describe multi-perspectival research methods, not just as the usage of mixed methods but to acknowledge that using methods from different disciplines enables the researcher to compare and contrast multiple points of view. Just as design objects have prescribed affordances, methods automatically imply ontological and epistemological affordances.

The bricolage notion is a powerful concept for qualitative researchers as it allows them to deploy available and established strategies and methods, but also grants them the licence to create new tools and techniques in order to do so. In a similar manner to how designers approach design, it is solution rather than problem-focused. The bricoleur views research methods actively, rather than passively, meaning that the researcher actively constructs methods with tools at hand rather than accepting and using pre-existing and universally applicable methodologies (Kincheloe & McLaren, 2005, p. 317).

In Kincheloe's view, bricolage signifies interdisciplinarity and the term 'generally refers to a process where disciplinary boundaries are crossed and the analytical frames of more than one discipline are employed by the researcher' (2001, p. 685). The act of sourcing, comparing and combining different elements from different origins reflects the crossing of disciplinary boundaries. It also means that the bricoleur must be acutely aware of the different theoretical and philosophical assumptions of the existing elements in order to construct a robust and sound application of methods. It in fact requires researchers to step back from the assumption that research methods are purely procedural, and instead to see them as a 'technology of justification, meaning a way of defending what we assert we know and the process by which we know it' (Kincheloe & McLaren, 2005, p. 318).

Criticism levied at bricoleurs centers on the idea that the bricolage approach only skims the surface of research understanding and lacks any methodological rigor. It is in fact the opposite, as bricoleurs who have to study diverse disciplines must be knowledgeable in the differing epistemologies and social theoretical assumptions in order to confidently select, adapt and apply the methods in the appropriate context. Kincheloe (2001, p. 686) argues that such a critical form of rigor avoids the reductionism of many monological, mimetic research orientations.

Examples of bricolage in use

The multi-perspectival and interdisciplinary characteristics of bricolage lend itself well to the nature of design questions. Therefore, is it unsurprising to see evidence of this approach in design PhDs. Daria Loi's 2005 thesis on tools to foster collaborative practices uses a methodological bricolage that draws from a variety of approaches such as dialogic research, storytelling, play, creative action and action learning. She created a series of tools to foster meaningful relationships between people in collaborative working environments. In addition, she also employed a range of methods such as reflective practice, exploratory installations, multi-sensorial writing and experimental techniques in her research.

Ben Singleton's soon to be completed PhD thesis (see his forthcoming paper, 2011a), explores the development of critical perspectives on service design discourse. His thesis starts as a detailed discourse analysis of service design and through a process of writing-as-inquiry he begins to unravel the dominant discourse into revealing its shortcomings. The end result of his thesis is to offer a reasoned agenda to guide how services, design and empowerment are linked to theory and practice. Singleton describes his overarching research approach as a 'conceptual construction' in which he uses insights drawn from a range of disciplines (architecture, anthropology, the history of technology, philosophy, international development and activist politics) to interrogate aspects of service design. The expositions and discussions of these aspects results in a series of short texts, which are then condensed into five long thematic sections; the service design discourse, the differences in designing human encounters with objects and with other humans, the issue of participation and empowerment in design discourse and examples of new forms of human co-operations. The multi-perspectival and interdisciplinary characteristics of bricolage is evident by the range of research strategies that are used and the way they have been brought together, for example: discourse analysis, thought experiments, case studies, peer review, tied together through writing, which Singleton describes as itself an active practice of inquiry rather than a passive process of reportage on research that happened 'elsewhere'. As Singleton's openly described, 'I'm just searching through different discourses, finding different points of reference or angles of approach' (2011b).

Another interesting example comes from Helen Box's 2007 thesis that uses visual communication and visual research strategies to critique and understand unusual visual artifacts (she terms them 'homeless, sticky design'). The projects are termed 'homeless and sticky' because they are hard to categorize but are admired and engaging. Some examples include a project documenting different types of lipstick, and another that features a taxonomy of North American breakfast cereal. Box's research is practice-based, using conceptual design projects to explore the theoretical model of design that has emerged from the investigation of eleven visual communication projects. Box's design project was used to 'demonstrate and reflect on the experience' (2007, p. 74) of applying her model.

In the course of her research, Box had to draw from a number of different disciplines to find the appropriate language and theories to inform the theoretical framework of her model. The two main disciplines that brought considerable insight to her work were the fields of Visual Communication and Visual Research, but she also had to draw on description of material artifacts by looking at the 'anatomy of the human heart, the origins of the encyclopaedia, photographic archiving, natural sciences taxonomy and vernacular cartography' (2007, p. 18).

CONVERSATIONS THROUGH WRITING AND MAKING

Link between practice and theory

The emergence of practice-based research has been a hotly debated issue in design scholarship. Discussions in this topic have included the relevance of practice activity to design research (Gray & Pirie, 1995; Newbury, 1996), the validity of practice-based knowledge in academic contexts (Candlin, 2000; Durling, 2002) and the translation of practice-based knowledge (know-how) into research (know-that) (Dilnot, 1998; Schön, 1983). Additionally, these scholarly debates have been supplemented by a specially commissioned UK research council report on the state and value of practice-based research in art, design and architecture (Rust, Mottram, & Till, 2007), as well as the presence of specialist conferences dedicated to practice-based knowledge such as the Experiential Knowledge Special Interest Group (EKSIG) conference held biannually in the UK[1].

In recent years, a growing number of PhDs have been described as 'practice-based' or 'practice-led'. I would argue that Design PhDs are inherently practice-based (i.e. deriving from the practice of design through studying the people, processes or products [Cross, 1999]) and the approach has become more widely accepted within the academic community. Durling, Friedman, & Guntherson (2002, p. 82) describe practice-led research as 'a study where practice is used as an interrogative process' while Rust et al. (2007, p. 11) emphasize that design practice has to play an instrumental part in the enquiry.

Knowledge translation through critical reflection

Design theorists (see Archer, 1995; Cross, 1982; Dilnot, 1998) agree that practice alone does not constitute research, and that reflection on the work must take place in order for design knowledge to be considered as research. Dilnot (1998, p. 27) emphasizes that in order for practice to become knowledge-productive, an additional further step must be taken toward critical reflection and analytical translation of practice into knowledge. Consequently, almost all practice-based research contains some element of critical reflection as a part of its process to derive knowledge from practice.

Reflective enquiry within a practice-based environment has been influenced by Donald Schön's theory of reflective practice (1983). Schön's description of reflective practice is particularly attractive to designers because it bridges the worlds of university and practice by 'finding research practices and learning tactics at the core of designing itself, avoiding the need for designers to borrow methodologies and pedagogies from other academic fields' (Tonkinwise, 2004, p. 223). In professional practice, Schön argues that a practitioner's knowledge is tacit and implicit in his/her patterns of action. He describes this as 'knowing-in-action'. The process of carrying out a course of acting, intervening, observing changes and reflecting on their effect, is described as 'reflection-in-action'. This process allows practitioners to make explicit their implicit knowledge. Schön's reflective practice method is generally carried out through the use of reflexive writing, mostly in journal form. Normally, a reflective model template is developed in accordance to the needs of the research and used as a site for initially descriptive data, moving eventually through several levels of reflection and analysis.

Conversations through writing

Although Schön's model of reflective practice has been the dominant methodology to reveal tacit knowledge implicit in our actions, there have been studies that have extended the use of the reflective practice model. Kaye Shumack, in her doctoral thesis titled 'Design and the Conversational Self' (2009), uses the journal format as the primary research methodology to enable her to generate conversational pieces between herself and her work by adopting several voices (I, You, Me, We). Her thesis regards the designer as an active agency and uses the designer as a site for exploring how ideas are located and how new insights or perspectives might be meaningfully introduced. Shumack uses her own design practice and examines her role as a designer in the research, viewing conversations as 'phenomenological events of exchange and learning, which are firmly grounded in human social and experiential experience' (p. 66). Although Schön (1992) regards the act of designing as 'conversations with the materials of the situation', the adoption of multiple voices and the requirement of the designer to take different roles required a combination of methods that not only exposed the design activity, but also how knowledge is constructed, exchanged and negotiated.

Shumack's 'conversational self' method is presented as an extension of Schön's levels[2] of 'reflection through design'. It involves 'naming and framing one's self as a situated and reflective actor within the design process' (2010). Shumack draws from theories of creative conversational learning contexts (Glanville, 2007; Pask, 1975), personal construct theory (Kelly, 1991; Thomas & Harri-Augstein, 1991), the self as forms as agency (Archer, 2003), experiential learning and knowledge creation through conversations (Baker, Jensen, and Kolb, 2002) and social knowledge as networks, flows and exchange processes (Boisot, 1994, 1995). She writes that 'these theories provide a means by which to clarify and make more explicit the ways that Schön's three reflective types can be mapped working both together, and separately, within a design process' (Shumack, 2010)[3].

Conversations through making

The idea of designing artifacts as a form of critique was first popularized and articulated at a doctoral level study by Anthony Dunne, whose PhD thesis (1997) explores how critical response to the ideological nature of design can inform the development of aesthetic possibilities for electronic products. The initial premise is based on critiquing and drawing attention to the role designers play in designing objects that perpetuate a culture of consumerism.

This idea was further expanded on by Dunne and Raby (2001) who set out to differentiate between the *affirmative* and *critical* natures of designed objects. Affirmative design perpetuates the existing norms of societal expectations, while critical design challenges the norm by expressing alternative values and ideologies. The term 'critical design' has now been adopted as an umbrella term for any type of design practice which suggests that design offers possibilities beyond the solving of design problems (Blauvelt, 2003).

A more recent study by Jayne Wallace (2007) in the field of digital jewellery has used a combination of reflective practice in the context of craft practice with tools that elicit emphatic connection between the designer and the user. Wallace's research, which she describes as 'open, exploratory and evolving' (p. 181), explores the possible integration of digital technologies and contemporary jewellery toward the development of personal and emotionally significant digital jewellery. Her research involves the creation of person-specific digital jewellery for four individuals using a combination of reflective practice and design probes. Her purpose was to reveal insights into 'opposing expectations and assumptions of digital objects and jewellery objects and also how the digital jewellery proposals were interpreted and appropriated in a personally emotionally significant context' (p. 5). Wallace's research can be divided into three sections: the first involves the creation of design probes to stimulate and reveal inspirational information from the participants, the second involves the creation of the digital jewellery proposals (in the form of objects and films) and finally, the third involves reflecting and analyzing the responses of the participants to their individually designed pieces.

An explicit goal for Wallace was to establish a jewellery methodology that was creative and reflexive, framed in Schön's view of reflective practice (p. 84). Unusually for a craft practitioner, Wallace moved away from personal expression and personal autonomy, to share dialog between the designer-maker and participants. Her approach of encouraging a shared dialog with participants and exploring personal expressive dimensions is evident in the development of her research methods. In developing a specific methodology for her thesis, she has been inspired by the contemporary jewellery practice of Bartels and Lindmark Vrijman, probe methods from Interaction Design (Gaver, Dunne, & Pacenti, 1999) and theoretical perspectives around the experiences of technology in HCI (McCarthy & Wright, 2004). Probe methods involve presenting participants with creative tools, description of task and questions designed to provoke inspirational response. An example probe pack might contain a disposable camera, a diary log and a specific task that the participant has to respond to using the given materials.

Bartels, Lindmark and Gaver were focused on opening dialog with participants, though Gaver was more concern with provoking rather than eliciting. Wallace makes a distinction between the two and instead states that her aim is to stimulate, rather than to provoke or probe. Rather than taking a snapshot of a particular context, group or place (which was Wallace's critique of design probes) she used her objects a way of building relationships with her participants over a period of time. She views the objects as a co-creative endeavor between herself and her participants, in her words 'I start them and they complete them'. The probes also acted as icebreakers for follow-on conversations with her participants where intimate things like feelings, sense of self and relationships with others are explored. These conversations were facilitated with the use of ten different probes, in addition to the text-based answers collected through vignettes and short questionnaires. Figures 26.1–26.6 show a selection of the probes used and accompanying instructions. (Figures 26.1–26.6 are from Wallace's thesis, pp. 115–120.)

For both Dunne and Wallace, critical reflection not only takes place between the designer and the artifact, but the critically designed artifact becomes a source of reflection for the users. The fact that Wallace's participants were asked to record their own reflections through writing and photographs after receiving their respective digital jewellery proposal highlights the importance of using the designed artifacts to facilitate conversations with users around issues arising from the values embodied by the artifacts. It became reflexive objects where participants return to reflect on their initial responses, often adding new layers of understanding and insight.

Figure 26.1 *Pot of clay* **stimulus**

Please use the clay inside this pot to make an impression or leave a trace of an object dear to you.

Figure 26.2 **Instructions accompanying** *Pot of Clay* **stimulus**

Figure 26.3 *Dream* **stimulus**

> Please keep this pillow by your bed or in your bag. Use the fold out piece of fabric to write on about a dream, a daydream or an aspiration.

Figure 26.4 **Instructions accompanying** *Dream* **stimulus**

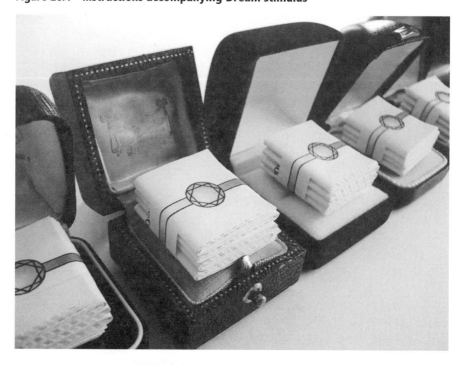

Figure 26.5 *Lost object* **stimulus**

Questions:
1. Have you ever lost an object that you treasured?
2. Please describe this object.
3. Could the item be replaced?
4. ...if it was replaced would it mean the same to you?
5. What is it that you remember about the object?
6. Why was it special to you?

Figure 26.6   Instructions accompanying *Lost Object* stimulus

THE ROLE OF THE VISUAL

Using images, graphics and diagrams as a way to think and learn

Mapping knowledge through images, graphics and diagrams is essentially a way of envisaging information. Tufte (1990) describes this process as a way of creating a multi-dimensional model of different worlds (physical, biological, imaginary or human) in order to better understand them. The usage of visual methods to facilitate thinking and learning is not particular to the visual arts discipline, for example, scientists have long used diagrams to present their theories or describe their research process. However, I would like to posit that the visual mode of communication features much more prominently in design research for three reasons: the questions that design ask are more likely to be concerned with things visual (Langrish, 2000), it is a communicative mode that suits designers' cognitive styles (Durling, Cross, & Johnson, 1996) and a high level of visual communication skill is required to effectively communicate concepts, process and method visually.

Visualizing knowledge is particularly conducive to visual–spatial learners (Gardner, 1985; Silverman, 1989) who tend to think in pictures rather than words. They learn better visually and spatially, 'involving synthesis, intuitive grasp of complex systems, simultaneous processing of concepts, inductive reasoning, active use of imagery, and idea generation by combining disparate elements in new ways' (Silverman, 2002). Research carried out by Durling et al. (1996) into the thinking and learning styles of designers using the Myers Briggs Type Indicator® suggests that designers prefer a pedagogic style that begins with the larger picture before moving into details and facts. They would rather explore data using a loose framework, rather than being presented with a rigid sequence of data. They are intuitive learners, preferring to focus on ideas and associations. Studies by Lawson (1990), Akin (1990) and Steadman (1972) on how designers work suggest a cyclical process. During the sketching process, the cyclical model of 'seeing–moving–seeing' is often used to externalize design thinking. Additionally, designers use these visualizations as a way of having a 'reflective conversation' (Schön, 1983) with their ideas in order to develop their design solutions. These characteristics closely echo descriptions of visual–spatial thinkers, suggesting that designers generally favor a visual–spatial approach to learning.

Visuals are generally used in design research for three purposes: (a) for reflection and exploration, (b) as an analysis and knowledge generation tool and (c) as a communication, facilitation and discussion tool. They can also be described as either an internal process which is used to facilitate a researcher's understanding or as an external process used to communicate or generate conversations around the research outcomes.

Reflection and exploration

The primary value of visual mapping is its ability to transform discrete sets of implicit knowledge into an explicit set of relational knowledge quickly and directly. It is useful to explore connections between ideas, concepts and theories of a given subject. Examples of this can be seen in my own PhD work (Yee, 2006) which explored an alternative pedagogic framework for teaching typography in a digital context. The study was a practice-led mixed method study into current typographic teaching practices, framed by action research methodology. As part of my literature review, the literature around the topic of typography and digital media was mapped to identify the construction of prior knowledge in relation to the research enquiry (see the paper by Yee [2003] for a more in-depth description of the mapping process). The visual mapping process enabled me to make explicit connections between concepts, stances and theories in different subjects as well as using the map to elicit feedback from other researchers on the connections that I had drawn from my initial literature review. The literature map (Figure 26.7) was an evolving entity, a tool that enabled me to track my understanding of the field but also to help me narrow my eventual research focus on specific areas of convergence. As Borg (2007) observes, the map was not simply a representation of a concept or process; it *is* the process (my emphasis). He suggest that the use of the map is more akin to scientific representations where diagrams are used to make explicit the data collection and interpretation process.

Analysis and knowledge generation

The role of visual mapping has featured heavily in the research process of Emma Jefferies' PhD (2010) on how visual skills in designers are developed and fostered. Her study employed a 'qualitative approach and a strategy of design-based research to externalize the underlying attributes and processes of developing and fostering visual practices through the designing, and testing, of teaching-learning artefacts' (2010, p. iii). Her research consisted of two research phases: design experiments with design students, and user testing with design educators.

In conversations around her educational experiences, Jefferies acknowledged that she relied heavily on the creation of visual diagrams to help her analyze and

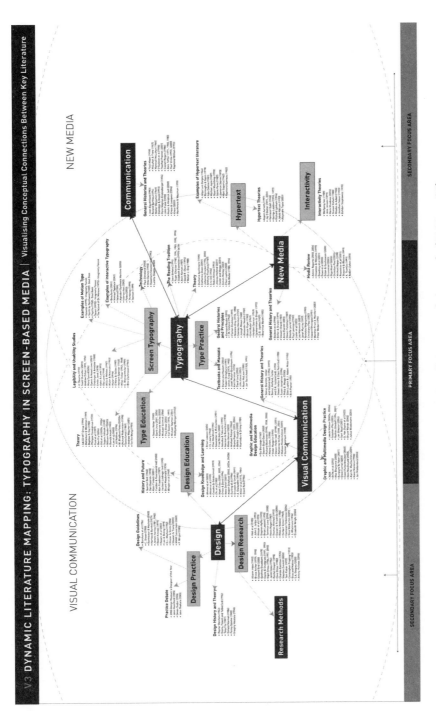

Figure 26.7   Yee's final version of her map documenting key literature of the study (2006, p. 24)

interrogate her textual data (2008). A key example was during the examination and analysis of her fieldwork data collected from classroom trials. She was able to extract insights into how designers' visual practices were fostered through qualitative data, but then had problems understanding how they related to the different elements of the model that included the design brief, the learning community and the learner. Through the process of visualization, she was able to draw connections between the different elements of her model, which in turn helped her to articulate her textual statement in a more precise manner. This way of working has similarities with how a designer would have a 'reflective conversation' (Schön, 1983) with their ideas through the process of sketching.

Designers commonly use visual strategies to help them organize and understand the relationship between data in their design practice. The power of data visualization is that it enables researchers to spot emerging patterns and themes in data. This use of visual analysis is effectively exemplified in Joe Eastwood's PhD thesis. Eastwood's (2007) study explores the relationship between text-based messages and audio-based communication within the contemporary urban environment. His practice-based study was divided into three stages: a contextual review through a series of interviews with designers to identify key questions, fieldwork studies of six public sites and the parallel development of exploratory design projects throughout the study. The data collection of his fieldwork studies comprised a combination of notes, sketches, photographs and audio recordings of typographic and audio communication. These observations were then visually analyzed through the creation of a series of charts and macroscopic drawings, to provide a visual account of each space investigated (see Figures 26.8 and 26.9). By choosing to represent the data visually, Eastwood was able to very quickly compare the different sites in terms of audio and typographic data. This form of visual analysis is not unlike comparative research that is often conducted by designers during the early part of a design process. Apart from its analysis and knowledge generation purposes, the final drawings acted as visual representation of the different sites; when reviewed as a set, the viewer is immediately struck by the distinctiveness of each site.

Communication, facilitation and discussion

Borg (2007) suggests that design researchers use visual communication in their research as an attempt to address their professional colleagues in the semiotic mode in which they are most comfortable. For example, he posits that 'a visual map engages the designers in a similar way to that of the scientists: the information is not primarily mediated by text, and can be grasped holistically'. This is an important point to consider, as the audience of research outcomes will most likely be designers or design educators. This case has been highlighted by Jefferies' experience in using concept maps as a way to facilitate iscussion with her supervisors during the course of her study. For example (see Figure 26.10), during her thesis construction she placed the chapter's key points on a white board to

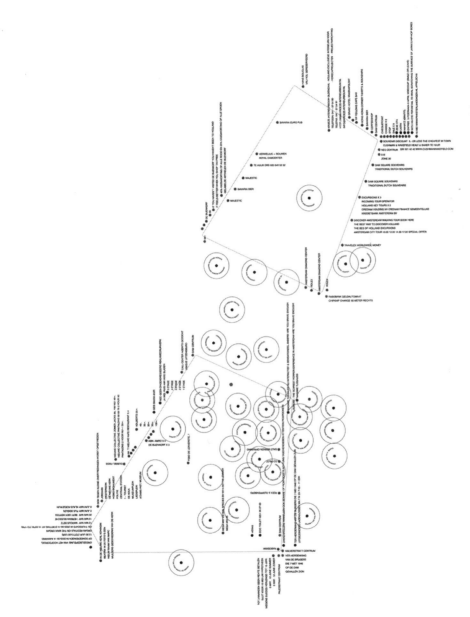

Figure 26.8 First example of visual documentation of Dam Square in Amsterdam extracted from Eastwood's thesis (2007)

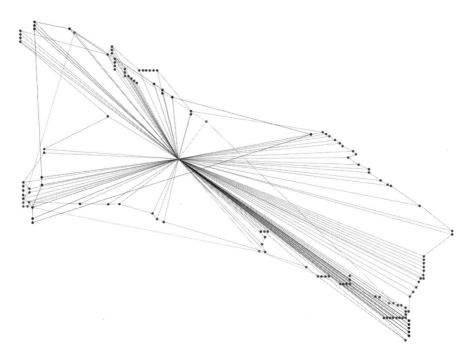

Figure 26.9   Second example of visual documentation of Dam Square in Amsterdam extracted from Eastwood's thesis (2007)

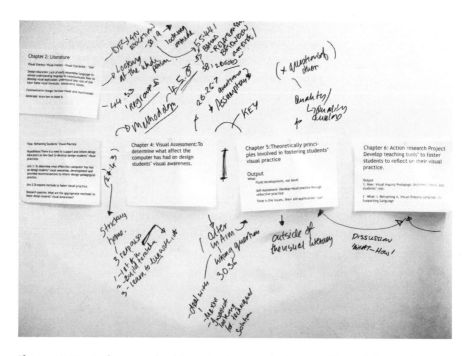

Figure 26.10   A photograph of the visual presentation of Jefferies' thesis chapters. Image supplied by Emma Jefferies

facilitate discussions with her supervisors, while noting down their comments on the board. This enabled her to visually see the connections between the chapters and also present an overview of the thesis to her supervisors. The use of a visual communication mode also helped Jefferies in her viva examination when she was able to clearly articulate her framework through a series of diagrams, without which the viva discussion would have proven much more difficult. Questions her examiners had prior to the session were immediately answered by the visual representation of her research (see Figures 26.11 and 26.12). As a result, they grasped the key concepts of the thesis and were confident of Jefferies' understanding of the framework, which had not been very evident in the textual narrative of the thesis.

THESIS-STRUCTURAL INNOVATION

Borg (2007) has posited that Design theses demonstrate innovative changes in what is generally assumed to be a very conservative text genre. Structural innovations in design PhDs can be observed in three areas: the narrative structure, the role of visual devices and the actual physical representation of the thesis.

Narrative structure: a non-linear approach

There are many different models and conventions of thesis presentation. Dunleavy (2003, p. 63) proposes that there are generally four fundamental ways of handling long, text-based explanations in social science and humanities theses: descriptive, analytical, argumentative and a matrix pattern, combining elements of any two or three other approaches. Additionally, the accepted format for a PhD thesis is linear, describing and sustaining a continued argument in a step-by-step format. However, non-linear forms have been experimented with successfully, as evidenced by Mazé (2007) and Von Busch (2008).

Ramia Mazé's (2007) thesis was an enquiry into issues of time in interaction design, and argued that a central concern of interaction design must be the 'temporal form' of interactive objects and their form of 'interactions' as they are used over time. Her study was a combination of a contextual review of past case studies of projects that she was involved in, and the use of current design projects to explore theoretical themes of the study. Her thesis is divided into three sections representing three research themes. Each theme is then sub-divided into three areas that describe the concept, the context in which the concept resides and an exploratory project that demonstrates the concept in use. Instead of presenting the projects sequentially or by types, she has chosen to illustrate her argument through three different viewpoints of historical, practical and critical stances. I observed that she has also chosen to move the discussion from theory to practice, comparing this movement with Frayling's (1993) framework of investigating 'into', 'for the purpose of' and 'through' design. Figure 26.13 is my

DISCUSSION MAP:
Characteristics of a Meaningful Visual Pedagogy in Design Education

Research Question	Research Opportunity	Hypothesis
'How can visual pedagogy in design education become meaningful to design students and educators?'	a. Understanding how students' visual practices are currently fostered in design education. b. Understanding how students' visual practices can be fostered in design education.	Developing characteristics of a visual pedagogy that promote explicit and student-centred approaches to fostering students' visual practices will contribute to meaningful learning experiences.

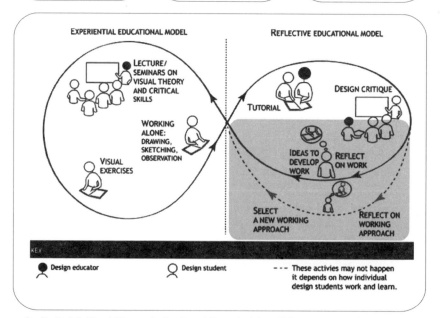

Studio Model: Visual literacy is developed through doing, dialogue, questioning, self-reflection and self-awareness

Figure 26.11   First example of Jefferies' representation of her framework as used in her viva examination. Images supplied by Emma Jefferies

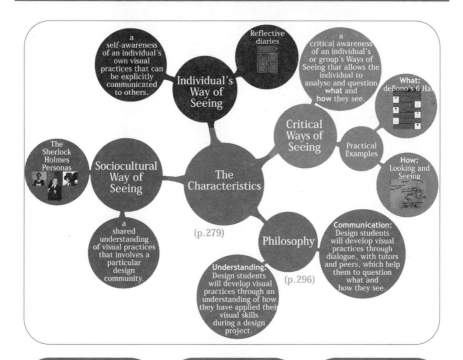

A response to the research question:
Characteristics of a Meaningful Visual Pedagogy in Design Education

The Characteristics	Aid Educational Objectives	Design Process
The characteristics provide a structure, processes and practical examples to inform the act of fostering students' visual practices in design education.	The philosophy that underlies the characteristics provides the beneficiaries involved in design education with a clear picture of how design students can develop their visual practices.	The design process aids engagement with the *characteristics;* which enables the research to become a usable piece of knowledge, aiding questioning of how students' visual practices are fostered and how they wish to develop them.
(Section 8.4)	(Section 8.5.1)	(Section 8.5.2)

Figure 26.12   Second example of Jefferies' representation of her framework as used in her viva examination. Images supplied by Emma Jefferies

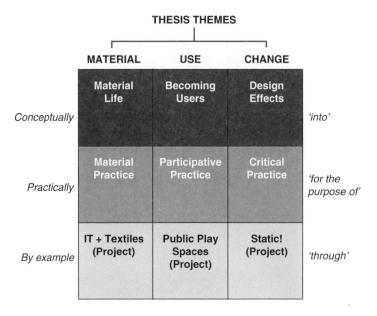

Figure 26.13 Mazé's research design represented by a 3 x 3 matrix showing the relationship between chapters

interpretation of Mazé's research design, which she described textually but not diagrammatically.

Her thesis structure reflects not only the approach and method of her enquiry but also the institutional circumstance in which the study was conducted. Although her work uses practice-based projects as the subject of enquiry, it differs from other practice-based theses. Unlike other typical practice-based theses that closely interweave practical project work and written reflection, her practice-based projects were conducted over several years and prior to her PhD. She became a PhD student when offered one year of funding from the Interactive Institute to write up her ongoing research as a dissertation and as a published book. Thus, practice-based projects are a subject of enquiry within the overall structure and are reflected upon in retrospect:

> I have tried to reflect the particular conditions of my research work in the form of the thesis – for example, the 'matrix' is intended to introduce a tension between research 'into'/'through' sections. This evades the more typical chronological account and provides a frame into which the 'practice' sections are inserted as portfolio-formatted pieces that disrupt the flow of the theoretical argument. (Mazé, 2010)

Von Busch's thesis (2008) on fashion hacktivism is unapologetically nonlinear. His PhD thesis explores a new designer role for fashion by adopting a social design practice that he termed as 'hacktivism of fashion'. It is a participatory, collective and enabling practice that involves the designer engaging actively with participants to create or reinterpret clothing, in Von Busch's words to make them *fashion'able*. He frames his research as not based on answering questions or positing a research model, but one that is about presenting unknown possibilities. His thesis consists of a series of individual projects interwoven with theory. The non-linear process that he has adopted in his practical project has been reflected in the narrative structure of his thesis. Unlike the usual structure of presenting research aims, objectives and methods, Von Busch's thesis does not have a strict beginning or end, nor does it conform to a progressive or deductive format. He describes his methodology as a series of intersecting process lines framed by participatory action research with an interventionist purpose, using a critical design approach to interrogate design practice. He is explicitly 'designerly' in his approach and presentation of his research. He suggests that the reader view the thesis as 'a series of journeys, pulled together by the "gravity" of an attractor and condensed into a prism' (p. 29) (see Figure 26.14 where he has laid out his content pages as a series of bifurcating routes in a rhizomatic structure). In terms of the purpose and role the design projects played in his work, he emphasized that they were not case studies built progressively but instead are applications of different lines of enquiry and understanding from other practices.

Visual narrative devices

Zoe Sadokierski's thesis (2010) presents an analysis of hybrid novels, which are defined as 'novels in which graphic devices like photographs, drawings and experimental typography are integrated into the written text' (2010, p. ix). She distinguishes hybrid novels from picture books, graphic novels or artists' books in that they are clearly categorized as novels. In hybrid text, word and image combine to create text that is neither purely written, nor purely visual, in effect it is a symbiotic relationship used for storytelling. Her thesis posits that visual communication designers possess the verbal and visual skills to offer useful analytical tools and critique strategy for the study of hybrid texts. The study is essentially a study on the interplay between image and text. And it is this interplay that Sadokierski chooses to explore, not only through her design practice, but also in the creation of her thesis. As a clear indication that the structure of the thesis demonstrates concepts in her research, she states explicitly that her 'thesis aims to present an argument *about* visual communication design, *through* visual communication design' (p. 12). Throughout the thesis, the use of graphic devices (graphic images and typography) plays an important role in forming the thesis argument alongside conventional text. An example of how these devices are used can be seen in Figures 26.15 and 26.16.

Physical structure

In the previous two examples, innovation in the PhD thesis was linked to its narrative structure. However, Daria Loi has taken the thesis-structural innovation to its logical end by changing the physical thesis itself (see Figures 26.17 and 26.18). Her thesis was presented as a suitcase containing participatory devices to

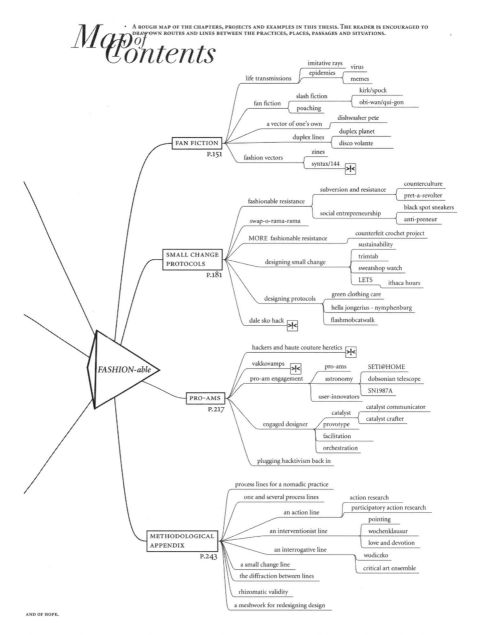

Figure 26.14   An image from Von Busch's content page of his thesis (2008, p. 25)

enable readers to have a discourse with the thesis, while at the same time actively demonstrating the concepts discussed in the research. The contents of the suitcase consisted of custom-made objects, CDs, images and instructional notes. Although it is fairly common for an artefact to accompany a written thesis within Art and Design, it was unprecedented that an artefact alone should act as the thesis. This unusual format has brought up issues of production, accessibility,

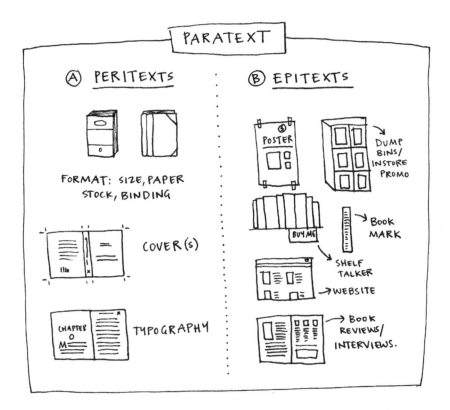

Paratext: threshold to interpretation[3]

Genette argues that paratext is an important and often neglected aspect of textual production and reception; although supplementary, Genette does not consider paratext superfluous. Paratext is more than a physical vessel for a primary text – it is a 'threshold to interpretation'. Genette states:

> [Paratexts] surround and extend [the text] precisely in order to *present* it, in the usual sense of this verb but also in the strongest sense: to *make present*, to ensure the text's presence in the world, its 'reception' and consumption in the form … of a book … the paratext is what enables a text to become a book and to be offered as such to its readers." (1)

Figure 26.15   First example of an image from Sadokierski's thesis (2010, p. 18)

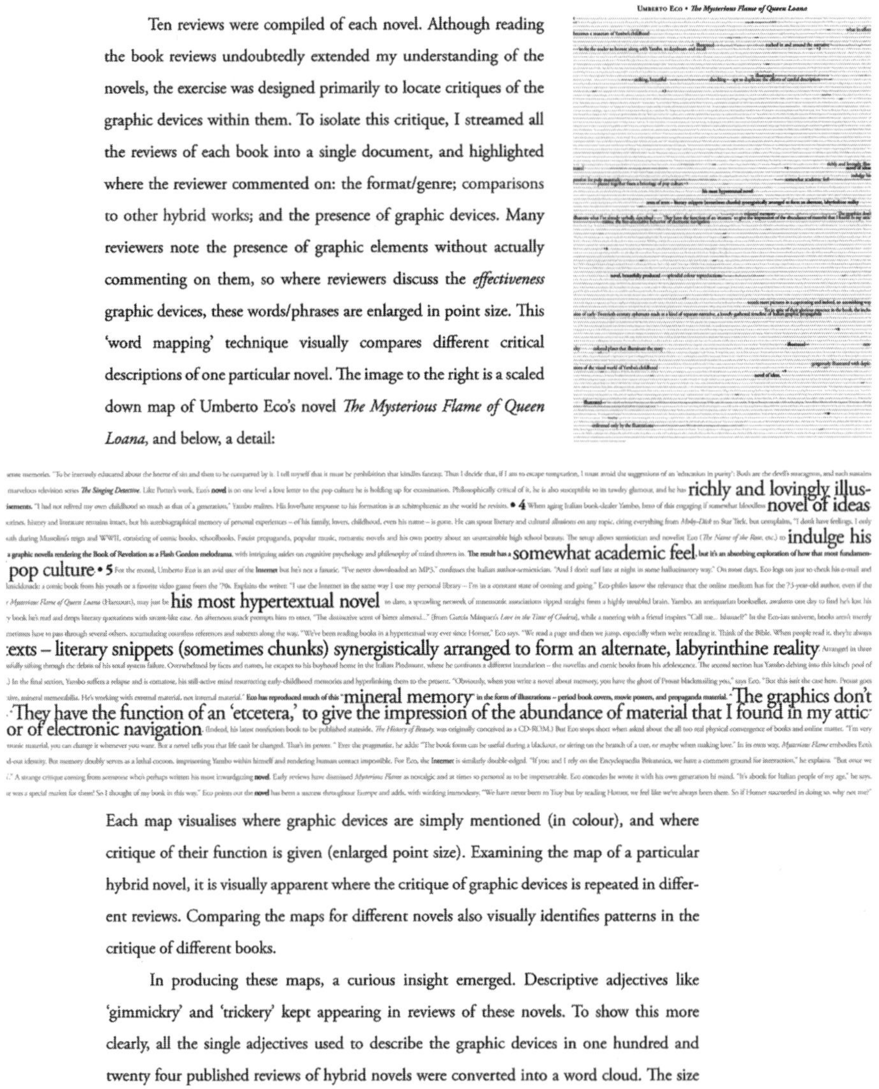

Ten reviews were compiled of each novel. Although reading the book reviews undoubtedly extended my understanding of the novels, the exercise was designed primarily to locate critiques of the graphic devices within them. To isolate this critique, I streamed all the reviews of each book into a single document, and highlighted where the reviewer commented on: the format/genre; comparisons to other hybrid works; and the presence of graphic devices. Many reviewers note the presence of graphic elements without actually commenting on them, so where reviewers discuss the *effectiveness* graphic devices, these words/phrases are enlarged in point size. This 'word mapping' technique visually compares different critical descriptions of one particular novel. The image to the right is a scaled down map of Umberto Eco's novel *The Mysterious Flame of Queen Loana*, and below, a detail:

Each map visualises where graphic devices are simply mentioned (in colour), and where critique of their function is given (enlarged point size). Examining the map of a particular hybrid novel, it is visually apparent where the critique of graphic devices is repeated in different reviews. Comparing the maps for different novels also visually identifies patterns in the critique of different books.

In producing these maps, a curious insight emerged. Descriptive adjectives like 'gimmickry' and 'trickery' kept appearing in reviews of these novels. To show this more clearly, all the single adjectives used to describe the graphic devices in one hundred and twenty four published reviews of hybrid novels were converted into a word cloud. The size

Figure 26.16   Second example of an image from Sadokierski's thesis (2010, p. 55)

control, supervision, institutional and examination issues that had to be addressed by Loi and her supervision team (see Loi's paper (2004) for a detailed description). I would also like to stress that the artefact as thesis is different from the presentation of an artefact as knowledge. The form of the thesis is intrinsically linked to the aims of the research and the combination of text, visuals and objects were intentionally 'designed' to present a coherent (if not entirely conventional) academic argument.

Figure 26.17   First example from Loi's thesis-in-a-suitcase. Image supplied by Daria Loi

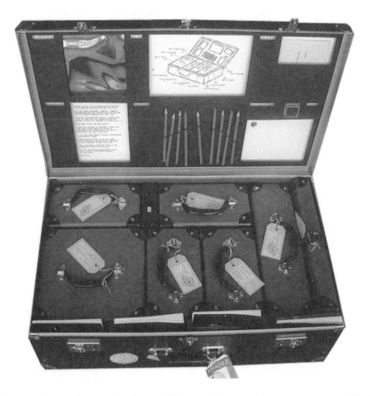

Figure 26.18   Second example from Loi's thesis-in-a-suitcase. Image supplied by Daria Loi

IMPLICATIONS FOR RESEARCH TRAINING AND EXAMINATION

In a previous paper (Yee, 2010), I touched on how the nature of design research and the approach to research by designers (termed as 'designerly' enquiry) should influence the content of design research training. I would like to expand a little more on that here by suggesting some guiding principles, as well as practical skills required. Additionally, the question of examination criteria will be discussed.

Understanding the nature of design questions

Harfield describes the field of design as one that 'generally constitutes a practice-based knowledge-utilization discipline, aimed at providing service to an external world ...' (Harfield, 2008, p. 151). He suggests that design is essentially normative rather than explanatory–descriptive. Unlike the natural sciences or humanities, design is not focused on descriptive or explanatory knowledge but instead focuses on offering possible future solutions (Dilnot, 1998). The idea of the third discipline has been proposed as a way to reframe and define design's position as an academic discipline. However, in offering up this 'third' discipline, it is important to consider how this ontological and epistemological stance influences the methodologies, methods and assessment of the discipline. This position brings all sorts of implications for design, particularly the role of rigor in design research.

A question of rigor

Rigor is an accepted and expected tenet of academic research. In academic practice, it is often described generally as a set of practices that denotes being thorough, exact, meticulous, objective, transparent and consistent in the pursuit of knowledge. However, not all of these scientifically derived characteristics sit well within design.

The question of rigor in design research is questioned by Wood as he argues that an overemphasis on rigor in academic writing is 'neither fitting nor helpful to the emergence of a new design culture that must accommodate rapid change, and which must encourage practitioners to become more entrepreneurial, self-reflexive, and socially responsible' (2000, p. 47). Wood provides a very detailed account of the origins of the idea of rigor, and how it came to be a defining characteristic of academic research. Rigor, he goes on to explain, stands for 'logical accuracy and exactitude', having been derived from the Latin word 'rigere' – to be stiff – and linking to the monastic truth-oriented knowledge rather than the craft guilds' results-oriented knowledge. Woods calls for a more 'emphatic' approach to design writing, in which he means to treat writing as a 'design task' with a tangible future outcome and an immediate effect. For example, we should concentrate on situated context and change over permanence and ideals; notions of 'discovery' over notions of 'truths'/'facts'; adaptability over a fixed plan and a holistic approach over a narrow focus. Woods call for a re-evaluation of the fixed notion of an 'ideal' world which has formed the western view of rigor into one that is dynamic and interrelated.

Spencer (2009) takes a less extreme stance toward the idea of rigor and instead discusses in more practical terms how rigor can be achieved through a more reflective and reflexive stance. Like many others before him (Buchanan, 1995; Cross, 1982; Dilnot, 1998; Glanville, 1999), Spencer takes the position that design's ontology is distinct from a natural science approach hence our understanding of rigor in design must be informed by the nature of design practice. Spencer's research is focused on design practice and not design research per se, but the discussions around how the standards of rigor are accepted by the discipline as well as academia is undeniably important for doctoral research, especially practice-based studies. Spencer suggests that a useful understanding of rigor can be achieved by examining the practise of Reflective Practice design practitioners. He reasons that rigor helps to define a practitioner's ideology and pre-structured thinking, and illustrates how designers manage and undertake a reflective enquiry. The role of reflective practice through conversations with making and writing has featured heavily in design PhDs, hence it would be useful to understand how reflective practice contributes to our understanding of rigor in design. Spencer suggests that reflective practice contributes to rigor in design by:

> … exposing and exploring ones ideologically conditioned thinking structure, developed by managing the thinking structure's coherence, through an iterative process of undermining stability – creating chaos events by propositional exploration of the situation of practice and exposure to feedback – and reforming the thinking structure by engaging creative and critical thinking to integrate insight and develop a refined understanding of the situation of practice. (2009, pp. 2398–2399)

Both Spencer and Woods highlight the importance of evaluating and making relevant the accepted academic tenets for design. Another area which I would like to examine is the idea of validity.

Useful instead of valid knowledge

Research methodologies are built around questioning and determining validity, which is linked to the larger question of rigor. Validity of research outcomes is often discussed in relation to the relevance of the data collected with the manner in which the research was conducted, and whether it was appropriate for the original research question. Validity refers to 'the best available approximation to the truth or falsity of propositions' (Cook & Campbell, 1979, p. 37). As discussed previously, design questions are focused more on future propositions than truth finding. If we assume this to be the purpose of design research, then the question of validity has reduced relevance. Instead, what might perhaps be a constructive guiding principle to follow is the evaluation of how *useful* a research outcome is to its intended audience. We should be focused on 'does it work?' rather than 'is it true?' Usefulness of design knowledge relates to how it benefits the understanding of the field, moving from factual knowledge to tacit knowledge, and the application of knowledge. Although ensuring 'valid' research design and research outcomes are essential, it is also important to focus on the usefulness of knowledge in relation to the research audience. This care for the reader/audience has been demonstrated in the use of visual devices in theses that address fellow design researchers in a familiar semantic mode.

Encouraging bricolage as a research attitude

The idea of the bricolage research attitude introduced earlier in this chapter is to encourage students to engage actively with the research methods. Research methods should not be seen as passive and rigid constructs that can be 'picked off the shelf' to fit a research question, but instead must be explored, negotiated and adapted. While it might be easier for a supervisor to advise a student to use 'this or that' method, it is far riskier to ask them to adopt a bricolage approach. First, supervisors need to be more conversant in different models of research. This can happen in numerous ways, for example, through exposure to different research traditions by being involved in interdisciplinary research supervision. Second, supervision training offered at institutional level should also be offered at subject level. Characteristics of 'designerly inquiring' should be addressed and discussed alongside the established academic understanding of research. Conversely, students need to be exposed to as many different research models as possible, and evaluate their appropriateness to design. They have to be conversant in the onto-logical, epistemological and methodological standpoints of the different research traditions through the study of diverse disciplines in order to confidently select, adapt and ultimately defend the methods they choose to utilize.

Visual communication training

On a practical level, the use of visual devices to help design researchers commu-nicate ideas and concepts should be explicitly taught in design doctoral training. Although the usage of visual devices is more common in Art and Design theses, it is mostly candidates with a visual communication background that have used visuals to support the presentation of their argument. I would argue that not all design students have the ability to visually communicate well, and that basic training workshops around the use of visual devices to facilitate either thinking, reflection or communication should be offered to design doctoral students.

CONCLUSION

This chapter has presented four characteristics of design research approaches that illustrate how designers are currently practising research. The practices of other disciplines tell us that methodological reinvention reflects a discipline in trouble (see Law & Urry, 2004). Design, I believe, is not a discipline in trouble but rather one in a transitory phase. It is breaking away from the crutches of a scientific model and building its own disciplinary foundation. The interdisciplinary nature of the PhDs discussed here also suggests that design does not exist as a discrete discipline but one that bridges other disciplines.

There is a lack of reference to design history in the thesis examples, which suggests that either the researchers are asking questions outside of the discipline or that current design history is inappropriate for the type of questions asked. Without this historical foundation, I suggest that methodology is used instead to build a research platform. One could argue that design, as a young academic discipline, is still asking 'new' questions and therefore requires new methods to explore them. I will offer an alternative response, which is that the variation in methods has more to do with the nature of a designerly approach adopted by designers due to the indeterminate quality of a future world. A designer often has to respond to differing and unpredictable contexts, resulting in the adoption and use of different methods. Designers are simply extending this approach to research.

The various design research approaches described here demonstrate the richness of the field, which is not currently reflected in the training provision for design researchers. Assessment criteria (which include discussion of thesis format) should address the multiplicity of format evidenced by the examples. Precedents set in terms of thesis format (as in Loi's case), the role of visual research and the skill of methods bricolage should be explicitly acknowledged by examiners and supervisors. Methodological innovation should be seen as one of the key components of design research. Each design PhD is methodologically unique, with some more explicitly different than others. This points to a growing confidence in the expression of a study as a 'design PhD', and not a PhD in the subject of design.

NOTES

1. This conference is a special interest group of the Design Research Society and is dedicated to discussions on the clarification of practice-based knowledge and research. The link to its website is http://www.experiential knowledge.org

2. Schön distinguishes between four different levels of reflection in an attempt to address the problem of self-reflexivity. They are:
   - *Fourth*: Reflection on reflection on description of designing
   - *Third*: Reflection on description of designing
   - *Second*: Description of designing
   - *First*: Designing (1987: 115)

3. Refer to the Shumack (2010) paper for a more detail description of the framework used in her journal template.

REFERENCES

Akin, O. (1990). Necessary conditions for design expertise and creativity. *Design Studies, 11*, 107–113.

Archer, B. (1995). The nature of research. *Co-design, Interdisciplinary Journal of Design* (January), 6–13.

Archer, M. S. (2003). *Structure, Agency and the Internal Conversation*. Cambridge: Cambridge University Press.

Baker, A., Jensen, P., & Kolb, D. (2002). *Conversational Learning: An Experiential Approach to Knowledge Creation*. London: Quorum Books.

Blauvelt, A. (Ed.). (2003). *Strangely Familiar – Design and Everyday Life*. Minneapolis, MN: Walker Art Centre.

Boisot, M. (1994). *Information and Organizations. The Manager as Anthropologist*. London: Harper Collins.

Boisot, M. (1995). *Information Space: A Framework for Learning in Organizations, Institutions and Culture*. London: Routledge.

Borg, E. (2007). *Evolution and change in academic genres*. Talk presented at the Discourse and Disciplinarity Conference, University of Leeds.

Box, H. (2007). Homeless, sticky design. Strategies for visual, creative, investigative projects. PhD dissertation, University of Technology, Sydney.

Buchanan, R. (1995). *The changing culture of communication design*. Paper presented at the Charting the Future of Graphic Design Education conference, Edmonton, Canada.

Candlin, F. (2000). Practice-based doctorates and questions of academic legitimacy. *International Journal of Art and Design Education, 19*(1), 96–101.

Cook, T. D. & Campbell, D. T. (1979). *Quasi-experimentation: Design and Analysis for Field Settings*. Chicago, IL: Rand McNally.

Cross, N. (1982). Designerly ways of knowing. *Design Studies, 3*(4), 221–227.

Cross, N. (1999). Design research: A discipline conversation. *Design Issues, 15*(2), 5–10.

Cross, N. (2006). *Designerly ways of knowing*. London: Springer.

Denzin, N. & Lincoln, Y. (2000). *Handbook of Qualitative Research* (2nd Ed.), Thousand Oaks, CA: Sage.

Dilnot, C. (1998). *The science of uncertainty: The potential contribution of design to knowledge*. Paper presented at the Doctoral Education in Design conference, Carnegie Mellon University, Pittsburgh.

Dunleavy, P. (2003). *Authoring a PhD: How to Plan, Draft, Write, and Finish a Doctoral Thesis*. Basingstoke: Palgrave Macmillan.

Dunne, A. (1997). Hertzian tales: An investigation into the critical and aesthetic potential of the electronic product as a post-optimal object. PhD dissertation, Royal College of Art, London.

Dunne, A. (1999). *Hertzian tales. Electronic products, aesthetic experience and critical design* (1st edn.). Cambridge, Massachussetts: The MIT Press.

Dunne, A. & Raby, F. (2001). *Design Noir: The Secret Life of Electronic Objects*. London, Basel: August/ Birkhauser.

Durling, D. (2002). Discourses on research and the PhD in design. *Quality Assurance in Education, 10*(2), 79–85.

Durling, D., Cross, N., & Johnson, J. (1996). *Personality and learning preferences of students in design and design-related disciplines*. Paper presented at the IDATER 96 International Conference on Design and Technology, Loughborough University.

Durling, D., Friedman, K., & Guntherson, P. (2002). Editorial: Debating the practise-based PhD. *International Journal of Design Sciences and Technology, 10*(2), 7–18.

Eastwood, J. (2007). An investigation of the relationship between typography and audio-based communication in the urban environment, with particular regard to pedestrian wayfinding. PhD dissertation, University of the Arts, London.

Fallman, D. (2008). The interaction design research triangle of design practice, design studies, and design exploration. *Design Issues, 24*(3), 4–18.

Fisher, T., Christer, K., & Mottram, J. (2005). ADIT: Art and Design Index to Thesis, retrieved 1st August 2010, from http://www.shu.ac.uk/research/c3ri/adit/index.cfm

Frayling, C. (1993). Research in art and design. *RCA Research Papers, 1*(1).

Gardner, H. (1985). *Frames of Mind: The Theory of Multiple Intelligences*. New York: McGraw-Hill.

Gaver, W. H., Dunne, A., & Pacenti, E. (1999). Design: Cultural probes. *Interactions, 6*(1), 21–29.

Glanville, R. (1998). *Keeing the faith with the design in design research*. Paper presented at the Designing Design Research 2: The Design Research Publication, Cyberbridge 4-D, De Montfort University, Leicester.

Glanville, R. (1999). Design and designing research. *Design Issues, 15*(2), 80–91.

Glanville, R. (2007). Conversation and Design. In R. Luppicini (Ed.), *The Handbook of Conversation Design for Instructional Applications*. Hershey, PA: Idea Group.

Gray, C. & Pirie, I. (1995). *Artistic research procedure: Research at the edge of chaos*? Paper presented at Design Interfaces: The European Academy of Design conference, University of Salford, Salford.

Harfield, S. (2008). *On the roots of undiscipline*. Paper presented at the Undisipline: Design Research Society Conference, Sheffield Hallam University, Sheffield.

Jefferies, E. (2008). Conversation with Joyce Yee, 14 March.

Jefferies, E. (2010). Fostering designers' visual practices through a sociocultural approach. PhD dissertation, University of Northumbria, Newcastle upon Tyne.

Jencks, C. & Silver, N. (1972). *Adhocism: The Case for Improvisation*. London: Secker and Warburg.

Kelly, G. A. (1991). *The Psychology of Personal Construct*. London: Routledge.

Kincheloe, J. (2001). Describing the bricolage: Conceptualizing a new rigor in qualitative research. *Qualitative Inquiry, 11*(3), 679–692.

Kincheloe, J. & McLaren, P. (2005). Rethinking critical theory and qualitative research. In N. Denzin & Y. Lincoln (Eds.), *The Landscape of Qualitative Research. Theories and Issues* (3rd Edn.) (pp. 303–342). Thousand Oaks, CA: Sage.

Langrish, J. (2000). *Not everything made of steel is a battleship*. Paper presented at the Foundations: Doctoral Education in Design Conference, La Clusaz, France.

Law, J. & Urry, J. (2004). Enacting the social. *Economy and Society, 33*(3), 390–410.

Lawson, B. (1990). *How Designers Think: The Design Process Demystified* (2nd Ed.). Oxford: Butterworth Architecture.

Lévi-Strauss, C. (1966). *The Savage Mind*. Chicago, IL: University of Chicago Press.

Loi, D. (2004). A suitcase as a PhD? Exploring the potential of travelling containers to articulate the multiple facets of a research thesis. *Working Papers in Art and Design, 3*.

Loi, D. (2005). Lavoretti per bimbi: Playful triggers as keys to foster collaborative practices and workspaces where people learn, wonder and play. PhD dissertation, RMIT, Melbourne.

Mazé, R. (2007). *Occupying Time: Design, Technology and the Form of Interaction*. Stockholm: Axl Books.

Mazé, R. (2010). Email to Joyce Yee, 1 November.

McCarthy, J. C. & Wright, P. C. (2004). *Technology as Experience*. Cambridge, MA: The MIT Press.

Nelson, C., Treichler, P. A., & Grossberg, L. (1992). Cultural studies: An introduction, in L. Grossberg, C. Nelson & P. A. Treichler (eds.), *Cultural studies*. New York: Routledge, pp. 1–16.

Newbury, D. (1996). *Research Perspectives in Art and Design: Introductory Essay*. Birmingham: University of Central England.

Pask, G. (1975). *Conversation, Cognition and Learning*. Amsterdam: Elsevier.

Rust, C., Mottram, J., & Till, J. (2007) *AHRC research review practice-led research in art, design and architecture*: Arts and Humanities Research Council.

Sadokierski, Z. (2010). Visual writing: A critique of graphic devices in hybrid novels, from a visual communication design perspective. PhD dissertation, University of Technology, Sydney.

Schön, D. (1992). Designing as reflective conversation with materials of a design situation. *Research in Engineering Design, 3*, 131–147.

Schön, D. A. (1983). *The Reflective Practitioner*. London: Temple–Smith.

Schön, D. A. (1987). *Educating the Reflective Practitioner: Toward a New Design for Teaching and Learning in the Professions*. London: Jossey-Bass.

Shumack, K. (2009). Design and the conversational self. PhD dissertation, University of Canberra, Canberra.

Shumack, K. (2010). The conversational self: Reflection-through-design using journal writings. *Journal of Research Practice, 6*(2) Article M17. Retrieved 28 February 2011, from http://jrp.icaap.org/index.php/jrp/article/view/195/192

Silverman, L. K. (1989). The visual–spatial learner. *Preventing School Failure, 34*, 15–20.

Singleton, B. (2011a). Crafty ecologies. *Design Ecologies, 1*(2) (in press).

Singleton, B. (2011b). E-mail to Joyce Yee, 17 March.

Spencer, N. (2009). *The relevance of rigour for design practise.* Paper presented at the Rigor and Relevance in Design: International Association of Society of Design Research Conference, Seoul, Korea.

Steadman, P. (1972). *The Evolution of Design: Biological Analogy in Architecture and the Applied Arts.* Cambridge: Cambridge University Press.

Thomas, L. & Harri-Augstein, S. (1991) *Learning Conversations.* London: Routledge.

Tonkinwise, C. (2004). *The idealist practice of reflection: Typologies, techniques and ideologies for design researchers.* Paper presented at the Futureground: Design Research Society Conference, Melbourne, Australia.

Tufte, E. R. (1990). *Envisioning Information.* Cheshire, CT: Graphic Press.

Von Busch, O. (2008). *Fashion-able. Hacktivism and engaged Fashion Design.* Gothenburg: Art Monitor, University of Gothenburg.

Wallace, J. (2007). Emotionally charged: A practice-centred enquiry of digital jewellery and personal emotional significance. PhD dissertation, Sheffield Hallam University, Sheffield.

Wood, J. (2000). The culture of academic rigour: Does design research really need it? *Design Journal, 3.1*, 44–57.

Yee, J. S. R. (2003). *Dynamic literature mapping: Typography in screen-based media.* Paper presented at the 5th European Academy of Design Conference, Barcelona.

Yee, J. S. R. (2006). Developing a practice-led framework to promote the practise and understanding of typography across different media. PhD dissertation, University of Northumbria, Newcastle upon Tyne.

Yee, J. S. R. (2010). Methodological innovation in practice-based design doctorates. *Journal of Research Practice, 6*(2), Article M15. Retrieved 28 February, 2011, from http://jrp.icaap.org/index.php/jrp/article/view/196/193

27

UNCAGED Boxed-up

Ralf Nuhn

INTRODUCTION

In this chapter, I reflect on my personal experience of working towards a 'mixed-mode' PhD in Electronic Arts, which has been completed in 2006 and was funded by an AHRC doctoral award. In particular, I will look at the relationships between the theoretical and reflective dimension of my thesis and the making, exhibition and documentation of my artworks. This will include a discussion of issues arising from the combination of physical and digital outputs used for the formal delivery of my thesis. Interestingly, this area of inquiry also lies at the very heart of my PhD research, both written and practical, which is an exploration of relationships and transitions between the physical world and the digital world of computers. Hence, within the context of *Digital Dissertations*, I felt it pertinent to provide a detailed account of my PhD research activity; starting with my quest to create novel ways to link the physical with the digital domain and leading towards a philosophical examination of the ontological difference between the 'real' and the 'virtual'. The chapter will conclude with a critical evaluation of my PhD project and make some suggestions how it might have been improved.

While there is an abundance of terms applied, more or less interchangeably, to various modes of research involving a combination of practical and a written outputs – such as practice-led, practice-based, practice-as-research, research-through-practice, etc. – I have chosen the, arguably, more neutral term 'mixed-mode research' to refer to my own approach. For me, this term best captures the notion that the practical and theoretical parts of my research are deeply intertwined and advance in a constant dialogue. Importantly, while theoretical concerns and critical evaluations of my artworks feed back into the process of creation, my practice is never a means to respond to a construct of primarily theoretical issues or questions.

MOTIVATION

Regarding my PhD project, the initial motivation to focus on the exploration of relationships between the physical world and the virtual world of computers can probably be linked to several practical and theoretical inputs. However, I believe there is one key event, which has helped to concretise a formerly rather subconscious artistic inclination towards this direction. During a conference on computer music in Barcelona in November 2001[1], a EU project officer introduced a new research initiative which, on the whole, was concerned with improving the relationships between virtual technologies and physical spaces. The presentation introduced the concepts of 'Mixed Reality'[2] and 'Presence Research'[3] and, in particular focused on the scenario of video conferences, with the question of how to enhance the notion of 'being there' (in the physical space) of those participating in a conference via a remotely linked video screen. I was immediately fascinated by the underlying idea of the presentation, to look for novel ways to extend the virtual world into the physical world and vice versa, and to mix the two domains more or less seamlessly.

Certainly, the conference presentation in Spain provided an academic research context, including an appropriate vocabulary, which would at least initially serve as a framework for my new artistic endeavours. On the other hand, I believe that on a more subconscious level, I had already been working towards the notion of combining physical elements with the virtual world of computers. In particular, I would argue that my new artistic approach was a direct development – at least from a perceptual and technical point of view – of my sound installation *Staccato Death/Life*, created in April 2001.

Staccato Death/Life features various household objects which are 'sonified' by electromechanical beaters controlled by a computer. The computer functions as a dual interface: in 'composer mode', the different beaters can be triggered directly by participants via an on-screen push-button interface; in 'automatic play mode', the computer randomly selects from different (musical) algorithms which have been created by composers from all over the world as a response to an online call for contributions.

Even though *Staccato Death/Life* was originally conceived with a different idea in mind, that is, to create a 'performance situation' focused on the relationships between everyday objects and their sonic characteristics rather than on the (musical) gestures and interpretations of a live player, I became over time more and more interested in the relationship between the computer and the physical sculpture.

My new interest was partially triggered by my observations and discussions with audiences during the initial exhibition at the 291 Gallery in London during May 2001. Despite the fact that the user interaction of *Staccato Death/Life* is very basic, I would argue that participants were simply fascinated, at that time, by the fact that their action in the virtual domain causes an event in the physical domain. In fact, people appeared to be more intrigued by the 'magical' relationship between the computer and the physical sculpture than by the sounds themselves; an assumption which has often been confirmed in conversations with participants.

FIRST IDEAS

Almost immediately after the conference presentation in Barcelona, I had some initial ideas as to how I could approach the notion of Mixed Reality. I feel it is useful to briefly outline at least one of the initial practical studies I designed on the basis of these ideas. This will provide a background for the subsequent section, in which I will briefly discuss the theoretical considerations that would, to some extent, inform the progression from these first ideas towards *UNCAGED*, a series of six 'telesymbiotic'[4] installations, constituting the primary practical output of my PhD investigations[5].

From a technical point of view, my initial studies were based on a very similar hardware and software set-up as *Staccato Death/Life*. For me this is an important fact, because it reflects the notion that my artistic ideas are often based on the scope of my technical horizon. I do not mean this in a restrictive sense, nor to say that my creations are simply an application of my technical skills. Rather, it underlines my conviction that as an artist working with and about technology, it can be advantageous to have a strong command of a certain set of tools in order to realise ideas more or less spontaneously – that is, without the mediation through technical experts or having first to acquire the necessary skills in order to realise a particular idea.

One of those studies, which would later be developed into the exhibit *PONG* (*telesymbiotic version*), features a virtual ball moving back and forth from the left to the right edge of the computer screen. Two thrust-pin type solenoids are positioned in close proximity to the left and right edge of the screen. Whenever the ball bounces against either edge of the screen, a trigger impulse is sent to the respective solenoid and its thrust-pin hits the edge of the screen where the ball is positioned. The combination of the sound produced by the impact of the solenoid's thrust-pin on the computer housing and its clearly visible mechanical action, gives the observer the impression that the virtual ball is being kicked from one side to the other side by the activity of the solenoids.

After I had transformed my initial ideas into concrete practical examples and had time to reflect on my creations, I became increasingly interested in the physico-philosophical implications of my approach. For instance, I could sense a certain relationship of my experiments to the quantum physical notion of non-locality, as proposed by the physicist Niels Bohr, and its implications for the existence of an invisible reality that supports our world – or to put it in different terms, its implication that an action in one part of the world could cause an instantaneous effect in another remote part of the world without there being a perceivable connection (cf. McEvoy & Zarate, 1999, pp. 168–170). For me the idea of traversing the distance between the physical and the screen-based world of computers is an assertion of this idea, even though in my approach the link between the two worlds is of course only 'make-believe'. Further, I considered that by implying a direct physical impact on the virtual image and vice versa, my approach seemed to challenge – at least in a metaphorical sense – Jean Baudrillard's concept of a 'hyperrealist' world where any direct experiences of the world are replaced by televised virtual images (cf. Baudrillard, 1993, pp. 79 and 80; Baudrillard, 1988, p. 11). Arguably, these contemplations would not directly impact on the further development of my approach into the final *UNCAGED* series. However, I feel mentioning them at this point is necessary with regards to a later section, where I will discuss the contextualisation of my approach within a socio-philosophical discourse about the relationships between the 'real' and the 'virtual'.

METHODOLOGY AND CREATION OF *UNCAGED*

The methodological approach for the further development of my initial studies into *UNCAGED* could be best described as experimentation and reconfiguration of existing technologies which result in new creative inventions and designs. This 'blue-sky research' was primarily led by my artistic taste and intuition that is informed by my professional expertise. Underlying this, however, was a variety of theoretical guidelines, ranging from formal and aesthetic considerations, the particular role of sound, aspects of HCI to social interaction.

While a detailed discussion of this theoretical framework would go far beyond the scope of this chapter I would like to summarise that the primary motivation behind my approach was to 'uncage' screen-based realities from the confines of their digital existence and to bring the remote computer world closer to our human experience. In particular, my work was opposed to the notion of immersive Virtual Reality where the physical world is more or less excluded from the participants, but instead attempted to situate the virtual domain within the physical world. Further, unlike most other work in the area of Mixed Reality which combines the 'real' and the 'virtual' in rather complex ways – often involving video capturing devices, novel projection platforms, electronic tags or mobile computing technology – *UNCAGED* aimed at extending conventional screen displays into their physical surroundings (and vice versa) in very immediate ways. One of the ideas behind this approach was to be more referential to and explicitly challenge our normal experience of engaging with 'virtual media'.

The creation of *UNCAGED* can be separated into a research and development phase and a production phase. The former was primarily led by playful exploration of different possibilities to combine on-screen and off-screen events using a familiar technical set-up. By contrast, the production phase was led by more specific practical considerations, that is, bearing in mind the eventual exhibition of the work at the V&A – National Museum of Childhood in London.

Throughout the creation of *UNCAGED* there has been a certain amount of collaboration on an artistic as well as on a technical level. While it is not always easy or appropriate to identify specific reasons for decisions concerning the artistic way of working, I would argue that my desire to collaborate with other artists is in some ways an organic extension from my group performance practice. With *UNCAGED*, I wanted to create an open platform where other artists could explore their ideas in the framework of my installation set-up.

My decision to collaborate with a team of technical experts is, of course, primarily a pragmatic decision, but at the same time it is grounded in my belief that with a multidisciplinary work, such as *UNCAGED*, it is problematic for the lead artist to become an expert in all of the areas involved, for example, software programming, electronics, etc. This is because by getting too deeply involved in all the technical details of the work, it is in my view very easy for the artist to lose focus of the work's overall artistic unity. At the same time, I believe that it is important for the lead artist to have a certain level of expertise in all of the areas involved, and to be able identify what is technically possible and to communicate her requirements clearly to the technical experts. If this is not the case, the artwork can often be transformed into a mere showcase for technological possibilities, or, in the other extreme, not be realised to its full technical potential.

During the research and development phase around fifteen preliminary studies were developed which in many ways were quite similar to that already described. These potential exhibits were based on video loops and simple animations interacting with different computer controlled electronic devices placed around a screen display. In particular, all studies established transitions between the screen-based domain and the surrounding physical environment in a very direct or literal way.

More or less right from the start, I was convinced that *UNCAGED* could be interesting for a wide range of audiences, including children. I therefore felt it appropriate to approach the V&A – National Museum of Childhood in London (MOC) with regards to my project. After several meetings with the exhibition curator at the MOC during summer 2003, an exhibition of *UNCAGED*, featuring six exhibits based on my preliminary studies, was agreed for May and June 2004. The commission of my work for an exhibition at this particular space imposed certain requirements and, in a sense, marked the transition from the research and development phase to the production phase. For instance, the exhibits would have to be of relatively low height so they would be accessible to children. Furthermore, I felt inclined to emphasise on the playful character of my work and to develop exhibits reminiscent of familiar games or childhood themes. In order to increase the engagement with the eventual exhibits, I also figured that the introduction of user-interactive elements might be useful even though most studies were conceived without this possibility. However, I should point out that my primary interest was concerned with the audiovisual relationship between the on-screen and off-screen events of the exhibits and not with user-interaction as such. In particular, I did not want to introduce highly complex user-interfaces, but instead make the user interaction as intuitive and evocative (of everyday interaction) as possible.

In this respect, I was very much stimulated by the approach taken by the Tangible Media Group at the MIT Media Laboratory. They advocate the use of every day objects as a basis for input devices with the rationale to look 'towards the bounty of richly-afforded physical devices of the last few millennia and inventing ways to reapply these elements of "tangible media" augmented by digital technology' (Ishii & Ullmer, 1997, p. 236). Even though, my own approach did not involve everyday objects as such, it was designed to be evocative of familiar forms of interaction. For instance, I reasoned that, where appropriate, a simple push-button interface allowing participants to activate or play with an exhibit would be preferable to a more complex interface, like a motion capture device. This approach was also an important feature in the overall research design of the project because one of my research questions was to find out whether the, at least at the time, rather unusual onscreen/off-screen relationships of my work could generate 'sufficient' interest to capture a large audience without their being any complex forms of user-interaction.

On the whole, one could say that during the research and development phase there was a notion of divergence in terms of inventing a great number of possible exhibits. By contrast, the production phase was characterised by a notion of convergence, meaning that the most appropriate studies were selected and developed into high-quality exhibits, which could be presented to a public audience.

UNCAGED AT THE V&A MUSEUM OF CHILDHOOD

For the exhibition at the MOC, *UNCAGED* has been developed into a series of six interactive installations which are linked by the common theme, to explore interrelationships and transitions between screen-based digital environments and their physical surroundings. *UNCAGED* incorporates different electromechanical devices and automated sculptures which interact, visually and acoustically, with computer generated animations and video images. Participants can playfully engage with the installations via touch screens, tangible custom-made interfaces and simple pushbuttons. As a detailed description of the exhibits is not possible within the context of this chapter I refer the reader to the *UNCAGED* website (www.telesymbiosis.com), which features photos and digital video recordings of the exhibits at the MOC. While the digitisation of the practical output of my thesis provides a convenient way to convey an overall idea about the work, I would like to point out that the video recordings and photos do not replace the direct experience of the actual exhibits; an epistemological problematic which I will discuss further in the final section of this chapter.

UNCAGED was exhibited over seven weeks during May and June 2004 at the MOC. According to the museum's statistics over 30,000 visitors from a wide social, ethnic and educational background participated in the exhibition. For me, the wide range of audiences and the museum's policy that 'everything can be touched by the audience' – which is nurtured by the exceptionally discrete conduct of the museum's attendants and security staff – provided an ideal context to exhibit *UNCAGED*, as I was interested to find out if the exhibits would work on different levels and stimulate playful and explorative engagement by different types of audiences.

During the exhibition, I spent about three full days within the space to observe visitors' conduct with the exhibits and to attempt to speak with visitors about their impressions and experiences. Unfortunately, in many cases, it proved to be extremely difficult or inappropriate to initiate (in-depth) conversations with visitors about the work. This might have been due to the fact that many visitors arrived in groups with small children and were too preoccupied with keeping the group together, or the fact that in the fairly large museum space there were many other interesting exhibits which had to be visited within a limited time span. In particular, discussions about the conceptual aspects of *UNCAGED* frequently turned out to be not very fruitful.

As noted earlier, artistically, I was mainly interested in the perceptual, 'telesymbiotic' interaction between on-screen and off-screen events. However, I felt it would be useful to observe visitors' conduct from a user-interactive perspective in order to evaluate the extent to which the exhibits were able to engage audiences. I reasoned that from these general findings obtained I would be able to deduce more specific conclusions regarding my approach to combine the digital world of computers with the physical world.

While working on the theoretical framework of my approach, which paralleled the research and development phase of *UNCAGED,* I discovered that, in a public exhibition context, *UNCAGED* might resonate with recent findings by the Work Interaction and Technology (WIT) research group at King's College, London. In particular, I was interested to find out if my approach could avoid the problem of inhibiting social interaction amongst gallery audiences, which, according to the WIT group, is a major problem with many contemporary computer mediated museum exhibits. The group's research is primarily based on observations of audiences in museums and they have a particular interest in studying computer-mediated artworks[6].

In spring 2003, I contacted Jon Hindmarsh, a senior researcher at the WIT group, to present my preliminary studies and ideas about *UNCAGED,* and invited him to conduct a study of audience behaviour during a possible exhibition of my work. Hindmarsh showed great interest in *UNCAGED*, and once I had arranged the exhibition at the MOC, he agreed to conduct a qualitative study of audience behaviour at the museum. In line with their broader research programme, their analysis of the audio–visual material paid particular attention to social interaction between visitors and how groups of visitors organise their collaborative exploration of the exhibits. At the same time, it includes comments about more general qualities of *UNCAGED* and about its presentation in the exhibition space.

The findings of the WIT group, which were published in an internal report, proved to be an invaluable resource for the evaluation of my own observations. In particular, it enabled me to read my findings against theirs and, thus, increase the validity of my conclusions. I will demonstrate this approach with an example relating to the manner in which *UNCAGED* was presented in the exhibition space. Despite my strong reservations, the curator at the MOC insisted upon installing display notes next to the exhibits which explained, in a rather instructive manner, 'how to interact' with the artworks. Personally, I rejected this type of note, because I wanted to encourage intuitive engagement and felt that it would be more rewarding for participants to playfully discover the exhibits rather than to follow some instructions. At first sight, this particular issue might seem rather peripheral and, indeed, my own observations during the exhibition revealed that most visitors would simply ignore the display notes. By contrast, the WIT researchers noted that children who were accompanied by adults would often demand some sort of explanation about how to 'operate' the exhibits. In many cases, the adults would then immediately refer to the labels for some help.

'However by the time the adults had read an appropriate section of the label the children were often very much engaged in "playing" with the exhibit. Therefore the adults then tended to attempt to strictly structure the child's activities in order to get them to follow the instructions from the labels. Directions such as "stop doing that for a moment" often featured heavily in these sequences' (Best & Hindmarsh, 2004, p. 9).

Despite the apparent demand for an explanation about how to operate an exhibit, I would argue that the above scenario illustrates above all that visitors (in this case the children) were perfectly able to engage with the exhibits by intuitively starting to play with them. It appears to me that the presence of the display notes distracted some adults from exploring the exhibits 'hands-on' together with their children and, instead, led them to rigorously instruct their children.

Obviously, in the context of my intention to stimulate explorative behaviour in audiences, this observation is extremely disappointing. Further, as I have pointed out before, the main focus for me was the perceptual interaction of the exhibits' on-screen and off-screen events and artefacts, and I believe that this notion was still conveyed even if participants made some wrong assumption about the user-interactive parts. Surely, one cannot rule out that in some cases people might have simply turned away from the exhibits if – due to the lack of instructive notes – they would not have been able to make sense of them. However, in my view, it is less of a problem to lose some part of the audience than to limit playful exploration of the work by offering manuals for the exhibits.

In further support of my aversion against instructive labels for *UNCAGED*, I would like to add that shortly after the exhibition at the MOC, I was invited to present one of the exhibits (*Glitchy & Scratchy*) at the ZKM – Centre for Art and

Media in Karlsruhe, Germany[7]. In this case, no instructions were given on the display note and I did not record a single case of visitors not knowing how to interact with the exhibit. According to reports from the ZKM staff, the exhibit has since become a favourite with audiences and in 2007 the ZKM purchased the exhibit for inclusion in their collection of interactive art (followed by the acquisition of two further *UNCAGED* exhibits in 2009).

For further details regarding my qualitative study of audience behaviour at the MOC, I refer the reader to my PhD thesis (Nuhn, 2006). For now, I would like to sum up that the overall level and quality of user interaction as well as social interaction was extremely encouraging. This, arguably, subjective interpretation, has been reflected in observations made by the observers of the WIT group:

> Whereas many pieces of interactive art fail to engage their audience by being overly complex or badly explained, or situated in institutions which normatively seem to discourage hands-on engagement, much of the interaction we recorded in the Museum of Childhood could be deemed successful. They supported playful engagement with complex technologies – a rare feat in contemporary museum. Moreover the exhibits supported and encouraged many forms of participation and gave rise to numerous forms of innovative engagement (e.g. the development of multi-party games around *Square Pusher*; the imitation of DJ-ing in *Glitchy & Scratchy,* etc.) (ibid, pp. 11 and 12).

Certainly, on the basis of my own and the WIT group's observations, one cannot be certain about what exactly made *UNCAGED* such a success with the audiences. However, I would argue that in the light of a ubiquitous presence and accessibility of – in terms of complexity of (games) design, user-responsive graphics and sounds, etc. – far more elaborate interactive entertainment media, for example, arcade games, game consoles, commercial multimedia applications, the fascination with *UNCAGED* cannot be explained by the possibilities of user interaction as such. In my view, this fascination is mainly related to how the user interaction affects the 'telesymbiotic' dimension of the work, namely the interaction between the on-screen and off-screen elements of the exhibits. I would therefore suggest that, on the whole, my ultimately very simple approach to perceptually bridge the gap between screen-based realities and their immediate physical surroundings has been successful.

REVISED VIEW OF *UNCAGED*

Thus far, the underlying tenor of this chapter has strongly resonated with the initial motivation behind *UNCAGED*, to uncage computer based realities from the confines of their digital existence and to bring the remote computer world closer to our human experience. This very motivation certainly expresses some degree of critical awareness about mainstream developments within digital technology industries at the time. In particular, my own approach can be seen as an attempt to provide a possible alternative to the, widely pursued area of immersive Virtual Reality, where the physical world is more or less excluded from the participants.

However, as a whole, my argumentations so far, have not questioned the potential of digital technology to be incorporated within our lives in meaningful and satisfying ways, but, if anything, sought to undermine the dominant paradigm of their developments and applications. I must confess, though, that this relatively optimistic narrative only reflects in part my attitude towards the project. In reality, things have been much more ambiguous and, in part, the *UNCAGED* project (including the previous theoretical account of it) has been a struggle to give meaning and understanding to an idea which began to crumble before it was even fully realised.

Already, during the early stages of the research and development phase of *UNCAGED*, but in particular after the work had been completed, I began to question the initial motivation behind the project. I believe that my reservations towards this, with hindsight, rather starry-eyed agenda arose from two coinciding, arguably interrelated, notions. First, my critical examination of the work itself nourished the impression that despite the perceptual fusion between the digital and the physical world, *UNCAGED* actually seems to highlight the distance between the two domains. In my view, all six exhibits bear an underlying absurdity, which arises from the very fusion between their physical and digital components. For me, this absurdity ultimately hints at the fallacy of the initial motivation behind *UNCAGED* and, in a wider context, questions the very idea to seek in virtual worlds a place for meaningful human exchange and experiences.

Second, temporally coinciding with, but not necessarily causally linked to the creation of *UNCAGED*, my former enthusiasm for the computer as a working tool was clouded by a growing frustration and, to put it bluntly, my reluctance to spend a good deal of my life (isolated) in front of the computer screen.

Admittedly, in the light of my original motivation, one could argue that the very objective of *UNCAGED* was precisely about improving our relationship with digital technology, and that therefore *UNCAGED* could be regarded as a step towards overcoming my own frustration with the computer. I do believe that *UNCAGED* is successful in bridging the gap between the digital world and the physical world on a perceptual basis, and I feel the six installations certainly incorporate digital technology in a rather enjoyable and stimulating way. However, for me the fusion between the digital and the physical world in *UNCAGED* only seems to work within the context of installation art or simply games, but ultimately, applied to 'real life', it does not offer much hope to make the digital world a more satisfying space to engage with.

This negative, or at least disillusioned, evaluation might come as a surprise for the observer of *UNCAGED* and/or reader of the preceding sections of this chapter. Retrospectively, it is difficult for me to trace whether the absurdity perceived in the work appeared to me as a sudden revelation, or whether it was not always inherent in the conception of the work. I was always aware that the fusion in *UNCAGED*, between the virtual and the physical world, would be some kind of make-believe situation. Right from the start, there was surely a certain amount of humour, maybe even irony, within my approach, and I did not claim to offer 'real' solutions for improving our relationship with the computer. At the same time, there was also a great deal of personal amazement regarding the effectiveness of this very simple and direct way to link the physical and the virtual world, and, if at all, I did not perceive the absurdity of my experiments as a problem regarding the initial, 'humane' motivation behind the project. Whereas in most other Mixed Reality approaches this absurdity might be veiled or distracted from the participants through greater technological sophistication or an overall subtler approach in mixing the virtual with the physical elements, I would now suggest that the simplicity of my approach brings to light an intrinsic absurdity of the very idea to fuse the physical with the virtual world.

As mentioned earlier, since the beginnings of *UNCAGED* I had been interested in the writings of Jean Baudrillard. Initially, I took his rather apocalyptic 'prophecy' of a total virtualisation of our world, or the 'murder of the real'[8] as he has put it, as a challenge against which to measure my own approach. However, in the light of my shrinking optimism in the possibilities of humanising the virtual world of computers, I felt it useful to revisit and deepen my understanding of his texts, relevant to the issues at stake, with the hope to find some clues or answers to exactly why I had the impression that my project had failed. In particular, I was interested to explore further his accounts on the specific nature of the virtual and how it differs from the 'real'.

In summary, from my understanding of Baudrillard, one could argue that there are four different notions of reality. First, there is 'primary reality', the realm we commonly refer to as the real world. According to Baudrillard, our primary reality is a world of appearances and we are only experiencing it as the 'true real', because we seem to have succeeded in objectivising these appearances and, in this way, brought into existence a 'reality effect'. Importantly, in Baudrillard's view, this reality effect is merely a simulation of a true real as it is based on an ontological simplification of the world, which ignores its ultimate strangeness or otherness (cf. Baudrillard, 2003). Second, there is a hyperreal universe, produced by our contemporary mediascape, that is, television, advertisement and (real-time) digital technologies. Both realities seem to seamlessly overlap and it is increasingly difficult for us to make a difference between the two. What is more, it is actually the hyperreal which engenders primary reality (cf. Baudrillard, 1994). Third, underlying primary reality, there is a more profound reality, a kind of 'hinterworld', which hides behind the world of appearances through the 'radical illusion' of the world. Importantly, for Baudrillard it is this radical illusion of the world which is the opposite of simulation and not the real, or primary world. To this third kind of reality we do not have direct access, but it is vital to keep alive the world's mystery, the notion of the Other. Baudrillard suggests that, in our artificial universe the illusion of the world is being destroyed by simulation and that the Other is now only experienced through forms of Evil (cf. Baudrillard, 1993). The fourth notion of reality would be a perfected form of hyperreality, a kind of fully immersive Virtual Reality, where these last vestiges of the Other are lost, because in Virtual Reality, there is no place for an underlying profound reality. This is because Virtual Reality is a completely simulated world based solely on the actualisation of computational data (cf. Baudrillard, 2005).

When applying the above framework directly to *UNCAGED,* one could consider the screen-based domain of the exhibits as being an instance of the second notion of reality, that is, hyperreality and the physical domain as being an instance of primary reality, the world of appearances. In this light, then, the idea behind *UNCAGED* to bridge the gap between the physical or primary world and the screen-based world of computers seems rather naïve. Not, though, in the sense that this project would be doomed to fail because of an unbridgeable distance between the two domains, as implied in my initial critical interpretation of *UNCAGED.* On the contrary, it seems naïve, because, according to Baudrillard, the virtual, hyperreal world is already inextricably linked with primary reality. In a sense, the perceptual fusion between the physical and the virtual artefacts of *UNCAGED* reiterates, at least in a metaphorical way, Baudrillard's idea about the sameness between the real and the hyperreal; the idea that, ultimately, both are simulations.

Even though I do not fully subscribe to the extremity of Baudrillard's assertion that primary reality amounts nowadays to nothing but simulation, I would argue that the problem with *UNCAGED* and, by extension, the very idea of Mixed Reality, is that by combining the virtual world with primary reality, the latter seems to be reduced to the same ontological level as the former. On the other hand, maybe in a more positive light, one could claim that *UNCAGED* actually puts a very ironic slant on Baudrillard's ideas. This is because, once we consider *UNCAGED* as a reflection of our simulated universe – comprising a nexus of virtual artefacts and physical appearances – we are confronted with a grotesque exaggeration of the matter. In my view, this irony is engendered by the extremely direct and simple approach of *UNCAGED,* or better, by reducing the rather complex technical–scientific–psychological–sociological–historical nexus between the real and the hyperreal to a series of straightforward one-to-one relationships.

With hindsight, I would contend that the real problem with *UNCAGED* is not related to the work itself, but rather to my motivation to make the virtual computer world a more 'humane' place to engage with, and my concern to offer new directions to overcome our difficulties to engage with computers in a satisfying way. I now hold the view that my research approach should instead have been more open. In particular, it should have been guided by a more neutral question, that is, to ask for the consequences of combining the physical domain with the virtual domain in a very direct way.

Not surprisingly, my critical evaluation of *UNCAGED* demanded a radical rethinking of my practical approach. Originally, I had the intention to create a subsequent body of work, where the transitions between the physical and the virtual world as well as the user interaction would be more seamless and technically sophisticated. I assume that it is obvious from my post-*UNCAGED* reflections that a development in this direction would have been extremely inappropriate.

Instead I figured that my new artistic projects should not be concerned with perfecting the perceptual and interactive level of *UNCAGED* but with exploring further the socio-philosophical issues implied in *UNCAGED*.

While there is no room in this chapter to discuss my subsequent practical work I would like to point out that, at the very least, my theoretical reflections on *UNCAGED* – based on Baudrillard's ideas about the real and the virtual – have provided me with a new heightened sensitivity with regards to the role of (digital) technology in my artistic work.

RETROSPECTIVE REFLECTION ON MIXED-MODE PHDS

While I believe that my PhD project, to some extent, serves as good example of how practical and theoretical research can be combined successfully I also have some strong reservations about the validity and relevance of this kind of approach. In the remainder of this chapter, I will discuss some issues that have arisen from a critical reflection on the very idea of mixed-mode PhDs.

To begin with, I would like to address a problem concerning the actual format of presentation of mixed-mode PhDs. My own thesis comprises a book of about 150 pages with text and images accompanied by a DVD (attached to the back cover of the book) featuring a video recording of *UNCAGED* at the Museum of Childhood. I have little doubt that the vast majority of people consulting my thesis in a library will initially access the work by reading through (parts of) the text and only if they are highly interested in the subject, might make the effort to locate a DVD player and engage with the audiovisual part provided. Consequently, the presentation format of my PhD foregrounds the written part of the project and sidelines any audiovisual engagement with its practical dimension. In the light of the very topic of my PhD, to combine physical and digital events and artefacts in new engaging ways, this rather inelegant way of presenting the outcomes of my research seems retrospectively very unimaginative, conventional and, in some ways, even ironic.

A very straightforward attempt to achieve a better balance between the written and the audiovisual parts of the thesis might have been to get rid of the paper version and simply provide all information on a single medium, that is, a DVD containing both the *UNCAGED* video and an electronic version of the written thesis. Banal as this might seem, this format would certainly have encouraged viewer-readers to pay more, possibly primary, attention to the audiovisual part of the thesis and to consult the written part in a more or less complimentary manner. Unfortunately, PhD regulations at Middlesex University do not permit this kind of submission format but require a bound paper copy adhering to precise formatting specifications. With this in mind, there is an immediate need to revise research regulations at Middlesex and, supposedly, many other research institutions.

Having said this, the digitisation of the written text might engender other, maybe more severe problems. In the specific case of my own thesis, following the successful viva, I have been led to provide a PDF version of the paper-based part of my submission. This PDF now circulates 'freely' on the Internet and access to the audiovisual dimension is provided through web addresses within the text pointing at online video recordings of the *UNCAGED* exhibits. Whereas it requires not much of an effort for the reader to follow up the links while studying the PDF on an online computer, it is also very likely that the audiovisual dimension is, in this form of presentation, even further reduced to a mere addition or illustration of the theoretical arguments. Further, in an even more depressing scenario, the downloadable PDF might be read in offline mode making immediate consultation of the videos impossible or the respective computer might not have installed the necessary plug-ins to view the videos, making their consultation much less attractive and, hence, less likely. Finally, the idea of digitising the book of my thesis seems somewhat incoherent with my critical view on the pervasion of digital technology through our lives that has emerged from my PhD research. Apart from the argument that a paper-based dissertation, unlike a digital dissertation, does not bear the risk of becoming inaccessible in the future due to changes in digital formats, I would also contend that the printed book is simply more pleasurable to read and encourages 'deeper' engagement with the material than does a digital document to be read on-screen. This is, I believe, a view shared by many readers but is also often criticised as being an overly nostalgic attitude. As a very concrete example suggesting an irreplaceable quality of paper-based material I would like to mention that a great number of academics – who, on the whole, are 'perfectly happy' to carry out many tasks at the computer – tend to print out (important) digital documents in order to study them in depth[9]. What is more, some of the features often readily accepted as being clear advantages of digital documents, such as being easily searchable and globally accessible via the Internet, pose at closer inspection some serious problems. For instance, the facility by which electronic books can be searched for specific keywords might encourage superficial engagement with the material and promote referencing of fragments 'instead of considering whole expressions or arguments'. Seen in the wider context of current trends in online culture, for example, the idea of 'the noosphere, which is a supposed global brain formed by the sum of all brains connected through the Internet', fragmentation of material can even lead to anonymity of authorship, which 'is what happens today with a lot of content; often you don't know where a quoted fragment from a news story came from, who wrote a comment, or who shot a video' (Lanier, 2011, pp. 45–47).

Either way, the idea of the practical part having become sidelined in the submission format of my thesis, is extremely frustrating because, for me, it constitutes the more important part of my research, that is, it is my primary contribution of knew knowledge and understanding to the (research) community. In line with Stephen Scrivener, I would argue that the practical dimension of my project 'already contains the activity of research, understood as that function which expands [its] field's potential and relevance'[10]. Further, while the written part certainly facilitates very direct access to issues and insights embedded within the practical dimension, it provides only one of many other possible perspectives of understanding it and, thus, is likely to limit the perceptual, affective and epistemological potential of the practical work. This more or less prescriptive way of understanding the work resonates with the aforementioned problem of displaying instructive notes next to the exhibits discouraging intuitive and exploratory engagement with the work and impeding on 'new discoveries' to be made.

In turn, the emphasis on the practical part of the thesis raises questions concerning the presentation and documentation of the artworks. Whereas the video recording of *UNCAGED* might convey some overall idea about the work, it differs profoundly from a first-hand experience of it. Given the initial motivation behind *UNCAGED*, to extend the digital domain into the physical domain and vice versa, it seems almost absurd having 'boxed up' the artworks within a conventional video frame for examination and archiving purposes. While it might be difficult to conceive of better, alternative ways for creating an audio–visual record of the practical work, a fundamentally different route to challenge the above problem of representation might be to consider more creative ways of writing (about) the artworks. Rather than trying to provide a more or less neutral description of the artistic outputs, which I have attempted in my thesis, a more phenomenological approach accounting for the conscious experience and subjective perception of *UNCAGED* might have been preferable. This might include the use of metaphors and an overall more poetic way of writing, capable of engendering the same kind of immediate sensibility as the actual experience of the physical artworks.

The problem of representation also has implications for the importance that should be given to the PhD viva, both from the student's perspective and the examiners' perspective. Coincidently, in the case of my own project, the external examiner had visited the exhibition at the MOC and was therefore able to base his evaluation on actual experience rather than on the provided recordings only. However, this was pure chance (the external examiner had not yet been chosen at the time of the exhibition, nor was I aware that he had visited the show) and will of course not be the case for the majority of people consulting my PhD. While it would have certainly been a considerable effort to install *UNCAGED* at the viva, I now feel that the creation of a dialogue between the theoretical account given in my thesis and the direct physical experience of the work by the examination board would have added an invaluable epistemological validity to the examination process and emphasised my standpoint of the practical work being the central outcome and contribution to knowledge and understanding of my research project. Further, in order to increase the impact and relevance of the viva, in particular where a live and/or physical component is central to the research, the opening up to a wider (academic) public should be more seriously considered and encouraged. Obviously, these considerations become more or less irrelevant where the practical component of the research activity as well as its outcomes take place within the digital domain, such as Net Art, Software Art, Digital Video and Electronic Music.

With regards to the 'truth value' of the written part of my PhD, I would like to make one final point. While I don't want to suggest that I have been lying in my thesis, I have to admit that in order to construct a coherent narrative, I have often felt obliged to present certain issues, especially regarding the development of my artistic work, in drastically simplified, possibly distorted ways. Most importantly, I have omitted the fact that since 2003 – coinciding with the research and development phase of *UNCAGED* – I have started to develop a shared artistic practice with Cécile Colle. While this collaboration might not have had a major impact on the final outcome of *UNCAGED,* it certainly played a key role in the critical assessment of *UNCAGED* and, obviously, radically changed my, or better *our,* post-*UNCAGED* practice. What is more, it also undermines my rather linear account I have provided regarding the development of my artistic practice. This is because, in collaboration with Cécile, I had produced a body of work before *UNCAGED* had been completed, which implies a much more critical view on 'new technologies' and the notion of interactivity than my motivation for *UNCAGED* might suggest.

CONCLUSION

In the light of this retrospective evaluation of my PhD project, both the written part and the representation of the artworks by means video recording might be viewed as a quasi-interface to the original, physical artistic output. Like an

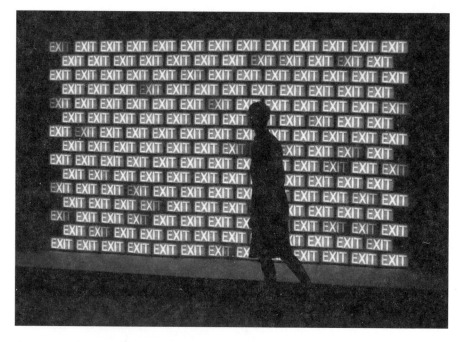

Figure 27.1   Exit-Wall (2010) by Cécile Colle}{Ralf Nuhn
Dimensions: 406 cm x 225 cm x 10 cm
200 exit sign boxes, permanent magnets, multi-sockets, metal structure

interface the thesis provides direct, and more or less standardised, access to some knowledge and understanding embedded within *UNCAGED*. At the same time, though, it also constitutes a barrier hiding away or distracting from other possible perspectives and physical experiences of the work. This viewpoint is in line with my theoretical and artistic research on the intrinsic nature of the interface and has been resumed paradigmatically in my recent collaboration with Cécile Colle, *Exit-Wall* (Figure 27.1).

NOTES

1. 'MOSART Workshop on Current Research Directions in Computer Music' held in Barcelona at the Pompeu Fabra University from 15 to 17 November 2001.

2. 'Mixed Reality' has now become a standard notion in areas like media art, architectural design as well as medicine. It refers to environments that mix computer generated realities with (representations of) the physical or 'real' world.

3. 'Presence research' is concerned with the notion of 'being there'. It is often applied to the area of virtual reality with the rationale to measure how much a participant is immersed within a virtual environment.

4. The term 'telesymbiosis' is used in biological research and literally means 'symbiosis at a distance'. It has been adopted to describe the quasi-symbiotic relationships – between the physical world and the distant computer world – in *UNCAGED*. Admittedly, the term might be misleading as it is also used (synonymously with the term 'telepresence') in the context of virtual reality, where it refers to a person's feeling of being present in a virtual or remote environment.

5. Photos and video recordings of *UNCAGED* can be accessed at: www.telesymbiosis.com

6. See the WIT group's website at http://www.kcl.ac.uk/depsta/pse/mancen/witrg/ for more detailed information about their research.

7. For details about *Glitchy & Scratchy* at the ZKM please visit http://www01.zkm.de/algorithmische-revolution/index.php?module=pagemaster&PAGE_user_op=view_page&PAGE_id=88 (accessed 10 October 2006).

8. cf. Baudrillard (2000, p. 61).

9. One should bear in mind that printing out documents involves considerable costs and might not be a viable option for readers who do not have free access to printing facilities.

10. cf. Stephen Scrivener's webpage at: http://www.chelsea.arts.ac.uk/17858.htm (last accessed on 25 March 2011).

REFERENCES

Baudrillard, J. (1988, c 1987). *The Ecstasy of Communiation.* New York: Semiotext(e).

Baudrillard, J. (1993, c 1990). *The Transparency of Evil.* London: Verso.

Baudrillard, J. (1994, c 1981). *Simulacra and Simulations.* Ann Arbor, MI: University of Michigan Press.

Baudrillard, J. (2000). *The Vital Illusion.* New York: Columbia University Press.

Baudrillard, J. (2003, c 2000). *Passwords.* London: Verso.

Baudrillard, J. (2005, c 2004). *The Intelligence of Evil or the Lucidity Pact.* Oxford: Berg.

Best, K. & Hindmarsh, J. (2004). *A report of preliminary findings from a study of visitor behaviour during the exhibition of 'UNCAGED'* by Ralf Nuhn in the Museum of Childhood at Bethnal Green, unpublished internal report, 13 pages.

Ishii, H. & Ullmer, B. (1997). Tangible bits: Towards seamless interfaces between people, bits and atoms. *Proc. CHI'97,* pp. 234–241.

Lanier, J. (2011). *You are not a Gadget.* London: Penguin Books.

McEvoy, J. P. & Zarate, O. (1999). *Introducing Quantum Theory.* Duxford: Icon Books.

Nuhn, R. (2006). UNCAGED: A novel, 'telesymbiotic' approach to bridge the divide between the physical world and the virtual world of computers? PhD thesis, Middlesex University (http://eprints.mdx.ac.uk/4472/).

Index